Forward Planner 2020

MAY	JUNE	JULY	AUGUST
1 F Philip and James	1 M Visitation of the BVM (transferred)	1 W	
2 Sa	2 Tu		
3 S Easter 4	3 W		
4 M	4 Th		
5 Tu	5 F		
6 W	6 Sa	6	6 Th Transfiguration
7 Th	7 S **Trinity Sunday**	7 Tu	7 F
8 F	8 M	8 W	8 Sa
9 Sa	9 Tu	9 Th	9 S Trinity 9
10 S Easter 5	10 W	10 F	10 M
11 M	11 Th Corpus Christi	11 Sa	11 Tu
12 Tu	12 F Barnabas (transferred)	12 S Trinity 5	12 W
13 W	13 Sa	13 M	13 Th
14 Th Matthias	14 S Trinity 1	14 Tu	14 F
15 F	15 M	15 W	15 Sa The Blessed Virgin Mary
16 Sa	16 Tu	16 Th	16 S Trinity 10
17 S Easter 6	17 W	17 F	17 M
18 M	18 Th	18 Sa	18 Tu
19 Tu	19 F	19 S Trinity 6	19 W
20 W	20 Sa	20 M	20 Th
21 Th **Ascension Day**	21 S Trinity 2	21 Tu	21 F
22 F	22 M	22 W Mary Magdalene	22 Sa
23 Sa	23 Tu	23 Th	23 S Trinity 11
24 S Easter 7	24 W Birth of John the Baptist	24 F	24 M Bartholomew
25 M	25 Th	25 Sa James	25 Tu
26 Tu	26 F	26 S Trinity 7	26 W
27 W	27 Sa	27 M	27 Th
28 Th	28 S Trinity 3	28 Tu	28 F
29 F	29 M Peter and Paul	29 W	29 Sa
30 Sa	30 Tu	30 Th	30 S Trinity 12
31 S **Pentecost**		31 F	31 M

Forward Planner 2020

SEPTEMBER	OCTOBER	NOVEMBER	DECEMBER
1 Tu	1 Th	1 S 4th before Advent, **All Saints' Day**	1 Tu
2 W	2 F	2 M All Souls	2 W
3 Th	3 Sa	3 Tu	3 Th
4 F	4 S Trinity 17	4 W	4 F
5 Sa	5 M	5 Th	5 Sa
6 S Trinity 13	6 Tu	6 F	6 S Advent 2
7 M	7 W	7 Sa	7 M
8 Tu	8 Th	8 S 3rd before Advent, Remembrance Sunday	8 Tu
9 W	9 F	9 M	9 W
10 Th	10 Sa	10 Tu	10 Th
11 F	11 S Trinity 18	11 W	11 F
12 Sa	12 M	12 Th	12 Sa
13 S Trinity 14	13 Tu	13 F	13 S Advent 3
14 M Holy Cross Day	14 W	14 Sa	14 M
15 Tu	15 Th	15 S 2nd before Advent	15 Tu
16 W	16 F	16 M	16 W
17 Th	17 Sa	17 Tu	17 Th
18 F	18 S Luke	18 W	18 F
19 Sa	19 M	19 Th	19 Sa
20 S Trinity 15	20 Tu	20 F	20 S Advent 4
21 M Matthew	21 W	21 Sa	21 M
22 Tu	22 Th	22 S Christ the King	22 Tu
23 W	23 F	23 M	23 W
24 Th	24 Sa	24 Tu	24 Th
25 F	25 S Last Sunday after Trinity	25 W	25 F **Christmas Day**
26 Sa	26 M	26 Th	26 Sa Stephen
27 S Trinity 16	27 Tu	27 F	27 S John
28 M	28 W Simon and Jude	28 Sa	28 M The Holy Innocents
29 Tu Michael and All Angels	29 Th	29 S **Advent Sunday**	29 Tu
30 W	30 F	30 M Andrew	30 W
	31 Sa		31 Th

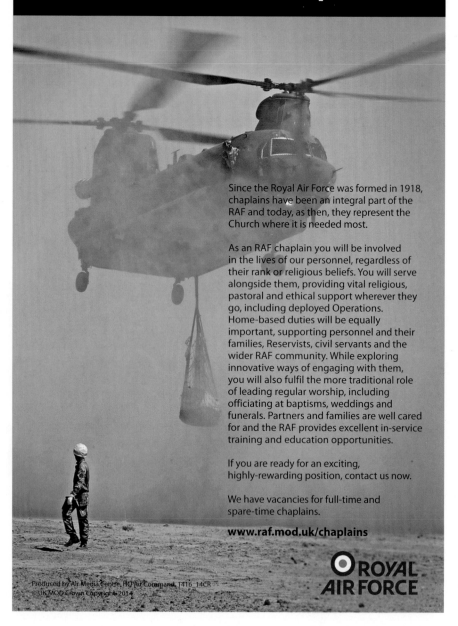

Could You Be Their Chaplain?

Since the Royal Air Force was formed in 1918, chaplains have been an integral part of the RAF and today, as then, they represent the Church where it is needed most.

As an RAF chaplain you will be involved in the lives of our personnel, regardless of their rank or religious beliefs. You will serve alongside them, providing vital religious, pastoral and ethical support wherever they go, including deployed Operations. Home-based duties will be equally important, supporting personnel and their families, Reservists, civil servants and the wider RAF community. While exploring innovative ways of engaging with them, you will also fulfil the more traditional role of leading regular worship, including officiating at baptisms, weddings and funerals. Partners and families are well cared for and the RAF provides excellent in-service training and education opportunities.

If you are ready for an exciting, highly-rewarding position, contact us now.

We have vacancies for full-time and spare-time chaplains.

www.raf.mod.uk/chaplains

ROYAL
AIR FORCE

Produced by Air Media Centre, HQ Air Command. 1416_14CR
© UK MOD Crown Copyright 2014

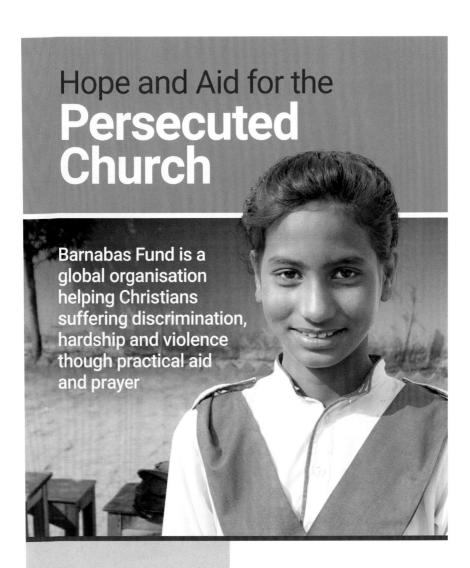

Hope and Aid for the
Persecuted Church

Barnabas Fund is a global organisation helping Christians suffering discrimination, hardship and violence though practical aid and prayer

To donate online please visit
www.barnabasfund.org

Barnabas Fund, 9 Priory Row,
Coventry, UK, CV1 5EX
02476 231 923 | info@barnabasfund.org

barnabasfund
hope and aid for the persecuted church

"A wonderful place for a wonderful retirement"

The College of St Barnabas is a residential community of retired Anglican clergy, set in beautiful Surrey countryside. Married couples are very welcome, as are those who have been widowed. Admission is open to licensed Church Workers and Readers. There are facilities for visitors and guests. Occasional quiet days and private retreats can be accommodated.

Residents are encouraged to lead active, independent lives. There is a Nursing Wing, to which both internal and direct admission are possible, providing domiciliary, residential and full nursing care for those who need it. This enables most residents to remain members of the College for the rest of their lives. It is sometimes possible to offer respite care here.

Sheltered 'Cloister' flats all have separate sitting rooms, bedrooms and en suite facilities. There are two Chapels; the Eucharist and Evensong are celebrated daily. We have three Libraries and a well-equipped Common Room. Meals are served in the Refectory or may be taken privately when necessary.

For further details or to arrange a preliminary visit, please see our website or contact the Warden, The Rev'd Kevin Scully, at

The College of St Barnabas,
Blackberry Lane, Lingfield, Surrey, RH7 6NJ
Tel: 01342 870260   Fax: 01342 871672
Email: warden@collegeofstbarnabas.com
Website: www.st-barnabas.org.uk

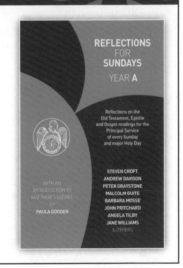

PBS
Prayer Book Society

THE PRAYER BOOK SOCIETY is a charity whose members represent a wide diversity of background, tradition and churchmanship, united by a determination to promote and preserve the use of the 1662 Book of Common Prayer for this and future generations.

Our many activities include:

- Forging links with and between clergy and churches
- Supporting clergy and laity
- Publishing books on relevant topics
- Promoting the prestigious Cranmer Awards for young people

Members receive five magazines a year and are invited to the annual residential conference featuring high calibre speakers from religious backgrounds, the media and the arts.

**Please contact Ian Woodhead on 01380 870384
or join online at www.pbs.org.uk**

The Prayer Book Society: Reg Charity No. 1099295;
Co. Limited by Guarantee No. 4786973; IOM Charity No 952

 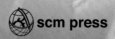

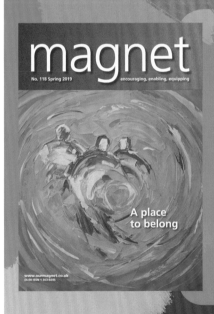

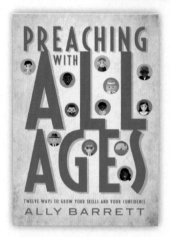
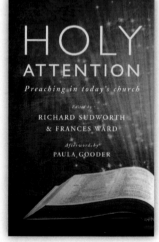
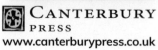

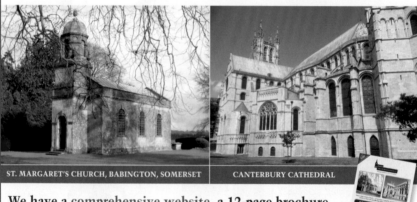

THE CANTERBURY
CHURCH
BOOK&
DESK DIARY
2020

including references for the Calendar, Lectionary and Collects for Year A

Name:..

Address:..

....

....

Telephone: ....

CANTERBURY
PRESS
Norwich

Canterbury Press Norwich, 13A Hellesdon Park Road, Norwich NR6 5DR

Canterbury Press Norwich is an imprint of Hymns Ancient and Modern Limited.
Registered Charity No. 270060

Acknowledgements

The Revised Common Lectionary is copyright © the Consultation on Common Texts,
1992 and is reproduced with permission. The Church of England's adapted form of
The Revised Common Lectionary, published as the Principal Service Lectionary in
Common Worship: Services and Prayers for the Church of England, the Second and
Third Service Lectionaries and the *Common Worship* Calendar, also published in the
same publication, and the Lectionaries for Certain Lesser Festivals, Common of the
Saints and Special Occasions, published in the annual *Common Worship Lectionary*,
are copyright ©The Archbishops' Council of the Church of England, 1995, 1997. The
Common Worship Weekday Lectionary is copyright ©The Archbishops' Council,
2005. The authorized amendments to the *Common Worship* calendar for use with
the *Book of Common Prayer* are copyright © The Archbishops' Council, 2000.
Material from these works is reproduced with permission.

Extracts from The Book of Common Prayer, the rights in which are invested in
the Crown, are reproduced by permission of the Crown's Patentee, Cambridge
University Press.

The sunset/sunrise times, based on the Cambridge area denoted on the first day of
each week, are reproduced with permission from data supplied by H.M. Nautical
Almanac Office. © Council for the Central Laboratory of the Research Councils.

Details of organisations and of office holders in the Church of England, the
Church in Wales, the Scottish Episcopal Church and the Church in Ireland, and of
other Churches and Provinces of the Anglican Communion, are reproduced with
permission from Crockfords Clerical Directory online and the various diocesan
websites.

Parochial Fees are reproduced with permission of the Church Commissioners.

First published 1983

© Compilation, *Canterbury Press Norwich 2019*

ISBN
Hardback edition: 978 1 78622 144 5
A5 Personal organiser: 978 1 78622 145 2

Printed and bound by CPI Group (UK) Ltd, Croydon, CR0 4YY

CONTENTS

PUBLISHER'S NOTE

1. The information given in the diary and pre-diary section is believed to be correct at the time of going to press in April 2019. Subsequently some vacancies will have been filled and new appointments made.
2. Following the final approval by General Synod in February 2000 of the *Common Worship* prayer book from Advent Sunday 2000 we have included the references for the appropriate Year A. CW references are laid out **Principal Service, Third Service, Second Service** so that they more appropriately link up with **Holy Communion, Morning Prayer** and **Evening Prayer** of the BCP prayer book 1928 which is also included. Some brief but important extra notes appear on page 25 and CW tables of Saints and Collect Readings appear on pp 28–33.
3. Principal Feasts and other Principal Holy Days are printed in **BOLD UPPER CASE**; Festivals are printed in *larger bold italic*; Lesser Festivals are printed in ordinary roman text typeface; and Commemorations are printed in ordinary *italic* text typeface.
4. For all dioceses in England (pp 8–13), Scotland, Wales and Ireland (pp 14–15) a postal address for either a Diocesan Office or Centre is included, together with a telephone number and website which will provide contact details for relevant departments and personnel. For overseas dioceses (pp 15–18) postal addresses are given for provincial offices, with a telephone number and website where possible.
5. The publisher welcomes suggestions for improvements to the diary and will consider those which are both practical and useful.

Calendar 2019

	JANUARY	FEBRUARY	MARCH	APRIL
Sun.	· 6 13 20 27 ·	· 3 10 17 24 ·	· 3 10 17 24 31	· 7 14 21 28 ·
Mon.	· 7 14 21 28 ·	· 4 11 18 25 ·	· 4 11 18 25 ·	1 8 15 22 29 ·
Tue.	1 8 15 22 29 ·	· 5 12 19 26 ·	· 5 12 19 26 ·	2 9 16 23 30 ·
Wed.	2 9 16 23 30 ·	· 6 13 20 27 ·	· 6 13 20 27 ·	3 10 17 24 · ·
Thu.	3 10 17 24 31	· 7 14 21 28 ·	· 7 14 21 28 ·	4 11 18 25 · ·
Fri.	4 11 18 25 · ·	1 8 15 22 · ·	1 8 15 22 29 ·	5 12 19 26 · ·
Sat.	5 12 19 26 · ·	2 9 16 23 · ·	2 9 16 23 30 ·	6 13 20 27 · ·

	MAY	JUNE	JULY	AUGUST
Sun.	· 5 12 19 26 ·	· 2 9 16 23 30	· 7 14 21 28 ·	· 4 11 18 25 ·
Mon.	· 6 13 20 27 ·	· 3 10 17 24 ·	1 8 15 22 29 ·	· 5 12 19 26 ·
Tue.	· 7 14 21 28 ·	· 4 11 18 25 ·	2 9 16 23 30 ·	· 6 13 20 27 ·
Wed.	1 8 15 22 29 ·	· 5 12 19 26 ·	3 10 17 24 31 ·	· 7 14 21 28 ·
Thu.	2 9 16 23 30 ·	· 6 13 20 27 ·	4 11 18 25 · ·	1 8 15 22 29 ·
Fri.	3 10 17 24 31 ·	· 7 14 21 28 ·	5 12 19 26 · ·	2 9 16 23 30 ·
Sat.	4 11 18 25 · ·	1 8 15 22 29 ·	6 13 20 27 · ·	3 10 17 24 31 ·

	SEPTEMBER	OCTOBER	NOVEMBER	DECEMBER
Sun.	1 8 15 22 29 ·	· 6 13 20 27 ·	· 3 10 17 24 ·	1 8 15 22 29 ·
Mon.	2 9 16 23 30 ·	· 7 14 21 28 ·	· 4 11 18 25 ·	2 9 16 23 30 ·
Tue.	3 10 17 24 · ·	1 8 15 22 29 ·	· 5 12 19 26 ·	3 10 17 24 31 ·
Wed.	4 11 18 25 · ·	2 9 16 23 30 ·	· 6 13 20 27 ·	4 11 18 25 · ·
Thu.	5 12 19 26 · ·	3 10 17 24 31 ·	· 7 14 21 28 ·	5 12 19 26 · ·
Fri.	6 13 20 27 · ·	4 11 18 25 · ·	1 8 15 22 29 ·	6 13 20 27 · ·
Sat.	7 14 21 28 · ·	5 12 19 26 · ·	2 9 16 23 30 ·	7 14 21 28 · ·

Calendar 2021 (See pages 501–512 for 2021 Forward Planner and back endpapers for 2022)

	JANUARY	FEBRUARY	MARCH	APRIL
Sun.	· 3 10 17 24 31	· 7 14 21 28 ·	· 7 14 21 28	· 4 11 18 25 ·
Mon.	· 4 11 18 25 ·	1 8 15 22 · ·	1 8 15 22 29 ·	· 5 12 19 26 ·
Tue.	· 5 12 19 26 ·	2 9 16 23 · ·	2 9 16 23 30 ·	· 6 13 20 27 ·
Wed.	· 6 13 20 27 ·	3 10 17 24 · ·	3 10 17 24 31 ·	· 7 14 21 28 ·
Thu.	· 7 14 21 28 ·	4 11 18 25 · ·	4 11 18 25 · ·	1 8 15 22 29 ·
Fri.	1 8 15 22 29 ·	5 12 19 26 · ·	5 12 19 26 · ·	2 9 16 23 30 ·
Sat.	2 9 16 23 30 ·	6 13 20 27 · ·	6 13 20 27 · ·	3 10 17 24 · ·

	MAY	JUNE	JULY	AUGUST
Sun.	· 2 9 16 23 30	· 6 13 20 27 ·	· 4 11 18 25 ·	1 8 15 22 29 ·
Mon.	· 3 10 17 24 31	· 7 14 21 28 ·	· 5 12 19 26 ·	2 9 16 23 30 ·
Tue.	· 4 11 18 25 ·	1 8 15 22 29 ·	· 6 13 20 27 ·	3 10 17 24 31 ·
Wed.	· 5 12 19 26 ·	2 9 16 23 30 ·	· 7 14 21 28 ·	4 11 18 25 · ·
Thu.	· 6 13 20 27 ·	3 10 17 24 · ·	1 8 15 22 29 ·	5 12 19 26 · ·
Fri.	· 7 14 21 28 ·	4 11 18 25 · ·	2 9 16 23 30 ·	6 13 20 27 · ·
Sat.	1 8 15 22 29 ·	5 12 19 26 · ·	3 10 17 24 31 ·	7 14 21 28 · ·

	SEPTEMBER	OCTOBER	NOVEMBER	DECEMBER
Sun.	· 5 12 19 26 ·	· 3 10 17 24 31	· 7 14 21 28 ·	· 5 12 19 26 ·
Mon.	· 6 13 20 27 ·	· 4 11 18 25 ·	1 8 15 22 29 ·	· 6 13 20 27 ·
Tue.	· 7 14 21 28 ·	· 5 12 19 26 ·	2 9 16 23 30 ·	· 7 14 21 28 ·
Wed.	1 8 15 22 29 ·	· 6 13 20 27 ·	3 10 17 24 · ·	1 8 15 22 29 ·
Thu.	2 9 16 23 30 ·	· 7 14 21 28 ·	4 11 18 25 · ·	2 9 16 23 30 ·
Fri.	3 10 17 24 · ·	1 8 15 22 29 ·	5 12 19 26 · ·	3 10 17 24 31 ·
Sat.	4 11 18 25 · ·	2 9 16 23 30 ·	6 13 20 27 · ·	4 11 18 25 · ·

Calendar 2020

	JANUARY					
Sun.	·	5	12	19	26	·
Mon.	·	6	13	20	27	·
Tue.	·	7	14	21	28	·
Wed.	1	8	15	22	29	·
Thu.	2	9	16	23	30	·
Fri.	3	10	17	24	31	·
Sat.	4	11	18	25	·	·

	FEBRUARY					
Sun.	·	2	9	16	23	·
Mon.	·	3	10	17	24	·
Tue.	·	4	11	18	25	·
Wed.	·	5	12	19	26	·
Thu.	·	6	13	20	27	·
Fri.	·	7	14	21	28	·
Sat.	1	8	15	22	29	·

	MARCH					
Sun.	1	8	15	22	29	
Mon.	2	9	16	23	30	·
Tue.	3	10	17	24	31	·
Wed.	4	11	18	25	·	·
Thu.	5	12	19	26	·	·
Fri.	6	13	20	27	·	·
Sat.	7	14	21	28	·	·

	APRIL					
Sun.	·	5	12	19	26	·
Mon.	·	6	13	20	27	·
Tue.	·	7	14	21	28	·
Wed.	1	8	15	22	29	·
Thu.	2	9	16	23	30	·
Fri.	3	10	17	24	·	·
Sat.	4	11	18	25	·	·

	MAY					
Sun.	·	3	10	17	24	31
Mon.	·	4	11	18	25	·
Tue.	·	5	12	19	26	·
Wed.	·	6	13	20	27	·
Thu.	·	7	14	21	28	·
Fri.	1	8	15	22	29	·
Sat.	2	9	16	23	30	·

	JUNE					
Sun.	·	7	14	21	28	·
Mon.	1	8	15	22	29	·
Tue.	2	9	16	23	30	·
Wed.	3	10	17	24	·	·
Thu.	4	11	18	25	·	·
Fri.	5	12	19	26	·	·
Sat.	6	13	20	27	·	·

	JULY					
Sun.	·	5	12	19	26	·
Mon.	·	6	13	20	27	·
Tue.	·	7	14	21	28	·
Wed.	1	8	15	22	29	·
Thu.	2	9	16	23	30	·
Fri.	3	10	17	24	31	·
Sat.	4	11	18	25	·	·

	AUGUST					
Sun.	·	2	9	16	23	30
Mon.	·	3	10	17	24	31
Tue.	·	4	11	18	25	·
Wed.	·	5	12	19	26	·
Thu.	·	6	13	20	27	·
Fri.	·	7	14	21	28	·
Sat.	1	8	15	22	29	·

	SEPTEMBER					
Sun.	·	6	13	20	27	·
Mon.	·	7	14	21	28	·
Tue.	1	8	15	22	29	·
Wed.	2	9	16	23	30	·
Thu.	3	10	17	24	·	·
Fri.	4	11	18	25	·	·
Sat.	5	12	19	26	·	·

	OCTOBER					
Sun.	·	4	11	18	25	·
Mon.	·	5	12	19	26	·
Tue.	·	6	13	20	27	·
Wed.	·	7	14	21	28	·
Thu.	1	8	15	22	29	·
Fri.	2	9	16	23	30	·
Sat.	3	10	17	24	31	·

	NOVEMBER					
Sun.	1	8	15	22	29	·
Mon.	2	9	16	23	30	·
Tue.	3	10	17	24	·	·
Wed.	4	11	18	25	·	·
Thu.	5	12	19	26	·	·
Fri.	6	13	20	27	·	·
Sat.	7	14	21	28	·	·

	DECEMBER					
Sun.	·	6	13	20	27	·
Mon.	·	7	14	21	28	·
Tue.	1	8	15	22	29	·
Wed.	2	9	16	23	30	·
Thu.	3	10	17	24	31	·
Fri.	4	11	18	25	·	·
Sat.	5	12	19	26	·	·

MOVEABLE FEASTS AND FASTS

2019

Advent Sunday	December 1

2020

Baptism of Christ	January 12
Septuagesima (Third Sunday before Lent)	February 9
Ash Wednesday	February 26
First Sunday of Lent	March 1
Fourth Sunday of Lent (Mothering Sunday)	March 22
Palm Sunday	April 5
Maundy Thursday	April 9
Good Friday	April 10
Easter Day	April 12
Ascension Day	May 21
Pentecost (Whit-Sunday)	May 31
Trinity Sunday	June 7
Fourth Sunday before Advent	November 1
Advent Sunday	November 29

GENERAL SYNOD OF THE CHURCH OF ENGLAND
Church House, Great Smith Street, London SW1P 3NZ. *Tel:* 020 7898 1000

OFFICERS

Presidents: The Archbishop of Canterbury and The Archbishop of York

Prolocutor of the Lower House of the Convocation of Canterbury: Rev. Canon Simon Butler

Prolocutor of the Lower House of the Convocation of York: Ven. Cherry Vann

Secretary-General: William Nye

Clerk to the Synod: Dr Jacqui Philips

Chief Legal Adviser and Joint Registrar of the Provinces of Canterbury and York (Registrar of the General Synod): Rev. Alexander McGregor

Standing Counsel: Christopher Packer

Officers of the Convocations

Synodical Secretary of the Convocation of Canterbury: Rev. Stephen Trott

Synodal Secretary of the Convocation of York: Rev. Paul Benfield

Administrative Secretary, House of Bishops: Mr William Nye. *Tel:* 020 7898 1361
email: william.nye@churchofengland.org

Secretary, House of Clergy: Mr Jonathan Neil-Smith. *Tel:* 020 7898 1373
email: jonathan.neil-smith@churchofengland.org.uk

Secretary, House of Laity: Mr Andrew Brown, *Tel:* 020 7898 1374
email: andrewj.brown@churchofengland.org

COMPOSITION OF THE GENERAL SYNOD

	Canterbury	York	Either Province	Totals
House of Bishops .... Diocesan and Suffragan Bishops	37	16		53
House of Clergy Deans, Service Chaplains and Chaplain-General of Prisons, Elected Proctors and Dean of Guernsey or Jersey, University Proctors, Religious Communities and Co-opted places	141	61	4	206
House of Laity .... Elected Laity, Religious Communities, Lay Armed Services, Co-opted places, Ex-officio (First and Second Church Estate Commissioners)	136	59	12	207
Either House of Bishops, **House of Clergy or House of Laity** .... Ex-officio: Dean of the Arches, the two Vicars General, Third Church Estates Commissioner and the Chairman of the Pensions Board and six Appointed Members of the Archbishops' Council	4	1	7	12
Maximum totals	318	137	23	478

Eight representatives of other Churches have been appointed to the Synod under its Standing Orders with speaking but not voting rights.

SESSIONS OF GENERAL SYNOD
Projected dates for 2020

LONDON	Monday 10 February – Saturday 15 February
YORK	Friday 10 July – Tuesday 14 July
LONDON	Monday 23 November – Wednesday 25 November

(subject to confirmation)

PROVINCES OF CANTERBURY AND YORK

BATH AND WELLS

BISHOP: Rt Rev. Peter Hancock, The Palace, Wells, Somerset BA5 2PD [2014]

Suffragan Bishop—**Taunton:** Rt Rev. Ruth Worsley

Assistant Bishops: Rt Rev. W. Persson, Rt Rev. P. Barber, Rt Rev. B. Rogerson, Rt Rev. R. Sainsbury, Rt Rev. G. Cassidy, Rt Rev. J. Perry, Rt Rev. B. C. Castle; Rt Rev. J. Goodall (PEV)

Archdeacons—**Wells:** Ven. A. Gell
   Bath: Ven. A. Youings **Taunton:** Ven. S. J. Hill

Cathedral Church of St Andrew in Wells
Dean: Very Rev. Dr J. Davies
Canons Residentiary: Canon N. Jepson-Biddle, Canon R. Paul, Vacancy, Ven. A. Gell

Organist: Mr M. Owens

Diocesan Office: The Old Deanery, Wells, Somerset BA5 2UG *Tel:* 01749 670777
website: www.bathandwells.org.uk

BIRMINGHAM

BISHOP: Rt Rev. David Urquhart, Bishop's Croft, Old Church Road, Harborne, Birmingham B17 0BG [2006]

Suffragan Bishop—**Aston:** Rt Rev. Anne Hollinghurst

Hon. Assistant Bishops: Rt Rev. M. W. Sinclair, Rt Rev. M. Santer, Rt Rev. I. Mottahedeh; Rt Rev. J. Goodall, Rt Rev. R. Thomas (PEVs)

Archdeacons—**Aston:** Ven. S. Heathfield
   Birmingham: Ven J. Tomlinson

Cathedral Church of St Philip
Dean: Very Rev. M. Thompson, Birmingham Cathedral, Colmore Row, Birmingham B3 2QB
Canons Residentiary: Canon N. Hand, Canon J. Houghton

Director of Music: Mr D. Hardie

Diocesan Office: 1 Colmore Row, Birmingham B3 2BJ
Tel: 0121 426 0400
website: www.cofebirmingham.com

BLACKBURN

BISHOP: Rt Rev. Julian Henderson, Bishop's House, Ribchester Road, Clayton-le-Dale, Blackburn, Lancs BB1 9EF [2013]

Suffragan Bishops—**Lancaster:** Rt Rev. Jillian Duff
   Burnley: Rt Rev. Philip North CMP

Assistant Bishops: Rt Rev. C. G. Ashton

Archdeacons: **Blackburn:** Ven. M. C. Ireland
   Lancaster: Ven. M. Everitt

Cathedral Church of St Mary the Virgin
Dean: Very Rev. P. Howell-Jones
Canons Residentiary: Canon A. Horsfall, Rt Rev. P. North, Canon R. Pailing

Director of Music: Mr S. Hudson

Diocesan Office: Clayton House, Walker Office Park, Blackburn BB1 2QE; *Tel:* 01254 503070
website: www.blackburn.anglican.org

BRISTOL

BISHOP: Rt Rev. Vivienne Faull, Bishop's Office, Church Lane, Winterbourne, Bristol BS36 1SG
Tel: (01454) 777728 [2018]

Suffragan Bishop—**Swindon:** Rt Rev. Dr Lee Rayfield

Assistant Bishops: Rt Rev. P. J. Firth, Rt Rev. P. St G. Vaughan; Rt Rev. J. Goodall, Rt Rev. R. Thomas (PEVs)

Archdeacon—**Bristol:** Ven N. Warwick
   Malmesbury: Ven. C. Bryan

Cathedral Church of the Holy and Undivided Trinity
Dean: Very Rev. Dr D. Hoyle *Office:* 0117 926 4879
Canons Residentiary: Canon N. Stanley, Canon M. Roden

Organist: Mr M. Lee

Diocesan Office: First Floor, Hillside House, 1500 Parkway North, Newbrick Road, Stoke Gifford, Bristol BS34 8YU *Tel:* 0117 906 0100
website: www.bristol.anglican.org

CANTERBURY

ARCHBISHOP: Most Rev. and Rt Hon. Justin Welby, Primate of all England and Metropolitan, Lambeth Palace, London SE1 7JU and Old Palace, Canterbury, Kent CT1 2EE [2012]

CHIEF OF STAFF: Mr D. Porter *Tel:* 020 7898 1223 (for provincial and communion matters)

Bishop at Lambeth: Rt Rev. T. Thornton

Suffragan Bishops—**Dover:** Vacancy (for all diocesan matters)

Hon. Assistant Bishops: Rt Rev. M. Gear, Rt Rev. R. Llewellin, Rt Rev. A. M. Turnbull

Archdeacons—**Canterbury:** Ven. J. Kelly-Moore
   Maidstone: Ven. S. Taylor **Ashford:** Ven. D. Miller

Provincial Episcopal Visitors—**Ebbsfleet:** Rt Rev. J. Goodall
   Richborough: Rt Rev. N. Banks
   Maidstone: Rt Rev. R. Thomas

Cathedral and Metropolitical Church of Christ
Dean: Very Rev. R. Willis *Office:* 01227 762862
Canons Residentiary: Ven. J. Kelly-Moore, Canon T. Naish, Canon E. Pennington

Organist: Dr D. Flood

Diocesan Office: Diocesan House, Lady Wootton's Green, Canterbury, Kent CT1 1NQ *Tel:* 01227 459401
website: www.canterburydiocese.org

CARLISLE

BISHOP: Rt Rev. James Newcome, Bishop's House, Ambleside Road, Keswick CA12 4DD [2009]

Suffragan Bishop—**Penrith:** Rt Rev. Emma Ineson

Hon. Assistant Bishops: Rt Rev. I. M. Griggs, Rt Rev. G. L. Hacker, Rt Rev. A. A. K. Graham, Rt Rev. H. Thompson, Rt Rev. R. Hardy, Rt Rev. J. Richardson, Rt Rev. P. S. Ramsden, Rt Rev. N. McCulloch, Rt Rev. C. Ashton, Rt Rev. J. Bell

Archdeacons—**Carlisle:** Ven. L. Townend
   West Cumberland: Ven. R. Pratt
   Westmorland and Furness: Ven. V. Ross

Cathedral Church of the Holy and Undivided Trinity
Dean: Very Rev. Mark Boyling *Office:* 01228 548151
Canons Residentiary: Canon M. A. Manley, Canon J. Kearton, Canon P. Clement

Director of Music: Mr M. Duthie

Diocesan Office: Church House, 19–24 Friargate, Penrith, Cumbria CA11 7XR *Tel:* 01768 807777
website: www.carlislediocese.org.uk

CHELMSFORD

BISHOP: Rt Rev. S. Cottrell, Bishopscourt, Margaretting, Ingatestone CM4 0HD [2010]

Area Bishops—**Barking:** Rt Rev. P. Hill
   Bradwell: Rt Rev. J. Perumbalath
   Colchester: Rt Rev. R. Morris

Hon. Assistant Bishops: Rt Rev. M. T. S. Mwamba, Rt Rev. R. Thomas, Rt Rev. N. Banks (PEVs)

Archdeacons—**Colchester:** Ven. R. Patten
   Harlow: Ven. V. Herrick **West Ham:** Ven. E. W. Cockett
   Barking: Ven. C. Burke **Southend:** Ven. M. Lodge
   Stansted: Ven. R. L. C. King
   Chelmsford: Ven. E. Snowden

Cathedral Church of St Mary the Virgin, St Peter and St Cedd
Dean: Very Rev. N. Henshall *Office:* (01245) 294489
Canons Residentiary: Canon I. Moody, Canon A. Kennedy, Vacancy

Director of Music: Mr J. Davy

Diocesan Office: 53 New Street, Chelmsford, Essex CM1 1AT *Tel:* 01245 294400
website: www.chelmsford.anglican.org

CHESTER

BISHOP: Rt Rev. Dr Peter Forster, Bishop's House, Abbey Square, Chester CH1 2JD [1996]

*Suffragan Bishops—***Birkenhead:** Rt Rev. Keith Sinclair **Stockport:** Vacancy

Hon. Assistant Bishops: Rt Rev. W. A. Pwaisiho, Rt Rev. C. F. Bazeley, Rt Rev. J. Hayden, Rt Rev. G. Dow, Rt Rev. A. L. Winstanley; Rt Rev. G. Webster, Rt Rev. R. Thomas (PEVs)

*Archdeacons—***Chester:** Ven. M. Gilbertson **Macclesfield:** Ven. I. G. Bishop

Cathedral Church of Christ and the Blessed Virgin Mary
Dean: Very Rev. T. Stratford *Office:* (01244) 324756
Canons Residentiary: Canon J. Brooke, Canon J. Dussek

Director of Music: Mr P. Rushforth

Diocesan Office: Church House, 5500 Daresbury Park, Daresbury, Warrington WA4 4GE *Tel:* 01928 718834
website: www.chester.anglican.org

CHICHESTER

BISHOP: Rt Rev. Dr M. Warner, The Palace, Chichester, West Sussex PO19 1PY [2012]

*Area Bishops—***Horsham:** Rt Rev. M. Sowerby **Lewes:** Rt Rev. R. Jackson

Hon. Assistant Bishops: Rt Rev. K. L. Barham, Rt Rev. A. D. Chesters, Rt Rev. L. A. Green, Rt Rev. C. H. Morgan, Rt Rev. N. S. Reade, Rt Rev. M. L. Langrish, Rt Rev. D. P. Wilcox, Rt Rev. P. Wheatley

*Archdeacons—***Chichester:** Vacancy
Brighton and Lewes: Ven. M. C. Lloyd Williams
Horsham: Ven. J. F. Windsor
Hastings: Ven. R. E. M. Dowler

Cathedral Church of the Holy Trinity
Dean: Very Rev. S. Waine *Office:* (01243) 782595
Canons: Canon N. T. Schofield, Canon S. Ferns, Vacancy

Organist: Mr C. Harrison

Diocesan Office: Diocesan Church House, 211 New Church Road, Hove, East Sussex BN3 4ED *Tel:* 01273 421021
website: www.chichester.anglican.org

COVENTRY

BISHOP: Rt Rev. Dr Christopher Cocksworth, Bishop's House, 23 Davenport Road, Coventry CV5 6PW [2008]

*Suffragan Bishop—***Warwick:** Rt Rev. John Stroyan

Hon Assistant Bishops: Rt Rev. D. R. J. Evans; Rt Rev. Jonathan Goodall (PEV)

*Archdeacons—***Coventry:** Ven. S. Field
Warwick: Ven. M. Rodham

Cathedral Church of St Michael

Dean: Very Rev. John Witcombe *Office:* (024) 7652 1200

Canons Residentiary: Canon D. A. Stone, Canon K. C. Fleming, Vacancy

Director of Music: Mr K. Beaumont

Diocesan Office: 1 Hill Top, Coventry CV1 5AB
Tel: 024 7652 1200
website: www.coventry.anglican.org

DERBY

BISHOP: Rt Rev. Elizabeth Lane, The Bishop's House, 6 King Street, Duffield, Derby DE56 4EU [2019]

*Suffragan Bishop—***Repton:** Rt Rev. Janet McFarlane

Hon. Assistant Bishops: Rt Rev. J. Nicholls, Rt Rev. R. Inwood

*Archdeacons—***Chesterfield:** Ven. C. Coslett
Derby: Ven. Dr C. J. Cunliffe

Cathedral Church of All Saints
Dean: Very Rev. Stephen Hance *Office:* (01332) 341201
Canons Residentiary: Canon R. Andrews, Canon E. Thomson, Canon S. Taylor

Master of Music and Organist: Mr. E Turner (acting)

Diocesan Office: Derby Church House, 1 Full Street, Derby DE1 3DR *Tel:* 01332 388650
website: www.derby.anglican.org

DURHAM

BISHOP: Rt Rev. Paul Butler, Auckland Castle, Bishop Auckland, Co. Durham DL14 7QJ [2014]

*Suffragan Bishop—***Jarrow:** Rt Rev. Sarah Clark

Hon. Assistant Bishops: Rt Rev. J. L. Pritchard, Rt Rev. D. S. Stancliffe; Rt Rev. G. H. Webster (PEV)

*Archdeacons—***Durham:** Vacancy
Auckland: Ven. R. Simpson **Sunderland:** Ven. R. Cooper

Cathedral Church of Christ and Blessed Mary the Virgin, and St Cuthbert of Durham
Dean: Very Rev. A. Tremlett *Office:* (0191) 384 7500
Canons Residentiary: Canon Prof. S. Oliver, Canon S. Jelley, Canon C. Allen, Canon M. Hampel

Organist: Mr D. Cook

Diocesan Office: Cuthbert House, Stonebridge, Durham DH1 3RY *Tel:* 01388 604515
email: diocesan.office@durham.anglican.org
website: www.durhamdiocese.org

ELY

BISHOP: Rt Rev. Stephen Conway, The Bishop's House, Ely, Cambs CB7 4DW [2010]

*Suffragan Bishop—***Huntingdon:** Vacancy

Hon. Assistant Bishops. Rt Rev. S. Barrington-Ward, Rt Rev. P. Dawes, Rt Rev. and Rt Hon Lord Williams of Oystermouth, Rt Rev. G. Knowles, Rt Rev. M. A. Seeley; Rt Rev. N. Banks (PEV)

*Archdeacons—***Cambridge:** Ven. A. J. Hughes
Huntingdon and Wisbech: Ven. H. K. McCurdy

Cathedral Church of the Holy and Undivided Trinity
Dean: Very Rev. M. Bonney *Office:* (01353) 667735
Canons Residentiary: Canon V. L. Johnson, Canon J. H. Martin, Canon J. Garrard

Director of Music: Mr E. Aldhouse

Diocesan Office: Bishop Woodford House, Barton Road, Ely, Cambs CB7 4DX *Tel:* 01353 652701
website: www.elydiocese.org

EUROPE

BISHOP OF GIBRALTAR IN EUROPE:
Rt Rev. R. Innes, 47 rue Capitaine Crespel – boite 49, 1050 Brussels, Belgium [2014]

*Suffragan Bishop—*Rt Rev. D. Hamid

Hon. Assistant Bishops: Rt Rev. J. Flack, Rt Rev. M. Colclough, Rt Rev. R. Garrard, Rt Rev. E. Holland, Rt Rev. D. S. Stancliffe, Rt Rev. D. J. Smith, Rt Rev. N. S. Reade, Rt Rev. S. Venner, Rt Rev. P. Whalon, Rt Rev. H. Rein, Rt Rev. J. Tavares de Pina Cabral, Rt Rev. M Turnbull, Rt Rev. M. Wharton; Rt Rev. N. Banks (PEV)

*Archdeacons—***Eastern Archdeaconry:** (Acting) Ven. A. Kelham **Germany and Northern Europe:** (Acting) Revd. J. Newsome **North West Europe:** Ven. P. D. Vrolijk **France:** Ven. M. Williams **Gibraltar and (Acting) Italy and Malta:** Ven. G. S. Johnston **Switzerland:** Ven. A. Kelham

Cathedral Church of the Holy Trinity, Gibraltar
Dean: Vacancy *Office:* (00 350) 2007 5745

Pro-Cathedral of St Paul Valletta, Malta
Dean: Canon S. H. M. Godfrey *Office:* 00 356 2122 5714

Pro-Cathedral of the Holy Trinity Brussels
Dean: Ven. P. D. Vrolijk *Office:* 02 511 7183

Diocesan Office: 14 Tufton Street, London SW1P 3QZ
Tel: 020 7898 1155
website: www.europe.anglican.org

EXETER

BISHOP Rt Rev. Robert Atwell, The Palace, Exeter, Devon EX1 1HY [2014]

Suffragan Bishops—**Crediton:** Rt Rev. Jacqueline Searle
Plymouth: Rt Rev. Nicholas McKinnel

Hon. Assistant Bishops: Rt Rev. R. S. Hawkins,
Rt Rev. A. M. Shaw, Rt Rev. M Rylands;
Rt Rev. J. Goodall (PEV)

Archdeacons—**Exeter:** Ven A. Beane
Plymouth: Ven. I. N. Chandler
Barnstaple: Ven. M. A. Butchers
Totnes: Ven. D. J. Dettmer

Cathedral Church of St Peter
Dean: Very Rev. J. Greener *Office:* (01392) 273509
Canons Residentiary: Canon J. Mustard,
Canon M. Williams, Canon B. Totterdell,
Canon C. Palmer

Director of Music: Mr T. Noon

Diocesan Office: The Old Deanery, The Cloisters, Exeter
EX1 1HS *Tel:* 01392 272686
website: www.exeter.anglican.org

GLOUCESTER

BISHOP: Rt Rev. Rachel Treweek, Church House,
College Green, Gloucester GL1 2LY [2015]

Suffragan Bishop—**Tewkesbury:** Rt Rev. Robert Springett

Hon. Assistant Bishops: Rt Rev. R. Evens,
Rt Rev. J. Priddis, Rt Rev. D. Jennings, Rt Rev. C. Hill,
Rt Rev. P. Harris, Rt Rev. P. J. Firth, Rt Rev. J. R. G. Neale

Archdeacons—**Gloucester:** Ven. H. Dawson
Cheltenham: Ven. P. Andrew

Cathedral Church of St Peter and the Holy and Indivisible Trinity
Dean: Very Rev. Stephen Lake *Office:* (01452) 528095
Canons Residentiary: Canon N. M. Arthy,
Canon C. S. M. Thomson, Canon A. J. Braddock,
Ven. H. Dawson; Canon R. Mitchell

Director of Music: Mr A. Partington

Diocesan Office: Church House, College Green,
Gloucester GL1 2LY *Tel:* 01452 410022
website: www.gloucester.anglican.org.

GUILDFORD

BISHOP: Rt Rev. Andrew Watson, Willow Grange,
Woking Road, Guildford, Surrey GU4 7QS [2014]

Suffragan Bishop—**Dorking:** Rt Rev. Jo Bailey Wells

Hon. Assistant Bishops: Rt Rev. C. W. Herbert,
Rt Rev. M. A. Baughen; Rt Rev. N. Banks (PEV)

Archdeacons—**Surrey:** Ven. P. Davies
Dorking: Vacancy

Cathedral Church of the Holy Spirit
Dean: Very Rev. D. L. Gwilliams *Office:* (01483) 547860
Canons Residentiary: Canon P. Smith, Canon J. Gittoes,
Ven. S. Beake

Master of Choristers and Cathedral Organist:
Mrs K. Dienes-Williams

Diocesan Office: Church House, 20 Alan Turing Road,
Guildford GU2 7YF *Tel:* 01483 790300
website: www.cofeguildford.org.uk

HEREFORD

BISHOP: Rt Rev. Richard Frith, The Bishop's House,
Hereford HR4 9BN [2014]

Suffragan Bishop—**Ludlow:** Rt Rev. Alistair Magowan

Hon. Assistant Bishops: Rt Rev. M. Bourke,
Rt Rev. R. Paterson, Rt Rev. M. Westall

Archdeacons—**Hereford:** Ven. D. C. Chedzey
Ludlow: Rt Rev. A. J. Magowan

Cathedral Church of the Blessed Virgin Mary and St Ethelbert
Dean: Very Rev. M. E. Tavinor *Office:* (01432) 374201
Canons Residentiary: Canon A. Piper, Canon C. Pullin

Organist and Director of Music: Mr G. Bowen

Diocesan Office: The Palace, Hereford HR4 9BL
Tel: 01432 374200
website: www.hereford.anglican.org

LEEDS

Bishop of Leeds: Rt Rev. Nicholas Baines, Hollin House,
Weetwood Avenue, Leeds LS16 5NG [2014]

Area Suffragan Bishops: **Bradford:** Rt Rev. Toby Howarth
Ripon: Rt Rev. Dr Helen-Ann Hartley
Huddersfield: Rt Rev. Jonathan Gibbs
Wakefield: Rt Rev. Anthony Robinson
Kirkstall: Rt Rev. Paul Slater

Hon. Assistant Bishops: Rt Rev. C. O. Buchanan,
Rt Rev. J. Flack, Rt Rev. C. Handford, Rt Rev. T. Butler,
Rt Rev. C. P. Edmondson, Rt Rev. D. Hawkins;
Rt Rev. G. Webster (PEV)

Archdeacons—**Richmond and Craven:** Ven. J. Gough
Bradford: Ven. A. J. Jolley **Leeds:** Ven. P. Ayers
Halifax: Ven. A. F. Dawtry **Pontefract:** Ven. P. K. Townley

Cathedral Church of St Peter (Bradford)
Dean: Very Rev. Jeremy Lepine *Office:* (01274) 777720
Canons Residentiary: Canon P. Maybury, Canon M. Coutts

Organist: Mr A. Berry

Cathedral Church of St Peter and St Wilfrid (Ripon)
Dean: Very Rev. J. Dobson *Office:* (01765) 603462
Canons Residentiary: Canon M. Gisbourne, Canon B. Pyke,
Canon A. Newby

Director of Music: Mr A. Bryden

Cathedral Church of All Saints (Wakefield)
Dean: Very Rev. S. Cowling *Office:* (01924) 373923
Canons Residentiary: Canon D. Walmsley,
Canon Dr J. Lawson, Canon A. Macpherson,
Canon L. Vesey-Saunders

Director of Music: Mr T. Moore

Diocesan Office: 17/19 York Place, Leeds LS1 2EX
Tel: 0113 2000 540
website: www.leeds.anglican.org

LEICESTER

BISHOP: Rt Rev. Martyn Snow, Bishop's Lodge Annexe,
12 Springfield Road, Leicester LE2 3BD [2016]

Suffragan Bishop—
Loughborough: Rt Rev. Guli Francis-Dehkani

Archdeacons—**Leicester:** Ven. R. Worsfold
Loughborough: Ven. C. Wood

Cathedral Church of St Martin
Dean: Very Rev. D. Monteith *Office:* (0116) 261 5200
Canons Residentiary: Canon P. Rattigan, Canon J. Arens,
Canon K. Rooms, Canon A. Adams

Director of Music: Dr C. Ouvry-Johns

Diocesan Office: St Martin's House, 7 Peacock Lane,
Leicester LE1 5PZ *Tel:* 0116 261 5200
website: www.leicester.anglican.org

LICHFIELD

BISHOP: Rt Rev. Michael Ipgrave, Bishop's House,
22 The Close, Lichfield, Staffs WS13 7LG [2016]

Area bishops—**Shrewsbury:** Vacancy
Stafford: Rt Rev. Geoffrey Annas
Wolverhampton: Rt Rev. Clive Gregory

Hon. Assistant Bishops: Rt Rev. D. Bentley,
Rt Rev. I. Mottahedeh; Rt Rev. J. Goodall,
Rt Rev. R. Thomas (PEVs)

Archdeacons—**Lichfield:** Ven. S. N. H. Baker
Stoke-on-Trent: Ven. M. J. Parker
Salop: Ven. P. W. Thomas **Walsall:** Ven. S. Weller

Cathedral Church of the Blessed Virgin Mary and St Chad
Dean: Very Rev. A. J. Dorber *Office:* (01543) 306250
Canons Residentiary: Canon A. Stead, Canon P. Hawkins

Director of Music: Mr B. Lamb

Diocesan Office: St Mary's House, The Close, Lichfield,
Staffs WS13 7LD *Tel:* 01543 306030
website: www.lichfield.anglican.org

LINCOLN

BISHOP: Rt Rev. Christopher Lowson, The Old Palace,
Minster Yard, Lincoln LN2 1PU [2011]

Suffragan Bishops—**Grimsby:** Rt Rev. David Court
Grantham: Rt Rev. Nicholas Chamberlain

Hon. Assistant Bishops: Rt Rev. D. Rossdale,
Rt Rev. T. Ellis, Rt Rev. D. Tustin, the Rt Rev. N. Peyton;
the Rt Rev. N. Banks (PEV)

Archdeacons: **Lincoln:** Ven. G. J. Kirk
Stow and Lindsey: Ven. M. J. Steadman
Boston: Ven. Dr J. P. H. Allain Chapman

Cathedral Church of the Blessed Virgin Mary
Dean: Very Rev. C. Wilson
Canons Residentiary: Canon J. Patrick,
Canon S. McDougall, Canon Dr P. Overend

Director of Music: Mr A. Prentice

Diocesan Office: Edward King House, Minster Yard,
Lincoln LN2 1PU Tel: 01522 504050
website: www.lincoln.anglican.org

LIVERPOOL

BISHOP: Rt Rev. Paul Bayes, Bishop's Lodge, Woolton
Park, Woolton, Liverpool L25 6DT [2014]

Suffragan Bishop—**Warrington:** Rt Rev. Beverley Mason

Hon. Assistant Bishops: Rt Rev. C. Ashton,
Rt Rev. G. Pearson; Rt Rev. G. Webster (PEV)

Archdeacons—**Liverpool:** Ven. M. McGurk
St Helens and Warrington: Ven. R. M. H. Preece
Knowsley and Sefton: Ven. P. H. Spiers
Wigan and West Lancashire: Ven. J. G. McKenzie

Cathedral Church of Christ
Dean: Very Rev. S. Jones Office: (0151) 705 2112
Canons Residentiary: Canon M. C. Davies,
Canon E. Loudon, Canon B. Lewis

Director of Music: Mr L. Ward

Diocesan Office: St James' House, 20 St James Road,
Liverpool L1 7BY Tel: 0151 709 9722
website: www.liverpool.anglican.org

LONDON

BISHOP: Rt Rev. Dame Sarah Mullally, The Old Deanery,
Dean's Court, London EC4V 5AA [2018]

Area Bishops—**Stepney:** Vacancy
Edmonton: Rt Rev. Robert Wickham
Willesden: Rt Rev. Peter Broadbent
Kensington: Rt Rev. Graham Tomlin

Suffragan Bishops— **Fulham:** Rt Rev. Jonathan Baker
Islington: Rt Rev. Richard Thorpe

Hon. Assistant Bishops: Rt Rev. M. Colclough,
Rt Rev. E. Holland, Rt Rev. S. Platten, Rt Rev. R. Ladds,
Rt Rev. W. Makhulu, Rt Rev. M. Marshall, Rt Rev. A.
Millar, Rt Rev. P. Wheatley, Rt Rev. J. Idowu-Fearon,
Rt Rev. M. Wharton, Rt Rev. Lord Harries of Pentregarth;
Rt Rev. R. Thomas (PEV)

Archdeacons—**London:** Ven. L. J. Miller
Charing Cross: Ven. R. Lain-Priestley
Hackney: Ven. E. Adekunle **Middlesex:** Ven. S. J. Welch
Hampstead: Ven. J. E. I. Hawkins
Northolt: Ven. D. J. Green

Cathedral Church of St Paul
Dean: Very Rev. Dr D. J. Ison Office: (020) 7246 8360
Canons Residentiary: Canon P. D. Hillas,
Canon J. Brewster, Canon S. Watson, Dr Paula Gooder

Director of Music: Mr A. Carwood

Diocesan Office: London Diocesan House, 36 Causton
Street, London SW1P 4AU Tel: 020 7932 1100
website: www.london.anglican.org

MANCHESTER

BISHOP: Rt Rev. David Walker, Bishopscourt,
Bury New Road, Manchester M7 4LE [2013]

Suffragan Bishops—**Bolton:** Rt Rev. Mark Ashcroft
Middleton: Rt Rev. Mark Davies

Hon. Assistant Bishops: Rt Rev. J. Nicholls,
Rt Rev. R. W. N. Hoare; Rt Rev. G. Webster (PEV)

Archdeacons—**Manchester:** Ven. K. Lund
Rochdale: Ven. C. E. Vann **Bolton:** Ven. J. Burgess
Salford: Ven. D. J. Sharples

**Cathedral and Collegiate Church of St Mary, St Denys
and St George**
Dean: Very Rev. R. Govender Office: (0161) 833 2220
Canons Residentiary: Canon D. Holgate,
Canon D. Sharples, Canon M. Wall

Organist and Master of the Choristers: Mr C. Stokes

Diocesan Office: Diocesan Church House, 90 Deansgate,
Manchester M3 2GH Tel: 0161 828 1400
website: www.manchester.anglican.org

NEWCASTLE

BISHOP: Rt Rev. Christine Hardman, The Bishop's House,
29 Moor Road South, Newcastle upon Tyne NE3 1PA
[2016]

Suffragan Bishop—**Berwick:** Rt Rev. Mark Tanner

Hon. Assistant Bishops: Rt Rev. S. Pedley,
Rt Rev. S. Platten, Rt Rev. J. Packer,
Rt Rev. J. Richardson; Rt Rev. G. Webster (PEV)

Archdeacons—**Lindisfarne:** Ven. P. J. A. Robinson
Northumberland: Ven. M. Wroe

Cathedral Church of St Nicholas
Dean: Ven. G. V. Miller Office: (0191) 2357554
Canons Residentiary: Canon C. McLaren,
Canon S. Harvey, Ven. M. Wroe

Director of Music: Mr I. Roberts

Diocesan Office: Church House, St John's Terrace,
North Shields NE29 6HS. Tel: 0191 232 1939
website: www.newcastle.anglican.org

NORWICH

BISHOP: Rt Rev. Graham Usher, Bishop's House, Norwich,
Norfolk NR3 1SB [2019]

Suffragan Bishops—**Thetford:** Rt Rev. Alan Winton
Lynn: Rt Rev. Jonathan Meyrick

Hon. Assistant Bishops: Rt Rev. A. Footitt, Rt Rev. P. Fox,
Rt Rev. R. Garrard, Rt Rev. D. Gillett, Rt Rev. D. Leake,
Rt Rev. M. Menin; Rt Rev. R. Thomas, Rt Rev. N. Banks
(PEVs)

Archdeacons—**Norwich:** Ven. K. E. Hutchinson
Lynn: Ven I. Bentley **Norfolk:** Ven. S. Betts

Cathedral Church of the Holy and Undivided Trinity
Dean: Very Rev. J. Hedges Office: (01603 218300)
Canons Residentiary: Canon Dr P. Doll, Canon K. James,
Canon A. W. Bryant, Canon A. Platten

Master of Music: Mr A. Grote

Diocesan Office: Diocesan House, 109 Dereham Rd,
Easton, Norwich, Norfolk NR9 5ES Tel: 01603 880853
website: www.dioceseofnorwich.org

OXFORD

BISHOP: Rt Rev. Steven Croft, Church House Oxford,
Langford Locks, Kidlington OX5 1GF [2016]

Area Bishops—**Reading:** Rt Rev. Andrew. Proud
Buckingham: Rt Rev. Dr Alan Wilson
Dorchester: Rt Rev. Colin Fletcher

Hon. Assistant Bishops: Rt Rev. K. Arnold,
Rt Rev. W. Down, Rt Rev. J. Johnson,
Rt Rev. H. Scriven, Rt Rev. H. Southern,
Rt Rev. J. Went, Rt Rev. D. Jennings;
Rt Rev. J. M. Goodall (PEV)

Archdeacons—**Oxford:** Ven. M. C. W. Gorick
Berkshire: Ven. O. J. Graham
Buckingham: Ven. G. C. Elsmore
Dorchester: Ven. J. D. French

Cathedral Church of Christ
Dean: Very Rev. M. Percy Office: (01865) 286829
Canons Residentiary: Canon E. Newey,
Canon Prof. N. Biggar, Canon S. Foot,
Canon C. Harrison, Canon Prof. G. Ward, Ven. M. Gorick

Organist: Mr. S. Grahl

Diocesan Office: Church House, Langford Locks,
Kidlington OX5 1GF Tel: 01865 208200
website: www.oxford.anglican.org

PETERBOROUGH

BISHOP: Rt Rev. Donald Allister, Bishop's Lodgings,
The Palace, Peterborough, Cambs PE1 1YA [2010]

Suffragan Bishop—**Brixworth:** Rt Rev. John Holbrook

Hon. Assistant Bishop: Rt Rev. J. Flack

Archdeacons—**Northampton:** Ven. R. J. Ormston
Oakham: Ven. G. J. Steele

Cathedral Church of St Peter, St Paul and St Andrew
Dean: Very Rev. C. Dalliston
Canons Residentiary: Canon I. Black, Canon S. Brown,
 Canon T. Alban-Jones, Canon R. Williams

Director of Music: Ms Tansy Castledine

Diocesan Office: The Palace, Peterborough PE1 1YB
 Tel: 01733 887000
 website: www.peterborough-diocese.org.uk

PORTSMOUTH
BISHOP: Rt Rev. Dr Christopher Foster, Bishopsgrove,
 26 Osborn Road, Fareham, Hants PO16 7DQ [2010]

Hon. Assistant Bishops: Rt Rev. J. Hind, Rt Rev. T. Bavin,
 Rt Rev. T. Thornton, Rt Rev. J. Frost, Rt Rev. I. Brackley

*Archdeacons—***Portsdown:** Ven. J. W. Grenfell
 The Meon: Ven. G. A. Collins
 Isle of Wight: Ven. P. Leonard

Cathedral Church of St Thomas of Canterbury
Dean: Very Rev. A. Cane *Office:* (023) 9282 3300
Canons Residentiary: Canon J. Spreadbury,
 Canon A. C. Rustell, Canon N. Ralph

Organist and Master of Choristers: Mr D. Price

Diocesan Office: First Floor, Peninsular House,
 Wharf Road, Portsmouth, Hampshire PO2 8HB
 Tel: 023 9289 9650
 website: www.portsmouth.anglican.org

ROCHESTER
BISHOP: Rt Rev. James Langstaff, Bishopcourt,
 St Margaret's Street, Rochester ME1 1TS [2010]

*Suffragan Bishop—***Tonbridge:** Rt Rev. Simon
 Burton-Jones

Hon. Assistant Bishops— Rt Rev. M. Turnbull,
 Rt Rev. M. Nazir-Ali, Rt Rev. S. Edozie-Okeke;
 Rt Rev. N. Banks, Rt Rev. R. Thomas (PEVs)

*Archdeacons—***Bromley and Bexley:** Ven. P. Wright
 Rochester: Ven. A. Wooding Jones
 Tonbridge: Ven. J. Conalty

Cathedral Church of Christ and the Blessed Virgin Mary
Dean: Very Rev. P. Hesketh *Office:* (01634) 810060
Canons Residentiary: Canon R. Phillips, Rev. M. Rushton,
 Canon S. Brewer, Canon C. Dench

Organist and Director of Music (Interim): Mr. A. Bawtree

Diocesan Office: St Nicholas Church, Boley Hill, Rochester,
 Kent ME1 1SL *Tel:* 01634 560000
 website: www.rochester.anglican.org

ST ALBANS
BISHOP: Rt Rev. Dr Alan Smith, Abbey Gate House,
 St Albans, Herts AL3 4HD [2009]

*Suffragan Bishops—***Hertford:** Rt Rev. M. Beasley
 Bedford: Rt Rev. R. Atkinson

Hon. Assistant Bishops: Rt Rev. R. J. N. Smith,
 Rt Rev. S. Venner, Rt Rev. J. Gladwin;
 Rt Rev. N. Banks (PEV)

*Archdeacons—***St Albans:** Ven. J. P. Smith
 Bedford: Ven. D. Middlebrook
 Hertford: Ven. J. McKenzie

Cathedral and Abbey Church of St Alban
Dean: Very Rev. J. John *Office:* (01727) 890208
Canons Residentiary: Canon A. Thompson,
 Canon T. Bull, Canon K. Walton, Canon T. Lomax

Master of the Music: Mr A. Lucas

Diocesan Office: Holywell Lodge, 41 Holywell Hill,
 St Albans, Herts AL1 1HE *Tel:* 01727 854532
 website: www.stalbans.anglican.org

ST EDMUNDSBURY AND IPSWICH
BISHOP: Rt Rev. Martin Seeley, Bishop's House,
 4 Park Road, Ipswich, Suffolk IP3 3ST [2015]

*Suffragan Bishop—***Dunwich:** Rt Rev. Michael Harrison

Hon. Assistant Bishops: Rt Rev. J. A. K. Millar,
 Rt Rev. G. P. Knowles, Rt Rev. J. Waine,
 Rt Rev. G. D. J. Walsh, Rt Rev. G. H. Reid;
 Rt Rev. N. Banks (PEV)

*Archdeacons—***Sudbury:** Ven. D. H. Jenkins
 Suffolk: Ven. I. D. J. Morgan Ipswich: Ven R. King

Cathedral Church of St James, Bury St Edmunds
Dean: Very Rev. J. P. Hawes *Office:* (01284) 748720
Canons Residentiary: Canon P. Banks, Canon M. Vernon,
 Ven S. Gaze

Director of Music: Mr J. Thomas

Diocesan Office: St Nicholas Centre, 4 Cutler Street,
 Ipswich, Suffolk IP1 1UQ *Tel:* 01473 298500
 website: www.cofesuffolk.org

SALISBURY
BISHOP: Rt Rev. Nicholas Holtam, South Canonry,
 71 The Close, Salisbury, Wiltshire SP1 2ER [2011]

*Area Bishops—***Sherborne:** Rt Rev. Karen Gorham
 Ramsbury: Rt Rev. Andrew Rumsey

Hon. Assistant Bishops: Rt Rev. J. D. G. Kirkham,
 Rt Rev. D. M. Hallatt, Rt Rev. B. Ind

*Archdeacons—***Sherborne:** Ven. P. Sayer
 Dorset: Ven. A. C. Macrow-Wood
 Sarum: Ven. A. P. Jeans **Wilts:** Ven. S. A. Groom

Cathedral Church of the Blessed Virgin Mary
Dean: Very Rev. N. Papadopulos *Office:* (01722) 555110
Canons Residentiary: Canon E. Probert, Canon R. J. Titley,
 Canon A. Macham

Organist: Mr D. Halls

Diocesan Office: Church House, Crane Street, Salisbury,
 Wiltshire SP1 2QB *Tel:* 01722 411922
 website: www.salisbury.anglican.org.uk

SHEFFIELD
BISHOP: Rt Rev. Peter Wilcox, Bishopcroft, Snaithing
 Lane, Sheffield S10 3LG [2017]

*Suffragan Bishop—***Doncaster:** Rt Rev. Peter Burrows

Hon. Assistant Bishops: Rt Rev. D. Hawtin,
 Rt Rev. T. W. Ellis; Rt Rev. G. Webster,
 Rt Rev. R. Thomas (PEVs)

*Archdeacons—***Sheffield and Rotherham:** Ven. M. L.
 Chamberlain **Doncaster:** Ven. S. A. Wilcockson

Cathedral Church of St Peter and St Paul
Dean: Very Rev. P. E. Bradley *Office:* (0114) 275 3434
Canons Residentiary: Vacancy, Canon K. Farrow

Director of Music: Mr T. Corns

Diocesan Office: Diocesan Church House, 95–99 Effingham
 Street, Rotherham S65 1BL *Tel:* 01709 309100
 website: www.sheffield.anglican.org

SODOR AND MAN
BISHOP: Rt Rev. Peter Eagles, Thie Yn Aspick, The Falls,
 Tromode Road, Douglas, Isle of Man IM4 4PZ [2017]

*Archdeacon—***Isle of Man:** Ven. A. Brown

Cathedral Church of St German, Peel
Dean: Very Rev. N. Godfrey *Office:* 01624 844830
Canons: Canon C. Burgess, Canon J. Coldwell,
 Canon J. Heaton, Canon J. Ward

Diocesan Office: Bishop's House (as above)
 Tel: 01624 622108
 website: www.sodorandman.im

SOUTHWARK
BISHOP: Rt Rev. Christopher Chessun, Bishop's House,
 38 Tooting Bec Gardens, London SW16 1QZ [2011]

*Area Bishops—***Croydon:** Rt Rev. Jonathan Clark
 Kingston: Rt Rev. Richard Cheetham
 Woolwich: Rt Rev. Karowei Dorgu

Hon. Assistant Bishops: Rt Rev. D. J. Atkinson,
 Rt Rev. J. Baker, Rt Rev. M. Doe, Rt Rev. P. Selby,
 Rt Rev. N. Stock, Rt Rev. P. Wheatley, Rt Rev. G. Kings,
 Rt Rev. Lord Harries of Pentregarth, Rt Rev. S. Platten,
 Rt Rev. P. Sontoye Omuku, Rt Rev. T. Thornton,
 Rt Rev. M. Thornton, Most Rev. Josiah Idowu-Fearon,
 Rt Rev. A. Poggo; Rt Rev. R. Thomas (PEV)

*Archdeacons—***Croydon:** Ven. C. J. Skilton
 Lambeth: Ven. S. P. Gates,
 Lewisham and Greenwich: Ven. A. M. Cutting
 Reigate: Ven. M. A. E. Astin
 Southwark: Ven. Dr J. E. Steen
 Wandsworth: Ven. J. Kiddle

Cathedral and Collegiate Church of St Saviour and St Mary Overie
Dean: Very Rev. Andrew Nunn *Office:* (020) 7367 6700
Canons Residentiary: Canon M. Rawson,
 Canon A. K. Ford, Canon G. M. Myers,
 Canon L. K. Roberts, Canon J. Colwill
Organist: Mr P. Wright
Diocesan Office: Trinity House, 4 Chapel Court, Borough
 High Street, London SE1 1HW *Tel:* 020 7939 9400
website: www.southwark.anglican.org

SOUTHWELL AND NOTTINGHAM
BISHOP: Rt Rev. Paul Williams, Bishop's Manor,
 Southwell, Nottinghamshire NG25 0JR [2015]
Suffragan Bishop—Sherwood: Rt Rev. Anthony Porter
Hon. Assistant Bishops: Rt Rev. J. Finney,
 Rt Rev. M. Jarrett, Rt Rev. R. Milner, Rt Rev. R.
 Williamson; Rt Rev. G. Webster (PEV)
Archdeacons—Nottingham: Vacancy
 Newark: Ven. D. A. Picken
Cathedral and Parish Church of the Blessed Virgin Mary
Dean: Very Rev. N. Sullivan *Office:* (01636) 812649/817810
Canons Residentiary: Vacancy, Canon N. Coates
Rector Chori: Mr P. Provost
Diocesan Office: Jubilee House, Westgate, Southwell,
 Notts NG25 0JH *Tel:* 01636 814331
website: www.southwell.anglican.org

TRURO
BISHOP: Rt Rev. Philip Mountstephen, Lis Escop, Feock,
 Truro, Cornwall TR3 6QQ [2018]
Suffragan Bishop—St Germans: Rt Rev. Christopher
 Goldsmith
Archdeacons—Cornwall: Ven P. Bryer
 Bodmin: Ven. A. A. Elkington
Cathedral Church of the Blessed Virgin Mary in Truro
Dean: Very Rev. R. Bush *Office:* (01872) 276782
Canons Residentiary: Canon L. Barley,
 Canon A. Bashforth, Canon S. Griffiths
Director of Music: Mr C. Gray
Diocesan Office: Church House, Woodlands Court,
 Truro Business Park, Truro TR4 9NH *Tel:* 01872 274351
website: www.truro.anglican.org

WINCHESTER
BISHOP: Rt Rev. Timothy Dakin, Wolvesey, Winchester
 SO23 9ND [2011]
Suffragan Bishops—Southampton: Vacancy
 Basingstoke: Rt Rev. David Williams
Hon. Assistant Bishops: Rt Rev. J. Dennis,
 Rt Rev. T. J. Bavin, Rt Rev. J. Ellison, Rt Rev. C. Herbert,
 Rt Rev. H. Scriven, Rt Rev. T. Wilmott,
 Rt Rev. Dom G. Hill
Archdeacons—Winchester: Ven. R. H. G. Brand
 Bournemouth: Ven. P. B. Rouch;
Cathedral Church of the Holy Trinity and of St Peter, St Paul and of St Swithun
Dean: Very Rev. C. Ogle *Office:* 01962 857200
Canon Residentiary: Canon M. P. C. Collinson;
 Canon R. Riem
Director of Music: Mr A. Lumsden
Diocesan Office: Old Alresford Place, Alresford,
 Hampshire SO24 9DH *Tel:* 01962 737300
website: www.winchester.anglican.org

WORCESTER
BISHOP: Rt Rev. John Inge, The Bishop's Office, The Old
 Palace, Deansway, Worcester WR1 2JE [2007]
Suffragan Bishop—Dudley: Rt Rev. Graham Usher
Hon. Assistant Bishops: Rt Rev. M. Hooper,
 Rt Rev. C. Mayfield, Rt Rev. H. Taylor, Rt Rev. M. Santer,
 Rt Rev. A. Priddis, Rt Rev. R. Paterson;
 Rt Rev. J. Goodall (PEV)
Archdeacons—Worcester: Ven. R. G. Jones
 Dudley: Ven. N. J. Groarke

Cathedral Church of Christ and the Blessed Virgin Mary
Dean: Very Rev. P. Atkinson *Office:* (01905) 732900
Canons Residentiary: Canon Dr G. Byrne,
 Canon M. Brierley
Director of Music (Interim): Dr James Lancelot
Diocesan Office: The Old Palace, Deansway, Worcester
 WR1 2JE *Tel:* 01905 20537
website: www.cofe-worcester.org.uk

YORK
ARCHBISHOP: Most Rev. and Rt Hon Dr John Sentamu,
 Primate of England and Metropolitan, Bishopthorpe
 Palace, Bishopthorpe, York, N. Yorks YO23 2GE [2005]
Suffragan Bishops—Hull: Rt Rev. Alison White
 Whitby: Rt Rev. Paul Ferguson
 Selby: Rt Rev. John Thomson
 Beverley: Rt Rev. G. Webster (PEV)
Hon. Assistant Bishops: Rt Rev. N. Baines,
 Rt Rev. D. J. Smith, Rt Rev. G. Bates, Rt Rev. G. Cray,
 Rt Rev. J. S. Jones, Rt Rev. D. G. Galliford,
 Rt Rev. M. Wallace, Rt Rev. D. Wilbourne
Archdeacons—York: Ven. S. R. Bullock
 East Riding: Ven. A. C. Broom
 Cleveland: Ven. S. J. Rushton
Cathedral Church of St Peter
Dean: Rt Rev. J. Frost *Office:* (01904) 557200
Canons Residentiary: Canon P. Moger,
 Canon C. Collingwood, Canon M. Smith
Director of Music: Mr R. Sharpe
Diocesan Office: The Diocese of York, Amy Johnson Way,
 Clifton Moor, York YO30 4XT *Tel:* 01904 699500
website: www.dioceseofyork.org.uk

Chaplains in Her Majesty's Services
Bishop to H.M. Forces: Rt Rev. Timothy Thornton
 Office: 020 7898 1200
ROYAL NAVY. Archdeacon for the Royal Navy, Vacancy,
 2 Leach Building, Whale Island, Portsmouth PO2 8BY
 Tel: 02392 625508
ARMY. Archdeacon for the Army, Ven. C. Langston,
 Ministry of Defence Chaplains (Army), Blenheim
 Building, Marlborough Lines, Monxton Road,
 Andover SP11 8HT *Tel:* 01264 383430
ROYAL AIR FORCE. Archdeacon for the RAF, Ven. J.
 Ellis, Chaplaincy Services (RAF), RAF High Wycombe
 HP14 4UE *Tel:* 01494 493802

Chaplains in the Prison Service
Chaplain General: Rev. J. Ridge, HMPPS Chaplaincy HQ,
 Post Point 8.34, Ministry of Justice, 102 Petty France,
 London SW1H 9AJ *Tel (mob):* 07394 715223

Chaplains in the National Health Service
The Hospitals Chaplaincies Council, Church House,
 Great Smith Street, London SW1P 3NZ
 Tel: 020 7898 1895

ROYAL PECULIARS
WESTMINSTER ABBEY
Collegiate Church of St Peter
Dean: Very Rev. John Hall
Sub-Dean and Canon Treasurer: Ven. D. Stanton
Rector of St Margaret's Church: Rev. J. Sinclair
Canon Steward: Canon A. Ball
Organist and Master of the Choristers: Mr J. O'Donnell
Administration: The Chapter Office, 20 Dean's Yard,
 Westminster, London SW1P 3PA *Tel:* 020 72222 5152
 website: www.westminster-abbey.org

The Queen's Free Chapel of St George Within Her Castle of Windsor
Dean: Rt Rev. David Conner
Canons: Canon M. Poll, Canon Dr H. Finlay,
 Canon Dr M. Powell
The College of St George, Windsor Castle, Windsor,
 Berkshire SL4 1NJ
 Tel: Chapter Office (General Enquiries) 01753 848888

THE CHURCH IN SCOTLAND, WALES AND IRELAND

THE SCOTTISH EPISCOPAL CHURCH

Primus: Most Rev. Mark Strange
  email: bishop@moray.anglican.org
Secretary General: Mr J. Stuart, 21 Grosvenor Crescent,
  Edinburgh EH12 5EE Tel: 0131 225 6357
website: www.scotland.anglican.org

Aberdeen and Orkney
Bishop: Rt Rev. Anne Dyer, Ashley House,
  6 Ashley Gardens, Aberdeen AB10 6RQ
Dean: Very Rev. I. M. Poobalan
Diocesan Office: University of Aberdeen,
  Marischal College, Broad Street, Aberdeen AB10 1YS
  email: office@aberdeen.anglican.org Tel: 01224 662247

Argyll and the Isles
Bishop: Rt Rev. Kevin Pearson
Dean: Very Rev. M. R. Campbell
Diocesan Office: St Moluag's Diocesan Centre,
  Croft Avenue, Oban, Argyll PA34 5JJ Tel: 01631 570 870
website: www.argyll.anglican.org

Brechin
Bishop: Rt Rev. Andrew Swift, Bishop's House,
  5 Ballumbie View, Dundee DD4 0NQ
Dean: Very Rev. J. R. Auld
Diocesan Office: 38 Langlands Street, Dundee DD4 6SZ
  Tel: 01382 459569
website: www.brechin.anglican.org

Edinburgh
Bishop: Rt Rev. John Armes, Bishop's Office,
  21A Grosvenor Crescent, Edinburgh EH12 5EL
Dean: Very Rev. J. A. Conway
Diocesan Centre: 21a Grosvenor Crescent,
  Edinburgh EH12 5EL Tel: 0131 538 7033
website: www.edinbugh.anglican.org

Glasgow and Galloway
Bishop: Vacancy, Bishop's Office, Diocesan Centre,
  5 St Vincent Place, Glasgow G1 2DH
Dean: Very Rev. K. Holdsworth
Diocesan Centre: 5 St Vincent Place, Glasgow G1 2DH
  Tel: 0141 221 5720
website: www.glasgow.anglican.org

Moray, Ross, and Caithness
Bishop: Rt Rev. Mark J. Strange, Bishop's House, St
  John's, Arpafeelie, North Kessock, Inverness IV1 3XD
Dean: Very Rev. S. Murray
Diocesan Office: 9–11 Kenneth Street, Inverness IV3 5NR
  Tel: 01463 237503
website: www.morayepiscopalchurch.scot

St Andrews, Dunkeld and Dunblane
Bishop: Rt Rev. Ian Paton
Provost: Very Rev. H. B. Farquharson
Diocesan Office: 28a Balhousie Street, Perth PH1 5HJ
  Tel: 01738 443173
website: www.standrews.anglican.org

THE CHURCH IN WALES

Archbishop of Wales: Rt Rev. J. D. E. Davies (Bishop of
  Swansea and Brecon)
Provincial Offices: 2 Callaghan Square, Cardiff CF10 5BT
  Tel: 029 2034 8200
website: www.churchinwales.org.uk

Bangor
Bishop: Rt Rev. Andrew John, Tŷ'r Esgob,
  Upper Garth Road, Bangor, Gwynedd LL57 2SS
Dean: Very Rev. K. Jones
Diocesan Office: Cathedral Close, Bangor,
  Gwynedd LL57 1RL Tel: 01248 354999
website: bangor.eglwysyngnghymru.org.uk

Llandaff
Bishop: Rt Rev. June Osborne, Llys Esgob, The Cathedral
  Green, Llandaff, Cardiff, S. Glamorgan CF5 2YE
Dean: Very Rev. G. H. Capon
Diocesan Office: The Court, Coychurch, Bridgend
  CF35 5EH Tel: 01656 868868
website: llandaff.churchinwales.org.uk

Monmouth
Bishop: Rt Rev. Richard Pain, Bishopstow, 91a Stow Hill,
  Newport, Gwent NP20 4EA
Dean: Very Rev. L. Tonge
Diocesan Office: 64 Caerau Road, Newport, Gwent
  NP20 4HJ Tel: 01633 267490
website: monmouth.churchinwales.org.uk

St Asaph
Bishop: Rt Rev. Gregory Cameron, Esgobty,
  Upper Denbigh Road, St Asaph, Denbighshire LL17 0TW
Dean: Very Rev. N. H. Williams
Diocesan Office: High Street, St Asaph, Denbighshire
  LL17 0RD Tel: 01745 582245
website: dioceseofstasaph.org.uk

St Davids
Bishop: Rt Rev. Joanna Penberthy, Llys Esgob, Abergwili,
  Carmarthen, Dyfed SA31 2JG
Dean: Very Rev. S. C. Rowland Jones
Diocesan Office: Llys Esgob, Abergwili, Dyfed SA31 2JG
  Tel: 01267 236145
website: stdavids.churchinwales.org.uk

Swansea and Brecon
Bishop: Rt Rev. John Davies, Ely Tower, Brecon,
  Powys LD3 9DJ
Dean: Very Rev. A. P. Shackerley
Diocesan Office: Cathedral Close, Brecon, Powys LD3 9DP
  Tel: 01874 623716
website: swanseaandbrecon.churchinwales.org.uk

THE CHURCH OF IRELAND

The Primate of All Ireland and Metropolitan:
  Most Rev. M. G. St A. Jackson
Central Office of the Church of Ireland: Church of
  Ireland House, Church Avenue, Rathmines, Dublin 6,
  Republic of Ireland Tel: 00353 (1) 4978 422
  website: www.ireland.anglican.org

National Cathedral: St. Patrick's
Dean: Very Rev. W. Morton, The Deanery,
  Upper Kevin Street, Dublin 8, Republic of Ireland
  website: stpatrickscathedral.ie

PROVINCE OF ARMAGH
Armagh
Archbishop: Most Rev. Richard Clark, Church House,
  46 Abbey Street, Armagh BT61 7DZ
Dean: Very Rev. G. J. O. Dunstan
Diocesan Office: Church House, 46 Abbey Street, Armagh
  BT61 7DZ Tel: 028 3752 2858
website: armagh.anglican.org

Clogher
Bishop: Rt Rev. John McDowell, The See House,
  Fivemiletown, Co. Tyrone BT75 0QP
Dean: Very Rev. K. R. J. Hall
Diocesan Office: St Macartin's Cathedral Hall, Hall's Lane,
  Enniskillen BT74 7DR Tel: 028 6634 7879
website: www.clogher.anglican.org

Connor
Bishop: Rt Rev. Alan Abernethy, Bishop's House,
  3 Upper Malone Road, Belfast BT9 6TD
Deans: Very Rev. S. Wright; St. Anne's Cathedral
  (shared with Down and Dromore) Very Rev. S. Forde
Diocesan Office: Church of Ireland House, 61–67 Donegall
  Street, Belfast, BT1 2QH Tel: 028 9032 8830
  website: www.connor.anglican.org

Derry and Raphoe
Bishop: Rt Rev. Kenneth Good, The See House, 112
  Culmore Road, Londonderry, Co. Londonderry BT48 8JF
Deans: Very Rev. R. J. Stewart (Derry), Very Rev. K. A. R.
  Barrett (Raphoe)
Diocesan Office: 24 London Street, Londonderry BT48 6RQ
  Tel: 028 7126 2440
website: www.derryandraphoe.org

Down and Dromore
Bishop: Rt Rev. Harold Miller, The See House,
32 Knockdene Park South, Belfast, BT5 7AB
Deans: Very Rev. H. Hull (Down), Very Rev. S. G. Wilson
(Dromore)
Diocesan Office: Church of Ireland House, 61–67 Donegall
Street, Belfast, BT1 2QH *Tel:* 028 9082 8830
website: www.downanddromore.org

Kilmore, Elphin and Ardagh
Bishop: Rt Rev. Ferran Glenfield, The See House, Kilmore,
Upper Cavan, Co. Cavan, Republic of Ireland
Deans: Very Rev. N. N. Crossey (Kilmore),
Very Rev. A. Williams (Sligo)
Diocesan Offices: 20A Market Street, Cootehill, Cavan ROI
Tel: 00353 (49) 5559954
website: www.dkea.ie

Tuam, Killala and Achonry
Bishop: Rt Rev. Patrick Rooke, Bishop's House,
Breaffy Woods, Castlebar, Co. Mayo, ROI
Tel: 00353 (94) 903 5703
Dean: Very Rev. A. J. Grimason (Tuam and Killala)
Diocesan Office: 11 Ros Ard, Cappagh Road, Barna,
Galway *Tel:* 086 8336666
website: tuam.anglican.org

PROVINCE OF DUBLIN
Cashel, Waterford, Lismore, Ossory, Ferns and Leighlin
Bishop: Rt Rev. Michael Burrows, Bishop's House,
Troy's Gate, Co. Kilkenny, Republic of Ireland
Deans: Very Revd. G.G. Field, (Cashel), Very Rev. T. W.
Gordon (Leighlin), Very Rev. M. Jansson (Waterford),
Very Rev. P. Draper (Lismore), Very Rev. D. McDonnell
(Kilkenny), Very Rev. P. Mooney (Ferns)
Diocesan Office: The Palace Coach House, Church Lane,
Kilkenny, ROI *Tel:* 00353 (56) 7761910
website: cashel.anglican.org

Cork, Cloyne and Ross
Bishop: Rt Rev. Paul Colton, The See House, Ballagh Road,
Fivemiletown BT75 0QP
Deans: Very Rev. N. Dunne (Cork), Very Rev. A. Marley
(Cloyne), Very Rev. C. L. Peters (Ross)
Diocesan Office: St Nicholas House, 14 Cove Street, Cork,
Co. Cork, ROI *Tel:* 00353 (21) 500 5080

Dublin and Glendalough
Archbishop: Most Rev. Michael Jackson
(*Primate of Ireland and Metropolitan*), The See House, 17
Temple Road, Dartry, Dublin 6, ROI
Dean: Very Rev. D. Dunne (Christchurch, Dublin),
Diocesan Office: Church of Ireland House, Church Ave,
Rathmines, Dublin 6 ROI *Tel:* 00353 (1) 496 6981
website: www.dublin.anglican.org

Limerick, Ardfert, Aghadoe, Killaloe, Kilfenora, Clonfert,
Kilmacduagh and Emly
Bishop: Rt Rev. Kenneth Kearon, Bishop's House, Kilbane
House, Golf Links Road, Castletroy, Limerick, V94 X0EF,
Republic of Ireland
Deans: Very Rev. N. Sloane, (Limerick), Very Rev. G. A.
Paulsen (Killaloe & Clonfert)
Diocesan Office: St John's Rectory, Ashe Street, Tralee,
Co. Kerry, ROI *Tel:* 00353 (66) 712 3182
website: www.limerick.anglican.org

Meath and Kildare
Bishop: Most Rev. Patricia Storey, Bishop's House,
Moyglare, Maynooth, Co. Kildare, ROI
Deans: Very Rev. P. Bogle (Clonmacnoise),
Very Rev. T. Wright (Kildare)
Diocesan Office: Moyglare, Maynooth, Co. Kildare, ROI
Tel: 00353 (1) 6292163
website: www.meathandkildare.org

PROVINCES AND CHURCHES
IN COMMUNION WITH THE SEE OF CANTERBURY

ANGLICAN CHURCH IN AOTEAROA, NEW ZEALAND AND POLYNESIA
Primates/Archbishops: Most Rev. Philip .
Richardson, PO Box 547, New Plymouth 4621,
New Zealand
email: bishop@taranakianglican.org.nz
Most Rev. Don Tamihere, PO Box 568, Gisborne,
4040, New Zealand
Office: +64 (0)6 867 8856
website: www.anglican.org.nz

ANGLICAN CHURCH OF AUSTRALIA
Archbishop of Melbourne and Primate of Australia:
Most Rev. Dr Philip Freier
Office: General Synod Office, Suite 4 Level 5, 189
Kent Street, Sydney, NSW, 2000, Australia
Tel: +61 (0)3 9653 4204
email: generalsecretary@anglican.org.au
website: www.anglican.org.au

THE CHURCH OF BANGLADESH
*Moderator, Church of Bangladesh and Bishop of
Dhaka:* Most Rev. P. S. Sarker, 54/1 Barobagh,
Mirpur-2, Dhaka, 1216, Bangladesh
Office: +880 2 805 3729

THE EPISCOPAL ANGLICAN CHURCH
OF BRAZIL (Igreja Episcopal Anglicana do
Brasil)
Primate: Most Rev. Naudal A. Gomes
(*Bishop of Curitiba*)
email: naudal321@gmail.com

Provincial Offices Praça Olavo Bilac, 63, Campos
Elíseos, CEP 01201–050, São Paulo, SP
Tel and fax: 55 11 3 667 8161
email: magda_cgp@yahoo.com.b
website: www.ieab.org.br

THE CHURCH OF THE PROVINCE OF BURUNDI
Primate: Most Rev. M.B. Nyaboho (*Archbishop of
Burundi and Bishop of Makamba*)
Provincial Secretary: Rev. F. Ndintore, BP 2098,
Bujumbura, Burundi
Office email: eabdiocmak@yahoo.fr
website: www.anglicanburundi.org

THE ANGLICAN CHURCH OF CANADA
Primate of the Anglican Church of Canada:
Most Rev. Frederick. J. Hiltz
email: primate@national.anglican.ca
*Offices of the General Synod and of its
Departments:* Anglican Church of Canada,
80 Hayden Street, Toronto, ON, M4Y 3G2
email: mthompson@national.anglican.ca
website: www.anglican.ca

THE CHURCH OF THE PROVINCE OF CENTRAL AFRICA
Archbishop of the Province: Rt Rev. Albert Chama,
PO Box 20798, Kitwe, Zambia
Office email: chama_albert@yahoo.ca
Provincial Treasurer: Mr E. Mwewa, CPCA,
PO Box 22317, Kitwe, Zambia

THE ANGLICAN CHURCH OF THE CENTRAL AMERICAN REGION (Iglesia Anglicana de la Region Central de America)

Primate: Most Rev. J. Murray Thompson Downs
(Bishop of Panama)
email: bpmurray@hotmail.com
Provincial Secretary: Mr H. Charles, Apartado R,
Balboa, Republic of Panama
email: invcat@yahoo.com

THE CHURCH OF THE PROVINCE OF THE CONGO

(Province de L'Eglise Anglicane Du Congo)
Archbishop of the Province and Bishop of Kindu:
Most Rev. Zacharie M. Katanda, Av. Penemisenga,
No 4, C/ Kasuku, Kindu Maniema, Rwanda
Provincial Secretary: Ven. A. Kibwela,
11 AV Basalakala, Commune de Kalamu,
Kinshasa, DR CONGO,
Office email: anthoniokibwela@gmail.com

IGLESIA ANGLICANA DE CHILE

Primate and Bishop of Santiago: Most Revd. Hector
Z, Muñoz
Office: Victoria Subercaseaux 41, RM Casilla
50675, Correo Central, Santiago, 6200732, Chile
email: tzavala@iach.cl *website:* www.iach.cl

THE HONG KONG HOLY CATHOLIC CHURCH (Hong Kong Sheng Kung Hui)

Primate and Bishop of Hong Kong Island:
Most Rev. Paul Kwong
Provincial Office, 16/F Tung Wai Commercial
Building, 109–111 Gloucester Road, Wanchai,
Hong Kong, SAR
email: peter.koon@hkskh.org

THE CHURCH OF THE PROVINCE OF THE INDIAN OCEAN

Archbishop of the Province and Bishop of
Seychelles: Most Rev. James. R. W. Y. Song
Address: PO Box 44, Victoria, Mahe, Seychelles
Office: +248 321 977
Provincial Secretary: Rev. Stephan Y.R.Raharojaona,
PO Box 44, Victoria, Mahe, Seychelles
email: stpsecacio@gmail.com

THE ANGLICAN COMMUNION IN JAPAN (Nippon Sei Ko Kai)

Primate: Most Rev. Nathaniel. M. Uematsu
(Bishop of Hokkaido)
email: nathaniel.m.u@nifty.com
General Secretary: Rev. J. Shin-Ichi Yahagi,
Nippon Sei Ko Kai, 65–3 Yarai-cho, Shinjuku-ku,
Tokyo 162–0805, Japan
email: general-sec.po@nskk.org
website: www.nskk.org

THE EPISCOPAL CHURCH IN JERUSALEM AND THE MIDDLE EAST

President-Bishop: Most Rev. Suheil Dawani
Address: St George's Cathedral Close, Nablus Road,
Box 19122, Jerusalem, 91191, Israel
email: bishop@j-diocese.org
Provincial Secretary: Ms G. Katsantonis, 2, Grigori
Afxentiou, Nicosia 1515, PO Box 22075, Cyprus
email: georgia@spidernet.com.cy

THE ANGLICAN CHURCH OF KENYA

Primate and Archbishop of All Kenya: Most Rev.
Jackson. O. Sapit, PO Box 678, Kericho, 20200,
Kenya
Office email: archoffice@ackenya.org
Provincial Secretary Rev. Canon R. Mbogo,
PO Box 40502 00100, Nairobi
email: ackpsoffice@ackenya.org
website: www.ackenya.org

ANGLICAN CHURCH IN KOREA

Primate: Most Rev. Moses N. Yoo *(Bishop of*
Daejeon) *email:* primate.ack@gmail.com
Provincial Offices: Rev. P.J.G.Choi 16, Sejon–daero
19–gil, Jung-gu, Seoul 100–120
email: freevayu@gmail.com
website: www.djdio.or.kr

THE CHURCH OF THE PROVINCE OF MELANESIA

Archbishop of the Province: Rt Rev. George Takeli
(Bishop of Central Melanesia)
email: g.takeli@comphq.org.sb
General Secretary: Mr A. Hauriasi, PO Box1 9,
Honiara, Solomon Islands
Tel: +677 20470

THE ANGLICAN CHURCH OF MEXICO

(La Iglesia Anglicana de Mexico)
Archbishop Rt Rev. Francisco Moreno
(Bishop of Northern Mexico)
email: primado@anglicanmx.org
Provincial Secretary Rev. Canon A. Walls, Acatlán
102 Oriente, Col Mitras Centro, Monterrey,
Nuevo Leon, 64460, Mexico
email: awalls@mexico-anglican.org

THE CHURCH OF THE PROVINCE OF MYANMAR (BURMA)

Archbishop of the Province: Most Rev. Stephen T.
M. Oo, *(Bishop of Yangon)*
email: stephenthan777@gmail.com
Provincial Secretary: Rev. Paul M. H. H. Ya, No 140,
Pyidaungsu Yeiktha Street, PO Box 11191,
Yangon, Myanmar
email: myinthtet@gmail.com

THE CHURCH OF NIGERIA

Metropolitan and Primate of All Nigeria Most Revd
Nicholas Okoh *(Archbishop of the Province of*
Abuja and Bishop of Abuja)
Provincial Secretary Episcopal House, 24 Douala
Street, Wuse District, Zone 5, PO Box 212, Abuja,
ADCP, Abuja
email: communicator1@anglican-nig.org

THE CHURCH OF NORTH INDIA (United)

Primate: Most Rev. Prem C. Singh *(Moderator of CNI*
and Bishop of Jabalpur)
Provincial Secretary: Rev. A. Masih, CNI Synod, PO
Box 311, 16, Pandit Pant Marg, New Delhi, 110 001
website: www.cnisynod.org

THE CHURCH OF PAKISTAN (United)

Moderator and Bishop of Peshawar: Most Rev.
Humphrey Peters
Provincial Secretary Mr A. Lamuel, Bishopsbourne,
Cathedral Close, The Mall, Lahore, 54000, Pakistan
email: anthony.lamuel00@gmail.com

THE ANGLICAN CHURCH OF PAPUA NEW GUINEA

Archbishop Most Rev. A. Migi (*Primate of ACPNG*)
email: archbishopmigi95@gmail.com
General Secretary Mr D. Kabekabe, PO Box 673, Lae 411, Morobe Province, Papua New Guinea
email: dpk07jan@gmail.com

EPISCOPAL CHURCH IN THE PHILIPPINES

Prime Bishop: Most Rev. Joel A. Pachao
email: bpjoelpachao@yahoo.com
Provincial Office: PO Box 10321, Broadway Centrum, 1112 Quezon City, Philippines
email: flaw997@gmail.com

THE CHURCH OF THE PROVINCE OF RWANDA (L'Eglise Anglicane au Rwanda)

Archbishop of the Province: Most Rev. Laurent Mbanda (*Bishop of Shyira*)
Provincial Secretary: Rev. F. Karemera, BP 2487, Kigali, Rwanda
email: frkaremera@ear-acr.org

THE ANGLICAN CHURCH OF SOUTHERN AFRICA

Primate: Most Rev. Thabo Makgoba (*Archbishop of Cape Town*)
email: archpa@anglicanchurchsa.org.za
Provincial Executive Officer: Ven. H. Arenz, 20 Bishopscourt Drive, Bishopscourt, Claremont, Western Cape 7708, South Africa
email: peo@anglicanchurchsa.org.za
website: www.anglicanchurchsa.org.za

THE ANGLICAN CHURCH OF SOUTH AMERICA

Presiding Bishop: Most Rev. Gregory Venables (*Bishop of Argentina*), 25 de Mayo 282, Capital Federal, Buenos Aires, 1001, Argentina
email: bpgreg@fibertel.com.ar
Provincial Secretary: C. Daly
email: cristindaly@gmail.com

THE PROVINCE OF THE ANGLICAN CHURCH IN SOUTH-EAST ASIA

Primate: Most Rev. Ng M. B. Hing (*Bishop of West Malaysia*), 16 Jalan Pudu, Kuala Lumpur, 50200, Malaysia
Provincial Secretary: Rev. Kenneth Thien Su Yin, PO Box 10811, 88809 Kota Kinabalu, Sabah, 88809, Malaysia
email: kenneththien@gmail.com

THE CHURCH OF SOUTH INDIA (United)

Moderator of CSI and Bishop of Madhya Kerala: Most Rev. Thomas Oommen, CSI Bishop's House, Cathedral Road, Kottayam, Kerala State, 686 001, India
email: csimkdbishopsoffice@gmail.com
Provincial Secretary: Rev. D. Sadananda, CSI Centre, No 5 Whites Road, Royapettah, Chennai, 6000 014, India
email: synodcsi@gmail.com
website: csisynod.com

THE EPISCOPAL CHURCH OF SOUTH SUDAN

Primate and Bishop of Juba: Most Rev. Justin Arama, C/O ECS Office, PO Box 7576, Kampala, Uganda
email: archbishop@southsudan.anglican.org
Provincial Secretary: Mr John A. Lumori, PO Box 110, Juba, South Sudan
email: provincialsecretary@southsudan.anglican.org *website:* www.juba.anglican.org

THE CHURCH OF THE PROVINCE OF THE SUDAN

Archbishop and Bishop of Khartoum: Most Rev. Ezekel Kondo, PO Box 65, Omdurman, Sudan
email: bishop@khartoum.anglican.org
Acting Provincial Secretary: Rev. M. Abujam
email: msabujam@gmail.com
website: www.khartoum.anglican.org

THE ANGLICAN CHURCH OF TANZANIA

Archbishop: Most Rev. Maimbo Mndolwa (*Bishop of Tanga*)
Provincial Secretary: Rev. Canon M. Ogunde, PO Box 899, Dodoma, Tanzania
email: act@anglican.or.tz
website: www.anglican.or.tz

THE CHURCH OF THE PROVINCE OF UGANDA

Archbishop of the Province: Most Rev. Stanley Ntagali (*Bishop of Kampala*)
email: abpcou@gmail.com
Acting Provincial Secretary: Rev. Canon Titus Baraka, PO Box 14123, Kampala
email: pschurchofuganda@gmail.com

THE EPISCOPAL CHURCH (IN THE UNITED STATES OF AMERICA)

Presiding Bishop and Primate: Most Rev. Michael Curry *email:* sjones@episcopalchurch.org
Offices of the Episcopal Church and its Departments: Episcopal Church Center, 815 Second Ave, New York, NY 10017, USA
email: mbarlowe@episcopalchurch.org
website: www.episcopalchurch.org
Convocation of American Churches in Europe, *Bishop-in-charge:* Rt Rev. Pierre. Whalon
Office: 23 Avenue George V. F-75008, Paris, France.
Tel: +33 1 53 23 84 06
email: bppwhalon@aol.com
website: www.tec-europe.org

THE CHURCH OF THE PROVINCE OF WEST AFRICA

Archbishop and Primate: Most Rev. Dr Daniel Sarfo (*Bishop of Kumasi and Archbishop of the internal province of Ghana*)
Provincial Secretary: Rev. Canon A. M. Eiwuley, PO Box KN 2023, Kaneshie, Accra, Ghana
email: morkeiwuley@gmail.com

THE CHURCH IN THE PROVINCE OF THE WEST INDIES

Archbishop and Bishop of Barbados: Vacancy
Provincial Secretary: Mrs E. Lawrence, Bamford House, Society Hill, St John, Barbados, West Indies
email: cpwi@caribsurf.wi

CHURCH OF BERMUDA (Extra Provincial – Canterbury)
Bishop Rt Rev. Nicholas Dill
  email: bishop@anglican.bm
Office: PO Box HM 769, Hamilton HM CX, Bermuda
  email: diocese@anglican.bm

THE CHURCH OF CEYLON (Extra-Provincial – Canterbury)
Bishop of Colombo: Rt Rev. D. R. Canagasabey,
  Bishop's Office, 368/3A Bauddhaloka Mawatha,
  Colombo - 07, Sri Lanka
  email: anglican@sltnet.lk
Bishop elect of Kurunegala: Rt Rev. K. Fernando,
  Bishop's House, 31 Kandy Road, Kurunegala,
  60000, Sri Lanka
  email: bishopkg@sltnet.lk

ANGLICAN CHURCH OF CUBA (Extra Provincial –Metropolitan Council)
Office: Mr F. de Arazoza, Calle 6 No 273 Vedado,
  Plaza de la revolucion, Ciudad de la Habana,
  CUBA Tel: +53 7 832 1120
  email: episcopal@enet.cu

THE LUSITANIAN CHURCH (Extra Provincial – Canterbury)
Provincial Treasurer: Rev. Sergio Alves
Office: Rua Afonso de Albuquerque, No 86,
  4430–003 Vila Nova de Gaia, Portugal
  email: sergioalves@igreja-lusitana.org
  website: www.igreja-lusitana.org

THE REFORMED EPISCOPAL CHURCH OF SPAIN (Extra Provincial – Canterbury)
Provincial Treasurer: Señor Jose Rodriguez, Calle
  Beneficencia 18, Madrid, 28004, Spain
  email: secretario@anglicanos.org
  website: www.anglicanos.org

OTHER CHRISTIAN DENOMINATIONS

Baptist Union of Great Britain
Baptist House, PO Box 44, 129 Broadway, Didcot,
  Oxfordshire OX11 8RT
Tel: 01235 517700
email: info@baptist.org.uk
website: www.baptist.org.uk

Catholic Bishops' Conference of England and Wales
39 Eccleston Square, London SW1V 1BX
Tel: 020 7630 8220
email: cnn@lifecbcew.uk
website: http://www.catholic-ew.org.uk/

Catholic Bishops' Conference of Scotland
General Secretariat: 64 Aitken Street, Airdrie,
  ML6 6LT
Tel: 01236 764061
website: www.bcos.org.uk

Church of Scotland (Presbyterian)
Administrative offices: 121 George Street,
  Edinburgh EH2 4YN
Tel: 0131 225 5722
Website: churchofscotland.org.uk

Evangelical Alliance
Registered Office: 176 Copenhagen Street,
  London N1 0ST
Tel: 020 7520 3830
email: info@aeuk.org
website: www.eauk.org

Evangelical Lutheran Church in England
28 Huntingdon Road, Cambridge CB3 0HH
Tel: 01223 355265 Fax: 01223 355265
email: info@lutheran.co.uk
website: www.lutheran.co.uk

Greek Orthodox Church in Great Britain
Thyateira House, 5 Craven Hill, London W2 3EN
Tel: 020 7723 4787 Fax: 020 7224 9301
email: mail@thyateira.org.uk
website: www.thyateira.org.uk

Methodist Church in Great Britain
Methodist Church House, 25 Marylebone Road,
  London NW1 5JR
Tel: 020 7486 5502
email: enquiries@methodistchurch.org.uk
website: www.methodist.org.uk

Moravian Church in Great Britain and Ireland
Moravian Church House, 5 Muswell Hill,
  London N10 3TJ
Tel: 020 8883 3409
website: www.moravian.org.uk

New Frontiers
Apostolic Leader: David Devenish, Woodside
  Church, Dover Crescent, Bedford MK41 8QH
email: office@newfrontierstogether.org
website: www.newfrontierstogether.org

Quakers (Religious Society of Friends)
Friends House, 173 Euston Road, London NW1 2BJ
Tel: 020 7663 1000
email: enquiries@quaker.org.uk
website: www.quaker.org.uk

Russian Orthodox Church in Great Britain and Ireland (Diocese of Sourozh – Patriarchate of Moscow)
Bishop Matthew of Sourozh, Cathedral of the
  Domitian of the Mother of God and All Saints,
  67 Ennismore Gardens, London SW7 1NH
Tel: 020 7584 0096
website: www.sourozh.org

Archdiocese of Orthodox Parishes of Russian Tradition in Western Europe (Patriarchate of Constantinople)
Dean: Archpriest Patrick Hodson, Folly Acre, Swaffham Road, Wendling, Dereham, Norfolk NR19 2AB
Tel: 01362 687 031
email: mail@exarchate-uk.org
website: www.exarchate.org

Russian Orthodox church outside Russia (ROCOR)
Bishop Administrator: His Grace Bishop Irenei of Richmond
Tel: (07926) 194 031

Diocesan Chancellery: 58 Shrewsbury Road, Prenton, Birkenhead, CH43 2HY
email: frpaulelliott@aol.com
website: www.rocor.org.uk

Salvation Army
101 Newington Causeway, Elephant and Castle, London SE1 6BN
Tel: 020 7367 4500
e-mail: info@salvationarmy.org.uk
website: www.salvationarmy.org.uk

United Reformed Church
Church House, 86 Tavistock Place, London WC1H 9RT
Tel: 020 7916 2020
email: urc@urc.org.uk
website: www.urc.org.uk

OTHER FAITH ORGANISATIONS

Bahá'i Community of the United Kingdom
27 Rutland Gate, London SW7 1PD
Tel: 020 7584 2566
email: nsa@bahai.org.uk
website: www.bahai.org.uk

Board of Deputies of British Jews
1 Torriano Mews, London NW5 2RZ
Tel: 020 7543 5400
email: info@bod.org.uk
website: www.bod.org.uk

Buddhist Society
58 Eccleston Square, London SW1V 1PH
Tel: 020 7834 5858
email: info@the buddhistsociety.org.uk
website: www.the buddhistsociety.org

Hindu Council UK
22 King Street, Southall UB2 4DA
Tel: 07903216291
email: admin@hinducounciluk.org
website: www.hinducounciluk.org

Muslim Association of Britain (Sunni)
24 Harrowdene Road, Wembley, Middlesex HA0 2JF
Tel: 020 8908 9109
email: office@mabonline.net

Muslim Council of Britain
PO Box 57330, London E1 2WJ
Tel: 0845 2622 786
email: admin@mcb.org.uk
website: www.mcb.org.uk

Sikh Council UK
Station House, G46 Old Warwick Road, Leamington Spa, Warwickshire CV31 3NS
Tel: 07867 698417
website: sikhcounciluk.org

ORGANISATIONS AND USEFUL CONTACTS

Action on Hearing Loss (formerly RNID), Chief Exec: Paul Breckell, 1–3 Highbury Station Road, London N11SE
Tel: 020 7359 4442 Textphone: 020 7296 8001
website: www.actiononhearingloss.org.uk

Additional Curates Society, Sec: Fr. Darren Smith, 16, Commercial Road, Birmingham, West Midlands B1 1RS
Tel: 0121 382 5533
website: www.additionalcurates.co.uk

Age UK, Tavis House, 1–6 Tavistock Square, London WC1H 9NA
Tel: 0800 169 8787   0800 678 1602 (Helpline)
website: www.ageuk.org.uk

Alcuin Club, Sec: Mr J. Ryding, 5 Saffron Street, Royston SG8 9TR
Tel: 01763 248676
website: www.alcuinclub.org.uk

Alpha International, Holy Trinity Brompton, Brompton Road, London SW7 1JA
Tel: 02070 520200
website: www.alpha.org

Anglican Centre in Rome, Palazzo Doria Pamphilj, Piazza Collegio Romano 2, 00186 Rome, Italy
Tel: 0039 066 780 302
website: www.anglicancentreinrome.org

Anglican Society for the Welfare of Animals, Sec: Mrs S. J. Chandler, PO Box 7193, Hook, Hampshire RG27 8GT
Tel: 01252 843093
website: www.aswa.org.uk

Archbishops' Secretary for Appointments, Canon Caroline Boddington, Church House, 27 Great Smith Street, London SW1P 3AZ
Tel: 020 7898 1876

ARCHWAY (Anglican Retreat and Conference House Wardens Association), Administrator: Jeff Witts
email: admin@archwaywardens.org.uk
website: www.archwaywardens.org.uk

Arthur Rank Centre see **Germinate: The Arthur Rank Centre**

The Arts Society (NADFAS) *Chief Exec:* Dr. Florian Schweizer, *Office:* 8 Guilford Street, London WC1N 1DA
Tel: 020 7430 0730
website: theartssociety.org

Association for Promoting Retreats, *Administrator:* 2 Brookfield Cottages, The Strand, Lympstone, Exmouth EX8 5ES
Tel: 01395 272243
website: www.promotingretreats.org

Association of Christian Teachers, The Doddridge Centre,109 St James Road, Northampton NN5 5LD
Tel: 01604 632046
website: www.christian-teachers.org.uk

Association of English Cathedrals, *Co-ordinator:* Mrs S. King, PO Box 53506, London SE19 1ZL
Tel: 020 8761 5130
website: www.englishcathedrals.co.uk

Barnardo's, *Chief Exec:* Javed Khan, Tanners Lane, Barkingside, Ilford, Essex IG6 1QG
Tel: 020 8550 8822
website: www.barnados.org.uk

Bat Conservation Trust, *Enquiries:* Quadrant House, 250 Kennington Lane, London SE11 5RD
Tel: 020 7820 7183
website: www.bats.org.uk

Bible Society, *Chief Executive:* Paul Williams, Bible Society, Stonehill Green, Westlea, Swindon SN5 7DG
Tel: 01793 418100
website: www.biblesociety.org.uk

Book-Aid Charitable Trust, Bromley House, Kangley Bridge Road, Lower Sydenham, London SE26 5AQ
Tel: 020 8778 2145
website: www.book-aid.org

Boys' Brigade, *Brigade Sec:* S. Dickinson, Felden Lodge, Hemel Hempstead, Herts HP3 0BL
Tel: 01442 231681
website: www.boysbrigade.org.uk

British Deaf Association, 356 Holloway Road, London N7 6PA
Tel: 020 7697 4140
website: www.bda.org.uk

Caring for God's Acre, 11 Drover's House, The Auction Yard, Craven Arms, Shropshire SY7 9BZ
Tel: 01588 673041
website: www.caringforgodsacre.org.uk

Cathedral and Church Shops Association, *Hon Sec:* Liz Lowrie, c/o St Patrick's Cathedral Dublin
Tel: 00 353 (0)1 4539472
website: www.cathedralandchurchshops.com

Cathedrals Plus, Sec: Paul Hammans, 3 Park Road, Southolt, Eye, Suffolk IP23 7QW
Tel: 07724 168 644
email: secretary@cathedralsplus.org.uk

Central Council of Church Bell Ringers, *Hon. Sec:* Mary Bone, 11 Bullfields, Sawbridgeworth CM21 9DB UK
Tel: 01279 726159
website: www.cccbr.org.uk

Central Readers' Council, *Sec:* Mr Andrew Walker, Church House, Great Smith Street, London SW1P 3NZ
Tel: 020 7898 1417
website: www.readers.cofe.anglican.org *email:* crcsec@btinternet.com

Changing Attitude *see* **OneBodyOneFaith**

Charity Commissioners, *CEO:* Mrs Helen Stephenson, PO Box 211, Bootle, L20 7YX
Tel: 0300 066 9197
website: www.charitycommission.gov.uk

Children's Society, *Interim Chief Exec:* Nicholas Roseveare, Edward Rudolf House, Margery Street, London WC1X 0JL
Tel: 0300 303 7000
website: www.childrenssociety.org.uk

Choir Schools Association, *Information Officer:* Jane Capon, Village Farm, The Street, Market Weston, Diss IP22 2NZ
email: info@choirschools.org.uk
website: www.choirschools.org.uk

Christian Aid, *Director:* Amanda Khozi Mukwashi, Inter-Church House, 35–41 Lower Marsh, London SE1 7RL
Tel: 020 7620 4444
website: www.christian-aid.org.uk

Christian Copyright Licensing International, Chantry House, 22 Upperton Road, Eastbourne BN21 1BF
Tel: 01323 436100
website: www.ccli.co.uk

Christian Education, *Director:* P. Fishpool, 5/6 Imperial Court, 12 Sovereign Road, Birmingham B30 3FH
Tel: 0121 458 3313
email: sales@christianeducation.org.uk
website: www.christianeducation.org.uk

Christians in Library and Information Services (formerly the Librarians' Christian Fellowship), *Hon Sec:* Graham Hedges, 176 Copenhagen Street, London N1 0ST
email: secretary@christianlis.org
website: christianlis.org

Christians in Secular Ministry (CHRISM), *Contact:* Sue Cossey, 1 Bye Mead, Emerson's Green, Bristol BS16 7DL
mobile: 07496047277
email: sue.cossey@yahoo.co.uk
website: www.chrism.org.uk

Church Army, *CEO:* Mark Russell, Headquarters: Wilson Carlile Centre, 50 Cavendish Street, Sheffield S3 7RZ
Tel: 0300 123 2113 *Direct number:* 0114 252 1656
email: n.thomson@churcharmy.org.uk
website: www.churcharmy.org.uk

Church Commissioners for England, *Sec:* Andrew Brown, Church House, Great Smith Street, London SW1P 3AZ
Tel: 020 7898 1661
website: www.churchofengland.org

Church House, The Corporation of the, *Sec:* Christopher Palmer, Church House, Great Smith Street, London SW1P 3AZ
Tel: 020 7898 1311
website: www.churchhouse.org.uk

Church Housing Trust, 49–51 East Road, London N1 6AH
Tel: 020 7269 1630
website: www.churchhousingtrust.org.uk

Church Lads' and Church Girls' Brigade, *National Coordinator:* Perry Gunn, 2 Barnsley Road, Wath upon Dearne, Rotherham, South Yorks S63 6PY
Tel: 01709 876535
website: www.clcgb.org.uk

Church Mission Society, *Deputy Executive Leader:* Debbie James, Watlington Road, Oxford OX4 6BZ *Tel:* 01865 787400 *website:* www.cms-uk.org

Church Music Society, *Treasurer:* John Roch, 39 Pine Croft, Chapeltown, Sheffield S35 1EB *website:* www.church-music.org.uk

Church of England Flower Arrangers Association, *Sec:* Mr L. Little, 36 Potters Lane, New Barnet EN5 5BE *Tel:* 0208 441 119 *website:* www.cefaa.org.uk

Church of England Guild of Vergers, *Gen Sec:* Stephen Stokes, Kemp House, 152–160 City Road, London EC1V 2NX *email:* CEGVGenSec@gmail.com *website:* cofgv.org.uk

Church of England Pensions Board, *Sec and Chief Exec:* John Ball, 29 Great Smith Street, London SW1P 3AZ *Tel:* 020 7898 1800

Church of England Record Society, *Hon Sec:* Mary Clare Martin, Department of Education and Community Studies, University of Greenwich, Avery Hill Campus, Mansion Site, Bexley Road, London SE9 2PQ *website:* www.coers.org

Church Pastoral Aid Society, *Gen Director:* John Dunnett, CPAS, Sovereign Court One (Unit 3), Sir William Lyons Road, University of Warwick Science Park, Coventry CV4 7EZ *Tel:* 0300 123 0780 *email:* info@cpas.org.uk *website:* www.cpas.org.uk

Church Society, *Gen Sec:* Rev. Lee Gatiss, Ground Floor, Centre Block, Hille Business Estate.132 St Albans Road, Watford WD24 4AE *Tel:* 01923 255410 *website:* www.churchsociety.org

Church Union, *Chairman:* Fr. Darren Smith, 16 Commercial Street, Birmingham B1 1RS *email:* membership@churchunion.co.uk *Tel:* 0121 382 5533 *website:* www.churchunion.co.uk

Churches Together in Britain and Ireland, *Sec:* Bob Fyffe, Interchurch House,35 Lower Marsh, London SE1 7RL 1BX *Tel:* 020 3794 2288 *website:* www.ctbi.org.uk

Clergy Support Trust, *Senior Treasurer:* Canon Simon Butler, 1 Dean Trench Street, London SW1P 3HB *Tel:* 020 7799 3696

College of Preachers, c /o Hymns Ancient & Modern Ltd,13a Hellesdon Park Road, Norwich NR6 5DR *Tel:* 03331 30228 *website:* www.collegeofpreachers.org.uk

Commonwealth War Graves Commission, *Enquiries:* 2 Marlow Road, Maidenhead SL6 7DX *Tel:* 01628 507138 *website:* www.cwgc.org

Compassionate Friends, *Chief Exec:* Carolyn Brice, *Office:* Kilburn Grange, Priory Park Road, London NW6 7UJ *Tel:* 0845 123 2304 (National Helpline); 0345 120 3785 (Admin) *website:* www.tcf.org.uk

Conservation Foundation, *Director:* David Shreeve, 1 Kensington Gore, London SW7 2AR *Tel:* 020 7591 3111 *website:* www.conservationfoundation.co.uk

The Conservation Volunteers, Sedum House, Mallard Way, Doncaster DN4 8DB *Tel:* 01302 388883 *website:* www.tcv.org.uk

Culham St Gabriel's, *CEO:* Dr. Kathryn Wright, 60–62 Banbury Road, Oxford OX2 6PN *Tel:* 01865 612035 *email:* enquiries@cstg.org.uk *website:* www.ctg.org.uk

Day One Christian Ministries *(incorporating The Lord's Day Observance Society),* *Contact:* Mr J. Holmes, Ryelands Road, Leominster, Herefordshire HR6 8NZ *Tel:* 01568 613740 *website:* www.dayone.co.uk

Department for Environment, Food and Rural Affairs (DEFRA), *Customer Contact Unit:* Eastbury House, 30–34 Albert Embankment, London SE1 7TL *Tel:* 08459 335577 (helpline) *website:* www.defra.gov.uk

Ecclesiastical Insurance Office PLC, Beaufort House, Brunswick Road, Gloucester GL1 1JZ *Tel:* 0345 777 3322 *website:* www.ecclesiastical.com

Embroiderers' Guild, *CEO:* Terry Murphy *Office:* Bucks County Museum, Church Street, Aylesbury, Bucks HP20 2QPE *email:* administrator@embroiderersguild.com *Tel:* 07455 597039

English Heritage, *Chief Exec:* Kate Mavor, The Engine House, Fire Fly Avenue, Swindon SN2 2EH *Tel:* 0870 3331181 *website:* www.english-heritage.org.uk

Fairtrade Foundation, 5.7 The Loom, 14 Gower's Walk, London E1 8PY *Tel:* 020 7405 5942 *website:* www.fairtrade.org.uk

Federation of Catholic Priests, *Sec Gen:* Rev. Peter Walsh, St Andrew's Vicarage, 2 Lingdale Road, Wirral CH48 5DQ *Tel:* 0151 632 4728

Feed the Minds, *Director:* Josephine Carlson, The Foundry, 17 Oval Way, London SE11 5RR *Tel:* 020 3752 5800 *website:* www.feedtheminds.org

Fellowship of St Alban and St. Sergius, 1 Canterbury Road, Oxford OX2 6LU *Tel:* 01865 552991 *email:* gensec@sobornost.org

Flag Institute, HQS Wellington, Victoria Embankment, London WC2R 2PN *email:* info@flaginstitute.org *website:* www.flaginstitute.org

Forward in Faith, 2a The Cloisters, Gordon Square, London WC1H 0AG *Tel:* 020 7388 3588 *website:* www.forwardinfaith.com

Friends of Friendless Churches, *Hon Dir:* Rachel Morley, St Anne's Vestry Hall, 2 Church Entry, London EC4V 5HB *Tel:* 020 7236 3934 *website:* www.friendsoffriendlesschurches.org.uk

Germinate: The Arthur Rank Centre
National Rural Officer: Dr Jill Hopkinson,
Stoneleigh Park, Warwickshire CV8 2LG
Tel: 024 7685 3060
website: http://www.germinate.net

Gift Aid (HM Revenue and Customs),
HMRC Charities, St Johns House, Merton Road,
Liverpool L75 1BB
Tel: 0845 302 0203 (helpline)
website: www.hmrc.gov.uk/charities/gift-aid

Girlguiding UK, *Chief Guide:* Amanda Medler,
17/19 Buckingham Palace Road, London
SW1W 0PT
Tel: 020 7834 6242/0800 169 5901
website: www.girlguiding.org.uk

Girl's Brigade, *Director:* Ruth Gilson, The Girls'
Brigade England & Wales, Cliff College, Calver,
Hope Valley, Derbyshire, S32 3XG.
Tel: 01246 582322
website: www.girlsbrigadeew.org.uk

Greenbelt Festivals (23–26 August 2019),
The Nest, Church House, 86 Tavistock Place,
London WC1H 9RT
Tel: 020 7329 0038
website: www.greenbelt.org.uk

Green Christian (Christian Ecology Link),10 Kiln
Gardens, Hartley Wintney, Hampshire RG27 8RG,
Tel: 0345 459 8460
website: www.greenchristian.org.uk

Guild of Church Musicians, *Gen Sec:* Dr A.
M. D. G. Walsh, 5 Lime Close, Chichester,
West Sussex PO19 6SW
Tel: 01243 788315
website: www.churchmusicians.org

Health and Safety Executive, Rose Court,
2 Southwark Bridge, London SE1 9HS
Tel: 0845 345 0055 (Infoline)
website: www.hse.gov.uk

Hymn Society of Great Britain and Ireland,
Sec: Rev. Robert Canham, Wind rush, Braithwaite,
Keswick CAI2 5SZ
website: www.hymnsocietygbi.org.uk

Inclusive Church, *National Coordinator:* Ruth Wilde
email: office@inclusive-church.org
website: inclusive-church.org.uk

Institute of Conservation (buildings etc)
CEO: Sara Crofts *Office:* Radisson Court, Unit
2,219 Long Lane London SE1 4PR
Tel: 020 3142 6799
email: admin@icon.org.uk
website: www.icon.org.uk

Intercontinental Church Society,
Mission Dir: Richard Bromley, Unit 11,
Ensign Business Centre, Westwood Way,
Westwood Business Park, Coventry CV4 8JA
Tel: 024 7646 3940
email: enquiries@ics-uk.org
website: www.ics-uk.org

Lambeth Palace, Lambeth Palace, London SE1 7JU
Tel: 020 7898 1200

Langley House Trust (helping ex-offenders), Langley
House Trust, PO Box 6364, Coventry CV6 9LL
Tel: 03330 035025
website: www.langleyhousetrust.org

Librarians' Christian Fellowship *see* **Christians in
Library and Information Services**

PRS for Music (music copyright), *Office:* 2 Pancras
Square, London N1C 4AG
Tel: 020 7580 5544
website: www.prsformusic.com

Mediawatch-UK, *Chairman:* David Chesney,
3 Willow House, Kennington Road, Ashford,
Kent TN24 0NR
Tel: 01233 633936
website: www.mediawatchuk.org

Meteorological Office, Fitzroy Road, Exeter EX1 3PB
Tel: 0870 900 0100
website: www.metoffice.gov.uk

Mission to Seafarers, *Sec Gen:* Rev. Andrew Wright,
St Michael Paternoster Royal, College Hill,
London EC4R 2RL
Tel: 020 7248 5202
website: www.missiontoseafarers.org

MODEM, 39 Eccleston Square, London SW1V 1BX
Tel: 020 7901 4890
website: www.modem-uk.com

Modern Church *Administrator:* Diane Kutar,
22 The Kiln, Burgess Hill, West Sussex RH15 0LU
email: office@modernchurch.org.uk
Tel: 0845 345 1909

Mothers' Union, *Chief Exec:* Beverley Julien,
Mary Sumner House, 24 Tufton Street,
London SW1P 3RB
Tel: 020 7222 5533
website: www.themothersunion.org

National Archives, Kew, Richmond-upon-Thames,
London TW9 4DU
Tel: 020 8876 3444
website: www.nationalarchives.gov.uk

**National Association of Flower Arrangement
Societies (NAFAS),** Osborne House,12 Devonshire
Square, London EC2M 4TE
Tel: 020 7247 5567
website: www.nafas.org.uk

National Association of Funeral Directors,
618 Warwick Road, Solihull, W. Midlands B91 1AA
Tel: 0845 230 1343
website: www.nafd.org.uk

National Association of Local Councils,
Chief Exec: Jonathan Owen, *Office:* 109 Great
Russell Street, London WC1B 3LD
Tel: 020 7637 1865
website: www.nalc.gov.uk

National Association of Memorial Masons,
1 Castle Mews, Rugby, Warwickshire CV21 2XL
Tel: 01788 542264
website: www.namm.org.uk

National Churches Trust, *Chief Exec:* Claire Walker,
7 Tufton Street, London SW1P 3QB
Tel: 020 7222 0605
website: www.nationalchurchestrust.org.uk

National Lottery Good Causes, 5th Floor,
1 Plough Place, London EC4A 1DE
Tel: 020 7211 3991
website: www.lotterygoodcauses.org.uk

National Rail Enquiries,
Tel: 08457 48 49 50 or 0845 60 50 600 (textphone)
website: www.nationalrail.co.uk

Natural England, *Interim Chief Exec:* Marion Spain
Office: County Hall, Spetchley Road, Worcester
WR5 2NP
Tel: 0300 060 3900
website: www.naturalengland.org.uk

OneBodyOneFaith, *Chief Exec:* Tracey Byrne,
Office: South Church House, 25 Market Place,
Newark, Notts NG24 1EA, *Tel:* 01636 673072

Ordinands' Association, *Chair:* Kevin Andersson –
Ripon College Cuddesdon
email: chair@ordinands.org.uk
website: www.ordinands.org.uk

Plainsong and Medieval Music Society, *Sec:* Prof Owen Rees, Faculty of Music, University of Oxford, St Aldgate's, Oxford OX1 1DB
Tel: 01865 276125
email: owen.rees@queens.ox.ac.uk
website: www.plainsong.org.uk

Prayer Book Society, *Chairman of Trustees:* Prudence Dailey, The Studio, Copyhold Farm, Goring Heath RG8 7RT
Tel: 0118 984 2582
website: www.pbs.org.uk

Reform *see* **Church Society**

Relate, Premier House, Carolina Court, Lakeside, Doncaster DN4 5RA
Tel: 0300 100 1234
website: www.relate.org.uk

Retired Clergy Association, *Hon Sec:* Revd. Malcolm Liles 473 City Road, Sheffield S2 1GF
Tel: 0114–453 7964 4
email: secretary@rcacoe.org
website: rcacoe.org

Retreat Association, *Exec Dir:* Alison McTier
Office: PO Box 1130, Princes Risborough, Buckinghamshire HP22 9RP
Tel: 01494 569 056
email: info@retreats.org.uk
website: www.retreats.org.uk

RNIB, *Interim Chief Exec:* Eliot Lyne
Office: 105 Judd Street, London WC1H 9NE
Tel: 020 7388 1266 (helpline: 0303 123 9999)
website: www.rnib.org.uk

RNID *see* **Action on Hearing Loss**

Royal British Legion, 199 Borough High Street, London SE1 1AA
Tel: 0808 802 8080
website: ww.britishlegion.org.uk

Royal College of Organists, *Dir:* Sir Andrew Parmley
Office: PO Box 7328, New Milton, Hampshire BH25 9DU
Tel: 020 3865 6998
website: www.rco.org.uk

Royal School of Church Music, 19 The Close, Salisbury SP1 2EB
Tel: 01722 424848, 424841
Membership website: www.rscm.com

St George's House, *Clergy Course Administrator:* Mrs Christine Chamberlain, St George's House, Windsor Castle, Windsor SL4 1NJ
Tel: 01753 848848; 01753 848850
website: www.stgeorgeshouse.org

St Luke's Healthcare for the Clergy, Room 201, Church House, Great Smith Street, London SW1P 3AZ
Tel: 020 7898 1700
website: www.stlukeshealtcare.org.uk

Samaritans, *Chief Exec:* Ruth Sutherland
Office: The Upper Mill, Kingston Road, Ewell, Surrey KT17 2AF
Tel: 020 8394 8300 (admin); 08457 909090 (helpline)
website: www.samaritans.org

Scout Association, *Chief Scout:* Bear Grylls
Contact: Scout Information Centre, Gilwell Park, Bury Road, Chingford, London E4 7QW
Tel: 0845 300 1818
website: www.scouts.org.uk

Scripture Union, Trinity House, Opal Court, Opal Drive, Fox Milne, Milton Keynes MK15 0DF
Tel: 01908 856000
website: www.scriptureunion.org.uk

Society of Catholic Priests, *Sec:* Fr. Chris.Reaney, 12 Cwrt y Fedwen, Maesteg CF34 9GH
Tel: 01656 734142
website: www.societyofcatholicpriests.com

Society for Church Archaeology, *Sec and Publicity Officer:* Norma Oldfield, c/o Council for British Archeology, St Mary's House, 66 Bootham, York YO30 7BZ
email: churcharcheology@gmail.com
website: www.churcharcheology.org

Society for Promoting Christian Knowledge, *Office:* 36 Causton Street, London SW1P 4ST
Tel: 020 7592 3900
website: www.spck.org.uk

Sons and Friends of the Clergy *see* **Clergy Support Trust**

Tearfund, *Chief Exec:* Mr N. Harris, 100 Church Road, Teddington, Middlesex TW11 8QE
Tel: 020 3906 3906
website: www.tearfund.org

TocH, PO Box 15824, Birmingham B13 3JU
Tel: 0121 443 3552
website: www.toch.org.uk

Traidcraft plc, Kingsway, Gateshead NE11 0NE
Tel: 0191 491 0591
website: www.traidcraft.co.uk

Train a Priest (TAP) Fund, *Contact:* c/o Church Times, Hymns Ancient & Modern, 13a Hellesdon Park Road, Norwich NR6 5DR
website: www.hymnsam.co.uk/train-a-priest

WATCH, *Sec:* Claire Creese, *Office:* St John's Church, Waterloo Road, London SE1 8TY
email: admin@womenandthechurch.org

William Temple Foundation, Park House, 200 Drake Street, Rochdale, Lancashire OL16 1PJ.
Director of Research: Chris Baker
Tel: 07779 000 021
website: www.williamtemplefoundation.org.uk

Women's Institute, *National Office:* 104 New King's Road, London SW6 4LY
Tel: 020 7371 9300
website: www.womens-institute.co.uk

World Council of Churches, *Gen. Sec:* Dr Olav Fykse Tveit, 150 route de Fernay, PO Box 2100, 1211 Geneva-2, Switzerland
Tel: 0041 22 791 6111
website: www.oikoumene.org

PAROCHIAL FEES

As the fees for 2020 have yet to be agreed, the total fee payable at the time of going to press (Incumbent and Parochial Church Council combined) is shown, with space for the revised figures to be added when available.

	1 Total fee payable for 2020	2 Fee payable to Incumbent	3 Fee payable to PCC	4 Total fee payable
	£ p	£ p	£ p	£ p
Baptisms				
There is no fee for the service of baptism				
Certificate issued at the time of baptism	14.00			
Short certificate of baptism given under Section 2, Baptismal Registers Measure 1961	14.00			
Marriages				
Publication of banns of marriage	30.00			
Certificate of banns issued at the time of publication	14.00			
Marriage service	455.00			
(Marriage certificate—See Note 6)				
Funerals and burials (of persons aged 16 years or more)				
Service in church				
Funeral service in church	195.00			
Burial of body in churchyard immediately before or after service	313.00			
Burial of cremated remains in churchyard	134.00			
Burial in cemetery or cremation immediately before or after service (See Note 3(ii))	28.00			
Burial of body in churchyard on separate occasion (See Note 3(iii))	341.00			
Burial of cremated remains in churchyard on separate occasion	162.00			
Burial in cemetery on separate occasion (See Note 3(ii))	69.00			
No service in church				
Service in crematorium or cemetery (See Note 3(ii))	195.00			
Burial of body in churchyard (See Note 3(iv))	341.00			
Burial of cremated remains in churchyard (See Note 3(iv))	162.00			
Certificate issued at the time of burial (See Note 3(v))	14.00			
Monuments in churchyards				
Erected with consent of incumbent under Chancellor's general directions:				
Small cross of wood	44.00			
Small vase not exceeding 305mm × 203mm × 203mm (12"× 8"× 8")	73.00			
Tablet, plaque or other marker commemorating person cremated	73.00			
Any other monument (the above fees to include original inscription)	140.00			
Additional inscription on existing monument (See Note 4)	27.00			
Searches in church registers, etc				
Searching registers of marriages prior to 1 July 1837 (See Note 5) (up to 1 hour)	30.00			
(each subsequent hour or part of an hour)	30.00			
Searching registers of baptisms and burials (See Note 5) (including the provision of one copy of an entry therein) (up to 1 hour)	30.00			
(each subsequent hour or part of an hour)	30.00			
Each additional copy of an entry in a register of baptisms or burials	14.00			
Inspection of instrument of apportionment or agreement for exchange of land for tithes deposited under Tithe Act 1836	Nil			
Furnishing copies of above (for every 72 words)	14.00			

Extras—The fees shown in this table are the statutory fees payable. It is stressed that the figures do not include charges for extras such as music (e.g. organist, choir), bells and flowers, which are fixed by the Parochial Church Council.

Notes on the Common Worship Calendar, Lectionary and Collects references (amended) 1997 and Weekday Lectionary references, approved 2005

The Common Worship lectionary for Sundays, Holy Days and Principal Feast days owes its origin to the Revised Common Lectionary originally developed by the Roman Catholic Church in 1969. The full Calendar, Lectionary and Collects were published by Church House Publishing, London and available for use from Advent 1997. An explanation of the background to the lectionary can be found in the introduction to the 1992 Report.

The following notes for guidance derived from the General Synod report GS1161A and revisions.

1 The year's lectionary follows **Year A** of the three-year cycle beginning on Advent Sunday 2019 and the Gospel readings are primarily taken from Mathew. (In Year B the Gospel readings are from Mark and in C from Luke.) John is read each year, especially around Christmas, Lent and Easter and also in the Year of Luke. References are to the New Revised Standard Version of the Bible and, in the case of psalms to the Common Worship Psalter. In the readings of psalms and other portions of Holy Scripture any version of Holy Scripture which is not prohibited by lawful authority may be used.

2 When there are only **two readings** at the Principal Service and that service is Holy Communion, the second reading is always the Gospel reading. When the Principal Service lectionary is used at a service other than the Holy Communion, the Gospel reading need not always be chosen. If there are only two readings at the Principal Service on Easter Day, the Second, Third, Fourth, Fifth, Sixth or Seventh Sunday of Easter, Ascension Day, Pentecost, the Conversion of Paul or the Festivals of Matthias, Barnabas, James and Stephen, the reading from the Acts of the Apostles must always be used.

3 In the choice of readings other than the Gospel reading, the minister must ensure that, in any year, a balance is maintained between readings from the Old and New Testaments and that, where a particular biblical book is appointed to be read over several weeks, the choice ensures that this continuity of one book is not lost.

4 Where a reading from the **Apocrypha** is offered an alternative Old Testament reading is always provided.

5 During the period from Advent Sunday to the Presentation of Christ in the Temple, during the period from Ash Wednesday to Trinity Sunday, and on All Saints' Day, the readings shall come from an authorized lectionary. During Ordinary Time (i.e. between the Presentation and Ash Wednesday and between Trinity Sunday and Advent Sunday), authorized lectionary provision remains the norm but, after due consultation with the Parochial Church Council, the minister may, from time to time, depart from the lectionary provision for pastoral reasons or preaching or teaching purposes.

6 Three sets of psalms and readings are provided for each Sunday as follows:
Principal Service (whether this service is Holy Communion or some other authorized form) which is likely to be the mid-morning service. A *Second Service*, an afternoon or evening service. A Gospel reading is always provided so that this lectionary can, if necessary, be used at Holy Communion. A *Third Service*, with short readings, intended for use when a third set of psalms and readings is needed. It is most appropriate for use at an Office, not a Eucharist.

7 On the Sundays between the Presentation of Christ in the Temple and the Second Sunday before Lent, and again on the Sundays after Trinity, the readings and Collects follow independent courses. The Collects and Post Communions are attached to the Sunday title (the Fifth/Fourth/Third Sunday before Lent, the First/Second/Third Sunday after Trinity, etc), but the sets of proper readings (Propers 4, 5, 6 etc.) belong to particular calendar dates (i.e. the Sunday between two dates).

8 On the Sundays after Trinity, the Principal Service Lectionary provides alternative Old Testament readings and psalms. Those under the heading 'Continuous' allow the Old Testament reading and its complementary psalm to stand independently of the other readings. Those under the heading 'Related' relate the Old Testament reading and the psalm to the Gospel reading. It is unhelpful to move from week to week from one column to another.

The **Weekday Lectionary** provided is that authorized by General Synod as revised by the Liturgical Commission (GS1520A as amended by GS1520B). The Daily Eucharistic Lectionary derives, with some adaption, from the *Ordo Lectionum Missae* of the Roman Catholic Church.

To this provision, since 2010, a further set of readings, the Common Worship Additional Weekday Lectionary, has been introduced. It provides two readings one a one-year cycle for each day (except for Sundays, Principal Feasts and Principal Holy Days). It is intended particularly for use in those churches and cathedrals which attract occasional rather than regular congregations, and each reading is designed to stand alone. They are shown in italics immediately below the Common Worship morning and evening readings.

Notes to Parochial Fees on page 24

1. Definitions: *Burial:* Includes deposit in a vault or brick grave and the interment or deposit of cremated remains. *Churchyard:* Includes the curtilage of a church and a burial ground of a church whether or not immediately adjoining such church. (NOTE: This includes any area used for the interment of cremated remains within such a curtilage or burial ground, whether consecrated or not.) *Cemetery:* Means a burial ground maintained by a burial authority. *Monument:* Includes headstones, cross, kerb, border, vas, chain, railing, tablet, plaque, marker, flatstone, tombstone or monument or tomb of any other kind.

2. Incumbent's Fee: Incumbents declare their fees to the Diocese, which takes them into account in determining the stipend paid to the incumbent.

3. Funerals and Burials: (i) No fee is payable in respect of a burial of a still-born infant, or for the funeral or burial of an infant dying within one year after birth. (ii) The fees prescribed by this table for a funeral service in any cemetery or crematorium are mandatory except where a cemetery or cremation authority has itself fixed different charges for these services, in which case the authority's charges apply. (iii) The fee for a burial in a churchyard on a separate occasion applies when burial does not follow on from a service in church. (iv) If a full funeral service is held at the graveside in a churchyard the incumbent's fee is increased to that payable where the service is held in church. (v) The certificate issued at the time of burial is a copy of the entry in the register of burials kept under the Parochial Registers and Records Measure 1978.

4. Monuments in Churchyards: The fee for an additional inscription on a small cross of wood, or a small vase, shall not exceed the current fee payable to the incumbent for the erection of such a monument.

5. Searches in Church Registers: The search fee relates to a particular search where the approximate date of the baptism, marriage or burial is known. The fee for a more general search of a church register would be negotiable.

6. Fee for Marriage Certificate: The following fees are currently payable to the incumbent under the Registration of Births, Deaths and Marriages (Fees) Order 2014: certificate of marriage at registration £4.00; subsequently £10.00. These fees may be increased from 1 April 2019.

For further information about this table and associated matters, see 'A Guide to Church of England Fees' issued by the Church Commissioners.

THEOLOGICAL COLLEGES

All Saints Centre for Mission and Ministry (formerly SNWTP), Aiken Hall, University of Chester, Crab Lane, Warrington WA2 0BD
Tel: 01925 534303 *email:* snwtpprincipal@chester.ac.uk

Church of Ireland Theological College, Braemor Park, Dublin 14, Republic of Ireland
Tel: 00353 (1) 492 3506

College of the Resurrection, Stocks Bank Road, Mirfield, West Yorks WF14 0BW
Tel: 01924 490441 *website:* college.mirfield.org.uk

Cranmer Hall, St John's College, 3 South Bailey, Durham DH1 3RJ
Tel: 0191 334 3924 *website:* www.dur.ac.uk/st-johns.college

Cumbria Christian Learning, Church House, 19–24 Friargate, Penrith, Cumbria CA11 7XR
Tel: 01768 807765 *website:* www.cumbriachristianlearning.org.uk

Eastern Region Ministry Course, 1A The Bounds, Lady Margaret Road, Cambridge CB3 0BJ
Tel: 01223 760444 *email:* asj43@cam.ac.uk

Lincoln School of Theology, Edward King House, Minster Yard LN2 1PU
Tel: 01522 504050 *email:* sally.myers@lincoln.anglican.org

Lindisfarne Regional Training Partnership, St John's Terrace, North Shields NE29 6HS
Tel: 0191 2704144 *email:* davidbryan@lindisfarnertp.org

Local Ministry Programme, Guildford, Church House Guildford, 20 Alan Turing Road, Guildford GU2 7YF *Tel:* 01483 790319 *email:* steve.summers@cofeguildford.org.uk

Oak Hill Theological College, Chase Side, Southgate, London N14 4PS
Tel: 020 8449 0467 *Website:* www.oakhill.ac.uk

Oxford Local Ministry Programme, Church House Oxford, Langford Locks, Kidlington OX5 1GF
Tel: 01865 208282 *email:* phil.cooke@oxford.anglican.org

Queen's Foundation for Ecumenical Theological Education, The Queen's Foundation, Somerset Road, Edgbaston, Birmingham B15 2QH
Tel: 0121 454 1527 *website:* www.queens.ac.uk

Ridley Hall, Ridley Hall Road, Cambridge CB3 9HG
Tel: 01223 741080 *website:* www.ridley.cam.ac.uk

Ripon College, Cuddesdon, Oxford OX44 9EX
Tel: 01865 874404 *website:* www.rcc.ac.uk

St Augustine's College of Theology, 52 Swan Street, West Malling ME19 6JX
Tel: 01732 252656 *website:* staugustines.college.ac.uk

St Hild College, Stocks Bank Road, Mirfield WF14 0BW
Tel: 01924 481924 *email:* enquiries@sthild.org

St John's College, Nottingham, Chilwell Lane, Bramcote, Nottingham NG9 3DS
Tel: 0115 925 1114 *website:* www.stjohns-nottm.ac.uk

St Mellitus College (non-residential), St Jude's Church, 24 Collingham Road, London SW5 0LX
Tel: 020 7052 0573 *website:* http://www.stmellitus.ac.uk/

St Padarn's Institute, 54 Cardiff Road, Llandaff, Cardiff CF5 2YJ
Tel: 029 2056 3379 *email:* via website

St Stephen's House, 16 Marston Street, Oxford OX4 1JX
Tel: 01865 613500 *website:* www.ssho.ox.ac.uk

Sarum College, 19, The Close, Salisbury SP1 2EE
Tel: 01722 424820 *website:* www.sarum.ac.uk

Scottish Episcopal Institute, Forbes House, 21 Grosvenor Crescent, Edinburgh EH12 5EE
Tel: 0131 2256357 *email:* tisec@scotland.anglican.org

South West Ministry Training Course, Riverside Church and Conference Centre, 13–14 Okehampton Street, St Thomas, Exeter EX4 1DU
Tel: 01392 272544 *website:* SWTC.org.uk

Trinity College, Stoke Hill, Stoke Bishop, Bristol BS9 1JP
Tel: 0117 968 2803 *website:* www.trinitycollegebristol.ac.uk

Westcott House, Jesus Lane, Cambridge CB5 8BP
Tel: 01223 741000 *website:* www.westcott.cam.ac.uk

Wycliffe Hall, 54 Banbury Road, Oxford OX2 6PW
Tel: 01865 274200 *website:* www.wycliffehall.org.uk

FLAGS FOR CHURCHES
Guidance issued by The Flag Institute for the Church of England
(reproduced by kind permission)

There are no legal restrictions on the flags which may be flown from a church, but there are some customs which should be followed. In general, any appropriate flag may be flown, subject to Diocesan guidance and the wishes of the Incumbent and Parochial Church Council (PCC). There is precedence for flying foreign, national, regional, civic, organisational, historical, or personal flags from a church with agreement. However it should be noted that there are certain legal and ceremonial restrictions placed upon some flags. For instance Royal Standards (British or foreign) may only be flown while the royal personage is actually within the building or grounds, being hoisted ('broken') on their arrival and lowered following their departure.

In the United Kingdom there are no legal timings for the raising and lowering of flags. Tradition has been to raise the flag first thing in the morning and lower it at sunset. There are no legislated dates when flags must, or must not, be flown. However each year the Lord Chamberlain, through the Department of Culture, Media and Sport, issues a list of days on which UK Government buildings should fly the national flag. Combining this with other appropriate civil and religious days, the Flag Institute has compiled a list of suitable dates for churches to fly flags (see table below). These suggestions in no way prohibit the flying of flags on any other day, such as local festivals or other occasions. Indeed it may be appropriate for a PCC to draw up their own list of dates for flying flags from their churches.

On occasion it will be necessary to fly a flag at half-mast. The correct procedure is to raise the flag to the top of the pole ('close-up'), held there for a moment, and then lowered to about two-thirds of the way up (to avoid being obscured by buildings, trees or parapets etc). This procedure is reversed when the flag is lowered.

If a national or other flag is to be placed on a coffin, the top left corner of the flag should be placed over the deceased's left shoulder. It should be removed before interment.

For further advice, guidance and information, e-mail the Flag Institute on **ecclesiastical@flaginstitute. org** or check the website on **www.flaginstitute.org**

The following is a suggested list of dates for flags to be flown from a church, which is neither mandatory nor exhaustive. The prime flag would be the most appropriate for each day, but an alternative suggestion is made. Other national flags also apply where *St George* is shown as an alternative.

Date	Occasion	Prime Flag	Alternative
20 January	Birthday of HRH The Countess of Wessex	Union Flag	St George
6 February	Her Majesty's Accession	Union Flag	St George
19 February	Birthday of HRH The Duke of York	Union Flag	St George
1 March	St David's Day	Wales	Union Flag
2nd Mon in March	Commonwealth Day	Union Flag	St George
10 March	Birthday of HRH The Earl of Wessex	Union Flag	St George
17 March	St Patrick's Day	St Patrick	Union Flag
March/April	Easter Sunday and following seven days	Diocesan Flag	St George
21 April	Birthday of HM The Queen	Union Flag	St George
23 April	St George's Day	St George	Diocesan Flag
May	Ascension Day	Diocesan Flag	St George
9 May	Europe Day	EU Flag	Union Flag
May/June	Trinity Sunday	Diocesan Flag	St George
2 June	Coronation Day	Union Flag	St George
June	HM The Queen's Official Birthday	Union Flag	St George
10 June	Birthday of HRH The Duke of Edinburgh	Union Flag	St George
15 August	Birthday of HRH The Princess Royal	Union Flag	St George
3 September	Merchant Navy Day	Red Ensign	Union Flag
3rd Sun in Sept.	Battle of Britain Day	Union Flag	St George
21 October	Trafalgar Day	Union Flag	St George
24 October	United Nations Day	UN Flag	Union Flag
1 November	All Saints Day	Diocesan Flag	St George
2nd Sun in Nov.	Remembrance Sunday	Union Flag	St George
11 November	Remembrance Day	Union Flag	St George
14 November	Birthday of HRH The Prince of Wales	Union Flag	St George
20 November	HM The Queen's Wedding Anniversary	Union Flag	St George
30 November	St Andrew's Day	St Andrew	Union Flag
25 December	Christmas Day – until Epiphany	Diocesan Flag	St George
As appropriate	Dedication Sunday	Diocesan Flag	St George
As appropriate	Patronal Festival	Diocesan Flag	St George
As appropriate	Local/Regional Days	Regional Flag	St George

COMMON OF THE SAINTS
Readings

The Blessed Virgin Mary
Genesis 3.8–15,20; Isaiah 7.10–14; Micah 5.1–4
Acts 1.12–14; Romans 8.18–30; Galatians 4.4–7
Psalms 45.10–17; 113; 131
Luke 1.26–38; Luke 1.39–47; John 19.25–27

Martyrs
2 Chronicles 24.17–21; Isaiah 43.1–7; Jeremiah 11.18–20;
Wisdom 4.10–15
Romans 8.35–39; 2 Corinthians 4.7–15; 2 Timothy
2.3–7[8–13];
Hebrews 11.32–40; 1 Peter 4.12–19; Revelation 12.10–12a
Psalms 3; 11; 31.1–5; 44.18–24; 126
Matthew 10.16–22, Matthew 10.28–39; Matthew 16.24–26;
John 12.24–26; John 15.18–21
For Agnes: also Revelation 7.13–17
*For Charles: also Ecclesiasticus 2.12–17; 1 Timothy
6.12–16*
*For Janani Luwum: also Ecclesiasticus 4.20–28; John
12.24–32*
For Polycarp: also Revelation 2.8–11
*For Perpetua: especially Revelation 12.10–12a; also
Wisdom 3.1–7*
For Alphege: also Hebrews 5.1–4
*For Justin: especially John 15.18–21; also 1 Maccabees
2.15–22; 1 Corinthians 1.18–25*
For Boniface: also Acts 20.24–28
For Alban: especially 2 Timothy 2.3–13; John 12.24–26
For Oswald: especially 1 Peter 4.12–19; John 16.29–33
For Laurence: also 2 Corinthians 9.6–10
*For Cyprian: especially 1 Peter 4.12–19; also Matthew
18.18–22*
*For John Coleridge Patteson: especially 2 Chronicles
24.17–21; also Acts 7.55–60*
*For William Tyndale: also Proverbs 8.4–11; 2 Timothy
3.12–17*
For Ignatius: also Philippians 3.7–12; John 6.52–58
For James Hannington: especially Matthew 10.28–39
For Edmund: also Proverbs 20.28; 21.1–4,7
*For Clement: also Philippians 3.17–4.3; Matthew
16.13–19*
For Lucy: also Wisdom 3.1–7; 2 Corinthians 4.6–15
*For Thomas Becket: especially Matthew 10.28–33, also
Ecclesiasticus 51.1–8*

Teachers of the Faith and Spiritual Writers
1 Kings 3.[6–10]11–14; Proverbs 4.1–9; Wisdom
7.7–10,15–16;
Ecclesiasticus 39.1–10
1 Corinthians 1.18–25; 1 Corinthians 2.1–10; 1 Corinthians
2.9–16; Ephesians 3.8–12; 2 Timothy 4.1–8; Titus 2.1–8
Psalms 19.7–10; 34.11–17; 37.30–35; 119.89–96; 119.97–104
Matthew 5.13–19; Matthew 13.52–58; Matthew 23.8–12;
Mark 4.1–9; John 16.12–15
*For Basil and Gregory: especially 2 Timothy 4.1–8;
Matthew 5.13–19*
For Hilary: also 1 John 2.18–25; John 8.25–32
*For Francis de Sales: also Proverbs 3.13–18; John
3.17–21*
*For Thomas Aquinas: especially Wisdom 7.7–10,15–16; 1
Corinthians 2.9–16; John 16.12–15*
*For William Law: especially 1 Corinthians 2.9–16; also
Matthew 17.1–9*
For Anselm: also Wisdom 9.13–18; Romans 5.8–11
*For Catherine of Siena: also Proverbs 8.1,6–11; John
17.12–26*
*For Athanasius: also Ecclesiasticus 4.20–28; also
Matthew 10.24–27*
For Irenæus: also 2 Peter 1.16–21
*For Gregory and Macrina of Nyssa: especially
1 Corinthians 2.9–13; also Wisdom 9.13–17*
For Jeremy Taylor: also Titus 2.7–8,11–14
For Bernard: especially Revelation 19.5–9
*For Augustine of Hippo: especially Ecclesiasticus
39.1–10; also Romans 13.11–13*
For John Bunyan: also Hebrews 12.1–2; Luke 21.21,34–36
For Gregory the Great: also 1 Thessalonians 2.3–8
*For John Chrysostom: especially Matthew 5.13–19; also
Jeremiah 1.4–10*
For Teresa of Avila: also Romans 8.22–27
*For Richard Hooker: especially John 16.12–15; also
Ecclesiasticus 44.10–15*

For Leo: also 1 Peter 5.1–11
For Ambrose: also Isaiah 41.9b–13; Luke 22.24–30
*John of the Cross: especially 1 Corinthians 2.1–10; also
John 14.18–23*

Bishops and Other Pastors
1 Samuel 16.1,6–13; Isaiah 6.1–8; Jeremiah 1.4–10;
Ezekiel 3.16–21; Malachi 2.5–7
Acts 20.28–35; 1 Corinthians 4.1–5; 2 Corinthians 4.1–10
(or 1,2,5–7); 2 Corinthians 5.14–20; 1 Peter 5.1–4
Psalms 1; 15; 16.5–11; 96; 110
Matthew 11.25–30; Matthew 24.42–46; John 10.11–16;
John 15.9–17; John 21.15–17
For Wulfstan: especially Matthew 24.42–46
*For George Herbert: especially Malachi 2.5–7; Matthew
11.25–30; also Revelation 19.5–9*
For David: also 2 Samuel 23.1–4; Psalm 89.19–22,24
For Edward King: also Hebrews 13.1–8
*For Dunstan: especially Matthew 24.42–46; also Exodus
31.1–5*
For John and Charles Wesley: also Ephesians 5.15–20
*For Augustine of Canterbury: also 1 Thessalonians
2.2b–8; Matthew 13.31–33*
*For Thomas Ken: especially 2 Corinthians 4.1–10;
Matthew 24.42–46*
For Richard: also John 21.15–19
*For John Keble: also Lamentations 3.19–26; Matthew
5.1–8*
For Swithun: also James 5.7–11,13–18
For Lancelot Andrewes: especially Isaiah 6.1–8
*For Martin of Tours: also 1 Thessalonians 5.1–11;
Matthew 25.34–40*
*For Charles Simeon: especially Malachi 2.5–7; also
Colossians 1.3–8; Luke 8.4–8*
For Hugh: also 1 Timothy 6.11–16
*For Nicholas: also Isaiah 61.1–3; 1 Timothy 6.6–11; Mark
10.13–16*

Members of Religious Communities
1 Kings 19.9–18; Proverbs 10.27–32; Song of Solomon
8.6–7;
Isaiah 61.10–62.5; Hosea 2.14–15,19–20
Acts 4.32–35; 2 Corinthians 10.17–11.2; Philippians 3.7–14;
1 John 2.15–17; Revelation 19.1,5–9
Psalms 34.1–8; 112.1–9; 119.57–64; 123; 131
Matthew 11.25–30; Matthew 19.3–12; Matthew 19.23–30;
Luke 9.57–62; Luke 12.32–37
For Aelred: also Ecclesiasticus 15.1–6
*For Antony: especially Philippians 3.7–14; also Matthew
19.16–26*
*For Julian of Norwich: also 1 Corinthians 13.8–13;
Matthew 5.13–16*
For Alcuin: also Colossians 3.12–16; John 4.19–24
For Bede: also Ecclesiasticus 39.1–10
For Etheldreda: also Matthew 25.1–13
For Benedict: also 1 Corinthians 3.10,11; Luke 18.18–22
For Dominic: also Ecclesiasticus 39.1–10
For Clare: especially Song of Solomon 8.6–7
For Hildegard: also 1 Corinthians 2.9–13; Luke 10.21–24
*For Vincent de Paul: also 1 Corinthians 1.25–31; Matthew
25.34–40*
*For Francis of Assisi: also Galatians 6.14–18; Luke
12.22–34*
For Hilda: especially Isaiah 61.10–62.5

Missionaries
Isaiah 52.7–10; Isaiah 61.1–3a; Ezekiel 34.11–16; Jonah
3.1–5
Acts 2.14,22–36; Acts 13.46–49; Acts 16.6–10; Acts
26.19–23;
Romans 15.17–21; 2 Corinthians 5.11–6.2
Psalms 67; 87; 97; 100; 117
Matthew 9.35–38; Matthew 28.16–20; Mark 16.15–20;
Luke 5.1–11; Luke 10.1–9
*For Anskar: also Isaiah 52.7–10; also Romans
10.11–15*
*For Cyril and Methodius: especially Isaiah 52.7–10; also
Romans 10.11–15*
For Chad: also 1 Timothy 6.11b–16
For Patrick: also Psalm 91.1–4,13–16; Luke 10.1–12,17–20
*For Cuthbert: especially Ezekiel 34.11–16; also Matthew
18.12–14*
For Columba: also Titus 2.11–15
For Aidan: also 1 Corinthians 9.16–19
For Ninian: especially Acts 13.46–49; Mark 16.15–20
For Paulinus: especially Matthew 28.16–20
*For Wilfrid: especially Luke 1.5–11; also 1 Corinthians
1.18–25*

For Henry Martyn: especially Mark 16.15–20; also Isaiah 55.6–11
For Willibrord: especially Isaiah 52.7–10; Matthew 28.16–20

Any Saint
General
Genesis 12.1–4; Proverbs 8.1–11; Micah 6.6–8;
Ecclesiasticus 2.7–13[14–17]
Ephesians 3.14–19; Ephesians 6.11–18; Hebrews 13.7–8,15–16; James 2.14–17; 1 John 4.7–16; Revelation 21.[1–4]5–7
Psalms 32; 33.1–5; 119.1–8; 139.1–4[5–12]; 145.8–14
Matthew 19.16–21; Matthew 25.1–13; Matthew 25.14–30;
John 15.1–8; John 17.20–26
Christian rulers
1 Samuel 16.1–13a; 1 Kings 3.3–14
1 Timothy 2.1–6
Psalms 72.1–7; 99
Mark 10.42–45; Luke 14.27–33
For Edward the Confessor: also 2 Samuel 23.1–5; 1 John 4.13–16
For Alfred the Great: also 2 Samuel 23.1–5; John 18.33–37
For Margaret of Scotland: also Proverbs 31.10–12,20, 26–31; 1 Corinthians 12.13–13.3; Matthew 25.34–46
Those working for the poor and underprivileged
Isaiah 58.6–11
Hebrews 13.1–3; 1 John 3.14–18
Psalms 82; 146.5–12
Matthew 5.1–12; Matthew 25.31–46
For Josephine Butler: especially Isaiah 58.6–11; also 1 John 3.18–23; Matthew 9.10–13
For William Wilberforce: also Job 31.16–23; Galatians 3.26–29; 4.6–7; Luke 4.16–21
For Elizabeth of Hungary: especially Matthew 25.31–46; also Proverbs 31.10–31
Men and women of learning
Proverbs 8.22–31; Ecclesiasticus 44.1–15
Philippians 4.7–8
Psalms 36.5–10; 49.1–4
Matthew 13.44–46,52;
John 7.14–18
Those whose holiness was revealed in marriage and family life
Proverbs 31.10–31 (*or* 10–13,19–20,30–31); Tobit 8.4–7
1 Peter 3.1–9
Psalms 127; 128
Mark 3.31–35; Luke 10.38–42
For Mary Sumner: also Hebrews 13.1–5
For Monica: also Ecclesiasticus 26.1–3,13–16

SPECIAL OCCASIONS

The Guidance of the Holy Spirit
Proverbs 24.3–7; Isaiah 30.15–21; Wisdom 9.13–17
Acts 15.23–29; Romans 8.22–27; 1 Corinthians 12.4–13
Psalms 25.1–9; 104.26–33; 143.8–10
Luke 14.27–33; John 14.23–26; John 16.13–15

Rogation Days
Deuteronomy 8.1–10; 1 Kings 8.35–40; Job 28.1–11
Philippians 4.4–7; 2 Thessalonians 3.6–13; 1 John 5.12–15
Psalms 104.21–30; 107.1–9; 121
Matthew 6.1–15; Mark 11.22–24; Luke 11.5–13

Harvest Thanksgiving
Year A
Deuteronomy 8.7–18 or Deuteronomy 28.1–14
Psalm 65
2 Corinthians 9.6–15
Luke 12.16–30 or Luke 17.11–19
Year B
Joel 2.21–27
Psalm 126
1 Timothy 2.1–7 or 1 Timothy 6.6–10
Matthew 6.25–33
Year C
Deuteronomy 26.1–11
Psalm 100
Philippians 4.4–9 or Revelation 14.14–18
John 6.25–35

Mission and Evangelism
Isaiah 49.1–6; Isaiah 52.7–10; Micah 4.1–5
Acts 17.12–34; 2 Corinthians 5.14–6.2; Ephesians 2.13–22
Psalms 2; 46; 67
Matthew 5.13–16; Matthew 28.16–20; John 17.20–26

The Unity of the Church
Jeremiah 33.6–9a; Ezekiel 36.23–28; Zephaniah 3.16–20
Ephesians 4.1–6; Colossians 3.9–17; 1 John 4.9–15
Psalms 100; 122; 133
Matthew 18.19–22; John 11.45–52; John 17.11b–23

The Peace of the World
Isaiah 9.1–6; Isaiah 57.15–19; Micah 4.1–5
Philippians 4.6–9; 1 Timothy 2.1–6; James 3.13–18
Psalms 40.14–17; 72.1–7; 85.8–13
Matthew 5.43–48; John 14.23–29; John 15.9–17

Social Justice and Responsibility
Isaiah 32.15–20; Amos 5.21–24; Amos 8.4–7; Acts 5.1–11
Colossians 3.12–15; James 2.1–4
Psalms 31.21–24; 85.1–7; 146.5–10
Matthew 5.1–12; Matthew 25.31–46; Luke 16.19–31

Ministry (including Ember Days)
Numbers 11.16–17,24–29; Numbers 27.15–23;
1 Samuel 16.1–13a; Isaiah 6.1–8; Isaiah 61.1–3;
Jeremiah 1.4–10 Acts 20.28–35; 1 Corinthians 3.3–11;
Ephesians 4.4–16; Philippians 3.7–14
Psalms 40.8–13; 84.8–12; 89.19–25; 101.1–5,7; 122
Luke 4.16–21; Luke 12.35–43; Luke 22.24–27; John 4.31–38;
John 15.5–17

In Time of Trouble
Genesis 9.8–17; Job 1.13–22; Isaiah 38.6–11
Romans 3.21–26; Romans 8.18–25; 2 Corinthians 8.1–5,9
Psalms 86.1–7; 107.4–15; 142.1–7
Mark 4.35–41; Luke 12.1–7; John 16.31–33

For the Sovereign
Joshua 1.1–9; Proverbs 8.1–16
Romans 13.1–10; Revelation 21.22–22.4
Psalms 20; 101; 121
Matthew 22.16–22; Luke 22.24–30

COMMON OF THE SAINTS

The Blessed Virgin Mary   *White*
Collect

Almighty and everlasting God,
who stooped to raise fallen humanity
through the child-bearing of blessed Mary;
grant that we, who have seen your glory
revealed in our human nature
and your love made perfect in our weakness,
may daily be renewed in your image
and conformed to the pattern of your Son
Jesus Christ our Lord,
who is alive and reigns with you,
in the unity of the Holy Spirit,
one God, now and for ever.

Post Communion

God most high,
whose handmaid bore the Word made flesh:
we thank you that in this sacrament of our redemption
you visit us with your Holy Spirit
and overshadow us by your power;
strengthen us to walk with Mary the joyful path of obedience
and so to bring forth the fruits of holiness;
through Jesus Christ our Lord.

Apostles and Evangelists   *Red*
Collect

Almighty God,
who built your Church upon the foundation
of the apostles and prophets,
with Jesus Christ himself as the chief corner-stone:
so join us together in unity of spirit by their doctrine,
that we may be made a holy temple acceptable to you;

through Jesus Christ your Son our Lord,
who is alive and reigns with you,
in the unity of the Holy Spirit, one God,
now and for ever.

Post Communion

Almighty God,
who on the day of Pentecost
sent your Holy Spirit to the apostles
with the wind from heaven and in tongues of flame,
filling them with joy and boldness to preach the gospel:
by the power of the same Spirit
strengthen us to witness to your truth
and to draw everyone to the fire of your love;
through Jesus Christ our Lord.

or

Lord God, the source of truth and love,
keep us faithful to the apostles' teaching and fellowship,
united in prayer and the breaking of bread,
and one in joy and simplicity of heart,
in Jesus Christ our Lord.

Martyrs *Red*

Collect

Almighty God,
by whose grace and power your holy martyr N
triumphed over suffering and was faithful unto death:
strengthen us with your grace,
that we may endure reproach and persecution
and faithfully bear witness to the name
of Jesus Christ your Son our Lord,
who is alive and reigns with you,
in the unity of the Holy Spirit,
one God, now and for ever.

Post Communion

Eternal God,
who gave us this holy meal
in which we have celebrated the glory of the cross
and the victory of your martyr N:
by our communion with Christ
in his saving death and resurrection,
give us with all your saints the courage to conquer evil
and so to share the fruit of the tree of life;
through Jesus Christ our Lord.

or

God our redeemer,
whose Church was strengthened by the blood of your
    martyr N:
so bind us, in life and death, to Christ's sacrifice
that our lives, broken and offered with his,
may carry his death and proclaim his resurrection in the
world;
through Jesus Christ our Lord.

Teachers of the Faith *White*

Collect

Almighty God,
who enlightened your Church
by the teaching of your servant N:
enrich it evermore with your heavenly grace
and raise up faithful witnesses
who, by their life and teaching,
may proclaim the truth of your salvation;
through Jesus Christ your Son our Lord,
who is alive and reigns with you,
in the unity of the Holy Spirit,
one God, now and for ever.

Post Communion

God of truth,
whose Wisdom set her table
and invited us to eat the bread and drink the wine
of the kingdom:
help us to lay aside all foolishness
and to live and walk in the way of insight,
that we may come with N
to the eternal feast of heaven;
through Jesus Christ our Lord.

Bishops and Other Pastors *White*

Collect

Eternal God,
you called N to proclaim your glory
in a life of prayer and pastoral zeal:
keep the leaders of your Church faithful
and bless your people through their ministry,
that the Church may grow into the full stature
of your Son Jesus Christ our Lord,
who is alive and reigns with you,
in the unity of the Holy Spirit,
one God, now and for ever.

or, for a Bishop

Almighty God,
the light of the faithful and shepherd of souls,
who set your servant N to be a bishop in the Church,
to feed your sheep by the word of Christ
and to guide them by good example:
give us grace to keep the faith of the Church
and to follow in the footsteps
of Jesus Christ your Son our Lord,
who is alive and reigns with you,
in the unity of the Holy Spirit,
one God, now and for ever.

Post Communion

God, shepherd of your people,
whose servant N revealed the loving service of Christ
in his/her ministry as a pastor of your people:
by this eucharist in which we share
awaken within us the love of Christ
and keep us faithful to our Christian calling;
through him who laid down his life for us,
but is alive and reigns with you, now and for ever.

Members of Religious Communities *White*

Collect

Almighty God,
by whose grace N, kindled with the fire of your love,
became a burning and a shining light in the Church:
inflame us with the same spirit of discipline and love,
that we may ever walk before you as children of light;
through Jesus Christ your Son our Lord,
who is alive and reigns with you,
in the unity of the Holy Spirit,
one God, now and for ever.

Post Communion

Merciful God,
who gave such grace to your servant N
that he/she served you with singleness of heart
and loved you above all things:
help us, whose communion with you
has been renewed in this sacrament,
to forsake all that holds us back from following Christ
and to grow into his likeness from glory to glory;
through Jesus Christ our Lord.

Missionaries *White*

Collect

Everlasting God,
whose servant N carried the good news of your Son
to the people of . . . :
grant that we who commemorate his/her service
may know the hope of the gospel in our hearts
and manifest its light in all our ways;
through Jesus Christ your Son our Lord,
who is alive and reigns with you,
in the unity of the Holy Spirit,
one God, now and for ever.

Post Communion

Holy Father,
who gathered us here around the table of your Son
to share this meal with the whole household of God:
in that new world where you reveal
the fullness of your peace,
gather people of every race and language
to share with N and all your saints
in the eternal banquet of Jesus Christ our Lord.

Any Saint *White*

Collect (general)

Almighty Father,
you have built up your Church
through the love and devotion of your saints:
inspire us to follow the example of *N*,
whom we commemorate today,
that we in our generation may rejoice with him/her
in the vision of your glory;
through Jesus Christ your Son our Lord,
who is alive and reigns with you,
in the unity of the Holy Spirit,
one God, now and for ever.

or (for Christian rulers)

Sovereign God,
who called *N* to be a ruler among his/her people
and gave him/her grace to be their servant:
help us, following our Saviour Christ
in the path of humble service,
to see his kingdom set forward on earth
and to enjoy its fullness in heaven;
who is alive and reigns with you,
in the unity of the Holy Spirit,
one God, now and for ever.

or (for those working with the poor and underprivileged)

Merciful God,
you have compassion on all that you have made
and your whole creation is enfolded in your love:
help us to stand firm for your truth,
to struggle against poverty,
and to share your love with our neighbour,
that with your servant *N*
we may be instruments of your peace;
through Jesus Christ your Son our Lord,
who is alive and reigns with you,
in the unity of the Holy Spirit,
one God, now and for ever.

or

God, the source of all holiness
and giver of all good things:
may we who have shared at this table
as strangers and pilgrims here on earth
be welcomed with all your saints
to the heavenly feast on the day of your kingdom;
through Jesus Christ our Lord.

or (for men and women of learning)

God our Father,
who gave wisdom and insight to your servant *N*
to fathom the depths of your love
and to understand your design for the world you
have made:
grant us the help of your Holy Spirit
that we also may come to a full knowledge of your
purposes
revealed in your Son Jesus Christ, our wisdom and
our life;
who is alive and reigns with you,
in the unity of the Holy Spirit,
one God, now and for ever.

*or (for those whose holiness was revealed in marriage and
family life)*

Eternal God,
whose love is revealed in the mystery of the Trinity:
help us, like your servant *N*,
to find in our human loving a mirror of your divine love
and to see in all your children our brothers and sisters
in Christ,
who is alive and reigns with you,
in the unity of the Holy Spirit,
one God, now and for ever.

Post Communion

Faithful God,
who called *N* to serve you
and gave him/her joy in walking the path of holiness:
by this eucharist
in which you renew within us the vision of your glory,
strengthen us all to follow the way of perfection
until we come to see you face to face;
through Jesus Christ our Lord.

or

God our redeemer,
who inspired *N* to witness to your love
and to work for the coming of your kingdom:
may we, who in this sacrament share the bread of heaven,
be fired by your Spirit to proclaim the gospel in our
daily living
and never to rest content until your kingdom come,
on earth as it is in heaven;
through Jesus Christ our Lord.

or

Father,
from whom every family in heaven and on earth takes
its name,
your servant *N* revealed your goodness
in a life of tranquillity and service:
grant that we who have gathered in faith around this table
may like him/her know the love of Christ
that surpasses knowledge
and be filled with all your fullness;
through Jesus Christ our Lord.

or

God, the source of all holiness and giver of all good things:
may we who have shared at this table
as stranger and pilgrims here on earth
be welcomed with all your saints
to the heavenly feast on the day of your kingdom;
through Jesus christ our Lord.

SPECIAL OCCASIONS

The Guidance of the Holy Spirit *Red*

Collect

God, who from of old
taught the hearts of your faithful people
by sending to them the light of your Holy Spirit:
grant us by the same Spirit
to have a right judgement in all things
and evermore to rejoice in his holy comfort;
through the merits of Christ Jesus our Saviour,
who is alive and reigns with you,
in the unity of the Holy Spirit,
one God, now and for ever.

or

Almighty God,
you have given your Holy Spirit to the Church
to lead us into all truth:
bless with the Spirit's grace and presence
the members of this . . . *(synod/PCC/etc.);*
keep us/them steadfast in faith and united in love,
that we/they may manifest your glory
and prepare the way of your kingdom;
through Jesus Christ your Son our Lord,
who is alive and reigns with you,
in the unity of the Holy Spirit,
one God, now and for ever.

Post Communion

God of power,
whose Holy Spirit renews your people
in the bread and wine we bless and share:
may the boldness of the Spirit transform us,
the gentleness of the Spirit lead us,
and the gifts of the Spirit equip us
to serve and worship you;
through Jesus Christ our Lord.

Rogation Days *White*

Collect

Almighty God,
whose will it is that the earth and the sea
should bear fruit in due season:
bless the labours of those who work on land and sea,
grant us a good harvest
and the grace always to rejoice in your fatherly care;
through Jesus Christ your Son our Lord,
who is alive and reigns with you,
in the unity of the Holy Spirit,
one God, now and for ever.

or

Almighty God and Father,
you have so ordered our life
that we are dependent on one another:
prosper those engaged in commerce and industry
and direct their minds and hands
that they may rightly use your gifts in the service of others;
through Jesus Christ your Son our Lord,
who is alive and reigns with you,
in the unity of the Holy Spirit,
one God, now and for ever.

or

God our Father,
you never cease the work you have begun
and prosper with your blessing all human labour:
make us wise and faithful stewards of your gifts
that we may serve the common good,
maintain the fabric of our world
and seek that justice where all may share
the good things you pour upon us;
through Jesus Christ your Son our Lord,
who is alive and reigns with you,
in the unity of the Holy Spirit,
one God, now and for ever.

Post Communion

God our creator,
you give seed for us to sow and bread for us to eat:
as you have blessed the fruit of our labour in this
eucharist,
so we ask you to give all your children their daily bread,
that the world may praise you for your goodness;
through Jesus Christ our Lord.

Harvest Thanksgiving *Green*

Collect

Eternal God,
you crown the year with your goodness
and you give us the fruits of the earth in their season:
grant that we may use them to your glory,
for the relief of those in need
and for our own well-being;
through Jesus Christ your Son our Lord,
who is alive and reigns with you,
in the unity of the Holy Spirit,
one God now and for ever.

Post Communion

Lord of the harvest,
with joy we have offered thanksgiving
for your love in creation
and have shared in the bread and the wine of the kingdom:
by your grace plant within us a reverence for all that you
give us
and make us generous and wise stewards
of the good things we enjoy;
through Jesus Christ our Lord.

Mission and Evangelism *Colour of the Season*

Collect

Almighty God,
who called your Church to witness
that you were in Christ reconciling the world to yourself:
help us to proclaim the good news of your love,
that all who hear it may be drawn to you;
through him who was lifted up on the cross,
and reigns with you
in the unity of the Holy Spirit,
one God, now and for ever.

Post Communion

Eternal God, giver of love and power,
your Son Jesus Christ has sent us into all the world
to preach the gospel of his kingdom:
confirm us in this mission,
and help us to live the good news we proclaim;
through Jesus Christ our Lord.

The Unity of the Church *Colour of the Season*

Collect

Heavenly Father,
you have called us in the Body of your Son Jesus Christ
to continue his work of reconciliation
and reveal you to the world:
forgive us the sins which tear us apart;
give us the courage to overcome our fears
and to seek that unity which is your gift and your will;
through Jesus Christ your Son our Lord,
who is alive and reigns with you,
in the unity of the Holy Spirit,
one God, now and for ever.

or

Lord Jesus Christ,
who said to your apostles,
'Peace I leave with you, my peace I give to you':
look not on our sins but on the faith of your Church
and grant it the peace and unity of your kingdom;
where you are alive and reign with the Father
in the unity of the Holy Spirit,
one God, now and for ever.

Post Communion

Eternal God and Father,
whose Son at supper prayed that his disciples might be
one,
as he is one with you:
draw us closer to him,
that in common love and obedience to you
we may be united to one another
in the fellowship of the one Spirit,
that the world may believe that he is Lord, to your
eternal glory;
through Jesus Christ our Lord.

The Peace of the World *Colour of the Season*

Collect

Almighty God,
from whom all thoughts of truth and peace proceed:
kindle, we pray, in the hearts of all, the true love of peace
and guide with your pure and peaceable wisdom
those who take counsel for the nations of the earth
that in tranquillity your kingdom may go forward,
till the earth is filled with the knowledge of your love;
through Jesus Christ your Son our Lord,
who is alive and reigns with you,
in the unity of the Holy Spirit,
one God, now and for ever.

Post Communion

God our Father,
your Son is our peace
and his cross the sign of reconciliation:
help us, who share the broken bread,
to bring together what is scattered
and to bind up what is wounded,
that Christ may bring in the everlasting kingdom of
his peace;
who is alive and reigns, now and for ever.

Social Justice and Responsibility *Colour of the Season*

Collect

Eternal God,
in whose perfect realm
no sword is drawn but the sword of righteousness,
and no strength known but the strength of love:
so guide and inspire the work of those who seek your
kingdom
that all your people may find their security
in that love which casts out fear
and in the fellowship revealed to us

in Jesus Christ our Saviour,
who is alive and reigns with you,
in the unity of the Holy Spirit,
one God, now and for ever.

or

Almighty and eternal God,
to whom we must all give account:
guide with your Spirit the . . . of this *(city, society, etc.)*,
that we/they may be faithful to the mind of Christ
and seek in all our/their purposes to enrich our
common life;
through Jesus Christ your Son our Lord,
who is alive and reigns with you,
in the unity of the Holy Spirit,
one God, now and for ever.

Post Communion

Blessed God,
help us, whom you have fed and satisfied in this eucharist,
to hunger and thirst for what is right,
help us, who here have rejoiced and been glad,
to stand with those who are persecuted and reviled;
help us, who here have glimpsed the life of heaven,
to strive for the cause of right
and for the coming of the kingdom of Jesus Christ,
who is alive and reigns, now and for ever.

Ministry (including Ember Days) *Red or*

Colour of the Season

Collect (for the ministry of all Christian people)

Almighty and everlasting God,
by whose Spirit the whole body of the Church
is governed and sanctified:
hear our prayer which we offer for all your faithful people,
that in their vocation and ministry
they may serve you in holiness and truth
to the glory of your name;
through our Lord and Saviour Jesus Christ,
who is alive and reigns with you,
in the unity of the Holy Spirit,
one God, now and for ever.

or (for those to be ordained)

Almighty God, the giver of all good gifts,
by your Holy Spirit you have appointed
various orders of ministry in the Church:
look with mercy on your servants
now called to be deacons and priests;
maintain them in truth and renew them in holiness,
that by word and good example they may faithfully
serve you
to the glory of your name and the benefit of your Church;
through the merits of our Saviour Jesus Christ,
who is alive and reigns with you,
in the unity of the Holy Spirit,
one God, now and for ever.

or (for vocations)

Almighty God,
you have entrusted to your Church
a share in the ministry of your Son our great high priest:
inspire by your Holy Spirit the hearts of many
to offer themselves for the ministry of your Church,
that strengthened by his power,
they may work for the increase of your kingdom
and set forward the eternal praise of your name;
through Jesus Christ your Son our Lord,
who is alive and reigns with you,
in the unity of the Holy Spirit,
one God, now and for ever.

or (for the inauguration of a new ministry)

God our Father, Lord of all the world,
through your Son you have called us into the fellowship
of your universal Church:
hear our prayer for your faithful people
that in their vocation and ministry
each may be an instrument of your love,

and give to your servant *N* now to be . . . *(installed,
inducted, etc.)*
the needful gifts of grace;
through our Lord and Saviour Jesus Christ,
who is alive and reigns with you,
in the unity of the Holy Spirit,
one God, now and for ever.

Post Communion

Heavenly Father,
whose ascended Son gave gifts of leadership and service
to the Church:
strengthen us who have received this holy food
to be good stewards of your manifold grace,
through him who came not to be served but to serve,
and give his life as a ransom for many,
Jesus Christ our Lord.

or

Lord of the harvest,
you have fed your people in this sacrament
with the fruits of creation made holy by your Spirit:
by your grace raise up among us faithful labourers
to sow your word and reap the harvest of souls;
through Jesus Christ our Lord.

In Time of Trouble *Colour of the Season*

Collect

Sovereign God,
the defence of those who trust in you
and the strength of those who suffer:
look with mercy on our affliction
and deliver us through our mighty Saviour Jesus Christ,
who is alive and reigns with you,
in the unity of the Holy Spirit,
one God, now and for ever.

Post Communion

Almighty God,
whose Son gave us in this meal a pledge of your saving
love
and a foretaste of your kingdom of justice and peace:
strengthen your people in their faith
that they may endure the sufferings of this present time
in expectation of the glory to be revealed;
through Jesus Christ our Lord.

For the Sovereign *Colour of the Season*

Collect

Almighty God,
the fountain of all goodness,
bless our Sovereign Lady, Queen Elizabeth,
and all who are in authority under her;
that they may order all things
in wisdom and equity, righteousness and peace,
to the honour and glory of your name
and the good of your Church and people;
through Jesus Christ your Son our Lord,
who is alive and reigns with you,
in the unity of the Holy Spirit,
one God, now and for ever.

Post Communion

O God, the Father of our Lord Jesus Christ,
our only Saviour, the prince of peace:
give us grace seriously to lay to heart
the great dangers we are in by our unhappy divisions;
take away our hatred and prejudice
and whatever else may hinder us from godly union
and concord,
that, as there is but one body, one Spirit
and one hope of our calling,
one Lord, one faith, one baptism,
one God and Father of us all,
so may we henceforth be all of one heart and of one soul,
united in one holy bond of truth and peace, of faith
and charity,
and may with one mind and one mouth glorify you;
through Jesus Christ our Lord.

ABBREVIATIONS
The list of Abbreviations of the Bible sometimes used in this diary

The Books of the Old Testament

Genesis	Gen.	1 Kings	1 Kgs	Ecclesiastes	Eccles.	Obadiah	Obad.
Exodus	Exod.	2 Kings	2 Kgs	Song of Solomon	S of Sol.	Jonah	Jonah
Leviticus	Lev.	1 Chronicles	1 Chr.	Isaiah	Isa.	Micah	Mic.
Numbers	Num.	2 Chronicles	2 Chr.	Jeremiah	Jer.	Nahum	Nahum
Deuteronomy	Deut.	Ezra	Ezra	Lamentations	Lam.	Habakkuk	Hab.
Joshua	Josh.	Nehemiah	Neh.	Ezekiel	Ezek.	Zephaniah	Zeph.
Judges	Judg.	Esther	Esther	Daniel	Dan.	Haggai	Hag.
Ruth	Ruth	Job	Job	Hosea	Hos.	Zechariah	Zech.
1 Samuel	1 Sam.	Psalms	Ps.	Joel	Joel	Malachi	Mal.
2 Samuel	2 Sam.	Proverbs	Prov.	Amos	Amos		

Apocrypha

1 Esdras	1 Esd.	Additions to Esther	Rest of Esth.	Baruch	Baruch	Bel and the Dragon	Bel & Dr
2 Esdras	2 Esd.			Song of the Three Holy Children	Song of the Three	Prayer of Manasseh	Pr of Man
Tobit	Tobit	Wisdom of Solomon	Wisd.			1 Maccabees	1 Macc.
Judith	Judith	Ecclesiasticus	Ecclus	Susanna	Sus.	2 Maccabees	2 Macc.

The Books of the New Testament

Matthew	Matt.	2 Corinthians	2 Cor.	1 Timothy	1 Tim.	2 Peter	2 Pet.
Mark	Mark	Galatians	Gal.	2 Timothy	2 Tim.	1 John	1 John
Luke	Luke	Ephesians	Eph.	Titus	Titus	2 John	2 John
John	John	Philippians	Phil.	Philemon	Philem.	3 John	3 John
The Acts	Acts	Colossians	Col.	Hebrews	Heb.	Jude	Jude
Romans	Rom.	1 Thessalonians	1 Thess.	James	Jas	Revelation	Rev.
1 Corinthians	1 Cor.	2 Thessalonians	2 Thess.	1 Peter	1 Pet.		

Sundays

CW Title ➝ **THE BAPTISM OF CHRIST**

BCP Title ➝ *The First Sunday of Epiphany*

(*White or* Gold)

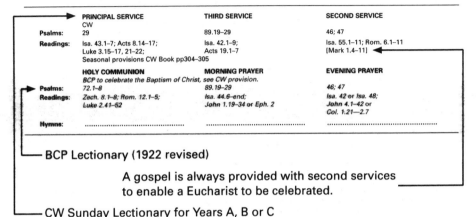

	PRINCIPAL SERVICE CW	THIRD SERVICE	SECOND SERVICE
Psalms:	29	89.19–29	46; 47
Readings:	Isa. 43.1–7; Acts 8.14–17; Luke 3.15–17, 21–22; Seasonal provisions CW Book pp304–305	Isa. 42.1–9; Acts 19.1–7	Isa. 55.1–11; Rom. 6.1–11 [Mark 1.4–11]
	HOLY COMMUNION BCP to celebrate the Baptism of Christ, see CW provision.	MORNING PRAYER	EVENING PRAYER
Psalms:	72.1–8	89.19–29	46; 47
Readings:	Zech. 8.1–8; Rom. 12.1–5; Luke 2.41–52	Isa. 44.6–end; John 1.19–34 or Eph. 2	Isa. 42 or Isa. 48; John 4.1–42 or Col. 1.21—2.7
Hymns:	....	....	....

— BCP Lectionary (1922 revised)

A gospel is always provided with second services to enable a Eucharist to be celebrated.

— CW Sunday Lectionary for Years A, B or C

Weekdays

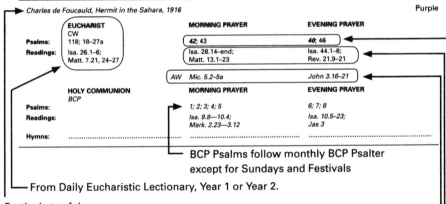

Charles de Foucauld, Hermit in the Sahara, 1916   Purple

	EUCHARIST CW	MORNING PRAYER	EVENING PRAYER
Psalms:	118; 18–27a	42; 43	40; 46
Readings:	Isa. 26.1–6; Matt. 7.21, 24–27	Isa. 28.14–end; Matt. 13.1–23	Isa. 44.1–8; Rev. 21.9–21
		AW Mic. 5.2–5a	John 3.16–21
	HOLY COMMUNION BCP	MORNING PRAYER	EVENING PRAYER
Psalms:		1; 2; 3; 4; 5	6; 7; 8
Readings:		Isa. 9.8—10.4; Mark 2.23—3.12	Isa. 10.5–23; Jas 3
Hymns:	....	....	....

— BCP Psalms follow monthly BCP Psalter except for Sundays and Festivals

— From Daily Eucharistic Lectionary, Year 1 or Year 2.

Festival etc of day:
Principal Feasts and other Principal Holy Days are printed in **BOLD UPPER CASE**;
Festivals are printed in ***larger bold italic***; lesser Festivals are printed in
ordinary roman text typeface; and Commemorations are printed in ordinary
italic text typeface. All BCP entries (including liturgical colours) are in italic.

Additional Weekday Lectionary readings —

Readings from CW weekday Lectionary, Years 1 or 2, seasonal or Ordinary time. —

Psalms at MP and EP follow the Common Worship Weekday Lectionary,
giving seasonal provisions where appropriate. N.B. Psalm numbering
in CW differs from that in BCP.

THE FIRST SUNDAY OF ADVENT

CW Year A begins   (Purple)

CW Weekday Lectionary Year 2 BCP 1922 Revised tables of Lessons or CW with variations.

	PRINCIPAL SERVICE CW	**THIRD SERVICE**	**SECOND SERVICE**
Psalms:	122	44	9* [9.1–8]
Readings:	Isa. 2.1–5; Rom. 13.11–end; Matt. 24.36–44	Mic. 4.1–7 [BCP Var. Isa. 2.1–5]; 1 Thess. 5.1–11	Isa. 52.1–12; Matt. 24.15–28

Seasonal provisions including Eucharistic prefaces until Christmas Eve. CW Book pp 300–301

	HOLY COMMUNION BCP	**MORNING PRAYER**	**EVENING PRAYER**
Psalms:	25.1–9	44	9
Readings:	Mic. 4.1–4, 6–7; Rom. 13.8–end; Matt. 21.1–13	Isa. 1.1–20; John 3.1–21 or 1 Thess. 4.13–5.11	Isa. 2 or Isa. 1.18–end; Matt. 24.1–28 or Rev. 14.13—15.4 Advent Coll. until Dec. 24
Hymns:	....	....	....

Explanatory Notes

[BCP Var.] Variations in CW Lectionary for use with BCP Lectionary.
( ) Psalms printed in brackets may be omitted. (i.e. when used as opening canticle).
On weekdays, the Psalm printed in *Bold Italics* may be used as the sole psalm.
* Longer psalms are marked with an asterisk. These may be shortened if desired.
[ ] Psalms printed in square brackets are alternatives.
A 7 week cycle of Psalms (Week 1 Ord) starts in Ordinary time on the day after the Presentation of Christ in the Temple until Shrove Tuesday and resumes on the day after Pentecost.
To enable the Second Service Lectionary to be used in Holy Communion, a Gospel is always included.

Diary users please note that main headings, psalms, readings, collects for both Sundays and weekdays are from the COMMON WORSHIP (CW) Calendar, Lectionary and Collect year A, and further reading references and collects can be found in "Common of the Saints."

N.B. Have you transferred your December notes from your 2019 Diary?

2020

	January					February					March					April					May						June			
S		5	12	19	26			2	9	16	23		1	8	15	22	29		5	12	19	26			3	10	17	24	31			7	14	21	28
M		6	13	20	27			3	10	17	24		2	9	16	23	30		6	13	20	27			4	11	18	25			1	8	15	22	29
T		7	14	21	28			4	11	18	25		3	10	17	24	31		7	14	21	28			5	12	19	26			2	9	16	23	30
W	1	8	15	22	29			5	12	19	26		4	11	18	25		1	8	15	22	29			6	13	20	27			3	10	17	24
T	2	9	16	23	30			6	13	20	27		5	12	19	26		2	9	16	23	30			7	14	21	28			4	11	18	25
F	3	10	17	24	31			7	14	21	28		6	13	20	27		3	10	17	24			1	8	15	22	29			5	12	19	26
S	4	11	18	25			1	8	15	22	29		7	14	21	28		4	11	18	25			2	9	16	23	30			6	13	20	27

CW COLLECTS

Almighty God,
give us grace to cast away the works of darkness
and to put on the armour of light,
now in the time of this mortal life,
in which your Son Jesus Christ
    came to us in great humility;
that on the last day,
when he shall come again in his glorious majesty
    to judge the living and the dead,
we may rise to the life immortal;
through him who is alive and reigns with you,
in the unity of the Holy Spirit, one God, now and
    for ever.

*This Collect may be used as the Post Communion
on any day from the Second Sunday of Advent
until Christmas Eve instead of the Post Communion
provided.*

or

Almighty God,
as your kingdom dawns,
turn us from the darkness of sin to the light
    of holiness,
that we may be ready to meet you
in our Lord and Saviour, Jesus Christ.

POST COMMUNION

O Lord our God,
make us watchful and keep us faithful
as we await the coming of your Son our Lord;
that, when he shall appear,
he may not find us sleeping in sin
but active in his service
and joyful in his praise;
through Jesus Christ our Lord.

BCP COLLECT

*Almighty God, give us grace that we may cast away
the works of darkness, and put upon us the armour of
light, now in the time of this mortal life, in which thy
Son Jesus Christ came to visit us in great humility;
that in the last day, when he shall come again in
his glorious Majesty, to ,judge both the quick and
the dead, we may rise to the ,life immortal; through
him who liveth and reigneth with thee and the Holy
Ghost, now and ever.*

2020

July				
S		5	12	19	26
M		6	13	20	27
T		7	14	21	28
W	1	8	15	22	29
T	2	9	16	23	30
F	3	10	17	24	31
S	4	11	18	25

August				
S		2	9	16	23	30
M		3	10	17	24	31
T		4	11	18	25
W		5	12	19	26
T		6	13	20	27
F		7	14	21	28
S	1	8	15	22	29

September				
S		6	13	20	27
M		7	14	21	28
T	1	8	15	22	29
W	2	9	16	23	30
T	3	10	17	24
F	4	11	18	25
S	5	12	19	26

October				
S		4	11	18	25
M		5	12	19	26
T		6	13	20	27
W		7	14	21	28
T	1	8	15	22	29
F	2	9	16	23	30
S	3	10	17	24	31

November				
S	1	8	15	22	29
M	2	9	16	23	30
T	3	10	17	24
W	4	11	18	25
T	5	12	19	26
F	6	13	20	27
S	7	14	21	28

December				
S		6	13	20	27
M		7	14	21	28
T	1	8	15	22	29
W	2	9	16	23	30
T	3	10	17	24	31
F	4	11	18	25
S	5	12	19	26

Purple

	EUCHARIST	**MORNING PRAYER**	**EVENING PRAYER**
	CW		
Psalms:	122	*50*; 54	70; *71*
Readings:	Isa. 4.2–end;	Isa. 25.1–9;	Isa. 42.18–end;
	Matt. 8.5–11	Matt. 12.1–21	Rev. 19

AW *Mal. 3.1–6*   *Matt. 3.1–6*

	HOLY COMMUNION	**MORNING PRAYER**	**EVENING PRAYER**
	BCP		
Psalms:		*9; 10; 11*	*12; 13; 14*
Readings:		*Isa. 3.1–15;*	*Isa. 4.2–end;*
		Mark 1.1–20	*Jas 1*
Hymns:	....	....	....

Sunrise 07.47; Sunset 15.50

2020

	January					February					March					April					May					June			
S		5	12	19	26		2	9	16	23		1	8	15	22	29		5	12	19	26		3	10	17	24	31		7	14	21	28
M		6	13	20	27		3	10	17	24		2	9	16	23	30		6	13	20	27		4	11	18	25		1	8	15	22	29
T		7	14	21	28		4	11	18	25		3	10	17	24	31		7	14	21	28		5	12	19	26		2	9	16	23	30
W	1	8	15	22	29		5	12	19	26		4	11	18	25		1	8	15	22	29		6	13	20	27		3	10	17	24	
T	2	9	16	23	30		6	13	20	27		5	12	19	26		2	9	16	23	30		7	14	21	28		4	11	18	25	
F	3	10	17	24	31		7	14	21	28		6	13	20	27		3	10	17	24		1	8	15	22	29		5	12	19	26	
S	4	11	18	25		1	8	15	22	29		7	14	21	28		4	11	18	25		2	9	16	23	30		6	13	20	27	

Francis Xavier, Missionary, Apostle of the Indies, 1552 — Purple

	EUCHARIST	MORNING PRAYER	EVENING PRAYER
	CW		
Psalms:	72.1–4, 18–19	*80*; 82	*74*; 75
Readings:	Isa. 11.1–10; Luke 10.21–24	Isa. 26.1–13; Matt. 12.22–37	Isa. 43.1–13; Rev. 20

AW *Zeph. 3.14–end*   *1 Thess. 4.13–end*

	HOLY COMMUNION	MORNING PRAYER	EVENING PRAYER
	BCP		
Psalms:		15; 16; 17	18
Readings:		Isa. 5.1–17; Mark 1.21–end	Isa. 5.18–end; Jas 2.1–13
Hymns:	....	....	....

2020

	July					August						September					October					November					December			
S		5	12	19	26		2	9	16	23	30		6	13	20	27		4	11	18	25	1	8	15	22	29		6	13	20	27
M		6	13	20	27		3	10	17	24	31		7	14	21	28		5	12	19	26	2	9	16	23	30		7	14	21	28
T		7	14	21	28		4	11	18	25		1	8	15	22	29		6	13	20	27	3	10	17	24		1	8	15	22	29
W	1	8	15	22	29		5	12	19	26		2	9	16	23	30		7	14	21	28	4	11	18	25		2	9	16	23	30
T	2	9	16	23	30		6	13	20	27		3	10	17	24		1	8	15	22	29	5	12	19	26		3	10	17	24	31
F	3	10	17	24	31		7	14	21	28		4	11	18	25		2	9	16	23	30	6	13	20	27		4	11	18	25
S	4	11	18	25		1	8	15	22	29		5	12	19	26		3	10	17	24	31	7	14	21	28		5	12	19	26

John of Damascus, Monk, Teacher of the Faith, c.749
Nicholas Ferrar, Deacon, Founder of the Little Gidding Community, 1637

Purple

	EUCHARIST CW	**MORNING PRAYER**	**EVENING PRAYER**
Psalms:	23	5; *7*	76; *77*
Readings:	Isa. 25.6–10a; Matt. 15.29–37	Isa. 28.1–13; Matt. 12.38–end	Isa. 43.14–end; Rev. 21.1–8
		AW Isa. 65.17—66.2	Matt. 24.1–14

	HOLY COMMUNION BCP	**MORNING PRAYER**	**EVENING PRAYER**
Psalms:		19; 20; 21	22; 23
Readings:		Isa. 6; Mark 2.1–22	Isa. 8.16—9.7; Jas 2.14–end
Hymns:	....	....	....

Purple

	EUCHARIST CW	**MORNING PRAYER**	**EVENING PRAYER**
Psalms:	118.18–27a	*42*; 43	*40*; 46
Readings:	Isa. 26.1–6; Matt. 7.21, 24–27	Isa. 28.14–end; Matt. 13.1–23	Isa. 44.1–8; Rev. 21.9–21
		AW *Mic. 5.2–5a*	*John 3.16–21*

	HOLY COMMUNION BCP	**MORNING PRAYER**	**EVENING PRAYER**
Psalms:		24; 25; 26	27; 28; 29
Readings:		Isa. 9.8—10.4; Mark 2.23—3.12	Isa. 10.5–23; Jas 3
Hymns:	....	....	....

2020

July					August						September					October					November						December				
S		5	12	19	26	S		2	9	16	23	30	S		6	13	20	27	S		4	11	18	25	S	1	8	15	22	29	S		6	13	20	27
M		6	13	20	27	M		3	10	17	24	31	M		7	14	21	28	M		5	12	19	26	M	2	9	16	23	30	M		7	14	21	28
T		7	14	21	28	T		4	11	18	25		T	1	8	15	22	29	T		6	13	20	27	T	3	10	17	24		T	1	8	15	22	29
W	1	8	15	22	29	W		5	12	19	26		W	2	9	16	23	30	W		7	14	21	28	W	4	11	18	25		W	2	9	16	23	30
T	2	9	16	23	30	T		6	13	20	27		T	3	10	17	24		T	1	8	15	22	29	T	5	12	19	26		T	3	10	17	24	31
F	3	10	17	24	31	F		7	14	21	28		F	4	11	18	25		F	2	9	16	23	30	F	6	13	20	27		F	4	11	18	25	
S	4	11	18	25		S	1	8	15	22	29	S	5	12	19	26		S	3	10	17	24	31	S	7	14	21	28		S	5	12	19	26	

Nicholas, Bishop of Myra, c.326 (CW Readings see Common of the Saints also Isa. 61.1–13; 1 Tim. 6.6–11;   Purple *or* White
Mark 10.13–16) *(also BCP)*

	EUCHARIST	MORNING PRAYER	EVENING PRAYER
	CW		
Psalms:	27.1–4, 16–17	*25*; 26	16; *17*
Readings:	Isa. 29.17–end; Matt. 9.27–31	Isa. 29.1–14; Matt. 13.24–43	Isa. 44.9–23; Rev. 21.22—22.5
		AW *Isa. 66.18–end*	*Luke 13.22–30*

	HOLY COMMUNION	MORNING PRAYER	EVENING PRAYER
	BCP Com. Bishop		
Psalms:	99	30; 31	32; 33; 34
Readings:	Ezek. 34.11–16; 1 Tim. 3.15–16; Mark 4.26–32	Isa. 10.24—11.9; Mark 3.13–end	Isa. 11.1—end of 12; Jas 4
Hymns:	....	....	....

CW COLLECT
Almighty Father, lover of souls,
who chose your servant Nicholas
to be a bishop in the Church,
that he might give freely out of the treasures of
   your grace:
make us mindful of the needs of others
and, as we have received,
so teach us also to give;
through Jesus Christ your Son our Lord,
who is alive and reigns with you,
in the unity of the Holy Spirit,
one God, now and for ever.

POST COMMUNION
God, shepherd of your people,
whose servant Nicholas revealed the loving service
   of Christ in his ministry as a pastor of your people:
by this eucharist in which we share
awaken within us the love of Christ
and keep us faithful to our Christian calling;
through him who laid down his life for us,
but is alive and reigns with you, now and for ever.

BCP COLLECT
*O God, the light of the faithful, and shepherd of souls,
who didst set blessed Nicholas to be a Bishop in the
Church, that he might feed thy sheep by his word and
guide them by his example: Grant us, we pray thee,
to keep the faith which he taught, and to follow in his
footsteps; through Jesus Christ our Lord. Amen.*

Ambrose, Bishop of Milan, Teacher of the Faith, 397 (CW Readings see Common of the Saints, also Isa. 41.9b–13; Luke 22.24–30) Purple or White

	EUCHARIST	MORNING PRAYER	EVENING PRAYER
	CW		
Psalms:	146.4–9	9; (10)	27; 28
Readings:	Isa. 30.19–21, 23–26; Matt. 9.35—10.1, 6–8	Isa. 29.15–end; Matt. 13.44–end	Isa. 44.24—45.13; Rev. 22.6–end
		AW Mic. 7.8–15	Rom. 15.30—16.7, 25–end
	HOLY COMMUNION	MORNING PRAYER	EVENING PRAYER
	BCP		
Psalms:		35; 36	37
Readings:		Isa. 13.1—14.2; Mark 4.1–20	Isa. 14.3–27; Jas 5; E. Coll. (1) Advent 2, (2) Advent 1
Hymns:	....	....	....

CW COLLECT
God of hosts,
who called Ambrose from the governor's throne
to be a bishop in your Church
and an intrepid champion of your faithful people:
mercifully grant that, as he did not fear to
    rebuke rulers,
so we, with like courage,
    may contend for the faith we have received;
through Jesus Christ your Son our Lord,
who is alive and reigns with you,
in the unity of the Holy Spirit,
one God, now and for ever.

POST COMMUNION
God of truth,
whose Wisdom set her table
and invited us to eat the bread and drink the wine
    of the kingdom:
help us to lay aside all foolishness
and to live and walk in the way of insight,
that we may come with Ambrose to the eternal feast
    of heaven;
through Jesus Christ our Lord.

THE SECOND SUNDAY OF ADVENT

(Purple)

	PRINCIPAL SERVICE CW	**THIRD SERVICE**	**SECOND SERVICE**
Psalms:	72.1–7, 18–19 [72.1–7]	80	11 [28]
Readings:	Isa. 11.1–10; Rom. 15.4–13; Matt. 3.1–12	Amos 7; Luke 1.5–20	1 Kgs 18.17–39; John 1.19–28 [BCP Var. Matt. 3.1–12]

Seasonal provisions CW Book pp 300–301

	HOLY COMMUNION BCP	**MORNING PRAYER**	**EVENING PRAYER**
Psalms:	50.1–6	80	11 [28]
Readings:	2 Kgs 22.8–10; 23.1–3; Rom. 15.4–13; Luke 21.25–33	Isa. 5; John 5.19–40 or 2 Pet. 3.1–14	Isa. 10.33—11.9 or Isa. 11.10—end of 12; Matt. 24.29—end or Rev. 20 and 21.1–8
Hymns:	....	....	....

2020

	January	February	March	April	May	June
S	5 12 19 26	2 9 16 23	1 8 15 22 29	5 12 19 26	3 10 17 24 31	7 14 21 28
M	6 13 20 27	3 10 17 24	2 9 16 23 30	6 13 20 27	4 11 18 25	1 8 15 22 29
T	7 14 21 28	4 11 18 25	3 10 17 24 31	7 14 21 28	5 12 19 26	2 9 16 23 30
W	1 8 15 22 29	5 12 19 26	4 11 18 25	1 8 15 22 29	6 13 20 27	3 10 17 24
T	2 9 16 23 30	6 13 20 27	5 12 19 26	2 9 16 23 30	7 14 21 28	4 11 18 25
F	3 10 17 24 31	7 14 21 28	6 13 20 27	3 10 17 24	1 8 15 22 29	5 12 19 26
S	4 11 18 25	1 8 15 22 29	7 14 21 28	4 11 18 25	2 9 16 23 30	6 13 20 27

CW COLLECTS

O Lord, raise up, we pray, your power
and come among us,
and with great might succour us;
that whereas, through our sins and wickedness
we are grievously hindered
in running the race that is set before us,
your bountiful grace and mercy
may speedily help and deliver us;
through Jesus Christ your Son our Lord,
to whom with you and the Holy Spirit,
be honour and glory, now and for ever.

or

Almighty God,
purify our hearts and minds,
that when your Son Jesus Christ comes again as
    judge and saviour
we may be ready to receive him,
who is our Lord and our God.

POST COMMUNION

Father in heaven,
who sent your Son to redeem the world
and will send him again to be our judge:
give us grace so to imitate him
in the humility and purity of his first coming
that, when he comes again,
we may be ready to greet him
with joyful love and firm faith;
through Jesus Christ our Lord.

BCP COLLECT

*Blessed Lord, who hast caused all holy Scriptures
to be written for our learning: Grant that we may in
such wise hear them, read, mark, learn, and inwardly
digest them, that by patience, and comfort of thy
holy Word, we may embrace and ever hold fast the
blessed hope of everlasting life, which thou hast
given us in our Saviour Jesus Christ.*

2020

July				
S		5	12	19	26
M		6	13	20	27
T		7	14	21	28
W	1	8	15	22	29
T	2	9	16	23	30
F	3	10	17	24	31
S	4	11	18	25

August				
S		2	9	16	23	30
M		3	10	17	24	31
T		4	11	18	25
W		5	12	19	26
T		6	13	20	27
F		7	14	21	28
S	1	8	15	22	29

September				
S		6	13	20	27
M		7	14	21	28
T	1	8	15	22	29
W	2	9	16	23	30
T	3	10	17	24
F	4	11	18	25
S	5	12	19	26

October				
S		4	11	18	25
M		5	12	19	26
T		6	13	20	27
W		7	14	21	28
T	1	8	15	22	29
F	2	9	16	23	30
S	3	10	17	24	31

November				
S	1	8	15	22	29
M	2	9	16	23	30
T	3	10	17	24
W	4	11	18	25
T	5	12	19	26
F	6	13	20	27
S	7	14	21	28

December				
S		6	13	20	27
M		7	14	21	28
T	1	8	15	22	29
W	2	9	16	23	30
T	3	10	17	24	31
F	4	11	18	25
S	5	12	19	26

Purple

	EUCHARIST	**MORNING PRAYER**	**EVENING PRAYER**
	CW		
Psalms:	85.7–end	*44*	*144*; 146
Readings:	Isa. 35;	Isa. 30.1–18;	Isa. 45.14–end;
	Luke 5.17–26	Matt. 14.1–12	1 Thess. 1

AW *Jer. 7.1–11* *Phil. 4.4–9*

	HOLY COMMUNION	**MORNING PRAYER**	**EVENING PRAYER**
	BCP		
Psalms:		44; 45; 46	47; 48; 49
Readings:		Isa. 17;	Isa. 18;
		Mark 4.21–end	1 Pet. 1.1–21
Hymns:	....	....	....

Sunrise 07.56; Sunset 15.47

2020

January					February					March					April					May						June				
S		5	12	19	26			2	9	16	23		1	8	15	22	29			5	12	19	26			3	10	17	24	31	
M		6	13	20	27			3	10	17	24		2	9	16	23	30			6	13	20	27			4	11	18	25		
T		7	14	21	28			4	11	18	25		3	10	17	24	31			7	14	21	28			5	12	19	26		
W	1	8	15	22	29			5	12	19	26		4	11	18	25		1	8	15	22	29			6	13	20	27		
T	2	9	16	23	30			6	13	20	27		5	12	19	26		2	9	16	23	30			7	14	21	28		
F	3	10	17	24	31			7	14	21	28		6	13	20	27		3	10	17	24		1	8	15	22	29		
S	4	11	18	25		1	8	15	22	29		7	14	21	28		4	11	18	25		2	9	16	23	30		6	13	20	27

Purple

	EUCHARIST	**MORNING PRAYER**	**EVENING PRAYER**
	CW		
Psalms:	96.1, 10–end	*56*; 57	*11*; 12; 13
Readings:	Isa. 40.1–11;	Isa. 30.19–end;	Isa. 46;
	Matt. 18.12–14	Matt. 14.13–end	1 Thess. 2.1–12

AW *Dan. 7.9–14* *Matt. 24.15–28*

	HOLY COMMUNION	**MORNING PRAYER**	**EVENING PRAYER**
	BCP		
Psalms:		*50; 51; 52*	*53; 54; 55*
Readings:		Isa. 19.1–17;	Isa. 19.18–end;
		Mark 5.1–20	1 Pet. 1.22—2.10
Hymns:			

DECEMBER
11 Wednesday

Ember Day (CW – see Common of the Saints)   Purple *or* Red

	EUCHARIST	**MORNING PRAYER**	**EVENING PRAYER**
	CW		
Psalms:	103.8–13	*62*; 63	*10*; 14
Readings:	Isa. 40.25–end;	Isa. 31;	Isa. 47;
	Matt. 11.28–end	Matt. 15.1–20	1 Thess. 2.13–end
		AW Amos 9.11–end	Rom. 13.8–end

	HOLY COMMUNION	**MORNING PRAYER**	**EVENING PRAYER**
	BCP		
Psalms:		56; 57; 58	59; 60; 61
Readings:		Isa. 21.1–12;	Isa. 22.1–14;
		Mark 5.21–end	1 Pet. 2.11—3.7
Hymns:	....	....	....

Purple

	EUCHARIST	**MORNING PRAYER**	**EVENING PRAYER**
	CW		
Psalms:	145.1, 8–13	53; *54*; 60	*73*
Readings:	Isa. 41.13–20;	Isa. 32;	Isa. 48.1–11;
	Matt. 11.11–15	Matt. 15.21–28	1 Thess. 3

AW *Jer. 23.5–8* *Mark 11.1–11*

	HOLY COMMUNION	**MORNING PRAYER**	**EVENING PRAYER**
	BCP		
Psalms:		*62; 63; 64*	*65; 66; 67*
Readings:		*Isa. 24;*	*Isa. 28.1–13;*
		Mark 6.1–13	*1 Pet. 3.8—4.6*
Hymns:	....	....	....

Full Moon

2020

	July				August					September				October				November				December			
S		5	12	19	26		2	9	16	23	30		6	13	20	27		4	11	18	25		1	8	15	22	29		6	13	20	27
M		6	13	20	27		3	10	17	24	31		7	14	21	28		5	12	19	26		2	9	16	23	30		7	14	21	28
T		7	14	21	28		4	11	18	25		1	8	15	22	29		6	13	20	27		3	10	17	24		1	8	15	22	29
W	1	8	15	22	29		5	12	19	26		2	9	16	23	30		7	14	21	28		4	11	18	25		2	9	16	23	30
T	2	9	16	23	30		6	13	20	27		3	10	17	24		1	8	15	22	29		5	12	19	26		3	10	17	24	31
F	3	10	17	24	31		7	14	21	28		4	11	18	25		2	9	16	23	30		6	13	20	27		4	11	18	25
S	4	11	18	25		1	8	15	22	29		5	12	19	26		3	10	17	24	31		7	14	21	28		5	12	19	26

Lucy, Martyr at Syracuse, 304 *(Also Lucy, V & M, BCP)*
(CW see Common of the Saints also Wisdom 3.1–7; 2 Cor. 4.6–15)
Samuel Johnson, Moralist, 1784
Ember Day (CW see Common of the Saints)

Purple *or* Red

	EUCHARIST	**MORNING PRAYER**	**EVENING PRAYER**
	CW		
Psalms:	1	85; *86*	82; *90*
Readings:	Isa. 48.17–19;	Isa. 33.1–22;	Isa. 48.12–end;
	Matt. 11.16–19	Matt. 15.29–end	1 Thess. 4.1–12
AW		*Jer. 33.14–22*	*Luke 21.25–36*

	HOLY COMMUNION	**MORNING PRAYER**	**EVENING PRAYER**
	BCP *Virgin Martyr*		
Psalms:	*131*	*68*	*69; 70*
Readings:	*Ecclus 51.1–10; Phil. 3.7–14;*	*Isa. 28.14–end;*	*Isa. 29.1–14;*
	Matt. 25.1–13	*Mark 6.14–29*	*1 Pet. 4.7–end*
Hymns:	....	....	....

CW COLLECT
God our redeemer,
who gave light to the world that was in darkness
by the healing power of the Saviour's cross:
shed that light on us, we pray,
that with your martyr Lucy
we may, by the purity of our lives,
reflect the light of Christ
and, by the merits of his passion,
come to the light of everlasting life;
through Jesus Christ your Son our Lord,
who is alive and reigns with you,
in the unity of the Holy Spirit,
one God, now and for ever.

POST COMMUNION
Eternal God,
who gave us this holy meal
in which we have celebrated the glory of the cross
and the victory of your martyr Lucy:
by our communion with Christ
in his saving death and resurrection,
give us with all your saints the courage to
    conquer evil
and so to share the fruit of the tree of life;
through Jesus Christ our Lord.

BCP COLLECT
*O God, who didst endue the holy Virgin Lucy with
grace to witness a good confession (and to suffer
gladly for thy sake): Grant that we, after her example,
may be found ready when the Bridegroom cometh
and enter with him to the marriage feast; through the
same thy Son Jesus Christ our Lord.*

2020

January					February					March					April					May						June				
S		5	12	19	26	**S**		2	9	16	23	**S**	1	8	15	22	29	**S**		5	12	19	26	**S**		3	10	17	24	31	**S**		7	14	21	28
M		6	13	20	27	**M**		3	10	17	24	**M**	2	9	16	23	30	**M**		6	13	20	27	**M**		4	11	18	25		**M**	1	8	15	22	29
T		7	14	21	28	**T**		4	11	18	25	**T**	3	10	17	24	31	**T**		7	14	21	28	**T**		5	12	19	26		**T**	2	9	16	23	30
W	1	8	15	22	29	**W**		5	12	19	26	**W**	4	11	18	25		**W**	1	8	15	22	29	**W**		6	13	20	27		**W**	3	10	17	24	
T	2	9	16	23	30	**T**		6	13	20	27	**T**	5	12	19	26		**T**	2	9	16	23	30	**T**		7	14	21	28		**T**	4	11	18	25	
F	3	10	17	24	31	**F**		7	14	21	28	**F**	6	13	20	27		**F**	3	10	17	24		**F**	1	8	15	22	29		**F**	5	12	19	26	
S	4	11	18	25		**S**	1	8	15	22	29	**S**	7	14	21	28		**S**	4	11	18	25		**S**	2	9	16	23	30		**S**	6	13	20	27	

John of the Cross, Poet, Teacher of the Faith, 1591
(CW Readings see Common of the Saints esp. 1 Cor. 2.1–10 also John 14.18–23)
Ember Day (CW see Common of the Saints)

Purple *or* White *or* Red

	EUCHARIST CW	**MORNING PRAYER**	**EVENING PRAYER**
Psalms:	80.1–4, 18–19	*145*	93; *94*
Readings:	Ecclus 48.1–4, 9–11 *or* 2 Kgs 2.9–12; Matt. 17.10–13	Isa. 35; Matt. 16.1–12	Isa. 49.1–13; 1 Thess. 4.13–end

	AW		*Zech. 14.4–11*	*Rev. 22.1–7*

	HOLY COMMUNION BCP	**MORNING PRAYER**	**EVENING PRAYER**
Psalms:		71; 72	73; 74
Readings:		Isa. 29.15–end; Mark 6.30–end	Isa. 30.1–18; 1 Pet. 5
Hymns:	....	....	....

CW COLLECT

O God, the judge of all,
who gave your servant John of the Cross
a warmth of nature, a strength of purpose
    and a mystical faith
that sustained him even in the darkness:
shed your light on all who love you
and grant them union of body and soul
in your Son Jesus Christ our Lord,
who is alive and reigns with you,
in the unity of the Holy Spirit,
one God, now and for ever.

POST COMMUNION

God of truth,
whose Wisdom set her table
and invited us to eat the bread and drink the
    wine of the kingdom:
help us to lay aside all foolishness
and to live and walk in the way of insight,
that we may come with John of the Cross to the
    eternal feast of heaven;
through Jesus Christ our Lord.

2020

	July					August						September					October					November					December			
S		5	12	19	26		2	9	16	23	30		6	13	20	27		4	11	18	25	1	8	15	22	29		6	13	20	27
M		6	13	20	27		3	10	17	24	31		7	14	21	28		5	12	19	26	2	9	16	23	30		7	14	21	28
T		7	14	21	28		4	11	18	25		1	8	15	22	29		6	13	20	27	3	10	17	24		1	8	15	22	29
W	1	8	15	22	29		5	12	19	26		2	9	16	23	30		7	14	21	28	4	11	18	25		2	9	16	23	30
T	2	9	16	23	30		6	13	20	27		3	10	17	24		1	8	15	22	29	5	12	19	26		3	10	17	24	31
F	3	10	17	24	31		7	14	21	28		4	11	18	25		2	9	16	23	30	6	13	20	27		4	11	18	25
S	4	11	18	25		1	8	15	22	29		5	12	19	26		3	10	17	24	31	7	14	21	28		5	12	19	26

THE THIRD SUNDAY OF ADVENT

(Purple)

	PRINCIPAL SERVICE CW	**THIRD SERVICE**	**SECOND SERVICE**
Psalms:	146.4–10 *or Canticle:* Magnificat	68.1–19	12 [14]
Readings:	Isa. 35.1–10; Jas 5.7–10; Matt. 11.2–11	Zeph. 3.14–end; Phil. 4.4–7 [BCP Var. Jas 5.7–10]	Isa. 5.8–end; Acts 13.13–41; [John 5.31–40]

Seasonal provisions CW Book pp 300–301

	HOLY COMMUNION BCP	**MORNING PRAYER**	**EVENING PRAYER**
Psalms:	80.1–7	68.1–20	12
Readings:	*Isa. 35.1–10;* *1 Cor. 4.1–5;* *Matt. 11.2–10*	*Isa. 25.1–9;* *Luke 3.1–17 or* *1 Tim. 1.12—2.7*	*Isa. 26 or Isa. 28.1–22;* *Matt. 25.1–30 or* *Rev. 21.9—22.5*
Hymns:	....	....	....

CW COLLECTS

O Lord Jesus Christ,
who at your first coming sent your messenger
to prepare your way before you:
grant that the ministers and stewards of your
    mysteries
may likewise so prepare and make ready your way
by turning the hearts of the disobedient
to the wisdom of the just,
that at your second coming to judge the world
we may be found an acceptable people in your sight;
for you are alive and reign with the Father
in the unity of the Holy Spirit,
one God, now and for ever.

or

God for whom we watch and wait,
you sent John the Baptist to prepare the way of
    your Son:
give us courage to speak the truth,
to hunger for justice,
and to suffer for the cause of right,
with Jesus Christ our Lord.

POST COMMUNION

We give you thanks, O Lord, for these heavenly gifts;
kindle in us the fire of your Spirit
that when your Christ comes again
we may shine as lights before his face;
who is alive and reigns now and for ever.

BCP COLLECT

*O Lord Jesu Christ, who at thy first coming didst send
thy messenger to prepare thy way before thee: Grant
that the ministers and stewards of thy mysteries
may likewise so prepare and make ready thy way, by
turning the hearts of the disobedient to the wisdom
of the just, that at thy second coming to judge the
world we may be found an acceptable people in thy
sight, who livest and reignest with the Father and the
Holy Spirit, ever one God, world without end.*

2020

	July					August						September					October					November					December			
S		5	12	19	26	S		2	9	16	23	30	S		6	13	20	27	S		4	11	18	25	S	1	8	15	22	29	S		6	13	20	27
M		6	13	20	27	M		3	10	17	24	31	M		7	14	21	28	M		5	12	19	26	M	2	9	16	23	30	M		7	14	21	28
T		7	14	21	28	T		4	11	18	25		T	1	8	15	22	29	T		6	13	20	27	T	3	10	17	24		T	1	8	15	22	29
W	1	8	15	22	29	W		5	12	19	26		W	2	9	16	23	30	W		7	14	21	28	W	4	11	18	25		W	2	9	16	23	30
T	2	9	16	23	30	T		6	13	20	27		T	3	10	17	24		T	1	8	15	22	29	T	5	12	19	26		T	3	10	17	24	31
F	3	10	17	24	31	F		7	14	21	28		F	4	11	18	25		F	2	9	16	23	30	F	6	13	20	27		F	4	11	18	25
S	4	11	18	25		S	1	8	15	22	29	S	5	12	19	26		S	3	10	17	24	31	S	7	14	21	28		S	5	12	19	26

DECEMBER
16 Monday

O Sapientia (BCP)
Note: BCP follows the medieval practice of using an eighth antiphon "O Virgin of Virgins" on December 23 and so commences one day before the CW (Roman) version.

Purple

	EUCHARIST CW	**MORNING PRAYER**	**EVENING PRAYER**
Psalms:	25.3–8	*40*	25; *26*
Readings:	Num. 24.2–7, 15–17; Matt. 21.23–27	Isa. 38.1–8, 21–22; Matt. 16.13–end	Isa. 49.14–25; 1 Thess. 5.1–11

		AW	*Isa. 40.1–11*	*Matt. 3.1–12*

	HOLY COMMUNION BCP	**MORNING PRAYER**	**EVENING PRAYER**
Psalms:		*79; 80; 81*	*82; 83; 84; 85*
Readings:		*Isa. 30.19–end; Mark 7.1–23*	*Isa. 31; 1 John 1.1—2.6*
Hymns:	....	....	....

Sunrise 08.03; Sunset 15.47

2020

	January					February					March					April					May						June			
S		5	12	19	26			2	9	16	23		1	8	15	22	29			5	12	19	26			3	10	17	24	31			7	14	21	28
M		6	13	20	27		3	10	17	24		2	9	16	23	30			6	13	20	27		4	11	18	25		1	8	15	22	29
T		7	14	21	28		4	11	18	25		3	10	17	24	31			7	14	21	28		5	12	19	26		2	9	16	23	30
W	1	8	15	22	29		5	12	19	26		4	11	18	25		1	8	15	22	29		6	13	20	27		3	10	17	24
T	2	9	16	23	30		6	13	20	27		5	12	19	26		2	9	16	23	30		7	14	21	28		4	11	18	25
F	3	10	17	24	31		7	14	21	28		6	13	20	27		3	10	17	24		1	8	15	22	29		5	12	19	26
S	4	11	18	25		1	8	15	22	29		7	14	21	28		4	11	18	25		2	9	16	23	30		6	13	20	27

Eglantyne Jebb, Social Reformer, Founder of 'Save the Children', 1928   Purple
O Sapientia (CW)
O Wisdom, coming forth from the mouth of the Most High,
reaching from one end to the other mightily,
and sweetly ordering all things:
Come and teach us the way of prudence

	EUCHARIST	**MORNING PRAYER**	**EVENING PRAYER**
	CW		
Psalms:	72.1–5, 18–19	*70*; 74	*50*; 54
Readings:	Gen. 49.2, 8–10;	Isa. 38.9–20;	Isa. 50;
	Matt. 1.1–17	Matt. 17.1–13	1 Thess. 5.12–end

		MORNING PRAYER	**EVENING PRAYER**
	AW	*Ecclus 24.1–9* or *Prov. 8.22–31*	*1 Cor. 2.1–13*

	HOLY COMMUNION	**MORNING PRAYER**	**EVENING PRAYER**
	BCP		
Psalms:		86; 87; 88	89
Readings:		Isa. 38.1–20;	Isa. 40.1–11;
		Mark 7.24—8.10	1 John 2.7–end
Hymns:	....	....	....

2020

July					August						September					October					November					December			
S		5	12	19	26		2	9	16	23	30		6	13	20	27		4	11	18	25		1	8	15	22	29		6	13	20	27
M		6	13	20	27		3	10	17	24	31		7	14	21	28		5	12	19	26		2	9	16	23	30		7	14	21	28
T		7	14	21	28		4	11	18	25		1	8	15	22	29		6	13	20	27		3	10	17	24		1	8	15	22	29
W	1	8	15	22	29		5	12	19	26		2	9	16	23	30		7	14	21	28		4	11	18	25		2	9	16	23	30
T	2	9	16	23	30		6	13	20	27		3	10	17	24		1	8	15	22	29		5	12	19	26		3	10	17	24	31
F	3	10	17	24	31		7	14	21	28		4	11	18	25		2	9	16	23	30		6	13	20	27		4	11	18	25
S	4	11	18	25		1	8	15	22	29		5	12	19	26		3	10	17	24	31		7	14	21	28		5	12	19	26

DECEMBER
18 Wednesday

2019

O Adonai, and leader of the House of Israel,
who appeared to Moses in the fire of the burning bush Purple
and gave him the law on Sinai:
Come and redeem us with an outstretched arm.
Ember Day (BCP)

Purple (*or Red*)

	EUCHARIST	MORNING PRAYER	EVENING PRAYER
	CW		
Psalms:	72.1–2, 12–13, 18–end	*75*; 96	25; *82*
Readings:	Jer. 23.5–8;	Isa. 39;	Isa. 51.1–8;
	Matt. 1.18–24	Matt. 17.14–21	2 Thess. 1
	AW	*Exod. 3.1–6*	*Acts 7.20–36*
	HOLY COMMUNION	MORNING PRAYER	EVENING PRAYER
	BCP Ember CEG		
Psalms:		90; 91; 92	93; 94
Readings:	Jer. 1.4–10 or	Isa. 40.12–end;	Isa. 41;
	Num. 11.16–17, 24–29 or	Mark 8.11—9.1	1 John 3
	Num. 27.15–end;		
	Acts 13.44–49 or Acts 20.28–35 or		
	Eph. 4.7–16; Matt. 9.35–38 or		
	Luke 4.16–21 or John 10.1–16		
Hymns:	....	....	....

BCP COLLECTS For Ember Days
Almighty God, our heavenly Father, who hast purchased to thyself an universal Church by the precious blood of thy dear Son: Mercifully look upon the same, and so guide and govern the minds of thy servants the Bishops and Pastors of thy flock, that they may lay hands suddenly on no man, but faithfully and wisely make choice of fit persons to serve in the sacred ministry of thy Church. And to those which shall be ordained to any holy function give thy grace and heavenly benediction; that both by their life and doctrine they may set forth thy glory, and set forward the salvation of all men; through Jesus Christ our Lord.

2020

	January	February	March	April	May	June
S	5 12 19 26	2 9 16 23	1 8 15 22 29	5 12 19 26	3 10 17 24 31	7 14 21 28
M	6 13 20 27	3 10 17 24	2 9 16 23 30	6 13 20 27	4 11 18 25	1 8 15 22 29
T	7 14 21 28	4 11 18 25	3 10 17 24 31	7 14 21 28	5 12 19 26	2 9 16 23 30
W	1 8 15 22 29	5 12 19 26	4 11 18 25	1 8 15 22 29	6 13 20 27	3 10 17 24
T	2 9 16 23 30	6 13 20 27	5 12 19 26	2 9 16 23 30	7 14 21 28	4 11 18 25
F	3 10 17 24 31	7 14 21 28	6 13 20 27	3 10 17 24	1 8 15 22 29	5 12 19 26
S	4 11 18 25	1 8 15 22 29	7 14 21 28	4 11 18 25	2 9 16 23 30	6 13 20 27

O Root of Jesse, standing as a sign among the peoples;
before you kings will shut their mouths,
to you the nations will make their prayer:
Come and deliver us, and delay no longer

Purple

	EUCHARIST	**MORNING PRAYER**	**EVENING PRAYER**
	CW		
Psalms:	71.3–8	144; *146*	10; *57*
Readings:	Judg. 13.2–7, 24–end;	Zeph. 1.1—2.3;	Isa. 51.9–16;
	Luke 1.5–25	Matt. 17.22–end	2 Thess. 2

AW	*Isa. 11.1–9*		*Rom. 15.7–13*

	HOLY COMMUNION	**MORNING PRAYER**	**EVENING PRAYER**
	BCP		
Psalms:		*95; 96; 97*	*98; 99; 100; 101*
Readings:		*Isa. 42.1–17;*	*Isa. 42.18—43.13;*
		Mark 9.2–32	*1 John 4*
Hymns:	....	....	....

2020

	July					August						September					October					November					December			
S		5	12	19	26		2	9	16	23	30		6	13	20	27		4	11	18	25		1	8	15	22	29		6	13	20	27
M		6	13	20	27		3	10	17	24	31		7	14	21	28		5	12	19	26		2	9	16	23	30		7	14	21	28
T		7	14	21	28		4	11	18	25			1	8	15	22	29		6	13	20	27		3	10	17	24		1	8	15	22	29
W	1	8	15	22	29		5	12	19	26		2	9	16	23	30		7	14	21	28		4	11	18	25		2	9	16	23	30
T	2	9	16	23	30		6	13	20	27		3	10	17	24		1	8	15	22	29		5	12	19	26		3	10	17	24	31
F	3	10	17	24	31		7	14	21	28		4	11	18	25		2	9	16	23	30		6	13	20	27		4	11	18	25
S	4	11	18	25		1	8	15	22	29		5	12	19	26		3	10	17	24	31		7	14	21	28		5	12	19	26

O Key of David and sceptre of the House of Israel;
you open and no one can shut;
you shut and no one can open:
Come and lead the prisoners from the prison house,
those who dwell in darkness and the shadow of death.
Ember Day (BCP)

Purple (*or Red*)

	EUCHARIST CW	**MORNING PRAYER**	**EVENING PRAYER**
Psalms:	24.1–6;	*46*; 95	*4*; 9
Readings:	Isa. 7.10–14; Luke 1.26–38	Zeph. 3.1–13; Matt. 18.1–20	Isa. 51.17–end; 2 Thess. 3
	AW	*Isa. 22.21–23*	*Rev. 3.7–13*

	HOLY COMMUNION BCP Ember CEG (See Dec. 18)	**MORNING PRAYER**	**EVENING PRAYER**
Psalms:		*102; 103*	*104*
Readings:		Isa. 43.14—44.5; Mark 9.33–end	Isa. 44.6–23; 1 John 5 or First Evensong for St Thomas 2 Sam. 15.17–21; John 11.1–16
Hymns:	....	....	....

BCP COLLECTS For Ember Days
Almighty God, the giver of all good gifts, who of thy divine providence hast appointed divers Orders in thy Church: Give thy grace, we humbly beseech thee, to all those who are to be called to any office or administration in the same; and so replenish them with the truth of thy doctrine, and endue them with innocency of life, that they may faithfully serve before thee, to the glory of thy great name, and the benefit of thy Holy Church; through Jesus Christ our Lord.

St Thomas the Apostle (BCP) Purple (or Red)
O Morning Star,
splendour of light eternal and sun of righteousness:
Come and enlighten those who dwell in darkness and the shadow of death.
Ember Day (BCP)

	EUCHARIST CW	**MORNING PRAYER**	**EVENING PRAYER**
Psalms:	33.1–4, 11–12, 20–end;	*121*; 122; 123	80; *84*
Readings:	Zech. 3.14–18; Luke 1.39–45	Zeph. 3.14–end; Matt. 18.21–end	Isa. 52.1–12; Jude

		MORNING PRAYER	**EVENING PRAYER**
	AW	Num. 24.15b–19	Rev. 22.10–21

	HOLY COMMUNION BCP St Thomas	**MORNING PRAYER**	**EVENING PRAYER**
Psalms:	139.1–11	105	106
Readings:	Job 42.1–6; Eph. 2.19–end; John 20.24–end	Job 42.1–6; John 14.1–7	Isa. 35; 1 Pet. 1.3–9; E. Coll. (1) Advent 4; (2) Advent 1
	(For BCP Ember CEG See Dec. 18)		
Hymns:	....	....	....

BCP COLLECT
Almighty and everliving God, who for the more
confirmation of the faith didst suffer thy holy
Apostle Thomas to be doubtful in thy Son's
resurrection: Grant us so perfectly, and without
all doubt, to believe in thy Son Jesus Christ that
our faith in thy sight may never be reproved.
Hear us, O Lord, through the same Jesus Christ,
to whom, with thee and the Holy Ghost, be all
honour and glory, now and for evermore.

2020

July					August						September					October					November						December				
S		5	12	19	26	S		2	9	16	23	30	S		6	13	20	27	S		4	11	18	25	S	1	8	15	22	29	S		6	13	20	27
M		6	13	20	27	M		3	10	17	24	31	M		7	14	21	28	M		5	12	19	26	M	2	9	16	23	30	M		7	14	21	28
T		7	14	21	28	T		4	11	18	25		T	1	8	15	22	29	T		6	13	20	27	T	3	10	17	24		T	1	8	15	22	29
W	1	8	15	22	29	W		5	12	19	26		W	2	9	16	23	30	W		7	14	21	28	W	4	11	18	25		W	2	9	16	23	30
T	2	9	16	23	30	T		6	13	20	27		T	3	10	17	24		T	1	8	15	22	29	T	5	12	19	26		T	3	10	17	24	31
F	3	10	17	24	31	F		7	14	21	28		F	4	11	18	25		F	2	9	16	23	30	F	6	13	20	27		F	4	11	18	25	
S	4	11	18	25		S	1	8	15	22	29		S	5	12	19	26		S	3	10	17	24	31	S	7	14	21	28		S	5	12	19	26	

THE FOURTH SUNDAY OF ADVENT

(Purple)

O King of the nations, and their desire,
the cornerstone making both one:
Come and save the human race,
which you fashioned from clay

	PRINCIPAL SERVICE CW	**THIRD SERVICE**	**SECOND SERVICE**
Psalms:	80.1–8, 18–20 [1–8]	144	113 [126]
Readings:	Isa. 7.10–16; Rom. 1.1–7; Matt. 1.18–end	Mic. 5.2–5a; Luke 1.26–38	1 Sam. 1.1–20; Rev. 22.6–end; [Luke 1.39–45]

Seasonal provisions CW Book pp 300–301

	HOLY COMMUNION BCP	**MORNING PRAYER**	**EVENING PRAYER**
Psalms:	*145.17–end*	*144*	*113 [126]*
Readings:	*Isa. 40.1–9; Phil. 4.4–7;* *John 1.19–28*	*Isa. 32.1–18;* *Luke 1.26–45 or* *2 Tim. 3.14—4.8*	*Isa. 33.2–22 or Isa. 35;* *Matt. 25.31–end or Rev. 22.6–end*
Hymns:	....	....	....

2020

January					February					March					April					May						June				
S		5	12	19	26	S		2	9	16	23	S	1	8	15	22	29	S		5	12	19	26	S		3	10	17	24	31	S		7	14	21	28
M		6	13	20	27	M		3	10	17	24	M	2	9	16	23	30	M		6	13	20	27	M		4	11	18	25	M	1	8	15	22	29
T		7	14	21	28	T		4	11	18	25	T	3	10	17	24	31	T		7	14	21	28	T		5	12	19	26	T	2	9	16	23	30
W	1	8	15	22	29	W		5	12	19	26	W	4	11	18	25	W	1	8	15	22	29	W		6	13	20	27	W	3	10	17	24
T	2	9	16	23	30	T		6	13	20	27	T	5	12	19	26	T	2	9	16	23	30	T		7	14	21	28	T	4	11	18	25
F	3	10	17	24	31	F		7	14	21	28	F	6	13	20	27	F	3	10	17	24	F	1	8	15	22	29	F	5	12	19	26
S	4	11	18	25	S	1	8	15	22	29	S	7	14	21	28	S	4	11	18	25	S	2	9	16	23	30	S	6	13	20	27

CW COLLECTS

God our redeemer,
who prepared the Blessed Virgin Mary
to be the mother of your Son:
grant that, as she looked for his coming as
    our saviour,
so we may be ready to greet him
when he comes again as our judge;
who is alive and reigns with you,
in the unity of the Holy Spirit,
one God, now and for ever.

or

Eternal God,
as Mary waited for the birth of your Son,
so we wait for his coming in glory;
bring us through the birth pangs of this present age
to see, with her, our great salvation
in Jesus Christ our Lord.

POST COMMUNION

Heavenly Father,
who chose the Blessed Virgin Mary
to be the mother of the promised saviour:
fill us your servants with your grace,
that in all things we may embrace your holy will
and with her rejoice in your salvation;
through Jesus Christ our Lord.

BCP COLLECT

*O Lord, raise up (we pray thee) thy power, and come
among us, and with great might succour us; that
whereas, through our sins and wickedness, we are
sore let and hindered in running the race that is
set before us, thy bountiful grace and mercy may
speedily help and deliver us; through the satisfaction
of thy Son our Lord, to whom with thee and the Holy
Ghost be honour and glory, world without end.*

2020

	July					August						September					October					November					December			
S		5	12	19	26	S		2	9	16	23	30	S		6	13	20	27	S		4	11	18	25	S	1	8	15	22	29	S		6	13	20	27
M		6	13	20	27	M		3	10	17	24	31	M		7	14	21	28	M		5	12	19	26	M	2	9	16	23	30	M		7	14	21	28
T		7	14	21	28	T		4	11	18	25		T	1	8	15	22	29	T		6	13	20	27	T	3	10	17	24		T	1	8	15	22	29
W	1	8	15	22	29	W		5	12	19	26		W	2	9	16	23	30	W		7	14	21	28	W	4	11	18	25		W	2	9	16	23	30
T	2	9	16	23	30	T		6	13	20	27		T	3	10	17	24		T	1	8	15	22	29	T	5	12	19	26		T	3	10	17	24	31
F	3	10	17	24	31	F		7	14	21	28		F	4	11	18	25		F	2	9	16	23	30	F	6	13	20	27		F	4	11	18	25
S	4	11	18	25		S	1	8	15	22	29	S	5	12	19	26		S	3	10	17	24	31	S	7	14	21	28		S	5	12	19	26

O Emmanuel, our king and our lawgiver,
the hope of the nations and their Saviour:
Come and save us, O Lord our God.

Purple

If the "Great O" Antiphons were commenced on Dec. 16, the following is used today:

O Virgin of virgins, how shall this be?
For neither before thee was any like thee, nor shall there be after.
Daughters of Jerusalem, why marvel ye at me?
The thing which ye behold is a divine mystery.

	EUCHARIST CW	**MORNING PRAYER**	**EVENING PRAYER**
Psalms:	25.3–9	128; 129; *130*; 131	*89.1–37*
Readings:	Mal. 3.1–4, 4.5–end; Luke 1.57–66	Mal. 1.1, 6–end; Matt. 19.1–12	Isa. 52.13—end of 53; 2 Pet. 1.1–15

		MORNING PRAYER	**EVENING PRAYER**
AW		*Isa. 7.10–15*	*Matt. 1.18–23*

	HOLY COMMUNION BCP	**MORNING PRAYER**	**EVENING PRAYER**
Psalms:		*110; 111; 112*	*113; 114; 115*
Readings:		*Isa. 46;* *Mark 10.32–end*	*Isa. 47;* *3 John*
Hymns:	....	....	....

Sunrise 08.07; Sunset 15.50

Christmas Eve   Purple

	MORNING EUCHARIST	MORNING PRAYER	EVENING PRAYER
	CW		
Psalms:	89.2, 19–27	*45*; 113	*85*
Readings:	2 Sam. 7.1–5, 8–11, 16;	Mal. 2.1–16;	Zech. 2;
	Acts 13.16–26;	Matt. 19.13–15	Rev. 1.1–8
	Luke 1.67–79		

AW: At Evening Prayer the readings for Christmas Eve are used.
At other services, the following readings are used:
Isa. 29.13–18   1 John 4.7–16

	HOLY COMMUNION	MORNING PRAYER	EVENING PRAYER
	BCP		
Psalms	24	116; 117; 118	119.1–32
Readings	Mic. 5.2–5a;	Isa. 48;	Zech. 2.10–end;
	Titus 3.3–7;	Mark 11.1–26	Titus 2.11—3.7
	Luke 2.1–14		
Hymns:	....	....	....

CW COLLECTS
Almighty God,
you make us glad with the yearly remembrance
of the birth of your Son Jesus Christ:
grant that, as we joyfully receive him as our redeemer,
so we may with sure confidence behold him
when he shall come to be our judge;
who is alive and reigns with you,
in the unity of the Holy Spirit,
one God, now and for ever.

or

Almighty God,
as we prepare with joy
to celebrate the gift of the Christ-child,
embrace the earth with your glory
and be for us a living hope
in Jesus Christ our Lord.

POST COMMUNION
Eternal God, for whom we wait,
you have fed us with the bread of eternal life:
keep us ever watchful,
that we may be ready to stand before the Son of Man,
Jesus Christ our Lord.

CHRISTMAS NIGHT COLLECTS
Eternal God,
who made this most holy night
to shine with the brightness of your one true light:
bring us, who have known the revelation
of that light on earth,
to see the radiance of your heavenly glory;
through Jesus Christ your Son our Lord,
who is alive and reigns with you,
in the unity of the Holy Spirit,
one God, now and for ever.

or

Eternal God,
in the stillness of this night
you sent your almighty Word
to pierce the world's darkness with the light of salvation:
give to the earth the peace that we long for
and fill our hearts with the joy of heaven
through our Saviour, Jesus Christ.

POST COMMUNION
God our Father,
in this night you have made known to us again
the coming of our Lord Jesus Christ:
confirm our faith and fix our eyes on him
until the day dawns
and Christ the Morning Star rises in our hearts.
To him be glory both now and for ever.

BCP COLLECT
O God, who makest us glad with the yearly
remembrance of the birth of thy only Son, Jesus Christ:
Grant that as we joyfully receive him for our redeemer,
so we may with sure confidence behold him, when he
shall come to be our judge; who liveth and reigneth with
thee and the Holy Ghost, one God, world without end.

2020

	July					August						September					October					November					December			
S		5	12	19	26		2	9	16	23	30		6	13	20	27		4	11	18	25	1	8	15	22	29		6	13	20	27
M		6	13	20	27		3	10	17	24	31		7	14	21	28		5	12	19	26	2	9	16	23	30		7	14	21	28
T		7	14	21	28		4	11	18	25		1	8	15	22	29		6	13	20	27	3	10	17	24		1	8	15	22	29
W	1	8	15	22	29		5	12	19	26		2	9	16	23	30		7	14	21	28	4	11	18	25		2	9	16	23	30
T	2	9	16	23	30		6	13	20	27		3	10	17	24		1	8	15	22	29	5	12	19	26		3	10	17	24	31
F	3	10	17	24	31		7	14	21	28		4	11	18	25		2	9	16	23	30	6	13	20	27		4	11	18	25
S	4	11	18	25		1	8	15	22	29		5	12	19	26		3	10	17	24	31	7	14	21	28		5	12	19	26

CHRISTMAS DAY Bank Holiday (UK)

White *or* Gold

PRINCIPAL SERVICE

Any of the following sets of readings may be used on the evening of Christmas Eve and on Christmas Day.
Set III should be used at some service during the celebration.

	I CW	II	III
Psalms:	96	97	98
Readings:	Isa. 9.2–7; Titus 2.11–14; Luke 2.1–14 [15–20]	Isa. 62.6–end; Titus 3.4–7; Luke 2.[1–7] 8–20	Isa. 52.7–10; Heb. 1.1–4 [5–12]; John 1.1–14

Seasonal provisions including Eucharistic preface until Jan 5. CW Book pp 302–303

		THIRD SERVICE	SECOND SERVICE
Psalms:		*110*; 117	8
Readings:		Isa. 62.1–5; Matt. 1.18–end	Isa. 65.17–25; Phil. 2.5–11 *or* Luke 2.1–20 if it has not been used at the Principal Service of the day

	HOLY COMMUNION BCP	MORNING PRAYER	EVENING PRAYER
Psalms:	98	110; 117	8
Readings:	Isa. 9.2–7; Heb. 1.1–12; John 1.1–14; Pr. Pref. until Jan. 1	Isa. 9.2–7; Luke 2.1–20	Isa. 7.10–14; 1 John 4.7–end
Hymns:	....	....	....

CW COLLECTS
Almighty God,
you have given us your only-begotten Son
to take our nature upon him
and as at this time to be born of a pure virgin:
grant that we, who have been born again
and made your children by adoption and grace,
may daily be renewed by your Holy Spirit;
through Jesus Christ your Son our Lord,
who is alive and reigns with you,
in the unity of the Holy Spirit,
one God, now and for ever.

or

Lord Jesus Christ,
your birth at Bethlehem
draws us to kneel in wonder at heaven touching earth:
accept our heartfelt praise,
as we worship you,
our Saviour and our eternal God.

POST COMMUNION
God our Father,
whose Word has come among us
in the Holy Child of Bethlehem:
may the light of faith illumine our hearts
    and shine in our words and deeds;
through him who is Christ the Lord.

BCP COLLECT
Almighty God, who hast given us thy only-begotten Son to take our nature upon him, and as at this time to be born of a pure Virgin: Grant that we being regenerate, and made thy children by adoption and grace, may daily be renewed by thy Holy Spirit; through the same our Lord Jesus Christ, who liveth and reigneth with thee and the same Spirit, ever one God, world without end.

Notes for Christmas

_____

_____

_____

_____

_____

_____

_____

_____

_____

_____

_____

_____

_____

_____

_____

_____

_____

_____

_____

_____

_____

_____

_____

_____

_____

_____

_____

_____

2020

	July					August						September					October					November						December			
S		5	12	19	26	S		2	9	16	23	30	S		6	13	20	27	S		4	11	18	25	S	1	8	15	22	29	S		6	13	20	27
M		6	13	20	27	M		3	10	17	24	31	M		7	14	21	28	M		5	12	19	26	M	2	9	16	23	30	M		7	14	21	28
T		7	14	21	28	T		4	11	18	25		T	1	8	15	22	29	T		6	13	20	27	T	3	10	17	24		T	1	8	15	22	29
W	1	8	15	22	29	W		5	12	19	26		W	2	9	16	23	30	W		7	14	21	28	W	4	11	18	25		W	2	9	16	23	30
T	2	9	16	23	30	T		6	13	20	27		T	3	10	17	24		T	1	8	15	22	29	T	5	12	19	26		T	3	10	17	24	31
F	3	10	17	24	31	F		7	14	21	28		F	4	11	18	25		F	2	9	16	23	30	F	6	13	20	27		F	4	11	18	25	
S	4	11	18	25		S	1	8	15	22	29		S	5	12	19	26		S	3	10	17	24	31	S	7	14	21	28		S	5	12	19	26	

Notes for Christmas

Stephen, Deacon, First Martyr Bank Holiday (UK)   Red

	PRINCIPAL SERVICE	**THIRD SERVICE**	**SECOND SERVICE**
	CW		
Psalms:	119.161–168	*13*; 31.1–8; 150	57; *86*
Readings:	2 Chr. 24.20–22;	Jer. 26.12–15;	Gen. 4.1–10;
	Acts 7.51–end;	Acts 6	Matt. 23.34–end
	Matt. 10.17–22		[BCP Var. Matt. 10.17–22]
	or		
	Acts 7.51–end;		
	Gal. 2.16b–20;		
	Matt. 10.17–22		

	HOLY COMMUNION	**MORNING PRAYER**	**EVENING PRAYER**
	BCP St Stephen		
Psalms:	*119.161–168*	*119.105–144*	*119.145–end*
Readings:	2 Chr. 24.20–22;	Gen. 4.1–10;	2 Chr. 24.15–22;
	Acts 7.55–end;	Acts 6	Acts 7.54—8.4;
	Matt. 23.34–end;		E. Coll: (1) St John (2) St Stephen
	Coll: (1)St Stephen, (2) Christmas:		(3) Christmas
Hymns:	....	....	....

CW COLLECT

Gracious Father,
who gave the first martyr Stephen
grace to pray for those who took up stones
    against him:
grant that in all our sufferings for the truth
we may learn to love even our enemies
and to seek forgiveness for those who desire
    our hurt,
looking up to heaven to him who was crucified for us,
Jesus Christ, our mediator and advocate,
who is alive and reigns with you,
in the unity of the Holy Spirit,
one God, now and for ever.

POST COMMUNION

Merciful Lord,
we thank you for the signs of your mercy
revealed in birth and death:
save us by the coming of your Son,
and give us joy in honouring Stephen,
first martyr of the new Israel;
through Jesus Christ our Lord.

BCP COLLECT

*Grant, O Lord, that in all our sufferings here upon
earth, for the testimony of thy truth, we may
stedfastly look up to heaven, and by faith behold
the glory that shall be revealed; and, being filled
with the Holy Ghost, may learn to love and bless
our persecutors, by the example of thy first Martyr
Saint Stephen, who prayed for his murderers to thee,
O blessed Jesus, who standest at the right hand of
God to succour all those that suffer for thee, our only
Mediator and Advocate.*

Collect of the Nativity is used until Dec. 31

2020

	July					August						September					October					November					December			
S		5	12	19	26	S		2	9	16	23	30	S		6	13	20	27	S		4	11	18	25	S	1	8	15	22	29	S		6	13	20	27
M		6	13	20	27	M		3	10	17	24	31	M		7	14	21	28	M		5	12	19	26	M	2	9	16	23	30	M		7	14	21	28
T		7	14	21	28	T		4	11	18	25		T	1	8	15	22	29	T		6	13	20	27	T	3	10	17	24		T	1	8	15	22	29
W	1	8	15	22	29	W		5	12	19	26		W	2	9	16	23	30	W		7	14	21	28	W	4	11	18	25		W	2	9	16	23	30
T	2	9	16	23	30	T		6	13	20	27		T	3	10	17	24		T	1	8	15	22	29	T	5	12	19	26		T	3	10	17	24	31
F	3	10	17	24	31	F		7	14	21	28		F	4	11	18	25		F	2	9	16	23	30	F	6	13	20	27		F	4	11	18	25	
S	4	11	18	25		S	1	8	15	22	29		S	5	12	19	26		S	3	10	17	24	31	S	7	14	21	28		S	5	12	19	26	

John, Apostle and Evangelist

White

	PRINCIPAL SERVICE	THIRD SERVICE	SECOND SERVICE
	CW		
Psalms:	117	*21*; 147.13–end	*97*
Readings:	Exod. 33.7–11a; 1 John 1; John 21.19b–end	Exod. 33.12–end [BCP Var. Exod. 33.7–11a] 1 John 2.1–11	Isa. 6.1–8; 1 John 5.1–12

Seasonal provisions: CW Book pp 328–329

	HOLY COMMUNION	MORNING PRAYER	EVENING PRAYER
	BCP St John Ev.		
Psalms:	92.11–end	120; 121; 122; 123; 124; 125	126; 127; 128; 129; 130; 131
Readings:	Exod. 33.18–end; 1 John 1; John 21.19b–end; Collects: (1) St John (2) Christmas	Exod. 33.9–19; John 13.21–35	Isa. 6.1–8; 1 John 5.1–12; E. Coll: (1) Holy Innocents (2) St John (3) Christmas
Hymns:	....	....	....

CW COLLECT

Merciful Lord,
cast your bright beams of light upon the Church:
that, being enlightened by the teaching
    of your blessed apostle and evangelist Saint John,
we may so walk in the light of your truth
that we may at last attain to the light of
    everlasting life;
through Jesus Christ
your incarnate Son our Lord,
who is alive and reigns with you,
in the unity of the Holy Spirit,
one God, now and for ever.

POST COMMUNION

Grant, O Lord, we pray,
that the Word made flesh
proclaimed by your apostle John
may, by the celebration of these holy mysteries,
ever abide and live within us;
through Jesus Christ our Lord.

BCP COLLECT

*Merciful Lord, we beseech thee to cast thy bright
beams of light upon thy Church, that it being
enlightened by the doctrine of thy blessed Apostle
and Evangelist Saint John may so walk in the light
of thy truth, that it may at length attain to the light of
everlasting life; through Jesus Christ our Lord.*

The Holy Innocents Red

	PRINCIPAL SERVICE	THIRD SERVICE	SECOND SERVICE
	CW		
Psalms:	124	*36*; 146	123; *128* [BCP Var. 124; 128]
Readings:	Jer. 31.15–17; 1 Cor. 1.26–29; Matt. 2.13–18	Baruch 4.21–27 *or* Gen. 37.13–20; Matt. 18.1–10	Isa. 49.14–25; Mark 10.13–16
	HOLY COMMUNION	MORNING PRAYER	EVENING PRAYER
	BCP Holy Innocents		
Psalms:	123	*132; 133; 134; 135*	*136; 137; 138*
Readings:	Jer. 31.10–17; Rev. 14.1–5; Matt. 2.13–18; Coll. (1) Holy Innocents, (2) Christmas	*Jer. 31.1–17;* *Matt. 18.1–10*	*Isa. 49.14–25; Mark 10.13–16* *E. Coll. (1) Holy Innocents,* *(2) Christmas*
Hymns:			

CW COLLECT

Heavenly Father,
whose children suffered at the hands of Herod,
though they had done no wrong:
by the suffering of your Son
and by the innocence of our lives
frustrate all evil designs
and establish your reign of justice and peace;
through Jesus Christ your Son our Lord,
who is alive and reigns with you,
in the unity of the Holy Spirit,
one God, now and for ever.

POST COMMUNION

Lord Jesus Christ,
in your humility you have stooped to share our
    human life
with the most defenceless of your children:
may we who have received these gifts of
    your passion
rejoice in celebrating the witness
of the Holy Innocents to the purity of your sacrifice
    made once for all upon the cross;
for you are alive and reign, now and for ever.

BCP COLLECT

O Almighty God, who out of the mouths of babes and
sucklings hast ordained strength, and madest infants
to glorify thee by their deaths; Mortify and kill all
vices in us, and so strengthen us by thy grace, that by
the innocency of our lives, and constancy of our faith,
even unto death, we may glorify thy holy Name;
through Jesus Christ our Lord.

2020

July					August						September					October					November					December				
S		5	12	19	26	S		2	9	16	23	30	S		6	13	20	27	S		4	11	18	25	S	1	8	15	22	29	S		6	13	20	27
M		6	13	20	27	M		3	10	17	24	31	M		7	14	21	28	M		5	12	19	26	M	2	9	16	23	30	M		7	14	21	28
T		7	14	21	28	T		4	11	18	25		T	1	8	15	22	29	T		6	13	20	27	T	3	10	17	24		T	1	8	15	22	29
W	1	8	15	22	29	W		5	12	19	26		W	2	9	16	23	30	W		7	14	21	28	W	4	11	18	25		W	2	9	16	23	30
T	2	9	16	23	30	T		6	13	20	27		T	3	10	17	24		T	1	8	15	22	29	T	5	12	19	26		T	3	10	17	24	31
F	3	10	17	24	31	F		7	14	21	28		F	4	11	18	25		F	2	9	16	23	30	F	6	13	20	27		F	4	11	18	25	
S	4	11	18	25		S	1	8	15	22	29		S	5	12	19	26		S	3	10	17	24	31	S	7	14	21	28		S	5	12	19	26	

THE FIRST SUNDAY OF CHRISTMAS

(White)

	PRINCIPAL SERVICE CW	**THIRD SERVICE**	**SECOND SERVICE**
Psalms:	148 [148.7–end]	105.1–11	132
Readings:	Isa. 63.7–9; Heb. 2.10–end; Matt. 2.13–end	Isa. 35.1–6; Gal. 3.23–end	· Isa. 49.7–13; Phil. 2.1–11; [Luke 2.41–end]

Seasonal Provisions: CW Book pp 302–303

	HOLY COMMUNION BCP	**MORNING PRAYER**	**EVENING PRAYER**
Psalms:	45.1–7	105.1–11	132
Readings:	Isa. 62.10–12; Gal. 4.1–7 Matt. 1.18–end	Isa. 40.1–11; Luke 2.22–40 or Col. 1.1–20	Isa. 40.12–end or Isa. 41.1–20; John 10.1–16 or Phil. 2.1–11
Hymns:	....	....	....

2020

	January					February					March					April					May						June			
S		5	12	19	26		2	9	16	23		1	8	15	22	29		5	12	19	26		3	10	17	24	31		7	14	21	28
M		6	13	20	27		3	10	17	24		2	9	16	23	30		6	13	20	27		4	11	18	25		1	8	15	22	29
T		7	14	21	28		4	11	18	25		3	10	17	24	31		7	14	21	28		5	12	19	26		2	9	16	23	30
W	1	8	15	22	29		5	12	19	26		4	11	18	25		1	8	15	22	29		6	13	20	27		3	10	17	24
T	2	9	16	23	30		6	13	20	27		5	12	19	26		2	9	16	23	30		7	14	21	28		4	11	18	25
F	3	10	17	24	31		7	14	21	28		6	13	20	27		3	10	17	24	1	8	15	22	29		5	12	19	26
S	4	11	18	25	1	8	15	22	29		7	14	21	28		4	11	18	25	2	9	16	23	30		6	13	20	27

CW COLLECTS

Almighty God,
who wonderfully created us in your own image
and yet more wonderfully restored us
through your Son Jesus Christ:
grant that, as he came to share in our humanity,
so we may share the life of his divinity;
who is alive and reigns with you,
in the unity of the Holy Spirit,
one God, now and for ever.

or

God in Trinity,
eternal unity of perfect love:
gather the nations to be one family,
and draw us into your holy life
through the birth of Emmanuel,
our Lord Jesus Christ.

POST COMMUNION

Heavenly Father,
whose blessed Son shared at Nazareth
   the life of an earthly home:
help your Church to live as one family,
united in love and obedience,
and bring us all at last to our home in heaven;
through Jesus Christ our Lord.

BCP COLLECT

Almighty God, who hast given us thy only begotten son to take our nature upon him, and as at this time to be born of a pure Virgin; Grant that we being regenerate, and made thy children by adoption and grace, may daily be renewed by thy Holy Spirit; through the same our Lord Jesus Christ, who liveth and reigneth with thee and the same Spirit, ever one God, world without end.

2020

July					August						September					October					November					December			
S		5	12	19	26	S		2	9	16	23	30	S		6	13	20	27	S		4	11	18	25	S	1	8	15	22	29	S		6	13	20	27
M		6	13	20	27	M		3	10	17	24	31	M		7	14	21	28	M		5	12	19	26	M	2	9	16	23	30	M		7	14	21	28
T		7	14	21	28	T		4	11	18	25		T	1	8	15	22	29	T		6	13	20	27	T	3	10	17	24		T	1	8	15	22	29
W	1	8	15	22	29	W		5	12	19	26		W	2	9	16	23	30	W		7	14	21	28	W	4	11	18	25		W	2	9	16	23	30
T	2	9	16	23	30	T		6	13	20	27		T	3	10	17	24		T	1	8	15	22	29	T	5	12	19	26		T	3	10	17	24	31
F	3	10	17	24	31	F		7	14	21	28		F	4	11	18	25		F	2	9	16	23	30	F	6	13	20	27		F	4	11	18	25
S	4	11	18	25		S	1	8	15	22	29	S	5	12	19	26		S	3	10	17	24	31	S	7	14	21	28		S	5	12	19	26

White

	EUCHARIST	MORNING PRAYER	EVENING PRAYER
	CW		
Psalms:	96.7–10	111; 112; *113*	*65*; 84
Readings:	1 John 2.12–17;	Jonah 2;	Isa. 59.1–15a;
	Luke 2.36–40	Col. 1.15–23	John 1.19–28

AW   *Isa. 9.2–7*   *John 8.12–20*

	HOLY COMMUNION	MORNING PRAYER	EVENING PRAYER
	BCP		
Psalms:		*144; 145; 146*	*147; 148; 149; 150*
Readings:		*Isa. 60.13–end;*	*Isa. 61;*
		Luke 12.22–34	*Col. 3.1–17*
Hymns:	....	....	....

Sunrise 08.09; Sunset 15.55

2020

	January					February					March					April					May						June			
S		5	12	19	26		2	9	16	23		1	8	15	22	29		5	12	19	26		3	10	17	24	31		7	14	21	28
M		6	13	20	27		3	10	17	24		2	9	16	23	30		6	13	20	27		4	11	18	25		1	8	15	22	29
T		7	14	21	28		4	11	18	25		3	10	17	24	31		7	14	21	28		5	12	19	26		2	9	16	23	30
W	1	8	15	22	29		5	12	19	26		4	11	18	25		1	8	15	22	29		6	13	20	27		3	10	17	24	
T	2	9	16	23	30		6	13	20	27		5	12	19	26		2	9	16	23	30		7	14	21	28		4	11	18	25	
F	3	10	17	24	31		7	14	21	28		6	13	20	27		3	10	17	24		1	8	15	22	29		5	12	19	26	
S	4	11	18	25		1	8	15	22	29		7	14	21	28		4	11	18	25		2	9	16	23	30		6	13	20	27	

John Wyclif, Reformer, 1384 Silvester, Bishop of Rome (BCP)   White

	EUCHARIST	**MORNING PRAYER**	**EVENING PRAYER**
	CW		
Psalms:	96.1, 11–end	*102*	*90*; 148
Readings:	1 John 2.18–21; John 1.1–18	Jonah 3—4; Col. 1.24—2.7	Is. 59.15b–end; John 1.29–34 *or* Evening Prayer for the Naming and Circumcision of Jesus: Ps. 148; Jer. 23.1–6; Col. 2.6–15

		AW	*Eccles. 3.1–13;*	*Rev. 21.1–8*

	HOLY COMMUNION	**MORNING PRAYER**	**EVENING PRAYER**
	BCP Com. bishop		
Psalms:	*99*	*144; 145; 146*	*147; 148; 149; 150*
Readings:	*Ezek. 34.11–16;* *1 Tim. 3.15–16;* *Mark 4.26–32*	*Isa. 62;* *Luke 12.35–48*	*Deut. 10.12—11.1;* *Luke 21.25–36*
Hymns:	....	....	....

BCP COLLECT

*O God, the light of the faithful, and shepherd of souls,
who didst set blessed Silvester to be a Bishop in the
Church, that he might feed thy sheep by his word and
guide them by his example: Grant us, we pray thee,
to keep the faith which he taught, and to follow in his
footsteps; through Jesus Christ our Lord. Amen.*

The Naming and Circumcision of Jesus Bank Holiday (UK)   White

	PRINCIPAL SERVICE CW	THIRD SERVICE	SECOND SERVICE
Psalms:	8	*103*; 150	*115*
Readings:	Num. 6.22–end; Gal. 4.4–7; Luke 2.15–21	Gen. 17.1–13; Rom. 2.17–end	Deut. 30.[1–10]11–end; Acts 3.1–16
	HOLY COMMUNION BCP Circumcision	MORNING PRAYER	EVENING PRAYER
Psalms:	98	103	115
Readings:	Gen. 17.3b–10; Rom. 4.8–13 or Eph. 2.11–18; Luke 2.15–21 *This CE&G may be used on each day until the Epiphany.*	Gen. 17.1–13; Rom. 2.17–end	Deut. 30; Rom. 13
Hymns:	....	....	....

CW COLLECT
Almighty God,
whose blessed Son was circumcised
in obedience to the law for our sake
and given the Name that is above every name:
give us grace faithfully to bear his Name,
to worship him in the freedom of the Spirit,
and to proclaim him as the Saviour of the world;
who is alive and reigns with you,
in the unity of the Holy Spirit,
one God, now and for ever.

POST COMMUNION
Eternal God,
whose incarnate Son was given the Name of Saviour:
grant that we who have shared
   in this sacrament of our salvation
may live out our years in the power
of the Name above all other names,
Jesus Christ our Lord.

BCP COLLECT
*Almighty God, who madest thy blessed Son to
be circumcised, and obedient to the law for man:
Grant us the true circumcision of the Spirit; that, our
hearts, and all our members, being mortified from
all worldly and carnal lusts, we may in all things
obey thy blessed will; through the same thy Son
Jesus Christ our Lord.*

BCP COLLECT FOR NEW YEAR'S DAY
*O Eternal Lord God, who hast brought thy servants
to the beginning of another year: Pardon, we humbly
beseech thee, our transgressions in the past, and
graciously abide with us all the days of our life;
through Jesus Christ our Lord.*

2020

	January					February					March					April					May						June			
S		5	12	19	26		2	9	16	23		1	8	15	22	29		5	12	19	26		3	10	17	24	31		7	14	21	28
M		6	13	20	27		3	10	17	24		2	9	16	23	30		6	13	20	27		4	11	18	25		1	8	15	22	29
T		7	14	21	28		4	11	18	25		3	10	17	24	31		7	14	21	28		5	12	19	26		2	9	16	23	30
W	1	8	15	22	29		5	12	19	26		4	11	18	25		1	8	15	22	29		6	13	20	27		3	10	17	24
T	2	9	16	23	30		6	13	20	27		5	12	19	26		2	9	16	23	30		7	14	21	28		4	11	18	25
F	3	10	17	24	31		7	14	21	28		6	13	20	27		3	10	17	24		1	8	15	22	29		5	12	19	26
S	4	11	18	25		1	8	15	22	29		7	14	21	28		4	11	18	25		2	9	16	23	30		6	13	20	27

Basil the Great and Gregory of Nazianzus, Bishops, Teachers of the Faith, 379 and 389   White
(CW Readings see Common of the Saints especially 2 Tim. 4.1–8; Matt. 5.13–19)
Seraphim, Monk of Sarov, Spiritual Guide, 1833.
Vedanayagam Samuel Azariah, Bishop in South India, Evangelist, 1945   Bank Holiday (Scotland)

	EUCHARIST	**MORNING PRAYER**	**EVENING PRAYER**
	CW		
Psalms:	98.1–4	*18.1–30*	45; *46*
Readings:	1 John 2.22–28;	Ruth 1;	Isa. 60.1–12;
	John 1.19–28	Col. 2.8–end	John 1.35–42
	AW	*Isa. 66.6–14*	*Matt. 12.46–50*

	HOLY COMMUNION	**MORNING PRAYER**	**EVENING PRAYER**
	BCP		
Psalms:		9; 10; 11	12; 13; 14
Readings:		Isa. 63.1–6;	Isa. 63.7–end;
		Matt. 1.18–end	1 Thess. 1
Hymns:	....	....	....

CW COLLECT
Lord God,
whose servants Basil and Gregory
proclaimed the mystery of your Word made flesh,
to build up your Church in wisdom and strength:
grant that we may rejoice in his presence
among us,
and so be brought with them to know
the power of your unending love;
through Jesus Christ your Son our Lord,
who is alive and reigns with you,
in the unity of the Holy Spirit,
one God, now and for ever.

POST COMMUNION
God of truth,
whose Wisdom set her table
and invited us to eat the bread and drink the wine of
the kingdom:
help us to lay aside all foolishness
and to live and walk in the way of insight,
that we may come with Basil and Gregory to the
eternal feast of heaven;
through Jesus Christ our Lord

2020

	July					August					September					October					November					December			
S		5	12	19	26		2	9	16	23	30		6	13	20	27		4	11	18	25		1	8	15	22	29		6	13	20	27
M		6	13	20	27		3	10	17	24	31		7	14	21	28		5	12	19	26		2	9	16	23	30		7	14	21	28
T		7	14	21	28		4	11	18	25		1	8	15	22	29		6	13	20	27		3	10	17	24		1	8	15	22	29
W	1	8	15	22	29		5	12	19	26	2	9	16	23	30		7	14	21	28		4	11	18	25		2	9	16	23	30
T	2	9	16	23	30		6	13	20	27	3	10	17	24		1	8	15	22	29		5	12	19	26		3	10	17	24	31
F	3	10	17	24	31		7	14	21	28	4	11	18	25		2	9	16	23	30		6	13	20	27		4	11	18	25
S	4	11	18	25		1	8	15	22	29	5	12	19	26		3	10	17	24	31		7	14	21	28		5	12	19	26

White

	EUCHARIST	**MORNING PRAYER**	**EVENING PRAYER**
	CW		
Psalms:	98.2–7	*127*; 128; 131	2; 110
Readings:	1 John 2.29—3.6; John 1.29–34	Ruth 2; Col. 3.1–11	Isa. 60.13–end; John 1.43–end

	AW	Deut. 6.4–15	John 10.31–end

	HOLY COMMUNION	**MORNING PRAYER**	**EVENING PRAYER**
	BCP		
Psalms:		15; 16; 17	18
Readings:		Isa. 64; Matt. 2	Isa. 65.1–16; 1 Thess. 2.1–16
Hymns:	....	....	....

2020

January	February	March	April	May	June
S 5 12 19 26	S 2 9 16 23	S 1 8 15 22 29	S 5 12 19 26	S 3 10 17 24 31	S 7 14 21 28
M 6 13 20 27	M 3 10 17 24	M 2 9 16 23 30	M 6 13 20 27	M 4 11 18 25	M 1 8 15 22 29
T 7 14 21 28	T 4 11 18 25	T 3 10 17 24 31	T 7 14 21 28	T 5 12 19 26	T 2 9 16 23 30
W 1 8 15 22 29	W 5 12 19 26	W 4 11 18 25	W 1 8 15 22 29	W 6 13 20 27	W 3 10 17 24
T 2 9 16 23 30	T 6 13 20 27	T 5 12 19 26	T 2 9 16 23 30	T 7 14 21 28	T 4 11 18 25
F 3 10 17 24 31	F 7 14 21 28	F 6 13 20 27	F 3 10 17 24	F 1 8 15 22 29	F 5 12 19 26
S 4 11 18 25	S 1 8 15 22 29	S 7 14 21 28	S 4 11 18 25	S 2 9 16 23 30	S 6 13 20 27

White

	EUCHARIST CW	**MORNING PRAYER**	**EVENING PRAYER**
Psalms:	98.1, 8–end	*89.1–37*	85; *87*
Readings:	1 John 3.7–10; John 1.35–42	Ruth 3; Col. 3.12—4.1	Isa. 61; John 2.1–12

AW *Isa. 63.7–16* *Gal. 3.23—4.7*

	HOLY COMMUNION BCP	**MORNING PRAYER**	**EVENING PRAYER**
Psalms:		*19; 20; 21*	*22; 23*
Readings:		Isa. 65.17–end; Matt. 3.1—4.11	Isa. 66.1–9; 1 Thess. 2.17—end of 3; E. Coll: Christmas 2
Hymns:	....	....	....

2020

	July					August						September					October					November					December			
S		5	12	19	26	S		2	9	16	23	30	S		6	13	20	27	S		4	11	18	25	S	1	8	15	22	29	S		6	13	20	27
M		6	13	20	27	M		3	10	17	24	31	M		7	14	21	28	M		5	12	19	26	M	2	9	16	23	30	M		7	14	21	28
T		7	14	21	28	T		4	11	18	25		T	1	8	15	22	29	T		6	13	20	27	T	3	10	17	24		T	1	8	15	22	29
W	1	8	15	22	29	W		5	12	19	26		W	2	9	16	23	30	W		7	14	21	28	W	4	11	18	25		W	2	9	16	23	30
T	2	9	16	23	30	T		6	13	20	27		T	3	10	17	24		T	1	8	15	22	29	T	5	12	19	26		T	3	10	17	24	31
F	3	10	17	24	31	F		7	14	21	28		F	4	11	18	25		F	2	9	16	23	30	F	6	13	20	27		F	4	11	18	25
S	4	11	18	25		S	1	8	15	22	29	S	5	12	19	26		S	3	10	17	24	31	S	7	14	21	28		S	5	12	19	26

THE SECOND SUNDAY OF CHRISTMAS

(White)

CW: Where celebration of The Epiphany is preferred, see January 6.

	PRINCIPAL SERVICE CW	**THIRD SERVICE**	**SECOND SERVICE**
Psalms:	147.13–21 *or Canticle:* Wisd. of Sol 10.15–21	87	96; 97
Readings:	Jer. 31.7–14 *or* Ecclus 24.1–12; Eph. 1.3–14; John 1.[1–9] 10–18	Jer. 31.15–17; 2 Cor. 1.3–12	Isa. 49.1–13; John 4.7–26

	HOLY COMMUNION BCP	**MORNING PRAYER**	**EVENING PRAYER**
Psalms:	93	87	135
Readings:	Exod. 24.12–18; 2 Cor. 8.9; John 1.14–18	Isa. 42.1–16; Matt. 6.19–end or Eph. 1	Isa. 43.1–13; or Isa. 43.14—44.5; Matt. 7.13–27 or 1 John 3
Hymns:	....	....	....

2020

	January					February					March					April					May					June				
S		5	12	19	26		2	9	16	23		1	8	15	22	29		5	12	19	26		3	10	17	24	31		7	14	21	28
M		6	13	20	27		3	10	17	24		2	9	16	23	30		6	13	20	27		4	11	18	25		1	8	15	22	29
T		7	14	21	28		4	11	18	25		3	10	17	24	31		7	14	21	28		5	12	19	26		2	9	16	23	30
W	1	8	15	22	29		5	12	19	26		4	11	18	25		1	8	15	22	29		6	13	20	27		3	10	17	24	
T	2	9	16	23	30		6	13	20	27		5	12	19	26		2	9	16	23	30		7	14	21	28		4	11	18	25	
F	3	10	17	24	31		7	14	21	28		6	13	20	27		3	10	17	24		1	8	15	22	29		5	12	19	26	
S	4	11	18	25		1	8	15	22	29		7	14	21	28		4	11	18	25		2	9	16	23	30		6	13	20	27		

CW COLLECTS

Almighty God,
in the birth of your Son
you have poured on us the new light of your
    incarnate Word,
and shown us the fullness of your love:
help us to walk in his light and dwell in his love
that we may know the fullness of his joy;
who is alive and reigns with you,
in the unity of the Holy Spirit,
one God, now and for ever.

or

God our Father,
in love you sent your Son
that the world may have life:
lead us to seek him among the outcast
and find him in those in need,
for Jesus Christ's sake.

POST COMMUNION

All praise to you,
almighty God and heavenly King,
who sent your Son into the world
to take our nature upon him
and to be born of a pure virgin:
grant that, as we are born again in him,
so he may continually dwell in us
and reign on earth as he reigns in heaven,
now and for ever.

BCP COLLECT

Almighty God, who didst wonderfully create man in thine own image, and didst yet more wonderfully restore him: Grant, we beseech thee, that as thy Son our Lord Jesus Christ was made in the likeness of men, so we may be made partakers of the divine nature; through the same thy Son, who with thee and the Holy Ghost liveth and reigneth, one God, world without end.

2020

July				
S		5	12	19	26
M		6	13	20	27
T		7	14	21	28
W	1	8	15	22	29
T	2	9	16	23	30
F	3	10	17	24	31
S	4	11	18	25

August				
S		2	9	16	23	30
M		3	10	17	24	31
T		4	11	18	25
W		5	12	19	26
T		6	13	20	27
F		7	14	21	28
S	1	8	15	22	29

September				
S		6	13	20	27
M		7	14	21	28
T	1	8	15	22	29
W	2	9	16	23	30
T	3	10	17	24
F	4	11	18	25
S	5	12	19	26

October				
S		4	11	18	25
M		5	12	19	26
T		6	13	20	27
W		7	14	21	28
T	1	8	15	22	29
F	2	9	16	23	30
S	3	10	17	24	31

November				
S	1	8	15	22	29
M	2	9	16	23	30
T	3	10	17	24
W	4	11	18	25
T	5	12	19	26
F	6	13	20	27
S	7	14	21	28

December				
S		6	13	20	27
M		7	14	21	28
T	1	8	15	22	29
W	2	9	16	23	30
T	3	10	17	24	31
F	4	11	18	25
S	5	12	19	26

THE EPIPHANY

Gold *or* White

	PRINCIPAL SERVICE CW	THIRD SERVICE	SECOND SERVICE
Psalms:	72.[1–9] 10–15	132; 113	98; 100 [BCP Var. 72; 98]
Readings:	Isa. 60.1–6; Eph. 3.1–12; Matt. 2.1–12	Jer. 31.7–14; John 1.29–34	Baruch 4.36—5.end *or* Isa. 60.1–9; John 2.1–11

If The Epiphany was celebrated on Sunday January 5, the following readings are used:

	EUCHARIST	MORNING PRAYER	EVENING PRAYER
Psalms:	2.7–end	8; *48*	96; *97*
Readings:	1 John 3.22—4.6; Matt. 4.12–17, 23–end	Ruth 4.1–17; Col. 4.2–end	Isa. 62; John 2.13–end

	HOLY COMMUNION BCP Epiphany	MORNING PRAYER	EVENING PRAYER
Psalms:	100	30; 31	32; 33; 34
Readings:	Isa. 60.1–9; Eph. 3.1–12; Matt. 2.1–12	Isa. 60; Luke 3.15–22	Isa. 61; John 2.1–11
Hymns:	....	....	....

CW COLLECTS
O God,
who by the leading of a star
manifested your only Son to the peoples of the earth:
mercifully grant that we,
who know you now by faith,
may at last behold your glory face to face;
through Jesus Christ your Son our Lord,
who is alive and reigns with you,
in the unity of the Holy Spirit,
one God, now and for ever.

or

Creator of the heavens,
who led the Magi by a star
to worship the Christ-child:
guide and sustain us,
that we may find our journey's end
in Jesus Christ our Lord.

POST COMMUNION
Lord God,
the bright splendour whom the nations seek:
may we who with the wise men
    have been drawn by your light
discern the glory of your presence in your Son,
the Word made flesh, Jesus Christ our Lord.

BCP COLLECT
*O God, who by the leading of a star didst manifest
thy only-begotten Son to the Gentiles: Mercifully
grant, that we, which know thee now by faith,
may after this life have the fruition of thy glorious
Godhead; through Jesus Christ our Lord.*

Sunrise 08.08; Sunset 16.03

2020

	January	February	March	April	May	June
S	5 12 19 26	2 9 16 23	1 8 15 22 29	5 12 19 26	3 10 17 24 31	7 14 21 28
M	6 13 20 27	3 10 17 24	2 9 16 23 30	6 13 20 27	4 11 18 25	1 8 15 22 29
T	7 14 21 28	4 11 18 25	3 10 17 24 31	7 14 21 28	5 12 19 26	2 9 16 23 30
W	1 8 15 22 29	5 12 19 26	4 11 18 25	1 8 15 22 29	6 13 20 27	3 10 17 24
T	2 9 16 23 30	6 13 20 27	5 12 19 26	2 9 16 23 30	7 14 21 28	4 11 18 25
F	3 10 17 24 31	7 14 21 28	6 13 20 27	3 10 17 24	1 8 15 22 29	5 12 19 26
S	4 11 18 25	1 8 15 22 29	7 14 21 28	4 11 18 25	2 9 16 23 30	6 13 20 27

White

EUCHARIST	MORNING PRAYER	EVENING PRAYER
CW		
Psalms: 2.7–end	*99*; 147.1–12	*118*
Readings: 1 John 3.22—4.6; Matt. 4.12–17, 23–end	Baruch 1.15—2.10 *or* Jer. 23.1–8; Matt. 20.1–16	Isa. 63.7–end; 1 John 3

If for pastoral reasons Epiphany is celebrated on January 5th. the following readings are used for the Eucharist

Psalms: 72.1–18

Readings: 1 John 4.7–10;
Mark 6.34–44

	AW	*Gen. 25.19–end*	*Eph. 1.1–6*

HOLY COMMUNION	MORNING PRAYER	EVENING PRAYER
BCP		
Psalms:	*35; 36*	*37*
Readings:	Hos. 5.8—6.6; Matt. 6.1–18	Hos. 8; 1 Thess. 4.13—5.11
Hymns:		

2020

	July					August					September					October					November					December			
S		5	12	19	26		2	9	16	23	30		6	13	20	27		4	11	18	25		1	8	15	22	29		6	13	20	27
M		6	13	20	27		3	10	17	24	31		7	14	21	28		5	12	19	26		2	9	16	23	30		7	14	21	28
T		7	14	21	28		4	11	18	25		1	8	15	22	29		6	13	20	27		3	10	17	24		1	8	15	22	29
W	1	8	15	22	29		5	12	19	26		2	9	16	23	30		7	14	21	28		4	11	18	25		2	9	16	23	30
T	2	9	16	23	30		6	13	20	27		3	10	17	24		1	8	15	22	29		5	12	19	26		3	10	17	24	31
F	3	10	17	24	31		7	14	21	28		4	11	18	25		2	9	16	23	30		6	13	20	27		4	11	18	25
S	4	11	18	25		1	8	15	22	29		5	12	19	26		3	10	17	24	31		7	14	21	28		5	12	19	26

Lucian, Priest and Martyr, 390 (BCP)

White (*or Red*)

	EUCHARIST	**MORNING PRAYER**	**EVENING PRAYER**
	CW		
Psalms:	72.1–8	*46*; 147.13–end	*145*
Readings:	1 John 4.7–10; Mark 6.34–44	Baruch 2.11–end *or* Jer. 30.1–17; Matt. 20.17–28	Isa. 64; 1 John 4.7–end

Alt. if The Epiphany was celebrated on Sunday January 5 these readings are used for the Eucharist:

Psalms:	72.1, 10–13
Readings:	1 John 4.11–18; Mark 6.45–52

		AW	Joel 2.28–end	Eph. 1.7–14

	HOLY COMMUNION	**MORNING PRAYER**	**EVENING PRAYER**
	BCP Com. Martyr		
Psalms:	*3*	*38; 39; 40*	*41; 42; 43*
Readings:	*Jer. 11.18–20;* *Heb. 11.32—12.2;* *Matt. 16.24–27*	*Hos. 9;* *Matt. 6.19–end*	*Hos. 10;* *1 Thess. 5.12–end*
Hymns:	....	....	....

BCP COLLECT
Almighty God, by whose grace and power thy holy Martyr Lucian triumphed over suffering and despised death: Grant, we beseech thee, that enduring hardness and waxing valiant in fight, we may with the noble army of martyrs received the crown of everlasting life; through Jesus Christ our Lord.

2020

	January					February					March					April					May					June			
S		5	12	19	26		2	9	16	23		1	8	15	22	29		5	12	19	26		3	10	17	24	31		7	14	21	28
M		6	13	20	27		3	10	17	24		2	9	16	23	30		6	13	20	27		4	11	18	25		1	8	15	22	29
T		7	14	21	28		4	11	18	25		3	10	17	24	31		7	14	21	28		5	12	19	26		2	9	16	23	30
W	1	8	15	22	29		5	12	19	26		4	11	18	25		1	8	15	22	29		6	13	20	27		3	10	17	24	
T	2	9	16	23	30		6	13	20	27		5	12	19	26		2	9	16	23	30		7	14	21	28		4	11	18	25	
F	3	10	17	24	31		7	14	21	28		6	13	20	27		3	10	17	24		1	8	15	22	29		5	12	19	26	
S	4	11	18	25		1	8	15	22	29		7	14	21	28		4	11	18	25		2	9	16	23	30		6	13	20	27	

White

	EUCHARIST	MORNING PRAYER	EVENING PRAYER
	CW		
Psalms:	72.1, 10–13	2; *148*	*67*; 72
Readings:	1 John 4.11–18; Mark 6.45–52	Baruch 3.1–8 *or* Jer. 30.18—31.9; Matt. 20.29–end	Isa. 65.1–16; 1 John 5.1–12

If The Epiphany was celebrated on Sunday January 5 these readings are used for the Eucharist:

Psalms:	72.1, 17–end		
Readings:	1 John 4.19–5.4; Luke 4.14–22		

		AW	*Prov. 8.12–21*		*Eph. 1.15–end*

	HOLY COMMUNION	MORNING PRAYER	EVENING PRAYER
	BCP		
Psalms:		*44; 45; 46*	*47; 48; 49*
Readings:		*Hos. 11;* *Matt. 7*	*Hos. 12;* *2 Thess. 1*
Hymns:	....	....	....

2020

	July					August						September					October					November					December			
S		5	12	19	26		2	9	16	23	30		6	13	20	27		4	11	18	25		1	8	15	22	29		6	13	20	27
M		6	13	20	27		3	10	17	24	31		7	14	21	28		5	12	19	26		2	9	16	23	30		7	14	21	28
T		7	14	21	28		4	11	18	25		1	8	15	22	29		6	13	20	27		3	10	17	24		1	8	15	22	29
W	1	8	15	22	29		5	12	19	26	2	9	16	23	30		7	14	21	28		4	11	18	25		2	9	16	23	30
T	2	9	16	23	30		6	13	20	27	3	10	17	24		1	8	15	22	29		5	12	19	26		3	10	17	24	31
F	3	10	17	24	31		7	14	21	28	4	11	18	25		2	9	16	23	30		6	13	20	27		4	11	18	25
S	4	11	18	25		1	8	15	22	29	5	12	19	26		3	10	17	24	31		7	14	21	28		5	12	19	26

William Laud, Archbishop of Canterbury, 1645   White

	EUCHARIST CW	**MORNING PRAYER**	**EVENING PRAYER**
Psalms:	72.1, 17–end	97; *149*	27; *29*
Readings:	1 John 4.19—5.4; Luke 4.14–22	Baruch 3.9—4.4 *or* Jer. 31.10–17; Matt. 23.1–12	Isa. 65.17–end; 1 John 5.13–end

If the Epiphany was celebrated on Sunday January 5 these readings are used for the Eucharist:

Psalms:	147.13–end
Readings:	1 John 5.5–13; Luke 6.12–16

		AW	Gen. 19.15–29		Eph. 2.1–10
	HOLY COMMUNION BCP		**MORNING PRAYER**		**EVENING PRAYER**
Psalms:			50; 51; 52		53; 54; 55
Readings:			Hos. 13.1–14; Matt. 8.1–17		Hos. 14; 2 Thess. 2
Hymns:	....		....		....

Full Moon

2020

	January				February				March				April				May					June			
S		5	12	19	26		2	9	16	23		1	8	15	22	29		5	12	19	26		3	10	17	24	31		7	14	21	28
M		6	13	20	27		3	10	17	24		2	9	16	23	30		6	13	20	27		4	11	18	25		1	8	15	22	29
T		7	14	21	28		4	11	18	25		3	10	17	24	31		7	14	21	28		5	12	19	26		2	9	16	23	30
W	1	8	15	22	29		5	12	19	26		4	11	18	25		1	8	15	22	29		6	13	20	27		3	10	17	24
T	2	9	16	23	30		6	13	20	27		5	12	19	26		2	9	16	23	30		7	14	21	28		4	11	18	25
F	3	10	17	24	31		7	14	21	28		6	13	20	27		3	10	17	24		1	8	15	22	29		5	12	19	26
S	4	11	18	25		1	8	15	22	29		7	14	21	28		4	11	18	25		2	9	16	23	30		6	13	20	27

Mary Slessor, Missionary in West Africa, 1915   White

	EUCHARIST	**MORNING PRAYER**	**EVENING PRAYER**
	CW		
Psalms:	147.13–end	98; *150*	*93*; 132
Readings:	1 John 5.5–13;	Baruch 4.21–30 *or*	Isa. 66.1–11;
	Luke 5.12–16	Jer. 33.14–end;	2 John
		Matt. 23.13–28	*or* Eve of Baptism of Christ:
			Ps. 36; Isa. 61;
			Titus 2.11–14; 3.4–7

If The Epiphany was celebrated on Sunday January 5th these readings are used for the Eucharist:

Psalms:	149.1–5
Readings:	1 John 5.14–end;
	John 3.22–30

		AW	*Gen. 17.1–14*		*Eph. 2.11–end*
	HOLY COMMUNION		**MORNING PRAYER**		**EVENING PRAYER**
	BCP				
Psalms:			*56; 57; 58*		*59; 60; 61*
Readings:			Joel 1;		Joel 2.1–14;
			Matt. 8.18–end		2 Thess. 3;
					E. Coll. Epiphany 1, Baptism

Hymns:

THE BAPTISM OF CHRIST
The First Sunday after Epiphany

(White *or* Gold)

	PRINCIPAL SERVICE CW	**THIRD SERVICE**	**SECOND SERVICE**
Psalms:	29	89.19–29	46; 47
Readings:	Isa. 42.1–9; Acts 10.34–43; Matt. 3.13–end;	Exod. 14.15–22; 1 John 5.6–9	Josh. 3.1–8, 14–end; Heb. 1.1–12; [Luke 3.15–22]

	HOLY COMMUNION BCP *To celebrate the Baptism of Christ, see CW provision.*	**MORNING PRAYER**	**EVENING PRAYER**
Psalms:	72.1–8	89.21–30	46
Readings:	Zech. 8.1–8; Rom. 12.1–5; Luke 2.41–52	Isa. 44.6–end; John 1.19–34 or Eph. 2	Isa. 45 or Isa. 48; John 4.1–42 or Col. 1.21—2.7
Hymns:	....	....	....

CW COLLECTS

Eternal Father,
who at the baptism of Jesus
revealed him to be your Son,
anointing him with the Holy Spirit:
grant to us, who are born again by water and
  the Spirit,
that we may be faithful to our calling
through Jesus Christ your Son our Lord,
who is alive and reigns with you,
in the unity of the Holy Spirit,
one God, now and for ever.

or

Heavenly Father
at the Jordan you revealed Jesus as your Son:
may we recognize him as our Lord
and know ourselves to be your beloved children;
through Jesus Christ our Saviour.

POST COMMUNION

Lord of all time and eternity,
you opened the heavens
  and revealed yourself as Father
in the baptism of Jesus your beloved Son:
by the power of your Spirit
complete the heavenly work of our rebirth
through the waters of the new creation;
through Jesus Christ our Lord.

BCP COLLECT

*O Lord, we beseech thee mercifully to receive the
prayers of thy people which call upon thee; and
grant that they may both perceive and know what
things they ought to do, and also may have grace
and power faithfully to fulfil the same; through
Jesus Christ our Lord.*

2020

July					August						September					October					November					December				
S		5	12	19	26	S		2	9	16	23	30	S		6	13	20	27	S		4	11	18	25	S	1	8	15	22	29	S		6	13	20	27
M		6	13	20	27	M		3	10	17	24	31	M		7	14	21	28	M		5	12	19	26	M	2	9	16	23	30	M		7	14	21	28
T		7	14	21	28	T		4	11	18	25		T	1	8	15	22	29	T		6	13	20	27	T	3	10	17	24		T	1	8	15	22	29
W	1	8	15	22	29	W		5	12	19	26		W	2	9	16	23	30	W		7	14	21	28	W	4	11	18	25		W	2	9	16	23	30
T	2	9	16	23	30	T		6	13	20	27		T	3	10	17	24		T	1	8	15	22	29	T	5	12	19	26		T	3	10	17	24	31
F	3	10	17	24	31	F		7	14	21	28		F	4	11	18	25		F	2	9	16	23	30	F	6	13	20	27		F	4	11	18	25	
S	4	11	18	25		S	1	8	15	22	29		S	5	12	19	26		S	3	10	17	24	31	S	7	14	21	28		S	5	12	19	26	

Hilary, Bishop of Poitiers, Teacher of the Faith, 367 (CW Readings see Common of the Saints
also 1 John 2.18–25; John 8.25–32) (also BCP)
Kentigern (Mungo), Missionary Bishop in Strathclyde and Cumbria, 603
George Fox, Founder of the Society of Friends (the Quakers), 1691

White

	EUCHARIST		MORNING PRAYER	EVENING PRAYER
DEL Wk 1	CW			
Psalms:	116.10–15		*2*; 110	*34*; 36
Readings:	1 Sam. 1.1–8;		Gen. 1.1–19;	Amos 1;
	Mark 1.14–20		Matt. 21.1–17	1 Cor. 1.1–17
		AW	*Isa.* 41.14–20	John 1.29–34

	HOLY COMMUNION	MORNING PRAYER	EVENING PRAYER
	BCP Com. Doctor		
Psalms:	37.30–35	68	69; 70
Readings:	Wisd. 7.7–14;	Joel 2.15–end;	Joel 3;
	1 Cor. 2.6–13;	Matt. 9.1–17	Gal. 1
	Matt. 13.51–52		
Hymns:	....	....	....

CW COLLECT
Everlasting God,
whose servant Hilary
steadfastly confessed your Son Jesus Christ
   to be both human and divine:
grant us his gentle courtesy
to bring to all the message of redemption
   in the incarnate Christ,
who is alive and reigns with you,
in the unity of the Holy Spirit,
one God, now and for ever.

POST COMMUNION
God of truth,
whose Wisdom set her table
and invited us to eat the bread and drink the wine
   of the kingdom:
help us to lay aside all foolishness
and to live and walk in the way of insight,
that we may come with Hilary
to the eternal feast of heaven;
through Jesus Christ our Lord.

BCP COLLECT
*O God, who hast enlightened thy Church by the
teaching of thy servant Hilary: Enrich it evermore, we
beseech thee, with thy heavenly grace and raise up
faithful witnesses, who by their life and doctrine may
set forth to all men the truth of thy salvation; through
Jesus Christ our Lord*

Sunrise 08.04; Sunset 16.13

2020

January				February				March				April				May					June			
S		5	12	19	26	S		2	9	16	23	S	1	8	15	22	29	S		5	12	19	26	S		3	10	17	24	31	S		7	14	21	28
M		6	13	20	27	M		3	10	17	24	M	2	9	16	23	30	M		6	13	20	27	M		4	11	18	25	M	1	8	15	22	29
T		7	14	21	28	T		4	11	18	25	T	3	10	17	24	31	T		7	14	21	28	T		5	12	19	26	T	2	9	16	23	30
W	1	8	15	22	29	W		5	12	19	26	W	4	11	18	25	W	1	8	15	22	29	W		6	13	20	27	W	3	10	17	24
T	2	9	16	23	30	T		6	13	20	27	T	5	12	19	26	T	2	9	16	23	30	T		7	14	21	28	T	4	11	18	25
F	3	10	17	24	31	F		7	14	21	28	F	6	13	20	27	F	3	10	17	24	F	1	8	15	22	29	F	5	12	19	26
S	4	11	18	25	S	1	8	15	22	29	S	7	14	21	28	S	4	11	18	25	S	2	9	16	23	30	S	6	13	20	27

White

	EUCHARIST	**MORNING PRAYER**	**EVENING PRAYER**
	CW		
Psalms:	*Canticle:* 1 Sam. 2.1, 4–8; *or* Mag.	8; *9*	*45*; 46
Readings:	1 Sam. 1.9–20;	Gen. 1.20–2.3;	Amos 2;
	Mark 1.21–28	Matt. 21.18–32	1 Cor. 1.18–end

AW		*Exod. 17.1–7*	*Acts 8.26–end*

	HOLY COMMUNION	**MORNING PRAYER**	**EVENING PRAYER**
	BCP		
Psalms:		71; 72	73; 74
Readings:		*Amos 1;*	*Amos 2;*
		Matt. 9.18–34	*Gal. 2*
Hymns:	....	....	....

2020

	July				August					September					October				November					December			
S		5	12	19	26	**S**		2	9	16	23	30	**S**		6	13	20	27	**S**		4	11	18	25	**S**	1	8	15	22	29	**S**		6	13	20	27
M		6	13	20	27	**M**		3	10	17	24	31	**M**		7	14	21	28	**M**		5	12	19	26	**M**	2	9	16	23	30	**M**		7	14	21	28
T		7	14	21	28	**T**		4	11	18	25	**T**	1	8	15	22	29	**T**		6	13	20	27	**T**	3	10	17	24	**T**	1	8	15	22	29
W	1	8	15	22	29	**W**		5	12	19	26	**W**	2	9	16	23	30	**W**		7	14	21	28	**W**	4	11	18	25	**W**	2	9	16	23	30
T	2	9	16	23	30	**T**		6	13	20	27	**T**	3	10	17	24	**T**	1	8	15	22	29	**T**	5	12	19	26	**T**	3	10	17	24	31
F	3	10	17	24	31	**F**		7	14	21	28	**F**	4	11	18	25	**F**	2	9	16	23	30	**F**	6	13	20	27	**F**	4	11	18	25
S	4	11	18	25	**S**	1	8	15	22	29	**S**	5	12	19	26	**S**	3	10	17	24	31	**S**	7	14	21	28	**S**	5	12	19	26

White

	EUCHARIST	**MORNING PRAYER**	**EVENING PRAYER**
	CW		
Psalms:	40.1–4, 7–10	19; *20*	*47*; 48
Readings:	1 Sam. 3.1–10, 19–20;	Gen. 2.4–end;	Amos 3;
	Mark 1.29–39	Matt. 21.33–end	1 Cor. 2

	AW	*Exod. 15.1–19*	*Col. 2.8–15*

	HOLY COMMUNION	**MORNING PRAYER**	**EVENING PRAYER**
	BCP		
Psalms:		*75; 76; 77*	*78*
Readings:		*Amos 3;*	*Amos 4;*
		Matt. 9.35—10.23	*Gal. 3*
Hymns:	....	....	....

White

	EUCHARIST CW	MORNING PRAYER	EVENING PRAYER
Psalms:	44.10–15, 24–25	*21*; 24	*61*; 65
Readings:	1 Sam. 4.1–11; Mark 1.40–end	Gen. 3; Matt. 22.1–14	Amos 4; 1 Cor. 3

		AW	Zech. 6.9–15	1 Pet. 2.4–10

	HOLY COMMUNION BCP	MORNING PRAYER	EVENING PRAYER
Psalms:		*79; 80; 81*	*82; 83; 84; 85*
Readings:		Amos 5; Matt. 10.24–end	Amos 6; Gal. 4.1—5.1
Hymns:	....	....	....

2020

	July				August					September				October				November					December			
S		5	12	19	26		2	9	16	23	30		6	13	20	27		4	11	18	25		1	8	15	22	29		6	13	20	27
M		6	13	20	27		3	10	17	24	31		7	14	21	28		5	12	19	26		2	9	16	23	30		7	14	21	28
T		7	14	21	28		4	11	18	25		1	8	15	22	29		6	13	20	27		3	10	17	24		1	8	15	22	29
W	1	8	15	22	29		5	12	19	26	2	9	16	23	30		7	14	21	28		4	11	18	25		2	9	16	23	30
T	2	9	16	23	30		6	13	20	27	3	10	17	24		1	8	15	22	29		5	12	19	26		3	10	17	24	31
F	3	10	17	24	31		7	14	21	28	4	11	18	25	2	9	16	23	30		6	13	20	27		4	11	18	25
S	4	11	18	25		1	8	15	22	29	5	12	19	26	3	10	17	24	31		7	14	21	28		5	12	19	26

Antony of Egypt, Hermit, Abbot, 356 (CW readings see Common of the Saints especially Phil. 3.7–14 also Matt. 19.16–26) *Charles Gore, Bishop, Founder of the Community of the Resurrection, 1932*

White

	EUCHARIST		**MORNING PRAYER**		**EVENING PRAYER**
	CW				
Psalms:	89.15–18		*67*; 72		*68*
Readings:	1 Sam. 8.4–7, 10–end; Mark 2.1–12		Gen. 4.1–16, 25–26; Matt. 22.15–33		Amos 5.1–17; 1 Cor. 4
		AW	*Isa. 51.7–16*		*Gal. 6.14–18*
	HOLY COMMUNION		**MORNING PRAYER**		**EVENING PRAYER**
	BCP				
Psalms:			*86; 87; 88*		*89*
Readings:			*Amos 7;* *Matt. 11*		*Amos 8;* *Gal. 5.2–end*
Hymns:	....		....		....

CW COLLECT
Most gracious God,
who called your servant Antony to sell all that he had
    and to serve you in the solitude of the desert:
by his example may we learn to deny ourselves
and to love you before all things;
through Jesus Christ your Son our Lord,
who is alive and reigns with you,
in the unity of the Holy Spirit,
one God, now and for ever.

POST COMMUNION
Merciful God,
who gave such grace to your servant Antony
that he served you with singleness of heart
and loved you above all things:
help us, whose communion with you
    has been renewed in this sacrament,
to forsake all that holds us back from following Christ
and to grow into his likeness from glory to glory;
through Jesus Christ our Lord.

Beginning of the Week of Prayer for Christian Unity. Prisca, Roman Virgin and Martyr (BCP) White (*or Red*)
Amy Carmichael, Founder of the Dohnavur Fellowship, spiritual writer, 1951

	EUCHARIST	MORNING PRAYER	EVENING PRAYER
	CW		
Psalms:	21.1–6	29; *33*	84; *85*
Readings:	1 Sam. 9.1–4, 17–19; 10.1a;	Gen. 6.1–10;	Amos 5.18–end;
	Mark 2.13–17	Matt. 22.34–end	1 Cor. 5

	AW	Lev. 16.11–22	Heb. 10.19–25	

	HOLY COMMUNION	MORNING PRAYER	EVENING PRAYER
	BCP Virgin Martyr		
Psalms:	131	90; 91; 92	93; 94
Readings:	Ecclus 51.10–12; Phil. 3.7–14;	Amos 9;	Obad.; Gal. 6;
	Matt. 25.1–13	Matt. 12.1–21	E. Coll. Epiphany 2
Hymns:	....	....	....

BCP COLLECT
O God, who didst endue the holy Virgin Prisca with grace to witness a good confession (and to suffer gladly for thy sake): Grant that we, after her example, may be found ready when the Bridegroom cometh and enter with him to the marriage feast; through the same thy Son Jesus Christ our Lord.

THE SECOND SUNDAY OF EPIPHANY

(White)

	PRINCIPAL SERVICE	THIRD SERVICE	SECOND SERVICE
	CW		
Psalms:	40.1–12	145.1–12	96
Readings:	Isa. 49.1–7;	Jer. 1.4–10;	Ezek. 2.1—3.4;
	1 Cor. 1.1–9;	Mark 1.14–20	Gal. 1.11–end;
	John 1.29–42		[John 1.43–end]
	Seasonal provisions CW Book pp 304–305		

	HOLY COMMUNION	MORNING PRAYER	EVENING PRAYER
	BCP		
Psalms:	107.13–22	145.1–12	96
Readings:	2 Kgs 4.1–17;	Isa. 49.1–13;	Isa. 49.14–end or Isa. 50.4–10;
	Rom. 12.6–16a;	Luke 4.16–30 or	John 12.20–end or
	John 2.1–11	Jas 1	1 Thess. 1.1—2.12
Hymns:	....	....	....

CW COLLECTS

Almighty God,
in Christ you make all things new:
transform the poverty of our nature
    by the riches of your grace,
and in the renewal of our lives
make known your heavenly glory;
through Jesus Christ your Son our Lord,
who is alive and reigns with you,
in the unity of the Holy Spirit,
one God, now and for ever.

or

Eternal Lord,
our beginning and our end:
bring us with the whole creation
to your glory, hidden through past ages
and made known
in Jesus Christ our Lord.

POST COMMUNION

God of glory,
you nourish us with your Word
who is the bread of life:
fill us with your Holy Spirit
that through us the light of your glory
may shine in all the world.
We ask this in the name of Jesus Christ our Lord.

BCP COLLECT

Almighty and everlasting God, who dost govern
all things in heaven and earth: Mercifully hear the
supplications of thy people, and grant us thy peace
all the days of our life; through Jesus Christ our Lord.

2020

	July					August						September					October					November					December			
S		5	12	19	26		2	9	16	23	30		6	13	20	27		4	11	18	25		1	8	15	22	29		6	13	20	27
M		6	13	20	27		3	10	17	24	31		7	14	21	28		5	12	19	26		2	9	16	23	30		7	14	21	28
T		7	14	21	28		4	11	18	25			1	8	15	22	29		6	13	20	27		3	10	17	24			1	8	15	22	29
W	1	8	15	22	29		5	12	19	26			2	9	16	23	30		7	14	21	28		4	11	18	25		2	9	16	23	30
T	2	9	16	23	30		6	13	20	27			3	10	17	24			1	8	15	22	29		5	12	19	26		3	10	17	24	31
F	3	10	17	24	31		7	14	21	28			4	11	18	25			2	9	16	23	30		6	13	20	27		4	11	18	25
S	4	11	18	25		1	8	15	22	29			5	12	19	26			3	10	17	24	31		7	14	21	28		5	12	19	26

Richard Rolle of Hampole, Spiritual Writer, 1349
Fabian, Bishop of Rome and Martyr 250 (BCP)

White (*or Red*)

DEL Wk 2	EUCHARIST CW	MORNING PRAYER	EVENING PRAYER
Psalms:	50.8–10, 16–17, 24	145; *146*	*71*
Readings:	1 Sam. 15, 16–23; Mark 2.18–22	Gen. 6.11—7.10; Matt. 24.1–14	Amos 6; 1 Cor. 6.1–11

AW 1 Kgs 17.8–16   Mark 8.1–10

	HOLY COMMUNION BCP Com Martyr	MORNING PRAYER	EVENING PRAYER
Psalms:	3	102; 103	104
Readings:	Jer. 11.18–20; Heb. 11.32—12.2; Matt. 16.24–27	Jonah 1 and 2; Matt. 12.22–end	Jonah 3 and 4; 1 Cor. 1.1–25
Hymns:	....	....	....

BCP COLLECT
Almighty God, by whose grace and power thy holy Martyr Fabian triumphed over suffering and despised death: Grant, we beseech thee, that enduring hardness and waxing valiant in fight, we may with the noble army of martyrs received the crown of everlasting life; through Jesus Christ our Lord.

Sunrise 07.57; Sunset 16.24

2020

January					February					March					April					May						June				
S		5	12	19	26	S		2	9	16	23	S	1	8	15	22	29	S		5	12	19	26	S		3	10	17	24	31	S		7	14	21	28
M		6	13	20	27	M		3	10	17	24	M	2	9	16	23	30	M		6	13	20	27	M		4	11	18	25	M	1	8	15	22	29
T		7	14	21	28	T		4	11	18	25	T	3	10	17	24	31	T		7	14	21	28	T		5	12	19	26	T	2	9	16	23	30
W	1	8	15	22	29	W		5	12	19	26	W	4	11	18	25	W	1	8	15	22	29	W		6	13	20	27	W	3	10	17	24
T	2	9	16	23	30	T		6	13	20	27	T	5	12	19	26	T	2	9	16	23	30	T		7	14	21	28	T	4	11	18	25
F	3	10	17	24	31	F		7	14	21	28	F	6	13	20	27	F	3	10	17	24	F	1	8	15	22	29	F	5	12	19	26
S	4	11	18	25	S	1	8	15	22	29	S	7	14	21	28	S	4	11	18	25	S	2	9	16	23	30	S	6	13	20	27

Agnes, Child Martyr at Rome, 304 (*Agnes, V&M, BCP*)   White *or* Red (*or Red*)

	EUCHARIST	**MORNING PRAYER**	**EVENING PRAYER**
	CW		
Psalms:	89.19–27	*132*; 147.1–12	*89.1–37*
Readings:	1 Sam. 16.1–13;	Gen. 7.11–end;	Amos 7;
	Mark 2.23–end	Matt. 24.15–28	1 Cor. 6.12–end
		AW *1 Kgs 19.1–9a*	*Mark 1.9–15*
	HOLY COMMUNION	**MORNING PRAYER**	**EVENING PRAYER**
	BCP Com. Virgin Martyr		
Psalms:	131	105	106
Readings:	Ecclus 51.10–12;	Mic. 1;	Mic. 2;
	Phil. 3.7–14;	Matt. 13.1–23	1 Cor. 1.26—2–end
	Matt. 25.1–13		
Hymns:			

CW COLLECT
Eternal God, shepherd of your sheep,
whose child Agnes was strengthened to bear witness
in her living and her dying
to the true love of her redeemer:
grant us the power to understand, with all
your saints,
what is the breadth and length and height and depth
and to know the love that surpasses knowledge,
even Jesus Christ your Son our Lord,
who is alive and reigns with you,
in the unity of the Holy Spirit,
one God, now and for ever.

POST COMMUNION
God our redeemer,
whose Church was strengthened by the blood of
your martyr Agnes:
so bind us, in life and death, to Christ's sacrifice
that our lives, broken and offered with his,
may carry his death and proclaim his resurrection
in the world;
through Jesus Christ our Lord.

BCP COLLECT
*O God, who didst endue the holy Virgin Agnes with
grace to witness a good confession (and to suffer
gladly for thy sake): Grant that we, after her example,
may be found ready when the Bridegroom cometh
and enter with him to the marriage feast; through the
same thy Son Jesus Christ our Lord.*

2020

July						August						September						October						November						December				
S		5	12	19	26	S		2	9	16	23	30	S		6	13	20	27	S		4	11	18	25	S	1	8	15	22	29	S		6	13	20	27
M		6	13	20	27	M		3	10	17	24	31	M		7	14	21	28	M		5	12	19	26	M	2	9	16	23	30	M		7	14	21	28
T		7	14	21	28	T		4	11	18	25		T	1	8	15	22	29	T		6	13	20	27	T	3	10	17	24		T	1	8	15	22	29
W	1	8	15	22	29	W		5	12	19	26		W	2	9	16	23	30	W		7	14	21	28	W	4	11	18	25		W	2	9	16	23	30
T	2	9	16	23	30	T		6	13	20	27		T	3	10	17	24		T	1	8	15	22	29	T	5	12	19	26		T	3	10	17	24	31
F	3	10	17	24	31	F		7	14	21	28		F	4	11	18	25		F	2	9	16	23	30	F	6	13	20	27		F	4	11	18	25	
S	4	11	18	25		S	1	8	15	22	29		S	5	12	19	26		S	3	10	17	24	31	S	7	14	21	28		S	5	12	19	26	

Vincent of Saragossa, Deacon, First Martyr of Spain, 304 (Vincent, M, BCP)

White *or* Red (*or* Red)

	EUCHARIST	**MORNING PRAYER**	**EVENING PRAYER**
	CW		
Psalms:	144.1–2, 9–10	*81*; 147.13–end	*97*; 98
Readings:	1 Sam. 17.32–33, 37, 40–51;	Gen. 8.1–14;	Amos 8;
	Mark 3.1–6	Matt. 24.29–end	1 Cor. 7.1–24
		AW 1 Kgs 19.9b–18	Mark 9.2–13

	HOLY COMMUNION	**MORNING PRAYER**	**EVENING PRAYER**
	BCP Com. Martyr		
Psalms:	3	107	108; 109
Readings:	Jer. 11.18–20;	Mic. 3;	Mic. 4.1—5.1;
	Heb. 11.32—12.2;	Matt. 13.24–43	1 Cor. 3
	Matt. 16.24–27		
Hymns:	....	....	....

BCP COLLECT
*Almighty God, by whose grace and power thy
holy Martyr Vincent triumphed over suffering,
and despised death: Grant, we beseech thee, that
enduring hardness, and waxing valiant in fight,
we may with the noble army of martyrs received
the crown of everlasting life; through Jesus Christ
our Lord.*

2020

	January				February				March				April				May				June			
S		5	12	19	26		2	9	16	23		1	8	15	22	29		5	12	19	26		3	10	17	24	31		7	14	21	28
M		6	13	20	27		3	10	17	24		2	9	16	23	30		6	13	20	27		4	11	18	25		1	8	15	22	29
T		7	14	21	28		4	11	18	25		3	10	17	24	31		7	14	21	28		5	12	19	26		2	9	16	23	30
W	1	8	15	22	29		5	12	19	26		4	11	18	25		1	8	15	22	29		6	13	20	27		3	10	17	24
T	2	9	16	23	30		6	13	20	27		5	12	19	26		2	9	16	23	30		7	14	21	28		4	11	18	25
F	3	10	17	24	31		7	14	21	28		6	13	20	27		3	10	17	24		1	8	15	22	29		5	12	19	26
S	4	11	18	25		1	8	15	22	29		7	14	21	28		4	11	18	25		2	9	16	23	30		6	13	20	27

White

	EUCHARIST	MORNING PRAYER	EVENING PRAYER
	CW		
Psalms:	56.1–2, 8–end	*76*; 148	99; 100; *111*
Readings:	1 Sam. 18.6–9, 19.1–7; Mark 3.7–12	Gen. 8.15—9.7; Matt. 25.1–13	Amos 9; 1 Cor. 7.25–end

AW   *Lev. 11.1–8, 13–19, 41–45*   *Acts 10.9–16*

	HOLY COMMUNION	MORNING PRAYER	EVENING PRAYER
	BCP		
Psalms:		*110; 111; 112; 113*	*114; 115*
Readings:		*Mic. 5.2–end;* *Matt. 13.44–end*	*Mic. 6;* *1 Cor. 4.1–17*
Hymns:	....	....	....

2020

	July					August					September					October					November					December			
S		5	12	19	26		2	9	16	23	30		6	13	20	27		4	11	18	25		1	8	15	22	29		6	13	20	27
M		6	13	20	27		3	10	17	24	31		7	14	21	28		5	12	19	26		2	9	16	23	30		7	14	21	28
T		7	14	21	28		4	11	18	25		1	8	15	22	29		6	13	20	27		3	10	17	24		1	8	15	22	29
W	1	8	15	22	29		5	12	19	26		2	9	16	23	30		7	14	21	28		4	11	18	25		2	9	16	23	30
T	2	9	16	23	30		6	13	20	27		3	10	17	24		1	8	15	22	29		5	12	19	26		3	10	17	24	31
F	3	10	17	24	31		7	14	21	28		4	11	18	25		2	9	16	23	30		6	13	20	27		4	11	18	25
S	4	11	18	25		1	8	15	22	29		5	12	19	26		3	10	17	24	31		7	14	21	28		5	12	19	26

Francis de Sales, Bishop of Geneva, Teacher of the Faith, 1622   White
(CW Reading see Common of the Saints also Prov. 3.13–18; John 3.17–21)

	EUCHARIST CW	**MORNING PRAYER**	**EVENING PRAYER**
Psalms:	57.1–2, 8–end	*27*; 149	*73*
Readings:	1 Sam. 24.3–22a; Mark 3.13–19	Gen. 9.8–19; Matt. 25.14–30	Hos. 1.1—2.1; 1 Cor. 8 *or* Eve of The Conversion of St Paul: Ps. 149; Isa. 49.1–13; Acts 22.3–16

AW   *Isa. 49.8–13*   *Acts 10.34–43*

	HOLY COMMUNION BCP	**MORNING PRAYER**	**EVENING PRAYER**
Psalms:		*116; 117; 118*	*119.1–32*
Readings:		*Mic. 7; Matt. 14*	*Nahum 1; 1 Cor. 4.18—5–end or First Evensong of St Paul: Jer. 1.4–10; Acts 26.1–23*

Hymns: ....

CW COLLECT
Holy God,
who called your bishop Francis de Sales
to bring many to Christ
    through his devout life
and to renew your Church
    with patience and understanding:
grant that we may, by word and example,
reflect your gentleness and love to all we meet;
through Jesus Christ our Saviour,
who is alive and reigns with you,
in the unity of the Holy Spirit,
one God, now and for ever.

POST COMMUNION
God, shepherd of your people,
whose servant Francis revealed the loving service of
    Christ in his ministry as a pastor of your people: by
    this eucharist in which we share
awaken within us the love of Christ
and keep us faithful to our Christian calling;
through him who laid down his life for us,
but is alive and reigns with you, now and for ever.

2020

	January	February	March	April	May	June
S	5 12 19 26	2 9 16 23	1 8 15 22 29	5 12 19 26	3 10 17 24 31	7 14 21 28
M	6 13 20 27	3 10 17 24	2 9 16 23 30	6 13 20 27	4 11 18 25	1 8 15 22 29
T	7 14 21 28	4 11 18 25	3 10 17 24 31	7 14 21 28	5 12 19 26	2 9 16 23 30
W	1 8 15 22 29	5 12 19 26	4 11 18 25	1 8 15 22 29	6 13 20 27	3 10 17 24
T	2 9 16 23 30	6 13 20 27	5 12 19 26	2 9 16 23 30	7 14 21 28	4 11 18 25
F	3 10 17 24 31	7 14 21 28	6 13 20 27	3 10 17 24	1 8 15 22 29	5 12 19 26
S	4 11 18 25	1 8 15 22 29	7 14 21 28	4 11 18 25	2 9 16 23 30	6 13 20 27

The Conversion of Paul   White

	PRINCIPAL SERVICE	THIRD SERVICE	SECOND SERVICE
	CW		
Psalms:	67	66; 147.13–end	119.41–56
Readings:	Jer. 1.4–10; Acts 9.1–22; Matt. 19.27–end *or* Acts 9.1–22; Gal. 1.11–16a; Matt. 19.27–end	Ezek. 3.22–end; Phil. 3.1–14	Ecclus 39.1–10 *or* Isa. 56.1–8; Col. 1.24—2.7

Displaced readings may be added to the preceding day's portion:

	EUCHARIST	MORNING PRAYER	EVENING PRAYER
	CW		
Readings:	2 Sam. 1.1–4, 11–12, 17–19, 23–end; Mark 3.20–21	Gen. 11.1–9; Matt. 25.31–end	Hos. 2.2–17; 1 Cor. 9.1–14

	HOLY COMMUNION	MORNING PRAYER	EVENING PRAYER
	BCP St Paul		
Psalms:	67	119.33–72	119.73–104
Readings:	Josh. 5.13–end; Acts 9.1–22; Matt. 19.27–end	Isa. 49.1–13; Gal. 1.11–end	Isa. 45.18–end; Phil. 3.1–14
Hymns:	....	....	....

CW COLLECT
Almighty God,
who caused the light of the gospel
to shine throughout the world
through the preaching of your servant Saint Paul:
grant that we who celebrate his wonderful
    conversion
may follow him in bearing witness to your truth;
through Jesus Christ your Son our Lord,
who is alive and reigns with you,
in the unity of the Holy Spirit,
one God, now and for ever.

POST COMMUNION
Almighty God,
who on the day of Pentecost
sent your Holy Spirit to the apostles
with the wind from heaven and in tongues of flame,
filling them with joy and boldness to preach
    the gospel:
by the power of the same Spirit
strengthen us to witness to your truth
and to draw everyone to the fire of your love;
through Jesus Christ our Lord.

BCP COLLECT
O God, who, through the preaching of the blessed
Apostle Saint Paul, hast caused the light of the
Gospel to shine throughout the world: Grant,
we beseech thee, that we, having his wonderufl
conversion in remembrance, may shew forth our
thankfulness unto thee for the same, by following the
holy doctrine which he taught; through Jesus Christ
our Lord.

2020

	July					August						September					October					November					December			
S		5	12	19	26		2	9	16	23	30		6	13	20	27		4	11	18	25		1	8	15	22	29		6	13	20	27
M		6	13	20	27		3	10	17	24	31		7	14	21	28		5	12	19	26		2	9	16	23	30		7	14	21	28
T		7	14	21	28		4	11	18	25		1	8	15	22	29		6	13	20	27		3	10	17	24		1	8	15	22	29
W	1	8	15	22	29		5	12	19	26		2	9	16	23	30		7	14	21	28		4	11	18	25		2	9	16	23	30
T	2	9	16	23	30		6	13	20	27		3	10	17	24		1	8	15	22	29		5	12	19	26		3	10	17	24	31
F	3	10	17	24	31		7	14	21	28		4	11	18	25		2	9	16	23	30		6	13	20	27		4	11	18	25	
S	4	11	18	25		1	8	15	22	29		5	12	19	26		3	10	17	24	31		7	14	21	28		5	12	19	26	

THE THIRD SUNDAY OF EPIPHANY

(White)

	PRINCIPAL SERVICE	**THIRD SERVICE**	**SECOND SERVICE**
	CW		
Psalms:	27.1, 4–12 (27.1–11)	113	33 (33.1–12)
Readings:	Isa. 9.1–4; 1 Cor. 1.10–18; Matt. 4.12–23	Amos 3.1–8; 1 John 1.1–4	Eccles. 3.1–11; 1 Pet. 1.3–12; [Luke 4.14–21]
	Seasonal provisions CW Book pp 304–305		

	HOLY COMMUNION	**MORNING PRAYER**	**EVENING PRAYER**
	BCP		
Psalms:	102.15–22	113	33 (or 33.1–12)
Readings:	2 Kgs 6.14b–23; Rom. 12.16b–end; Matt. 8.1–13	Hos. 11.1—12.6; John 2 or Jas 2	Hos. 14 or Joel 2.15–end; John 6.22–40 or Gal. 1
Hymns:	....	....	....

2020

	January					February					March					April					May						June			
S		5	12	19	26			2	9	16	23		1	8	15	22	29			5	12	19	26			3	10	17	24	31			7	14	21	28
M		6	13	20	27			3	10	17	24		2	9	16	23	30			6	13	20	27			4	11	18	25			1	8	15	22	29
T		7	14	21	28			4	11	18	25		3	10	17	24	31			7	14	21	28			5	12	19	26			2	9	16	23	30
W	1	8	15	22	29			5	12	19	26		4	11	18	25			1	8	15	22	29			6	13	20	27			3	10	17	24	
T	2	9	16	23	30			6	13	20	27		5	12	19	26			2	9	16	23	30			7	14	21	28			4	11	18	25	
F	3	10	17	24	31			7	14	21	28		6	13	20	27			3	10	17	24		1	8	15	22	29			5	12	19	26	
S	4	11	18	25			1	8	15	22	29		7	14	21	28			4	11	18	25		2	9	16	23	30			6	13	20	27	

CW COLLECTS

Almighty God,
whose Son revealed in signs and miracles
the wonder of your saving presence:
renew your people with your heavenly grace,
and in all our weakness
sustain us by your mighty power;
through Jesus Christ your Son our Lord,
who is alive and reigns with you,
in the unity of the Holy Spirit,
one God, now and for ever.

or

God of all mercy
your Son proclaimed good news to the poor,
release to the captives,
and freedom to the oppressed:
anoint us with your Holy Spirit
and set all your people free
to praise you in Christ our Lord.

POST COMMUNION

Almighty Father,
whose Son our Saviour Jesus Christ
   is the light of the world:
may your people,
illumined by your word and sacraments,
shine with the radiance of his glory,
that he may be known, worshipped, and obeyed
   to the ends of the earth;
for he is alive and reigns, now and for ever.

BCP COLLECT

*Almighty and everlasting God, mercifully look upon
our infirmities, and in all our dangers and necessities
stretch forth thy right hand to help and defend us;
through Jesus Christ our Lord.*

2020

	July					August						September					October					November					December			
S		5	12	19	26		2	9	16	23	30		6	13	20	27		4	11	18	25		1	8	15	22	29		6	13	20	27
M		6	13	20	27		3	10	17	24	31		7	14	21	28		5	12	19	26		2	9	16	23	30		7	14	21	28
T		7	14	21	28		4	11	18	25		1	8	15	22	29		6	13	20	27		3	10	17	24		1	8	15	22	29
W	1	8	15	22	29		5	12	19	26		2	9	16	23	30		7	14	21	28		4	11	18	25		2	9	16	23	30
T	2	9	16	23	30		6	13	20	27		3	10	17	24		1	8	15	22	29		5	12	19	26		3	10	17	24	31
F	3	10	17	24	31		7	14	21	28		4	11	18	25		2	9	16	23	30		6	13	20	27		4	11	18	25
S	4	11	18	25		1	8	15	22	29		5	12	19	26		3	10	17	24	31		7	14	21	28		5	12	19	26

(Timothy and Titus, Companions of St Paul may be celebrated on this day at the Minister's discretion where there is sufficient reason.)

White

CW Lesser Festival EUCHARIST: Ps. 100; Isa. 61.1–3a; 2 Tim. 2.1–8 *or* Titus 1.1–5; Luke 10.1–9)

DEL Wk 3	EUCHARIST CW	MORNING PRAYER	EVENING PRAYER
Psalms:	89.19–27	40; *108*	*138*; 144
Readings:	2 Sam. 5.1–7, 10; Mark 3.22–30	Gen. 11.27—12.9; Matt. 26.1–16	Hos. 2.18—end of 3; 1 Cor. 9.15–end
AW		*Ezek. 37.15–end*	*John 17.1–19*

	HOLY COMMUNION BCP	MORNING PRAYER	EVENING PRAYER
Psalms:		*120; 121; 122; 123; 124; 125*	*126; 127; 128; 129; 130; 131*
Readings:		*Hab. 1;* *1 Cor. 7*	*Hab. 2;* *1 Cor. 8;*
Hymns:	....	....	....

CW COLLECT (if used)
Heavenly Father,
who sent your apostle Paul to preach the gospel,
and gave him Timothy and Titus to be his
    companions in faith:
grant that our fellowship in the Holy Spirit
may bear witness to the name of Jesus,
who is alive and reigns with you,
in the unity of the Holy Spirit,
one God, now and for ever.

POST COMMUNION
Holy Father,
who gathered us here around the table of your
    Son to share this meal with the whole
household of God: in that new world where you
    reveal the fullness of your peace,
gather people of every race and language
to share with Timothy and Titus and all your
    saints in the eternal banquet of Jesus Christ
    our Lord.

Sunrise 07.49; Sunset 16.36

2020

	January					February					March					April					May						June			
S		5	12	19	26	S		2	9	16	23	S	1	8	15	22	29	S		5	12	19	26	S		3	10	17	24	31	S		7	14	21	28
M		6	13	20	27	M		3	10	17	24	M	2	9	16	23	30	M		6	13	20	27	M		4	11	18	25	M	1	8	15	22	29
T		7	14	21	28	T		4	11	18	25	T	3	10	17	24	31	T		7	14	21	28	T		5	12	19	26	T	2	9	16	23	30
W	1	8	15	22	29	W		5	12	19	26	W	4	11	18	25	W	1	8	15	22	29	W		6	13	20	27	W	3	10	17	24
T	2	9	16	23	30	T		6	13	20	27	T	5	12	19	26	T	2	9	16	23	30	T		7	14	21	28	T	4	11	18	25
F	3	10	17	24	31	F		7	14	21	28	F	6	13	20	27	F	3	10	17	24	F	1	8	15	22	29	F	5	12	19	26
S	4	11	18	25	S	1	8	15	22	29	S	7	14	21	28	S	4	11	18	25	S	2	9	16	23	30	S	6	13	20	27

Thomas Aquinas, Priest, Philosopher, Teacher of the Faith, 1274   White
(CW Readings see Common of the Saints especially Wisd. 77–10, 15–16; 1 Cor. 2.9–16; John 16.12–15)

	EUCHARIST CW	**MORNING PRAYER**	**EVENING PRAYER**
Psalms:	24.7–end	34; **36**	**145**
Readings:	2 Sam. 6.12–15, 17–19; Mark 3.31–end	Gen. 13.2–end; Matt. 26.17–35	Hos. 4.1–16; 1 Cor. 10.1–13

	AW	Ezek. 20.39–44	John 17.20–end

	HOLY COMMUNION BCP	**MORNING PRAYER**	**EVENING PRAYER**
Psalms:		132; 133; 134; 135	136; 137; 138
Readings:		Hab. 3.2–end; 1 Cor. 9	Zeph. 1; 1 Cor. 10.1—11.1
Hymns:	....	....	....

CW COLLECT
Eternal God,
who enriched your Church with the learning and
    holiness of your servant Thomas Aquinas:
give to all who seek you
a humble mind and a pure heart
that they may know your Son Jesus Christ
as the way, the truth and the life;
who is alive and reigns with you,
in the unity of the Holy Spirit,
one God, now and for ever.

POST COMMUNION
God of truth,
whose Wisdom set her table
and invited us to eat the bread and drink the wine
    of the kingdom:
help us to lay aside all foolishness
and to live and walk in the way of insight,
that we may come with Thomas Aquinas to the
    eternal feast of heaven;
through Jesus Christ our Lord.

2020

July	August	September	October	November	December
S 5 12 19 26	S 2 9 16 23 30	S 6 13 20 27	S 4 11 18 25	S 1 8 15 22 29	S 6 13 20 27
M 6 13 20 27	M 3 10 17 24 31	M 7 14 21 28	M 5 12 19 26	M 2 9 16 23 30	M 7 14 21 28
T 7 14 21 28	T 4 11 18 25	T 1 8 15 22 29	T 6 13 20 27	T 3 10 17 24	T 1 8 15 22 29
W 1 8 15 22 29	W 5 12 19 26	W 2 9 16 23 30	W 7 14 21 28	W 4 11 18 25	W 2 9 16 23 30
T 2 9 16 23 30	T 6 13 20 27	T 3 10 17 24	T 1 8 15 22 29	T 5 12 19 26	T 3 10 17 24 31
F 3 10 17 24 31	F 7 14 21 28	F 4 11 18 25	F 2 9 16 23 30	F 6 13 20 27	F 4 11 18 25
S 4 11 18 25	S 1 8 15 22 29	S 5 12 19 26	S 3 10 17 24 31	S 7 14 21 28	S 5 12 19 26

White

	EUCHARIST		MORNING PRAYER	EVENING PRAYER
	CW			
Psalms:	89.19–27		45; *46*	21; *29*
Readings:	2 Sam. 7.4–17;		Gen. 14;	Hos. 5.1–7;
	Mark 4.1–20		Matt. 26.36–46	1 Cor. 10.14—11.1
		AW	*Neh. 2.1–10*	*Rom. 12.1–8*

	HOLY COMMUNION	MORNING PRAYER	EVENING PRAYER
	BCP		
Psalms:		*139; 140; 141*	*142; 143*
Readings:		*Zeph. 2;*	*Zeph. 3;*
		1 Cor. 11.2–end	*1 Cor. 12.1–27*
Hymns:	....	....	....

2020

	January						February						March						April						May						June				
S		5	12	19	26			2	9	16	23			1	8	15	22	29			5	12	19	26			3	10	17	24	31			7	14	21	28
M		6	13	20	27			3	10	17	24			2	9	16	23	30			6	13	20	27			4	11	18	25			1	8	15	22	29
T		7	14	21	28			4	11	18	25			3	10	17	24	31			7	14	21	28			5	12	19	26			2	9	16	23	30
W	1	8	15	22	29			5	12	19	26			4	11	18	25			1	8	15	22	29			6	13	20	27			3	10	17	24
T	2	9	16	23	30			6	13	20	27			5	12	19	26			2	9	16	23	30			7	14	21	28			4	11	18	25
F	3	10	17	24	31			7	14	21	28			6	13	20	27			3	10	17	24		1	8	15	22	29			5	12	19	26
S	4	11	18	25			1	8	15	22	29			7	14	21	28			4	11	18	25		2	9	16	23	30			6	13	20	27

Charles, King and Martyr, 1649 (CW Readings see Common of the Saints especially Ecclus 2.12–17; 1 Tim. 6.12–16)

White *or* Red

	EUCHARIST CW	MORNING PRAYER	EVENING PRAYER
Psalms:	132.1–5, 11–15	47; *48*	24; *33*
Readings:	2 Sam. 7.18–19, 24–end; Mark 4.21–25	Gen. 15; Matt. 26.47–56	Hos. 5.8—6.6; 1 Cor. 11.2–16

		AW	*Deut. 26.16–end*	*Rom. 14.1–9*

	HOLY COMMUNION BCP	MORNING PRAYER	EVENING PRAYER
Psalms:		*144; 145; 146*	*147; 148; 149; 150*
Readings:		Zech. 11; 1 Cor. 12.27—end of 13	Zech. 13; 1 Cor. 14.1–19
Hymns:	....	....	....

CW COLLECT
King of kings and Lord of lords,
whose faithful servant Charles
prayed for those who persecuted him
and died in the living hope of your eternal kingdom:
grant us by your grace so to follow his example
that we may love and bless our enemies,
through the intercession of your Son, our Lord
   Jesus Christ,
who is alive and reigns with you, in the unity of the
   Holy Spirit, one God, now and for ever.

POST COMMUNION
Eternal God,
who gave us this holy meal
in which we have celebrated the glory of the cross
and the victory of your martyr Charles:
by our communion with Christ
in his saving death and resurrection,
give us with all your saints the courage to
   conquer evil
and so to share the fruit of the tree of life;
through Jesus Christ our Lord.

2020

	July					August						September					October					November					December			
S		5	12	19	26	S		2	9	16	23	30	S		6	13	20	27	S		4	11	18	25	S	1	8	15	22	29	S		6	13	20	27
M		6	13	20	27	M		3	10	17	24	31	M		7	14	21	28	M		5	12	19	26	M	2	9	16	23	30	M		7	14	21	28
T		7	14	21	28	T		4	11	18	25	T	1	8	15	22	29	T		6	13	20	27	T	3	10	17	24	T	1	8	15	22	29
W	1	8	15	22	29	W		5	12	19	26	W	2	9	16	23	30	W		7	14	21	28	W	4	11	18	25	W	2	9	16	23	30
T	2	9	16	23	30	T		6	13	20	27	T	3	10	17	24	T	1	8	15	22	29	T	5	12	19	26	T	3	10	17	24	31
F	3	10	17	24	31	F		7	14	21	28	F	4	11	18	25	F	2	9	16	23	30	F	6	13	20	27	F	4	11	18	25
S	4	11	18	25	S	1	8	15	22	29	S	5	12	19	26	S	3	10	17	24	31	S	7	14	21	28	S	5	12	19	26

John Bosco, Priest, Founder of the Salesian Teaching Order, 1888   White

	EUCHARIST CW	**MORNING PRAYER**	**EVENING PRAYER**
Psalms:	51.1–6, 9	61; *65*	*67*; 77
Readings:	2 Sam. 11.1–10, 13–17; Mark 4.26–34	Gen. 16; Matt. 26.57–end	Hos. 6.7—7.2; 1 Cor. 11.17–end
		AW Lev. 19.9–28	*Rom. 15.1–7*

	HOLY COMMUNION BCP	**MORNING PRAYER**	**EVENING PRAYER**
Psalms:		144; 145; 146	147; 148; 149; 150
Readings:		Mal. 1; 1 Cor. 14.20–end	Mal. 2.1–16; 1 Cor. 15.1–34
Hymns:	....	....	....

2020

	January				February				March				April				May				June			
S		5	12	19	26		2	9	16	23		1	8	15	22	29		5	12	19	26		3	10	17	24	31		7	14	21	28
M		6	13	20	27		3	10	17	24		2	9	16	23	30		6	13	20	27		4	11	18	25		1	8	15	22	29
T		7	14	21	28		4	11	18	25		3	10	17	24	31		7	14	21	28		5	12	19	26		2	9	16	23	30
W	1	8	15	22	29		5	12	19	26		4	11	18	25		1	8	15	22	29		6	13	20	27		3	10	17	24
T	2	9	16	23	30		6	13	20	27		5	12	19	26		2	9	16	23	30		7	14	21	28		4	11	18	25
F	3	10	17	24	31		7	14	21	28		6	13	20	27		3	10	17	24		1	8	15	22	29		5	12	19	26
S	4	11	18	25		1	8	15	22	29		7	14	21	28		4	11	18	25		2	9	16	23	30		6	13	20	27

Brigid, Abbess of Kildare, c.525　　　　　　　　　　　　　　White

	EUCHARIST	MORNING PRAYER	EVENING PRAYER
	CW		
Psalms:	51.11–16	*68*	118
Readings:	2 Sam. 12.1–7, 10–17;	Gen. 17.1–22;	1 Sam. 1.19b–end;
	Mark 4.35–end	Matt. 27.1–10	Heb. 4.11–end
			Eve of the Presentation of Christ in the Temple.

		MORNING PRAYER	EVENING PRAYER
AW		*Jer. 33.1–11*	*1 Peter 5.5b–end*

	HOLY COMMUNION	MORNING PRAYER	EVENING PRAYER
	BCP		
Psalms:		1; 2; 3; 4; 5	6; 7; 8
Readings:		*Mal. 2.17—3.12;*	*First Evensong of Purification of*
		1 Cor. 15.35–end	*the Virgin Mary: Exod. 13.11–16;*
			Gal. 4.1–7;
			E. Coll., Purification
Hymns:	....	....	....

2020

	July					August					September					October					November					December			
S		5	12	19	26		2	9	16	23	30		6	13	20	27		4	11	18	25		1	8	15	22	29		6	13	20	27
M		6	13	20	27		3	10	17	24	31		7	14	21	28		5	12	19	26		2	9	16	23	30		7	14	21	28
T		7	14	21	28		4	11	18	25		1	8	15	22	29		6	13	20	27		3	10	17	24		1	8	15	22	29
W	1	8	15	22	29		5	12	19	26		2	9	16	23	30		7	14	21	28		4	11	18	25		2	9	16	23	30
T	2	9	16	23	30		6	13	20	27		3	10	17	24		1	8	15	22	29		5	12	19	26		3	10	17	24	31
F	3	10	17	24	31		7	14	21	28		4	11	18	25		2	9	16	23	30		6	13	20	27		4	11	18	25
S	4	11	18	25		1	8	15	22	29		5	12	19	26		3	10	17	24	31		7	14	21	28		5	12	19	26

THE PRESENTATION OF CHRIST IN THE TEMPLE
(Candlemas)
Purification of the Virgin Mary
(Gold *or* White)

	PRINCIPAL SERVICE	**THIRD SERVICE**	**SECOND SERVICE**
	CW		
Psalms:	24.[1–6] 7–end	48; 146	122; 132
Readings:	Mal. 3.1–5;	Exod. 13.1–16;	Hag. 2.1–9;
	Heb. 2.14–end;	Rom. 12.1–5	John 2.18–22
	Luke 2.22–40		
	Seasonal provisions CW Book pp 306–307		

	HOLY COMMUNION	**MORNING PRAYER**	**EVENING PRAYER**
	BCP Purification		
Psalms:	*48.1–7*	*48; 146*	*122; 132*
Readings:	*Mal. 3.1–5;*	*1 Sam. 1.21–end;*	*Hag. 2.1–9;*
	Gal. 4.1–7;	*Heb. 10.1–10*	*Rom. 12.1–5*
	Luke 2.22–40		
Hymns:	....	....	....

2020

	January	February	March	April	May	June
S	5 12 19 26	2 9 16 23	1 8 15 22 29	5 12 19 26	3 10 17 24 31	7 14 21 28
M	6 13 20 27	3 10 17 24	2 9 16 23 30	6 13 20 27	4 11 18 25	1 8 15 22 29
T	7 14 21 28	4 11 18 25	3 10 17 24 31	7 14 21 28	5 12 19 26	2 9 16 23 30
W	1 8 15 22 29	5 12 19 26	4 11 18 25	1 8 15 22 29	6 13 20 27	3 10 17 24
T	2 9 16 23 30	6 13 20 27	5 12 19 26	2 9 16 23 30	7 14 21 28	4 11 18 25
F	3 10 17 24 31	7 14 21 28	6 13 20 27	3 10 17 24	1 8 15 22 29	5 12 19 26
S	4 11 18 25	1 8 15 22 29	7 14 21 28	4 11 18 25	2 9 16 23 30	6 13 20 27

CW COLLECTS

Almighty and ever-living God,
clothed in majesty,
whose beloved Son
    was this day presented in the Temple,
in substance of our flesh:
grant that we may be presented to you
with pure and clean hearts,
by your Son Jesus Christ our Lord,
who is alive and reigns with you,
in the unity of the Holy Spirit,
one God, now and for ever.

or

Lord Jesus Christ,
light of the nations and glory of Israel:
make your home among us,
and present us pure and holy
to your heavenly Father,
your God, and our God.

POST COMMUNION

Lord, you fulfilled the hope of Simeon and Anna,
who lived to welcome the Messiah:
may we, who have received these gifts
    beyond words,
prepare to meet Christ Jesus when he comes
    to bring us to eternal life;
for he is alive and reigns, now and for ever.

BCP COLLECT

Almighty and everliving God, we humbly beseech thy Majesty, that, as thy only-begotten Son was this day presented in the temple in substance of our flesh, so we may be presented unto thee with pure and clean hearts, by the same thy Son Jesus Christ our Lord.

2020

	July					August						September					October					November					December			
S		5	12	19	26	S		2	9	16	23	30	S		6	13	20	27	S		4	11	18	25	S	1	8	15	22	29	S		6	13	20	27
M		6	13	20	27	M		3	10	17	24	31	M		7	14	21	28	M		5	12	19	26	M	2	9	16	23	30	M		7	14	21	28
T		7	14	21	28	T		4	11	18	25		T	1	8	15	22	29	T		6	13	20	27	T	3	10	17	24		T	1	8	15	22	29
W	1	8	15	22	29	W		5	12	19	26		W	2	9	16	23	30	W		7	14	21	28	W	4	11	18	25		W	2	9	16	23	30
T	2	9	16	23	30	T		6	13	20	27		T	3	10	17	24		T	1	8	15	22	29	T	5	12	19	26		T	3	10	17	24	31
F	3	10	17	24	31	F		7	14	21	28		F	4	11	18	25		F	2	9	16	23	30	F	6	13	20	27		F	4	11	18	25	
S	4	11	18	25		S	1	8	15	22	29		S	5	12	19	26		S	3	10	17	24	31	S	7	14	21	28		S	5	12	19	26	

Anskar, Archbishop of Hamburg, Missionary in Denmark and Sweden, 865   Green, White (*or Red*)
(CW Readings see Common of the Saints especially Isa. 52.7–10 also Rom. 10.11–15)
Blasius, Armenian Bishop and Martyr (BCP). **Ordinary time starts today**

DEL Wk 4	**EUCHARIST**		**MORNING PRAYER**	**EVENING PRAYER**
	CW			
Psalms:	3		*1;* 2; 3 (Week 1 Ord)	*4;* 7
Readings:	2 Sam. 15.13–14, 30, 16.5–13;		Lev. 19.1–18, 30–end;	Joel 1.1–14;
	Mark 5.1–20		1 Tim. 1.1–17	John 15.1–11
		AW	*Gen. 1.26–end*	*Mark 10.1–16*
	HOLY COMMUNION		**MORNING PRAYER**	**EVENING PRAYER**
	BCP Com. Martyr			
Psalms:	*3*		*15; 16; 17*	*18*
Readings:	*Jer. 11.18–20; Heb. 11.3—12.2;*		*Jer. 1;*	*Jer. 2.1–13;*
	Matt. 16.24–27		*2 Cor. 1.1—2.11*	*2 Cor. 2.12—end of 3*
Hymns:	....		....	....

CW COLLECT
God of grace and might,
who sent your servant Anskar
to spread the gospel to the Nordic peoples:
raise up, we pray, in our generation
    messengers of your good news
    and heralds of your kingdom
that the world may come to know
    the immeasurable riches of our Saviour Jesus Christ,
who is alive and reigns with you,
in the unity of the Holy Spirit,
one God, now and for ever.

POST COMMUNION
Holy Father,
who gathered us here around the table of your Son
to share this meal with the whole household of God:
in that new world where you reveal
the fullness of your peace,
gather people of every race and language
to share with Anskar and all your saints
in the eternal banquet of Jesus Christ our Lord.

BCP COLLECT
*Almighty God, by whose grace and power thy holy
Martyr Blasius triumphed over suffering and despised
death: Grant, we beseech thee, that enduring hardness
and waxing valiant in fight, we may with the noble
army of martyrs received the crown of everlasting life;
through Jesus Christ our Lord.*

*The following are always used from the day after the
Presentation of Christ in the Temple until the first of the
Sundays before Lent.*

CW COLLECT
Almighty God,
by whose grace alone we are accepted
    and called to your service:
strengthen us by your Holy Spirit
and make us worthy of our calling;
through Jesus Christ your Son our Lord,
who is alive and reigns with you,
in the unity of the Holy Spirit,
one God, now and for ever.

or

God of our salvation,
help us to turn away from those habits which harm our
    bodies and poison our minds
and to choose again your gift of life,
revealed to us in Jesus Christ our Lord.

POST COMMUNION
God of truth,
we have seen with our eyes
    and touched with our hands the bread of life:
strengthen our faith
that we may grow in love for you and for each other;
through Jesus Christ our Lord.

Sunrise 07.38; Sunset 16.49

2020

	January	February	March	April	May	June
S	5 12 19 26	2 9 16 23	1 8 15 22 29	5 12 19 26	3 10 17 24 31	7 14 21 28
M	6 13 20 27	3 10 17 24	2 9 16 23 30	6 13 20 27	4 11 18 25	1 8 15 22 29
T	7 14 21 28	4 11 18 25	3 10 17 24 31	7 14 21 28	5 12 19 26	2 9 16 23 30
W	1 8 15 22 29	5 12 19 26	4 11 18 25	1 8 15 22 29	6 13 20 27	3 10 17 24
T	2 9 16 23 30	6 13 20 27	5 12 19 26	2 9 16 23 30	7 14 21 28	4 11 18 25
F	3 10 17 24 31	7 14 21 28	6 13 20 27	3 10 17 24	1 8 15 22 29	5 12 19 26
S	4 11 18 25	1 8 15 22 29	7 14 21 28	4 11 18 25	2 9 16 23 30	6 13 20 27

Gilbert of Sempringham, Founder of the Gilbertine Order, 1189 Green

	EUCHARIST	**MORNING PRAYER**	**EVENING PRAYER**
	CW		
Psalms:	86.1–6	*5*; 6(8)	*9*; 10*
Readings:	2 Sam. 18.9–10, 14, 24–25, 30—19.3; Mark 5.21–end	Lev. 23.1–22; 1 Tim. 1.18—end of 2	Joel 1.15–end; John 15.12–17

		AW	*Ruth 1.1–18*	*1 John 3.14–end*

	HOLY COMMUNION	**MORNING PRAYER**	**EVENING PRAYER**
	BCP		
Psalms:		*19; 20; 21*	*22; 23*
Readings:		*Jer. 4.1–18; 2 Cor. 4*	*Jer. 5.1–19; 2 Cor. 5*
Hymns:	....	....	....

2020

	July				August				September				October				November				December			
S		5	12	19	26	S		2	9	16	23	30	S		6	13	20	27	S		4	11	18	25	S	1	8	15	22	29	S		6	13	20	27
M		6	13	20	27	M		3	10	17	24	31	M		7	14	21	28	M		5	12	19	26	M	2	9	16	23	30	M		7	14	21	28
T		7	14	21	28	T		4	11	18	25	T	1	8	15	22	29	T		6	13	20	27	T	3	10	17	24	T	1	8	15	22	29
W	1	8	15	22	29	W		5	12	19	26	W	2	9	16	23	30	W		7	14	21	28	W	4	11	18	25	W	2	9	16	23	30
T	2	9	16	23	30	T		6	13	20	27	T	3	10	17	24	T	1	8	15	22	29	T	5	12	19	26	T	3	10	17	24	31
F	3	10	17	24	31	F		7	14	21	28	F	4	11	18	25	F	2	9	16	23	30	F	6	13	20	27	F	4	11	18	25
S	4	11	18	25	S	1	8	15	22	29	S	5	12	19	26	S	3	10	17	24	31	S	7	14	21	28	S	5	12	19	26

Agatha, Sicilian Virgin and Martyr (BCP)   Green (*or Red*)

	EUCHARIST	MORNING PRAYER	EVENING PRAYER
	CW		
Psalms:	32.1–8	*119.1–32*	*11*; 12; 13
Readings:	2 Sam. 24.2, 9–17;	Lev. 23.23–end;	Joel 2.1–17;
	Mark 6.1–6a	1 Tim. 3	John 15.18–end

AW   *1 Sam. 1.19b–end*   *Luke 2.41–end*

	HOLY COMMUNION	MORNING PRAYER	EVENING PRAYER
	BCP Com. Virgin Martyr		
Psalms:	131	24; 25; 26	27; 28; 29
Readings:	Ecclus 51.10–12; Phil. 3.7–14;	Jer. 5.20–end;	Jer. 6.1–21;
	Matt. 25.1–13	2 Cor. 5.20—7.1	2 Cor. 7.2–end
Hymns:	....	....	....

BCP COLLECT
O God, who didst endue the holy Virgin Agatha with grace to witness a good confession (and to suffer gladly for thy sake): Grant that we, after her example, may be found ready when the Bridegroom cometh and enter with him to the marriage feast; through the same thy Son Jesus Christ our Lord.

2020

	January				February				March				April				May					June			
S		5	12	19	26		2	9	16	23		1	8	15	22	29		5	12	19	26		3	10	17	24	31			7	14	21	28
M		6	13	20	27		3	10	17	24		2	9	16	23	30		6	13	20	27		4	11	18	25		1	8	15	22	29
T		7	14	21	28		4	11	18	25		3	10	17	24	31		7	14	21	28		5	12	19	26		2	9	16	23	30
W	1	8	15	22	29		5	12	19	26		4	11	18	25		1	8	15	22	29		6	13	20	27		3	10	17	24
T	2	9	16	23	30		6	13	20	27		5	12	19	26		2	9	16	23	30		7	14	21	28		4	11	18	25
F	3	10	17	24	31		7	14	21	28		6	13	20	27		3	10	17	24		1	8	15	22	29		5	12	19	26
S	4	11	18	25		1	8	15	22	29		7	14	21	28		4	11	18	25		2	9	16	23	30		6	13	20	27

The Martyrs of Japan, 1597   Green
Accession of Queen Elizabeth II, 1952

	EUCHARIST	**MORNING PRAYER**	**EVENING PRAYER**
	CW		
Psalms:	*Canticle:* 1 Chr. 29.10–12		
	or Psalm 145.1–5	14; *15*; 16	*18**
Readings:	1 Kgs 2.1–4, 10–12;	Lev. 24.1–9;	Joel 2.18–27;
	Mark 6.7–13	1 Tim. 4	John 16.1–15

AW   *Gen. 47.1–12*   *Eph. 3.14–end*

	HOLY COMMUNION	**MORNING PRAYER**	**EVENING PRAYER**
	BCP		
Psalms:		*30; 31*	*32; 33; 34*
Readings:		*Jer. 7.1–28;*	*Jer. 8;*
		2 Cor. 8	*2 Cor. 9*
Hymns:	....	....	....

2020

July					August					September					October					November					December			
S		5	12	19	26	S		2	9	16	23	30	S		6	13	20	27	S		4	11	18	25	S	1	8	15	22	29	S		6	13	20	27
M		6	13	20	27	M		3	10	17	24	31	M		7	14	21	28	M		5	12	19	26	M	2	9	16	23	30	M		7	14	21	28
T		7	14	21	28	T		4	11	18	25		T	1	8	15	22	29	T		6	13	20	27	T	3	10	17	24		T	1	8	15	22	29
W	1	8	15	22	29	W		5	12	19	26		W	2	9	16	23	30	W		7	14	21	28	W	4	11	18	25		W	2	9	16	23	30
T	2	9	16	23	30	T		6	13	20	27		T	3	10	17	24		T	1	8	15	22	29	T	5	12	19	26		T	3	10	17	24	31
F	3	10	17	24	31	F		7	14	21	28		F	4	11	18	25		F	2	9	16	23	30	F	6	13	20	27		F	4	11	18	25	
S	4	11	18	25		S	1	8	15	22	29		S	5	12	19	26		S	3	10	17	24	31	S	7	14	21	28		S	5	12	19	26	

FEBRUARY
7 Friday

	EUCHARIST CW	**MORNING PRAYER**	**EVENING PRAYER**
Psalms:	18.31–36, 50–end	17; *19*	*22*
Readings:	Ecclus 47.2–11; Mark 6.14–29	Lev. 25.1–24; 1 Tim. 5.1–16	Joel 2.28–end; John 16.16–22
		AW *2 Sam. 1.17–end*	*Rom. 8.28–end*

	HOLY COMMUNION BCP	**MORNING PRAYER**	**EVENING PRAYER**
Psalms:		*35; 36*	*37*
Readings:		*Jer. 9.1–24;* *2 Cor. 10*	*Jer. 10;* *2 Cor. 11*
Hymns:	....	....	....

January				February				March				April				May					June			
S		5	12	19	26	S			2	9	16	23	S	1	8	15	22	29	S		5	12	19	26	S		3	10	17	24	31	S		7	14	21	28
M		6	13	20	27	M		3	10	17	24	M	2	9	16	23	30	M		6	13	20	27	M		4	11	18	25	M	1	8	15	22	29
T		7	14	21	28	T		4	11	18	25	T	3	10	17	24	31	T		7	14	21	28	T		5	12	19	26	T	2	9	16	23	30
W	1	8	15	22	29	W		5	12	19	26	W	4	11	18	25	W	1	8	15	22	29	W		6	13	20	27	W	3	10	17	24
T	2	9	16	23	30	T		6	13	20	27	T	5	12	19	26	T	2	9	16	23	30	T		7	14	21	28	T	4	11	18	25
F	3	10	17	24	31	F		7	14	21	28	F	6	13	20	27	F	3	10	17	24	F	1	8	15	22	29	F	5	12	19	26
S	4	11	18	25	S	1	8	15	22	29	S	7	14	21	28	S	4	11	18	25	S	2	9	16	23	30	S	6	13	20	27

	EUCHARIST	MORNING PRAYER	EVENING PRAYER
	CW		
Psalms:	119.9–16	20; 21; *23*	*24*; 25
Readings:	1 Kgs 3.4–13; Mark 8.1–10	Num. 6.1–5, 21–end; 1 Tim. 5.17–end	Joel 3.1–3, 9–end; John 16.23–end

AW *S. of Sol 2.8–end* *1 Cor. 13*

	HOLY COMMUNION	MORNING PRAYER	EVENING PRAYER
	BCP		
Psalms:		*38; 39; 40*	*41; 42; 43*
Readings:		*Jer. 14;* *2 Cor. 12.1–13*	*Jer. 15; 2 Cor. 12.14—end of 13;* *E. Coll. 5th Sunday after Epiphany*
Hymns:	....	....	....

THE THIRD SUNDAY BEFORE LENT

(Green)

Septuagesima

(Purple)

	PRINCIPAL SERVICE **CW Proper 1**	**THIRD SERVICE**	**SECOND SERVICE**
Psalms:	112.1–9 [10]	5; 6	[1; 3]4
Readings:	Isa. 58.1–9a [9b–12]; 1 Cor. 2.1–12 [13–end]; Matt. 5.13–20	Jer. 26.1–16; Acts 3.1–10	Amos 2.4–end; Eph. 4.17–end; [Mark 1.29–39]

	HOLY COMMUNION *BCP*	**MORNING PRAYER**	**EVENING PRAYER**
Psalms:	*9.10–20*	*5; 6*	*[1; 3] 4*
Readings:	*Gen. 1.1–5;* *1 Cor. 9.24–27;* *Matt. 20.1–16*	*Gen. 1.1—2.3;* *John 1.1–18* *or Rev. 21.1–14*	*Gen. 2.4–end or Jer. 10.1–16;* *Mark 10.1–16* *or Rev. 21.15—22.5*
Hymns:	....	....	....

Full Moon

2020

	January					February					March					April					May						June			
S		5	12	19	26		2	9	16	23	**S**	1	8	15	22	29		5	12	19	26		3	10	17	24	31		7	14	21	28
M		6	13	20	27	**M**	3	10	17	24	**M**	2	9	16	23	30	**M**	6	13	20	27	**M**	4	11	18	25		**M**	1	8	15	22	29
T		7	14	21	28	**T**	4	11	18	25	**T**	3	10	17	24	31	**T**	7	14	21	28	**T**	5	12	19	26		**T**	2	9	16	23	30
W	1	8	15	22	29	**W**	5	12	19	26	**W**	4	11	18	25		**W**	1	8	15	22	29	**W**	6	13	20	27		**W**	3	10	17	24	
T	2	9	16	23	30	**T**	6	13	20	27	**T**	5	12	19	26		**T**	2	9	16	23	30	**T**	7	14	21	28		**T**	4	11	18	25	
F	3	10	17	24	31	**F**		7	14	21	28	**F**	6	13	20	27	**F**	3	10	17	24	**F**	1	8	15	22	29	**F**	5	12	19	26	
S	4	11	18	25		**S**	1	8	15	22	29	**S**	7	14	21	28	**S**	4	11	18	25	**S**	2	9	16	23	30	**S**	6	13	20	27	

CW COLLECTS

Almighty God,
who alone can bring order
to the unruly wills and passions of sinful humanity:
give your people grace
so to love what you command
and to desire what you promise,
that, among the many changes of this world,
our hearts may surely there be fixed
where true joys are to be found;
through Jesus Christ your Son our Lord,
who is alive and reigns with you,
in the unity of the Holy Spirit,
one God, now and for ever.

or

Eternal God,
whose Son went among the crowds
and brought healing with his touch:
help us to show his love,
in your Church as we gather together,
and by our lives as they are transformed
    into the image of Christ our Lord.

POST COMMUNION

Merciful Father,
who gave Jesus Christ to be for us the bread of life,
that those who come to him should never hunger:
draw us to the Lord in faith and love,
that we may eat and drink with him
at his table in the kingdom,
where he is alive and reigns, now and for ever.

BCP COLLECT

*O Lord, we beseech thee favourably to hear the
prayers of thy people; that we, who are justly
punished for our offences, may be mercifully
delivered by thy goodness, for the glory of thy Name;
through Jesus Christ our Saviour, who liveth and
reigneth with thee and the Holy Ghost, ever one God,
world without end.*

2020

	July					August						September					October					November					December			
S		5	12	19	26	S		2	9	16	23	30	S		6	13	20	27	S		4	11	18	25	S	1	8	15	22	29	S		6	13	20	27
M		6	13	20	27	M		3	10	17	24	31	M		7	14	21	28	M		5	12	19	26	M	2	9	16	23	30	M		7	14	21	28
T		7	14	21	28	T		4	11	18	25		T	1	8	15	22	29	T		6	13	20	27	T	3	10	17	24		T	1	8	15	22	29
W	1	8	15	22	29	W		5	12	19	26		W	2	9	16	23	30	W		7	14	21	28	W	4	11	18	25		W	2	9	16	23	30
T	2	9	16	23	30	T		6	13	20	27		T	3	10	17	24		T	1	8	15	22	29	T	5	12	19	26		T	3	10	17	24	31
F	3	10	17	24	31	F		7	14	21	28		F	4	11	18	25		F	2	9	16	23	30	F	6	13	20	27		F	4	11	18	25
S	4	11	18	25		S	1	8	15	22	29		S	5	12	19	26		S	3	10	17	24	31	S	7	14	21	28		S	5	12	19	26

FEBRUARY
10 Monday

2020

Scholastica, sister of Benedict, Abbess of Plombariola, c.543

Green (*or* Purple)

DEL Wk 5	**EUCHARIST** CW	**MORNING PRAYER**	**EVENING PRAYER**
Psalms:	132.1–9	27; *30* (Week 2 Ord)	26; *28*; 29
Readings:	1 Kgs 8.1–7, 9–13; Mark 6.53–end	Gen. 24.1–28; 1 Tim. 6.1–10	Eccles. 1; John 17.1–5

AW — *Exod. 23.1–13* — *Jas 2.1–13*

	HOLY COMMUNION BCP	**MORNING PRAYER**	**EVENING PRAYER**
Psalms:		50; 51; 52	53; 54; 55
Readings:		Gen. 3; Matt. 15.29—16.12	Gen. 4.1–16; Rom. 1
Hymns:	....	....	....

Sunrise 07.26; Sunset 17.03

2020

	January					February					March					April					May						June			
S		5	12	19	26		2	9	16	23		1	8	15	22	29		5	12	19	26		3	10	17	24	31		7	14	21	28
M		6	13	20	27		3	10	17	24		2	9	16	23	30		6	13	20	27		4	11	18	25		1	8	15	22	29
T		7	14	21	28		4	11	18	25		3	10	17	24	31		7	14	21	28		5	12	19	26		2	9	16	23	30
W	1	8	15	22	29		5	12	19	26		4	11	18	25		1	8	15	22	29		6	13	20	27		3	10	17	24	
T	2	9	16	23	30		6	13	20	27		5	12	19	26		2	9	16	23	30		7	14	21	28		4	11	18	25	
F	3	10	17	24	31		7	14	21	28		6	13	20	27		3	10	17	24		1	8	15	22	29		5	12	19	26	
S	4	11	18	25		1	8	15	22	29		7	14	21	28		4	11	18	25		2	9	16	23	30		6	13	20	27	

Green (*or* Purple)

	EUCHARIST	MORNING PRAYER	EVENING PRAYER
	CW		
Psalms:	84.1–10	32; *36*	*33*
Readings:	1 Kgs 8.22–23, 27–30; Mark 7.1–13	Gen. 24.29–end; 1 Tim. 6.11–end	Eccles. 2; John 17.6–19

		MORNING PRAYER	EVENING PRAYER
AW		*Deut. 10.12–end*	*Heb. 13.1–16*

	HOLY COMMUNION	MORNING PRAYER	EVENING PRAYER
	BCP		
Psalms:		*56; 57; 58*	*59; 60; 61*
Readings:		*Gen. 6.5–end;* *Matt. 16.13–end*	*Gen. 7;* *Rom. 2*
Hymns:	....	....	....

2020

	July					August						September					October					November					December			
S		5	12	19	26		2	9	16	23	30		6	13	20	27		4	11	18	25	1	8	15	22	29		6	13	20	27
M		6	13	20	27		3	10	17	24	31		7	14	21	28		5	12	19	26	2	9	16	23	30		7	14	21	28
T		7	14	21	28		4	11	18	25			1	8	15	22	29		6	13	20	27	3	10	17	24		1	8	15	22	29
W	1	8	15	22	29		5	12	19	26		2	9	16	23	30		7	14	21	28	4	11	18	25		2	9	16	23	30
T	2	9	16	23	30		6	13	20	27		3	10	17	24		1	8	15	22	29	5	12	19	26		3	10	17	24	31
F	3	10	17	24	31		7	14	21	28		4	11	18	25		2	9	16	23	30	6	13	20	27		4	11	18	25
S	4	11	18	25		1	8	15	22	29		5	12	19	26		3	10	17	24	31	7	14	21	28		5	12	19	26

Green (or Purple)

	EUCHARIST CW	**MORNING PRAYER**	**EVENING PRAYER**
Psalms:	37.3–6, 30–32	*34*	*119.33–56*
Readings:	1 Kgs 10.1–10; Mark 7.14–23	Gen. 25.7–11, 19–end; 2 Tim. 1.1–14	Eccles. 3.1–15; John 17.20–end

AW   *Isa. 58.6–end*   *Matt. 25.31–end*

	HOLY COMMUNION BCP	**MORNING PRAYER**	**EVENING PRAYER**
Psalms:		*62; 63; 64*	*65; 66; 67*
Readings:		Gen. 8.1–14; Matt. 17.1–23	Gen. 8.15—9.17; Rom. 3
Hymns:	....	....	....

2020

	January						February					March						April						May							June				
S		5	12	19	26			2	9	16	23		1	8	15	22	29			5	12	19	26			3	10	17	24	31				7	14	21	28
M		6	13	20	27			3	10	17	24		2	9	16	23	30			6	13	20	27			4	11	18	25				1	8	15	22	29
T		7	14	21	28			4	11	18	25		3	10	17	24	31			7	14	21	28			5	12	19	26				2	9	16	23	30
W	1	8	15	22	29			5	12	19	26		4	11	18	25			1	8	15	22	29			6	13	20	27				3	10	17	24	
T	2	9	16	23	30			6	13	20	27		5	12	19	26			2	9	16	23	30			7	14	21	28				4	11	18	25	
F	3	10	17	24	31			7	14	21	28		6	13	20	27			3	10	17	24			1	8	15	22	29				5	12	19	26	
S	4	11	18	25			1	8	15	22	29		7	14	21	28			4	11	18	25			2	9	16	23	30				6	13	20	27	

Green (*or Purple*)

	EUCHARIST	**MORNING PRAYER**	**EVENING PRAYER**
	CW		
Psalms:	106.3, 35–41	*37**	39; *40*
Readings:	1 Kgs 11.4–13; Mark 7.24–30	Gen. 26.34—27.40; 2 Tim. 1.15—2.13	Eccles. 3.16—end of 4; John 18.1–11

| | | | AW | *Isa. 42.1–9* | *Luke 4.14–21* |

	HOLY COMMUNION	**MORNING PRAYER**	**EVENING PRAYER**
	BCP		
Psalms:		68	69; 70
Readings:		Gen. 11.1–9; Matt. 17.24—18.14	Gen. 11.27—12.10; Rom. 4
Hymns:	....	....	....

Cyril and Methodius, Missionaries to the Slavs, 869 & 885
(CW Readings see Common of the Saints especially Isa. 52.7–10 also Rom. 10.11–15)
Valentine, Martyr at Rome, c.269 (BCP)

Green *or* White (*or* Purple *or* Red)

	EUCHARIST	MORNING PRAYER	EVENING PRAYER
	CW		
Psalms:	81.8.1–14	*31*	*35*
Readings:	1 Kgs 11.29–32, 12.19;	Gen. 27.41—end of 28;	Eccles. 5;
	Mark 7.31–end	2 Tim. 2.14–end	John 18.12–27

		AW	*Amos 5.6–15*	*Eph. 4.25–end*

	HOLY COMMUNION	MORNING PRAYER	EVENING PRAYER
	BCP Com. Martyr		
Psalms:	*3*	*71; 72*	*73; 74*
Readings:	Jer. 11.18–20;	Gen. 13;	Gen. 14;
	Heb. 11.32—12.2;	Matt. 18.15–end	Rom. 5
	Matt. 16.24–27		
Hymns:	....	....	....

CW COLLECT
Lord of all,
who gave to your servants Cyril and Methodius
the gift of tongues to proclaim the gospel to
    the Slavs:
make your whole Church one as you are one
that all Christians may honour one another,
and east and west acknowledge
    one Lord, one faith, one baptism,
and you, the God, and Father of all;
through Jesus Christ your Son our Lord,
who is alive and reigns with you,
in the unity of the Holy Spirit,
one God, now and for ever.

POST COMMUNION
Holy Father,
who gathered us here around the table of your Son
to share this meal with the whole household of God:
in that new world where you reveal
    the fullness of your peace,
gather people of every race and language
to share with Cyril and Methodius and all your saints
in the eternal banquet of Jesus Christ our Lord.

BCP COLLECT
*Almighty God, by whose grace and power thy
holy Martyr Valentine triumphed over suffering
and despised death: Grant, we beseech thee, that
enduring hardness and waxing valiant in fight,
we may with the noble army of martyrs received
the crown of everlasting life; through Jesus Christ
our Lord.*

2020

January					February					March					April					May						June				
S		5	12	19	26	S		2	9	16	23	S	1	8	15	22	29	S		5	12	19	26	S		3	10	17	24	31	S		7	14	21	28
M		6	13	20	27	M		3	10	17	24	M	2	9	16	23	30	M		6	13	20	27	M		4	11	18	25	M	1	8	15	22	29
T		7	14	21	28	T		4	11	18	25	T	3	10	17	24	31	T		7	14	21	28	T		5	12	19	26	T	2	9	16	23	30
W	1	8	15	22	29	W		5	12	19	26	W	4	11	18	25	W	1	8	15	22	29	W		6	13	20	27	W	3	10	17	24	
T	2	9	16	23	30	T		6	13	20	27	T	5	12	19	26	T	2	9	16	23	30	T		7	14	21	28	T	4	11	18	25	
F	3	10	17	24	31	F		7	14	21	28	F	6	13	20	27	F	3	10	17	24		F	1	8	15	22	29	F	5	12	19	26	
S	4	11	18	25		S	1	8	15	22	29	S	7	14	21	28		S	4	11	18	25		S	2	9	16	23	30	S	6	13	20	27	

Sigfrid, Bishop, Apostle of Sweden, 1045
Thomas Bray, Priest, Founder of the SPCK and the SPG, 1730

Green (*or Purple*)

	EUCHARIST	**MORNING PRAYER**	**EVENING PRAYER**
	CW		
Psalms:	106.6–7, 20–23	41; *42*; 43	45; *46*
Readings:	1 Kgs 12.26–32, 13.33–end; Mark 8.1–10	Gen. 29.1–30; 2 Tim. 3	Eccles. 6; John 18.28–end
		AW Amos 5.18–24	*John 2.13–22*

	HOLY COMMUNION	**MORNING PRAYER**	**EVENING PRAYER**
	BCP		
Psalms:		75; 76; 77	78
Readings:		Gen. 15; Matt. 19.1–15	Gen. 16; Rom. 6 E. Coll. Sexagesima
Hymns:	....	....	....

2020

	July				August					September				October				November				December			
S		5	12	19	26		2	9	16	23	30		6	13	20	27		4	11	18	25		1	8	15	22	29		6	13	20	27
M		6	13	20	27		3	10	17	24	31		7	14	21	28		5	12	19	26		2	9	16	23	30		7	14	21	28
T		7	14	21	28		4	11	18	25		1	8	15	22	29		6	13	20	27		3	10	17	24		1	8	15	22	29
W	1	8	15	22	29		5	12	19	26		2	9	16	23	30		7	14	21	28		4	11	18	25		2	9	16	23	30
T	2	9	16	23	30		6	13	20	27		3	10	17	24		1	8	15	22	29		5	12	19	26		3	10	17	24	31
F	3	10	17	24	31		7	14	21	28		4	11	18	25		2	9	16	23	30		6	13	20	27		4	11	18	25
S	4	11	18	25		1	8	15	22	29		5	12	19	26		3	10	17	24	31		7	14	21	28		5	12	19	26

THE SECOND SUNDAY BEFORE LENT

(Green)

Sexagesima

(Purple)

	PRINCIPAL SERVICE	THIRD SERVICE	SECOND SERVICE
	CW		
Psalms:	136 *or* 136.1–9, 23–26	100; 150	148
Readings:	Gen. 1.1—2.3;	Job 38.1–21;	Prov. 8.1, 22–31;
	Rom. 8.18–25;	Col. 1.15–20	Rev. 4;
	Matt. 6.25–34		[Luke 12.16–31]

	HOLY COMMUNION	MORNING PRAYER	EVENING PRAYER
	BCP		
Psalms:	83.1–2, 13–end	10	[7] 13
Readings:	Gen. 3.9–19; 2 Cor. 11.19–31;	Gen. 3;	Gen. 6.5–end or Gen. 8.15—9.17;
	Luke 8.4–15	Mark 9.33–end or 1 Cor. 6	or Ecclus 15.11–end
			Luke 17.20–end or 1 Cor. 10.1–24
Hymns:	....	....	....

2020

	January	February	March	April	May	June
S	5 12 19 26	2 9 16 23	1 8 15 22 29	5 12 19 26	3 10 17 24 31	7 14 21 28
M	6 13 20 27	3 10 17 24	2 9 16 23 30	6 13 20 27	4 11 18 25	1 8 15 22 29
T	7 14 21 28	4 11 18 25	3 10 17 24 31	7 14 21 28	5 12 19 26	2 9 16 23 30
W	1 8 15 22 29	5 12 19 26	4 11 18 25	1 8 15 22 29	6 13 20 27	3 10 17 24
T	2 9 16 23 30	6 13 20 27	5 12 19 26	2 9 16 23 30	7 14 21 28	4 11 18 25
F	3 10 17 24 31	7 14 21 28	6 13 20 27	3 10 17 24	1 8 15 22 29	5 12 19 26
S	4 11 18 25	1 8 15 22 29	7 14 21 28	4 11 18 25	2 9 16 23 30	6 13 20 27

CW COLLECTS

Almighty God,
you have created the heavens and the earth
and made us in your own image:
teach us to discern your hand in all your works
and your likeness in all your children;
through Jesus Christ your Son our Lord,
who with you and the Holy Spirit
  reigns supreme over all things,
now and for ever.

or

Almighty God,
give us reverence for all creation
and respect for every person,
that we may mirror your likeness
in Jesus Christ our Lord.

POST COMMUNION

God our creator,
by your gift
the tree of life
  was set at the heart of the earthly paradise,
and the bread of life at the heart of your Church:
may we who have been nourished
  at your table on earth
be transformed by the glory of the Saviour's cross
and enjoy the delights of eternity;
through Jesus Christ our Lord.

BCP COLLECT

*O Lord God, who seest that we put not our trust in
any thing that we do: Mercifully grant that by thy
power we may be defended against all adversity;
through Jesus Christ our Lord.*

2020

	July					August						September					October					November					December			
S		5	12	19	26		2	9	16	23	30		6	13	20	27		4	11	18	25		1	8	15	22	29		6	13	20	27
M		6	13	20	27		3	10	17	24	31		7	14	21	28		5	12	19	26		2	9	16	23	30		7	14	21	28
T		7	14	21	28		4	11	18	25			1	8	15	22	29		6	13	20	27		3	10	17	24			1	8	15	22	29
W	1	8	15	22	29		5	12	19	26		2	9	16	23	30		7	14	21	28		4	11	18	25		2	9	16	23	30
T	2	9	16	23	30		6	13	20	27		3	10	17	24			1	8	15	22	29		5	12	19	26		3	10	17	24	31
F	3	10	17	24	31		7	14	21	28		4	11	18	25		2	9	16	23	30		6	13	20	27		4	11	18	25
S	4	11	18	25		1	8	15	22	29		5	12	19	26		3	10	17	24	31		7	14	21	28		5	12	19	26

Janani Luwum, Archbishop of Uganda, Martyr, 1977 (CW Readings see Common of the Saints also Ecclus 4.20–28; John 12.24–32)

Green *or* Red (*or Purple*)

DEL Wk 6	**EUCHARIST** CW	**MORNING PRAYER**	**EVENING PRAYER**
Psalms:	119.65–72	*44* (Week 3 Ord.)	*47*; 49
Readings:	Jas 1.1–11; Mark 8.11–13	Gen. 29.31—30.24; 2 Tim. 4.1–8	Eccles. 7.1–14; John 19.1–16
		AW Isa. 61.1–9	Mark 6.1–13

	HOLY COMMUNION BCP	**MORNING PRAYER**	**EVENING PRAYER**
Psalms:		86; 87; 88	89
Readings:		Gen. 17.1–22; Matt. 19.16—20.16	Gen. 18; Rom. 7
Hymns:	....	....	....

CW COLLECT
God of truth,
whose servant Janani Luwum walked in the light,
and in his death defied the powers of darkness:
free us from fear of those who kill the body,
that we too may walk as children of light,
through him who overcame darkness
    by the power of the cross,
Jesus Christ your Son our Lord,
who is alive and reigns with you,
in the unity of the Holy Spirit,
one God, now and for ever.

POST COMMUNION
Eternal God,
who gave us this holy meal
in which we have celebrated the glory of the cross
and the victory of your martyr Janani Luwum:
by our communion with Christ
in his saving death and resurrection,
give us with all your saints the courage to
    conquer evil
and so to share the fruit of the tree of life;
through Jesus Christ our Lord.

Sunrise 07.12; Sunset 17.16

2020

	January					February					March					April					May						June			
S		5	12	19	26		2	9	16	23		1	8	15	22	29		5	12	19	26		3	10	17	24	31		7	14	21	28
M		6	13	20	27		3	10	17	24		2	9	16	23	30		6	13	20	27		4	11	18	25		1	8	15	22	29
T		7	14	21	28		4	11	18	25		3	10	17	24	31		7	14	21	28		5	12	19	26		2	9	16	23	30
W	1	8	15	22	29		5	12	19	26		4	11	18	25		1	8	15	22	29		6	13	20	27		3	10	17	24	
T	2	9	16	23	30		6	13	20	27		5	12	19	26		2	9	16	23	30		7	14	21	28		4	11	18	25	
F	3	10	17	24	31		7	14	21	28		6	13	20	27		3	10	17	24		1	8	15	22	29		5	12	19	26	
S	4	11	18	25		1	8	15	22	29		7	14	21	28		4	11	18	25		2	9	16	23	30		6	13	20	27	

Green (*or* Purple)

	EUCHARIST	**MORNING PRAYER**	**EVENING PRAYER**
	CW		
Psalms:	94.12–18	*48*; 52	*50*
Readings:	Jas 1.12–18;	Gen. 31.1–24;	Eccles. 7.15–end;
	Mark 8.14–21	2 Tim. 4.9–end	John 19.17–30

		AW	*Isa. 52.1–10*	*Rom. 10.5–21*

	HOLY COMMUNION	**MORNING PRAYER**	**EVENING PRAYER**
	BCP		
Psalms:		*90; 91; 92*	*93; 94*
Readings:		*Gen. 19.1–3, 12–29;*	*Gen. 21;*
		Matt. 20.17–end	*Rom. 8.1–17*
Hymns:	....	....	....

Green (*or Purple*)

	EUCHARIST	MORNING PRAYER	EVENING PRAYER
	CW		
Psalms:	15	*119.57–80*	*59*; 60; (67)
Readings:	Jas 1.19–end; Mark 8.22–26	Gen. 31.25—32.2; Titus 1	Eccles. 8; John 19.31–end
AW		*Isa. 52.13—53.6*	*Rom. 15.14–21*

	HOLY COMMUNION	MORNING PRAYER	EVENING PRAYER
	BCP		
Psalms:		*95; 96; 97*	*98; 99; 100; 101*
Readings:		Gen. 22.1–19; Matt. 21.1–22	Gen. 23; Rom. 8.18–end
Hymns:	....	....	....

Green (*or* Purple)

	EUCHARIST CW	**MORNING PRAYER**	**EVENING PRAYER**
Psalms:	34.1–7	56; *57*; (63*)	61; *62*; 64
Readings:	Jas 2.1–9; Mark 8.27–33	Gen. 32.3–30; Titus 2	Eccles. 9; John 20.1–10

| | | AW | *Isa. 53.4–12* | *2 Cor. 4.1–10* |

	HOLY COMMUNION BCP	**MORNING PRAYER**	**EVENING PRAYER**
Psalms:		*102; 103*	*104*
Readings:		*Gen. 24.1–28;* *Matt. 21.23–end*	*Gen. 24.29–end;* *Rom. 9*
Hymns:	....	....	....

Green (*or Purple*)

	EUCHARIST CW	**MORNING PRAYER**	**EVENING PRAYER**
Psalms:	112	*51*; 54	*38*
Readings:	Jas 2.14–24, 26; Mark 8.34—9.1	Gen. 33.1–17; Titus 3	Eccles. 11.1–8; John 20.11–18

AW   *Zech. 8.16–end*   *Matt. 10.1–15*

	HOLY COMMUNION BCP	**MORNING PRAYER**	**EVENING PRAYER**
Psalms:		*105*	*106*
Readings:		*Gen. 25.7–11, 19–end;* *Matt. 22.1–33*	*Gen. 26.1–5, 12–end;* *Rom. 10*
Hymns:	....	....	....

2020

	January						February					March					April					May						June			
S		5	12	19	26			2	9	16	23		1	8	15	22	29		5	12	19	26			3	10	17	24	31			7	14	21	28
M		6	13	20	27			3	10	17	24		2	9	16	23	30		6	13	20	27			4	11	18	25			1	8	15	22	29
T		7	14	21	28			4	11	18	25		3	10	17	24	31		7	14	21	28			5	12	19	26			2	9	16	23	30
W	1	8	15	22	29			5	12	19	26		4	11	18	25		1	8	15	22	29			6	13	20	27			3	10	17	24	
T	2	9	16	23	30			6	13	20	27		5	12	19	26		2	9	16	23	30			7	14	21	28			4	11	18	25	
F	3	10	17	24	31			7	14	21	28		6	13	20	27		3	10	17	24			1	8	15	22	29			5	12	19	26	
S	4	11	18	25			1	8	15	22	29		7	14	21	28		4	11	18	25			2	9	16	23	30			6	13	20	27	

Green (*or Purple*)

	EUCHARIST	**MORNING PRAYER**	**EVENING PRAYER**
	CW		
Psalms:	12.1–7	*68*	65; *66*
Readings:	Jas 3.1–10;	Gen. 35;	Eccles. 11.9—end of 12;
	Mark 9.2–13	Philemon	John 20.19–end

AW	*Jer. 1.4–10*	*Matt. 10.16–22*

	HOLY COMMUNION	**MORNING PRAYER**	**EVENING PRAYER**
	BCP		
Psalms:		107	108; 109
Readings:		Gen. 27.1–40;	Gen. 27.41—end of 28;
		Matt. 22.34—23.12	Rom. 11;
			E. Coll. Quinquagesima

Hymns: ....

THE SUNDAY NEXT BEFORE LENT

(Green)

Quinquagesima

(Purple)

	PRINCIPAL SERVICE CW	**THIRD SERVICE**	**SECOND SERVICE**
Psalms:	2 *or* 99	72	84
Readings:	Exod. 24.12–end; 2 Pet. 1.16–end; Matt. 17.1–9	Exod. 34.29–end; 2 Cor. 4.3–6	Ecclus 48.1–10 *or* 2 Kgs 2.1–12; Matt. 17.9–23 (*or* 1–23)
	HOLY COMMUNION BCP	**MORNING PRAYER**	**EVENING PRAYER**
Psalms:	77.11–end	72	84
Readings:	Gen. 9.8–17; 1 Cor. 13; Luke 18.31–43	Gen. 12.1–8 or Ecclus 1.1–13; Matt. 5.1–16 or 1 Cor. 12.4–end	Gen. 13 or Gen. 15.1–18 or Ecclus 1.14–end; Luke 10.25–37 or 2 Cor. 1.1–22 or First Evensong of St Matthias Isa. 22.15–22; John 15.1–16
Hymns:	....	....	....

2020

	January					February					March					April					May						June			
S		5	12	19	26		2	9	16	23		1	8	15	22	29		5	12	19	26		3	10	17	24	31		7	14	21	28
M		6	13	20	27		3	10	17	24		2	9	16	23	30		6	13	20	27		4	11	18	25		1	8	15	22	29
T		7	14	21	28		4	11	18	25		3	10	17	24	31		7	14	21	28		5	12	19	26		2	9	16	23	30
W	1	8	15	22	29		5	12	19	26		4	11	18	25		1	8	15	22	29		6	13	20	27		3	10	17	24	
T	2	9	16	23	30		6	13	20	27		5	12	19	26		2	9	16	23	30		7	14	21	28		4	11	18	25	
F	3	10	17	24	31		7	14	21	28		6	13	20	27		3	10	17	24		1	8	15	22	29		5	12	19	26	
S	4	11	18	25		1	8	15	22	29		7	14	21	28		4	11	18	25		2	9	16	23	30		6	13	20	27	

These collects are not used on or after Ash Wednesday

CW COLLECTS

Almighty Father,
whose Son was revealed in majesty
before he suffered death upon the cross:
give us grace to perceive his glory,
that we may be strengthened to suffer with him
and be changed into his likeness, from glory to glory;
who is alive and reigns with you,
in the unity of the Holy Spirit,
one God, now and for ever.

or

Holy God,
you know the disorder of our sinful lives:
set straight our crooked hearts,
and bend our wills to love your goodness
    and your glory
in Jesus Christ our Lord.

POST COMMUNION

Holy God,
we see your glory in the face of Jesus Christ:
may we who are partakers at his table
reflect his life in word and deed,
that all the world may know
his power to change and save.
This we ask through Jesus Christ our Lord.

BCP COLLECT

O Lord, who hast taught us that all our doings without charity are nothing worth; Send thy Holy Ghost, and pour into our hearts that most excellent gift of charity, the very bond of peace and of all virtues, without which whosoever liveth is counted dead before thee: Grant this for thine only Son Jesus Christ's sake.

2020

	July					August						September					October					November					December			
S		5	12	19	26	S		2	9	16	23	30	S		6	13	20	27	S		4	11	18	25	S	1	8	15	22	29	S		6	13	20	27
M		6	13	20	27	M		3	10	17	24	31	M		7	14	21	28	M		5	12	19	26	M	2	9	16	23	30	M		7	14	21	28
T		7	14	21	28	T		4	11	18	25		T	1	8	15	22	29	T		6	13	20	27	T	3	10	17	24		T	1	8	15	22	29
W	1	8	15	22	29	W		5	12	19	26		W	2	9	16	23	30	W		7	14	21	28	W	4	11	18	25		W	2	9	16	23	30
T	2	9	16	23	30	T		6	13	20	27		T	3	10	17	24		T	1	8	15	22	29	T	5	12	19	26		T	3	10	17	24	31
F	3	10	17	24	31	F		7	14	21	28		F	4	11	18	25		F	2	9	16	23	30	F	6	13	20	27		F	4	11	18	25	
S	4	11	18	25		S	1	8	15	22	29		S	5	12	19	26		S	3	10	17	24	31	S	7	14	21	28		S	5	12	19	26	

St Matthias, Ap. and M. (BCP)   Green (*or Purple or Red*)

DEL Week 7	**EUCHARIST** CW	**MORNING PRAYER**	**EVENING PRAYER**
Psalms:	19.7–end	**71** (Week 4 Ord)	**72**; 75
Readings:	Jas 3.13–end; Mark 9.14–29	Gen. 37.1–11 [BCP Var. Jonah 1.1–9] Gal. 1	Jer. 1; John 3.1–21

AW   2 Kgs 2.13–22   3 John

	HOLY COMMUNION BCP St Matthias	**MORNING PRAYER**	**EVENING PRAYER**
Psalms:	16.1–7	116; 117; 118	119.1–32
Readings:	1 Sam. 2.27–35; Acts 1.15–26; Matt. 11.25–30	1 Sam. 2.27–35; Matt. 7.15–27	1 Sam. 16.1–13; Acts 20.17–35
Hymns:	....	....	....

BCP COLLECT

O Almighty God, who into the place of the traitor Judas didst choose the faithful servant Matthias to be of the number of the twelve Apostles: Grant that thy Church, being always preserved from false Apostles, may be ordered and guided by faithful and true pastors: through Jesus Christ our Lord.

Sunrise 06.58; Sunset 17.29

Green (*or Purple*)

	EUCHARIST	MORNING PRAYER	EVENING PRAYER
	CW		
Psalms:	55.7–9, 24	*73*	*74*
Readings:	Jas 4.1–10; Mark 9.30–37	Gen. 37.12–end; Gal. 2.1–10	Jer. 2.1–13; John 3.22–end

AW   *Judg. 14.5–17*   *Rev. 10.4–11*

	HOLY COMMUNION	MORNING PRAYER	EVENING PRAYER
	BCP		
Psalms:		119.33–72	119.73–104
Readings:		Gen. 31.22—32.2; Matt. 24.1–28	Gen. 32.3–30; Rom. 13
Hymns:	....	....	....

2020

	July					August						September					October					November					December			
S		5	12	19	26		2	9	16	23	30		6	13	20	27		4	11	18	25		1	8	15	22	29		6	13	20	27
M		6	13	20	27		3	10	17	24	31		7	14	21	28		5	12	19	26		2	9	16	23	30		7	14	21	28
T		7	14	21	28		4	11	18	25		1	8	15	22	29		6	13	20	27		3	10	17	24		1	8	15	22	29
W	1	8	15	22	29		5	12	19	26		2	9	16	23	30		7	14	21	28		4	11	18	25		2	9	16	23	30
T	2	9	16	23	30		6	13	20	27		3	10	17	24		1	8	15	22	29		5	12	19	26		3	10	17	24	31
F	3	10	17	24	31		7	14	21	28		4	11	18	25		2	9	16	23	30		6	13	20	27		4	11	18	25
S	4	11	18	25		1	8	15	22	29		5	12	19	26		3	10	17	24	31		7	14	21	28		5	12	19	26

ASH WEDNESDAY

Purple *or* Lent array

	PRINCIPAL SERVICE	THIRD SERVICE	SECOND SERVICE
	CW		
Psalms:	51.1–18	*38*	*51 or* 102
Readings:	Joel 2.1–2, 12–17 *or* Isa. 58.1–12;	Dan. 9.3–6, 17–19;	Isa. 1.10–18;
	2 Cor. 5.20b—6.10;	1 Tim. 6.6–19	Luke 15.11–end
	Matt. 6.1–6, 16–21 *or* John 8.1–11		

Seasonal provisions CW Book pp 308–309

	HOLY COMMUNION	MORNING PRAYER	EVENING PRAYER
	BCP		
Psalms:	57	*119.105–144*	*119.145–end*
Readings:	*Joel 2.12–17; Jas 4.1–10;*	*Isa. 58;*	*Jonah 3 or Prayer of Manasses;*
	Matt. 6.16–21	*Mark 2.13–22*	*Heb. 3.12—4.13*
	Ash Wednesday collect until April 4.		
	The Commination may be used today.		

Hymns: ....

CW COLLECTS
Almighty and everlasting God,
you hate nothing that you have made
and forgive the sins of all those who are penitent:
create and make in us new and contrite hearts
that we, worthily lamenting our sins
and acknowledging our wretchedness,
may receive from you, the God of all mercy,
perfect remission and forgiveness;
through Jesus Christ your Son our Lord,
who is alive and reigns with you,
in the unity of the Holy Spirit,
one God, now and for ever.
*(This Collect may be used as the Post Communion on
any day from the First Sunday of Lent until the Saturday
after the Fourth Sunday of Lent instead of the Post
Communion provided.)*

or

Holy God,
our lives are laid open before you:
rescue us from the chaos of sin
and through the death of your Son
bring us healing and make us whole
in Jesus Christ our Lord.

POST COMMUNION
Almighty God,
you have given your only Son to be for us
both a sacrifice for sin
and also an example of godly life:
give us grace
that we may always most thankfully receive
these his inestimable gifts,
and also daily endeavour to follow
the blessed steps of his most holy life;
through Jesus Christ our Lord.

BCP COLLECT
*Almighty and everlasting God, who hatest nothing
that thou hast made, and dost forgive the sins of all
them that are penitent: Create and make in us new and
contrite hearts, that we worthily lamenting our sins, and
acknowledging our wretchedness, may obtain of thee,
the God of all mercy, perfect remission and forgiveness;
through Jesus Christ our Lord.*

George Herbert, Priest, Poet, 1633 (CW Readings see Common of the Saints especially Mal. 2.5–7; Matt. 11.25–30; also Rev. 19.5–9)

Purple *or* Lent array *or* White

	EUCHARIST CW	**MORNING PRAYER**	**EVENING PRAYER**
Psalms:	1	77	*74*
Readings:	Deut. 30.15–end; Luke 9.22–25	Gen. 39; Gal. 2.11–end	Jer. 2.14–32; John 4.1–26
AW		*Gen. 2.7–end*	*Heb. 2.5–end*
	HOLY COMMUNION BCP	**MORNING PRAYER**	**EVENING PRAYER**
Psalms:		*120; 121; 123; 124; 125*	*126; 127; 128; 129; 130; 131*
Readings:	Exod. 24.12–18; Matt. 8.5–13	Gen. 33; Matt. 24.29–end	Gen. 35.1–20; Rom. 14
Hymns:	....	....	....

CW COLLECT
King of glory, king of peace,
who called your servant George Herbert
from the pursuit of worldly honours
to be a priest in the temple of his God and king
grant us also the grace to offer ourselves
with singleness of heart
   in humble obedience to your service;
through Jesus Christ your Son our Lord,
who is alive and reigns with you,
in the unity of the Holy Spirit,
one God, now and for ever.

POST COMMUNION
God, shepherd of your people,
whose servant George Herbert revealed
the loving service of Christ
in his ministry as a pastor of your people:
by this eucharist in which we share
awaken within us the love of Christ
and keep us faithful to our Christian calling;
through him who laid down his life for us,
but is alive and reigns with you, now and for ever

2020

	July				August					September				October				November					December			
S		5	12	19	26		2	9	16	23	30			6	13	20	27			4	11	18	25		1	8	15	22	29			6	13	20	27
M		6	13	20	27		3	10	17	24	31			7	14	21	28			5	12	19	26		2	9	16	23	30			7	14	21	28
T		7	14	21	28		4	11	18	25		1	8	15	22	29			6	13	20	27		3	10	17	24		1	8	15	22	29
W	1	8	15	22	29		5	12	19	26		2	9	16	23	30			7	14	21	28		4	11	18	25		2	9	16	23	30
T	2	9	16	23	30		6	13	20	27		3	10	17	24		1	8	15	22	29		5	12	19	26		3	10	17	24	31
F	3	10	17	24	31		7	14	21	28		4	11	18	25		2	9	16	23	30		6	13	20	27		4	11	18	25
S	4	11	18	25		1	8	15	22	29		5	12	19	26		3	10	17	24	31		7	14	21	28		5	12	19	26

Purple *or* Lent array

	EUCHARIST	MORNING PRAYER	EVENING PRAYER
	CW		
Psalms:	51.1–5, 17–18	*3; 7*	*31*
Readings:	Isa. 58.1–9a;	Gen. 40;	Jer. 3.6–22;
	Matt. 9.14–15	Gal. 3.1–14	John 4.27–42

| | | AW | *Gen. 4.1–12* | *Heb. 4.12–end* |

	HOLY COMMUNION	MORNING PRAYER	EVENING PRAYER
	BCP		
Psalms:		*132; 133; 134; 135*	*136; 137; 138*
Readings:	*1 Kgs 19.3b–8;*	Gen. 37;	Gen. 40;
	Matt. 5.43—6.6	Matt. 25.1–30	Rom. 15
Hymns:	....	....	....

2020

	January					February				March					April					May						June			
S		5	12	19	26		2	9	16	23	S	1	8	15	22	29	S		5	12	19	26	S		3	10	17	24	31	S		7	14	21	28
M		6	13	20	27		3	10	17	24	M	2	9	16	23	30	M		6	13	20	27	M		4	11	18	25	M	1	8	15	22	29
T		7	14	21	28		4	11	18	25	T	3	10	17	24	31	T		7	14	21	28	T		5	12	19	26	T	2	9	16	23	30
W	1	8	15	22	29		5	12	19	26	W	4	11	18	25	W	1	8	15	22	29	W		6	13	20	27	W	3	10	17	24
T	2	9	16	23	30		6	13	20	27	T	5	12	19	26	T	2	9	16	23	30	T		7	14	21	28	T	4	11	18	25
F	3	10	17	24	31		7	14	21	28	F	6	13	20	27	F	3	10	17	24	F	1	8	15	22	29	F	5	12	19	26
S	4	11	18	25	S	1	8	15	22	29	S	7	14	21	28	S	4	11	18	25	S	2	9	16	23	30	S	6	13	20	27

Purple *or* Lent array

	EUCHARIST		**MORNING PRAYER**	**EVENING PRAYER**
	CW			
Psalms:	86.1–7		*71*	*73*
Readings:	Isa. 58.9b–end;		Gen. 41.1–24;	Jer. 4.1–18;
	Luke 5.27–32		Gal. 3.15–22	John 4.43–end
		AW	*2 Kgs 22.11–end*	*Heb. 5.1–10*

	HOLY COMMUNION	**MORNING PRAYER**	**EVENING PRAYER**
	BCP		
Psalms:		*139; 140; 141*	*142; 143*
Readings:	*Isa. 38.1–6a;*	*Gen. 41.1–40;*	*Gen. 41.41–end;*
	Mark 6.45–56	*Matt. 25.31–end*	*Rom. 16;*
			E. Coll. (1) Lent 1 (2) Ash Wednesday

Hymns: ....

THE FIRST SUNDAY OF LENT

(Purple or Lent array)

	PRINCIPAL SERVICE	THIRD SERVICE	SECOND SERVICE
	CW		
Psalms:	32	119.1–16	50.1–15
Readings:	Gen. 2.15–17; 3.1–7;	Jer. 18.1–11;	Deut. 6.4–9, 16–end;
	Rom. 5.12–19; Matt. 4.1–11	Luke 18.9–14	Luke 15.1–10
	Seasonal provisions CW Book pp 308–309		

	HOLY COMMUNION	MORNING PRAYER	EVENING PRAYER
	BCP		
Psalms:	91.1–12	119.1–16	50.1–75
Readings:	Gen. 3.1–6;	Gen. 18 or Ecclus 2;	Gen. 21.1–21 or Gen. 22.1–19
	2 Cor. 6.1–10;	Matt. 3 or Heb. 6	or Baruch 3.1–14;
	Matt. 4.1–11		Mark 14.1–26 or 2 Cor. 4
Hymns:	....	....	....

CW COLLECTS

Almighty God,
whose Son Jesus Christ fasted forty days
   in the wilderness,
and was tempted as we are, yet without sin:
give us grace to discipline ourselves
   in obedience to your Spirit;
and, as you know our weakness,
so may we know your power to save;
through Jesus Christ your Son our Lord,
who is alive and reigns with you,
in the unity of the Holy Spirit,
one God, now and for ever.

or

Heavenly Father,
your Son battled with the powers of darkness,
and grew closer to you in the desert:
help us to use these days to grow in wisdom
   and prayer
that we may witness to your saving love
in Jesus Christ our Lord.

POST COMMUNION

Lord God,
you have renewed us with the living bread
   from heaven;
by it you nourish our faith,
increase our hope,
and strengthen our love:
teach us always to hunger for him
   who is the true and living bread,
and enable us to live by every word
   that proceeds from out of your mouth;
through Jesus Christ our Lord.

BCP COLLECT

O Lord, who for our sake didst fast forty days and forty nights: Give us grace to use such abstinence, that, our flesh being subdued to the Spirit, we may ever obey thy godly motions in righteousness and true holiness, to thy honour and glory, who livest and reignest with the Father and the Holy Ghost, one God, world without end.

2020

July				
S		5	12	19	26
M		6	13	20	27
T		7	14	21	28
W	1	8	15	22	29
T	2	9	16	23	30
F	3	10	17	24	31
S	4	11	18	25

August				
S		2	9	16	23	30
M		3	10	17	24	31
T		4	11	18	25
W		5	12	19	26
T		6	13	20	27
F		7	14	21	28
S	1	8	15	22	29

September				
S		6	13	20	27
M		7	14	21	28
T	1	8	15	22	29
W	2	9	16	23	30
T	3	10	17	24
F	4	11	18	25
S	5	12	19	26

October				
S		4	11	18	25
M		5	12	19	26
T		6	13	20	27
W		7	14	21	28
T	1	8	15	22	29
F	2	9	16	23	30
S	3	10	17	24	31

November				
S	1	8	15	22	29
M	2	9	16	23	30
T	3	10	17	24
W	4	11	18	25
T	5	12	19	26
F	6	13	20	27
S	7	14	21	28

December				
S		6	13	20	27
M		7	14	21	28
T	1	8	15	22	29
W	2	9	16	23	30
T	3	10	17	24	31
F	4	11	18	25
S	5	12	19	26

Chad, Bishop of Lichfield, Missionary, 672
(CW Readings see Common of the Saints also 1 Tim. 6.11b–16)
CW (Chad may be celebrated with Cedd on October 26 instead of March 2)

Purple *or* Lent array *or* White

	EUCHARIST	MORNING PRAYER	EVENING PRAYER
	CW		
Psalms:	19.7–end	10; *11*	12; *13*; 14
Readings:	Lev. 19.1–2, 11–18;	Gen. 41.25–45;	Jer. 4.19–end;
	Matt. 25.31–end	Gal. 3.23—4.7	John 5.1–18

AW	Gen. 6.11–end, 7.11–16	Luke 4.14–21

	HOLY COMMUNION	MORNING PRAYER	EVENING PRAYER
	BCP Bishop		
Psalms:	99	9; 10; 11;	12; 13; 14
Readings:	Ezek. 34.11–16a;	Gen. 42;	Gen. 43;
	1 Tim. 3.15–16; Mark 4.26–32	Matt. 26.1–30	Phil. 1
	or Matt. 25.31–46		
Hymns:	....	....	....

CW COLLECT

Almighty God,
from the first fruits of the English nation
who turned to Christ,
you called your servant Chad
to be an evangelist and bishop of his own people:
give us grace so to follow his peaceable nature,
humble spirit and prayerful life,
that we may truly commend to others
the faith which we ourselves profess;
through Jesus Christ your Son our Lord,
who is alive and reigns with you,
in the unity of the Holy Spirit,
one God, now and for ever.

POST COMMUNION

Holy Father,
who gathered us here around the table of your Son
to share this meal with the whole household of God:
in that new world where you reveal
the fullness of your peace,
gather people of every race and language
to share with Chad and all your saints
in the eternal banquet of Jesus Christ our Lord.

BCP COLLECT

*O God, the light of the faithful, and shepherd of
souls, who didst set blessed Chad to be a Bishop in
the Church, that he might feed thy sheep by his word
and guide them by his example: Grant us, we pray
thee, to keep the faith which he taught, and to follow
in his footsteps; through Jesus Christ our Lord.*

Sunrise 06.43; Sunset 17.42

2020

	January					February					March					April					May						June			
S		5	12	19	26		2	9	16	23		1	8	15	22	29		5	12	19	26		3	10	17	24	31			7	14	21	28
M		6	13	20	27		3	10	17	24		2	9	16	23	30		6	13	20	27		4	11	18	25		1	8	15	22	29
T		7	14	21	28		4	11	18	25		3	10	17	24	31		7	14	21	28		5	12	19	26		2	9	16	23	30
W	1	8	15	22	29		5	12	19	26		4	11	18	25		1	8	15	22	29		6	13	20	27		3	10	17	24	
T	2	9	16	23	30		6	13	20	27		5	12	19	26		2	9	16	23	30		7	14	21	28		4	11	18	25	
F	3	10	17	24	31		7	14	21	28		6	13	20	27		3	10	17	24		1	8	15	22	29		5	12	19	26	
S	4	11	18	25		1	8	15	22	29		7	14	21	28		4	11	18	25		2	9	16	23	30		6	13	20	27	

David, Bishop of Menevia, Patron of Wales, c.60 may be kept on this day   Purple *or* Lent array *or* White
where there is sufficient reason at the discretion of the minister.
(CW Readings see Common of the Saints also 2 Sam. 23.1–4; Ps. 89.19–23, 25)

	EUCHARIST CW	MORNING PRAYER	EVENING PRAYER
Psalms:	34.4–6, 21–22	*44*	46; *49*
Readings:	Isa. 55.10–11; Matt. 6.7–15	Gen. 41.46—42.5; Gal. 4.8–20	Jer. 5.1–19; John 5.19–29
AW		*Deut. 31.7–13*	*1 John 3.1–10*
	HOLY COMMUNION BCP	MORNING PRAYER	EVENING PRAYER
Psalms:		*15; 16; 17*	*18*
	Isa. 55.6–11; Matt. 21.10–16	Gen. 44; Matt. 26.31–56	Gen. 45.1–15; Phil. 2
Hymns:	....	....	....

CW COLLECT (if used)
Almighty God,
who called your servant David
 to be a faithful and wise steward of your mysteries
 for the people of Wales:
in your mercy, grant that,
 following his purity of life
 and zeal for the gospel of Christ,
we may with him receive the crown of
 everlasting life;
through Jesus Christ your Son our Lord,
who is alive and reigns with you,
in the unity of the Holy Spirit,
one God, now and for ever.

POST COMMUNION
God, shepherd of your people,
whose servant David revealed the loving service of
 Christ in his ministry as a pastor of your people:
by this eucharist in which we share
awaken within us the love of Christ
and keep us faithful to our Christian calling;
through him who laid down his life for us,
but is alive and reigns with you, now and for ever.

2020

	July				August				September				October				November				December			
S		5	12	19	26		2	9	16	23	30		6	13	20	27		4	11	18	25		1	8	15	22	29		6	13	20	27
M		6	13	20	27		3	10	17	24	31		7	14	21	28		5	12	19	26		2	9	16	23	30		7	14	21	28
T		7	14	21	28		4	11	18	25		1	8	15	22	29		6	13	20	27		3	10	17	24		1	8	15	22	29
W	1	8	15	22	29		5	12	19	26		2	9	16	23	30		7	14	21	28		4	11	18	25		2	9	16	23	30
T	2	9	16	23	30		6	13	20	27		3	10	17	24		1	8	15	22	29		5	12	19	26		3	10	17	24	31
F	3	10	17	24	31		7	14	21	28		4	11	18	25		2	9	16	23	30		6	13	20	27		4	11	18	25
S	4	11	18	25		1	8	15	22	29		5	12	19	26		3	10	17	24	31		7	14	21	28		5	12	19	26

MARCH
4 Wednesday

Ember Day (CW for Ember Days see Common of the Saints) *(also BCP)*   Purple *or* Lent array *or* Red (*or Red*)

	EUCHARIST CW	**MORNING PRAYER**	**EVENING PRAYER**
Psalms:	51.1–5, 17–18	*6*; 17	9; *28*
Readings:	Jonah 3; Luke 11.29–32	Gen. 42.6–17; Gal. 4.21—5.1	Jer. 5.20–end; John 5.30–end

		AW	*Gen. 11.1–9*	*Matt. 24.15–28*

	HOLY COMMUNION BCP For Ember CEG see Dec 18	**MORNING PRAYER**	**EVENING PRAYER**
Psalms:		19; 20; 21	22; 23
Readings:	Isa. 58.1–9a; Matt. 12.38–50	Gen. 45.16—46.7; Matt. 26.57–end	Gen. 46.26—47.12; Phil. 3
Hymns:	....	....	....

2020

	January			
S		5	12	19	26
M		6	13	20	27
T		7	14	21	28
W	1	8	15	22	29
T	2	9	16	23	30
F	3	10	17	24	31
S	4	11	18	25	

February
S 2 9 16 23
M 3 10 17 24
T 4 11 18 25
W 5 12 19 26
T 6 13 20 27
F 7 14 21 28
S 1 8 15 22 29

March
S 1 8 15 22 29
M 2 9 16 23 30
T 3 10 17 24 31
W 4 11 18 25
T 5 12 19 26
F 6 13 20 27
S 7 14 21 28

April
S 5 12 19 26
M 6 13 20 27
T 7 14 21 28
W 1 8 15 22 29
T 2 9 16 23 30
F 3 10 17 24
S 4 11 18 25

May
S 3 10 17 24 31
M 4 11 18 25
T 5 12 19 26
W 6 13 20 27
T 7 14 21 28
F 1 8 15 22 29
S 2 9 16 23 30

June
S 7 14 21 28
M 1 8 15 22 29
T 2 9 16 23 30
W 3 10 17 24
T 4 11 18 25
F 5 12 19 26
S 6 13 20 27

Purple *or* Lent array

	EUCHARIST	MORNING PRAYER	EVENING PRAYER
	CW		
Psalms:	138	*42*; 43	137; 138; *142*
Readings:	Esther 14.1–5, 12–14	Gen. 42.18–28;	Jer. 6.9–21;
	or Isa. 55.6–9;	Gal. 5.2–15	John 6.1–15
	Matt. 7.7–12		

		AW	*Gen. 13.1–13*	*1 Pet. 2.13–end*

	HOLY COMMUNION	MORNING PRAYER	EVENING PRAYER
	BCP		
Psalms:		24; 25; 26	27; 28; 29
Readings:	Isa. 58.9b–14;	Gen. 47.13–end;	Gen. 48;
	John 8.31–45	Matt. 27.1–26	Phil. 4
Hymns:	....	....	....

2020

	July					August						September					October					November					December			
S		5	12	19	26	S		2	9	16	23	30	S		6	13	20	27	S		4	11	18	25	S	1	8	15	22	29	S		6	13	20	27
M		6	13	20	27	M		3	10	17	24	31	M		7	14	21	28	M		5	12	19	26	M	2	9	16	23	30	M		7	14	21	28
T		7	14	21	28	T		4	11	18	25		T	1	8	15	22	29	T		6	13	20	27	T	3	10	17	24		T	1	8	15	22	29
W	1	8	15	22	29	W		5	12	19	26		W	2	9	16	23	30	W		7	14	21	28	W	4	11	18	25		W	2	9	16	23	30
T	2	9	16	23	30	T		6	13	20	27		T	3	10	17	24		T	1	8	15	22	29	T	5	12	19	26		T	3	10	17	24	31
F	3	10	17	24	31	F		7	14	21	28		F	4	11	18	25		F	2	9	16	23	30	F	6	13	20	27		F	4	11	18	25
S	4	11	18	25	S	1	8	15	22	29		S	5	12	19	26		S	3	10	17	24	31	S	7	14	21	28		S	5	12	19	26

MARCH
6 Friday

2020

Ember Day (CW for Ember Days see Common of the Saints) *(also BCP)*   Purple *or* Lent array

	EUCHARIST	**MORNING PRAYER**	**EVENING PRAYER**
	CW		
Psalms:	130	*22*	54; *55*
Readings:	Ezek. 18.21–28; Matt. 5.20–26	Gen. 42.29–end; Gal. 5.16–end	Jer. 6.22–end; John 6.16–27

AW   *Gen. 21.1–8*   *Luke 9.18–27*

	HOLY COMMUNION	**MORNING PRAYER**	**EVENING PRAYER**
	BCP; for Ember CEG see Dec 18		
Psalms:	3	*30; 31*	*32; 33; 34*
Readings:	Ezek. 18.20–25; John 5.2–15	Gen. 49.1–32; Matt. 27.27–56	Gen. 49.33—end of 50; Col. 1.1–20
Hymns:	....	....	....

2020

	January					February					March					April					May						June			
S		5	12	19	26		2	9	16	23		1	8	15	22	29		5	12	19	26		3	10	17	24	31		7	14	21	28
M		6	13	20	27		3	10	17	24		2	9	16	23	30		6	13	20	27		4	11	18	25			1	8	15	22	29
T		7	14	21	28		4	11	18	25		3	10	17	24	31		7	14	21	28		5	12	19	26			2	9	16	23	30
W	1	8	15	22	29		5	12	19	26		4	11	18	25		1	8	15	22	29		6	13	20	27			3	10	17	24	
T	2	9	16	23	30		6	13	20	27		5	12	19	26		2	9	16	23	30		7	14	21	28			4	11	18	25	
F	3	10	17	24	31		7	14	21	28		6	13	20	27		3	10	17	24		1	8	15	22	29			5	12	19	26	
S	4	11	18	25		1	8	15	22	29		7	14	21	28		4	11	18	25		2	9	16	23	30			6	13	20	27	

Perpetua, Felicity and their Companions, Martyrs at Carthage, 203 (CW Readings see Common of the Saints especially Rev. 12.10–12a also Wisd. 3.1–7.) *Perpetua (BCP)* Ember Day (CW for Ember days see Common of the Saints) *(also BCP)*

Purple *or* Lent array *or* Red (*or Red*)

	EUCHARIST CW	MORNING PRAYER	EVENING PRAYER
Psalms:	119.1–8	59; *63*	*4*; 16
Readings:	Deut. 26.16–end; Matt. 5.43–end	Gen. 43.1–15; Gal. 6	Jer. 7.1–20; John 6.27–40

		MORNING PRAYER	EVENING PRAYER
	AW	*Gen. 32.22–32*	*2 Pet. 1.10–end*

	HOLY COMMUNION BCP Com Martyr For Ember CEG see Dec 18	MORNING PRAYER	EVENING PRAYER
Psalms:	*3*	*35; 36;*	*37*
Readings:	*Jer. 11.18–20; Heb. 11.32—12.2; Matt. 16.24–27 or Ezek. 18.26–32; Matt. 17.1–9 or Luke 4.16–21 or John 10.1–16*	*Exod. 1.1–14, 22—2.10; Matt. 27.57—end of 28*	*Exod. 2.11–22; Col. 1.21—2.7; E. Coll. (1) Lent 2 (2) Ash Wednesday*
Hymns:	....	....	....

CW COLLECT

Holy God,
who gave great courage to Perpetua, Felicity
    and their companions,
grant that we may be worthy
    to climb the ladder of sacrifice
and be received into the garden of peace;
through Jesus Christ your Son our Lord,
who is alive and reigns with you,
in the unity of the Holy Spirit,
One God, now and for ever.

POST COMMUNION

God our redeemer,
whose Church was strengthened by the blood of your
martyrs Perpetua, Felicity and their companions: so
bind us, in life and death, to Christ's sacrifice that
our lives, broken and offered with his, may carry his
death and proclaim his resurrection in the world;
through Jesus Christ our Lord

BCP COLLECT

Almighty God, by whose grace and power thy holy Martyr Perpetua triumphed over suffering, and despised death: Grant, we beseech thee, that enduring hardness, and waxing valiant in fight, we may with the noble army of martyrs receive the crown of everlasting life; through Jesus Christ our Lord.

2020

	July					August						September						October						November						December			
S		5	12	19	26	**S**		2	9	16	23	30	**S**		6	13	20	27	**S**		4	11	18	25	**S**	1	8	15	22	29	**S**		6	13	20	27
M		6	13	20	27	**M**		3	10	17	24	31	**M**		7	14	21	28	**M**		5	12	19	26	**M**	2	9	16	23	30	**M**		7	14	21	28
T		7	14	21	28	**T**		4	11	18	25		**T**	1	8	15	22	29	**T**		6	13	20	27	**T**	3	10	17	24		**T**	1	8	15	22	29
W	1	8	15	22	29	**W**		5	12	19	26		**W**	2	9	16	23	30	**W**		7	14	21	28	**W**	4	11	18	25		**W**	2	9	16	23	30
T	2	9	16	23	30	**T**		6	13	20	27		**T**	3	10	17	24		**T**	1	8	15	22	29	**T**	5	12	19	26		**T**	3	10	17	24	31
F	3	10	17	24	31	**F**		7	14	21	28		**F**	4	11	18	25		**F**	2	9	16	23	30	**F**	6	13	20	27		**F**	4	11	18	25	
S	4	11	18	25		**S**	1	8	15	22	29		**S**	5	12	19	26		**S**	3	10	17	24	31	**S**	7	14	21	28		**S**	5	12	19	26	

THE SECOND SUNDAY OF LENT

(Purple *or* Lent array)

	PRINCIPAL SERVICE CW	**THIRD SERVICE**	**SECOND SERVICE**
Psalms:	121	74	135 [135.1–14]
Readings:	Gen. 12.1–4a; Rom. 4.1–5, 13–17; John 3.1–17	Jer. 22.1–9; Matt. 8.1–13	Num. 21.4–9; Luke 14.27–33
	Seasonal provisions CW Book pp 308–309		

	HOLY COMMUNION BCP	**MORNING PRAYER**	**EVENING PRAYER**
Psalms:	25.13–end	74	135
Readings:	Jer. 17.5–10; 1 Thess. 4.1–8; Matt. 15.21–28	Gen. 27.1–40 or Ecclus 4.11–28; Matt. 9.1–17 or Heb. 9.11–end	Gen. 28.10–end or Gen. 32.3–30 or Ecclus 5.1–14; Mark 14.27–52 or 2 Cor. 5
Hymns:	....	....	....

....

....

....

....

....

....

....

....

....

....

....

....

....

....

....

....

....

....

....

....

....

....

2020

January	February	March	April	May	June
S　　5 12 19 26	S　　2　9 16 23	S　1　8 15 22 29	S　　5 12 19 26	S　　3 10 17 24 31	S　　　7 14 21 28
M　6 13 20 27	M　3 10 17 24	M　2　9 16 23 30	M　6 13 20 27	M　4 11 18 25	M　1　8 15 22 29
T　7 14 21 28	T　4 11 18 25	T　3 10 17 24 31	T　7 14 21 28	T　5 12 19 26	T　2　9 16 23 30
W 1　8 15 22 29	W　5 12 19 26	W　4 11 18 25	W 1　8 15 22 29	W　6 13 20 27	W　3 10 17 24
T　2　9 16 23 30	T　6 13 20 27	T　5 12 19 26	T　2　9 16 23 30	T　7 14 21 28	T　4 11 18 25
F　3 10 17 24 31	F　7 14 21 28	F　6 13 20 27	F　3 10 17 24	F 1　8 15 22 29	F　5 12 19 26
S　4 11 18 25	S 1　8 15 22 29	S　7 14 21 28	S　4 11 18 25	S　2　9 16 23 30	S　6 13 20 27

CW COLLECTS

Almighty God,
you show to those who are in error the light of
  your truth,
that they may return to the way of righteousness:
grant to all those who are admitted
  into the fellowship of Christ's religion,
that they may reject those things
  that are contrary to their profession,
and follow all such things as are agreeable to
  the same;
through our Lord Jesus Christ,
who is alive and reigns with you,
in the unity of the Holy Spirit,
one God, now and for ever.

or

Almighty God,
by the prayer and discipline of Lent
may we enter into the mystery of Christ's sufferings,
and by following in his Way
come to share in his glory;
through Jesus Christ our Lord.

POST COMMUNION

Almighty God,
you see that we have no power of ourselves to
  help ourselves:
keep us both outwardly in our bodies,
and inwardly in our souls;
that we may be defended from all adversities
  which may happen to the body,
and from all evil thoughts
  which may assault and hurt the soul;
through Jesus Christ our Lord.

BCP COLLECT

*Almighty God, who seest that we have no power of
ourselves to help ourselves: Keep us both outwardly
in our bodies, and inwardly in our souls; that we
may be defended from all adversities which may
happen to the body, and from all evil thoughts which
may assault and hurt the soul; through Jesus Christ
our Lord.*

2020

	July					August						September						October					November						December			
S		5	12	19	26	S		2	9	16	23	30	S		6	13	20	27	S		4	11	18	25	S	1	8	15	22	29	S		6	13	20	27
M		6	13	20	27	M		3	10	17	24	31	M		7	14	21	28	M		5	12	19	26	M	2	9	16	23	30	M		7	14	21	28
T		7	14	21	28	T		4	11	18	25		T	1	8	15	22	29	T		6	13	20	27	T	3	10	17	24		T	1	8	15	22	29
W	1	8	15	22	29	W		5	12	19	26		W	2	9	16	23	30	W		7	14	21	28	W	4	11	18	25		W	2	9	16	23	30
T	2	9	16	23	30	T		6	13	20	27		T	3	10	17	24		T	1	8	15	22	29	T	5	12	19	26		T	3	10	17	24	31
F	3	10	17	24	31	F		7	14	21	28		F	4	11	18	25		F	2	9	16	23	30	F	6	13	20	27		F	4	11	18	25	
S	4	11	18	25		S	1	8	15	22	29		S	5	12	19	26		S	3	10	17	24	31	S	7	14	21	28		S	5	12	19	26	

Purple *or* Lent array

	EUCHARIST	**MORNING PRAYER**	**EVENING PRAYER**
	CW		
Psalms:	79.8–9, 12, 14	26; *32*	70; *74*
Readings:	Dan. 9.4–10; Luke 6.36–38	Gen. 43.16–end; Heb. 1	Jer. 7.21–end; John 6.41–51

| | | AW | *1 Chr. 21.1–17* | *1 John 2.1–8* |

	HOLY COMMUNION	**MORNING PRAYER**	**EVENING PRAYER**
	BCP		
Psalms:		44; 45; 46	47; 48; 49
Readings:	Heb. 2.1–10; John 8.21–30	Exod. 2.23—end of 3; John 1.1–28	Exod. 4.1–23; Col. 2.8—3.11
Hymns:	....	....	....

Full Moon Sunrise 06.27; Sunset 17.54

2020

January				
S		5	12	19	26
M		6	13	20	27
T		7	14	21	28
W	1	8	15	22	29
T	2	9	16	23	30
F	3	10	17	24	31
S	4	11	18	25

February				
S		2	9	16	23
M		3	10	17	24
T		4	11	18	25
W		5	12	19	26
T		6	13	20	27
F		7	14	21	28
S	1	8	15	22	29

March				
S	1	8	15	22	29
M	2	9	16	23	30
T	3	10	17	24	31
W	4	11	18	25
T	5	12	19	26
F	6	13	20	27
S	7	14	21	28

April				
S		5	12	19	26
M		6	13	20	27
T		7	14	21	28
W	1	8	15	22	29
T	2	9	16	23	30
F	3	10	17	24
S	4	11	18	25

May				
S		3	10	17	24	31
M		4	11	18	25
T		5	12	19	26
W		6	13	20	27
T		7	14	21	28
F	1	8	15	22	29
S	2	9	16	23	30

June				
S		7	14	21	28
M	1	8	15	22	29
T	2	9	16	23	30
W	3	10	17	24
T	4	11	18	25
F	5	12	19	26
S	6	13	20	27

Purple *or* Lent array

	EUCHARIST CW	MORNING PRAYER	EVENING PRAYER
Psalms:	50.8, 16–end	**50**	**52**; 53; 54
Readings:	Isa. 1.10, 16–20; Matt. 23.1–12	Gen. 44.1–17; Heb. 2.1–9	Jer. 8.1–15; John 6.52–59

		AW	*Zech. 3*	*2 Pet. 2.1–10a*

	HOLY COMMUNION BCP	MORNING PRAYER	EVENING PRAYER
Psalms:		50; 51; 52	53; 54; 55
Readings:	Heb. 2.11–end; Matt. 23.1–12	Exod. 4.27—6.1; John 1.29–end	Exod. 6.2–13, 7.1–7; Col. 3.12—4.1
Hymns:	....	....	....

Purple *or* Lent array

	EUCHARIST	**MORNING PRAYER**	**EVENING PRAYER**
	CW		
Psalms:	31, 4–5, 14–18	*35*	*3*; 51
Readings:	Jer. 18.18–20; Matt. 20.17–28	Gen. 44.18–end; Heb. 2.10–end	Jer. 8.18—9.11; John 6.60–end

AW		*Job 1.1–22*	*Luke 21.34—22.6*

	HOLY COMMUNION	**MORNING PRAYER**	**EVENING PRAYER**
	BCP		
Psalms:		*56; 57; 58*	*59; 60; 61*
Readings:	*Heb. 3.1–6;* *Matt. 20.17–28*	*Exod. 7.8–end;* *John 2*	*Exod. 8.1–19;* *Col. 4.2–end*
Hymns:	....	....	....

2020

	January					February					March					April					May						June			
S		5	12	19	26	S		2	9	16	23	S	1	8	15	22	29	S		5	12	19	26	S		3	10	17	24	31	S		7	14	21	28
M		6	13	20	27	M		3	10	17	24	M	2	9	16	23	30	M		6	13	20	27	M		4	11	18	25	M	1	8	15	22	29
T		7	14	21	28	T		4	11	18	25	T	3	10	17	24	31	T		7	14	21	28	T		5	12	19	26	T	2	9	16	23	30
W	1	8	15	22	29	W		5	12	19	26	W	4	11	18	25	W	1	8	15	22	29	W		6	13	20	27	W	3	10	17	24	
T	2	9	16	23	30	T		6	13	20	27	T	5	12	19	26	T	2	9	16	23	30	T		7	14	21	28	T	4	11	18	25	
F	3	10	17	24	31	F		7	14	21	28	F	6	13	20	27	F	3	10	17	24		F	1	8	15	22	29	F	5	12	19	26	
S	4	11	18	25		S	1	8	15	22	29	S	7	14	21	28		S	4	11	18	25		S	2	9	16	23	30	S	6	13	20	27	

Gregory the Great, Bishop of Rome and Confessor (BCP)   Purple *or* Lent array (*or* White)

	EUCHARIST	**MORNING PRAYER**	**EVENING PRAYER**
	CW		
Psalms:	1	*34*	*71*
Readings:	Jer. 17.5–10;	Gen. 45.1–15;	Jer. 9.12–24;
	Luke 16.19–end	Heb. 3.1–6	John 7.1–13

AW   *2 Chr. 29.1–11*   *Mark 11.15–19*

	HOLY COMMUNION	**MORNING PRAYER**	**EVENING PRAYER**
	BCP Com. Confessor		
Psalms:	*37, 30–35*	*62; 63; 64*	*65; 66; 67*
Readings:	*Wisd. 7.7–14; 1 Cor. 2.6–13;.*	*Exod. 8.20—9.12;*	*Exod. 9.13–end;*
	Matt. 13.51–52 or	*John 3.1–21*	*Philemon*
	Heb. 3.7–19; John 5.30–47		
Hymns:	....	....	....

BCP COLLECT
*O God, who hast enlightened thy Church by the
teaching of thy servant Gregory: Enrich it evermore,
we beseech thee, with thy heavenly grace and raise
up faithful witnesses, who by their life and doctrine
may set forth to all men the truth of thy salvation;
through Jesus Christ our Lord.*

2020

	July						August						September						October						November						December			
S		5	12	19	26	S		2	9	16	23	30	S		6	13	20	27	S		4	11	18	25	S	1	8	15	22	29	S		6	13	20	27
M		6	13	20	27	M		3	10	17	24	31	M		7	14	21	28	M		5	12	19	26	M	2	9	16	23	30	M		7	14	21	28
T		7	14	21	28	T		4	11	18	25		T	1	8	15	22	29	T		6	13	20	27	T	3	10	17	24		T	1	8	15	22	29
W	1	8	15	22	29	W		5	12	19	26		W	2	9	16	23	30	W		7	14	21	28	W	4	11	18	25		W	2	9	16	23	30
T	2	9	16	23	30	T		6	13	20	27		T	3	10	17	24		T	1	8	15	22	29	T	5	12	19	26		T	3	10	17	24	31
F	3	10	17	24	31	F		7	14	21	28		F	4	11	18	25		F	2	9	16	23	30	F	6	13	20	27		F	4	11	18	25	
S	4	11	18	25		S	1	8	15	22	29	S	5	12	19	26		S	3	10	17	24	31	S	7	14	21	28		S	5	12	19	26	

Purple *or* Lent array

	EUCHARIST CW	**MORNING PRAYER**	**EVENING PRAYER**
Psalms:	105.16–22	40; *41*	*6*; 38
Readings:	Gen. 37.3–4, 12–13, 17–28; Matt. 21.33–43, 45–46	Gen. 45.16–end; Heb. 3.7–end	Jer. 10.1–16; John 7.14–24

		AW	*Exod. 19.1–9a*	*1 Pet. 1.1–9*

	HOLY COMMUNION *BCP*	**MORNING PRAYER**	**EVENING PRAYER**
Psalms:		68	69; 70
Readings:	*Heb. 4.1–end;* *Matt. 21.33–end*	*Exod. 10.1–20;* *John 3.22–end*	*Exod. 10.21—11.end;* *Eph. 1*
Hymns:	....	....	....

2020

January	February	March	April	May	June
S 5 12 19 26	S 2 9 16 23	S 1 8 15 22 29	S 5 12 19 26	S 3 10 17 24 31	S 7 14 21 28
M 6 13 20 27	M 3 10 17 24	M 2 9 16 23 30	M 6 13 20 27	M 4 11 18 25	M 1 8 15 22 29
T 7 14 21 28	T 4 11 18 25	T 3 10 17 24 31	T 7 14 21 28	T 5 12 19 26	T 2 9 16 23 30
W 1 8 15 22 29	W 5 12 19 26	W 4 11 18 25	W 1 8 15 22 29	W 6 13 20 27	W 3 10 17 24
T 2 9 16 23 30	T 6 13 20 27	T 5 12 19 26	T 2 9 16 23 30	T 7 14 21 28	T 4 11 18 25
F 3 10 17 24 31	F 7 14 21 28	F 6 13 20 27	F 3 10 17 24	F 1 8 15 22 29	F 5 12 19 26
S 4 11 18 25	S 1 8 15 22 29	S 7 14 21 28	S 4 11 18 25	S 2 9 16 23 30	S 6 13 20 27

Purple *or* Lent array

	EUCHARIST		**MORNING PRAYER**	**EVENING PRAYER**
	CW			
Psalms:	103.1–4, 9–12		3; *25*	*23*; 27
Readings:	Mic. 7.14–15, 18–20;		Gen. 46.1–7, 28–end;	Jer. 10.17–24;
	Luke 15.1–3, 11–end		Heb. 4.1–13	John 7.25–36
		AW	Exod. 19.9b–19	Acts 7.44–50

	HOLY COMMUNION	**MORNING PRAYER**	**EVENING PRAYER**
	BCP		
Psalms:		71; 72	73; 74
Readings:	Heb. 5.1–end;	Exod. 12.1–20;	Exod. 12.21–36; Eph. 2;
	Luke 15.11–end	John 4.1–26	E. Coll. (1) Lent 3, (2) Ash Wed.
Hymns:	....	....	....

2020

	July					August						September					October					November					December			
S		5	12	19	26	S		2	9	16	23	30	S		6	13	20	27	S		4	11	18	25	S	1	8	15	22	29	S		6	13	20	27
M		6	13	20	27	M		3	10	17	24	31	M		7	14	21	28	M		5	12	19	26	M	2	9	16	23	30	M		7	14	21	28
T		7	14	21	28	T		4	11	18	25		T	1	8	15	22	29	T		6	13	20	27	T	3	10	17	24		T	1	8	15	22	29
W	1	8	15	22	29	W		5	12	19	26		W	2	9	16	23	30	W		7	14	21	28	W	4	11	18	25		W	2	9	16	23	30
T	2	9	16	23	30	T		6	13	20	27		T	3	10	17	24		T	1	8	15	22	29	T	5	12	19	26		T	3	10	17	24	31
F	3	10	17	24	31	F		7	14	21	28		F	4	11	18	25		F	2	9	16	23	30	F	6	13	20	27		F	4	11	18	25
S	4	11	18	25		S	1	8	15	22	29	S	5	12	19	26		S	3	10	17	24	31	S	7	14	21	28		S	5	12	19	26

THE THIRD SUNDAY OF LENT

(Purple *or* Lent array)

	PRINCIPAL SERVICE	**THIRD SERVICE**	**SECOND SERVICE**
	CW		
Psalms:	95	46	40
Readings:	Exod. 17.1–7;	Amos 7.10–end;	Josh. 1.1–9;
	Rom. 5.1–11;	2 Cor. 1.1–11	Eph. 6.10–20;
	John 4.5–42		[John 2.13–22]
	Seasonal provisions CW Book pp 308–309		

	HOLY COMMUNION	**MORNING PRAYER**	**EVENING PRAYER**
	BCP		
Psalms:	*9.13–end*	*46*	*40*
Readings:	*Num. 22.21–31;*	*Gen. 37* or *Ecclus 10.12–24;*	*Gen. 39* or *Gen. 42* or
	Eph. 5.1–14;	*Matt. 18.1–14* or	*Ecclus 17.1–26; Mark 14.53–end*
	Luke 11.14–28	*Heb. 10.19–end*	or *2 Cor. 5.20—7.1*
Hymns:	....	....	....

	January					February					March					April					May						June			
S		5	12	19	26		2	9	16	23		1	8	15	22	29		5	12	19	26		3	10	17	24	31			7	14	21	28
M		6	13	20	27		3	10	17	24		2	9	16	23	30		6	13	20	27		4	11	18	25			1	8	15	22	29
T		7	14	21	28		4	11	18	25		3	10	17	24	31		7	14	21	28		5	12	19	26			2	9	16	23	30
W	1	8	15	22	29		5	12	19	26		4	11	18	25		1	8	15	22	29		6	13	20	27			3	10	17	24	
T	2	9	16	23	30		6	13	20	27		5	12	19	26		2	9	16	23	30		7	14	21	28			4	11	18	25	
F	3	10	17	24	31		7	14	21	28		6	13	20	27		3	10	17	24		1	8	15	22	29			5	12	19	26	
S	4	11	18	25		1	8	15	22	29		7	14	21	28		4	11	18	25		2	9	16	23	30			6	13	20	27	

CW COLLECTS

Almighty God,
whose most dear Son went not up to joy
but first he suffered pain,
and entered not into glory before he was crucified:
mercifully grant that we,
walking in the way of the cross,
may find it none other than the way of life and peace;
through Jesus Christ your Son our Lord,
who is alive and reigns with you,
in the unity of the Holy Spirit,
one God, now and for ever.

or

Eternal God,
give us insight
to discern your will for us,
to give up what harms us,
and to seek the perfection we are promised
in Jesus Christ our Lord.

POST COMMUNION

Merciful Lord,
grant your people grace to withstand the temptations
of the world, the flesh and the devil,
and with pure hearts and minds to follow you,
the only God;
through Jesus Christ our Lord.

BCP COLLECT

*We beseech thee, Almighty God, look upon the
hearty desires of thy humble servants, and stretch
forth the right hand of thy Majesty, to be our defence
against all our enemies; through Jesus Christ
our Lord.*

2020

	July					August						September					October					November					December			
S		5	12	19	26	**S**		2	9	16	23	30	**S**		6	13	20	27	**S**		4	11	18	25	**S**	1	8	15	22	29	**S**		6	13	20	27
M		6	13	20	27	**M**		3	10	17	24	31	**M**		7	14	21	28	**M**		5	12	19	26	**M**	2	9	16	23	30	**M**		7	14	21	28
T		7	14	21	28	**T**		4	11	18	25		**T**	1	8	15	22	29	**T**		6	13	20	27	**T**	3	10	17	24		**T**	1	8	15	22	29
W	1	8	15	22	29	**W**		5	12	19	26		**W**	2	9	16	23	30	**W**		7	14	21	28	**W**	4	11	18	25		**W**	2	9	16	23	30
T	2	9	16	23	30	**T**		6	13	20	27		**T**	3	10	17	24		**T**	1	8	15	22	29	**T**	5	12	19	26		**T**	3	10	17	24	31
F	3	10	17	24	31	**F**		7	14	21	28		**F**	4	11	18	25		**F**	2	9	16	23	30	**F**	6	13	20	27		**F**	4	11	18	25	
S	4	11	18	25		**S**	1	8	15	22	29		**S**	5	12	19	26		**S**	3	10	17	24	31	**S**	7	14	21	28		**S**	5	12	19	26	

Purple *or* Lent array

	EUCHARIST	**MORNING PRAYER**	**EVENING PRAYER**

CW The following readings may replace those provided for Holy Communion on any day (except St Joseph's day) during the Third Week of Lent: Exod. 17.1–7; Ps. 95.1–2, 6–end; John 4.5–42

Psalms:	42.1–2; 43.1–4	*5; 7*	*11; 17*
Readings:	2 Kgs 5.1–15;	Gen. 47.1–27;	Jer. 11.1–17;
	Luke 4.24–30	Heb. 4.14—5.10	John 7.37–52

		AW	*Josh. 4.1–13*	*Luke 9.1–11*

	HOLY COMMUNION	**MORNING PRAYER**	**EVENING PRAYER**
	BCP		
Psalms:		79; 80; 81	82; 83; 84; 85
Readings:	Heb. 6.1–10;	Exod. 12.37–end;	Exod. 13.1–16;
	Luke 4.23–30	John 4.27–end	Eph. 3
Hymns:	....	....	....

Sunrise 06.11; Sunset 18.07

Patrick, Bishop, Missionary, Patron of Ireland, c.460 Bank Holiday (NI)   Purple *or* Lent array *or* White
(CW Readings see Common of the Saints also Ps. 91.1–4, 13–16; Luke 10.1–12, 17–20)

	EUCHARIST	MORNING PRAYER	EVENING PRAYER
Psalms:	25.3–10	6; *9*	61; 62; *64*
Readings:	Song of the Three 2, 11–20	Gen. 47.28—end of 48;	Jer. 11.18—12.6;
	or Dan. 2.20–23;	Heb. 5.11—6.12	John 7.53—8.11
	Matt. 18.21–end		

		MORNING PRAYER	EVENING PRAYER
	AW	Exod. 15.22–27	Heb. 10.32–end
	HOLY COMMUNION	MORNING PRAYER	EVENING PRAYER
	BCP		
Psalms:		86; 87; 88	89
Readings:	Heb. 6.11–20;	Exod. 13.17—14.14;	Exod. 14.15–end;
	Matt. 18.15–22	John 5.1–23	Eph. 4.1–16
Hymns:	....	....	....

CW COLLECT

Almighty God,
who in your providence chose your servant Patrick
to be the apostle of the Irish people:
keep alive in us the fire of the faith he kindled
and strengthen us in our pilgrimage
    towards the light of everlasting life;
through Jesus Christ your Son our Lord,
who is alive and reigns with you,
in the unity of the Holy Spirit,
one God, now and for ever.

POST COMMUNION

Holy Father,
who gathered us here around the table of your Son
to share this meal with the whole household of God:
in that new world where you reveal
    the fullness of your peace,
gather people of every race and language
to share with Patrick and all your saints
in the eternal banquet of Jesus Christ our Lord.

Cyril, Bishop of Jerusalem, Teacher of the Faith, 386
Edward, King of the West Saxons (BCP)

Purple *or* Lent array (*or* Red)

	EUCHARIST	MORNING PRAYER	EVENING PRAYER
	CW		
Psalms:	147.13–end	*38*	36; *39*
Readings:	Deut. 4.1, 5–9;	Gen. 49.1–32;	Jer. 13.1–11;
	Matt. 5.17–19	Heb. 6.13–end	John 8.12–30 *or* Eve of Joseph of
			Nazareth:
			Ps. 132; Hos. 11.1–9; Luke 2.41–end

		AW	*Gen. 9.8–17*	*1 Pet. 3.18–end*

	HOLY COMMUNION	MORNING PRAYER	EVENING PRAYER
	BCP Com. Martyr		
Psalms:	3	90; 91; 92	93; 94
Readings:	Jer. 11.18–20; Heb. 11.32—12.2;	Exod. 15.1–26;	Exod. 15.27—16.35;
	Matt. 16.24–27 or	John 5.24–end	Eph. 4.17–30
	Heb. 7.1–10; Matt. 15.1–20		
Hymns:	....	....	....

BCP COLLECT
Almighty God, by whose grace and power thy holy Martyr Edward triumphed over suffering and despised death: Grant, we beseech thee, that enduring hardness and waxing valiant in fight, we may with the noble army of martyrs received the crown of everlasting life; through Jesus Christ our Lord.

Joseph of Nazareth   Purple *or* Lent array *or* White

	PRINCIPAL SERVICE	THIRD SERVICE	SECOND SERVICE
	CW		
Psalms:	89.26–36	25; 147.1–12	1; 112
Readings:	2 Sam. 7.4–16; Rom. 4.13–18; Matt. 1.18–end	Isa. 11.1–10; Matt. 13.54–end	Gen. 50.22–end; Matt. 2.13–end

Seasonal provisions for Saints Days: CW Book p 328

Displaced readings may be added to the previous or following day's portion:

	EUCHARIST	MORNING PRAYER	EVENING PRAYER
	CW		
Readings:	Jer. 7.23–28; Luke 11.14–23	Gen. 49.33—end of 50; Heb. 7.1–10	Jer. 14; John 8.31–47

	HOLY COMMUNION	MORNING PRAYER	EVENING PRAYER
	BCP for St Joseph use CW provision		
Psalms:		95; 96; 97	98; 99; 100; 101
Readings:	Heb. 7.11–25; John 6.26–35	Exod. 17; John 6.1–21	Exod. 18; Eph. 4.31—5.21
Hymns:	....	....	....

CW COLLECT
God our Father,
who from the family of your servant David
raised up Joseph the carpenter
to be the guardian of your incarnate Son
and husband of the Blessed Virgin Mary:
give us grace to follow him
in faithful obedience to your commands;
through Jesus Christ your Son our Lord,
who is alive and reigns with you,
in the unity of the Holy Spirit,
one God, now and for ever.

POST COMMUNION
Heavenly Father,
whose Son grew in wisdom and stature
in the home of Joseph the carpenter of Nazareth
and on the wood of the cross
perfected the work of the world's salvation:
help us, strengthened by this sacrament
  of his passion,
to count the wisdom of the world as foolishness,
and to walk with him in simplicity and trust;
through Jesus Christ our Lord.

2020

July					August					September					October					November					December			
S		5	12	19	26	S		2	9	16	23	30	S		6	13	20	27	S		4	11	18	25	S	1	8	15	22	29	S		6	13	20	27
M		6	13	20	27	M		3	10	17	24	31	M		7	14	21	28	M		5	12	19	26	M	2	9	16	23	30	M		7	14	21	28
T		7	14	21	28	T		4	11	18	25	T	1	8	15	22	29	T		6	13	20	27	T	3	10	17	24	T	1	8	15	22	29
W	1	8	15	22	29	W		5	12	19	26	W	2	9	16	23	30	W		7	14	21	28	W	4	11	18	25	W	2	9	16	23	30
T	2	9	16	23	30	T		6	13	20	27	T	3	10	17	24	T	1	8	15	22	29	T	5	12	19	26	T	3	10	17	24	31
F	3	10	17	24	31	F		7	14	21	28	F	4	11	18	25	F	2	9	16	23	30	F	6	13	20	27	F	4	11	18	25
S	4	11	18	25	S	1	8	15	22	29	S	5	12	19	26	S	3	10	17	24	31	S	7	14	21	28	S	5	12	19	26

Cuthbert, Bishop of Lindisfarne, Missionary, 687
(CW Readings see Common of the Saints, especially Ezek. 34.11–16 also Matt. 18.12–14)
May also be celebrated on September 4.

Purple *or* Lent array *or* White

	EUCHARIST	MORNING PRAYER	EVENING PRAYER
	CW		
Psalms:	81.6–10; 13; 16	*22*	*69*
Readings:	Hos. 14;	Exod. 1.1–14;	Jer. 15.10–end;
	Mark 12.28–34	Heb. 7.11–end	John 8.48–end
AW		Num. 20.1–13	1 Cor. 10.23–end

	HOLY COMMUNION	MORNING PRAYER	EVENING PRAYER
	BCP		
Psalms:		*102; 103*	*104*
Readings:	Heb. 7.26–end;	Exod. 19;	Exod. 20.1–21;
	John 4.5–26	John 6.22–40	Eph. 5.22—6.9
Hymns:	....	....	....

CW COLLECT
Almighty God,
who called your servant Cuthbert
   from following the flock
to follow your Son and to be a shepherd of
   your people:
in your mercy, grant that we, following his example,
may bring those who are lost home to your fold;
through Jesus Christ your Son our Lord,
who is alive and reigns with you,
in the unity of the Holy Spirit,
one God, now and for ever.

POST COMMUNION
Holy Father,
who gathered us here around the table of your Son
to share this meal with the whole household of God:
in that new world where you reveal
   the fullness of your peace,
gather people of every race and language
to share with Cuthbert and all your saints
in the eternal banquet of Jesus Christ our Lord.

2020

	January				February				March				April				May					June			
S		5	12	19	26		2	9	16	23		1	8	15	22	29		5	12	19	26		3	10	17	24	31		7	14	21	28
M		6	13	20	27		3	10	17	24		2	9	16	23	30		6	13	20	27		4	11	18	25		1	8	15	22	29
T		7	14	21	28		4	11	18	25		3	10	17	24	31		7	14	21	28		5	12	19	26		2	9	16	23	30
W	1	8	15	22	29		5	12	19	26		4	11	18	25		1	8	15	22	29		6	13	20	27		3	10	17	24
T	2	9	16	23	30		6	13	20	27		5	12	19	26		2	9	16	23	30		7	14	21	28		4	11	18	25
F	3	10	17	24	31		7	14	21	28		6	13	20	27		3	10	17	24		1	8	15	22	29		5	12	19	26
S	4	11	18	25		1	8	15	22	29		7	14	21	28		4	11	18	25		2	9	16	23	30		6	13	20	27

Thomas Cranmer, Archbishop of Canterbury, Reformation Martyr, 1556
(CW Readings see Common of the Saints) Benedict, Abbot (BCP)

Purple *or* Lent array *or* Red (*or White*)

	EUCHARIST CW	MORNING PRAYER	EVENING PRAYER
Psalms:	51.1–2, 17–end	*31*	*116*; 130
Readings:	Hos. 5.15—6.6; Luke 18.9–14	Exod. 1.22—2.10; Heb. 8	Jer. 16.10—17.4; John 9.1–17
AW		*Isa. 43.14–end*	*Heb. 3.1–15*

	HOLY COMMUNION BCP Com. Abbot	MORNING PRAYER	EVENING PRAYER
Psalms:	*1*	105	106
Readings:	*Prov. 10.27–32; 1 John 2.15–17; Luke 6.20–23a or Heb. 8.1–6; John 8.1–11*	*Exod. 22.20—23.17; John 6.41–end*	*Exod. 23.18–end; Eph. 6.10–end; E. Coll. (1) Lent 4, (2) Ash Wed.*
Hymns:	....	....	....

CW COLLECT
Father of all mercies,
who through the work of your servant Thomas
   Cranmer renewed the worship of your Church
and through his death
   revealed your strength in human weakness:
by your grace strengthen us to worship you
in spirit and in truth
and so to come to the joys of your everlasting
   kingdom;
through Jesus Christ our Mediator and Advocate,
who is alive and reigns with you,
in the unity of the Holy Spirit,
one God, now and for ever.

POST COMMUNION
Eternal God,
who gave us this holy meal
in which we have celebrated
   the glory of the cross
and the victory of your martyr Thomas Cranmer:
by our communion with Christ
in his saving death and resurrection,
give us with all your saints the courage to
   conquer evil
and so to share the fruit of the tree of life;
through Jesus Christ our Lord.

BCP COLLECT for St Benedict
O God, by whose grace the blessed Abbot Benedict,
enkindled with the fire of thy love, became a burning
and a shining light in thy Church: Grant that we may
be inflamed with the same spirit of discipline and
love, and ever walk before thee as children of light;
through Jesus Christ our Lord.

THE FOURTH SUNDAY OF LENT
Mothering Sunday

(Purple *or* Lent array)

	PRINCIPAL SERVICE	**THIRD SERVICE**	**SECOND SERVICE**
	CW		
Psalms:	23	19	31.1–16 *or* 31.1–8
Readings:	1 Sam. 16.1–13;	Isa. 43.1–7;	Mic. 7 *or* Pr. of Manasseh;
	Eph. 5.8–14; John 9.1–41	Eph. 2.8–14	Jas 5; [John 3.14–21]
	Seasonal provisions CW Book p 308–309		

**PRINCIPAL SERVICE FOR
MOTHERING SUNDAY**
Ps. 34.11–20 *or* 127.1–4;
Exod. 2.1–10 *or* 1 Sam. 1.20–end;
2 Cor. 1.3–7 *or* Col. 3.12–17;
Luke 33–35 *or* John 19.25b–27

If the Principal Service readings have been displaced by Mothering Sunday provisions, they may be used at the Second Service

	HOLY COMMUNION	**MORNING PRAYER**	**EVENING PRAYER**
	BCP		
Psalms:	122	19	31.1–16 *or* 31.1–8
Readings:	Exod. 16.2–7a;	Gen. 43 or	Gen. 44.1—45.8 or
	Gal. 4.21–end or	Ecclus 27.30—28.9;	Gen. 45.16—46.7 or
	Heb. 12.22–24;	Luke 15 or Heb. 12	Ecclus 34.13–end;
	John 6.1–14		Mark 15.1–21 or 2 Cor. 9
Hymns:	....	....	....

CW COLLECTS
Merciful Lord,
absolve your people from their offences,
that through your bountiful goodness
we may all be delivered from the chains of those sins
which by our frailty we have committed;
grant this, heavenly Father,
for Jesus Christ's sake, our blessed Lord and Saviour,
who is alive and reigns with you,
in the unity of the Holy Spirit,
one God, now and for ever.

or

Merciful Lord,
you know our struggle to serve you:
when sin spoils our lives
and overshadows our hearts,
come to our aid
and turn us back to you again;
through Jesus Christ our Lord.

POST COMMUNION
Lord God,
whose blessed Son our Saviour
gave his back to the smiters
and did not hide his face from shame:
give us grace to endure the sufferings
    of this present time
with sure confidence in the glory that shall be revealed;
through Jesus Christ our Lord.

BCP COLLECT
*Grant, we beseech thee, Almighty God, that we, who for
our evil deeds do worthily deserve to be punished, by the
comfort of thy grace may mercifully be relieved; through
our Lord and Saviour Jesus Christ.*
**Mothering Sunday may be celebrated in preference to the
provision for the Fourth Sunday of Lent.**

CW COLLECTS FOR MOTHERING SUNDAY
God of compassion,
whose Son Jesus Christ, the child of Mary,
shared the life of a home in Nazareth,
and on the cross
drew the whole human family to himself:
strengthen us in our daily living
that in joy and in sorrow
we may know the power of your presence
to bind together and to heal;
through Jesus Christ your Son our Lord,
who is alive and reigns with you,
in the unity of the Holy Spirit,
one God, now and for ever.

or

God of love,
passionate and strong,
tender and careful:
watch over us and hold us
all the days of our life;
through Jesus Christ our Lord.

POST COMMUNION
Loving God,
as a mother feeds her children at the breast
you feed us in this sacrament
    with the food and drink of eternal life:
help us who have tasted your goodness
to grow in grace within the household of faith;
through Jesus Christ our Lord.

2020

July					August						September					October					November					December				
S		5	12	19	26	S		2	9	16	23	30	S		6	13	20	27	S		4	11	18	25	S	1	8	15	22	29	S		6	13	20	27
M		6	13	20	27	M		3	10	17	24	31	M		7	14	21	28	M		5	12	19	26	M	2	9	16	23	30	M		7	14	21	28
T		7	14	21	28	T		4	11	18	25		T	1	8	15	22	29	T		6	13	20	27	T	3	10	17	24		T	1	8	15	22	29
W	1	8	15	22	29	W		5	12	19	26		W	2	9	16	23	30	W		7	14	21	28	W	4	11	18	25		W	2	9	16	23	30
T	2	9	16	23	30	T		6	13	20	27		T	3	10	17	24		T	1	8	15	22	29	T	5	12	19	26		T	3	10	17	24	31
F	3	10	17	24	31	F		7	14	21	28		F	4	11	18	25		F	2	9	16	23	30	F	6	13	20	27		F	4	11	18	25	
S	4	11	18	25		S	1	8	15	22	29		S	5	12	19	26		S	3	10	17	24	31	S	7	14	21	28		S	5	12	19	26	

Purple *or* Lent array

	EUCHARIST	MORNING PRAYER	EVENING PRAYER

CW The following readings may replace those provided for the Eucharist on any day (except the Annunciation) this week:
Ps. 27.1, 9–10, 16–17; Micah 7.7–9; John 9

Psalms: 30.1–5, 8, 11–end

70; *77*

25; 28

Readings: Isa. 65.17–21;
John 4.43–end

Exod. 2.11–22;
Heb. 9.1–14

Jer. 17.5–18;
John 9.18–end

AW   *2 Kgs 24.18—25.7*

1 Cor. 15.20–34

	HOLY COMMUNION	MORNING PRAYER	EVENING PRAYER

BCP

Psalms:

110; 111; 112; 113

114; 115

Readings: *Heb. 11.1–6;*
John 2.13–end

Exod. 24;
John 7.1–24

Exod. 25.1–22;
1 Tim. 1.1–17

Hymns: ....

Sunrise 05.54; Sunset 18.19

2020

	January				February				March				April				May					June			
S		5	12	19	26		2	9	16	23		1	8	15	22	29		5	12	19	26		3	10	17	24	31		7	14	21	28
M		6	13	20	27		3	10	17	24		2	9	16	23	30		6	13	20	27		4	11	18	25		1	8	15	22	29
T		7	14	21	28		4	11	18	25		3	10	17	24	31		7	14	21	28		5	12	19	26		2	9	16	23	30
W	1	8	15	22	29		5	12	19	26		4	11	18	25	1	8	15	22	29		6	13	20	27		3	10	17	24
T	2	9	16	23	30		6	13	20	27		5	12	19	26	2	9	16	23	30		7	14	21	28		4	11	18	25
F	3	10	17	24	31		7	14	21	28		6	13	20	27	3	10	17	24		1	8	15	22	29		5	12	19	26
S	4	11	18	25		1	8	15	22	29		7	14	21	28	4	11	18	25		2	9	16	23	30		6	13	20	27

Walter Hilton of Thurgarton, Augustinian Canon, Mystic, 1396
Paul Couturier, Priest, Ecumenist, 1953
Oscar Romero, Archbishop of San Salvador, Martyr, 1980

Purple *or* Lent array

	EUCHARIST CW	**MORNING PRAYER**	**EVENING PRAYER**
Psalms:	46.1–8	54; *79*	*80*; 82
Readings:	Ezek. 47.1–9, 12; John 5.1–3, 5–16	Exod. 2.23—3.20; Heb. 9.15–end	Eve of the Annunciation Ps. 85; Wisd. 9.1–12 *or* Gen. 3.8–15; Gal. 4.1–5

AW *Jer. 13.12–19*   *Acts 13.26–35*

	HOLY COMMUNION BCP	**MORNING PRAYER**	**EVENING PRAYER**
Psalms:		*116; 117; 118*	*119.1–32*
Readings:	*Heb. 11.13–16a; John 7.14–24*	*Exod. 28.1–4, 29–41; John 7.25–end*	*Exod. 29.38—30.16; 1 Tim. 1.18—end of 2 or 1st Evensong of Annunciation of our Lady: Gen. 3.1–15; Rom. 5.12–21*

| **Hymns:** | .... | .... | .... |

2020

	July					August					September					October					November					December			
S		5	12	19	26		2	9	16	23	30		6	13	20	27		4	11	18	25		1	8	15	22	29		6	13	20	27
M		6	13	20	27		3	10	17	24	31		7	14	21	28		5	12	19	26		2	9	16	23	30		7	14	21	28
T		7	14	21	28		4	11	18	25		1	8	15	22	29		6	13	20	27		3	10	17	24		1	8	15	22	29
W	1	8	15	22	29		5	12	19	26		2	9	16	23	30		7	14	21	28		4	11	18	25		2	9	16	23	30
T	2	9	16	23	30		6	13	20	27		3	10	17	24		1	8	15	22	29		5	12	19	26		3	10	17	24	31
F	3	10	17	24	31		7	14	21	28		4	11	18	25		2	9	16	23	30		6	13	20	27		4	11	18	25
S	4	11	18	25		1	8	15	22	29		5	12	19	26		3	10	17	24	31		7	14	21	28		5	12	19	26

THE ANNUNCIATION OF OUR LORD TO THE BLESSED VIRGIN MARY
White *or* Gold

	PRINCIPAL SERVICE	THIRD SERVICE	SECOND SERVICE
	CW		
Psalms:	40.5–11	111; 113 [BCP Var. 111 only]	131; 146
Readings:	Isa. 7.10–14;	1 Sam. 2.1–10;	Isa. 52.1–12;
	Heb. 10.4–10;	Rom. 5.12–end	Heb. 2.5–end
	Luke 1.26–38	[BCP Var. Heb. 10.4–10]	

Season provisions CW Book pp. 310–311

Displaced readings may be added to the previous or following day's portion:

	EUCHARIST	MORNING PRAYER	EVENING PRAYER
	CW		
Readings:	Isa. 49.8–15;	Exod. 4.1–23;	Jer. 18.13–end;
	John 5.17–30	Heb. 10.1–18	John 10.11–21

	HOLY COMMUNION	MORNING PRAYER	EVENING PRAYER
	BCP Com. Annunciation		
Psalms:	113	119.33–72	119.73–104
Readings:	Isa. 7.10–14[15]; Rom. 5.12–19;	Isa. 52.7–12;	1 Sam. 2.5–end;
	Luke 1.26–38	Heb. 2.5–end	Matt. 1.18–23
Hymns:	....	....	....

CW COLLECT
We beseech you, O Lord,
pour your grace into our hearts,
that as we have known the incarnation
of your Son Jesus Christ
by the message of an angel,
so by his cross and passion
we may be brought to the glory of his resurrection;
through Jesus Christ your Son our Lord,
who is alive and reigns with you,
in the unity of the Holy Spirit,
one God, now and for ever.

POST COMMUNION
God most high,
whose handmaid bore the Word made flesh:
we thank you that in this sacrament of
  our redemption
you visit us with your Holy Spirit
and overshadow us by your power;
strengthen us to walk with Mary
  the joyful path of obedience
and so to bring forth the fruits of holiness;
through Jesus Christ our Lord.

BCP COLLECT
We beseech thee, O Lord, pour thy grace into our hearts; that, as we have known the incarnation of thy Son Jesus Christ by the message of an angel, so by his cross and passion we may be brought unto the glory of his resurrection; through the same Jesus Christ our Lord.

2020

	January				February				March				April				May					June		
S		5	12	19	26		2	9	16	23		1	8	15	22	29		5	12	19	26		3	10	17	24	31			7	14	21	28
M		6	13	20	27		3	10	17	24		2	9	16	23	30		6	13	20	27		4	11	18	25		1	8	15	22	29
T		7	14	21	28		4	11	18	25		3	10	17	24	31		7	14	21	28		5	12	19	26		2	9	16	23	30
W	1	8	15	22	29		5	12	19	26		4	11	18	25		1	8	15	22	29		6	13	20	27		3	10	17	24
T	2	9	16	23	30		6	13	20	27		5	12	19	26		2	9	16	23	30		7	14	21	28		4	11	18	25
F	3	10	17	24	31		7	14	21	28		6	13	20	27		3	10	17	24		1	8	15	22	29		5	12	19	26
S	4	11	18	25		1	8	15	22	29		7	14	21	28		4	11	18	25		2	9	16	23	30		6	13	20	27

Harriet Monsell, Founder of the Community of St John the Baptist, Clewer, 1883   Purple *or* Lent array

	EUCHARIST	**MORNING PRAYER**	**EVENING PRAYER**
	CW		
Psalms:	106.19–23	53; *86*	*94*
Readings:	Exod. 32.7–14;	Exod. 4.27—6.1;	Jer. 19.1–13;
	John 5.31–end	Heb. 10.19–25	John 10.22–end

AW   *Jer. 22.11–19*   *Luke 11.37–52*

	HOLY COMMUNION	**MORNING PRAYER**	**EVENING PRAYER**
	BCP		
Psalms:		*119.105–144*	*119.145–end*
Readings:	Heb. *12.12–17;*	Exod. 34;	Exod. 35.20—36.7;
	John 5.17–27	John 8.31–end	1 Tim. *4*
Hymns:	....	....	....

Purple *or* Lent array

	EUCHARIST	MORNING PRAYER	EVENING PRAYER
	CW		
Psalms:	34.15–end	*102*	13; *16*
Readings:	Wisd. 2.1, 12–22 *or* Jer. 26.8–11; John 7.1–2, 10, 25–30	Exod. 6.2–13; Heb. 10.26–end	Jer. 19.14—20.6; John 11.1–16

AW		*Jer. 17.1–14*	*Luke 6.17–26*

	HOLY COMMUNION	MORNING PRAYER	EVENING PRAYER
	BCP		
Psalms:	99	120; 121; 122; 123; 124; 125	126; 127; 128; 129; 130; 131
Readings:	Heb. 12.22–end; John 11.33–46	Exod. 40.17–end; John 9	Lev. 6.8–end; 1 Tim. 5
Hymns:	....	....	....

2020

	January					February					March					April					May						June			
S		5	12	19	26		2	9	16	23		1	8	15	22	29		5	12	19	26		3	10	17	24	31			7	14	21	28
M		6	13	20	27		3	10	17	24		2	9	16	23	30		6	13	20	27		4	11	18	25			1	8	15	22	29
T		7	14	21	28		4	11	18	25		3	10	17	24	31		7	14	21	28		5	12	19	26			2	9	16	23	30
W	1	8	15	22	29		5	12	19	26		4	11	18	25		1	8	15	22	29		6	13	20	27			3	10	17	24	
T	2	9	16	23	30		6	13	20	27		5	12	19	26		2	9	16	23	30		7	14	21	28			4	11	18	25	
F	3	10	17	24	31		7	14	21	28		6	13	20	27		3	10	17	24		1	8	15	22	29			5	12	19	26	
S	4	11	18	25		1	8	15	22	29		7	14	21	28		4	11	18	25		2	9	16	23	30			6	13	20	27	

Purple *or* Lent array

	EUCHARIST	**MORNING PRAYER**	**EVENING PRAYER**
	CW		
Psalms:	7.1–2, 8–10	*32*	*140*; 141; 142
Readings:	Jer. 11.18–20; John 7.40–52	Exod. 7.8–end; Heb. 11.1–16	Jer. 20.7–end; John 11.17–27

	AW	*Ezra 1*	*2 Cor. 1.12–19*

	HOLY COMMUNION	**MORNING PRAYER**	**EVENING PRAYER**
	BCP		
Psalms:		*132; 133; 134; 135*	*136; 137; 138*
Readings:	Heb. 13.7–21; John 8.12–20	Lev. 19.1–18, 30–end; John 10.1–21	Lev. 25.1–24; 1 Tim. 6; E. Coll. (1) Lent 5, (2) Ash Wed.
Hymns:	....	....	....

THE FIFTH SUNDAY OF LENT

(Purple or Lent array)

Passiontide begins British Summertime begins Clocks go forward one hour

	PRINCIPAL SERVICE	THIRD SERVICE	SECOND SERVICE
	CW		
Psalms:	130	86	30
Readings:	Ezek. 37.1–14; Rom. 8.6–11; John 11.1–45	Jer. 31.27–37; John 12.20–33	Lam. 3.19–33; Matt. 20.17–end

Seasonal provisions until Wednesday of Holy Week CW Book pp 312–313

	HOLY COMMUNION	MORNING PRAYER	EVENING PRAYER
	BCP		
Psalms:	143	86	30
Readings:	Exod. 24.4–8; Heb. 9.11–15; John 8.46–end	Exod. 2.23—end of 3; Matt. 20.17–28 or Heb. 13.1–21	Exod. 4.1–23 or Exod. 4.27—6.1; Mark 15.22–end or 2 Cor. 11.16—12.10
Hymns:	....	....	....

CW COLLECTS
Most merciful God,
who by the death and resurrection of your Son
 Jesus Christ
delivered and saved the world:
grant that by faith in him who suffered on the cross
we may triumph in the power of his victory;
through Jesus Christ your Son our Lord,
who is alive and reigns with you,
in the unity of the Holy Spirit,
one God, now and for ever.

or

Gracious Father,
you gave up your Son
out of love for the world:
lead us to ponder the mysteries of his passion,
that we may know eternal peace
through the shedding of our Saviour's blood,
Jesus Christ our Lord.

POST COMMUNION
Lord Jesus Christ,
you have taught us
that what we do for the least of our brothers
 and sisters
we do also for you:
give us the will to be the servant of others
as you were the servant of all,
and gave up your life and died for us,
but are alive and reign, now and for ever.

BCP COLLECT
*We beseech thee, Almighty God, mercifully to look
upon thy people; that by thy great goodness they
may be governed and preserved evermore, both in
body and soul; through Jesus Christ our Lord.*

Purple *or* Lent array

	EUCHARIST	**MORNING PRAYER**	**EVENING PRAYER**
	CW The following readings may replace those provided for the Eucharist on any day this week: 2 Kgs 4.18–21, 32–37; Ps. 17.1–8, 16; John 11.1–45		
Psalms:	23	*73*; 121	*26*; 27
Readings:	Sus. 1–9, 15–17, 19–30, 33–62 or [41b–62] *or* Josh. 2.1–14; John 8.1–11	Exod. 8.1–19; Heb. 11.17–31	Jer. 21.1–10; John 11.28–44

AW	*Joel 2.12–17*		*2 John*

	HOLY COMMUNION	**MORNING PRAYER**	**EVENING PRAYER**
	BCP		
Psalms:		144; 145; 146	147; 148; 149; 150
Readings:	*Col. 1.13–23a; John 7.1–13*	*Num. 6; John 10.22–end*	*Num. 9.15–end and 10.29–end; Titus 1.1—2.8*
Hymns:	....	....	....

Sunrise 06.38; Sunset 19.31

John Donne, Priest, Poet, 1631   Purple *or* Lent array

	EUCHARIST	**MORNING PRAYER**	**EVENING PRAYER**
	CW		
Psalms:	102.1–3, 16–23	*35*; 123	*61*; 64
Readings:	Num. 21.4–9; John 8.21–30	Exod. 8.20–end; Heb. 11.32—12.2	Jer. 22.1–5, 13–19; John 11.45–end

AW   *Isa. 58.1–14*   *Mark 10.32–45*

	HOLY COMMUNION	**MORNING PRAYER**	**EVENING PRAYER**
	BCP		
Psalms:		*144; 145; 146*	*147; 148; 149; 150*
Readings:	Col. 2.8–12; John 7.32–39	Num. 11.10–33; John 11.1–44	Num. 12; Titus 2.9—end of 3
Hymns:	....	....	....

2020

	July				August					September				October				November				December			
S		5	12	19	26		2	9	16	23	30		6	13	20	27		4	11	18	25		1	8	15	22	29		6	13	20	27
M		6	13	20	27		3	10	17	24	31		7	14	21	28		5	12	19	26		2	9	16	23	30		7	14	21	28
T		7	14	21	28		4	11	18	25		1	8	15	22	29		6	13	20	27		3	10	17	24		1	8	15	22	29
W	1	8	15	22	29		5	12	19	26	2	9	16	23	30		7	14	21	28	4	11	18	25	2	9	16	23	30
T	2	9	16	23	30		6	13	20	27	3	10	17	24	1	8	15	22	29	5	12	19	26	3	10	17	24	31
F	3	10	17	24	31		7	14	21	28	4	11	18	25	2	9	16	23	30	6	13	20	27	4	11	18	25
S	4	11	18	25	1	8	15	22	29	5	12	19	26	3	10	17	24	31	7	14	21	28	5	12	19	26

Frederick Denison Maurice, Priest, Teacher of the Faith, 1872

Purple *or* Lent array

	EUCHARIST CW	**MORNING PRAYER**	**EVENING PRAYER**
Psalms:	*Canticle:* Bless the Lord	*55*; 124	56; *62*
Readings:	Dan. 3.14–20, 24–25, 28; John 8.31–42	Exod. 9.1–12; Heb. 12.3–13	Jer. 22.20—23.8; John 12.1–11

AW — *Job 36.1–12* — *John 14.1–14*

	HOLY COMMUNION BCP	**MORNING PRAYER**	**EVENING PRAYER**
Psalms:		1; 2; 3; 4; 5	6; 7; 8
Readings:	Col. 2.13–19; John 7.40–end	Num. 13.1–3, 17–end; John 11.45–end	Num. 14.1–25; 2 Tim. 1
Hymns:	....	....	....

2020

	January					February					March					April					May						June			
S		5	12	19	26		2	9	16	23		1	8	15	22	29		5	12	19	26		3	10	17	24	31			7	14	21	28
M		6	13	20	27		3	10	17	24		2	9	16	23	30		6	13	20	27		4	11	18	25			1	8	15	22	29
T		7	14	21	28		4	11	18	25		3	10	17	24	31		7	14	21	28		5	12	19	26			2	9	16	23	30
W	1	8	15	22	29		5	12	19	26		4	11	18	25		1	8	15	22	29		6	13	20	27			3	10	17	24	
T	2	9	16	23	30		6	13	20	27		5	12	19	26		2	9	16	23	30		7	14	21	28			4	11	18	25	
F	3	10	17	24	31		7	14	21	28		6	13	20	27		3	10	17	24		1	8	15	22	29			5	12	19	26	
S	4	11	18	25		1	8	15	22	29		7	14	21	28		4	11	18	25		2	9	16	23	30			6	13	20	27	

Purple *or* Lent array

	EUCHARIST	**MORNING PRAYER**	**EVENING PRAYER**
	CW		
Psalms:	105.4–9	*40*; 125	42; *43*
Readings:	Gen. 17.3–9;	Exod. 9.13–end;	Jer. 23.9–32;
	John 8.51–end	Heb. 12.14–end	John 12.12–19

AW   *Jer. 9.17–22*   *Luke 13.31–35*

	HOLY COMMUNION	**MORNING PRAYER**	**EVENING PRAYER**
	BCP		
Psalms:		*9; 10; 11*	*12; 13; 14*
Readings:	*Col. 3.8–11;*	*Num. 16.1–35;*	*Num. 16.36—end of 17;*
	John 10.22–38	*John 12.1–19*	*2 Tim. 2*
Hymns:	....	....	....

2020

July	August	September	October	November	December
S 5 12 19 26	S 2 9 16 23 30	S 6 13 20 27	S 4 11 18 25	S 1 8 15 22 29	S 6 13 20 27
M 6 13 20 27	M 3 10 17 24 31	M 7 14 21 28	M 5 12 19 26	M 2 9 16 23 30	M 7 14 21 28
T 7 14 21 28	T 4 11 18 25	T 1 8 15 22 29	T 6 13 20 27	T 3 10 17 24	T 1 8 15 22 29
W 1 8 15 22 29	W 5 12 19 26	W 2 9 16 23 30	W 7 14 21 28	W 4 11 18 25	W 2 9 16 23 30
T 2 9 16 23 30	T 6 13 20 27	T 3 10 17 24	T 1 8 15 22 29	T 5 12 19 26	T 3 10 17 24 31
F 3 10 17 24 31	F 7 14 21 28	F 4 11 18 25	F 2 9 16 23 30	F 6 13 20 27	F 4 11 18 25
S 4 11 18 25	S 1 8 15 22 29	S 5 12 19 26	S 3 10 17 24 31	S 7 14 21 28	S 5 12 19 26

Richard Bishop of Chichester (BCP)

Purple *or* Lent array (*or White*)

	EUCHARIST	MORNING PRAYER	EVENING PRAYER
	CW		
Psalms:	18.1–6	*22*; 126	*31*
Readings:	Jer. 20.10–13;	Exod. 10;	Jer. 24;
	John 10.31–end	Heb. 13.1–16	John 12.20–36a

| | | AW | *Lam. 5.1–3, 19–22* | *John 12.20–26* |

	HOLY COMMUNION	MORNING PRAYER	EVENING PRAYER
	BCP Com. Bishop		
Psalms:	99	*15; 16; 17*	*18*
Readings:	*Ezek. 34.11–16; 1 Tim. 3.15–16;*	*Num. 20;*	*Num. 22.1–35;*
	Mark 4.26–32 or	*John 12.20–end*	*2 Tim. 3*
	Col. 3.12–17; John 11.47–54		
Hymns:	....	....	....

BCP COLLECT

O God, the light of the faithful, and shepherd of souls, who didst set blessed Richard of Chichester to be a Bishop in the Church, that he might feed thy sheep by his word and guide them by his example: Grant us, we pray thee, to keep the faith which he taught, and to follow in his footsteps; through Jesus Christ our Lord.

St Ambrose Bishop of Milan (BCP)   Purple *or* Lent array (*or* White)

	EUCHARIST	**MORNING PRAYER**	**EVENING PRAYER**
	CW		
Psalms:	*Canticle: Jer. 31.10–13 or* Ps. 121	*23*; 127	128; 129; *130*
Readings:	Ezek. 37.21–28;	Exod. 11;	Jer. 25.1–14;
	John 11.45–end	Heb. 13.17–end	John 12.36b–end

		AW	*Job 17.6–end*	*John 12.27–36*

	HOLY COMMUNION	**MORNING PRAYER**	**EVENING PRAYER**
	BCP Com. Bishop		
Psalms:	99	19; 20; 21	22; 23
Readings:	Ezek. 34.11–16; 1 Tim. 3.15–16;	Num. 22.36—23.26;	Num. 23.27—end of 24; 2 Tim. 4
	Mark 4.26–32 or	John 13	E. Coll. (1) Ash Wednesday,
	Col. 4.2–6; John 6.35–end		(2) Sunday next before Easter
Hymns:	....	....	....

BCP COLLECT
*O God, the light of the faithful, and shepherd of souls,
who didst set blessed Ambrose to be a Bishop in the
Church, that he might feed thy sheep by his word and
guide them by his example: Grant us, we pray thee,
to keep the faith which he taught, and to follow in his
footsteps; through Jesus Christ our Lord.*

2020

July				
S		5	12	19	26
M		6	13	20	27
T		7	14	21	28
W	1	8	15	22	29
T	2	9	16	23	30
F	3	10	17	24	31
S	4	11	18	25

August				
S		2	9	16	23	30
M		3	10	17	24	31
T		4	11	18	25
W		5	12	19	26
T		6	13	20	27
F		7	14	21	28
S	1	8	15	22	29

September				
S		6	13	20	27
M		7	14	21	28
T	1	8	15	22	29
W	2	9	16	23	30
T	3	10	17	24
F	4	11	18	25
S	5	12	19	26

October				
S		4	11	18	25
M		5	12	19	26
T		6	13	20	27
W		7	14	21	28
T	1	8	15	22	29
F	2	9	16	23	30
S	3	10	17	24	31

November				
S	1	8	15	22	29
M	2	9	16	23	30
T	3	10	17	24
W	4	11	18	25
T	5	12	19	26
F	6	13	20	27
S	7	14	21	28

December				
S		6	13	20	27
M		7	14	21	28
T	1	8	15	22	29
W	2	9	16	23	30
T	3	10	17	24	31
F	4	11	18	25
S	5	12	19	26

PALM SUNDAY
Sunday next before Easter
(Red)

PRINCIPAL SERVICE	THIRD SERVICE	SECOND SERVICE
CW		
Liturgy of the Palms:		
Psalms: 118.1–2, 19–end (Alt. 118.19–24)	61; 62	80
Readings: Matt. 21.1–11	Zech. 9.9–12	Isa. 5.1–7;
	[BCP Var. Isa. 42.1–9]	Matt. 21.33–end
	Luke 16.19–end	
Liturgy of the Passion:		
Psalms: 31.9–16 (Alt. 31.9–18)		
Readings: Isa. 50.4–9a; Phil. 2.5–11;		
Matt. 26.14—27.end *or*		
Matt. 27.11–54		
Seasonal provisions CW Book pp 312–313		

HOLY COMMUNION	MORNING PRAYER	EVENING PRAYER
BCP		
Psalms: 73.22–end	61; 62	80
Readings: Zech. 9.9–12; Phil. 2.5–11;	Isa. 52.13—end of 53;	Exod. 10.21—end of 11 or
Matt. 27.1–54 or Matt. 21.1–13	Matt. 26	Isa. 59.12–end;
		Luke 19.29–end or John 12.1–19

The Passion according to St Matthew (Matt. 26.[1–35] and 27.1–60 [61–66]) may be read or sung at any celebration on this day.

Where there are more celebrations of the Holy Communion than one, and the Passion according to St Matthew is read at one of these celebrations, Matt. 21.1–13 may be substituted at any other celebration.

Hymns: ....

....

....

....

....

....

....

....

....

....

....

....

....

....

....

2020

	January					February					March					April					May						June			
S		5	12	19	26		2	9	16	23		1	8	15	22	29		5	12	19	26		3	10	17	24	31		7	14	21	28
M		6	13	20	27		3	10	17	24		2	9	16	23	30		6	13	20	27		4	11	18	25		1	8	15	22	29
T		7	14	21	28		4	11	18	25		3	10	17	24	31		7	14	21	28		5	12	19	26		2	9	16	23	30
W	1	8	15	22	29		5	12	19	26		4	11	18	25		1	8	15	22	29		6	13	20	27		3	10	17	24
T	2	9	16	23	30		6	13	20	27		5	12	19	26		2	9	16	23	30		7	14	21	28		4	11	18	25
F	3	10	17	24	31		7	14	21	28		6	13	20	27		3	10	17	24		1	8	15	22	29		5	12	19	26
S	4	11	18	25		1	8	15	22	29		7	14	21	28		4	11	18	25		2	9	16	23	30		6	13	20	27

CW COLLECTS

Almighty and everlasting God,
who in your tender love towards the human race
  sent your Son our Saviour Jesus Christ
to take upon him our flesh
and to suffer death upon the cross:
grant that we may follow the example
  of his patience and humility,
and also be made partakers of his resurrection;
through Jesus Christ your Son our Lord,
who is alive and reigns with you,
in the unity of the Holy Spirit,
one God, now and for ever.

or

True and humble King,
hailed by the crowd as Messiah:
grant us the faith to know you and love you,
that we may be found beside you
on the way of the cross,
which is the path of glory.

POST COMMUNION

Lord Jesus Christ,
you humbled yourself in taking the form of a servant,
and in obedience died on the cross for our salvation:
give us the mind to follow you
and to proclaim you as Lord and King,
to the glory of God the Father.

BCP COLLECT

*Almighty and everlasting God, who, of thy tender
love towards mankind, hast sent thy Son, our Saviour
Jesus Christ, to take upon him our flesh, and to suffer
death upon the cross, that all mankind should follow
the example of his great humility; Mercifully grant,
that we may both follow the example of his patience,
and also be made partakers of his resurrection;
through the same Jesus Christ our Lord.*

2020

July					August						September					October					November					December				
S		5	12	19	26	S		2	9	16	23	30	S		6	13	20	27	S		4	11	18	25	S	1	8	15	22	29	S		6	13	20	27
M		6	13	20	27	M		3	10	17	24	31	M		7	14	21	28	M		5	12	19	26	M	2	9	16	23	30	M		7	14	21	28
T		7	14	21	28	T		4	11	18	25		T	1	8	15	22	29	T		6	13	20	27	T	3	10	17	24		T	1	8	15	22	29
W	1	8	15	22	29	W		5	12	19	26		W	2	9	16	23	30	W		7	14	21	28	W	4	11	18	25		W	2	9	16	23	30
T	2	9	16	23	30	T		6	13	20	27		T	3	10	17	24		T	1	8	15	22	29	T	5	12	19	26		T	3	10	17	24	31
F	3	10	17	24	31	F		7	14	21	28		F	4	11	18	25		F	2	9	16	23	30	F	6	13	20	27		F	4	11	18	25
S	4	11	18	25		S	1	8	15	22	29	S	5	12	19	26		S	3	10	17	24	31	S	7	14	21	28		S	5	12	19	26

Monday of Holy Week

Red

	PRINCIPAL SERVICE CW	MORNING PRAYER	EVENING PRAYER
Psalms:	36.5–11	41	25
Readings:	Isa. 42.1–9; Heb. 9.11–15; John 12.1–11	Lam. 1.1–12a; Luke 22.1–23 [BCP Var. John 12.1–11]	Lam. 2.8–19; Col. 1.18–23
	HOLY COMMUNION BCP	MORNING PRAYER	EVENING PRAYER
Psalms:	55.1–8	30; 31	32; 33; 34
Readings:	Isa. 63.1–19; Gal. 6.1–11; Mark 14.1–end	Lam. 1.1–12; John 14.1–14	Lam. 3.1–42; John 14.15–end
Hymns:	....	....	....

Sunrise 06.22; Sunset 19.43

2020

January				February				March				April				May					June			
S		5	12	19	26	S		2	9	16	23	S	1	8	15	22	29	S		5	12	19	26	S		3	10	17	24	31	S		7	14	21	28
M		6	13	20	27	M		3	10	17	24	M	2	9	16	23	30	M		6	13	20	27	M		4	11	18	25	M	1	8	15	22	29
T		7	14	21	28	T		4	11	18	25	T	3	10	17	24	31	T		7	14	21	28	T		5	12	19	26	T	2	9	16	23	30
W	1	8	15	22	29	W		5	12	19	26	W	4	11	18	25	W	1	8	15	22	29	W		6	13	20	27	W	3	10	17	24
T	2	9	16	23	30	T		6	13	20	27	T	5	12	19	26	T	2	9	16	23	30	T		7	14	21	28	T	4	11	18	25
F	3	10	17	24	31	F		7	14	21	28	F	6	13	20	27	F	3	10	17	24	F	1	8	15	22	29	F	5	12	19	26
S	4	11	18	25	S	1	8	15	22	29	S	7	14	21	28	S	4	11	18	25	S	2	9	16	23	30	S	6	13	20	27

Tuesday of Holy Week   Red

	PRINCIPAL SERVICE	MORNING PRAYER	EVENING PRAYER
	CW		
Psalms:	71.1–14 or [71.1–8]	27	55.13–24
Readings:	Isa. 49.1–7;	Lam. 3.1–18;	Lam. 3.40–51;
	1 Cor. 1.18–31;	Luke 22.24–53 (or 39–53)	Gal. 6.11–end
	John 12.20–36	[BCP Var. John 12.20–36]	

	HOLY COMMUNION	MORNING PRAYER	EVENING PRAYER
	BCP		
Psalms:	13	35; 36	37
Readings:	Isa. 50.5–11; Rom. 5.6–19;	Isa. 42.1–9;	Wisd. 2.1, 12–end;
	Mark 15.1–39	John 15.1–16	John 15.17–end
Hymns:			

2020

	July					August						September					October					November					December			
S		5	12	19	26	S		2	9	16	23	30	S		6	13	20	27	S		4	11	18	25	S	1	8	15	22	29	S		6	13	20	27
M		6	13	20	27	M		3	10	17	24	31	M		7	14	21	28	M		5	12	19	26	M	2	9	16	23	30	M		7	14	21	28
T		7	14	21	28	T		4	11	18	25	T	1	8	15	22	29	T		6	13	20	27	T	3	10	17	24	T	1	8	15	22	29
W	1	8	15	22	29	W		5	12	19	26	W	2	9	16	23	30	W		7	14	21	28	W	4	11	18	25	W	2	9	16	23	30
T	2	9	16	23	30	T		6	13	20	27	T	3	10	17	24	T	1	8	15	22	29	T	5	12	19	26	T	3	10	17	24	31
F	3	10	17	24	31	F		7	14	21	28	F	4	11	18	25	F	2	9	16	23	30	F	6	13	20	27	F	4	11	18	25
S	4	11	18	25	S	1	8	15	22	29	S	5	12	19	26	S	3	10	17	24	31	S	7	14	21	28	S	5	12	19	26

Wednesday of Holy Week · Red

	PRINCIPAL SERVICE	MORNING PRAYER	EVENING PRAYER
	CW		
Psalms:	70	102 [102.1–18]	88
Readings:	Isa. 50.4–9a; Heb. 12.1–3; John 13.21–32	Wisd. 1.16—2.1, 12–22 *or* Jer. 11.18–20; Luke 22.54–end [BCP Var. John 13.21–32]	Isa. 63.1–9; Rev. 14.18—15.4

	HOLY COMMUNION	MORNING PRAYER	EVENING PRAYER
	BCP		
Psalms:	54	*38; 39; 40*	*41; 42; 43*
Readings:	Isa. 49.1–9a; Heb. 9.16–end; Luke 22	*Num. 21.4–9; John 16.1–15*	*Lev. 16.2–24; John 16.16–end*
Hymns:	....	....	....

Full Moon

2020

	January	February	March	April	May	June
S	5 12 19 26	2 9 16 23	1 8 15 22 29	5 12 19 26	3 10 17 24 31	7 14 21 28
M	6 13 20 27	3 10 17 24	2 9 16 23 30	6 13 20 27	4 11 18 25	1 8 15 22 29
T	7 14 21 28	4 11 18 25	3 10 17 24 31	7 14 21 28	5 12 19 26	2 9 16 23 30
W	1 8 15 22 29	5 12 19 26	4 11 18 25	1 8 15 22 29	6 13 20 27	3 10 17 24
T	2 9 16 23 30	6 13 20 27	5 12 19 26	2 9 16 23 30	7 14 21 28	4 11 18 25
F	3 10 17 24 31	7 14 21 28	6 13 20 27	3 10 17 24	1 8 15 22 29	5 12 19 26
S	4 11 18 25	1 8 15 22 29	7 14 21 28	4 11 18 25	2 9 16 23 30	6 13 20 27

MAUNDY THURSDAY

Red, *or* as in Lent; White at Holy Communion

	PRINCIPAL SERVICE	MORNING PRAYER	EVENING PRAYER
	CW		
Psalms:	116.1, 10–end *or* [116.9–end]	42; 43	39
Readings:	Exod. 12.1–4 [5–10], 11–14;	Lev. 16.2–24;	Exod. 11;
	1 Cor. 11.23–26;	Luke 23.1–25	Eph. 2.11–18
	John 13.1–17, 31b–35	[BCP Var. John 13.1–17, 31b–35]	
	Seasonal provisions CW Book pp 314–315		

	HOLY COMMUNION	MORNING PRAYER	EVENING PRAYER
	BCP		
Psalms:	43	44; 45; 46	47; 48; 49
Readings:	Exod. 12.1–11; 1 Cor. 11.17–end;	Exod. 24.1–11;	Exod. 16.2–15;
	Luke 23.1–49	John 17	John 13.1–35
Hymns:	....	....	....

CW COLLECTS

God our Father,
you have invited us to share in the supper
which your Son gave to his Church
to proclaim his death until he comes:
may he nourish us by his presence,
and unite us in his love;
who is alive and reigns with you,
in the unity of the Holy Spirit,
one God, now and for ever.

or

God our Father,
your Son Jesus Christ was obedient to the end
and drank the cup prepared for him:
may we who share his table
watch with him through the night of suffering
and be faithful.
*At Morning and Evening Prayer the Collect of
Palm Sunday is used.*

POST COMMUNION

Lord Jesus Christ,
we thank you that in this wonderful sacrament
you have given us the memorial of your passion:
grant us so to reverence the sacred mysteries
of your body and blood
that we may know within ourselves
and show forth in our lives
the fruit of your redemption,
for you are alive and reign, now and for ever.

2020

July				August					September				October				November					December			
S		5	12	19	26	S		2	9	16	23	30	S		6	13	20	27	S		4	11	18	25	S	1	8	15	22	29	S		6	13	20	27
M		6	13	20	27	M		3	10	17	24	31	M		7	14	21	28	M		5	12	19	26	M	2	9	16	23	30	M		7	14	21	28
T		7	14	21	28	T		4	11	18	25		T	1	8	15	22	29	T		6	13	20	27	T	3	10	17	24		T	1	8	15	22	29
W	1	8	15	22	29	W		5	12	19	26		W	2	9	16	23	30	W		7	14	21	28	W	4	11	18	25		W	2	9	16	23	30
T	2	9	16	23	30	T		6	13	20	27		T	3	10	17	24		T	1	8	15	22	29	T	5	12	19	26		T	3	10	17	24	31
F	3	10	17	24	31	F		7	14	21	28		F	4	11	18	25		F	2	9	16	23	30	F	6	13	20	27		F	4	11	18	25
S	4	11	18	25	S	1	8	15	22	29		S	5	12	19	26		S	3	10	17	24	31	S	7	14	21	28		S	5	12	19	26

GOOD FRIDAY Bank Holiday (UK)

Hangings removed: Red for Liturgy

	PRINCIPAL SERVICE CW	MORNING PRAYER	EVENING PRAYER
Psalms:	22 *or* [22.1–11 *or* 1–21]	69	130; 143
Readings:	Isa. 52.13—end of 53; Heb. 10.16–25 *or* Heb. 4.14–16; 5.7–9; John 18.1—end of 19	Gen. 22.1–18; A part of John 18–19 if not read at the Principal Service *or* Heb. 10.1–10 [BCP Var. John 18]	Lam. 5.15–end; A part of John 18–19 if not used at the Principal Service John 19.38–end *or* Col. 1.18–23; [BCP Var. John 19.38–end]

	HOLY COMMUNION BCP	MORNING PRAYER	EVENING PRAYER
Psalms:	*140.1–9*	50; 51; 52	*53; 54; 55*
Readings:	*Num. 21.4–9; Heb. 10.1–25; John 19.1–37*	*Gen. 22.1–18; John 18*	*Isa. 52.13—end of 53; John 19.31–end or 1 Pet. 2.11–end*

The Passion according to St John (John 18 and 19 to v37) may be read or sung on this day, immediately before the Gospel, which in that case should be John 19.38–end

Hymns: ....

CW COLLECTS

Almighty Father,
look with mercy on this your family for which our
    Lord Jesus Christ was content to be betrayed
    and given up into the hands of sinners
    and to suffer death upon the cross;
who is alive and glorified with you and the Holy Spirit, one
    God, now and for ever.

or

Eternal God,
in the cross of Jesus we see the cost of our sin
and the depth of your love:
in humble hope and fear may we place at his feet
all that we have and all that we are,
through Jesus Christ our Lord.

BCP COLLECTS

Almighty God, we beseech thee graciously to behold this thy family, for which our Lord Jesus Christ was contented to be betrayed, and given up into the hands of wicked men, and to suffer death upon the cross, who now liveth and reigneth with thee and the Holy Ghost, ever one God, world without end.

Almighty and everlasting God, by whose Spirit the whole body of the Church is governed and sanctified: Receive our supplications and prayers, which we offer before thee for all estates of men in thy holy Church, that every member of the same, in his vocation and ministry, may truly and godly serve thee; through our Lord and Saviour Jesus Christ.

Instead of the third collect may be said:

O merciful God, who hast made all men, and hatest nothing that thou hast made, nor wouldest the death of a sinner, but rather that he should be converted and live: Have mercy upon thine ancient people the Jews, and upon all who have not known thee, or who deny the faith of Christ crucified; take from them all ignorance, hardness of heart, and contempt of thy Word; and so fetch them home, blessed Lord, to thy fold, that they may be made one flock under one shepherd, Jesus Christ our Lord, who liveth and reigneth with thee and the Holy Spirit, one God, world without end.

2020

	January					February					March					April					May						June			
S		5	12	19	26		2	9	16	23		1	8	15	22	29		5	12	19	26		3	10	17	24	31		7	14	21	28
M		6	13	20	27		3	10	17	24		2	9	16	23	30		6	13	20	27		4	11	18	25			1	8	15	22	29
T		7	14	21	28		4	11	18	25		3	10	17	24	31		7	14	21	28		5	12	19	26			2	9	16	23	30
W	1	8	15	22	29		5	12	19	26		4	11	18	25		1	8	15	22	29		6	13	20	27			3	10	17	24	
T	2	9	16	23	30		6	13	20	27		5	12	19	26		2	9	16	23	30		7	14	21	28			4	11	18	25	
F	3	10	17	24	31		7	14	21	28		6	13	20	27		3	10	17	24		1	8	15	22	29			5	12	19	26	
S	4	11	18	25		1	8	15	22	29		7	14	21	28		4	11	18	25		2	9	16	23	30			6	13	20	27	

Easter Eve Hangings removed

PRINCIPAL SERVICE CW	MORNING PRAYER	EVENING PRAYER

These readings are for use at services other than the Easter Vigil

Psalms:	31.1–4, 15–16 *or* [31.1–5]	142	116
Readings:	Job. 14.1–14 *or* Lam. 3.1–9, 19–24; 1 Pet. 4.1–8; Matt. 27.57–end *or* John 19.38–end	Hos. 6.1–6; John 2.18–22	Job 19.21–27; 1 John 5.5–12

HOLY COMMUNION BCP	MORNING PRAYER	EVENING PRAYER

Psalms:		*56; 57; 58*	*59; 60; 61*
Readings:	*Job 14.1–14; 1 Pet. 3.17–22; Matt. 27.57–end*	*Zech. 9.9–12; Luke 23.50–end*	*Job 19.21–27; John 2.13–22 E. Coll. Easter Eve only*

EASTER VIGIL (CW Readings) White *or* Gold

A minimum of three Old Testament readings should be chosen.
The reading from Exodus 14 should always be used.

Gen. 1.1—2.4a	Ps. 136.1–9, 23–end
Gen. 7.1–5, 11–18; 8.6–18; 9.8–13	Ps. 46
Gen. 22.1–18	Ps. 16
Exod. 14.10–end; 15.20–21	*Canticle:* **Exod. 15.1b–13, 17–18**
Isa. 55.1–11	*Canticle:* Isa. 12.2–end
Baruch 3.9–15, 32—4.4 *or* Prov. 8.1–8, 19–21; 9.4b–6	Ps. 19
Ezek. 36.24–28	Ps. 42; 43
Ezek. 37.1–14	Ps. 143
Zeph. 3.14–end	Ps. 98
Rom. 6.3–11	**Ps. 114**
Matt. 28.1–10	

Hymns: ....

CW COLLECTS

Grant, Lord,
that we who are baptized into the death
of your Son our Saviour Jesus Christ
may continually put to death our evil desires
and be buried with him;
and that through the grave and gate of death
we may pass to our joyful resurrection;
through his merits, who died and was buried
and rose again for us,
your Son Jesus Christ our Lord.

or

In the depths of our isolation
we cry to you, Lord God:
give light in our darkness
and bring us out of the prison of our despair;
through Jesus Christ our Lord.

BCP COLLECT

Grant, O Lord, that as we are baptized into the death
of thy blessed Son our Saviour Jesus Christ, so by
continual mortifying our corrupt affections we may
be buried with him; and that, through the grave, and
gate of death, we may pass to our joyful resurrection;
for his merits, who died, and was buried, and rose
again for us, thy Son Jesus Christ our Lord.

EASTER VIGIL COLLECTS

Lord of all life and power,
who through the mighty resurrection of your Son
overcame the old order of sin and death
to make all things new in him:
grant that we, being dead to sin
and alive to you in Jesus Christ,
may reign with him in glory;
to whom with you and the Holy Spirit
be praise and honour, glory and might,
now and in all eternity.

or

God of Glory,
by the raising of your Son
you have broken the chains of death and hell:
fill your Church with faith and hope;
for a new day has dawned
and the way to life stands open
in our Saviour Jesus Christ.

2020

	July	August	September	October	November	December
S	5 12 19 26	2 9 16 23 30	6 13 20 27	4 11 18 25	1 8 15 22 29	6 13 20 27
M	6 13 20 27	3 10 17 24 31	7 14 21 28	5 12 19 26	2 9 16 23 30	7 14 21 28
T	7 14 21 28	4 11 18 25	1 8 15 22 29	6 13 20 27	3 10 17 24	1 8 15 22 29
W	1 8 15 22 29	5 12 19 26	2 9 16 23 30	7 14 21 28	4 11 18 25	2 9 16 23 30
T	2 9 16 23 30	6 13 20 27	3 10 17 24	1 8 15 22 29	5 12 19 26	3 10 17 24 31
F	3 10 17 24 31	7 14 21 28	4 11 18 25	2 9 16 23 30	6 13 20 27	4 11 18 25
S	4 11 18 25	1 8 15 22 29	5 12 19 26	3 10 17 24 31	7 14 21 28	5 12 19 26

2020

	January					February					March					April					May						June				
S		5	12	19	26		2	9	16	23		1	8	15	22	29		5	12	19	26		3	10	17	24	31			7	14	21	28
M		6	13	20	27		3	10	17	24		2	9	16	23	30		6	13	20	27		4	11	18	25			1	8	15	22	29
T		7	14	21	28		4	11	18	25		3	10	17	24	31		7	14	21	28		5	12	19	26			2	9	16	23	30
W	1	8	15	22	29		5	12	19	26		4	11	18	25		1	8	15	22	29		6	13	20	27			3	10	17	24	
T	2	9	16	23	30		6	13	20	27		5	12	19	26		2	9	16	23	30		7	14	21	28			4	11	18	25	
F	3	10	17	24	31		7	14	21	28		6	13	20	27		3	10	17	24		1	8	15	22	29			5	12	19	26	
S	4	11	18	25		1	8	15	22	29		7	14	21	28		4	11	18	25		2	9	16	23	30			6	13	20	27	

Notes for Easter

2020

July						August							September						October						November						December				
S		5	12	19	26	S		2	9	16	23	30	S		6	13	20	27	S		4	11	18	25	S	1	8	15	22	29	S		6	13	20	27
M		6	13	20	27	M		3	10	17	24	31	M		7	14	21	28	M		5	12	19	26	M	2	9	16	23	30	M		7	14	21	28
T		7	14	21	28	T		4	11	18	25		T	1	8	15	22	29	T		6	13	20	27	T	3	10	17	24		T	1	8	15	22	29
W	1	8	15	22	29	W		5	12	19	26		W	2	9	16	23	30	W		7	14	21	28	W	4	11	18	25		W	2	9	16	23	30
T	2	9	16	23	30	T		6	13	20	27		T	3	10	17	24		T	1	8	15	22	29	T	5	12	19	26		T	3	10	17	24	31
F	3	10	17	24	31	F		7	14	21	28		F	4	11	18	25		F	2	9	16	23	30	F	6	13	20	27		F	4	11	18	25	
S	4	11	18	25		S	1	8	15	22	29		S	5	12	19	26		S	3	10	17	24	31	S	7	14	21	28		S	5	12	19	26	

EASTER DAY

(White *or* Gold)

	PRINCIPAL SERVICE CW	**THIRD SERVICE**	**SECOND SERVICE**
Psalms:	118.1–2, 14–24 [118.14–24]	114; 117	105 *or* 66.1–11
Readings:	Acts 10.34–43 *or* Jer. 31.1–6; Col. 3.1–4 *or* Acts 10.34–43; John 20.1 18 *or* Matt. 28.1–10 The Reading from Acts must be used as either the first or second reading	Exod. 14.10–18, 26–15.2; Rev. 15.2–4	S. of Sol 3.2–5, 8.6–7; John 20.11–18 if not read at the Principal Service *or* Rev. 1.12–18

Seasonal provisions CW Book pp 316–317 until the Eve of Ascension (May 20)

	HOLY COMMUNION BCP	**MORNING PRAYER**	**EVENING PRAYER**
Psalms:	111	*Easter Anthems;*	105 or *66.1–11*
Readings:	*Exod. 12.21–28; Col. 3.1–7;* *John 20.1–10;* *Pr. Pref. until April 19*	*Exod. 12.1–14;* *Rev. 1.4–18*	*Isa. 51.1–16* or *Exod. 14;* *John 20.1–23* or *Rom. 6.1–13*
Hymns:	....	....	....

2020

	January	February	March	April	May	June
S	5 12 19 26	2 9 16 23	1 8 15 22 29	5 12 19 26	3 10 17 24 31	7 14 21 28
M	6 13 20 27	3 10 17 24	2 9 16 23 30	6 13 20 27	4 11 18 25	1 8 15 22 29
T	7 14 21 28	4 11 18 25	3 10 17 24 31	7 14 21 28	5 12 19 26	2 9 16 23 30
W	1 8 15 22 29	5 12 19 26	4 11 18 25	1 8 15 22 29	6 13 20 27	3 10 17 24
T	2 9 16 23 30	6 13 20 27	5 12 19 26	2 9 16 23 30	7 14 21 28	4 11 18 25
F	3 10 17 24 31	7 14 21 28	6 13 20 27	3 10 17 24	1 8 15 22 29	5 12 19 26
S	4 11 18 25	1 8 15 22 29	7 14 21 28	4 11 18 25	2 9 16 23 30	6 13 20 27

CW COLLECTS

Lord of all life and power,
who through the mighty resurrection of your Son
overcame the old order of sin and death
to make all things new in him:
grant that we, being dead to sin
and alive to you in Jesus Christ,
may reign with him in glory;
to whom with you and the Holy Spirit
be praise and honour, glory and might,
now and in all eternity.

or

God of Glory,
by the raising of your Son
you have broken the chains of death and hell:
fill your Church with faith and hope;
for a new day has dawned
and the way to life stands open
in our Saviour Jesus Christ.

POST COMMUNION

God of Life,
who for our redemption gave your only-begotten Son
    to the death of the cross,
and by his glorious resurrection
have delivered us from the power of our enemy:
grant us so to die daily to sin,
that we may evermore live with him
    in the joy of his risen life;
through Jesus Christ our Lord.

BCP COLLECTS

*Almighty God, who through thine only-begotten Son
Jesus Christ hast overcome death, and opened unto
us the gate of everlasting life: We humbly beseech
thee, that, as by thy special grace preventing us
thou dost put into our minds good desires, so by
thy continual help we may bring the same to good
effect; through Jesus Christ our Lord, who liveth and
reigneth with thee and the Holy Ghost, ever one God,
world without end.*

The following Collect may be used on Easter Day and seven days after:

*O God, who for our redemption didst give thine
only-begotten Son to the death of the cross, and by
his glorious resurrection hast delivered us from the
power of our enemy: Grant us to die daily unto sin,
that we may evermore live with him in the joy of his
resurrection; through the same Jesus Christ our Lord.*

2020

July					August						September					October					November					December				
S		5	12	19	26	S		2	9	16	23	30	S		6	13	20	27	S		4	11	18	25	S	1	8	15	22	29	S		6	13	20	27
M		6	13	20	27	M		3	10	17	24	31	M		7	14	21	28	M		5	12	19	26	M	2	9	16	23	30	M		7	14	21	28
T		7	14	21	28	T		4	11	18	25		T	1	8	15	22	29	T		6	13	20	27	T	3	10	17	24		T	1	8	15	22	29
W	1	8	15	22	29	W		5	12	19	26		W	2	9	16	23	30	W		7	14	21	28	W	4	11	18	25		W	2	9	16	23	30
T	2	9	16	23	30	T		6	13	20	27		T	3	10	17	24		T	1	8	15	22	29	T	5	12	19	26		T	3	10	17	24	31
F	3	10	17	24	31	F		7	14	21	28		F	4	11	18	25		F	2	9	16	23	30	F	6	13	20	27		F	4	11	18	25	
S	4	11	18	25		S	1	8	15	22	29		S	5	12	19	26		S	3	10	17	24	31	S	7	14	21	28		S	5	12	19	26	

Monday of Easter Week.   Bank Holiday (UK, not Scotland)

White *or* Gold

	EUCHARIST	MORNING PRAYER	EVENING PRAYER
	CW		
Psalms:	16.1–2, 6–end	*111*; 117; 146	*135*
Readings:	Acts 2.14, 22–32; Matt. 28.8–15	Exod. 12.1–14; 1 Cor. 15.1–11	S. of Sol. 1.9—2.7; Mark 16.1–8

	AW	*Isa. 54.1–14*	*Rom. 1.1–7*

	HOLY COMMUNION	MORNING PRAYER	EVENING PRAYER
	BCP		
Psalms:	*Easter Anthems*	*68*	*69; 70*
Readings:	*Hos. 6.1–6; Acts 10.34–43; Luke 24.13–35*	*Exod. 15.1–18; Luke 24.1–12*	*Isa. 12; 1 Pet. 1.1–12*
Hymns:	....	....	....

BCP Easter Day Collect.

Sunrise 06.06; Sunset 19.55

2020

	January	February	March	April	May	June
S	5 12 19 26	2 9 16 23	1 8 15 22 29	5 12 19 26	3 10 17 24 31	7 14 21 28
M	6 13 20 27	3 10 17 24	2 9 16 23 30	6 13 20 27	4 11 18 25	1 8 15 22 29
T	7 14 21 28	4 11 18 25	3 10 17 24 31	7 14 21 28	5 12 19 26	2 9 16 23 30
W	1 8 15 22 29	5 12 19 26	4 11 18 25	1 8 15 22 29	6 13 20 27	3 10 17 24
T	2 9 16 23 30	6 13 20 27	5 12 19 26	2 9 16 23 30	7 14 21 28	4 11 18 25
F	3 10 17 24 31	7 14 21 28	6 13 20 27	3 10 17 24	1 8 15 22 29	5 12 19 26
S	4 11 18 25	1 8 15 22 29	7 14 21 28	4 11 18 25	2 9 16 23 30	6 13 20 27

Tuesday of Easter Week   White *or* Gold

	EUCHARIST	**MORNING PRAYER**	**EVENING PRAYER**
	CW		
Psalms:	33.4–5, 18–end	*112*; 147.1–12	*136*
Readings:	Acts 2.36–41;	Exod. 12.14–36;	S. of Sol. 2.8–end;
	John 20.11–18	1 Cor. 15.12–19	Luke 24.1–12

AW   *Isa. 51.1–11*   *John 5.19–29*

	HOLY COMMUNION	**MORNING PRAYER**	**EVENING PRAYER**
	BCP		
Psalms:	16.9–end	71; 72	73; 74
Readings:	1 Kgs 17.17–end;	Isa. 25.1–9;	Isa. 26.1–19;
	Acts 13.26–41;	Matt. 28.1–10	1 Pet. 1.13–end
	Luke 24.36b–48		
Hymns:	....	....	....

BCP Easter Day Collect.

2020

	July				August					September				October				November				December			
S		5	12	19	26		2	9	16	23	30		6	13	20	27		4	11	18	25		1	8	15	22	29		6	13	20	27
M		6	13	20	27		3	10	17	24	31		7	14	21	28		5	12	19	26		2	9	16	23	30		7	14	21	28
T		7	14	21	28		4	11	18	25		1	8	15	22	29		6	13	20	27		3	10	17	24		1	8	15	22	29
W	1	8	15	22	29		5	12	19	26	2	9	16	23	30		7	14	21	28	4	11	18	25	2	9	16	23	30
T	2	9	16	23	30		6	13	20	27	3	10	17	24		1	8	15	22	29	5	12	19	26	3	10	17	24	31
F	3	10	17	24	31		7	14	21	28	4	11	18	25		2	9	16	23	30	6	13	20	27	4	11	18	25
S	4	11	18	25		1	8	15	22	29	5	12	19	26		3	10	17	24	31	7	14	21	28	5	12	19	26

Wednesday of Easter Week

White *or* Gold

	EUCHARIST		MORNING PRAYER	EVENING PRAYER
	CW			
Psalms:	105.1–9		*113*; 147.13–end	*105*
Readings:	Acts 3.1–10;		Exod. 12.37–end;	S. of Sol. 3;
	Luke 24.13–35		1 Cor. 15.20–28	Matt. 28.16–end
		AW	*Isa. 26.1–19*	*John 20.1–10*
	HOLY COMMUNION		MORNING PRAYER	EVENING PRAYER
	BCP			
Psalms:	*111*		75; 76; 77	78
Readings:	*Isa. 42.10–16;*		*Isa. 61;*	*S. of Sol. 2.8–end;*
	Acts 3.12–18;		*John 21.1–14*	*Rev. 7.9–end*
	John 20.11–18			
Hymns:	....		....	....

BCP Easter Day Collect.

2020

	January	February	March	April	May	June
S	5 12 19 26	2 9 16 23	1 8 15 22 29	5 12 19 26	3 10 17 24 31	7 14 21 28
M	6 13 20 27	3 10 17 24	2 9 16 23 30	6 13 20 27	4 11 18 25	1 8 15 22 29
T	7 14 21 28	4 11 18 25	3 10 17 24 31	7 14 21 28	5 12 19 26	2 9 16 23 30
W	1 8 15 22 29	5 12 19 26	4 11 18 25	1 8 15 22 29	6 13 20 27	3 10 17 24
T	2 9 16 23 30	6 13 20 27	5 12 19 26	2 9 16 23 30	7 14 21 28	4 11 18 25
F	3 10 17 24 31	7 14 21 28	6 13 20 27	3 10 17 24	1 8 15 22 29	5 12 19 26
S	4 11 18 25	1 8 15 22 29	7 14 21 28	4 11 18 25	2 9 16 23 30	6 13 20 27

Thursday of Easter Week

White *or* Gold

	EUCHARIST CW	MORNING PRAYER	EVENING PRAYER
Psalms:	8	*114*; 148	*106*
Readings:	Acts 3.11–end; Luke 24.35–48	Exod. 13.1–16; 1 Cor. 15.29–34	S. of Sol. 5.2—6.3; Luke 7.11–17

AW   *Isa. 43.14–21*   *Rev. 1.4–end*

	HOLY COMMUNION BCP	MORNING PRAYER	EVENING PRAYER
Psalms:	*113*	*79; 80; 81*	*82; 83; 84; 85*
Readings:	*Isa. 43.16–21; Acts 8.26–end; John 21.1–14*	*1 Kgs 17.8–end; Mark 5.21–end*	*Dan. 12; 1 Thess. 4.13–end*
Hymns:			

BCP Easter Day Collect.

Friday of Easter Week   White *or* Gold

	EUCHARIST		MORNING PRAYER	EVENING PRAYER
	CW			
Psalms:	118.1–4, 22–26		*115*; 149	*107*
Readings:	Acts 4.1–12;		Exod. 13.17—14.14;	S. of Sol. 7.10—8.4;
	John 21.1–14		1 Cor. 15.35–50	Luke 8.41–end
		AW	*Isa. 42.10–17*	*1 Thess. 5.1–11*
	HOLY COMMUNION		MORNING PRAYER	EVENING PRAYER
	BCP			
Psalms:	116.1–9		86; 87; 88	89
Readings:	Ezek. 37.1–14;		2 Kgs 4.8–37;	Zeph. 3.14–end;
	1 Pet. 3.18–22;		Luke 7.11–17	Acts 17.16–31
	Matt. 28.16–end			
Hymns:	....		....	....

BCP Easter Day Collect.

2020

	January					February					March					April					May						June			
S		5	12	19	26		2	9	16	23		1	8	15	22	29		5	12	19	26		3	10	17	24	31			7	14	21	28
M		6	13	20	27		3	10	17	24		2	9	16	23	30		6	13	20	27		4	11	18	25			1	8	15	22	29
T		7	14	21	28		4	11	18	25		3	10	17	24	31		7	14	21	28		5	12	19	26			2	9	16	23	30
W	1	8	15	22	29		5	12	19	26		4	11	18	25		1	8	15	22	29		6	13	20	27			3	10	17	24	
T	2	9	16	23	30		6	13	20	27		5	12	19	26		2	9	16	23	30		7	14	21	28			4	11	18	25	
F	3	10	17	24	31		7	14	21	28		6	13	20	27		3	10	17	24		1	8	15	22	29			5	12	19	26	
S	4	11	18	25		1	8	15	22	29		7	14	21	28		4	11	18	25		2	9	16	23	30			6	13	20	27	

Saturday of Easter Week   White *or* Gold

	EUCHARIST	**MORNING PRAYER**	**EVENING PRAYER**
	CW		
Psalms:	118.1–4, 14–21	*116*; 150	*145*
Readings:	Acts 4.13–21;	Exod. 14.15–end;	S. of Sol. 8.5–7;
	Mark 16.9–15	1 Cor. 15.51–end	John 11.17–44

AW   *Job 14.1–14*   *John 21.1–14*

	HOLY COMMUNION	**MORNING PRAYER**	**EVENING PRAYER**
	BCP		
Psalms:	118.*14–21*	*90; 91; 92*	*93; 94*
Readings:	Zech. 8.1–8;	Jer. 31.1–14;	Mic. 7.7–end;
	1 Pet. 2.1–10;	John 11.17–44	Acts 26.1–23;
	John 20.24–end		E. Coll. Easter 1
Hymns:	....	....	....

BCP Easter Day Collect.

THE SECOND SUNDAY OF EASTER
Easter 1

(White)

	PRINCIPAL SERVICE	THIRD SERVICE	SECOND SERVICE
	CW		
Psalms:	16	81.1–10	30.1–5
Readings:	Acts 2.14a, 22–32; Alt. O.T. Exod. 14.10–end, 15.20–21; The reading from Acts must be used as either the first or second reading. 1 Pet. 1.3–9; John 20.19–end	Exod. 12.1–17; 1 Cor. 5.6b–8	Dan. 6.1–23 *or* 6.6–23; Mark 15.46—16.8
	Seasonal provisions CW Book pp 316–317		

	HOLY COMMUNION	MORNING PRAYER	EVENING PRAYER
	BCP		
Psalms:	*81.1–4*	*81.1–11*	*30.1–5*
Readings:	*Ezek. 37.1–10; 1 John 5.4–12;* *John 20.19–23*	*Isa. 52.1–12;* *Luke 24.13–35* or *1 Cor. 15.1–28*	*Isa. 54* or *Ezek. 37.1–14;* *John 20.24–end* or *Rev. 5*
Hymns:	....	....	....

CW COLLECTS

Almighty Father,
you have given your only Son to die for our sins
and to rise again for our justification:
grant us so to put away the leaven of malice
    and wickedness
that we may always serve you in pureness of
    living and truth;
through the merits of your Son Jesus Christ our Lord,
who is alive and reigns with you,
in the unity of the Holy Spirit,
one God, now and for ever.

or

Risen Christ,
for whom no door is locked, no entrance barred:
open the doors of our hearts,
that we may seek the good of others
and walk the joyful road of sacrifice and peace,
to the praise of God the Father.

POST COMMUNION

Lord God our Father,
through our Saviour Jesus Christ
you have assured your children of eternal life
and in baptism have made us one with him:
deliver us from the death of sin
and raise us to new life in your love,
in the fellowship of the Holy Spirit,
by the grace of our Lord Jesus Christ.

BCP COLLECT

Almighty Father, who hast given thine only Son to
die for our sins, and to rise again for our justification:
Grant us so to put away the leaven of malice and
wickedness, that we may always serve thee in
pureness of living and truth; through the merits of
the same thy Son Jesus Christ our Lord.

2020

	July					August						September					October					November					December			
S		5	12	19	26	S		2	9	16	23	30	S		6	13	20	27	S		4	11	18	25	S	1	8	15	22	29	S		6	13	20	27
M		6	13	20	27	M		3	10	17	24	31	M		7	14	21	28	M		5	12	19	26	M	2	9	16	23	30	M		7	14	21	28
T		7	14	21	28	T		4	11	18	25		T	1	8	15	22	29	T		6	13	20	27	T	3	10	17	24		T	1	8	15	22	29
W	1	8	15	22	29	W		5	12	19	26		W	2	9	16	23	30	W		7	14	21	28	W	4	11	18	25		W	2	9	16	23	30
T	2	9	16	23	30	T		6	13	20	27		T	3	10	17	24		T	1	8	15	22	29	T	5	12	19	26		T	3	10	17	24	31
F	3	10	17	24	31	F		7	14	21	28		F	4	11	18	25		F	2	9	16	23	30	F	6	13	20	27		F	4	11	18	25
S	4	11	18	25		S	1	8	15	22	29		S	5	12	19	26		S	3	10	17	24	31	S	7	14	21	28		S	5	12	19	26

White

	EUCHARIST	MORNING PRAYER	EVENING PRAYER
	CW		
Psalms:	2.1–9	2; *19*	*139*
Readings:	Acts 4.23–31;	Exod. 15.1–21;	Deut. 1.3–18;
	John 3.1–8	Col. 1.1–14	John 20.1–10

AW *Ezek. 1.22* *Rev. 4*

	HOLY COMMUNION	MORNING PRAYER	EVENING PRAYER
	BCP		
Psalms:		102; 103	104
Readings:		Deut. 1.3–18;	Deut. 1.19–end;
		Acts 1.1–14	Acts 1.15–end
Hymns:	....	....	....

Sunrise 05.51; Sunset 20.07

2020

	January				February				March				April				May					June			
S		5	12	19	26		2	9	16	23		1	8	15	22	29		5	12	19	26			3	10	17	24	31			7	14	21	28
M		6	13	20	27		3	10	17	24		2	9	16	23	30		6	13	20	27			4	11	18	25			1	8	15	22	29
T		7	14	21	28		4	11	18	25		3	10	17	24	31		7	14	21	28			5	12	19	26			2	9	16	23	30
W	1	8	15	22	29		5	12	19	26		4	11	18	25		1	8	15	22	29			6	13	20	27			3	10	17	24
T	2	9	16	23	30		6	13	20	27		5	12	19	26		2	9	16	23	30			7	14	21	28			4	11	18	25
F	3	10	17	24	31		7	14	21	28		6	13	20	27		3	10	17	24		1	8	15	22	29			5	12	19	26
S	4	11	18	25		1	8	15	22	29		7	14	21	28		4	11	18	25		2	9	16	23	30			6	13	20	27

Anselm, Abbot of Le Bec, Archbishop of Canterbury, Teacher of the Faith 1109   White
(CW Readings see Common of the Saints also Wisd. 9.13–18; Rom. 5.8–11)

	EUCHARIST CW	**MORNING PRAYER**	**EVENING PRAYER**
Psalms:	93	*8*; 20; 21	*104*
Readings:	Acts 4.32–end; John 3.7–15	Exod. 15.22—16.10; Col. 1.15–end	Deut. 1.19–40; John 20.11–18

	AW	*Prov. 8.1–11*	*Acts 16.6–15*

	HOLY COMMUNION BCP	**MORNING PRAYER**	**EVENING PRAYER**
Psalms:		*105*	*106*
Readings:		*Deut. 2.1–25;* *Acts 2.1–21*	*Deut. 2.26—3.5;* *Acts 2.22–end*
Hymns:	....	....	....

CW COLLECT
Eternal God, who gave great gifts to your servant
Anselm as a pastor and teacher:
grant that we, like him, may desire you with our
whole heart and, so desiring, may seek you
and, seeking, may find you;
through Jesus Christ your Son our Lord,
who is alive and reigns with you,
in the unity of the Holy Spirit,
one God, now and for ever.

POST COMMUNION
God of truth,
whose Wisdom set her table
and invited us to eat the bread and drink the wine
  of the kingdom:
help us to lay aside all foolishness
and to live and walk in the way of insight,
that we may come with Anselm
to the eternal feast of heaven;
through Jesus Christ our Lord.

2020

	July				August					September				October				November					December			
S	5 12 19 26		S	2 9 16 23 30		S	6 13 20 27		S	4 11 18 25		S	1 8 15 22 29		S	6 13 20 27
M	6 13 20 27		M	3 10 17 24 31		M	7 14 21 28		M	5 12 19 26		M	2 9 16 23 30		M	7 14 21 28
T	7 14 21 28		T	4 11 18 25		T	1 8 15 22 29		T	6 13 20 27		T	3 10 17 24		T	1 8 15 22 29
W	1 8 15 22 29		W	5 12 19 26		W	2 9 16 23 30		W	7 14 21 28		W	4 11 18 25		W	2 9 16 23 30
T	2 9 16 23 30		T	6 13 20 27		T	3 10 17 24		T	1 8 15 22 29		T	5 12 19 26		T	3 10 17 24 31
F	3 10 17 24 31		F	7 14 21 28		F	4 11 18 25		F	2 9 16 23 30		F	6 13 20 27		F	4 11 18 25
S	4 11 18 25		S	1 8 15 22 29		S	5 12 19 26		S	3 10 17 24 31		S	7 14 21 28		S	5 12 19 26

White

	EUCHARIST	**MORNING PRAYER**	**EVENING PRAYER**
	CW		
Psalms:	34.1–8	16; *30*	*33*
Readings:	Acts 5.17–26; John 3.16–21	Exod. 16.11–end; Col. 2.1–15	Deut. 3.18–end; John 20.19–end *or* Evening Prayer of St George: Ps. 111, 116; Jer. 15.15–end; Heb. 11.32—12.2

		AW	*Hos. 5.15—6.6*	*1 Cor. 15.1–11*

	HOLY COMMUNION	**MORNING PRAYER**	**EVENING PRAYER**
	BCP		
Psalms:		*107*	*108; 109*
Readings:		*Deut. 3.18–end;* *Acts 3.1—4.4*	*Deut. 4.1–24;* *Acts 4.5–31*
Hymns:	....	....	....

2020

	January	February	March	April	May	June
S	5 12 19 26	2 9 16 23	1 8 15 22 29	5 12 19 26	3 10 17 24 31	7 14 21 28
M	6 13 20 27	3 10 17 24	2 9 16 23 30	6 13 20 27	4 11 18 25	1 8 15 22 29
T	7 14 21 28	4 11 18 25	3 10 17 24 31	7 14 21 28	5 12 19 26	2 9 16 23 30
W	1 8 15 22 29	5 12 19 26	4 11 18 25	1 8 15 22 29	6 13 20 27	3 10 17 24
T	2 9 16 23 30	6 13 20 27	5 12 19 26	2 9 16 23 30	7 14 21 28	4 11 18 25
F	3 10 17 24 31	7 14 21 28	6 13 20 27	3 10 17 24	1 8 15 22 29	5 12 19 26
S	4 11 18 25	1 8 15 22 29	7 14 21 28	4 11 18 25	2 9 16 23 30	6 13 20 27

George, Martyr. Patron of England, c.304   Red

	PRINCIPAL SERVICE	THIRD SERVICE	SECOND SERVICE
	CW		
Psalms:	126	5; 146	3; 11
Readings:	1 Macc. 2.59–64 *or* Rev. 12.7–12; 2 Tim. 2.3–13; John 15.18–21	Josh. 1.1–9; Eph. 6.10–20	Isa. 43.1–7; John 15.1–8

Seasonal provisions CW Book pp 328–329

Displaced readings may be added to the previous or following days' portion

	EUCHARIST	MORNING PRAYER	EVENING PRAYER
Readings:	Acts 5.27–33; John 3.31–end	Exod. 17; Col. 2.16—3.11	Deut. 4.1–14; John 21.1–14

	HOLY COMMUNION	MORNING PRAYER	EVENING PRAYER
	BCP Com. Martyr		
Psalms:	3	110; 111; 112; 113	114; 115
Readings:	*Jer. 1.1.18–20; Heb. 11.32—12.2;* *Matt. 16.24–27*	*Deut. 4.25–40;* *Acts 4.32—5.11*	*Deut. 5.1–21;* *Acts 5.12—6.7*
Hymns:	....	....	....

CW COLLECT

God of hosts,
who so kindled the flame of love
in the heart of your servant George
that he bore witness to the risen Lord
by his life and by his death:
give us the same faith and power of love
that we who rejoice in his triumphs
may come to share with him the fullness of
   the resurrection;
through Jesus Christ your Son our Lord,
who is alive and reigns with you,
in the unity of the Holy Spirit,
one God, now and for ever.

POST COMMUNION

Eternal God,
who gave us this holy meal
in which we have celebrated the glory of the cross
and the victory of your martyr George:
by our communion with Christ
in his saving death and resurrection,
give us with all your saints the courage to
   conquer evil
and so to share the fruit of the tree of life;
   through Jesus Christ our Lord.

BCP COLLECT

Almighty God, by whose grace and power thy
holy Martyr George triumphed over suffering
and despised death: Grant, we beseech thee, that
enduring hardness and waxing valiant in fight,
we may with the noble army of martyrs receive
the crown of everlasting life; through Jesus Christ
our Lord.

2020

July						August						September						October						November						December					
S		5	12	19	26	S		2	9	16	23	30	S		6	13	20	27	S		4	11	18	25	S	1	8	15	22	29	S		6	13	20	27
M		6	13	20	27	M		3	10	17	24	31	M		7	14	21	28	M		5	12	19	26	M	2	9	16	23	30	M		7	14	21	28
T		7	14	21	28	T		4	11	18	25		T	1	8	15	22	29	T		6	13	20	27	T	3	10	17	24		T	1	8	15	22	29
W	1	8	15	22	29	W		5	12	19	26		W	2	9	16	23	30	W		7	14	21	28	W	4	11	18	25		W	2	9	16	23	30
T	2	9	16	23	30	T		6	13	20	27		T	3	10	17	24		T	1	8	15	22	29	T	5	12	19	26		T	3	10	17	24	31
F	3	10	17	24	31	F		7	14	21	28		F	4	11	18	25		F	2	9	16	23	30	F	6	13	20	27		F	4	11	18	25	
S	4	11	18	25		S	1	8	15	22	29		S	5	12	19	26		S	3	10	17	24	31	S	7	14	21	28		S	5	12	19	26	

Mellitus, Bishop of London, first bishop at St Paul's 624
The Seven Martyrs of the Melanesian Brotherhood Solomon Islands 2003

White

	EUCHARIST CW	**MORNING PRAYER**	**EVENING PRAYER**
Psalms:	27.1–5, 16–17	57; *61*	*118*
Readings:	Acts 5.34–42; John 6.1–15	Exod. 18.1–12; Col. 3.12—4.1	Deut. 4.15–31; John 21.15–19 *or* Eve of St Mark: Ps. 19; Isa. 52.7–10; Mark 1.1–15

		AW	Gen. 6.9–end	1 Pet. 3.8–end

	HOLY COMMUNION BCP	**MORNING PRAYER**	**EVENING PRAYER**
Psalms:		116; 117; 118	119.1–32
Readings:		Deut. 5.22–end; Acts 6.8—7.16	Deut. 6; Acts 7.17–34 *or First Evensong of St Mark:* Ezek. 1; Acts 12.25—13.13
Hymns:	....	....	....

2020

	January					February					March					April					May						June			
S		5	12	19	26		2	9	16	23		1	8	15	22	29		5	12	19	26		3	10	17	24	31			7	14	21	28
M		6	13	20	27		3	10	17	24		2	9	16	23	30		6	13	20	27		4	11	18	25			1	8	15	22	29
T		7	14	21	28		4	11	18	25		3	10	17	24	31		7	14	21	28		5	12	19	26			2	9	16	23	30
W	1	8	15	22	29		5	12	19	26		4	11	18	25		1	8	15	22	29		6	13	20	27			3	10	17	24	
T	2	9	16	23	30		6	13	20	27		5	12	19	26		2	9	16	23	30		7	14	21	28			4	11	18	25	
F	3	10	17	24	31		7	14	21	28		6	13	20	27		3	10	17	24		1	8	15	22	29			5	12	19	26	
S	4	11	18	25		1	8	15	22	29		7	14	21	28		4	11	18	25		2	9	16	23	30			6	13	20	27	

Mark the Evangelist Red

	PRINCIPAL SERVICE	THIRD SERVICE	SECOND SERVICE
	CW		
Psalms:	119.9–16	37.23–41; 148	45
Readings:	Prov. 15.28–end *or*	Isa. 62.6–10 *or*	Ezek. 1.4–14;
	Acts 15.35–end;	Ecclus 51.13–end;	2 Tim. 4.1–11
	Eph. 4.7–16; Mark 13.5 –13	Acts 12.25—13.13	

Displaced readings may be added to the following days portion

	EUCHARIST	MORNING PRAYER	EVENING PRAYER
	CW		
Readings:	Acts 6.1–7;	Exod. 18.13–end;	Deut. 4.32–40;
	John 6.16–21	Col. 4.2–end	John 21.20–end

	HOLY COMMUNION	MORNING PRAYER	EVENING PRAYER
	BCP St Mark		
Psalms:	119.6–16	119.33–72	119.73–104
Readings:	Prov. 15.28–33;	Ecclus 51.13–end;	Isa. 62.6–end;
	Eph. 4.7–16; John 15.1–11	Acts 15.35–end	2 Tim. 4.1–11;
			E. Coll. Easter 2

Hymns:

CW COLLECT
Almighty God,
who enlightened your holy Church
through the inspired witness
    of your evangelist Saint Mark:
grant that we, being firmly grounded
    in the truth of the gospel,
may be faithful to its teaching both in word and deed;
through Jesus Christ your Son our Lord,
who is alive and reigns with you,
in the unity of the Holy Spirit,
one God, now and for ever.

POST COMMUNION
Lord God, the source of truth and love,
keep us faithful to the apostles' teaching and
    fellowship,
united in prayer and the breaking of bread,
and one in joy and simplicity of heart,
in Jesus Christ our Lord.

BCP COLLECT
*O almighty God, who hast instructed thy holy Church
with the heavenly doctrine of thy Evangelist Saint
Mark: Give us grace, that, being not like children
carried away with every blast of vain doctrine, we
may be established in the truth of thy holy Gospel;
through Jesus Christ our Lord.*

THE THIRD SUNDAY OF EASTER
Easter 2
(White)

	PRINCIPAL SERVICE	THIRD SERVICE	SECOND SERVICE
	CW		
Psalms:	116.1–3, 10–17 [116.1–7]	23	48
Readings:	Acts 2.14a, 36–41;	Isa. 40.1–11;	Hag. 1.13—2.9;
	Alt. O.T. Zeph. 3.14–end;	1 Pet. 5.1–11	1 Cor. 3.10–17;
	if used Acts must be second		[John 2.13–22]
	reading		
	1 Pet. 1.17–23;		
	Luke 24.13–35		

Seasonal provisions CW Book pp 316–317

	HOLY COMMUNION	MORNING PRAYER	EVENING PRAYER
	BCP		
Psalms:	23	23	48
Readings:	Ezek. 34.11–16a;	Exod. 16.2–15 or Isa. 55;	Exod. 32 or Exod. 33.7–end or
	1 Pet. 2.19–end;	John 5.19–29 or 1 Cor. 15.35–end	Isa. 56.1–8;
	John 10.11–16		John 21 or Phil. 3.7–end
Hymns:	....	....	....

CW COLLECTS

Almighty Father,
who in your great mercy gladdened the disciples
    with the sight of the risen Lord:
give us such knowledge of his presence with us,
that we may be strengthened and sustained
    by his risen life
and serve you continually in righteousness and truth;
through Jesus Christ your Son our Lord,
who is alive and reigns with you,
in the unity of the Holy Spirit,
one God, now and for ever.

or

Risen Christ,
you filled your disciples with boldness and
    fresh hope:
strengthen us also to proclaim your risen life
and fill us with your peace,
to the glory of God the Father.

POST COMMUNION

Living God,
your Son made himself known to his disciples
in the breaking of bread:
open the eyes of our faith,
that we may see him in all his redeeming work;
who is alive and reigns, now and for ever.

BCP COLLECT

Almighty God, who hast given thine only Son to be unto us both a sacrifice for sin, and also an ensample of godly life: Give us grace that we may always most thankfully receive that his inestimable benefit, and also daily endeavour ourselves to follow the blessed steps of his most holy life; through the same Jesus Christ our Lord.

2020

July				August					September				October				November					December			
S	5	12	19	26	**S**	2	9	16	23	30	**S**	6	13	20	27	**S**	4	11	18	25	**S**	1	8	15	22	29	**S**	6	13	20	27
M	6	13	20	27	**M**	3	10	17	24	31	**M**	7	14	21	28	**M**	5	12	19	26	**M**	2	9	16	23	30	**M**	7	14	21	28
T	7	14	21	28	**T**	4	11	18	25	**T**	1	8	15	22	29	**T**	6	13	20	27	**T**	3	10	17	24	**T**	1	8	15	22	29
W	1	8	15	22	29	**W**	5	12	19	26	**W**	2	9	16	23	30	**W**	7	14	21	28	**W**	4	11	18	25	**W**	2	9	16	23	30
T	2	9	16	23	30	**T**	6	13	20	27	**T**	3	10	17	24	**T**	1	8	15	22	29	**T**	5	12	19	26	**T**	3	10	17	24	31
F	3	10	17	24	31	**F**	7	14	21	28	**F**	4	11	18	25	**F**	2	9	16	23	30	**F**	6	13	20	27	**F**	4	11	18	25
S	4	11	18	25	**S**	1	8	15	22	29	**S**	5	12	19	26	**S**	3	10	17	24	31	**S**	7	14	21	28	**S**	5	12	19	26

Christina Rossetti, Poet, 1894

White

	EUCHARIST	**MORNING PRAYER**	**EVENING PRAYER**
	CW		
Psalms:	119.17–24	*96*; 97	*61*; 65
Readings:	Acts 6.8–15;	Exod. 19;	Deut. 5.1–22;
	John 6.22–29	Luke 1.1–25	Eph. 1.1–14

		AW	*Exod. 24.1–11*	*Rev. 5*

	HOLY COMMUNION	**MORNING PRAYER**	**EVENING PRAYER**
	BCP		
Psalms:		*120; 121; 122; 123; 124; 125*	*126; 127; 128; 129; 130; 131*
Readings:		*Deut. 8;*	*Deut. 9.1–10;*
		Acts 8.26–end	*Acts 9.1–31*
Hymns:	....	....	....

Sunrise 05.36; Sunset 20.19

Peter Chanel, Missionary in the South Pacific, Martyr 1841   White

	EUCHARIST	**MORNING PRAYER**	**EVENING PRAYER**
	CW		
Psalms:	31.1–5, 16	*98*; 99; 100	*71*
Readings:	Acts 7.51—8.1a;	Exod. 20.1–21;	Deut. 5.22–end;
	John 6.30–35	Luke 1.26–38	Eph. 1.15–end
	AW	*Lev. 19.9–18, 32–end*	*Matt. 5.38–end*

	HOLY COMMUNION	**MORNING PRAYER**	**EVENING PRAYER**
	BCP		
Psalms:		132; 133; 134; 135	136; 137; 138
Readings:		*Deut. 9.11–end;*	*Deut. 10;*
		Acts 9.32–end	*Acts 10.1–23*
Hymns:	....	....	....

2020

	July					August						September					October					November					December			
S		5	12	19	26		2	9	16	23	30		6	13	20	27		4	11	18	25		1	8	15	22	29		6	13	20	27
M		6	13	20	27		3	10	17	24	31		7	14	21	28		5	12	19	26		2	9	16	23	30		7	14	21	28
T		7	14	21	28		4	11	18	25		1	8	15	22	29		6	13	20	27		3	10	17	24		1	8	15	22	29
W	1	8	15	22	29		5	12	19	26		2	9	16	23	30		7	14	21	28		4	11	18	25		2	9	16	23	30
T	2	9	16	23	30		6	13	20	27		3	10	17	24		1	8	15	22	29		5	12	19	26		3	10	17	24	31
F	3	10	17	24	31		7	14	21	28		4	11	18	25		2	9	16	23	30		6	13	20	27		4	11	18	25
S	4	11	18	25		1	8	15	22	29		5	12	19	26		3	10	17	24	31		7	14	21	28		5	12	19	26

Catherine of Siena, Teacher of the Faith 1380 (CW Readings see Common of the Saints
also Prov. 8.1, 6–11; John 17.12–26)

White

	EUCHARIST CW	MORNING PRAYER	EVENING PRAYER
Psalms:	66.1–6	*105*	67; *72*
Readings:	Acts 8.1b–8; John 6.35–40	Exod. 24; Luke 1.39–56	Deut. 6; Eph. 2.1–10
AW		*Gen. 3.8–21*	*1 Cor. 15.12–28*

	HOLY COMMUNION BCP	MORNING PRAYER	EVENING PRAYER
Psalms:		139; 140; 141	*142; 143*
Readings:		*Deut. 11.1–12; Acts 10.24–end*	*Deut. 11.13–end; Acts 11.1–18*
Hymns:			

CW COLLECT

God of compassion,
who gave your servant Catherine of Siena
a wondrous love of the passion of Christ:
grant that your people
may be united to him in his majesty
and rejoice for ever in the revelation of his glory;
who is alive and reigns with you,
in the unity of the Holy Spirit,
one God, now and for ever.

POST COMMUNION

God of truth
whose Wisdom set her table
and invited us to eat the bread and drink the wine
of the kingdom:
help us to lay aside all foolishness
and to live and walk in the way of insight,
that we may come with Catherine
to the eternal feast of heaven;
through Jesus Christ our Lord.

2020					
January	**February**	**March**	**April**	**May**	**June**
S 5 12 19 26	S 2 9 16 23	S 1 8 15 22 29	S 5 12 19 26	S 3 10 17 24 31	S 7 14 21 28
M 6 13 20 27	M 3 10 17 24	M 2 9 16 23 30	M 6 13 20 27	M 4 11 18 25	M 1 8 15 22 29
T 7 14 21 28	T 4 11 18 25	T 3 10 17 24 31	T 7 14 21 28	T 5 12 19 26	T 2 9 16 23 30
W 1 8 15 22 29	W 5 12 19 26	W 4 11 18 25	W 1 8 15 22 29	W 6 13 20 27	W 3 10 17 24
T 2 9 16 23 30	T 6 13 20 27	T 5 12 19 26	T 2 9 16 23 30	T 7 14 21 28	T 4 11 18 25
F 3 10 17 24 31	F 7 14 21 28	F 6 13 20 27	F 3 10 17 24	F 1 8 15 22 29	F 5 12 19 26
S 4 11 18 25	S 1 8 15 22 29	S 7 14 21 28	S 4 11 18 25	S 2 9 16 23 30	S 6 13 20 27

Pandita Mary Ramabai, Translator of the Scriptures, 1922   White

	EUCHARIST	**MORNING PRAYER**	**EVENING PRAYER**
	CW		
Psalms:	66.7–8, 14–end	*136*	*73*
Readings:	Acts 8.26–end;	Exod. 25.1–22;	Deut. 7.1–11;
	John 6.44–51	Luke 1.57–end	Eph. 2.11–end *or* Eve of
			Philip and James
			Ps. 25 [BCP Var. 119.1–81];
			Isa. 40.27–end; John 12.20–26

		AW	*Isa. 33.13–22*	*Mark 6.47–end*

	HOLY COMMUNION	**MORNING PRAYER**	**EVENING PRAYER**
	BCP		
Psalms:		144; 145; 146	147; 148; 149; 150
Readings:		Deut. 12.1–14;	Deut. 15.1–18;
		Acts 11.19–end	Acts 12.1–24
			or *First Evensong of S. Philip and*
			S. James Prov. 4.10–18;
			John 1.43–end
Hymns:	....	....	....

2020

	July				August					September				October				November				December			
S		5	12	19	26		2	9	16	23	30		6	13	20	27		4	11	18	25		1	8	15	22	29		6	13	20	27
M		6	13	20	27		3	10	17	24	31		7	14	21	28		5	12	19	26		2	9	16	23	30		7	14	21	28
T		7	14	21	28		4	11	18	25		1	8	15	22	29		6	13	20	27		3	10	17	24		1	8	15	22	29
W	1	8	15	22	29		5	12	19	26	2	9	16	23	30		7	14	21	28		4	11	18	25		2	9	16	23	30
T	2	9	16	23	30		6	13	20	27	3	10	17	24		1	8	15	22	29		5	12	19	26		3	10	17	24	31
F	3	10	17	24	31		7	14	21	28	4	11	18	25		2	9	16	23	30		6	13	20	27		4	11	18	25
S	4	11	18	25	1	8	15	22	29	5	12	19	26		3	10	17	24	31		7	14	21	28		5	12	19	26

Philip and James, Apostles Red

	PRINCIPAL SERVICE	THIRD SERVICE	SECOND SERVICE
	CW		
Psalms:	119.1–8	139; 146	149
Readings:	Isa. 30.15–21; Eph. 1.3–10; John 14.1–14	Prov. 4.10–18 [BCP Var. Isa. 30.1–5] Jas 1.1–12 [BCP Var. John 12.20–26]	Job 23.1–12; John 1.43–end

Displaced readings may be added to the previous or next day's portion

	EUCHARIST	MORNING PRAYER	EVENING PRAYER
	CW		
Readings:	Acts 9.1–20; John 6.52–59	Exod. 28.1–4a, 29–38; Luke 2.1–20	Deut. 7.12–end; Eph. 3.1–13

	HOLY COMMUNION	MORNING PRAYER	EVENING PRAYER
	BCP SS Philip & James		
Psalms:	25.1–9	1; 2; 3; 4; 5	6; 7; 8
Readings:	Prov. 4.10–18; Jas 1, [1]2–12; John 14.1–14	Job 23.1–12; John 6.1–14	Isa. 30.15–21; John 17.1–8
Hymns:	....	....	....

CW COLLECT

Almighty Father,
whom truly to know is eternal life:
teach us to know your Son Jesus Christ
as the way, the truth, and the life;
that we may follow the steps
     of your holy apostles Philip and James,
and walk steadfastly in the way that leads to
     your glory;
through Jesus Christ your Son our Lord,
who is alive and reigns with you,
in the unity of the Holy Spirit,
one God, now and for ever.

POST COMMUNION

Almighty God,
who on the day of Pentecost
sent your Holy Spirit to the apostles
with the wind from heaven and in tongues of flame,
filling them with joy and boldness to preach
     the gospel:
by the power of the same Spirit
strengthen us to witness to your truth
and to draw everyone to the fire of your love;
through Jesus Christ our Lord.

BCP COLLECT

O Almighty God, whom truly to know is everlasting life: Grant us perfectly to know thy Son Jesus Christ to be the way, the truth, and the life; that, following the steps of thy holy Apostles, Saint Philip and Saint James, we may stedfastly walk in the way that leadeth to eternal life; through the same thy Son Jesus Christ our Lord.

2020

	January					February					March					April					May						June			
S		5	12	19	26		2	9	16	23		1	8	15	22	29		5	12	19	26			3	10	17	24	31		7	14	21	28
M		6	13	20	27		3	10	17	24		2	9	16	23	30		6	13	20	27			4	11	18	25		1	8	15	22	29
T		7	14	21	28		4	11	18	25		3	10	17	24	31		7	14	21	28			5	12	19	26		2	9	16	23	30
W	1	8	15	22	29		5	12	19	26		4	11	18	25		1	8	15	22	29			6	13	20	27		3	10	17	24	
T	2	9	16	23	30		6	13	20	27		5	12	19	26		2	9	16	23	30			7	14	21	28		4	11	18	25	
F	3	10	17	24	31		7	14	21	28		6	13	20	27		3	10	17	24		1	8	15	22	29			5	12	19	26	
S	4	11	18	25		1	8	15	22	29		7	14	21	28		4	11	18	25		2	9	16	23	30			6	13	20	27	

Athanasius, Bishop of Alexandria, Teacher of the Faith, 373 (CW Reading   White
see Common of the Saints also Ecclus 4.20–28 and Matt. 10.24–27

	EUCHARIST	**MORNING PRAYER**	**EVENING PRAYER**
	CW		
Psalms:	116.10–15	108; *110*; 111	23; *27*
Readings:	Acts 9.31–42;	Exod. 29.1–9;	Deut. 8;
	John 6.60–69	Luke 2.21–40	Eph. 3.14–end

			MORNING PRAYER	**EVENING PRAYER**
		AW	*Isa. 61.10—62.5*	*Luke 24.1–12*

	HOLY COMMUNION	**MORNING PRAYER**	**EVENING PRAYER**
	BCP		
Psalms:		*9; 10; 11*	*12; 13; 14*
Readings:		*Deut. 18.9–end;*	*Deut. 19;*
		Acts 13.44—14.7	*Acts 14.8–end*
Hymns:	....	....	....

CW COLLECT
Ever-living God,
whose servant Athanasius testified
to the mystery of the Word made flesh for
    our salvation:
help us, with all your saints,
to contend for the truth
and to grow into the likeness of your Son,
Jesus Christ our Lord,
who is alive and reigns with you,
in the unity of the Holy Spirit,
one God, now and for ever.

POST COMMUNION
God of truth,
whose Wisdom set her table
and invited us to eat the bread and drink the wine
    of the kingdom:
help us to lay aside all foolishness
and to live and walk in the way of insight,
that we may come with Athanasius
to the eternal feast of heaven;
through Jesus Christ our Lord.

2020

	July					August						September					October					November					December			
S		5	12	19	26	S		2	9	16	23	30	S		6	13	20	27	S		4	11	18	25	S	1	8	15	22	29	S		6	13	20	27
M		6	13	20	27	M		3	10	17	24	31	M		7	14	21	28	M		5	12	19	26	M	2	9	16	23	30	M		7	14	21	28
T		7	14	21	28	T		4	11	18	25	T	1	8	15	22	29	T		6	13	20	27	T	3	10	17	24	T	1	8	15	22	29
W	1	8	15	22	29	W		5	12	19	26	W	2	9	16	23	30	W		7	14	21	28	W	4	11	18	25	W	2	9	16	23	30
T	2	9	16	23	30	T		6	13	20	27	T	3	10	17	24	T	1	8	15	22	29	T	5	12	19	26	T	3	10	17	24	31
F	3	10	17	24	31	F		7	14	21	28	F	4	11	18	25	F	2	9	16	23	30	F	6	13	20	27	F	4	11	18	25
S	4	11	18	25	S	1	8	15	22	29	S	5	12	19	26	S	3	10	17	24	31	S	7	14	21	28	S	5	12	19	26

THE FOURTH SUNDAY OF EASTER
Easter 3
(White)

	PRINCIPAL SERVICE	THIRD SERVICE	SECOND SERVICE
	CW		
Psalms:	23	106.6–24	29.1–10
Readings:	Acts 2.42–end;	Neh. 9.6–15;	Ezra. 3.1–13;
	Alt. O.T. Gen. 7; if used, Acts	1 Cor. 10.1–13	Eph. 2.11–end;
	must be second reading		[Luke 19.37–48]
	1 Pet. 2.19–end; John 10.1–10		
	Seasonal provisions CW Book p 316–317		

	HOLY COMMUNION	MORNING PRAYER	EVENING PRAYER
	BCP		
Psalms:	57	106.6–24	29.1–10
Readings:	Gen. 45.3–10;	Num. 22.1–35 or Isa. 57.15–end;	Num. 22.36—23.26 or
	1 Pet. 2.11–17;	Mark 5.21–end or	Num. 23.27—end of 24 or
	John 16.16–22	Acts 2.22–end	Isa. 59; John 11.1–44 or
			Rev. 2.1–17
Hymns:	....	....	....

CW COLLECTS

Almighty God,
whose Son Jesus Christ is the resurrection and
  the life:
raise us, who trust in him,
from the death of sin to the life of righteousness,
that we may seek those things which are above,
where he reigns with you
in the unity of the Holy Spirit,
one God, now and for ever.

or

Risen Christ,
faithful shepherd of your Father's sheep:
teach us to hear your voice
and to follow your command,
that all your people may be gathered into one flock,
to the glory of God the Father.

POST COMMUNION

Merciful Father,
you gave your Son Jesus Christ to be the
  good shepherd,
and in his love for us to lay down his life and
  rise again:
keep us always under his protection,
and give us grace to follow in his steps;
through Jesus Christ our Lord.

BCP COLLECT

*Almighty God, who shewest to them that be in error
the light of thy truth, to the intent that they may
return into the way of righteousness: Grant unto all
them that are admitted into the fellowship of Christ's
religion, that they may eschew those things that
are contrary to their profession, and follow all such
things as are agreeable to the same; through our
Lord Jesus Christ.*

2020

	July					August						September					October					November					December			
S		5	12	19	26		2	9	16	23	30		6	13	20	27		4	11	18	25		1	8	15	22	29		6	13	20	27
M		6	13	20	27		3	10	17	24	31		7	14	21	28		5	12	19	26		2	9	16	23	30		7	14	21	28
T		7	14	21	28		4	11	18	25			1	8	15	22	29		6	13	20	27		3	10	17	24			1	8	15	22	29
W	1	8	15	22	29		5	12	19	26		2	9	16	23	30		7	14	21	28		4	11	18	25		2	9	16	23	30
T	2	9	16	23	30		6	13	20	27		3	10	17	24		1	8	15	22	29		5	12	19	26		3	10	17	24	31
F	3	10	17	24	31		7	14	21	28		4	11	18	25		2	9	16	23	30		6	13	20	27		4	11	18	25
S	4	11	18	25		1	8	15	22	29		5	12	19	26		3	10	17	24	31		7	14	21	28		5	12	19	26

English Saints and Martyrs of the Reformation Era   Bank Holiday (UK)   White
CW: **Lesser Festival EUCHARIST:** Isa. 43.1–7 *or* Ecclus 2.10–17; Ps. 87; 2 Cor. 4.5–12; John 12.20–26

	EUCHARIST CW	MORNING PRAYER	EVENING PRAYER
Psalms:	42.1–2; 43.1–4	*103*	112; 113; *114*
Readings:	Acts 11.1–18; John 10.1–10 [*or* 11–18]	Exod. 32.1–14; Luke 2.41–end	Deut. 9.1–21; Eph. 4.1–16

		AW	Jer. 31.10–17	Rev. 7.9–end

	HOLY COMMUNION BCP	MORNING PRAYER	EVENING PRAYER
Psalms:		19; 20; 21	22; 23
Readings:		Deut. 21.22—22.8; Acts 15.1–21	Deut. 24.5–end; Acts 15.22–35
Hymns:	....	....	....

CW COLLECT
Merciful God,
who, when your Church on earth was torn apart
    by the ravages of sin,
raised up men and women in this land
who witnessed to their faith with courage
    and constancy:
give to your Church that peace which is your will,
and grant that those who have been divided on earth
    may be reconciled in heaven,
and share together in the vision of your glory;
through Jesus Christ your Son our Lord,
who is alive and reigns with you,
in the unity of the Holy Spirit,
one God, now and for ever.

POST COMMUNION
God, the source of all holiness
and giver of all good things:
may we who have shared at this table
as strangers and pilgrims here on earth
be welcomed with all your saints
to the heavenly feast on the day of your kingdom;
through Jesus Christ our Lord.

Sunrise 05.23; Sunset 20.31

2020

January				February				March				April				May					June			
S	5	12	19	26	S		2	9	16	23	S	1	8	15	22	29	S		5	12	19	26	S		3	10	17	24	31	S		7	14	21	28
M	6	13	20	27	M		3	10	17	24	M	2	9	16	23	30	M		6	13	20	27	M		4	11	18	25	M	1	8	15	22	29
T	7	14	21	28	T		4	11	18	25	T	3	10	17	24	31	T		7	14	21	28	T		5	12	19	26	T	2	9	16	23	30
W	1	8	15	22	29	W		5	12	19	26	W	4	11	18	25	W	1	8	15	22	29	W		6	13	20	27	W	3	10	17	24
T	2	9	16	23	30	T		6	13	20	27	T	5	12	19	26	T	2	9	16	23	30	T		7	14	21	28	T	4	11	18	25
F	3	10	17	24	31	F		7	14	21	28	F	6	13	20	27	F	3	10	17	24	F	1	8	15	22	29	F	5	12	19	26
S	4	11	18	25	S	1	8	15	22	29	S	7	14	21	28	S	4	11	18	25	S	2	9	16	23	30	S	6	13	20	27

	EUCHARIST	MORNING PRAYER	EVENING PRAYER
	CW		
Psalms:	87	*139*	115; *116*
Readings:	Acts 11.19–26;	Exod. 32.15–34;	Deut. 9.23—10.5;
	John 10.22–30	Luke 3.1–14	Eph. 4.17–end

		AW	*Job 31.13–23*	*Matt. 7.1–12*

	HOLY COMMUNION	MORNING PRAYER	EVENING PRAYER
	BCP		
Psalms:		*24; 25; 26*	*27; 28; 29*
Readings:		*Deut. 26;*	*Deut. 28.58–end;*
		Acts 15.36—16.5	*Acts 16.6–end*
Hymns:	....	....	....

2020

	July				August					September				October				November					December			
S		5	12	19	26		2	9	16	23	30		6	13	20	27		4	11	18	25		1	8	15	22	29		6	13	20	27
M		6	13	20	27		3	10	17	24	31		7	14	21	28		5	12	19	26		2	9	16	23	30		7	14	21	28
T		7	14	21	28		4	11	18	25		1	8	15	22	29		6	13	20	27		3	10	17	24		1	8	15	22	29
W	1	8	15	22	29		5	12	19	26		2	9	16	23	30		7	14	21	28		4	11	18	25		2	9	16	23	30
T	2	9	16	23	30		6	13	20	27		3	10	17	24		1	8	15	22	29		5	12	19	26		3	10	17	24	31
F	3	10	17	24	31		7	14	21	28		4	11	18	25		2	9	16	23	30		6	13	20	27		4	11	18	25
S	4	11	18	25		1	8	15	22	29		5	12	19	26		3	10	17	24	31		7	14	21	28		5	12	19	26

St John the Evangelist ante portam Latinam (BCP)　　　　　　　　　　　White

	EUCHARIST	MORNING PRAYER	EVENING PRAYER
	CW		
Psalms:	67	*135*	*47*; 48
Readings:	Acts 12.24—13.5;	Exod. 33;	Deut. 10.12–end;
	John 12.44–end	Luke 3.15–22	Eph. 5.1–14

　　　　　　　　　　　　　　AW　　*Gen. 2.4b–9*　　　　　　　*1 Cor. 15.35–49*

	HOLY COMMUNION	MORNING PRAYER	EVENING PRAYER
	BCP CEG of Dec. 27		
Psalms:		30; 31	32; 33; 34
Readings:		Deut. 29.10–end;	Deut. 30;
		Acts 17.1–15	Acts 17.16–end
Hymns:	....	....	....

BCP COLLECT
Merciful Lord, we beseech thee to cast thy bright beams of light upon thy Church, that it being enlightened by the doctrine of thy blessed Apostle and Evangelist Saint John may so walk in the light of thy truth, that it may at length attain to the light of everlasting life; through Jesus Christ our Lord.

2020

	January	February	March	April	May	June
S	5 12 19 26	2 9 16 23	1 8 15 22 29	5 12 19 26	3 10 17 24 31	7 14 21 28
M	6 13 20 27	3 10 17 24	2 9 16 23 30	6 13 20 27	4 11 18 25	1 8 15 22 29
T	7 14 21 28	4 11 18 25	3 10 17 24 31	7 14 21 28	5 12 19 26	2 9 16 23 30
W	1 8 15 22 29	5 12 19 26	4 11 18 25	1 8 15 22 29	6 13 20 27	3 10 17 24
T	2 9 16 23 30	6 13 20 27	5 12 19 26	2 9 16 23 30	7 14 21 28	4 11 18 25
F	3 10 17 24 31	7 14 21 28	6 13 20 27	3 10 17 24	1 8 15 22 29	5 12 19 26
S	4 11 18 25	1 8 15 22 29	7 14 21 28	4 11 18 25	2 9 16 23 30	6 13 20 27

White

	EUCHARIST	MORNING PRAYER	EVENING PRAYER
	CW		
Psalms:	89.1–2, 20–26	*118*	81; *85*
Readings:	Acts 13.13–25; John 13.16–20	Exod. 34.1–10, 27–end; Luke 4.1–13	Deut. 11.8–end; Eph. 5.15–end

		AW	*Prov. 28.3–end*	*Mark 10.17–31*

	HOLY COMMUNION	MORNING PRAYER	EVENING PRAYER
	BCP		
Psalms:		*35; 36*	*37*
Readings:		Deut. 31.1–13; Acts 18.1–23	Deut. 31.14–29; Acts 18.24—19.7
Hymns:	....	....	....

Full Moon

Julian of Norwich, Spiritual Writer, c.1417 (CW Readings see Common of the Saints also 1 Cor. 13.8–13; Matt. 5.13–16)   White

	EUCHARIST CW	MORNING PRAYER	EVENING PRAYER
Psalms:	2	*33*	*36*; 40
Readings:	Acts 13.26–33; John 14.1–6	Exod. 35.20—36.7; Luke 4.14–30	Deut. 12.1–14; Eph. 6.1–9

		AW	*Eccles. 12.1–8*	*Rom. 6.1–11*

	HOLY COMMUNION BCP	MORNING PRAYER	EVENING PRAYER
Psalms:		*38; 39; 40*	*41; 42; 43*
Readings:		*Deut. 31.30—32.14; Acts 19.8–20*	*Deut. 32.15–47; Acts 19.21–end*
Hymns:	....	....	....

CW COLLECT

Most holy God, the ground of our beseeching,
who through your servant Julian
revealed the wonders of your love:
grant that as we are created in your nature
and restored by your grace,
our wills may be so made one with yours
that we may come to see you face to face
and gaze on you for ever;
through Jesus Christ your Son our Lord,
who is alive and reigns with you,
in the unity of the Holy Spirit,
one God, now and for ever.

POST COMMUNION

Merciful God,
who gave such grace to your servant Julian
that she served you with singleness of heart
and loved you above all things:
help us, whose communion with you
has been renewed in this sacrament,
to forsake all that holds us back from following Christ
and to grow into his likeness from glory to glory;
through Jesus Christ our Lord.

White

	EUCHARIST	**MORNING PRAYER**	**EVENING PRAYER**
	CW		
Psalms:	98.1–5	*34*	*84*; 86
Readings:	Acts 13.44–end;	Exod. 40.17–end;	Deut. 15.1–18;
	John 14.7–14	Luke 4.31–37	Eph. 6.10–end

		AW	*1 Chr. 29.10–13*	*Luke 24.13–35*

	HOLY COMMUNION	**MORNING PRAYER**	**EVENING PRAYER**
	BCP		
Psalms:		*44; 45; 46*	*47; 48; 49*
Readings:		*Deut. 33;*	*Deut. 32.48–end and 34;*
		Acts 20.1–16	*Acts 20.17–end;*
			E. Coll. Easter 4

Hymns: ....

2020

	July					August						September				October				November					December			
S		5	12	19	26		2	9	16	23	30		6	13	20	27		4	11	18	25		1	8	15	22	29		6	13	20	27
M		6	13	20	27		3	10	17	24	31		7	14	21	28		5	12	19	26		2	9	16	23	30		7	14	21	28
T		7	14	21	28		4	11	18	25		1	8	15	22	29		6	13	20	27		3	10	17	24		1	8	15	22	29
W	1	8	15	22	29		5	12	19	26		2	9	16	23	30		7	14	21	28		4	11	18	25		2	9	16	23	30
T	2	9	16	23	30		6	13	20	27		3	10	17	24		1	8	15	22	29		5	12	19	26		3	10	17	24	31
F	3	10	17	24	31		7	14	21	28		4	11	18	25		2	9	16	23	30		6	13	20	27		4	11	18	25
S	4	11	18	25		1	8	15	22	29		5	12	19	26		3	10	17	24	31		7	14	21	28		5	12	19	26

THE FIFTH SUNDAY OF EASTER
Easter 4

(White)

	PRINCIPAL SERVICE	THIRD SERVICE	SECOND SERVICE
	CW		
Psalms:	31.1–5, 15–16 [31.1–5]	30	147.1–12
Readings:	Acts 7.55–end;	Ezek. 37.1–12;	Zech. 4.1–10;
	Alt. O.T. Gen. 8.1–19; if used, Acts	John 5.19–29	Rev. 21.1–14;
	must be second reading		[Luke 2.25–32 [33–38]]
	1 Pet. 2.2–10; John 14.1–14		
	Seasonal provisions CW Book p 316–317		

	HOLY COMMUNION	MORNING PRAYER	EVENING PRAYER
	BCP		
Psalms:	*66.14–end*	*30*	*147.1–11*
Readings:	*Job 19.21–27a;*	*Deut. 4.1–24 or Isa. 60;*	*Deut. 4.25–40 or*
	Jas 1.17–21;	*Luke 16.19–end or*	*Deut. 5 or Isa. 61;*
	John 16.5–15	*Acts 3*	*Luke 7.1–35 or Rev. 2.18—3.6*
Hymns:	....	....	....

CW COLLECTS
Almighty God,
who through your only-begotten Son Jesus Christ
have overcome death and opened to us
   the gate of everlasting life:
grant that, as by your grace going before us
   you put into our minds good desires,
so by your continual help
we may bring them to good effect;
through Jesus Christ our risen Lord,
who is alive and reigns with you,
in the unity of the Holy Spirit,
one God, now and for ever.

or

Risen Christ,
your wounds declare your love for the world
and the wonder of your risen life:
give us compassion and courage
to risk ourselves for those we serve,
to the glory of God the Father.

POST COMMUNION
Eternal God,
whose Son Jesus Christ is the way,
   the truth, and the life:
grant us to walk in his way,
to rejoice in his truth,
and to share his risen life;
who is alive and reigns, now and for ever.

BCP COLLECT
*O Almighty God, who alone canst order the unruly
wills and affections of sinful men; Grant unto thy
people, that they may love the thing which thou
commandest, and desire that which thou dost
promise; that so, among the sundry and manifold
changes of the world, our hearts may surely there be
fixed, where true joys are to be found; through Jesus
Christ our Lord.*

2020

July					August						September					October					November					December			
S		5	12	19	26	S		2	9	16	23	30	S		6	13	20	27	S		4	11	18	25	S	1	8	15	22	29	S		6	13	20	27
M		6	13	20	27	M		3	10	17	24	31	M		7	14	21	28	M		5	12	19	26	M	2	9	16	23	30	M		7	14	21	28
T		7	14	21	28	T		4	11	18	25		T	1	8	15	22	29	T		6	13	20	27	T	3	10	17	24		T	1	8	15	22	29
W	1	8	15	22	29	W		5	12	19	26		W	2	9	16	23	30	W		7	14	21	28	W	4	11	18	25		W	2	9	16	23	30
T	2	9	16	23	30	T		6	13	20	27		T	3	10	17	24		T	1	8	15	22	29	T	5	12	19	26		T	3	10	17	24	31
F	3	10	17	24	31	F		7	14	21	28		F	4	11	18	25		F	2	9	16	23	30	F	6	13	20	27		F	4	11	18	25
S	4	11	18	25		S	1	8	15	22	29		S	5	12	19	26		S	3	10	17	24	31	S	7	14	21	28		S	5	12	19	26

White

EUCHARIST	MORNING PRAYER	EVENING PRAYER
CW		

Psalms: 118.1–3, 14–15   *145*   *105*

Readings: Acts 14.5–18;   Num. 9.15–end; 10.33–end;   Deut. 16.1–20;
John 14.21–26   Luke 4.38–end   1 Pet. 1.1–12

AW   *Gen. 15.1–18*   *Rom. 4.13–end*

HOLY COMMUNION	MORNING PRAYER	EVENING PRAYER
BCP		

Psalms: *56; 57; 58*   *59; 60; 61*

Readings: Josh. 1;   Josh. 2;
    Acts 21.1–16   Acts 21.17–36

Hymns: ....

Sunrise 05.11; Sunset 20.42

2020

	January					February					March					April					May						June			
S		5	12	19	26		2	9	16	23		1	8	15	22	29		5	12	19	26		3	10	17	24	31		7	14	21	28
M		6	13	20	27		3	10	17	24		2	9	16	23	30		6	13	20	27		4	11	18	25			1	8	15	22	29
T		7	14	21	28		4	11	18	25		3	10	17	24	31		7	14	21	28		5	12	19	26			2	9	16	23	30
W	1	8	15	22	29		5	12	19	26		4	11	18	25		1	8	15	22	29		6	13	20	27			3	10	17	24	
T	2	9	16	23	30		6	13	20	27		5	12	19	26		2	9	16	23	30		7	14	21	28			4	11	18	25	
F	3	10	17	24	31		7	14	21	28		6	13	20	27		3	10	17	24		1	8	15	22	29			5	12	19	26	
S	4	11	18	25		1	8	15	22	29		7	14	21	28		4	11	18	25		2	9	16	23	30			6	13	20	27	

	EUCHARIST CW	**MORNING PRAYER**	**EVENING PRAYER**
Psalms:	145.10–end	*19*; 147.1–12	96; *97*
Readings:	Acts 14.19–end; John 14.27–end	Num. 11.1–33; Luke 5.1–11	Deut. 17.8–end; 1 Pet. 1.13–end

AW   *Deut. 8.1–10*   *Matt. 6.19–end*

	HOLY COMMUNION BCP	**MORNING PRAYER**	**EVENING PRAYER**
Psalms:		*62; 63; 64*	*65; 66; 67*
Readings:		*Josh. 3;* *Acts 21.37—22.22*	*Josh. 4.1—5.1;* *Acts 22.23—23.11*
Hymns:	....	....	....

White

	EUCHARIST	**MORNING PRAYER**	**EVENING PRAYER**
	CW		
Psalms:	122.1–5	*30*; 147.13–end	98; *99*; 100
Readings:	Acts 15.1–6;	Num. 12;	Deut. 18.9–end;
	John 15.1–8	Luke 5.12–26	1 Pet. 2.1–10 *or* Eve of Matthias
			Ps. 147; Isa. 22.15–22; Phil. 3.13b–4.1

		AW	Hos. 13.4–14	1 Cor. 15.50–end

	HOLY COMMUNION	**MORNING PRAYER**	**EVENING PRAYER**
	BCP		
Psalms:		*68*	*69; 70*
Readings:		Josh. 5.13—6.20;	Josh. 7;
		Acts 23.12–end	Acts 24.1–23
Hymns:	....	....	....

2020

	January				February				March				April				May					June			
S		5	12	19	26		2	9	16	23		1	8	15	22	29		5	12	19	26		3	10	17	24	31		7	14	21	28
M		6	13	20	27		3	10	17	24		2	9	16	23	30		6	13	20	27		4	11	18	25		1	8	15	22	29
T		7	14	21	28		4	11	18	25		3	10	17	24	31		7	14	21	28		5	12	19	26		2	9	16	23	30
W	1	8	15	22	29		5	12	19	26		4	11	18	25	1	8	15	22	29		6	13	20	27		3	10	17	24
T	2	9	16	23	30		6	13	20	27		5	12	19	26	2	9	16	23	30		7	14	21	28		4	11	18	25
F	3	10	17	24	31		7	14	21	28		6	13	20	27	3	10	17	24		1	8	15	22	29		5	12	19	26
S	4	11	18	25		1	8	15	22	29		7	14	21	28	4	11	18	25		2	9	16	23	30		6	13	20	27

Matthias the Apostle (may be celebrated on February 24 BCP)   Red

	PRINCIPAL SERVICE CW	**THIRD SERVICE**	**SECOND SERVICE**
Psalms:	15	16; 147.1–12 [BCP Var. 15]	80
Readings:	Isa. 22.15–25; Acts 1.15–26; John 15.9–17 *or* Acts 1.15–26; 1 Cor. 4.1–7; John 15.9–17	1 Sam. 2.27–35 [BCP Var. Jonah 1.1–9]; Acts 2.37–47	1 Sam. 16.1–13a; Matt. 7.15–27

Displaced readings may be added to the previous or following day's portion:

	EUCHARIST CW	**MORNING PRAYER**	**EVENING PRAYER**
Readings:	Acts 15.7–21; John 15.9–11	Num. 13.1–3, 17–end; Luke 5.27–end	Deut. 19; 1 Pet. 2.11–end

	HOLY COMMUNION *BCP*	**MORNING PRAYER**	**EVENING PRAYER**
Psalms:		*71; 72*	*73; 74*
Readings:		*Josh. 9.3–end;* *Acts 24.24—25.12*	*Josh. 10.1–15;* *Acts 25.13–end*
Hymns:	....	....	....

CW COLLECT for Matthias
Almighty God,
who in the place of the traitor Judas
chose your faithful servant Matthias
to be of the number of the Twelve:
preserve your Church from false apostles
and, by the ministry of faithful pastors and teachers,
keep us steadfast in your truth;
through Jesus Christ your Son our Lord,
who is alive and reigns with you,
in the unity of the Holy Spirit,
one God, now and for ever.

POST COMMUNION
Lord God, the source of truth and love,
keep us faithful to the apostles' teaching
   and fellowship,
united in prayer and the breaking of bread,
and one in joy and simplicity of heart,
in Jesus Christ our Lord.

2020

July				August					September				October				November				December			
S		5	12	19	26	**S**		2	9	16	23	30	**S**		6	13	20	27	**S**		4	11	18	25	**S**	1	8	15	22	29	**S**		6	13	20	27
M		6	13	20	27	**M**		3	10	17	24	31	**M**		7	14	21	28	**M**		5	12	19	26	**M**	2	9	16	23	30	**M**		7	14	21	28
T		7	14	21	28	**T**		4	11	18	25		**T**	1	8	15	22	29	**T**		6	13	20	27	**T**	3	10	17	24		**T**	1	8	15	22	29
W	1	8	15	22	29	**W**		5	12	19	26		**W**	2	9	16	23	30	**W**		7	14	21	28	**W**	4	11	18	25		**W**	2	9	16	23	30
T	2	9	16	23	30	**T**		6	13	20	27		**T**	3	10	17	24		**T**	1	8	15	22	29	**T**	5	12	19	26		**T**	3	10	17	24	31
F	3	10	17	24	31	**F**		7	14	21	28		**F**	4	11	18	25		**F**	2	9	16	23	30	**F**	6	13	20	27		**F**	4	11	18	25	
S	4	11	18	25		**S**	1	8	15	22	29		**S**	5	12	19	26		**S**	3	10	17	24	31	**S**	7	14	21	28		**S**	5	12	19	26	

White

	EUCHARIST	MORNING PRAYER	EVENING PRAYER
	CW		
Psalms:	57.8–end	*138*; 149	*66*
Readings:	Acts 15.22–31; John 15.12–17	Num. 14.1–25; Luke 6.1–11	Deut. 21.22—22.8; 1 Pet. 3.1–12
AW		*Ezek. 36.33–end*	*Rom. 8.1–11*

	HOLY COMMUNION	MORNING PRAYER	EVENING PRAYER
	BCP		
Psalms:		75; 76; 77	78
Readings:		Josh. 21.43—22.8; Acts 26	Josh. 22.9–end; Acts 27
Hymns:	....	....	....

2020

	January					February					March					April					May						June			
S		5	12	19	26		2	9	16	23		1	8	15	22	29		5	12	19	26		3	10	17	24	31		7	14	21	28
M		6	13	20	27		3	10	17	24		2	9	16	23	30		6	13	20	27		4	11	18	25			1	8	15	22	29
T		7	14	21	28		4	11	18	25		3	10	17	24	31		7	14	21	28		5	12	19	26			2	9	16	23	30
W	1	8	15	22	29		5	12	19	26		4	11	18	25		1	8	15	22	29		6	13	20	27			3	10	17	24	
T	2	9	16	23	30		6	13	20	27		5	12	19	26		2	9	16	23	30		7	14	21	28			4	11	18	25	
F	3	10	17	24	31		7	14	21	28		6	13	20	27		3	10	17	24		1	8	15	22	29			5	12	19	26	
S	4	11	18	25		1	8	15	22	29		7	14	21	28		4	11	18	25		2	9	16	23	30			6	13	20	27	

Caroline Chisholm, Social Reformer, 1877   White

	EUCHARIST	**MORNING PRAYER**	**EVENING PRAYER**
	CW		
Psalms:	100	*146*; 150	*118*
Readings:	Acts 16.1–10;	Num. 14.26–end;	Deut. 24.5–end;
	John 15.18–21	Luke 6.12–26	1 Pet. 3.13–end

AW   *Isa. 38.9–20*   *Luke 24.33–end*

	HOLY COMMUNION	**MORNING PRAYER**	**EVENING PRAYER**
	BCP		
Psalms:		*79; 80; 81*	*82; 83; 84; 85*
Readings:		*Josh. 23;*	*Josh. 24.1–28;*
		Acts 28.1–15	*Acts 28.16–end;*
			E. Coll. Rogation Sunday

Hymns: ....

THE SIXTH SUNDAY OF EASTER
Rogation Sunday (Easter 5)
(White)

	PRINCIPAL SERVICE	THIRD SERVICE	SECOND SERVICE
	CW		
Psalms:	66.7–18	73.21–28	87; 36.5–10
Readings:	Acts 17.22–31;	Job. 14.1–2, 7–15; 19.23–27a;	Zech. 8.1–13;
	Alt. O.T. Gen. 8.20—9.17;	1 Thess. 4.13–18	Rev. 21.22—22.5;
	if used Acts must be second		[John 21.1–14]
	reading		
	1 Pet. 3.13–22; John 14.15–21		
	Seasonal provision CW Book pp 316–317		

	HOLY COMMUNION	MORNING PRAYER	EVENING PRAYER
	BCP		
Psalms:	*66.1–8*	*73.21–28*	*87; 36.5–10*
Readings:	*Joel 2.21–26; Jas 1.22–end;*	*Deut. 6 or Isa. 62;*	*Deut. 8 or Deut. 10.12—11.1 or*
	John 16.23b–end;	*Luke 20.27—21.4 or*	*Isa. 63.7–end;*
	Rogation Coll. until May 20	*Acts 4.1–33*	*John 6.47–69 or Rev. 3.7–end*
Hymns:	....	....	....

2020

January				February				March				April				May				June			
S	5	12	19	26	S		2	9	16	23	S	1	8	15	22	29	S		5	12	19	26
M	6	13	20	27	M		3	10	17	24	M	2	9	16	23	30	M		6	13	20	27
T	7	14	21	28	T		4	11	18	25	T	3	10	17	24	31	T		7	14	21	28
W	1	8	15	22	29	W		5	12	19	26	W	4	11	18	25	W	1	8	15	22	29
T	2	9	16	23	30	T		6	13	20	27	T	5	12	19	26	T	2	9	16	23	30
F	3	10	17	24	31	F		7	14	21	28	F	6	13	20	27	F	3	10	17	24	
S	4	11	18	25	S	1	8	15	22	29	S	7	14	21	28	S	4	11	18	25

May					June				
S		3	10	17	24	31	S		7	14	21	28
M		4	11	18	25	M	1	8	15	22	29
T		5	12	19	26	T	2	9	16	23	30
W		6	13	20	27	W	3	10	17	24
T		7	14	21	28	T	4	11	18	25
F	1	8	15	22	29	F	5	12	19	26
S	2	9	16	23	30	S	6	13	20	27

CW COLLECTS

God our redeemer,
you have delivered us from the power of darkness
and brought us into the kingdom of your Son:
grant, that as by his death he has recalled us to life,
so by his continual presence in us he may raise us
    to eternal joy;
through Jesus Christ your Son our Lord,
who is alive and reigns with you,
in the unity of the Holy Spirit,
one God, now and for ever.

or

Risen Christ,
by the lakeside you renewed your call to
    your disciples:
help your Church to obey your command
and draw the nations to the fire of your love,
to the glory of God the Father.

POST COMMUNION

God our Father,
whose Son Jesus Christ gives the water of
    eternal life:
may we thirst for you,
the spring of life and source of goodness,
through him who is alive and reigns, now and
    for ever.

BCP COLLECT

*O Lord, from whom all good things do come:
Grant to us thy humble servants, that by thy holy
inspiration we may think those things that be good,
and by thy merciful guiding may perform the same;
through our Lord Jesus Christ.*

2020

July					August						September					October					November					December				
S		5	12	19	26	S		2	9	16	23	30	S		6	13	20	27	S		4	11	18	25	S	1	8	15	22	29	S		6	13	20	27
M		6	13	20	27	M		3	10	17	24	31	M		7	14	21	28	M		5	12	19	26	M	2	9	16	23	30	M		7	14	21	28
T		7	14	21	28	T		4	11	18	25		T	1	8	15	22	29	T		6	13	20	27	T	3	10	17	24		T	1	8	15	22	29
W	1	8	15	22	29	W		5	12	19	26		W	2	9	16	23	30	W		7	14	21	28	W	4	11	18	25		W	2	9	16	23	30
T	2	9	16	23	30	T		6	13	20	27		T	3	10	17	24		T	1	8	15	22	29	T	5	12	19	26		T	3	10	17	24	31
F	3	10	17	24	31	F		7	14	21	28		F	4	11	18	25		F	2	9	16	23	30	F	6	13	20	27		F	4	11	18	25	
S	4	11	18	25		S	1	8	15	22	29		S	5	12	19	26		S	3	10	17	24	31	S	7	14	21	28		S	5	12	19	26	

White

Rogation Day For readings see Common of the Saints   Bank Holiday (UK)

	EUCHARIST	MORNING PRAYER	EVENING PRAYER
	CW		
Psalms:	149.1–5	*65*; 67	*121*; 122; 123
Readings:	Acts 16.11–15;	Num. 16.1–35;	Deut. 26;
	John 15.26—16.4	Luke 6.27–38	1 Pet. 4.1–11
		AW *Prov. 4.1–13*	*Phil. 2.1–11*

	HOLY COMMUNION	MORNING PRAYER	EVENING PRAYER
	BCP Rogation		
Psalms:	107.1–9	*90; 91; 92*	*93; 94*
Readings:	Job 28.1–11; Jas 5.7–11;	*Deut. 7.6–13;*	*Deut. 11.8–21;*
	Luke 6.36–42	*Matt. 6.5–18*	*Matt. 6.19–end*
Hymns:	....	....	....

CW ROGATION COLLECT

Almighty God,
whose will it is that the earth and the sea
    should bear fruit in due season:
bless the labours of those who work on land and sea,
grant us a good harvest
and the grace always to rejoice in your fatherly care;
through Jesus Christ your Son our Lord,
who is alive and reigns with you,
in the unity of the Holy Spirit,
one God, now and for ever.
This collect, or any from the following two days may
be used on any Rogation Day.

POST COMMUNION

God our creator,
you give seed for us to sow and bread for us to eat:
as you have blessed the fruit of our labour in
    this eucharist,
so we ask you to give all your children their
    daily bread,
that the world may praise you for your goodness;
through Jesus Christ our Lord.

Sunrise 05.00; Sunset 20.53

2020

January	February	March	April	May	June
S 5 12 19 26	S 2 9 16 23	S 1 8 15 22 29	S 5 12 19 26	S 3 10 17 24 31	S 7 14 21 28
M 6 13 20 27	M 3 10 17 24	M 2 9 16 23 30	M 6 13 20 27	M 4 11 18 25	M 1 8 15 22 29
T 7 14 21 28	T 4 11 18 25	T 3 10 17 24 31	T 7 14 21 28	T 5 12 19 26	T 2 9 16 23 30
W 1 8 15 22 29	W 5 12 19 26	W 4 11 18 25	W 1 8 15 22 29	W 6 13 20 27	W 3 10 17 24
T 2 9 16 23 30	T 6 13 20 27	T 5 12 19 26	T 2 9 16 23 30	T 7 14 21 28	T 4 11 18 25
F 3 10 17 24 31	F 7 14 21 28	F 6 13 20 27	F 3 10 17 24	F 1 8 15 22 29	F 5 12 19 26
S 4 11 18 25	S 1 8 15 22 29	S 7 14 21 28	S 4 11 18 25	S 2 9 16 23 30	S 6 13 20 27

Dunstan, Archbishop of Canterbury, Restorer of Monastic Life, 988 *(Also BCP)*   White
(CW Readings see Common of the Saints especially Matt. 24.42–46; also Exod. 31.1–5)
Rogation Day

	EUCHARIST	MORNING PRAYER	EVENING PRAYER
	CW		
Psalms:	138	124; 125; *126*; 127	*128*; 129; 130; 131
Readings:	Acts 16.22–34;	Num. 16.36–end;	Deut. 28.1–14;
	John 16.5–11	Luke 6.39–end	1 Pet. 4.12–end

AW		*Isa. 32.12–end*	*Rom. 5.1–11*

	HOLY COMMUNION	MORNING PRAYER	EVENING PRAYER
	BCP Rogation or Com. Bishop		
Psalms:	*121* or *99*	*95; 96; 97*	*98; 99; 100; 101*
Readings:	*Deut. 8.1–10 or Ezek. 34.11–16;*	*Deut. 28.1–14;*	*1 Kgs 8.22–43;*
	Jas 5.16–20 or 1 Tim. 3.15–16;	*Luke 5.1–11*	*Jas 5.1–18*
	Luke 11.5–13 or Mark 4.26–32		
Hymns:	....	....	....

CW COLLECT
Almighty God,
who raised up Dunstan to be a true shepherd of the
    flock, a restorer of monastic life
and a faithful counsellor to those in authority:
give to all pastors the same gifts of your Holy Spirit
that they may be true servants of Christ
    and of all his people;
through Jesus Christ your Son our Lord,
who is alive and reigns with you,
in the unity of the Holy Spirit,
one God, now and for ever.

POST COMMUNION
God, shepherd of your people,
whose servant Dunstan revealed the loving service of
    Christ in his ministry as a pastor of your people:
by this eucharist in which we share
awaken within us the love of Christ
and keep us faithful to our Christian calling;
through him who laid down his life for us,
but is alive and reigns with you, now and for ever.

BCP COLLECT
*O God, the light of the faithful and shepherd of souls,
who didst set blessed Dunstan to be a bishop in the
church, that he might feed thy sheep by his word and
guide them by his example: Grant us, we pray thee,
to keep the faith which he taught, and to follow in his
footsteps; through Jesus Christ our Lord*

CW ROGATION COLLECT
Almighty God and Father,
you have so ordered our life
    that we are dependent on one another:
prosper those engaged in commerce and industry
and direct their minds and hands
that they may rightly use your gifts in the service of
others; through Jesus Christ your Son our Lord,
who is alive and reigns with you, in the unity of the Holy
    Spirit, one God, now and for ever.

For alternative readings see Common of the Saints.

2020

July				
S		5	12	19	26
M		6	13	20	27
T		7	14	21	28
W	1	8	15	22	29
T	2	9	16	23	30
F	3	10	17	24	31
S	4	11	18	25	

August
S		2	9	16	23	30
M		3	10	17	24	31
T		4	11	18	25	
W		5	12	19	26	
T		6	13	20	27	
F		7	14	21	28	
S	1	8	15	22	29	

September
S		6	13	20	27
M		7	14	21	28
T	1	8	15	22	29
W	2	9	16	23	30
T	3	10	17	24	
F	4	11	18	25	
S	5	12	19	26	

October
S		4	11	18	25
M		5	12	19	26
T		6	13	20	27
W		7	14	21	28
T	1	8	15	22	29
F	2	9	16	23	30
S	3	10	17	24	31

November
S	1	8	15	22	29
M	2	9	16	23	30
T	3	10	17	24	
W	4	11	18	25	
T	5	12	19	26	
F	6	13	20	27	
S	7	14	21	28	

December
S		6	13	20	27
M		7	14	21	28
T	1	8	15	22	29
W	2	9	16	23	30
T	3	10	17	24	31
F	4	11	18	25	
S	5	12	19	26	

Alcuin of York, Deacon, Abbot of Tours, 804
(CW readings see Common of the Saints also Col. 3.12–16; John 4.19–24)
White

Rogation Day

	EUCHARIST CW	MORNING PRAYER	EVENING PRAYER
Psalms:	148.1–2, 11–end	*132*; 133	Ps. 15; 24
Readings:	Acts 17.15, 22—18.1; John 16.12–15	Num. 17.1–11; Luke 7.1–10	2 Sam. 23.1–5; Col. 2.20—3.4

At Evening Prayer the readings for the Eve of Ascension Day are used.
At other services, the following readings are used:

	AW	*Isa. 43.1–13*	*Titus 2.11—3.8*

	HOLY COMMUNION BCP Rogation	MORNING PRAYER	EVENING PRAYER
Psalms:	108.1–6	102; 103	104
Readings:	Deut. 34.1–7; Eph. 4.7–13; John 17.1–11	Joel. 2.21–27; John 6.22–40	Song of the Three 29–37; Luke 24.36–end; E. Coll. Ascension Day
Hymns:	....	....	....

CW COLLECT

God of wisdom, eternal light,
who shone in the heart of your servant Alcuin,
revealing to him your power and pity:
scatter the darkness of our ignorance
that, with all our heart and mind and strength,
we may seek your face
and be brought with all your saints
to your holy presence;
through Jesus Christ your Son our Lord,
who is alive and reigns with you,
in the unity of the Holy Spirit,
one God, now and for ever.

POST COMMUNION

Merciful God,
who gave such grace to your servant Alcuin
that he served you with singleness of heart
and loved you above all things:
help us, whose communion with you
   has been renewed in this sacrament,
to forsake all that holds us back from following Christ
and to grow into his likeness from glory to glory;
through Jesus Christ our Lord.

CW ROGATION COLLECT

God our Father,
you never cease the work you have begun
and prosper with your blessing all human labour:
make us wise and faithful stewards of your gifts
that we may serve the common good,
maintain the fabric of our world
and seek that justice where all may share
   the good things you pour upon us;
through Jesus Christ your Son our Lord,
who is alive and reigns with you,
in the unity of the Holy Spirit,
one God, now and for ever.
For alternative readings see Common of the Saints.

2020

January						February						March						April						May							June					
S		5	12	19	26	S		2	9	16	23	S	1	8	15	22	29	S		5	12	19	26	S		3	10	17	24	31	S		7	14	21	28
M		6	13	20	27	M		3	10	17	24	M	2	9	16	23	30	M		6	13	20	27	M		4	11	18	25		M	1	8	15	22	29
T		7	14	21	28	T		4	11	18	25	T	3	10	17	24	31	T		7	14	21	28	T		5	12	19	26		T	2	9	16	23	30
W	1	8	15	22	29	W		5	12	19	26	W	4	11	18	25		W	1	8	15	22	29	W		6	13	20	27		W	3	10	17	24	
T	2	9	16	23	30	T		6	13	20	27	T	5	12	19	26		T	2	9	16	23	30	T		7	14	21	28		T	4	11	18	25	
F	3	10	17	24	31	F		7	14	21	28	F	6	13	20	27		F	3	10	17	24		F	1	8	15	22	29		F	5	12	19	26	
S	4	11	18	25		S	1	8	15	22	29	S	7	14	21	28		S	4	11	18	25		S	2	9	16	23	30		S	6	13	20	27	

ASCENSION DAY

Gold *or* White

	PRINCIPAL SERVICE	THIRD SERVICE	SECOND SERVICE
	CW		
Psalms:	47 *or* 93	110; 150	8
Readings:	The reading from Acts must be used as first or second reading Acts 1.1–11 *or* Dan. 7.9–14; Eph. 1.15–end *or* Acts 1.1–11; Luke 24.44–end	Isa. 52.7–end; Heb. 7.[11–25] 26–end	Song of the Three 29–37 *or* 2 Kgs 2.1–15; Rev. 5; [Mark 16.14–20]
	Seasonal provisions CW Book pp 318–319		

	HOLY COMMUNION	MORNING PRAYER	EVENING PRAYER
	BCP		
Psalms:	68.1–6	110; 150	8
Readings:	Dan. 7.13–14; Acts 1.1–11; Mark 16.14–end or Luke 24.44–53; Pr. Pref. until May 27	2 Kgs 2.1–15; Eph. 4.1–16	Dan. 7.9–10, 13–14; Heb. 1
Hymns:	....	....	....

CW COLLECTS

Grant, we pray, almighty God,
that as we believe your only-begotten Son
  our Lord Jesus Christ
to have ascended into the heavens,
so we in heart and mind may also ascend
and with him continually dwell;
who is alive and reigns with you,
in the unity of the Holy Spirit,
one God, now and for ever.

or

Risen Christ,
you have raised our human nature to the throne
  of heaven:
help us to seek and serve you,
that we may join you at the Father's side,
where you reign with the Spirit in glory,
now and for ever.

POST COMMUNION

God our Father,
you have raised our humanity in Christ
and have fed us with the bread of heaven:
mercifully grant that, nourished
with such spiritual blessings,
we may set our hearts in the heavenly places;
through Jesus Christ our Lord.

BCP COLLECT

Grant, we beseech thee, Almighty God, that like as we do believe thy only-begotten Son our Lord Jesus Christ to have ascended into the heavens; so we may also in heart and mind thither ascend, and with him continually dwell, who liveth and reigneth with thee and the Holy Ghost, one God, world without end.

2020

	July					August					September					October					November					December			
S		5	12	19	26		2	9	16	23	30		6	13	20	27		4	11	18	25		1	8	15	22	29		6	13	20	27
M		6	13	20	27		3	10	17	24	31		7	14	21	28		5	12	19	26		2	9	16	23	30		7	14	21	28
T		7	14	21	28		4	11	18	25		1	8	15	22	29		6	13	20	27		3	10	17	24		1	8	15	22	29
W	1	8	15	22	29		5	12	19	26		2	9	16	23	30		7	14	21	28		4	11	18	25		2	9	16	23	30
T	2	9	16	23	30		6	13	20	27		3	10	17	24		1	8	15	22	29		5	12	19	26		3	10	17	24	31
F	3	10	17	24	31		7	14	21	28		4	11	18	25		2	9	16	23	30		6	13	20	27		4	11	18	25
S	4	11	18	25		1	8	15	22	29		5	12	19	26		3	10	17	24	31		7	14	21	28		5	12	19	26

White

EUCHARIST	MORNING PRAYER	EVENING PRAYER
CW		

Psalms:	47.1–6	20; *81*	*145*
Readings:	Acts 18.9–18;	Num. 20.1–13;	Deut. 29.2–15;
	John 16.20–23	Luke 7.11–17	1 John 1.1—2.6

The nine days after Ascension Day until Pentecost are days of prayer and preparation to celebrate the outpouring of the Spirit. The alternative sequence of daily readings may be used at either morning or evening prayer on these days or as readings at an Alternative Service

	AP/AW	*Exod. 35.30—36.1;*	*Gal. 5.13–end*
HOLY COMMUNION		MORNING PRAYER	EVENING PRAYER
BCP			

Psalms:		*107*	*108; 109*
Readings:		*Judg. 2.6–end;*	*Judg. 4;*
		Heb. 2	*Heb. 3*
Hymns:	....	....	....

CW COLLECT
Holy Spirit, sent by the Father,
ignite in us your holy fire;
strengthen your children with the gift of faith,
revive your Church with the breath of love,
and renew the face of the earth,
through Jesus Christ our Lord.

2020

	January	February	March	April	May	June
S	5 12 19 26	2 9 16 23	1 8 15 22 29	5 12 19 26	3 10 17 24 31	7 14 21 28
M	6 13 20 27	3 10 17 24	2 9 16 23 30	6 13 20 27	4 11 18 25	1 8 15 22 29
T	7 14 21 28	4 11 18 25	3 10 17 24 31	7 14 21 28	5 12 19 26	2 9 16 23 30
W	1 8 15 22 29	5 12 19 26	4 11 18 25	1 8 15 22 29	6 13 20 27	3 10 17 24
T	2 9 16 23 30	6 13 20 27	5 12 19 26	2 9 16 23 30	7 14 21 28	4 11 18 25
F	3 10 17 24 31	7 14 21 28	6 13 20 27	3 10 17 24	1 8 15 22 29	5 12 19 26
S	4 11 18 25	1 8 15 22 29	7 14 21 28	4 11 18 25	2 9 16 23 30	6 13 20 27

White

	EUCHARIST	MORNING PRAYER	EVENING PRAYER
	CW		
Psalms:	47.1–2, 7–end	21; *47*	84; *85*
Readings:	Acts 18.22–end;	Num. 21.4–9;	Deut. 30;
	John 16.23–28	Luke 7.18–35	1 John 2.7–17

	AP/AW	*Num. 11.16–17, 24–29*	*1 Cor. 2*
	HOLY COMMUNION	MORNING PRAYER	EVENING PRAYER
	BCP		
Psalms:		*110; 111; 112; 113*	*114; 115*
Readings:		*Judg. 5;*	*Judg. 6.1–24;*
		Heb. 4.1–13	*Heb. 4.14—5.10*
			E. Coll. Sunday after Ascension
Hymns:	....	....	....

2020

	July				August					September				October				November				December			
S		5	12	19	26		2	9	16	23	30		6	13	20	27		4	11	18	25		1	8	15	22	29		6	13	20	27
M		6	13	20	27		3	10	17	24	31		7	14	21	28		5	12	19	26		2	9	16	23	30		7	14	21	28
T		7	14	21	28		4	11	18	25		1	8	15	22	29		6	13	20	27		3	10	17	24		1	8	15	22	29
W	1	8	15	22	29		5	12	19	26		2	9	16	23	30		7	14	21	28		4	11	18	25		2	9	16	23	30
T	2	9	16	23	30		6	13	20	27		3	10	17	24		1	8	15	22	29		5	12	19	26		3	10	17	24	31
F	3	10	17	24	31		7	14	21	28		4	11	18	25		2	9	16	23	30		6	13	20	27		4	11	18	25
S	4	11	18	25		1	8	15	22	29		5	12	19	26		3	10	17	24	31		7	14	21	28		5	12	19	26

THE SEVENTH SUNDAY OF EASTER
Sunday after Ascension Day (Easter 6)
(White)

	PRINCIPAL SERVICE CW	**THIRD SERVICE**	**SECOND SERVICE**
Psalms:	68.1–10, 32–35 [68.1–10]	104.26–35	47
Readings:	Acts 1.6–14; Alt. O.T. Ezek. 36.24–28; if used, Acts must be second reading 1 Pet. 4.12–14; 5.6–11; John 17.1–11	Isa. 65.17–25; Rev. 21.1–8	2 Sam. 23.1–5; Eph. 1.15–23; [Mark 16.14–20]

Seasonal provisions CW Book p 320–321

	HOLY COMMUNION BCP	**MORNING PRAYER**	**EVENING PRAYER**
Psalms:	68.32–end	104.26–35	47
Readings:	2 Kgs 2.9–15; 1 Pet. 4.7–11; John 15.26—16.4a	Deut. 26 or Isa. 64; John 14.1–14 or Eph. 1.3–end	Deut. 30 or Deut. 34 or Isa. 65.17–end; John 16.5–end or Acts 1.1–14
Hymns:	....	....	....

2020

	January	February	March	April	May	June
S	5 12 19 26	2 9 16 23	1 8 15 22 29	5 12 19 26	3 10 17 24 31	7 14 21 28
M	6 13 20 27	3 10 17 24	2 9 16 23 30	6 13 20 27	4 11 18 25	1 8 15 22 29
T	7 14 21 28	4 11 18 25	3 10 17 24 31	7 14 21 28	5 12 19 26	2 9 16 23 30
W	1 8 15 22 29	5 12 19 26	4 11 18 25	1 8 15 22 29	6 13 20 27	3 10 17 24
T	2 9 16 23 30	6 13 20 27	5 12 19 26	2 9 16 23 30	7 14 21 28	4 11 18 25
F	3 10 17 24 31	7 14 21 28	6 13 20 27	3 10 17 24	1 8 15 22 29	5 12 19 26
S	4 11 18 25	1 8 15 22 29	7 14 21 28	4 11 18 25	2 9 16 23 30	6 13 20 27

CW COLLECTS

O God the King of glory,
you have exalted your only Son Jesus Christ
with great triumph to your kingdom in heaven:
we beseech you, leave us not comfortless,
but send your Holy Spirit to strengthen us
and exalt us to the place
  where our Saviour Christ is gone before,
who is alive and reigns with you,
in the unity of the Holy Spirit,
one God, now and for ever.

or

Risen, ascended Lord,
as we rejoice at your triumph,
fill your Church on earth with power and compassion,
that all who are estranged by sin
may find forgiveness and know your peace,
to the glory of God the Father.

POST COMMUNION

Eternal God, giver of love and power,
your Son Jesus Christ has sent us into all the world
to preach the gospel of his kingdom:
confirm us in this mission,
and help us to live the good news we proclaim;
through Jesus Christ our Lord.

BCP COLLECT

*O God the King of glory, who hast exalted thine
only Son Jesus Christ with great triumph unto thy
kingdom in heaven: We beseech thee, leave us not
comfortless; but send to us thine Holy Ghost to
comfort us, and exalt us unto the same place whither
our Saviour Christ is gone before, who liveth and
reigneth with thee and the Holy Ghost, one God,
world without end.*

2020

	July					August						September					October					November					December			
S		5	12	19	26	S		2	9	16	23	30	S		6	13	20	27	S		4	11	18	25	S	1	8	15	22	29	S		6	13	20	27
M		6	13	20	27	M		3	10	17	24	31	M		7	14	21	28	M		5	12	19	26	M	2	9	16	23	30	M		7	14	21	28
T		7	14	21	28	T		4	11	18	25		T	1	8	15	22	29	T		6	13	20	27	T	3	10	17	24		T	1	8	15	22	29
W	1	8	15	22	29	W		5	12	19	26		W	2	9	16	23	30	W		7	14	21	28	W	4	11	18	25		W	2	9	16	23	30
T	2	9	16	23	30	T		6	13	20	27		T	3	10	17	24		T	1	8	15	22	29	T	5	12	19	26		T	3	10	17	24	31
F	3	10	17	24	31	F		7	14	21	28		F	4	11	18	25		F	2	9	16	23	30	F	6	13	20	27		F	4	11	18	25
S	4	11	18	25	S	1	8	15	22	29		S	5	12	19	26		S	3	10	17	24	31	S	7	14	21	28		S	5	12	19	26

The Venerable Bede, Monk at Jarrow, Scholar, Historian, 735 (CW Readings see Common of the Saints   White
also Ecclus 39.1–10) *Aldhelm, Bishop of Sherborne, 709*   Bank Holiday (UK)

	EUCHARIST CW	MORNING PRAYER	EVENING PRAYER
Psalms:	68.1–6	*93*; 96; 97	*18*
Readings:	Acts 19.1–8; John 16.29–end	Num. 22.1–35; Luke 7.36–end	Deut. 31.1–13; 1 John 2.18–end
	AP/AW	Num. 27.15–end	1 Cor. 3

	HOLY COMMUNION BCP	MORNING PRAYER	EVENING PRAYER
		119.33–72	119.73–104
Readings:		Judg. 6.25–end; Heb. 5.11—end of 6	Judg. 7; Heb. 7
Hymns:	....	....	....

CW COLLECT

God our maker,
whose Son Jesus Christ gave to your servant Bede
grace to drink in with joy
   the word that leads us to know you and to love you:
in your goodness
grant that we also may come at length to you,
the source of all wisdom,
and stand before your face;
through Jesus Christ your Son our Lord,
who is alive and reigns with you,
in the unity of the Holy Spirit,
one God, now and for ever.

POST COMMUNION

Merciful God,
who gave such grace to your servant Bede
that he served you with singleness of heart
and loved you above all things:
help us, whose communion with you
   has been renewed in this sacrament,
to forsake all that holds us back from following Christ
and to grow into his likeness from glory to glory;
through Jesus Christ our Lord.

BCP COLLECT for St Aldhelm

*God, the light of the faithful, and shepherd of souls,
who didst set blessed Aldhelm to be a Bishop in the
Church, that he might feed thy sheep by his word and
guide them by his example: Grant us, we pray thee,
to keep the faith which he taught, and to follow in his
footsteps; through Jesus Christ our Lord.*

Sunrise 04.51; Sunset 21.03

2020

January	February	March	April	May	June
S 5 12 19 26	S 2 9 16 23	S 1 8 15 22 29	S 5 12 19 26	S 3 10 17 24 31	S 7 14 21 28
M 6 13 20 27	M 3 10 17 24	M 2 9 16 23 30	M 6 13 20 27	M 4 11 18 25	M 1 8 15 22 29
T 7 14 21 28	T 4 11 18 25	T 3 10 17 24 31	T 7 14 21 28	T 5 12 19 26	T 2 9 16 23 30
W 1 8 15 22 29	W 5 12 19 26	W 4 11 18 25	W 1 8 15 22 29	W 6 13 20 27	W 3 10 17 24
T 2 9 16 23 30	T 6 13 20 27	T 5 12 19 26	T 2 9 16 23 30	T 7 14 21 28	T 4 11 18 25
F 3 10 17 24 31	F 7 14 21 28	F 6 13 20 27	F 3 10 17 24	F 1 8 15 22 29	F 5 12 19 26
S 4 11 18 25	S 1 8 15 22 29	S 7 14 21 28	S 4 11 18 25	S 2 9 16 23 30	S 6 13 20 27

Augustine, first Archbishop of Canterbury, 605 (CW Readings see Common of the Saints   White
also 1 Thess. 2.2b–8, Matt. 13.31–33) *(also BCP)*
John Calvin, Reformer 1564. Philip Neri, Founder of the Oratorians, Spiritual Guide, 1595

	EUCHARIST	MORNING PRAYER	EVENING PRAYER
	CW		
Psalms:	68.9–10, 18–19	98; *99*; 100	*68*
Readings:	Acts 20.17–27; John 17.1–11	Num. 22.36—23.12; Luke 8.1–15	Deut. 31.14–29; 1 John 3.1–10

	AP/AW	*1 Sam. 10.1–10*	*1 Cor. 12.1–13*

	HOLY COMMUNION	MORNING PRAYER	EVENING PRAYER
	BCP Com. Bishop		
Psalms:	99	119.105–144	119.145–end
Readings:	Ezek. 34.11–16; 1 Tim. 3.15–16; Mark 4.26–32	Judg. 8.32—9.24; Heb. 8	Judg. 10.17—11.28; Heb. 9.1–14
Hymns:	....	....	....

CW COLLECT

Almighty God,
whose servant Augustine was sent as the apostle
  of the English people:
grant that as he laboured in the Spirit
to preach Christ's gospel in this land,
so all who hear the good news
may strive to make your truth known in all the world;
through Jesus Christ your Son our Lord,
who is alive and reigns with you,
in the unity of the Holy Spirit,
one God, now and for ever.

POST COMMUNION

God, shepherd of your people,
whose servant Augustine revealed the loving service
  of Christ in his ministry as a pastor of your people:
by this eucharist in which we share
awaken within us the love of Christ
and keep us faithful to our Christian calling;
through him who laid down his life for us,
but is alive and reigns with you, now and for ever.

BCP COLLECT

*O God, the light of the faithful, and shepherd of souls,
who didst set blessed Augustine to be a Bishop in the
Church, that he might feed thy sheep by his word and
guide them by his example: Grant us, we pray thee,
to keep the faith which he taught, and to follow in his
footsteps; through Jesus Christ our Lord. Amen.*

Venerable Bede, Presbyter (BCP) White

	EUCHARIST	**MORNING PRAYER**	**EVENING PRAYER**
	CW		
Psalms:	68.27–28, 32–end	2; *29*	36; *46*
Readings:	Acts 20.28–end;	Num. 23.13–end;	Deut. 31.30—32.14;
	John 17.11–19	Luke 8.16–25	1 John 3.11–end

	AP/AW	*1 Kgs 19.1–18*	*Matt. 3.13–end*

	HOLY COMMUNION	**MORNING PRAYER**	**EVENING PRAYER**
	BCP Com. Doctor		
Psalms:	37.30–35	120; 121; 122; 123; 124; 125	126; 127; 128; 129; 130; 131
Readings:	Wisd. 7.7–14; 1 Cor. 2.6–13;	Judg. 11.29—12.7;	Judg. 13;
	Matt. 13.51–52	Heb. 9.15–end	Heb. 10.1–18
Hymns:	....	....	....

BCP COLLECT

O God who hast enlightened thy Church by the teaching of thy servant Bede: Enrich it evermore, we beseech thee, with thy heavenly grace, and raise up faithful witnesses who by their life and doctrine may set forth to all men the truth of thy salvation; through Jesus Christ our Lord.

2020

	January				February				March				April				May					June			
S		5	12	19	26		2	9	16	23		1	8	15	22	29		5	12	19	26		3	10	17	24	31			7	14	21	28
M		6	13	20	27		3	10	17	24		2	9	16	23	30		6	13	20	27		4	11	18	25		1	8	15	22	29
T		7	14	21	28		4	11	18	25		3	10	17	24	31		7	14	21	28		5	12	19	26		2	9	16	23	30
W	1	8	15	22	29		5	12	19	26		4	11	18	25		1	8	15	22	29		6	13	20	27		3	10	17	24
T	2	9	16	23	30		6	13	20	27		5	12	19	26		2	9	16	23	30		7	14	21	28		4	11	18	25
F	3	10	17	24	31		7	14	21	28		6	13	20	27		3	10	17	24		1	8	15	22	29		5	12	19	26
S	4	11	18	25		1	8	15	22	29		7	14	21	28		4	11	18	25		2	9	16	23	30		6	13	20	27

Lanfranc, Prior of Le Bec, Archbishop of Canterbury, Scholar, 1089

White

	EUCHARIST	MORNING PRAYER	EVENING PRAYER
	CW		
Psalms:	16.1, 5–end	*24*; 72	*139*
Readings:	Acts 22.30; 23.6–11; John 17.20–end	Num. 24; Luke 8.26–39	Deut. 32.15–47; 1 John 4.1–6

		AP/AW	*Ezek. 11.14–20*	*Matt. 9.35—10.20*
	HOLY COMMUNION		MORNING PRAYER	EVENING PRAYER
	BCP			
Psalms:			132; 133; 134; 135	136; 137; 138
Readings:			Judg. 14; Heb. 10.19–end	Judg. 16.4–end; Heb. 11
Hymns:	....		....	....

2020

	July					August					September					October					November					December			
S		5	12	19	26		2	9	16	23	30		6	13	20	27		4	11	18	25		1	8	15	22	29		6	13	20	27
M		6	13	20	27		3	10	17	24	31		7	14	21	28		5	12	19	26		2	9	16	23	30		7	14	21	28
T		7	14	21	28		4	11	18	25		1	8	15	22	29		6	13	20	27		3	10	17	24		1	8	15	22	29
W	1	8	15	22	29		5	12	19	26		2	9	16	23	30		7	14	21	28		4	11	18	25		2	9	16	23	30
T	2	9	16	23	30		6	13	20	27		3	10	17	24		1	8	15	22	29		5	12	19	26		3	10	17	24	31
F	3	10	17	24	31		7	14	21	28		4	11	18	25		2	9	16	23	30		6	13	20	27		4	11	18	25
S	4	11	18	25		1	8	15	22	29		5	12	19	26		3	10	17	24	31		7	14	21	28		5	12	19	26

MAY
29 Friday

White

	EUCHARIST	**MORNING PRAYER**	**EVENING PRAYER**
	CW		
Psalms:	103.1–2, 11–12, 19–20	*28*; 30	*147*
Readings:	Acts 25.13–21; John 21.15–19	Num. 27.12–end; Luke 8.40–end	Deut. 33; 1 John 4.7–end
	AP/AW	*Ezek. 36.22–28*	*Matt. 12.22–32*
	HOLY COMMUNION	**MORNING PRAYER**	**EVENING PRAYER**
	BCP		
Psalms:		*139; 140; 141*	*142; 143*
Readings:		*Ruth 1;* *Heb. 12.1–13*	*Ruth 2;* *Heb. 12.14–end*
Hymns:	....	....	....

	January				February				March				April				May				June			
S		5	12	19	26		2	9	16	23		1	8	15	22	29		5	12	19	26			3	10	17	24	31			7	14	21	28
M		6	13	20	27		3	10	17	24		2	9	16	23	30		6	13	20	27		4	11	18	25		1	8	15	22	29
T		7	14	21	28		4	11	18	25		3	10	17	24	31		7	14	21	28		5	12	19	26		2	9	16	23	30
W	1	8	15	22	29		5	12	19	26		4	11	18	25		1	8	15	22	29		6	13	20	27		3	10	17	24
T	2	9	16	23	30		6	13	20	27		5	12	19	26		2	9	16	23	30		7	14	21	28		4	11	18	25
F	3	10	17	24	31		7	14	21	28		6	13	20	27		3	10	17	24		1	8	15	22	29		5	12	19	26
S	4	11	18	25		1	8	15	22	29		7	14	21	28		4	11	18	25		2	9	16	23	30		6	13	20	27

Josephine Butler, Social Reformer, 1906 (CW Readings see Common of the Saints
especially Isa. 58.6–11; also 1 John 3.18–23; Matt. 9.10–13).
Joan of Arc, Visionary, 1431. Apolo Kivebulaya, Priest, Evangelist in Central Africa, 1933

White

	EUCHARIST	MORNING PRAYER	EVENING PRAYER
	CW		
Psalms:	11.4–end	42; *43*	*48*
Readings:	Acts 28.16–20, 30–end;	Num. 32.1–27;	Deut. 16.9–15;
	John 21.20–end	Luke 9.1–7	John 15.26—16.15

At Evening Prayer the readings for the Eve of Pentecost are used.
At other services, the following readings are used:

	AP/AW	*Micah 3.1–8*	*Eph. 6.10–20*
	HOLY COMMUNION	MORNING PRAYER	EVENING PRAYER
	BCP		
Psalms:		*144; 145; 146*	*147; 148; 149; 150*
Readings:		*Ruth 4.1–17;*	*Deut. 16.9–12;*
		Heb. 13	*Luke 11.1–13*
Hymns:	....	....	....

CW COLLECT
God of compassion and love,
by whose grace your servant Josephine Butler
followed in the way of your Son
in caring for those in need:
help us like her to work with strength
for the restoration of all
to the dignity and freedom of those created in
  your image;
through Jesus Christ our Saviour,
who is alive and reigns with you,
in the unity of the Holy Spirit,
one God, now and for ever.

POST COMMUNION
God our redeemer,
who inspired Josephine Butler to witness to
  your love
and to work for the coming of your kingdom:
may we, who in this sacrament share the bread
  of heaven,
be fired by your Spirit to proclaim the gospel in our
  daily living
and never to rest content until your kingdom come,
on earth as it is in heaven;
through Jesus Christ our Lord.

2020

	July					August					September					October					November					December			
S		5	12	19	26		2	9	16	23	30		6	13	20	27		4	11	18	25		1	8	15	22	29		6	13	20	27
M		6	13	20	27		3	10	17	24	31		7	14	21	28		5	12	19	26		2	9	16	23	30		7	14	21	28
T		7	14	21	28		4	11	18	25		1	8	15	22	29		6	13	20	27		3	10	17	24		1	8	15	22	29
W	1	8	15	22	29		5	12	19	26		2	9	16	23	30		7	14	21	28		4	11	18	25		2	9	16	23	30
T	2	9	16	23	30		6	13	20	27		3	10	17	24		1	8	15	22	29		5	12	19	26		3	10	17	24	31
F	3	10	17	24	31		7	14	21	28		4	11	18	25		2	9	16	23	30		6	13	20	27		4	11	18	25
S	4	11	18	25		1	8	15	22	29		5	12	19	26		3	10	17	24	31		7	14	21	28		5	12	19	26

PENTECOST
Whit Sunday
(Red)

	PRINCIPAL SERVICE	THIRD SERVICE	SECOND SERVICE
	CW		
Psalms:	104.26–36; 37b [104.26–end]	87	67; 133
Readings:	The reading from Acts must be used as either the first or second reading.	Gen. 11.1–9; Acts 10.34–48	Joel 2.21–32 [BCP Var. Num. 11.24–30] Acts 2.14–21 [22–38] [Luke 24.44–53]
	Acts 2.1–21 *or* Num. 11.24–30; 1 Cor. 12.3b–13 *or* Acts 2.1–21; John 20.19–23 *or* John 7.37–39		
	Seasonal provision CW Book pp 320–321		

	HOLY COMMUNION	MORNING PRAYER	EVENING PRAYER
	BCP		
Psalms:	122	87	67; 133
Readings:	Deut. 16.9–12; Acts 2.1–11; John 14.15–31a; Pr. Pref. until June 7; Whit Sunday Coll. until June 7	Joel 2.28–end; Rom. 8.1–17	Isa. 11.1–9 or Ezek. 36.22–36; Rom. 8.18–end or Gal. 5.13–end
Hymns:	....	....	....

CW COLLECTS

God, who as at this time
taught the hearts of your faithful people
by sending to them the light of your Holy Spirit:
grant us by the same Spirit
to have a right judgement in all things
and evermore to rejoice in his holy comfort;
through the merits of Christ Jesus our Saviour,
who is alive and reigns with you,
in the unity of the Holy Spirit,
one God, now and for ever.

or

Holy Spirit, sent by the Father
Ignite in us your holy fire;
Strengthen your children with the gift of faith
Revive your Church with the breath of love,
And renew the fact of the earth,
Through Jesus Christ our Lord.

POST COMMUNION

Faithful God,
who fulfilled the promises of Easter
by sending us your Holy Spirit
and opening to every race and nation
the way of life eternal:
open our lips by your Spirit,
that every tongue may tell of your glory;
through Jesus Christ our Lord.

*This Collect and Post Communion are not used on the
weekdays after Pentecost.
The following are used on these weekdays.*

CW COLLECT

O Lord, from whom all good things come:
grant to us your humble servants,
that by your holy inspiration
we may think those things that are good,
and by your merciful guiding may perform the same;
through our Lord Jesus Christ,
who is alive and reigns with you,
in the unity of the Holy Spirit,
one God, now and for ever.

POST COMMUNION

Gracious God, lover of all,
in this sacrament
we are one family in Christ your Son,
one in the sharing of his body and blood
and one in the communion of his Spirit:
help us to grow in love for one another
and come to the full maturity of the Body of Christ.
We make our prayer through your Son our Saviour.

BCP COLLECT

*God, who as at this time didst teach the hearts of thy
faithful people, by the sending to them the light of thy
Holy Spirit; Grant us by the same Spirit to have a right
judgement in all things, and evermore to rejoice in his
holy comfort; through the merits of Christ Jesus our
Saviour, who liveth and reigneth with thee, in the unity of
the same Spirit, one God, world without end.*

2020

July					August						September					October					November					December				
S		5	12	19	26	S		2	9	16	23	30	S		6	13	20	27	S		4	11	18	25	S		1	8	15	22	29	S			6	13	20	27
M		6	13	20	27	M		3	10	17	24	31	M		7	14	21	28	M		5	12	19	26	M	2	9	16	23	30	M			7	14	21	28
T		7	14	21	28	T		4	11	18	25		T	1	8	15	22	29	T		6	13	20	27	T	3	10	17	24		T		1	8	15	22	29
W	1	8	15	22	29	W		5	12	19	26		W	2	9	16	23	30	W		7	14	21	28	W	4	11	18	25		W	2	9	16	23	30
T	2	9	16	23	30	T		6	13	20	27		T	3	10	17	24		T	1	8	15	22	29	T	5	12	19	26		T	3	10	17	24	31
F	3	10	17	24	31	F		7	14	21	28		F	4	11	18	25		F	2	9	16	23	30	F	6	13	20	27		F	4	11	18	25
S	4	11	18	25		S	1	8	15	22	29		S	5	12	19	26		S	3	10	17	24	31	S	7	14	21	28		S	5	12	19	26

The Visit of the Blessed Virgin Mary to Elizabeth (transferred)

White

	PRINCIPAL SERVICE	THIRD SERVICE	SECOND SERVICE
	CW		
Psalms:	113	85; 150	122; 127; 128
Readings:	Zeph. 3.14–18;	1 Sam. 2.1–10;	Zech. 2.10–13;
	Rom. 12.9–16;	Mark 3.31–end	John 3.25–30
	Luke 1.39–49[50–56]		

	HOLY COMMUNION	MORNING PRAYER	EVENING PRAYER
	BCP Visitation		
Psalms:	113	1; 2; 3; 4; 5	6; 7; 8
Readings:	1 Sam. 2.1–3;	Ezek. 11.14–20;	Wisd. 1.1–7;
	Gal. 4.1–5; Luke 1.39–45	Acts 2.12–36	Acts 2.37–end
Hymns:	....	....	....

CW COLLECT

Mighty God,
by whose grace Elizabeth rejoiced with Mary
and greeted her as the mother of the Lord:
look with favour on your lowly servants
that, with Mary, we may magnify your holy name
and rejoice to acclaim her Son our Saviour,
who is alive and reigns with you,
in the unity of the Holy Spirit,
one God, now and for ever.

POST COMMUNION

Gracious God,
who gave joy to Elizabeth and Mary
as they recognized the signs of redemption
    at work within them:
help us, who have shared in the joy of this eucharist,
to know the Lord deep within us
and his love shining out in our lives,
that the world may rejoice in your salvation;
through Jesus Christ our Lord.

BCP COLLECT

O God, who didst lead the Blessed Virgin Mary to
visit Elizabeth to their exceeding joy and comfort:
Grant unto they people, that as Mary did rejoice
to be called the Mother of the Lord, so they may
ever rejoice to believe the incarnation of thine only-
begotten Son; to whom with thee and the Holy Ghost
be all honour and glory, world without end.

Sunrise 04.44; Sunset 21.12

2020

	January				February				March				April				May					June			
S		5	12	19	26		2	9	16	23		1	8	15	22	29		5	12	19	26		3	10	17	24	31			7	14	21	28
M		6	13	20	27		3	10	17	24		2	9	16	23	30		6	13	20	27		4	11	18	25		1	8	15	22	29
T		7	14	21	28		4	11	18	25		3	10	17	24	31		7	14	21	28		5	12	19	26		2	9	16	23	30
W	1	8	15	22	29		5	12	19	26		4	11	18	25		1	8	15	22	29		6	13	20	27		3	10	17	24
T	2	9	16	23	30		6	13	20	27		5	12	19	26		2	9	16	23	30		7	14	21	28		4	11	18	25
F	3	10	17	24	31		7	14	21	28		6	13	20	27		3	10	17	24		1	8	15	22	29		5	12	19	26
S	4	11	18	25		1	8	15	22	29		7	14	21	28		4	11	18	25		2	9	16	23	30		6	13	20	27

JUNE

2020
Tuesday 2

Ordinary Time resumes. *Tuesday in Whitsun Week (BCP)*   Green (*or White*)

DEL Wk 9	**EUCHARIST**	**MORNING PRAYER**	**EVENING PRAYER**
	CW		
Psalms:	90.1–4, 10, 14, 16	*132*; 133 (Week 7 Ord)	(134) *135*
Readings:	2 Pet. 3.11a, 17 end;	Josh. 2;	Job 2;
	Mark 12.13–17	Luke 9.28–36	Rom. 1.18–end

| | | AW | *Gen. 13.1–12* | *Rom. 12.9–end* |

	HOLY COMMUNION	**MORNING PRAYER**	**EVENING PRAYER**
	BCP		
Psalms:		9; 10; 11	12; 13; 14
Readings:	*Acts 8.14–17;*	*Ezek. 37.1–14;*	*Wisd. 7.15—8.1;*
	John 10.1–10	*1 Cor. 12.1–13*	*1 Cor. 12.27—end of 13*
Hymns:	....	....	....

For CW Collects see Sunday June 1
BCP Whit Sunday Collect

2020

	July				August				September				October				November				December		
S	5 12 19 26		S	2 9 16 23 30		S	6 13 20 27		S	4 11 18 25		S	1 8 15 22 29		S	6 13 20 27
M	6 13 20 27		M	3 10 17 24 31		M	7 14 21 28		M	5 12 19 26		M	2 9 16 23 30		M	7 14 21 28
T	7 14 21 28		T	4 11 18 25		T	1 8 15 22 29		T	6 13 20 27		T	3 10 17 24		T	1 8 15 22 29
W	1 8 15 22 29		W	5 12 19 26		W	2 9 16 23 30		W	7 14 21 28		W	4 11 18 25		W	2 9 16 23 30
T	2 9 16 23 30		T	6 13 20 27		T	3 10 17 24		T	1 8 15 22 29		T	5 12 19 26		T	3 10 17 24 31
F	3 10 17 24 31		F	7 14 21 28		F	4 11 18 25		F	2 9 16 23 30		F	6 13 20 27		F	4 11 18 25
S	4 11 18 25		S	1 8 15 22 29		S	5 12 19 26		S	3 10 17 24 31		S	7 14 21 28		S	5 12 19 26

Wednesday in Whitsun Week also Ember Day (BCP)
The Martyrs of Uganda, 1885–7, 1977

Green (*or White or Red*)

	EUCHARIST	MORNING PRAYER	EVENING PRAYER
	CW		
Psalms:	123	*119.153–end*	*136*
Readings:	2 Tim. 1.1–3, 6–12;	Josh. 3;	Job 3;
	Mark 12.18–27	Luke 9.37–50	Rom. 2.1–16

AW *Gen. 15* *Rom. 4.1–8*

	HOLY COMMUNION	MORNING PRAYER	EVENING PRAYER
	BCP Ember CEG see Dec 18 or		
Psalms:		*15; 16; 17*	*18*
Readings:	*Acts 2.14–21;*	*1 Kgs 19.1–18;*	*Wisd. 9;*
	John 6.44–51	*1 Cor. 2*	*1 Cor. 3*
Hymns:	....	....	....

For CW Collects see Sunday June 1
BCP Whit Sunday Collect

Petroc, Abbot of Padstow 6th century
Thursday in Whitsun Week (BCP)

Green (*or White*)

	EUCHARIST	**MORNING PRAYER**	**EVENING PRAYER**
	CW		
Psalms:	25.4–12	*143*; 146	*138*; 140; 141
Readings:	2 Tim. 2.8–15;	Josh. 4.1—5.1;	Job 4;
	Mark 12.28–34	Luke 9.51–end	Rom. 2.17–end

AW *Gen. 22.1–18* *Heb. 11.8–19*

	HOLY COMMUNION	**MORNING PRAYER**	**EVENING PRAYER**
	BCP		
Psalms:		*19; 20; 21*	*22; 23*
Readings:	Acts 2.22–28;	2 Sam. 23.1–5;	Exod. 35.30—36.1;
	Luke 9.1–6	Eph. 6.10–20	Acts 18.24—19.7
Hymns:	....	....	....

For CW Collects see Sunday June 1
BCP Whit Sunday Collect

JUNE
5 Friday

Boniface (Wynfrith) of Crediton, Bishop, Apostle of Germany, Martyr, 754   Red *or* Green (*or* White)
(CW Readings see Common of the Saints also Acts 20.24–28) *(also BCP)*
(Friday in Whitsun Week also Ember Day BCP)

	EUCHARIST	**MORNING PRAYER**	**EVENING PRAYER**
	CW		
Psalms:	119.161–168	142; *144*	*145*
Readings:	2 Tim. 3.10–end;	Josh. 5.2–end;	Job 5;
	Mark 12.35–37	Luke 10.1–16	Rom. 3.1–20

	AW	Isa. 51.1–8	*John 8.48–end*

	HOLY COMMUNION	**MORNING PRAYER**	**EVENING PRAYER**
	BCP Ember CEG see Dec 18 or		
Psalms:		*24; 25; 26*	*27; 28; 29*
Readings:	Acts 8.5–8;	Num. 11.16–17, 24–29;	Jer. 31.31–34;
.	Luke 5.17–26	2 Cor. 5.14—6.10	2 Cor. 3
Hymns:	....	....	....

CW COLLECT
God our redeemer,
who called your servant Boniface
to preach the gospel among the German people
and to build up your Church in holiness:
grant that we may preserve in our hearts
that faith which he taught with his words
     and sealed with his blood,
and profess it in lives dedicated to your Son
Jesus Christ our Lord,
who is alive and reigns with you,
in the unity of the Holy Spirit, one God,
     now and for ever.

POST COMMUNION
God our redeemer,
whose Church was strengthened by the blood
     of your martyr Boniface:
so bind us, in life and death, to Christ's sacrifice
that our lives, broken and offered with his,
may carry his death and proclaim his
     resurrection in the world;
through Jesus Christ our Lord.

BCP COLLECT
*Almighty God, by whose grace and power thy
holy Martyr Boniface triumphed over suffering
and despised death: Grant, we beseech thee, that
enduring hardness and waxing valiant in fight,
we may with the noble army of martyrs receive
the crown of everlasting life; through Jesus Christ
our Lord.*

Full Moon

2020

	January					February					March					April					May						June				
S		5	12	19	26	S		2	9	16	23	S	1	8	15	22	29	S		5	12	19	26	S		3	10	17	24	31	S		7	14	21	28
M		6	13	20	27	M		3	10	17	24	M	2	9	16	23	30	M		6	13	20	27	M		4	11	18	25	M	1	8	15	22	29
T		7	14	21	28	T		4	11	18	25	T	3	10	17	24	31	T		7	14	21	28	T		5	12	19	26	T	2	9	16	23	30
W	1	8	15	22	29	W		5	12	19	26	W	4	11	18	25	W	1	8	15	22	29	W		6	13	20	27	W	3	10	17	24
T	2	9	16	23	30	T		6	13	20	27	T	5	12	19	26	T	2	9	16	23	30	T		7	14	21	28	T	4	11	18	25
F	3	10	17	24	31	F		7	14	21	28	F	6	13	20	27	F	3	10	17	24	F	1	8	15	22	29	F	5	12	19	26
S	4	11	18	25	S	1	8	15	22	29	S	7	14	21	28	S	4	11	18	25	S	2	9	16	23	30	S	6	13	20	27

Ini Kopuria, founder of the Melanesian Brotherhood, 1945
(Saturday in Whitsun Week also Ember Day BCP)

Green (*or White or Red*)

	EUCHARIST	MORNING PRAYER	EVENING PRAYER
	CW		
Psalms:	71.7–16	*147*	97; 98
Readings:	2 Tim. 4.1–8; Mark 12.38–end	Josh. 6.1–20; Luke 10.17–24	Exod. 34.1–10; Mark 1.1–13

At Evening Prayer the readings for the Eve of Trinity Sunday are used.
At other services, the following readings are used:

		Ecclus 44.19–23 or *Josh. 2.1–15*	*Jas 2.14–26*

	HOLY COMMUNION	MORNING PRAYER	EVENING PRAYER
	BCP Ember CEG see Dec 18		
Psalms:		30; 31	32; 33; 34
Readings:	Acts 13.44–end; Matt. 20.29–34	Num. 27.15–end; Matt. 9.35—10.20	Isa. 61; Acts 20.17–35; E. Coll. Trinity Sunday
Hymns:	....	....	....

For CW Collects see Sunday June 1
BCP Whit Sunday Collect

2020

July					August						September					October					November					December				
S		5	12	19	26	S		2	9	16	23	30	S		6	13	20	27	S		4	11	18	25	S	1	8	15	22	29	S		6	13	20	27
M		6	13	20	27	M		3	10	17	24	31	M		7	14	21	28	M		5	12	19	26	M	2	9	16	23	30	M		7	14	21	28
T		7	14	21	28	T		4	11	18	25	T	1	8	15	22	29	T		6	13	20	27	T	3	10	17	24	T	1	8	15	22	29
W	1	8	15	22	29	W		5	12	19	26	W	2	9	16	23	30	W		7	14	21	28	W	4	11	18	25	W	2	9	16	23	30
T	2	9	16	23	30	T		6	13	20	27	T	3	10	17	24	T	1	8	15	22	29	T	5	12	19	26	T	3	10	17	24	31
F	3	10	17	24	31	F		7	14	21	28	F	4	11	18	25	F	2	9	16	23	30	F	6	13	20	27	F	4	11	18	25
S	4	11	18	25	S	1	8	15	22	29	S	5	12	19	26	S	3	10	17	24	31	S	7	14	21	28	S	5	12	19	26

TRINITY SUNDAY

(White *or* Gold)

	PRINCIPAL SERVICE CW	THIRD SERVICE	SECOND SERVICE
Psalms:	8	86.8–13	93; 150
Readings:	Isa. 40.12–17, 27–31; 2 Cor. 13.11–13; Matt. 28.16–20	Exod. 3.1–6, 13–15; John 17.1–11	Isa. 6.1–8 [BCP Var. Isa. 40.12–17, 27–31] John 16.5–15

Seasonal provisions CW Book pp 322–323

	HOLY COMMUNION BCP	MORNING PRAYER	EVENING PRAYER
Psalms:	8	86.8–13	93; 150
Readings:	Isa. 6.1–8; Rev. 4; John 3.1–15; Pr. Pref. today only	Isa. 6.1–8; Mark 1.1–11 or 1 Pet. 1.1–12	Exod. 34.1–10 or Num. 6.22–end or Isa. 40.12–end; Matt. 28.16–end or Eph. 3
Hymns:	....	....	....

2020

January				February				March				April				May					June			
S		5	12	19	26	S		2	9	16	23	S	1	8	15	22	29	S		5	12	19	26	S		3	10	17	24	31	S		7	14	21	28
M		6	13	20	27	M		3	10	17	24	M	2	9	16	23	30	M		6	13	20	27	M		4	11	18	25	M	1	8	15	22	29
T		7	14	21	28	T		4	11	18	25	T	3	10	17	24	31	T		7	14	21	28	T		5	12	19	26	T	2	9	16	23	30
W	1	8	15	22	29	W		5	12	19	26	W	4	11	18	25	W	1	8	15	22	29	W		6	13	20	27	W	3	10	17	24
T	2	9	16	23	30	T		6	13	20	27	T	5	12	19	26	T	2	9	16	23	30	T		7	14	21	28	T	4	11	18	25
F	3	10	17	24	31	F		7	14	21	28	F	6	13	20	27	F	3	10	17	24	F	1	8	15	22	29	F	5	12	19	26
S	4	11	18	25	S	1	8	15	22	29	S	7	14	21	28	S	4	11	18	25	S	2	9	16	23	30	S	6	13	20	27

CW COLLECTS

Almighty and everlasting God,
you have given us your servants grace,
by the confession of a true faith,
to acknowledge the glory of the eternal Trinity
and in the power of the divine majesty to worship
the Unity:
keep us steadfast in this faith,
that we may evermore be defended from
all adversities;
through Jesus Christ your Son our Lord,
who is alive and reigns with you,
in the unity of the Holy Spirit,
one God, now and for ever.

or

Holy God, faithful and unchanging:
enlarge our minds with the knowledge of
your truth,
and draw us more deeply into the mystery of
your love,
that we may truly worship you,
Father, Son and Holy Spirit,
one God, now and for ever.

POST COMMUNION

Almighty and eternal God,
you have revealed yourself as Father, Son
and Holy Spirit,
and live and reign in the perfect unity of love:
hold us firm in this faith,
that we may know you in all your ways
and evermore rejoice in your eternal glory,
who are three Persons yet one God,
now and for ever.

BCP COLLECT

*Almighty and everlasting God, who hast given unto
us thy servants grace, by the confession of a true
faith, to acknowledge the glory of the eternal Trinity,
and in the power of the Divine Majesty to worship the
Unity; We beseech thee, that thou wouldest keep us
stedfast in this faith, and evermore defend us from all
adversities, who livest and reignest, one God, world
without end.*

2020

	July					August					September					October					November					December			
S		5	12	19	26		2	9	16	23	30		6	13	20	27		4	11	18	25		1	8	15	22	29		6	13	20	27
M		6	13	20	27		3	10	17	24	31		7	14	21	28		5	12	19	26		2	9	16	23	30		7	14	21	28
T		7	14	21	28		4	11	18	25		1	8	15	22	29		6	13	20	27		3	10	17	24		1	8	15	22	29
W	1	8	15	22	29		5	12	19	26		2	9	16	23	30		7	14	21	28	4	11	18	25		2	9	16	23	30
T	2	9	16	23	30		6	13	20	27		3	10	17	24		1	8	15	22	29		5	12	19	26		3	10	17	24	31
F	3	10	17	24	31		7	14	21	28		4	11	18	25		2	9	16	23	30		6	13	20	27		4	11	18	25
S	4	11	18	25		1	8	15	22	29		5	12	19	26		3	10	17	24	31		7	14	21	28		5	12	19	26

Thomas Ken, Bishop of Bath and Wells, Non-Juror, Hymn Writer, 1711
(CW Readings see Common of the Saints especially 2 Cor. 4.1–10; Matt. 24.42–46)

White *or* Green

DEL Wk 10	EUCHARIST CW	MORNING PRAYER	EVENING PRAYER
Psalms:	121	*1*; 2; 3 (Week 1 Ord.)	*4*; 7
Readings:	1 Kgs 17.1–6; Matt. 5.1–12	Josh. 7.1–15; Luke 10.25–37	Job 7; Rom. 4.1–12

		AW	*Exod. 2.1–10*	*Heb. 11.23–31*

	HOLY COMMUNION BCP	MORNING PRAYER	EVENING PRAYER
Psalms:		38; 39; 40	41; 42; 43
Readings:		1 Sam. 1; Jas 1	1 Sam. 2.1–21; Luke 1.1–23
Hymns:			

CW COLLECT

O God, from whom all blessings flow,
by whose providence we are kept
and by whose grace we are directed:
help us, through the example of your servant
    Thomas Ken,
faithfully to keep your word,
humbly to accept adversity
and steadfastly to worship you;
through Jesus Christ your Son our Lord,
who is alive and reigns with you,
in the unity of the Holy Spirit,
one God, now and for ever.

POST COMMUNION

God, shepherd of your people,
whose servant Thomas Ken revealed the loving
service of Christ in his ministry as a pastor of your
people: by this eucharist in which we share
awaken within us the love of Christ
and keep us faithful to our Christian calling;
through him who laid down his life for us,
but is alive and reigns with you, now and for ever.

Sunrise 04.40; Sunset 21.18

2020

	January					February					March					April					May						June			
S		5	12	19	26		2	9	16	23		1	8	15	22	29		5	12	19	26		3	10	17	24	31			7	14	21	28
M		6	13	20	27		3	10	17	24		2	9	16	23	30		6	13	20	27		4	11	18	25			1	8	15	22	29
T		7	14	21	28		4	11	18	25		3	10	17	24	31		7	14	21	28		5	12	19	26			2	9	16	23	30
W	1	8	15	22	29		5	12	19	26		4	11	18	25		1	8	15	22	29		6	13	20	27			3	10	17	24	
T	2	9	16	23	30		6	13	20	27		5	12	19	26		2	9	16	23	30		7	14	21	28			4	11	18	25	
F	3	10	17	24	31		7	14	21	28		6	13	20	27		3	10	17	24		1	8	15	22	29			5	12	19	26	
S	4	11	18	25		1	8	15	22	29		7	14	21	28		4	11	18	25		2	9	16	23	30			6	13	20	27	

Columba, Abbot of Iona, Missionary, 597 (CW Readings see Common of the Saints also Titus 2.11–15)   Green
Ephrem of Syria, Deacon, Hymn Writer, Teacher of the Faith, 373

	EUCHARIST	**MORNING PRAYER**	**EVENING PRAYER**
	CW		
Psalms:	4	*5*; 6; (8)	*9*; 10*
Readings:	1 Kgs 17.7–16;	Josh. 7.16–end;	Job 8;
	Matt. 5.13–16	Luke 10.38–end	Rom. 4.13–end
	AW	*Exod. 2.11–end*	*Acts 7.17–29*
	HOLY COMMUNION	**MORNING PRAYER**	**EVENING PRAYER**
	BCP		
Psalms:		*44; 45; 46*	*47; 48; 49*
Readings:		*1 Sam. 2.22–end;*	*1 Sam. 3;*
		Jas 2.1–13	*Luke 1.24–56*
Hymns:	....	....	....

CW COLLECT
Almighty God,
who filled the heart of Columba
with the joy of the Holy Spirit
and with deep love for those in his care:
may your pilgrim people follow him,
strong in faith, sustained by hope,
and one in the love that binds us to you;
through Jesus Christ your Son our Lord,
who is alive and reigns with you,
in the unity of the Holy Spirit,
one God, now and for ever.

POST COMMUNION
Holy Father,
who gathered us here around the table of your Son
to share this meal with the whole household of God:
in that new world where you reveal
    the fullness of your peace,
gather people of every race and language
to share with Columba and all your saints
in the eternal banquet of Jesus Christ our Lord.

2020

July				August					September				October				November					December			
S	5 12 19 26			S	2 9 16 23 30			S	6 13 20 27			S	4 11 18 25			S	1 8 15 22 29			S	6 13 20 27	
M	6 13 20 27			M	3 10 17 24 31			M	7 14 21 28			M	5 12 19 26			M	2 9 16 23 30			M	7 14 21 28	
T	7 14 21 28			T	4 11 18 25			T	1 8 15 22 29			T	6 13 20 27			T	3 10 17 24			T	1 8 15 22 29	
W	1 8 15 22 29			W	5 12 19 26			W	2 9 16 23 30			W	7 14 21 28			W	4 11 18 25			W	2 9 16 23 30	
T	2 9 16 23 30			T	6 13 20 27			T	3 10 17 24			T	1 8 15 22 29			T	5 12 19 26			T	3 10 17 24 31	
F	3 10 17 24 31			F	7 14 21 28			F	4 11 18 25			F	2 9 16 23 30			F	6 13 20 27			F	4 11 18 25	
S	4 11 18 25			S	1 8 15 22 29			S	5 12 19 26			S	3 10 17 24 31			S	7 14 21 28			S	5 12 19 26	

Green

	EUCHARIST	MORNING PRAYER	EVENING PRAYER
	CW		
Psalms:	16.1, 6–end	*119.1–32*	*11*; 12; 13
Readings:	1 Kgs 18.20–39; Matt. 5.17–19	Josh. 8.1–29; Luke 11.1–13	Job 9; Rom. 5.1–11 *or* Eve of Corpus Christi: Ps. 110, 111; Exod. 16.2–15; John 6.22–35 For Eve of Barnabas see June 11

		AW	*Exod. 3.1–12*	*Acts 7.30–38*

	HOLY COMMUNION	MORNING PRAYER	EVENING PRAYER
	BCP		
Psalms:		*50; 51; 52*	*53; 54; 55*
Readings:		*1 Sam. 4;* *Jas 2.14–end*	*1 Sam. 7;* *Luke 1.57–end* *or first Evensong of St Barnabas* *Job 29.11–16; Acts 4.32–end*
Hymns:	....	....	....

2020

	January	February	March	April	May	June
S	5 12 19 26	2 9 16 23	1 8 15 22 29	5 12 19 26	3 10 17 24 31	7 14 21 28
M	6 13 20 27	3 10 17 24	2 9 16 23 30	6 13 20 27	4 11 18 25	1 8 15 22 29
T	7 14 21 28	4 11 18 25	3 10 17 24 31	7 14 21 28	5 12 19 26	2 9 16 23 30
W	1 8 15 22 29	5 12 19 26	4 11 18 25	1 8 15 22 29	6 13 20 27	3 10 17 24
T	2 9 16 23 30	6 13 20 27	5 12 19 26	2 9 16 23 30	7 14 21 28	4 11 18 25
F	3 10 17 24 31	7 14 21 28	6 13 20 27	3 10 17 24	1 8 15 22 29	5 12 19 26
S	4 11 18 25	1 8 15 22 29	7 14 21 28	4 11 18 25	2 9 16 23 30	6 13 20 27

Day of Thanksgiving for Holy Communion (Corpus Christi) if observed   White

	PRINCIPAL SERVICE	THIRD SERVICE	SECOND SERVICE
	CW		
Psalms:	116.10–end	147	23; 42; 43
Readings:	Gen. 14.18–20; 1 Cor. 11.23–26;	Deut. 8.2–16;	Prov. 9.1–5;
	John 6.51–58	1 Cor. 10.1–17	Luke 9.11–17
			or Eve of Barnabas Ps. 1, 5;
			Isa. 42.5–12; Acts 14.8–28

Where the Thanksgiving for the Holy Communion is not observed, see tomorrow for Barnabas the Apostle

Displaced readings may be added to yesterday's portion:

	EUCHARIST	MORNING PRAYER	EVENING PRAYER
Readings:	1 Kgs 18.41–end;	Josh. 8.30–end;	Job 10;
	Matt. 5.20–26	Luke 11.14–28	Rom. 5.12–end

	HOLY COMMUNION	MORNING PRAYER	EVENING PRAYER
	BCP St Barnabas (for Corpus Christi use CW provisions)		
Psalms:	112	56; 57; 57	59; 60; 61
Readings:	Job 29.11–16; Acts 11.22–30;	Jer. 9.23, 24; Acts 9.26–31	Isa. 42.5–12; Acts 14.8–end
	John 15.12–16		
Hymns:	....	....	....

CW COLLECT FOR CORPUS CHRISTI
Lord Jesus Christ,
we thank you that in this wonderful sacrament
you have given us the memorial of your passion:
grant us so to reverence the sacred mysteries
    of your body and blood
that we may know within ourselves
and show forth in our lives
the fruits of your redemption;
for you are alive and reign with the Father
in the unity of the Holy Spirit
one God now and for ever.

POST COMMUNION
All praise to you, our God and Father,
for you have fed us with the bread of heaven
and quenched our thirst from the true vine:
hear our prayer that, being grafted into Christ,
we may grow together in unity
and feast with him in his kingdom;
through Jesus Christ our Lord.

BCP COLLECT FOR ST. BARNABAS
*O Lord God Almighty, who didst endue thy holy
Apostle Barnabas with singular gifts of the Holy
Ghost: Leave us not, we beseech thee, destitute of
thy manifold gifts, nor yet of grace to use them alway
to thine honour and glory; through Jesus Christ
our Lord.*

2020

	July					August					September					October					November					December			
S		5	12	19	26		2	9	16	23	30		6	13	20	27		4	11	18	25		1	8	15	22	29		6	13	20	27
M		6	13	20	27		3	10	17	24	31		7	14	21	28		5	12	19	26		2	9	16	23	30		7	14	21	28
T		7	14	21	28		4	11	18	25		1	8	15	22	29		6	13	20	27		3	10	17	24		1	8	15	22	29
W	1	8	15	22	29		5	12	19	26		2	9	16	23	30		7	14	21	28		4	11	18	25		2	9	16	23	30
T	2	9	16	23	30		6	13	20	27		3	10	17	24		1	8	15	22	29		5	12	19	26		3	10	17	24	31
F	3	10	17	24	31		7	14	21	28		4	11	18	25		2	9	16	23	30		6	13	20	27		4	11	18	25
S	4	11	18	25		1	8	15	22	29		5	12	19	26		3	10	17	24	31		7	14	21	28		5	12	19	26

Barnabas the Apostle (if transferred)   Red

	PRINCIPAL SERVICE CW	**THIRD SERVICE**	**SECOND SERVICE**
Psalms:	112	100; 101; 117	147
Readings:	Job 29.11–16; Acts 11.19–end; John 15.12–17 *or* Acts 11.19–end; Gal. 2.1–10; John 15.12–17 Reading from Acts must be either 1st or 2nd reading Seasonal provisions CW Book pp 328–329 Displaced readings may be added to tomorrow's portion	Jer. 9.23–24; Acts 4.32–end	Eccles. 12.9–end *or* Tobit 4.5–11; Acts 9.26–31

	EUCHARIST	**MORNING PRAYER**	**EVENING PRAYER**
Readings:	1 Kgs 19.9, 11–16; Matt. 5.27–32	Josh. 9.3–26; Luke 11.29–36	Job 11; Rom. 6.1–14
	If Barnabas is not transferred AW	Exod. 34.1–10	Mark 7.1–13

	HOLY COMMUNION BCP	**MORNING PRAYER**	**EVENING PRAYER**
Psalms:		62; 63; 64	65; 66; 67
Readings:		1 Sam. 9.26—10.16; Jas 4	1 Sam. 10.17–end; Luke 2.1–39
Hymns:	....	....	....

CW COLLECT
Bountiful God, giver of all gifts,
who poured your Spirit upon your servant Barnabas
and gave him grace to encourage others:
help us, by his example,
to be generous in our judgements
and unselfish in our service;
through Jesus Christ your Son our Lord,
who is alive and reigns with you,
in the unity of the Holy Spirit,
one God, now and for ever.

POST COMMUNION
Lord God, the source of truth and love,
keep us faithful to the apostles' teaching and
   fellowship,
united in prayer and the breaking of bread,
and one in joy and simplicity of heart,
in Jesus Christ our Lord.

Green

	EUCHARIST CW	**MORNING PRAYER**	**EVENING PRAYER**
Psalms:	16.1–7	20; 21; *23*	*24*; 25
Readings:	1 Kgs 19.9–end; Matt. 5.33–37	Josh. 10.1–15; Luke 11.37–end	Job 12; Rom. 6.15–end

		AW	*Exod. 34.27–end*	*2 Cor. 3.7–end*

	HOLY COMMUNION BCP	**MORNING PRAYER**	**EVENING PRAYER**
Psalms:		*68*	*69; 70*
Readings:		*1 Sam. 11;* *Jas 5*	*1 Sam. 12;* *Matt. 2*
Hymns:	....	....	....

2020

July					August						September					October					November					December			
S		5	12	19	26	S		2	9	16	23	30	S		6	13	20	27	S		4	11	18	25	S	1	8	15	22	29	S		6	13	20	27
M		6	13	20	27	M		3	10	17	24	31	M		7	14	21	28	M		5	12	19	26	M	2	9	16	23	30	M		7	14	21	28
T		7	14	21	28	T		4	11	18	25		T	1	8	15	22	29	T		6	13	20	27	T	3	10	17	24		T	1	8	15	22	29
W	1	8	15	22	29	W		5	12	19	26		W	2	9	16	23	30	W		7	14	21	28	W	4	11	18	25		W	2	9	16	23	30
T	2	9	16	23	30	T		6	13	20	27		T	3	10	17	24		T	1	8	15	22	29	T	5	12	19	26		T	3	10	17	24	31
F	3	10	17	24	31	F		7	14	21	28		F	4	11	18	25		F	2	9	16	23	30	F	6	13	20	27		F	4	11	18	25
S	4	11	18	25		S	1	8	15	22	29	S	5	12	19	26		S	3	10	17	24	31	S	7	14	21	28		S	5	12	19	26

THE FIRST SUNDAY AFTER TRINITY

(Green)

PRINCIPAL SERVICE	THIRD SERVICE	SECOND SERVICE

PRINCIPAL SERVICE
CW Proper 6
Readings and Psalms in Italics provide semi-continuous O.T. pattern. O.T. Readings in Roman type are closely related to the Epistle & Gospel for the day; which are common to both sets of O.T. readings.

Psalms: *116.1, 10–17 [116.9–17]* | 45 | [42] 43
100

Readings: *Gen. 18.1–15[21.1–7];* | Deut. 10.12—11.1; | 1 Sam. 21.1–15;
Exod. 19.2–8a; Rom. 5.1–8; | Acts 23.12–end | Luke 11.14–28
Matt. 9.35—10.8[9–23].

HOLY COMMUNION	MORNING PRAYER	EVENING PRAYER

HOLY COMMUNION
BCP

Psalms: *41.1–4* | 45 | *[42]; 43*

Readings: *2 Sam. 9.6–end;* | Josh. 1 or Job 1; | Josh. 5.13—6.20 or
1 John 4.7–end; | Mark 2.1–22 or | Josh. 24 or Job 2;
Luke 16.19–end | Rom. 1 | Matt. 1.18–end or Acts 8.26–end

Hymns: .... | .... | ....

CW COLLECTS

O God,
the strength of all those who put their trust in you,
mercifully accept our prayers
and, because through the weakness
of our mortal nature
we can do no good thing without you,
grant us the help of your grace,
that in the keeping of your commandments
we may please you both in will and deed;
through Jesus Christ your Son our Lord,
who is alive and reigns with you,
in the unity of the Holy Spirit,
one God, now and for ever.

or

God of truth,
help us to keep your law of love
and to walk in ways of wisdom,
that we may find true life
in Jesus Christ your Son.

POST COMMUNION

Eternal Father,
we thank you for nourishing us
with these heavenly gifts:
may our communion strengthen us in faith,
build us up in hope,
and make us grow in love;
for the sake of Jesus Christ our Lord.

BCP COLLECT

*O God, the strength of all them that put their trust
in thee, mercifully accept our prayers; and because
through the weakness of our mortal nature we can
do no good thing without thee, grant us the help of
thy grace, that in keeping of thy commandments we
may please thee both in will and deed; through Jesus
Christ our Lord.*

2020

July					August						September					October					November					December				
S		5	12	19	26	S		2	9	16	23	30	S		6	13	20	27	S		4	11	18	25	S	1	8	15	22	29	S		6	13	20	27
M		6	13	20	27	M		3	10	17	24	31	M		7	14	21	28	M		5	12	19	26	M	2	9	16	23	30	M		7	14	21	28
T		7	14	21	28	T		4	11	18	25		T	1	8	15	22	29	T		6	13	20	27	T	3	10	17	24		T	1	8	15	22	29
W	1	8	15	22	29	W		5	12	19	26		W	2	9	16	23	30	W		7	14	21	28	W	4	11	18	25		W	2	9	16	23	30
T	2	9	16	23	30	T		6	13	20	27		T	3	10	17	24		T	1	8	15	22	29	T	5	12	19	26		T	3	10	17	24	31
F	3	10	17	24	31	F		7	14	21	28		F	4	11	18	25		F	2	9	16	23	30	F	6	13	20	27		F	4	11	18	25	
S	4	11	18	25		S	1	8	15	22	29		S	5	12	19	26		S	3	10	17	24	31	S	7	14	21	28		S	5	12	19	26	

Evelyn Underhill, Spiritual Writer 1941

Green

DEL Wk 11	**EUCHARIST** CW	**MORNING PRAYER**	**EVENING PRAYER**
Psalms:	5.1–5	27; *30*; (Week 2 Ord)	26; *28*; 29
Readings:	1 Kgs 21.1–16; Matt. 5.38–42	Josh. 14; Luke 12.1–12	Job 13; Rom. 7.1–6

AW   *Gen. 37.1–11*   *Rom. 12.9–21*

	HOLY COMMUNION BCP	**MORNING PRAYER**	**EVENING PRAYER**
Psalms:		75; 76; 77	78
Readings:		1 Sam. 13; 1 Pet. 1.1–21	1 Sam. 14.1–23; Luke 2.40–end
Hymns:	....	....	....

Sunrise 04.38; Sunset 21.23

Richard, Bishop of Chichester, 1253 (CW Readings see Common of the Saints also John 21.15–19) Green *or* White
Joseph Butler, Bishop of Durham, Philosopher, 1752

	EUCHARIST	MORNING PRAYER	EVENING PRAYER
	CW		
Psalms:	51.1–9	32; *36*	*33*
Readings:	1 Kgs 21.17–end;	Josh. 21.43—22.8;	Job 14;
	Matt. 5.43–end	Luke 12.13–21	Rom. 7.7–end
	AW	*Gen. 41.15–40*	*Mark 13.1–13*
	HOLY COMMUNION	MORNING PRAYER	EVENING PRAYER
	BCP		
Psalms:		79; 80; 81	82; 83; 84; 85
Readings:		1 Sam. 14.24–48;	1 Sam. 15;
		1 Pet. 1.22—2.10	Luke 3.1–22
Hymns:	....	....	....

CW COLLECT

Most merciful redeemer,
who gave to your bishop Richard a love of learning,
a zeal for souls and a devotion to the poor:
grant that, encouraged by his example,
we may know you more clearly,
  love you more dearly,
  and follow you more nearly, day by day,
who with the Father and the Holy Spirit are alive
  and reign,
one God, now and for ever.

POST COMMUNION

God, shepherd of your people,
whose servant Richard revealed the loving service of
  Christ in his ministry as a pastor of your people:
by this eucharist in which we share
awaken within us the love of Christ
and keep us faithful to our Christian calling;
through him who laid down his life for us,
but is alive and reigns with you, now and for ever.

2020

	July					August						September					October					November					December				
S		5	12	19	26		2	9	16	23	30		6	13	20	27		4	11	18	25		1	8	15	22	29		6	13	20	27
M		6	13	20	27		3	10	17	24	31		7	14	21	28		5	12	19	26		2	9	16	23	30		7	14	21	28
T		7	14	21	28		4	11	18	25		1	8	15	22	29		6	13	20	27		3	10	17	24		1	8	15	22	29
W	1	8	15	22	29		5	12	19	26		2	9	16	23	30		7	14	21	28		4	11	18	25		2	9	16	23	30
T	2	9	16	23	30		6	13	20	27		3	10	17	24		1	8	15	22	29		5	12	19	26		3	10	17	24	31
F	3	10	17	24	31		7	14	21	28		4	11	18	25		2	9	16	23	30		6	13	20	27		4	11	18	25
S	4	11	18	25		1	8	15	22	29		5	12	19	26		3	10	17	24	31		7	14	21	28		5	12	19	26

Samuel and Henrietta Barnett, Social Reformers 1913 and 1936. St Alban, Martyr (BCP)   Green (or Red)

	EUCHARIST CW	MORNING PRAYER	EVENING PRAYER
Psalms:	31.21–end	*34*	*119.33–56*
Readings:	2 Kgs 2.1, 6–14; Matt. 6.1–6, 16–18	Josh. 22.9–end; Luke 12.22–31	Job 15; Rom. 8.1–11
AW		Gen. 42.17–end	Matt. 18.1–14

	HOLY COMMUNION BCP Com. Martyr	MORNING PRAYER	EVENING PRAYER
Psalms:	3	86; 87; 88	89
Readings:	Jer. 11.18–20; Heb. 11.32—12.2; Matt. 16.24–27	1 Sam. 16; 1 Pet. 2.11—3.7	1 Sam. 17.1–30; Luke 4.1–30
Hymns:	....	....	....

BCP COLLECT
Almighty God, by whose grace and power thy holy Martyr Alban triumphed over suffering and despised death: Grant, we beseech thee, that enduring hardness and waxing valiant in fight, we may with the noble army of martyrs receive the crown of everlasting life; through Jesus Christ our Lord.

Bernard Mizeki, Apostle of the Ma Shona, Martyr, 1896   Green

	EUCHARIST	**MORNING PRAYER**	**EVENING PRAYER**
	CW		
Psalms:	97.1–8	*37**	39; *40*
Readings:	Ecclus 48.1–14 *or* Isa. 63.7–9;	Josh. 23;	Job 16.1—17.2;
	Matt. 6.7–15	Luke 12.32–40	Rom. 8.12–17

AW   *Gen. 45.1–15*   *Acts 7.9–16*

	HOLY COMMUNION	**MORNING PRAYER**	**EVENING PRAYER**
	BCP		
Psalms:		*90; 91; 92*	*93; 94*
Readings:		*1 Sam. 17.31–54;*	*1 Sam. 17.55—18.16;*
		1 Pet. 3.8—4.6	*Luke 5.1–11*
Hymns:	....	....	....

2020

	July					August						September					October					November					December			
S		5	12	19	26		2	9	16	23	30		6	13	20	27		4	11	18	25		1	8	15	22	29		6	13	20	27
M		6	13	20	27		3	10	17	24	31		7	14	21	28		5	12	19	26		2	9	16	23	30		7	14	21	28
T		7	14	21	28		4	11	18	25		1	8	15	22	29		6	13	20	27		3	10	17	24		1	8	15	22	29
W	1	8	15	22	29		5	12	19	26		2	9	16	23	30		7	14	21	28		4	11	18	25		2	9	16	23	30
T	2	9	16	23	30		6	13	20	27		3	10	17	24		1	8	15	22	29		5	12	19	26		3	10	17	24	31
F	3	10	17	24	31		7	14	21	28		4	11	18	25		2	9	16	23	30		6	13	20	27		4	11	18	25
S	4	11	18	25		1	8	15	22	29		5	12	19	26		3	10	17	24	31		7	14	21	28		5	12	19	26

Sundar Singh of India, Sadhu (Holy Man), Evangelist, Teacher of the Faith, 1929

Green

	EUCHARIST CW	MORNING PRAYER	EVENING PRAYER
Psalms:	132.1–5, 11–13	*31*	*35*
Readings:	2 Kgs 11.1–4, 9–18, 20; Matt. 6.19–23;	Josh. 24.1–28; Luke 12.41–48	Job 17.3–end; Rom. 8.18–30
		AW Gen. 47.1–12	*1 Thess. 5.12–end*

	HOLY COMMUNION BCP	MORNING PRAYER	EVENING PRAYER
Psalms:		*95; 96; 97*	*98; 99; 100; 101*
Readings:		*1 Sam. 19;* *1 Pet. 4.7–end*	*1 Sam. 20.1–17;* *Mark 1.21–39*
Hymns:	....	....	....

2020

	January					February					March					April					May						June				
S		5	12	19	26		2	9	16	23		1	8	15	22	29		5	12	19	26		3	10	17	24	31		7	14	21	28
M		6	13	20	27		3	10	17	24		2	9	16	23	30		6	13	20	27		4	11	18	25		1	8	15	22	29
T		7	14	21	28		4	11	18	25		3	10	17	24	31		7	14	21	28		5	12	19	26		2	9	16	23	30
W	1	8	15	22	29		5	12	19	26		4	11	18	25		1	8	15	22	29		6	13	20	27		3	10	17	24	
T	2	9	16	23	30		6	13	20	27		5	12	19	26		2	9	16	23	30		7	14	21	28		4	11	18	25	
F	3	10	17	24	31		7	14	21	28		6	13	20	27		3	10	17	24		1	8	15	22	29		5	12	19	26	
S	4	11	18	25		1	8	15	22	29		7	14	21	28		4	11	18	25		2	9	16	23	30		6	13	20	27	

Translation of Edward, King of the West Saxons, 979 (BCP)   Green (*or Red*)

	EUCHARIST	**MORNING PRAYER**	**EVENING PRAYER**
	CW		
Psalms:	89.25–33	41; *42*; 43	45; *46*
Readings:	2 Chr. 24.17–25; Matt. 6.24–end	Josh. 24.29–end; Luke 12.49–end	Job 18; Rom. 8.31–end
	AW	Gen. 50.4–21	Luke 15.11–end

	HOLY COMMUNION	**MORNING PRAYER**	**EVENING PRAYER**
	BCP Com. Martyr		
Psalms:	3	102; 103	104
Readings:	Jer. 11.18–20; Heb. 11.32—12.2; Matt. 16.24–27	1 Sam. 20.18–end; 1 Pet. 5	1 Sam. 21.1—22.5; Mark 1.40—2.12; E. Coll. Trinity 2

Hymns: ....

BCP COLLECT
Almighty God, by whose grace and power thy holy Martyr Edward triumphed over suffering and despised death: Grant, we beseech thee, that enduring hardness and waxing valiant in fight, we may with the noble army of martyrs receive the crown of everlasting life; through Jesus Christ our Lord.

2020

July					August						September					October					November					December				
S		5	12	19	26	S		2	9	16	23	30	S		6	13	20	27	S		4	11	18	25	S	1	8	15	22	29	S		6	13	20	27
M		6	13	20	27	M		3	10	17	24	31	M		7	14	21	28	M		5	12	19	26	M	2	9	16	23	30	M		7	14	21	28
T		7	14	21	28	T		4	11	18	25		T	1	8	15	22	29	T		6	13	20	27	T	3	10	17	24		T	1	8	15	22	29
W	1	8	15	22	29	W		5	12	19	26		W	2	9	16	23	30	W		7	14	21	28	W	4	11	18	25		W	2	9	16	23	30
T	2	9	16	23	30	T		6	13	20	27		T	3	10	17	24		T	1	8	15	22	29	T	5	12	19	26		T	3	10	17	24	31
F	3	10	17	24	31	F		7	14	21	28		F	4	11	18	25		F	2	9	16	23	30	F	6	13	20	27		F	4	11	18	25	
S	4	11	18	25		S	1	8	15	22	29		S	5	12	19	26		S	3	10	17	24	31	S	7	14	21	28		S	5	12	19	26	

THE SECOND SUNDAY AFTER TRINITY

(Green)

	PRINCIPAL SERVICE	THIRD SERVICE	SECOND SERVICE
	CW Proper 7		
Psalms:	86.1–10, 16–end* [86.1–10]; 69.8–11 [12–17]18–20 (or 69.14–20)	49	46 [48]
Readings:	Gen. 21.8–21; Jer. 20.7–13; Rom. 6.1b–11; Matt. 10.24–39	Deut. 11.1–15; Acts 27.1–12	1 Sam. 24.1–17; Luke 14.12–24 [BCP Var. Luke 14.1–14]
	HOLY COMMUNION	MORNING PRAYER	EVENING PRAYER
	BCP		
Psalms:	120	49	46 [48]
Readings:	Gen. 12.1–4; 1 John 3.13–end; Luke 14.16–24	Judg. 4 or 5 or Job 3; Mark 2.23—3.19 or Rom. 5	Judg. 6.33—7.23 or Ruth 1 or Job 5.6–end; Matt. 2 or Acts 9.1–31
Hymns:	....	....	....

2020

	January					February					March					April					May					June			
S		5	12	19	26		2	9	16	23		1	8	15	22	29		5	12	19	26		3	10	17	24	31		7	14	21	28
M		6	13	20	27		3	10	17	24		2	9	16	23	30		6	13	20	27		4	11	18	25		1	8	15	22	29
T		7	14	21	28		4	11	18	25		3	10	17	24	31		7	14	21	28		5	12	19	26		2	9	16	23	30
W	1	8	15	22	29		5	12	19	26		4	11	18	25		1	8	15	22	29		6	13	20	27		3	10	17	24	
T	2	9	16	23	30		6	13	20	27		5	12	19	26		2	9	16	23	30		7	14	21	28		4	11	18	25	
F	3	10	17	24	31		7	14	21	28		6	13	20	27		3	10	17	24	1	8	15	22	29		5	12	19	26	
S	4	11	18	25		1	8	15	22	29		7	14	21	28		4	11	18	25	2	9	16	23	30		6	13	20	27	

CW COLLECTS

Lord, you have taught us
that all our doings without love are nothing worth:
  send your Holy Spirit
and pour into our hearts that most excellent gift of
  love, the true bond of peace and of all virtues,
without which whoever lives is counted dead
  before you.
Grant this for your only Son Jesus Christ's sake,
who is alive and reigns with you,
in the unity of the Holy Spirit,
one God, now and for ever.

or

Faithful Creator,
whose mercy never fails:
deepen our faithfulness to you
and to your living Word,
Jesus Christ our Lord.

POST COMMUNION

Loving Father,
we thank you for feeding us at the supper of
  your Son:
sustain us with your Spirit,
that we may serve you here on earth
until our joy is complete in heaven,
and we share in the eternal banquet
with Jesus Christ our Lord.

BCP COLLECT

*O Lord, who never failest to help and govern them
whom thou dost bring up in thy stedfast fear and
love: Keep us, we beseech thee, under the protection
of thy good providence, and make us to have a
perpetual fear and love of thy holy Name; through
Jesus Christ our Lord.*

2020

July					August						September					October					November					December			
S		5	12	19	26	S		2	9	16	23	30	S		6	13	20	27	S		4	11	18	25	S	1	8	15	22	29	S		6	13	20	27
M		6	13	20	27	M		3	10	17	24	31	M		7	14	21	28	M		5	12	19	26	M	2	9	16	23	30	M		7	14	21	28
T		7	14	21	28	T		4	11	18	25		T	1	8	15	22	29	T		6	13	20	27	T	3	10	17	24		T	1	8	15	22	29
W	1	8	15	22	29	W		5	12	19	26		W	2	9	16	23	30	W		7	14	21	28	W	4	11	18	25		W	2	9	16	23	30
T	2	9	16	23	30	T		6	13	20	27		T	3	10	17	24		T	1	8	15	22	29	T	5	12	19	26		T	3	10	17	24	31
F	3	10	17	24	31	F		7	14	21	28		F	4	11	18	25		F	2	9	16	23	30	F	6	13	20	27		F	4	11	18	25
S	4	11	18	25	S	1	8	15	22	29		S	5	12	19	26		S	3	10	17	24	31	S	7	14	21	28		S	5	12	19	26

Alban, First Martyr of Britain, c.250 (CW Readings see Common of the Saints
especially 2 Tim. 2.3–13; John 12.24–26)

Red *or* Green

DEL Wk 12	**EUCHARIST**	**MORNING PRAYER**	**EVENING PRAYER**
	CW		
Psalms:	60.1–5, 11–end	**44** (Week 3 Ord)	**47**; 49
Readings:	2 Kgs 17.5–8, 13–15, 18; Matt. 7.1–5	Judg. 2; Luke 13.1–9	Job 19; Rom. 9.1–18
		AW	*Isa. 32*	*Jas 3.13–end*

	HOLY COMMUNION	**MORNING PRAYER**	**EVENING PRAYER**
	BCP		
Psalms:		107	108; 109
Readings:		1 Sam. 22.6–end; 2 Pet. 1	1 Sam. 23; Luke 5.27–end
Hymns:			

CW COLLECT
Eternal Father,
when the gospel of Christ first came to our land
you gloriously confirmed the faith of Alban
by making him the first to win a martyr's crown:
grant that, following his example,
in the fellowship of the saints we may worship you,
the living God, and give true witness
to Jesus Christ your Son our Lord,
who is alive and reigns with you,
in the unity of the Holy Spirit,
one God, now and for ever.

POST COMMUNION
God our redeemer,
whose Church was strengthened
by the blood of your martyr Alban:
so bind us, in life and death, to Christ's sacrifice
that our lives, broken and offered with his,
may carry his death
and proclaim his resurrection in the world;
through Jesus Christ our Lord.

Sunrise 04.38; Sunset 21.25

2020

	July					August						September					October					November					December			
S		5	12	19	26	**S**		2	9	16	23	30	**S**		6	13	20	27	**S**		4	11	18	25	**S**	1	8	15	22	29	**S**		6	13	20	27
M		6	13	20	27	**M**		3	10	17	24	31	**M**		7	14	21	28	**M**		5	12	19	26	**M**	2	9	16	23	30	**M**		7	14	21	28
T		7	14	21	28	**T**		4	11	18	25		**T**	1	8	15	22	29	**T**		6	13	20	27	**T**	3	10	17	24		**T**	1	8	15	22	29
W	1	8	15	22	29	**W**		5	12	19	26		**W**	2	9	16	23	30	**W**		7	14	21	28	**W**	4	11	18	25		**W**	2	9	16	23	30
T	2	9	16	23	30	**T**		6	13	20	27		**T**	3	10	17	24		**T**	1	8	15	22	29	**T**	5	12	19	26		**T**	3	10	17	24	31
F	3	10	17	24	31	**F**		7	14	21	28		**F**	4	11	18	25		**F**	2	9	16	23	30	**F**	6	13	20	27		**F**	4	11	18	25	
S	4	11	18	25		**S**	1	8	15	22	29		**S**	5	12	19	26		**S**	3	10	17	24	31	**S**	7	14	21	28		**S**	5	12	19	26	

Etheldreda, Abbess of Ely c.678((CW Readings see Common of the Saints also Matt. 25.1–13)   White *or* Green

	EUCHARIST	MORNING PRAYER	EVENING PRAYER
	CW		
Psalms:	48.1–2, 8–end	*48*; 52	*50*
Readings:	2 Kgs 19.9b–11, 14–21, 31–36; Matt. 7.6, 12–14	Judg. 4.1–23; Luke 13.10–21	Job 21; Rom. 9.19–end *or* Evensong of The Birth of John the Baptist: Ps. 71; Judg. 13.2–7, 24–end; Luke 1.5–25

		AW	*Prov. 3.1–18*	*Matt. 5.1–12*
	HOLY COMMUNION		MORNING PRAYER	EVENING PRAYER
	BCP			
Psalms:			*110; 111; 112; 113*	*114; 115*
Readings			*1 Sam. 24; 2 Pet. 2*	*1 Sam. 25.2–42; Luke 6.1–19 or 1st Evensong for the Nativity of St John the Baptist: Mal. 3.1–6; Luke 1.5–23; E. Coll: Nativity of John the Baptist*

Hymns: ....

COLLECT
Eternal God,
who bestowed such grace upon your servant
   Etheldreda
that she gave herself wholly to the life of prayer
and to the service of your true religion:
grant that we, like her,
may so live our lives on earth seeking your kingdom
 that by your guiding we may be joined to the
glorious fellowship of your saints;
through Jesus Christ your Son our Lord,
who is alive and reigns with you,
in the unity of the Holy Spirit,
one God, now and for ever.

POST COMMUNION
Merciful God,
who gave such grace to your servant Julian
that she served you with singleness of heart
and loved you above all things:
help us, whose communion with you
has been renewed in this sacrament,
to forsake all that holds us back from following Christ
and to grow into his likeness from glory to glory;
through Jesus Christ our Lord.

2021

January				
S		3	10	17	24	31
M		4	11	18	25
T		5	12	19	26
W		6	13	20	27
T		7	14	21	28
F	1	8	15	22	29
S	2	9	16	23	30

February
S		7	14	21	28
M	1	8	15	22
T	2	9	16	23
W	3	10	17	24
T	4	11	18	25
F	5	12	19	26
S	6	13	20	27

March
S		7	14	21	28
M	1	8	15	22	29
T	2	9	16	23	30
W	3	10	17	24	31
T	4	11	18	25
F	5	12	19	26
S	6	13	20	27

April
S		4	11	18	25
M		5	12	19	26
T		6	13	20	27
W		7	14	21	28
T	1	8	15	22	29
F	2	9	16	23	30
S	3	10	17	24

May
S		2	9	16	23	30
M		3	10	17	24	31
T		4	11	18	25
W		5	12	19	26
T		6	13	20	27
F		7	14	21	28
S	1	8	15	22	29

June
S		6	13	20	27
M		7	14	21	28
T	1	8	15	22	29
W	2	9	16	23	30
T	3	10	17	24
F	4	11	18	25
S	5	12	19	26

The Birth of John the Baptist Ember Day (CW see Common of the Saints)   White

	PRINCIPAL SERVICE CW	THIRD SERVICE	SECOND SERVICE
Psalms:	85.7–end	50; 149	80; 82 [BCP Var. Ps. 82]
Readings:	Isa. 40.1–11; Acts 13.14b–26 or Gal. 3.23–end; Luke 1.57–66, 80	Ecclus 48.1–10 or Mal. 3.1–6; Luke 3.1–17	Mal. 4; Matt. 11.2–19

Displaced readings may be added to yesterday's or tomorrow's portion:

	EUCHARIST	MORNING PRAYER	EVENING PRAYER
Readings:	2 Kgs 22.8–13, 23.1–3; Matt. 7.15–20	Judg. 5; Luke 13.22–end	Job 22; Rom. 10–1–10

	HOLY COMMUNION BCP St John Baptist	MORNING PRAYER	EVENING PRAYER
Psalms:	80.1–7	116; 117; 118	119.1–32
Readings:	Isa. 40.1–11; Acts 13.22–26; Luke 1.57–end	Ecclus 48.1–10; Luke 3.1–20	Mal. 4; Matt. 11.2–19
Hymns:	....	....	....

CW COLLECT

Almighty God,
by whose providence your servant John the Baptist
was wonderfully born,
and sent to prepare the way of your Son our Saviour
by the preaching of repentance:
lead us to repent according to his preaching
and, after his example,
constantly to speak the truth, boldly to rebuke vice,
and patiently to suffer for the truth's sake;
through Jesus Christ your Son our Lord,
who is alive and reigns with you,
in the unity of the Holy Spirit,
one God, now and for ever.

POST COMMUNION

Merciful Lord,
whose prophet John the Baptist
proclaimed your Son as the Lamb of God
   who takes away the sin of the world:
grant that we who in this sacrament
have known your forgiveness
and your life-giving love may ever tell
of your mercy and your peace;
through Jesus Christ our Lord.

BCP COLLECT

*Almighty God, by whose providence thy servant
John Baptist was wonderfully born, and sent to
prepare the way of thy Son our Saviour, by preaching
of repentance: Make us so to follow his doctrine and
holy life, that we may truly repent according to his
preaching; and after his example constantly speak
the truth, boldly rebuke vice, and patiently suffer for
the truth's sake; through Jesus Christ our Lord.*

Green

	EUCHARIST	**MORNING PRAYER**	**EVENING PRAYER**
	CW		
Psalms:	79.1–9, 12	56; *57*; (63*)	61; *62*; 64
Readings:	2 Kgs 24.8–17; Matt. 7.21–end	Judg. 6.1–24; Luke 14.1–11	Job 23; Rom. 10.11–end

AW   *Jer. 6.9–15*   *1 Tim. 2.1–6*

	HOLY COMMUNION	**MORNING PRAYER**	**EVENING PRAYER**
	BCP		
Psalms:		119.33–72	119.73–104
Readings:		1 Sam. 31; Jude	2 Sam. 1; Matt. 5.17–end
Hymns:	....	....	....

2021

	January	February	March	April	May	June
S	3 10 17 24 31	7 14 21 28	7 14 21 28	4 11 18 25	2 9 16 23 30	6 13 20 27
M	4 11 18 25	1 8 15 22	1 8 15 22 29	5 12 19 26	3 10 17 24 31	7 14 21 28
T	5 12 19 26	2 9 16 23	2 9 16 23 30	6 13 20 27	4 11 18 25	1 8 15 22 29
W	6 13 20 27	3 10 17 24	3 10 17 24 31	7 14 21 28	5 12 19 26	2 9 16 23 30
T	7 14 21 28	4 11 18 25	4 11 18 25	1 8 15 22 29	6 13 20 27	3 10 17 24
F	1 8 15 22 29	5 12 19 26	5 12 19 26	2 9 16 23 30	7 14 21 28	4 11 18 25
S	2 9 16 23 30	6 13 20 27	6 13 20 27	3 10 17 24	1 8 15 22 29	5 12 19 26

Ember Day (CW see Common of the Saints)   Green *or* Red

	EUCHARIST		**MORNING PRAYER**	**EVENING PRAYER**
	CW			
Psalms:	137.1–6		*51*; 54	*38*
Readings:	2 Kgs 25.1–12;		Judg. 6.25–end;	Job 24;
	Matt. 8.1–4		Luke 14.12–24	Rom. 11.1–12
		AW	*1 Sam. 16.14–end*	*John 14.15–end*

	HOLY COMMUNION	**MORNING PRAYER**	**EVENING PRAYER**
	BCP		
Psalms:		*119.105–144*	*119.145–end*
Readings:		*2 Sam. 2.1—3.1;*	*2 Sam. 3.17–end;*
		1 John 1.1–2.6	*Matt. 6.1–23*
Hymns:	....	....	....

2020

July						August						September						October						November						December				
S		5	12	19	26	S		2	9	16	23	30	S		6	13	20	27	S		4	11	18	25	S	1	8	15	22	29	S		6	13	20	27
M		6	13	20	27	M		3	10	17	24	31	M		7	14	21	28	M		5	12	19	26	M	2	9	16	23	30	M		7	14	21	28
T		7	14	21	28	T		4	11	18	25		T	1	8	15	22	29	T		6	13	20	27	T	3	10	17	24		T	1	8	15	22	29
W	1	8	15	22	29	W		5	12	19	26		W	2	9	16	23	30	W		7	14	21	28	W	4	11	18	25		W	2	9	16	23	30
T	2	9	16	23	30	T		6	13	20	27		T	3	10	17	24		T	1	8	15	22	29	T	5	12	19	26		T	3	10	17	24	31
F	3	10	17	24	31	F		7	14	21	28		F	4	11	18	25		F	2	9	16	23	30	F	6	13	20	27		F	4	11	18	25	
S	4	11	18	25		S	1	8	15	22	29		S	5	12	19	26		S	3	10	17	24	31	S	7	14	21	28		S	5	12	19	26	

Cyril, Bishop of Alexandria, Teacher of the Faith, 444 Ember Day (CW see Common of the Saints)   Green *or* Red

	EUCHARIST CW	MORNING PRAYER	EVENING PRAYER
Psalms:	74.1–3, 21–end	*68*	65; *66*
Readings:	Lam. 2.10–14, 18–19; Matt. 8.5–17	Judg. 7; Luke 14.25–end	Job 25—26; Rom. 11.13–24

	AW	*Isa. 6.1–9*	*Rev. 19.9–end*

	HOLY COMMUNION BCP	MORNING PRAYER	EVENING PRAYER
Psalms:		*120; 121; 123; 124; 125*	*126; 127; 128; 129; 130; 131*
Readings:		*2 Sam. 5.1–12, 17–end; 1 John 2.7–end*	*2 Sam. 6; Matt. 7; E. Coll: Trinity 3*
Hymns:	....	....	....

(ruled blank lines)

2021

January		February		March		April		May		June	
S	3 10 17 24 31	S	7 14 21 28	S	7 14 21 28	S	4 11 18 25	S	2 9 16 23 30	S	6 13 20 27
M	4 11 18 25	M	1 8 15 22	M	1 8 15 22 29	M	5 12 19 26	M	3 10 17 24 31	M	7 14 21 28
T	5 12 19 26	T	2 9 16 23	T	2 9 16 23 30	T	6 13 20 27	T	4 11 18 25	T	1 8 15 22 29
W	6 13 20 27	W	3 10 17 24	W	3 10 17 24 31	W	7 14 21 28	W	5 12 19 26	W	2 9 16 23 30
T	7 14 21 28	T	4 11 18 25	T	4 11 18 25	T	1 8 15 22 29	T	6 13 20 27	T	3 10 17 24
F	1 8 15 22 29	F	5 12 19 26	F	5 12 19 26	F	2 9 16 23 30	F	7 14 21 28	F	4 11 18 25
S	2 9 16 23 30	S	6 13 20 27	S	6 13 20 27	S	3 10 17 24	S	1 8 15 22 29	S	5 12 19 26

THE THIRD SUNDAY AFTER TRINITY

(Green)

	PRINCIPAL SERVICE	THIRD SERVICE	SECOND SERVICE
	CW Proper 8		
Psalms:	13	52; 53	50 [or 50.1–15]
	89.1–4, 15–18 [or 89.8–18]		
Readings:	Gen. 22.1–14;	Deut. 15.1–11;	1 Sam. 28.3–19;
	Jer. 28.5–9;	Acts 27.[13–32] 33–end	Luke 17.20–end or
	Rom. 6.12–end;		Eve of Peter & Paul, Apostles:
	Matt. 10.40–end		Ps. 66, 67; Ezek. 3.4–11;
			Gal. 1.13—2.8
			or Peter alone: Acts 9.32–end

	HOLY COMMUNION	MORNING PRAYER	EVENING PRAYER
	BCP		
Psalms:	55.17–23	52; 53	50
Readings:	2 Chr. 33.9–13;	1 Sam. 1 or Job 19;	1 Sam. 2.1–21 or
	1 Pet. 5.5b–11;	Mark 4.1–29 or Rom. 6	1 Sam. 3 or Job 28;
	Luke 15.1–10		Matt. 4.23—5.16 or Acts 10
			or First Evensong of St Peter
			Ezek. 2.1–7; Acts 3
Hymns:	....	....	....

2020

	July					August					September					October					November					December			
S		5	12	19	26		2	9	16	23	30		6	13	20	27		4	11	18	25		1	8	15	22	29		6	13	20	27
M		6	13	20	27		3	10	17	24	31		7	14	21	28		5	12	19	26		2	9	16	23	30		7	14	21	28
T		7	14	21	28		4	11	18	25			1	8	15	22	29		6	13	20	27		3	10	17	24		1	8	15	22	29
W	1	8	15	22	29		5	12	19	26		2	9	16	23	30		7	14	21	28		4	11	18	25		2	9	16	23	30
T	2	9	16	23	30		6	13	20	27		3	10	17	24		1	8	15	22	29		5	12	19	26		3	10	17	24	31
F	3	10	17	24	31		7	14	21	28		4	11	18	25		2	9	16	23	30		6	13	20	27		4	11	18	25
S	4	11	18	25		1	8	15	22	29		5	12	19	26		3	10	17	24	31		7	14	21	28		5	12	19	26

CW COLLECTS

Almighty God,
you have broken the tyranny of sin
and have sent the Spirit of your Son into our hearts
  whereby we call you Father:
give us grace to dedicate our freedom to
  your service,
that we and all creation may be brought
  to the glorious liberty of the children of God;
through Jesus Christ your Son our Lord,
who is alive and reigns with you,
in the unity of the Holy Spirit,
one God, now and for ever.

or

God our Saviour,
look on this wounded world
in pity and in power;
hold fast to your promises of peace
won for us by your Son,
our Saviour Jesus Christ.

POST COMMUNION

O God, whose beauty is beyond our imagining
and whose power we cannot comprehend:
show us your glory as far as we can grasp it,
and shield us from knowing more than we can bear
until we may look upon you without fear;
through Jesus Christ our Saviour.

BCP COLLECT

*O Lord, we beseech thee mercifully to hear us; and
grant that we, to whom thou hast given an hearty
desire to pray, may by thy mighty aid be defended
and comforted in all dangers and adversities; through
Jesus Christ our Lord.*

2021

	January					February					March					April					May					June			
S		3	10	17	24	31		7	14	21	28		7	14	21	28		4	11	18	25		2	9	16	23	30		6	13	20	27
M		4	11	18	25		1	8	15	22		1	8	15	22	29		5	12	19	26		3	10	17	24	31		7	14	21	28
T		5	12	19	26		2	9	16	23		2	9	16	23	30		6	13	20	27		4	11	18	25		1	8	15	22	29
W		6	13	20	27		3	10	17	24		3	10	17	24	31		7	14	21	28		5	12	19	26		2	9	16	23	30
T		7	14	21	28		4	11	18	25		4	11	18	25		1	8	15	22	29		6	13	20	27		3	10	17	24
F	1	8	15	22	29		5	12	19	26		5	12	19	26		2	9	16	23	30		7	14	21	28		4	11	18	25
S	2	9	16	23	30		6	13	20	27		6	13	20	27		3	10	17	24		1	8	15	22	29		5	12	19	26

Peter and Paul, Apostles Peter the Apostle (BCP)   Red

	PRINCIPAL SERVICE CW	THIRD SERVICE	SECOND SERVICE
Psalms:	125	71; 113	124; 138
Readings:	Zech. 4.1–6a, 10b–end; Acts 12.1–11; Matt. 16.13–19 or Acts 12.1–11; 2 Tim. 4.6–8, 17–18; Matt. 16.13–19 or for Peter alone Ezek. 3.22–27; Acts 12.1–11; Matt. 16.13–19 or Acts 12.1–11; 1 Pet. 2.19–end; Matt. 16.13–19	Isa. 49.1–6; Acts 11.1–18	Ezek. 34.11–16; John 21.15–22

Displaced readings may be added to yesterday's or tomorrow's portion:

	EUCHARIST CW	MORNING PRAYER	EVENING PRAYER
Readings:	Amos 2.6–10, 13–end; Matt. 8.18–22	Judg. 8.22–end; Luke 15.1–10	Job 27; Rom. 11.25–end

	HOLY COMMUNION BCP St Peter	MORNING PRAYER	EVENING PRAYER
Psalms:	125	139; 140; 141	142; 143
Readings:	Ezek. 3.4–11; Acts 12.1–11; Matt. 16.13–19	Ezek. 3.4–11; Acts 11.1–18	Ezek. 34.11–16; John 21.15–22
Hymns:	....	....	....

CW COLLECTS for Peter and Paul

Almighty God,
whose blessed apostles Peter and Paul
glorified you in their death as in their life:
grant that your Church,
inspired by their teaching and example,
and made one by your Spirit,
may ever stand firm upon the one foundation,
Jesus Christ your Son our Lord,
who is alive and reigns with you,
in the unity of the Holy Spirit,
one God, now and for ever.

or, where Peter is celebrated alone

Almighty God,
who inspired your apostle Saint Peter
to confess Jesus as Christ and Son of the
    living God:
build up your Church upon this rock,
that in unity and peace it may proclaim one truth
and follow one Lord, your Son our Saviour Christ,
who is alive and reigns with you,
in the unity of the Holy Spirit,
one God, now and for ever.

POST COMMUNION

Almighty God,
who on the day of Pentecost
sent your Holy Spirit to the apostles
with the wind from heaven and in tongues of flame,
filling them with joy and boldness to preach
    the gospel:
by the power of the same Spirit
strengthen us to witness to your truth
and to draw everyone to the fire of your love;
through Jesus Christ our Lord.

BCP COLLECT

O Almighty God, who by thy Son Jesus Christ didst give to thy Apostle Saint Peter many excellent gifts, and commandedst him earnestly to feed thy flock: Make, we beseech thee, all Bishops and Pastors diligently to preach thy holy Word, and the people obediently to follow the same, that they may receive the crown of everlasting glory; through Jesus Christ our Lord.

Sunrise 04.42; Sunset 21.24

2020

	July					August					September					October					November					December			
S		5	12	19	26		2	9	16	23	30		6	13	20	27		4	11	18	25	1	8	15	22	29		6	13	20	27
M		6	13	20	27		3	10	17	24	31		7	14	21	28		5	12	19	26	2	9	16	23	30		7	14	21	28
T		7	14	21	28		4	11	18	25		1	8	15	22	29		6	13	20	27	3	10	17	24		1	8	15	22	29
W	1	8	15	22	29		5	12	19	26		2	9	16	23	30		7	14	21	28	4	11	18	25		2	9	16	23	30
T	2	9	16	23	30		6	13	20	27		3	10	17	24		1	8	15	22	29	5	12	19	26		3	10	17	24	31
F	3	10	17	24	31		7	14	21	28		4	11	18	25		2	9	16	23	30	6	13	20	27		4	11	18	25
S	4	11	18	25		1	8	15	22	29		5	12	19	26		3	10	17	24	31	7	14	21	28		5	12	19	26

Green

DEL Wk 13	**EUCHARIST**	**MORNING PRAYER**	**EVENING PRAYER**
	CW		
Psalms:	5.8–end	73 (Week 4 Ord)	74
Readings:	Amos 3.1–8, 4.11–12;	Judg. 9.1–21;	Job 28;
	Matt. 8.23–27	Luke 15.11–end	Rom. 12.1–8

		AW	*Prov. 1.20–end*	*Jas 5.13–end*

	HOLY COMMUNION	**MORNING PRAYER**	**EVENING PRAYER**
	BCP		
Psalms:		*144; 145; 146*	*147; 148; 149; 150*
Readings:		*2 Sam. 11;*	*2 Sam. 12.1–23;*
		1 John 3.13—4.6	*Matt. 11.2–end*
Hymns:	....	....	....

2021

	January					February					March					April					May					June			
S		3	10	17	24	31		7	14	21	28		7	14	21	28		4	11	18	25		2	9	16	23	30		6	13	20	27
M		4	11	18	25		1	8	15	22		1	8	15	22	29		5	12	19	26		3	10	17	24	31		7	14	21	28
T		5	12	19	26		2	9	16	23		2	9	16	23	30		6	13	20	27		4	11	18	25		1	8	15	22	29
W		6	13	20	27		3	10	17	24		3	10	17	24	31		7	14	21	28		5	12	19	26		2	9	16	23	30
T		7	14	21	28		4	11	18	25		4	11	18	25		1	8	15	22	29		6	13	20	27		3	10	17	24
F	1	8	15	22	29	5	12	19	26		5	12	19	26		2	9	16	23	30		7	14	21	28		4	11	18	25
S	2	9	16	23	30	6	13	20	27		6	13	20	27		3	10	17	24		1	8	15	22	29		5	12	19	26

Henry, John and Henry Venn the younger, Priests, Evangelical Divines 1797, 1813 and 1873   Green

	EUCHARIST CW	**MORNING PRAYER**	**EVENING PRAYER**
Psalms:	50.7–14	*77*	*119.81–104*
Readings:	Amos 5.14–15, 21–24; Matt. 8.28–end	Judg. 9.22–end; Luke 16.1–18	Job 29; Rom. 12.9–end
		AW *Isa. 5.8–24*	*Jas 1.17–25*

	HOLY COMMUNION BCP	**MORNING PRAYER**	**EVENING PRAYER**
Psalms:		1; 2; 3; 4; 5	6; 7; 8
Readings:		2 Sam. 13.38—14.24; 1 John 4.7–end	2 Sam. 14.25—15.12; Luke 7.36—8.3
Hymns:	....	....	....

2020

	July					August						September					October					November					December			
S		5	12	19	26		2	9	16	23	30		6	13	20	27		4	11	18	25		1	8	15	22	29		6	13	20	27
M		6	13	20	27		3	10	17	24	31		7	14	21	28		5	12	19	26		2	9	16	23	30		7	14	21	28
T		7	14	21	28		4	11	18	25		1	8	15	22	29		6	13	20	27		3	10	17	24		1	8	15	22	29
W	1	8	15	22	29		5	12	19	26		2	9	16	23	30		7	14	21	28		4	11	18	25		2	9	16	23	30
T	2	9	16	23	30		6	13	20	27		3	10	17	24		1	8	15	22	29		5	12	19	26		3	10	17	24	31
F	3	10	17	24	31		7	14	21	28		4	11	18	25		2	9	16	23	30		6	13	20	27		4	11	18	25
S	4	11	18	25		1	8	15	22	29		5	12	19	26		3	10	17	24	31		7	14	21	28		5	12	19	26

Visitation of Blessed Virgin Mary (BCP)   Green (*or White*)

EUCHARIST	**MORNING PRAYER**	**EVENING PRAYER**
CW		
Psalms: 19.7–10	*78.1–39**	*78.40–end**
Readings: Amos 7.10–end; Matt. 9.1–8	Judg. 11.1–11; Luke 16.19–end	Job 30; Rom. 13.1–7 *or* Eve of Thomas the Apostle: Ps. 27; Isa. 35; Heb. 10.35—11.1

		AW	*Isa. 57.14–end*	*John 13.1–17*

HOLY COMMUNION	**MORNING PRAYER**	**EVENING PRAYER**
BCP Visitation		
Psalms: 113	*9; 10; 11*	*12; 13; 14*
Readings: 1 Sam. 2.1–3; Gal. 4.1–5; Luke 1.39–45	2 Sam. 15.13–end; 1 John 5	2 Sam. 16.1–19; Matt. 12.22–end
Hymns:	....	....

BCP COLLECT for Visitation
God, who didst lead the blessed Virgin Mary to visit Elizabeth, to their exceedingly joy and comfort: Grant unto thy people, that as Mary did rejoice to be called the Mother of the Lord, so they may ever rejoice to believe the incarnation of thine only–begotten Son, to whom with thee and the Holy Ghost be all honour and glory, world without end.

2021

	January					February				March					April				May					June			
S		3	10	17	24	31	S			7	14	21	28	S		7	14	21	28	S		4	11	18	25	S		2	9	16	23	30	S		6	13	20	27
M		4	11	18	25		M		1	8	15	22		M	1	8	15	22	29	M		5	12	19	26	M		3	10	17	24	31	M		7	14	21	28
T		5	12	19	26		T		2	9	16	23		T	2	9	16	23	30	T		6	13	20	27	T		4	11	18	25	T	1	8	15	22	29
W		6	13	20	27		W		3	10	17	24		W	3	10	17	24	31	W		7	14	21	28	W		5	12	19	26	W	2	9	16	23	30
T		7	14	21	28		T		4	11	18	25		T	4	11	18	25		T	1	8	15	22	29	T		6	13	20	27	T	3	10	17	24	
F	1	8	15	22	29		F		5	12	19	26		F	5	12	19	26		F	2	9	16	23	30	F		7	14	21	28	F	4	11	18	25	
S	2	9	16	23	30		S		6	13	20	27		S	6	13	20	27		S	3	10	17	24		S	1	8	15	22	29	S	5	12	19	26	

Thomas the Apostle *(December 21 BCP)* Red

	PRINCIPAL SERVICE	THIRD SERVICE	SECOND SERVICE
	CW		
Psalms:	31.1–6	92; 146	139
Readings:	Hab. 2.1–4; Eph. 2.19–end; John 20.24–29	2 Sam. 15.17–21 *or* Ecclus 2; John 11.1–16	Job 42.1–6 [BCP Var. Hab. 2.1–4] 1 Pet. 1.3–12

For seasonal provisions CW Book p 328.

Displaced readings may be added to the previous or following day's portion

	EUCHARIST	MORNING PRAYER	EVENING PRAYER
	CW		
Readings:	Amos 8.4–6, 9–12; Matt. 9.9–13	Judg. 11.29–end; Luke 17.1–10	Job 31; Rom. 13.8–end

	HOLY COMMUNION	MORNING PRAYER	EVENING PRAYER
	BCP		
Psalms:		15; 16; 17	18
Readings:		2 Sam. 17.1–23; 2 John	2 Sam. 17.24—18.18; Matt. 13.1–23
Hymns:	....	....	....

CW COLLECT
Almighty and eternal God,
who, for the firmer foundation of our faith,
allowed your holy apostle Thomas
   to doubt the resurrection of your Son
till word and sight convinced him:
grant to us, who have not seen,
   that we also may believe
and so confess Christ as our Lord and our God;
who is alive and reigns with you,
in the unity of the Holy Spirit,
one God, now and for ever.

POST COMMUNION
Lord God, the source of truth and love,
keep us faithful to the apostles' teaching
   and fellowship,
united in prayer and the breaking of bread,
and one in joy and simplicity of heart,
in Jesus Christ our Lord.

2020

	July	August	September	October	November	December
S	5 12 19 26	2 9 16 23 30	6 13 20 27	4 11 18 25	1 8 15 22 29	6 13 20 27
M	6 13 20 27	3 10 17 24 31	7 14 21 28	5 12 19 26	2 9 16 23 30	7 14 21 28
T	7 14 21 28	4 11 18 25	1 8 15 22 29	6 13 20 27	3 10 17 24	1 8 15 22 29
W	1 8 15 22 29	5 12 19 26	2 9 16 23 30	7 14 21 28	4 11 18 25	2 9 16 23 30
T	2 9 16 23 30	6 13 20 27	3 10 17 24	1 8 15 22 29	5 12 19 26	3 10 17 24 31
F	3 10 17 24 31	7 14 21 28	4 11 18 25	2 9 16 23 30	6 13 20 27	4 11 18 25
S	4 11 18 25	1 8 15 22 29	5 12 19 26	3 10 17 24 31	7 14 21 28	5 12 19 26

Translation of St Martin, Bishop of Tours, c.397 (BCP) Green

	EUCHARIST	MORNING PRAYER	EVENING PRAYER
	CW		
Psalms:	85.8–end	*76*; 79	81; *84*
Readings:	Amos 9.11–end;	Judg. 12.1–7;	Job 32;
	Matt. 9.14–17	Luke 17.11–19	Rom. 14.1–12

| | | AW | *Isa. 25.1–9* | *Acts 2.22–33* |

	HOLY COMMUNION	MORNING PRAYER	EVENING PRAYER
	BCP		
Psalms:	*99*	*19; 20; 21*	*22; 23*
Readings:	*Ezek. 34.11–16; 1 Tim. 3.15–16;*	*2 Sam. 18.19–end;*	*2 Sam. 19.1–23; Matt. 13.24–43;*
	Mark 4.26–32	*3 John*	*E. Coll. Trinity 4*
Hymns:	....	....	....

BCP COLLECT
O God, the light of the faithful, and shepherd of souls, who didst set blessed Martin to be a Bishop in the Church, that he might feed thy sheep by his word and guide them by his example: Grant us, we pray thee, to keep the faith which he taught, and to follow in his footsteps; through Jesus Christ our Lord.

THE FOURTH SUNDAY AFTER TRINITY

(Green)

	PRINCIPAL SERVICE	THIRD SERVICE	SECOND SERVICE
	CW Proper 9		
Psalms:	*45.10–end or*	*55.1–15, 18–22*	*56[57]*
	Canticle: Song of Sol 2.8–13		
	145.8–15		
Readings:	*Gen. 24.34–38, 42–49, 58–end*	Deut. 24.10–end;	2 Sam. 2.1–11; 3.1;
	Zech. 9.9–12	Acts 28.1–16	Luke 18.31—19.10
	Rom. 7.15–25a;		
	Matt. 11.16–19, 25–end		

	HOLY COMMUNION	MORNING PRAYER	EVENING PRAYER
	BCP		
Psalms:	79.8–10	*55.1–15, 18–22*	*56 [57]*
Readings:	Gen. 3.17–19; Rom. 8.18–23;	*1 Sam. 12 or Job 29;*	*1 Sam. 15.1–31 or 1 Sam. 16 or*
	Luke 6.36–42	*Mark 6.1–32 or Rom. 12*	*Job 38; Matt. 5.17–end or*
			Acts 13.1–26
Hymns:	....	....	....

Full Moon

2020

	July					August						September					October					November					December			
S		5	12	19	26		2	9	16	23	30		6	13	20	27		4	11	18	25		1	8	15	22	29		6	13	20	27
M		6	13	20	27		3	10	17	24	31		7	14	21	28		5	12	19	26		2	9	16	23	30		7	14	21	28
T		7	14	21	28		4	11	18	25		1	8	15	22	29		6	13	20	27		3	10	17	24		1	8	15	22	29
W	1	8	15	22	29		5	12	19	26		2	9	16	23	30		7	14	21	28		4	11	18	25		2	9	16	23	30
T	2	9	16	23	30		6	13	20	27		3	10	17	24		1	8	15	22	29		5	12	19	26		3	10	17	24	31
F	3	10	17	24	31		7	14	21	28		4	11	18	25		2	9	16	23	30		6	13	20	27		4	11	18	25
S	4	11	18	25		1	8	15	22	29		5	12	19	26		3	10	17	24	31		7	14	21	28		5	12	19	26

CW COLLECTS

O God, the protector of all who trust in you,
without whom nothing is strong, nothing is holy:
increase and multiply upon us your mercy;
that with you as our ruler and guide
we may so pass through things temporal
that we lose not our hold on things eternal;
grant this, heavenly Father,
for our Lord Jesus Christ's sake,
who is alive and reigns with you,
in the unity of the Holy Spirit,
one God, now and for ever.

or

Gracious Father,
by the obedience of Jesus
you brought salvation to our wayward world:
draw us into harmony with your will,
that we may find all things restored in him,
our Saviour, Jesus Christ.

POST COMMUNION

Eternal God,
comfort of the afflicted and healer of the broken,
you have fed us at the table of life and hope:
teach us the ways of gentleness and peace,
that all the world may acknowledge
the kingdom of your Son Jesus Christ our Lord.

BCP COLLECT

*O God, the protector of all that trust in thee, without
whom nothing is strong, nothing is holy: Increase
and multiply upon us thy mercy; that, thou being
our ruler and guide, we may so pass through things
temporal, that we finally lose not the things eternal:
Grant this, O heavenly Father, for Jesus Christ's sake
our Lord.*

2021

January					February					March					April					May					June				
S		3	10	17	24	31	S			7	14	21	28	S			7	14	21	28	S		4	11	18	25	S		2	9	16	23	30	S		6	13	20	27
M		4	11	18	25	M	1	8	15	22	M	1	8	15	22	29	M		5	12	19	26	M		3	10	17	24	31	M		7	14	21	28
T		5	12	19	26	T	2	9	16	23	T	2	9	16	23	30	T		6	13	20	27	T		4	11	18	25	T	1	8	15	22	29
W		6	13	20	27	W	3	10	17	24	W	3	10	17	24	31	W		7	14	21	28	W		5	12	19	26	W	2	9	16	23	30
T		7	14	21	28	T	4	11	18	25	T	4	11	18	25	T	1	8	15	22	29	T		6	13	20	27	T	3	10	17	24
F	1	8	15	22	29	F	5	12	19	26	F	5	12	19	26	F	2	9	16	23	30	F		7	14	21	28	F	4	11	18	25
S	2	9	16	23	30	S	6	13	20	27	S	6	13	20	27	S	3	10	17	24	S	1	8	15	22	29	S	5	12	19	26

Thomas More, Scholar and John Fisher, Bishop of Rochester, Reformation Martyrs, 1535

Green

DEL Wk 14	**EUCHARIST** CW	**MORNING PRAYER**	**EVENING PRAYER**
Psalms:	145.2–9	*80*; 82 (Week 5 Ord)	*85*; 86
Readings:	Hos. 2.14–16, 19–20; Matt. 9.18–26	Judg. 13.1–24; Luke 17.20–end	Job 33; Rom. 14.13–end

	AW	*Exod. 20.1–17*	*Matt. 6.1–15*
	HOLY COMMUNION BCP	**MORNING PRAYER**	**EVENING PRAYER**
Psalms:		30; 31	32; 33; 34
Readings:		2 Sam. 19.24–end; 1 Thess. 1	2 Sam. 23.1–17; Matt. 13.44–end
Hymns:	....	....	....

Sunrise 04.47; Sunset 21.21

2020

	July					August						September					October					November					December			
S		5	12	19	26		2	9	16	23	30		6	13	20	27		4	11	18	25	S	1	8	15	22	29		6	13	20	27
M		6	13	20	27		3	10	17	24	31		7	14	21	28		5	12	19	26	M	2	9	16	23	30		7	14	21	28
T		7	14	21	28		4	11	18	25		1	8	15	22	29		6	13	20	27	T	3	10	17	24		1	8	15	22	29
W	1	8	15	22	29		5	12	19	26		2	9	16	23	30		7	14	21	28	W	4	11	18	25		2	9	16	23	30
T	2	9	16	23	30		6	13	20	27		3	10	17	24		1	8	15	22	29	T	5	12	19	26		3	10	17	24	31
F	3	10	17	24	31		7	14	21	28		4	11	18	25		2	9	16	23	30	F	6	13	20	27		4	11	18	25
S	4	11	18	25		1	8	15	22	29		5	12	19	26		3	10	17	24	31	S	7	14	21	28		5	12	19	26

Green

	EUCHARIST	**MORNING PRAYER**	**EVENING PRAYER**
	CW		
Psalms:	103.8–12	87; *89.1–18*	*89.19–end*
Readings:	Hos. 8.4–7, 11–13;	Judg. 14;	Job 38;
	Matt. 9.32–end	Luke 18.1–14	Rom. 15.1–13

AW *Prov. 6.6–19* *Luke 4.1–14*

	HOLY COMMUNION	**MORNING PRAYER**	**EVENING PRAYER**
	BCP		
Psalms:		*35; 36*	*37*
Readings:		2 Sam. 24;	1 Kgs 1.5–31;
		1 Thess. 2.1–16	Mark 4.35—5.20
Hymns:	....	....	....

2021

	January	February	March	April	May	June
S	3 10 17 24 31	7 14 21 28	7 14 21 28	4 11 18 25	2 9 16 23 30	6 13 20 27
M	4 11 18 25	1 8 15 22	1 8 15 22 29	5 12 19 26	3 10 17 24 31	7 14 21 28
T	5 12 19 26	2 9 16 23	2 9 16 23 30	6 13 20 27	4 11 18 25	1 8 15 22 29
W	6 13 20 27	3 10 17 24	3 10 17 24 31	7 14 21 28	5 12 19 26	2 9 16 23 30
T	7 14 21 28	4 11 18 25	4 11 18 25	1 8 15 22 29	6 13 20 27	3 10 17 24
F	1 8 15 22 29	5 12 19 26	5 12 19 26	2 9 16 23 30	7 14 21 28	4 11 18 25
S	2 9 16 23 30	6 13 20 27	6 13 20 27	3 10 17 24	1 8 15 22 29	5 12 19 26

Green

	EUCHARIST	MORNING PRAYER	EVENING PRAYER
	CW		
Psalms:	115.3–10	*119.105–128*	*91*; 93
Readings:	Hos. 10.1–3, 7–8, 12; Matt. 10.1–7	Judg. 15.1—16.3; Luke 18.15–30	Job 39; Rom. 15.14–21

AW	*Isa. 24.1–15*	*1 Cor. 6.1–11*

	HOLY COMMUNION	MORNING PRAYER	EVENING PRAYER
	BCP		
Psalms:		*38; 39; 40*	*41; 42; 43*
Readings:		*1 Kgs 1.32–end;* *1 Thess. 2.17—end of 3*	*1 Chr. 22.2–end;* *Mark 5.21–end*
Hymns:	....	....	....

2020

	July					August						September					October					November					December			
S		5	12	19	26	**S**		2	9	16	23	30	**S**		6	13	20	27	**S**		4	11	18	25	**S**	1	8	15	22	29	**S**		6	13	20	27
M		6	13	20	27	**M**		3	10	17	24	31	**M**		7	14	21	28	**M**		5	12	19	26	**M**	2	9	16	23	30	**M**		7	14	21	28
T		7	14	21	28	**T**		4	11	18	25		**T**	1	8	15	22	29	**T**		6	13	20	27	**T**	3	10	17	24		**T**	1	8	15	22	29
W	1	8	15	22	29	**W**		5	12	19	26		**W**	2	9	16	23	30	**W**		7	14	21	28	**W**	4	11	18	25		**W**	2	9	16	23	30
T	2	9	16	23	30	**T**		6	13	20	27		**T**	3	10	17	24		**T**	1	8	15	22	29	**T**	5	12	19	26		**T**	3	10	17	24	31
F	3	10	17	24	31	**F**		7	14	21	28		**F**	4	11	18	25		**F**	2	9	16	23	30	**F**	6	13	20	27		**F**	4	11	18	25
S	4	11	18	25		**S**	1	8	15	22	29		**S**	5	12	19	26		**S**	3	10	17	24	31	**S**	7	14	21	28		**S**	5	12	19	26

	EUCHARIST	**MORNING PRAYER**	**EVENING PRAYER**
	CW		
Psalms:	105.1–7	90; *92*	*94*
Readings:	Hos. 11.3–4, 8–9; Matt. 10.7–15	Judg. 16.4–end; Luke 18.31–end	Job 40; Rom. 15.22–end

AW   *Job 7*   *Matt. 7.21–29*

	HOLY COMMUNION	**MORNING PRAYER**	**EVENING PRAYER**
	BCP		
Psalms:		44; 45; 46	47; 48; 49
Readings:		1 Chr. 28.1–10; 1 Thess. 4.1–12	1 Chr. 28.20—29.9; Matt. 9.27—10.23
Hymns:	....	....	....

Green

	EUCHARIST	MORNING PRAYER	EVENING PRAYER
	CW		
Psalms:	80.1–7	*88*; (95)	*102*
Readings:	Hos. 14.2–end;	Judg. 17;	Job 41;
	Matt. 10.16–23	Luke 19.1–10	Rom. 16.1–16

		AW	*Jer. 20.7–end*	*Matt. 27.27–44*

	HOLY COMMUNION	MORNING PRAYER	EVENING PRAYER
	BCP		
Psalms:		*50; 51; 52*	*53; 54; 55*
Readings:		1 Chr. 29.10–end;	1 Kgs 3;
		1 Thess. 4.13—5.11	Matt. 10.24–end
Hymns:	....	....	....

2020

	July				August					September				October				November				December			
S		5	12	19	26		2	9	16	23	30			6	13	20	27			4	11	18	25		1	8	15	22	29			6	13	20	27
M		6	13	20	27		3	10	17	24	31			7	14	21	28			5	12	19	26		2	9	16	23	30			7	14	21	28
T		7	14	21	28		4	11	18	25			1	8	15	22	29			6	13	20	27		3	10	17	24		1	8	15	22	29
W	1	8	15	22	29		5	12	19	26			2	9	16	23	30			7	14	21	28		4	11	18	25		2	9	16	23	30
T	2	9	16	23	30		6	13	20	27			3	10	17	24		1	8	15	22	29		5	12	19	26		3	10	17	24	31
F	3	10	17	24	31		7	14	21	28			4	11	18	25		2	9	16	23	30		6	13	20	27		4	11	18	25
S	4	11	18	25	1	8	15	22	29			5	12	19	26		3	10	17	24	31		7	14	21	28		5	12	19	26

Benedict of Nursia, Abbot of Monte Cassino, Father of Western Monasticism, c.550
(CW Readings see Common of the Saints, also 1 Cor. 3.10, 11; Luke 18.18–22)

White *or* Green

	EUCHARIST CW	MORNING PRAYER	EVENING PRAYER
Psalms:	51.1–7	96; *97*; 100	*104*
Readings:	Isa. 6.1–8; Matt. 10.24–33	Judg. 18.1–20, 27–end; Luke 19.11–27	Job 42; Rom. 16.17–end

	AW	*Job 28*	*Heb. 11.32—12.2*

	HOLY COMMUNION BCP	MORNING PRAYER	EVENING PRAYER
Psalms:		*56; 57; 58*	*59; 60; 61*
Readings:		*1 Kgs 4.21–end; 1 Thess. 5.12–end*	*1 Kgs 5; Mark 6.7–44; E. Coll. Trinity 5*
Hymns:	....	....	....

CW COLLECT

Eternal God,
who made Benedict a wise master
in the school of your service
and a guide to many called into community
   to follow the rule of Christ:
grant that we may put your love before all else
and seek with joy the way
   of your commandments;
through Jesus Christ your Son our Lord,
who is alive and reigns with you,
in the unity of the Holy Spirit,
one God, now and for ever.

POST COMMUNION

Merciful God,
who gave such grace to your servant Benedict
that he served you with singleness of heart
and loved you above all things:
help us, whose communion with you
   has been renewed in this sacrament,
to forsake all that holds us back from following Christ
and to grow into his likeness from glory to glory;
through Jesus Christ our Lord.

THE FIFTH SUNDAY AFTER TRINITY

(Green)

	PRINCIPAL SERVICE CW Proper 10	**THIRD SERVICE**	**SECOND SERVICE**
Psalms:	119.105–112; 65. [1–7] 8–end	64; 65	60 [63]
Readings:	Gen. 25.19–end; Isa. 55.10–13; Rom. 8.1–11; Matt. 13.1–9, 18–23	Deut. 28.1–14; Acts 28.17–end	2 Sam. 7.18–end; Luke 19.41—20.8 [BCP Var. Luke 20.1–8]

	HOLY COMMUNION BCP	**MORNING PRAYER**	**EVENING PRAYER**
Psalms:	84.8–end	64; 65	60 [63]
Readings:	1 Kgs 19.19–21; 1 Pet. 3.8–15a; Luke 5.1–11	1 Sam. 17.1–54 or Wisd. 1; Mark 6.53—7.23 or Rom. 13	1 Sam. 20.1–17 or 1 Sam. 26 or Wisd. 2; Matt. 6 or Acts 14
Hymns:	....	....	....

2020

	July					August						September					October					November					December			
S		5	12	19	26		2	9	16	23	30		6	13	20	27		4	11	18	25		1	8	15	22	29		6	13	20	27
M		6	13	20	27		3	10	17	24	31		7	14	21	28		5	12	19	26		2	9	16	23	30		7	14	21	28
T		7	14	21	28		4	11	18	25		1	8	15	22	29		6	13	20	27		3	10	17	24		1	8	15	22	29
W	1	8	15	22	29		5	12	19	26		2	9	16	23	30		7	14	21	28		4	11	18	25		2	9	16	23	30
T	2	9	16	23	30		6	13	20	27		3	10	17	24		1	8	15	22	29		5	12	19	26		3	10	17	24	31
F	3	10	17	24	31		7	14	21	28		4	11	18	25		2	9	16	23	30		6	13	20	27		4	11	18	25
S	4	11	18	25		1	8	15	22	29		5	12	19	26		3	10	17	24	31		7	14	21	28		5	12	19	26

CW COLLECTS

Almighty and everlasting God,
by whose Spirit the whole body of the Church
  is governed and sanctified;
hear our prayer which we offer
for all your faithful people,
that in their vocation and ministry
they may serve you in holiness and truth
to the glory of your name;
through our Lord and Saviour Jesus Christ,
who is alive and reigns with you,
in the unity of the Holy Spirit,
one God, now and for ever.

or

Almighty God,
send down upon your Church
the riches of your Spirit,
and kindle in all who minister the gospel
your countless gifts of grace;
through Jesus Christ our Lord.

POST COMMUNION

Grant, O Lord, we beseech you,
that the course of this world may be
  so peaceably ordered by your governance,
that your Church may joyfully serve you
  in all godly quietness;
through Jesus Christ our Lord.

BCP COLLECT

*Grant, O Lord, we beseech thee, that the course
of this world may be so peaceably ordered by thy
governance, that thy Church may joyfully serve thee
in all godly quietness; through Jesus Christ our Lord.*

2021

	January		February		March		April		May		June
S	3 10 17 24 31	S	7 14 21 28	S	7 14 21 28	S	4 11 18 25	S	2 9 16 23 30	S	6 13 20 27
M	4 11 18 25	M	1 8 15 22	M	1 8 15 22 29	M	5 12 19 26	M	3 10 17 24 31	M	7 14 21 28
T	5 12 19 26	T	2 9 16 23	T	2 9 16 23 30	T	6 13 20 27	T	4 11 18 25	T	1 8 15 22 29
W	6 13 20 27	W	3 10 17 24	W	3 10 17 24 31	W	7 14 21 28	W	5 12 19 26	W	2 9 16 23 30
T	7 14 21 28	T	4 11 18 25	T	4 11 18 25	T	1 8 15 22 29	T	6 13 20 27	T	3 10 17 24
F	1 8 15 22 29	F	5 12 19 26	F	5 12 19 26	F	2 9 16 23 30	F	7 14 21 28	F	4 11 18 25
S	2 9 16 23 30	S	6 13 20 27	S	6 13 20 27	S	3 10 17 24	S	1 8 15 22 29	S	5 12 19 26

Green

Bank Holiday (NI Only)

DEL Wk 15	**EUCHARIST**	**MORNING PRAYER**	**EVENING PRAYER**
Psalm	50.7–15	*98*; 99; 101 (Ord. Week 6)	*105** (*or* 103)
Readings:	Isa. 1.11–17;	1 Sam. 1.1–20;	Ezek. 1.1–14;
	Matt. 10.34—11.1	Luke 19.28–40	2 Cor. 1.1–14

AW *Exod. 32.1–14*   *Col. 3.1–11*

	HOLY COMMUNION	**MORNING PRAYER**	**EVENING PRAYER**
	BCP		
Psalms:		*68*	*69; 70*
Readings:		1 Kgs 6.1–14;	1 Kgs 8.1–21;
		2 Thess. 1	Matt. 14.22–end
Hymns:	....	....	....

(ruled lines for notes)

Sunrise 04.55; Sunset 21.16

2020

July						August							September					October						November						December					
S		5	12	19	26	S		2	9	16	23	30	S		6	13	20	27	S		4	11	18	25	S	1	8	15	22	29	S		6	13	20	27
M		6	13	20	27	M		3	10	17	24	31	M		7	14	21	28	M		5	12	19	26	M	2	9	16	23	30	M		7	14	21	28
T		7	14	21	28	T		4	11	18	25		T	1	8	15	22	29	T		6	13	20	27	T	3	10	17	24		T	1	8	15	22	29
W	1	8	15	22	29	W		5	12	19	26		W	2	9	16	23	30	W		7	14	21	28	W	4	11	18	25		W	2	9	16	23	30
T	2	9	16	23	30	T		6	13	20	27		T	3	10	17	24		T	1	8	15	22	29	T	5	12	19	26		T	3	10	17	24	31
F	3	10	17	24	31	F		7	14	21	28		F	4	11	18	25		F	2	9	16	23	30	F	6	13	20	27		F	4	11	18	25
S	4	11	18	25		S	1	8	15	22	29		S	5	12	19	26		S	3	10	17	24	31	S	7	14	21	28		S	5	12	19	26

John Keble, Priest, Tractarian, Poet, 1866 (CW Readings see Common of the Saints
also Lam. 3.19–26; Matt. 5.1–8)

White *or* Green

	EUCHARIST CW	**MORNING PRAYER**	**EVENING PRAYER**
Psalms:	48.1–7	*106** (*or* 103)	107*
Readings:	Isa. 7.1–9; Matt. 11.20–24	1 Sam. 1.21—2.11; Luke 19.41–end	Ezek. 1.15—2.2; 2 Cor. 1.15—2.4
		AW *Prov. 9.1–12*	*2 Thess. 2.13—3.5*
	HOLY COMMUNION BCP	**MORNING PRAYER**	**EVENING PRAYER**
Psalms:		*71; 72*	*73; 74*
Readings:		*1 Kgs 8.22–53; 2 Thess. 2*	*1 Kgs 8.54—9.9; Mark 8.1–26*
Hymns:	....	....	....

CW COLLECT

Father of the eternal Word,
in whose encompassing love
all things in peace and order move:
grant that, as your servant John Keble
    adored you in all creation,
so we may have a humble heart of love
for the mysteries of your Church
and know your love to be new every morning,
in Jesus Christ your Son our Lord,
who is alive and reigns with you,
in the unity of the Holy Spirit,
one God, now and for ever.

POST COMMUNION

God, shepherd of your people,
whose servant John Keble revealed
the loving service of Christ in his ministry as a pastor
    of your people:
by this eucharist in which we share
awaken within us the love of Christ
and keep us faithful to our Christian calling;
through him who laid down his life for us,
but is alive and reigns with you, now and for ever.

Swithun, Bishop of Winchester, c.862 (CW Readings see Common of the Saints also Jas 5.7–11, 13–18)   White *or* Green
(also BCP); Bonaventure, Friar, Bishop, Teacher of the Faith, 1274

	EUCHARIST	MORNING PRAYER	EVENING PRAYER
	CW		
Psalms:	94.5–11	110; *111*; 112	*119.129–152*
Readings:	Isa. 10.5–7, 13–16;	1 Sam. 2.12–26;	Ezek. 2.3—3.11;
	Matt. 11.25–27	Luke 20.1–8	2 Cor. 2.5–end

	AW	*Isa. 26.1–9*	*Rom. 8.12–27*

	HOLY COMMUNION	MORNING PRAYER	EVENING PRAYER
	BCP Com. Bishop		
Psalms:	*99*	*75; 76; 77*	*78*
Readings:	*Ezek. 34.11–16; 1 Tim. 3.15–16;*	*1 Kgs 10;*	*1 Kgs 11.1–13;*
	Mark 4.26–32	*2 Thess. 3*	*Matt. 16.13–end*
Hymns:	....	....	....

CW COLLECT
Almighty God,
by whose grace we celebrate again
the feast of your servant Swithun:
grant that, as he governed with gentleness
  the people committed to his care,
so we, rejoicing in our Christian inheritance,
may always seek to build up your Church
  in unity and love;
through Jesus Christ your Son our Lord,
who is alive and reigns with you,
in the unity of the Holy Spirit,
one God, now and for ever.

POST COMMUNION
God, shepherd of your people,
whose servant Swithun revealed the loving service of
  Christ in his ministry
as a pastor of your people:
by this eucharist in which we share
awaken within us the love of Christ
and keep us faithful to our Christian calling;
through him who laid down his life for us,
but is alive and reigns with you, now and for ever.

BCP COLLECT
*O God, the light of the faithful, and shepherd of souls,
who didst set blessed Swithun to be a Bishop in the
Church, that he might feed thy sheep by his word and
guide them by his example: Grant us, we pray thee,
to keep the faith which he taught, and to follow in his
footsteps; through Jesus Christ our Lord.*

2020

July					August						September					October					November					December				
S	5	12	19	26	S	2	9	16	23	30	S	6	13	20	27	S	4	11	18	25	S	1	8	15	22	29	S	6	13	20	27
M	6	13	20	27	M	3	10	17	24	31	M	7	14	21	28	M	5	12	19	26	M	2	9	16	23	30	M	7	14	21	28
T	7	14	21	28	T	4	11	18	25		T	1	8	15	22	29	T	6	13	20	27	T	3	10	17	24		T	1	8	15	22	29
W	1	8	15	22	29	W	5	12	19	26	W	2	9	16	23	30	W	7	14	21	28	W	4	11	18	25	W	2	9	16	23	30
T	2	9	16	23	30	T	6	13	20	27	T	3	10	17	24	T	1	8	15	22	29	T	5	12	19	26	T	3	10	17	24	31
F	3	10	17	24	31	F	7	14	21	28	F	4	11	18	25	F	2	9	16	23	30	F	6	13	20	27	F	4	11	18	25
S	4	11	18	25	S	1	8	15	22	29	S	5	12	19	26	S	3	10	17	24	31	S	7	14	21	28	S	5	12	19	26

Osmund, Bishop of Salisbury, 1099   Green

	EUCHARIST	**MORNING PRAYER**	**EVENING PRAYER**
	CW		
Psalms:	102.14–21	113; *115*	114; *116*; 117
Readings:	Isa. 26.7–9, 16–19;	1 Sam. 2.27–end;	Ezek. 3.12–end;
	Matt. 11.28–end	Luke 20.9–19;	2 Cor. 3

AW   Jer. 8.18—9.6   *John 13.21–35*

	HOLY COMMUNION	**MORNING PRAYER**	**EVENING PRAYER**
	BCP		
Psalms:		*79; 80; 81*	*82; 83; 84; 85*
Readings:		*1 Kgs 11.26–end;*	*1 Kgs 12.1–24;*
		Gal. 1	*Matt. 17*
Hymns:	....	....	....

Green

	EUCHARIST	MORNING PRAYER	EVENING PRAYER
	CW		
Psalms:	*Canticle:* Isa. 38.10–16 *or* Ps. 32.1–8	*139*	*130*; 131; 137
Readings:	Isa. 38.1–6, 21–22, 7–8; Matt. 12.1–8	1 Sam. 3.1—4.1a; Luke 20.20–26	Ezek. 8; 2 Cor. 4

AW   *2 Sam. 5.1–12*   *Matt. 27.45–56*

	HOLY COMMUNION	MORNING PRAYER	EVENING PRAYER
	BCP		
Psalms:		*86; 87; 88*	*89*
Readings:		*1 Kgs 12.25—13.10;* *Gal. 2*	*1 Kgs 13.11–end;* *Mark 9.33–end*
Hymns:	....	....	....

Elizabeth Ferard, first Deaconess of the Church of England, Founder of the Community of St Andrew, 1883   Green

	EUCHARIST	**MORNING PRAYER**	**EVENING PRAYER**
	CW		
Psalms:	10.1–5a, 12	120; *121*; 122	*118*
Readings:	Mic. 2.1–5;	1 Sam. 4.1b–end;	Ezek. 9;
	Matt. 12.14–21	Luke 20.27–40;	2 Cor. 5

		AW	*Hos. 11.1–11*	*Matt. 28.1–7*

	HOLY COMMUNION	**MORNING PRAYER**	**EVENING PRAYER**
	BCP		
Psalms:		*90; 91; 92*	*93; 94*
Readings:		*1 Kgs 14.1–20;*	*2 Chr. 12;*
		Gal. 3	*Matt. 18.12–end*
Hymns:	....	....	....

2021

January					February					March					April					May					June				
S	3	10	17	24	31	S		7	14	21	28	S		7	14	21	28	S		4	11	18	25	S		2	9	16	23	30	S		6	13	20	27
M	4	11	18	25		M	1	8	15	22		M	1	8	15	22	29	M		5	12	19	26	M		3	10	17	24	31	M		7	14	21	28
T	5	12	19	26		T	2	9	16	23		T	2	9	16	23	30	T		6	13	20	27	T		4	11	18	25	T	1	8	15	22	29
W	6	13	20	27		W	3	10	17	24		W	3	10	17	24	31	W		7	14	21	28	W		5	12	19	26	W	2	9	16	23	30
T	7	14	21	28		T	4	11	18	25		T	4	11	18	25		T	1	8	15	22	29	T		6	13	20	27	T	3	10	17	24	
F	1	8	15	22	29	F	5	12	19	26		F	5	12	19	26		F	2	9	16	23	30	F		7	14	21	28	F	4	11	18	25	
S	2	9	16	23	30	S	6	13	20	27		S	6	13	20	27		S	3	10	17	24		S	1	8	15	22	29	S	5	12	19	26	

THE SIXTH SUNDAY AFTER TRINITY

(Green)

	PRINCIPAL SERVICE	THIRD SERVICE	SECOND SERVICE
	CW Proper 11		
Psalms:	*139.1–11, 23–24 [139.1–11];*	71	67 [70]
	86.11–17		
Readings:	*Gen. 28.10–19a;*	Deut. 30.1–10;	1 Kgs 2.10–12; 3.16–end;
	Wisd. 12.13, 16–19 or	1 Pet. 3.8–18	Acts 4.1–22;
	Isa. 44.6–8; Rom. 8.12–25;	[BCP Var. 1 Pet. 3.13–22]	[Mark 6.30–34, 53–end]
	Matt. 13.24–30, 36–43		

	HOLY COMMUNION	MORNING PRAYER	EVENING PRAYER
	BCP		
Psalms:	*90.12–end*	71	*67 [70]*
Readings:	*Gen. 4.2b–15;*	*2 Sam. 1* or	*2 Sam. 7* or
	Rom. 6.3–11;	*Wisd. 3.1–9;*	*2 Sam. 12.1–23* or *Wisd. 4.7–14;*
	Matt. 5.20–26	*Mark 7.24—8.10* or	*Matt. 7* or *Acts 15.1–31*
		Rom. 14.1—15.7	
Hymns:	....	....	....

2020

July					August					September					October					November					December				
S		5	12	19	26	S		2	9	16	23	30	S		6	13	20	27	S		4	11	18	25	S	1	8	15	22	29	S		6	13	20	27
M		6	13	20	27	M		3	10	17	24	31	M		7	14	21	28	M		5	12	19	26	M	2	9	16	23	30	M		7	14	21	28
T		7	14	21	28	T		4	11	18	25	T	1	8	15	22	29	T		6	13	20	27	T	3	10	17	24	T	1	8	15	22	29
W	1	8	15	22	29	W		5	12	19	26	W	2	9	16	23	30	W		7	14	21	28	W	4	11	18	25	W	2	9	16	23	30
T	2	9	16	23	30	T		6	13	20	27	T	3	10	17	24	T	1	8	15	22	29	T	5	12	19	26	T	3	10	17	24	31
F	3	10	17	24	31	F		7	14	21	28	F	4	11	18	25	F	2	9	16	23	30	F	6	13	20	27	F	4	11	18	25
S	4	11	18	25	S	1	8	15	22	29	S	5	12	19	26	S	3	10	17	24	31	S	7	14	21	28	S	5	12	19	26

CW COLLECTS

Merciful God,
you have prepared for those who love you
such good things as pass our understanding:
pour into our hearts such love toward you
that we, loving you in all things and above all things,
may obtain your promises,
which exceed all that we can desire;
through Jesus Christ your Son our Lord,
who is alive and reigns with you,
in the unity of the Holy Spirit,
one God, now and for ever.

or

Creator God,
you made us all in your image:
may we discern you in all that we see,
and serve you in all that we do;
through Jesus Christ our Lord.

POST COMMUNION

God of our pilgrimage,
you have led us to the living water:
refresh and sustain us
as we go forward on our journey,
in the name of Jesus Christ our Lord.

BCP COLLECT

*O God, who hast prepared for them that love thee
such good things as pass man's understanding: Pour
into our hearts such love toward thee, that we, loving
thee above all things, may obtain thy promises,
which exceed all that we can desire; through
Jesus Christ our Lord.*

2021

	January						February						March						April						May						June				
S	3	10	17	24	31			7	14	21	28			7	14	21	28			4	11	18	25			2	9	16	23	30			6	13	20	27
M	4	11	18	25			1	8	15	22			1	8	15	22	29			5	12	19	26			3	10	17	24	31			7	14	21	28
T	5	12	19	26			2	9	16	23			2	9	16	23	30			6	13	20	27			4	11	18	25			1	8	15	22	29
W	6	13	20	27			3	10	17	24			3	10	17	24	31			7	14	21	28			5	12	19	26			2	9	16	23	30
T	7	14	21	28			4	11	18	25			4	11	18	25			1	8	15	22	29			6	13	20	27			3	10	17	24	
F	1	8	15	22	29		5	12	19	26			5	12	19	26			2	9	16	23	30			7	14	21	28			4	11	18	25	
S	2	9	16	23	30		6	13	20	27			6	13	20	27			3	10	17	24			1	8	15	22	29			5	12	19	26	

Margaret of Antioch, Martyr, 4th century (also BCP)
Bartolomé de las Casas, Apostle to the Indies, 1566

Green (*or Red*)

		MORNING PRAYER	EVENING PRAYER
DEL Wk 16	**EUCHARIST** CW		
Psalms:	50.3–7, 14	123; 124; 125; *126* (Week 7 Ord)	*127*; 128; 129
Readings:	Mic. 6.1–4, 6–8; Matt. 12.38–42	1 Sam. 5; Luke 20.41—21.4	Ezek. 10.1–19; 2 Cor. 6.1—7.1
	AW	Exod. 40.1–16	Luke 14.15–24

	HOLY COMMUNION BCP Com. Martyr	MORNING PRAYER	EVENING PRAYER
Psalms:	3	102; 103	104
Readings	Jer. 11.18–20; Heb. 11.52—12.2; Matt. 16.24–27	2 Chr. 13; Gal. 4.1—5.1	2 Chr. 14; Luke 9.51–end
Hymns:	....	....	....

BCP COLLECT
Almighty God, by whose grace and power thy holy Martyr Margaret of Antioch triumphed over suffering and despised death: Grant, we beseech thee, that enduring hardness and waxing valiant in fight, we may with the noble army of martyrs receive the crown of everlasting life; through Jesus Christ our Lord.

Sunrise 05.03; Sunset 21.08

2020

	July					August						September					October					November					December				
S		5	12	19	26		2	9	16	23	30		6	13	20	27		4	11	18	25		1	8	15	22	29		6	13	20	27
M		6	13	20	27		3	10	17	24	31		7	14	21	28		5	12	19	26		2	9	16	23	30		7	14	21	28
T		7	14	21	28		4	11	18	25		1	8	15	22	29		6	13	20	27		3	10	17	24		1	8	15	22	29
W	1	8	15	22	29		5	12	19	26		2	9	16	23	30		7	14	21	28		4	11	18	25		2	9	16	23	30
T	2	9	16	23	30		6	13	20	27		3	10	17	24		1	8	15	22	29		5	12	19	26		3	10	17	24	31
F	3	10	17	24	31		7	14	21	28		4	11	18	25		2	9	16	23	30		6	13	20	27		4	11	18	25
S	4	11	18	25		1	8	15	22	29		5	12	19	26		3	10	17	24	31		7	14	21	28		5	12	19	26

Green

	EUCHARIST	**MORNING PRAYER**	**EVENING PRAYER**
	CW		
Psalms:	85.1–7	*132*; 133	(134); *135*
Readings:	Mic. 7.14–15, 18–20; Matt. 12.46–end	1 Sam. 6.1–16; Luke 21.5–19;	Ezek. 11.14–end; 2 Cor. 7.2–end *or* Eve of Mary Magdalene: Ps. 139; Isa. 25.1–9; 2 Cor. 1.3–7

		AW	*Prov. 11.1–12*		*Mark 12.38–44*

	HOLY COMMUNION	**MORNING PRAYER**	**EVENING PRAYER**
	BCP		
Psalms:		*105*	*106*
Readings:		*2 Chr. 15;* *Gal. 5.2–end*	*2 Chr. 16;* *Luke 10.1–22* or *First Evensong of Mary Magdalen:* *Prov. 31.10–end; Luke 8.1–3*
Hymns:	....	....	....

Mary Magdalene   White

	PRINCIPAL SERVICE	THIRD SERVICE	SECOND SERVICE
	CW		
Psalms:	42.1–10	30; 32; 150	63
Readings:	S. of Sol. 3.1–4; 2 Cor. 5.14–17; John 20.1–2, 11–18	1 Sam. 16.14–end; Luke 8.1–3	Zeph. 3.14–end; Mark 15.40—16.7 [BCP Var. S of Sol. 3.1–4]

Seasonal provisions including Eucharistic prefaces on Saints Days: CW Book p 328

Displaced readings may be added to the previous or following day's portion:

	EUCHARIST	MORNING PRAYER	EVENING PRAYER
	CW		
Readings:	Jer. 1.1, 4–10; Matt. 13.1–9	1 Sam. 7; Luke 21.20–28;	Ezek. 12.1–16; 2 Cor. 8.1–15

	HOLY COMMUNION	MORNING PRAYER	EVENING PRAYER
	BCP Mary Magdalen		
Psalms:	30.1–5	107	108; 109
Readings:	Zeph. 3.14–20; 2 Cor. 5.14–17; John 20.11–18	Isa. 52.7–10; John 20.1–20	Zeph. 3.14–end; Mark 15.40–end
Hymns:	....	....	....

CW COLLECT
Almighty God,
whose Son restored Mary Magdalene
   to health of mind and body
and called her to be a witness to his resurrection:
forgive our sins and heal us by your grace,
that we may serve you
in the power of his risen life;
who is alive and reigns with you,
in the unity of the Holy Spirit,
one God, now and for ever.

POST COMMUNION
God of life and love,
whose risen son called Mary Magdalene by name
and sent her to tell of his resurrection to his apostles:
in your mercy, help us,
who have been united with him in this eucharist,
to proclaim the good news
   that he is alive and reigns, now and for ever.

BCP COLLECT
O Almighty God, whose blessed Son didst call
and sanctify Mary Magdalen to be a witness to his
resurrection: Mercifully grant that by thy grace we
may be healed of all our infirmities, and always serve
thee in the power of his endless life, who with thee
and the Holy Ghost liveth and reigneth, one God,
world without end.

Bridget of Sweden, Abbess of Vadstena, 1373   Green

	EUCHARIST	MORNING PRAYER	EVENING PRAYER
	CW		
Psalms:	36.5–10	*143*; 146	*138*; 140; 141
Readings:	Jer. 2.1–3, 7–8, 12–13;	1 Sam. 8;	Ezek. 12.17–end;
	Matt. 13.10–17	Luke 21.29–end	2 Cor. 8.16—9.5

	AW	*Job 38*	*Luke 18.1–14*
	HOLY COMMUNION	MORNING PRAYER	EVENING PRAYER
	BCP		
Psalms:		110; 111; 112; 113	114; 115
Readings:		*1 Kgs 18.1–16;*	*1 Kgs 18.17–end;*
		1 Cor. 1.1–25	*Luke 12.1–34*
Hymns:	....	....	....

2021

	January					February					March					April					May					June			
S		3	10	17	24	31			7	14	21	28			7	14	21	28			4	11	18	25			2	9	16	23	30			6	13	20	27
M		4	11	18	25		1	8	15	22		1	8	15	22	29		5	12	19	26		3	10	17	24	31		7	14	21	28
T		5	12	19	26		2	9	16	23		2	9	16	23	30		6	13	20	27		4	11	18	25		1	8	15	22	29
W		6	13	20	27		3	10	17	24		3	10	17	24	31		7	14	21	28		5	12	19	26		2	9	16	23	30
T		7	14	21	28		4	11	18	25		4	11	18	25		1	8	15	22	29		6	13	20	27		3	10	17	24
F	1	8	15	22	29		5	12	19	26		5	12	19	26		2	9	16	23	30		7	14	21	28		4	11	18	25
S	2	9	16	23	30		6	13	20	27		6	13	20	27		3	10	17	24		1	8	15	22	29		5	12	19	26

Green

	EUCHARIST	MORNING PRAYER	EVENING PRAYER
	CW		
Psalms:	Ps. 23 *or Canticle:* Jer. 31.10–13	142; *144*	*145*
Readings:	Jer. 3.14–17;	1 Sam. 9.1–14;	Ezek. 13.1–6;
	Matt. 13.18–23	Luke 22.1–13	2 Cor. 9.6–end
			or Eve of James the Apostle:
			Ps. 144; Deut. 30.11–end;
			Mark 5.21–end

		AW	*Job 42.1–6*	*John 3.1–15*

	HOLY COMMUNION	MORNING PRAYER	EVENING PRAYER
	BCP		
Psalms:		116; 117; 118	119.1–32
Readings:		1 Kgs 19;	1 Kgs 21;
		1 Cor. 1.26—end of 2	Luke 12.35–end
			or First Evensong of St James:
			2 Kgs 1.1–15; Luke 9.46–56
Hymns:	....	....	....

2020

	July					August						September					October					November					December			
S		5	12	19	26	S		2	9	16	23	30	S		6	13	20	27	S		4	11	18	25	S	1	8	15	22	29	S		6	13	20	27
M		6	13	20	27	M		3	10	17	24	31	M		7	14	21	28	M		5	12	19	26	M	2	9	16	23	30	M		7	14	21	28
T		7	14	21	28	T		4	11	18	25		T	1	8	15	22	29	T		6	13	20	27	T	3	10	17	24		T	1	8	15	22	29
W	1	8	15	22	29	W		5	12	19	26		W	2	9	16	23	30	W		7	14	21	28	W	4	11	18	25		W	2	9	16	23	30
T	2	9	16	23	30	T		6	13	20	27		T	3	10	17	24		T	1	8	15	22	29	T	5	12	19	26		T	3	10	17	24	31
F	3	10	17	24	31	F		7	14	21	28		F	4	11	18	25		F	2	9	16	23	30	F	6	13	20	27		F	4	11	18	25	
S	4	11	18	25		S	1	8	15	22	29	S	5	12	19	26		S	3	10	17	24	31	S	7	14	21	28		S	5	12	19	26	

James the Apostle   Red

	PRINCIPAL SERVICE	THIRD SERVICE	SECOND SERVICE
	CW		
Psalms:	126	7; 29; 117	94
Readings:	Jer. 45.1–5; Acts 11.27—12.2; Matt. 20.20–28 *or* Acts 11.27—12.2; 2 Cor. 4.7–15; Matt. 20.20–28	2 Kgs 1.9–15 [BCP Var. Jer. 45.1–5]; Luke 9.46–56	Jer. 26.1–15; Mark 1.14–20

Seasonal provisions on Saints Days: CW Book p 328

Displaced readings may be added to the previous day's portion

	EUCHARIST	MORNING PRAYER	EVENING PRAYER
	CW		
Readings:	Jer. 7.1–11; Matt. 13.24–30	1 Sam. 9.15—10.1; Luke 22.14–23	Ezek. 14.1–11; 2 Cor. 10

	HOLY COMMUNION	MORNING PRAYER	EVENING PRAYER
	BCP		
Psalms:	*15*	*119.33–72*	*119.73–104*
Readings:	*2 Kgs 1.9–15; Acts 11.27—12.3a; Matt. 20.23–28*	*Jer. 45; Mark 1.14–20*	*Jer. 26.1–15; Mark 5.21–end; E. Coll. Trinity 7*
Hymns:	....	....	....

CW COLLECT FOR JAMES
Merciful God,
whose holy apostle Saint James,
leaving his father and all that he had,
was obedient to the calling of your Son Jesus Christ
and followed him even to death:
help us, forsaking the false attractions of the world,
to be ready at all times to answer your call
     without delay;
through Jesus Christ your Son our Lord,
who is alive and reigns with you,
in the unity of the Holy Spirit,
one God, now and for ever.

POST COMMUNION
Almighty God,
who on the day of Pentecost
sent your Holy Spirit to the apostles
with the wind from heaven and in tongues of flame,
filling them with joy and boldness
     to preach the gospel:
by the power of the same Spirit
strengthen us to witness to your truth
and to draw everyone to the fire of your love;
through Jesus Christ our Lord.

BCP COLLECT FOR ST JAMES
Grant, merciful God, that as thy holy Apostle Saint James, leaving his father and all that he had, without delay was obedient unto the calling of thy Son Jesus Christ, and followed him; so we, forsaking all worldly and carnal affections, may be evermore ready to follow thy holy commandments; through Jesus Christ our Lord.

2021

January				
S		3	10	17	24	31
M		4	11	18	25
T		5	12	19	26
W		6	13	20	27
T		7	14	21	28
F	1	8	15	22	29
S	2	9	16	23	30

February
S   7 14 21 28
M 1 8 15 22
T 2 9 16 23
W 3 10 17 24
T 4 11 18 25
F 5 12 19 26
S 6 13 20 27

March
S   7 14 21 28
M 1 8 15 22 29
T 2 9 16 23 30
W 3 10 17 24 31
T 4 11 18 25
F 5 12 19 26
S 6 13 20 27

April
S   4 11 18 25
M   5 12 19 26
T   6 13 20 27
W   7 14 21 28
T 1 8 15 22 29
F 2 9 16 23 30
S 3 10 17 24

May
S   2 9 16 23 30
M   3 10 17 24 31
T   4 11 18 25
W   5 12 19 26
T   6 13 20 27
F   7 14 21 28
S 1 8 15 22 29

June
S   6 13 20 27
M   7 14 21 28
T 1 8 15 22 29
W 2 9 16 23 30
T 3 10 17 24
F 4 11 18 25
S 5 12 19 26

THE SEVENTH SUNDAY AFTER TRINITY

(Green)

	PRINCIPAL SERVICE	THIRD SERVICE	SECOND SERVICE
	CW Proper 12		
Psalms:	*105.1–11; 45b [105.1–11]*	77	*75 [76]*
	or *128*		
	119.129–136		
Readings:	*Gen. 29.15–28;*	S. of Sol. 2 *or*	1 Kgs 6.11–14, 23–end;
	1 Kgs 3.5–12;	1 Macc. 2. [1–14] 15–22;	Acts 12.1–17;
	Rom. 8.26–end;	1 Pet. 4.7–14	[John 6.1–21]
	Matt. 13.31–33, 44–52		

	HOLY COMMUNION	MORNING PRAYER	EVENING PRAYER
	BCP		
Psalms:	*34.11–end*	77	*75 [76]*
Readings:	*1 Kgs 17.8–16;*	2 Sam. 18 or Wisd. 5.1–16;	1 Kgs 3 or 1 Kgs 8.22–61 or
	Rom. 6.19–end;	Mark 9.2–32 or	Wisd. 6.1–11; Matt. 9.35—10.23 or
	Matt. 8.1–10a	Phil. 1	Acts 16.6–end
Hymns:	....	....	....

2020

July					August						September					October					November					December				
S		5	12	19	26	S		2	9	16	23	30	S		6	13	20	27	S		4	11	18	25	S	1	8	15	22	29	S		6	13	20	27
M		6	13	20	27	M		3	10	17	24	31	M		7	14	21	28	M		5	12	19	26	M	2	9	16	23	30	M		7	14	21	28
T		7	14	21	28	T		4	11	18	25		T	1	8	15	22	29	T		6	13	20	27	T	3	10	17	24		T	1	8	15	22	29
W	1	8	15	22	29	W		5	12	19	26		W	2	9	16	23	30	W		7	14	21	28	W	4	11	18	25		W	2	9	16	23	30
T	2	9	16	23	30	T		6	13	20	27		T	3	10	17	24		T	1	8	15	22	29	T	5	12	19	26		T	3	10	17	24	31
F	3	10	17	24	31	F		7	14	21	28		F	4	11	18	25		F	2	9	16	23	30	F	6	13	20	27		F	4	11	18	25	
S	4	11	18	25	S	1	8	15	22	29		S	5	12	19	26		S	3	10	17	24	31	S	7	14	21	28		S	5	12	19	26	

CW COLLECTS

Lord of all power and might,
the author and giver of all good things:
graft in our hearts the love of your name,
increase in us true religion,
nourish us with all goodness,
and of your great mercy keep us in the same;
through Jesus Christ your Son our Lord,
who is alive and reigns with you,
in the unity of the Holy Spirit,
one God, now and for ever.

or

Generous God,
you give us gifts and make them grow:
though our faith is small as mustard-seed,
make it grow to your glory
and the flourishing of your kingdom;
through Jesus Christ our Lord.

POST COMMUNION

Lord God, whose Son is the true vine
and the source of life,
ever giving himself that the world may live:
may we so receive within ourselves
the power of his death and passion
that, in his saving cup, we may share his glory
and be made perfect in his love;
for he is alive and reigns, now and for ever.

BCP COLLECT

Lord of all power and might, who art the author and giver of all good things: Graft in our hearts the love of thy Name, increase in us true religion, nourish us with all goodness, and of thy great mercy keep us in the same; through Jesus Christ our Lord.

2021

	January						February					March					April					May					June			
S	3	10	17	24	31	S		7	14	21	28	S		7	14	21	28	S		4	11	18	25	S		2	9	16	23	30	S		6	13	20	27
M	4	11	18	25		M	1	8	15	22		M	1	8	15	22	29	M		5	12	19	26	M		3	10	17	24	31	M		7	14	21	28
T	5	12	19	26		T	2	9	16	23		T	2	9	16	23	30	T		6	13	20	27	T		4	11	18	25		T	1	8	15	22	29
W	6	13	20	27		W	3	10	17	24		W	3	10	17	24	31	W		7	14	21	28	W		5	12	19	26		W	2	9	16	23	30
T	7	14	21	28		T	4	11	18	25		T	4	11	18	25		T	1	8	15	22	29	T		6	13	20	27		T	3	10	17	24	
F	1	8	15	22	29	F	5	12	19	26		F	5	12	19	26		F	2	9	16	23	30	F		7	14	21	28		F	4	11	18	25	
S	2	9	16	23	30	S	6	13	20	27		S	6	13	20	27		S	3	10	17	24		S	1	8	15	22	29	S	5	12	19	26	

Anne and Joachim, Parents of the Blessed Virgin Mary may be celebrated on this day at the Minister's discretion where there is sufficient reason. *St Anne (BCP)*
CW Lesser Festival; EUCHARIST: *Ps. 127; Zeph. 3.14–18a; Rom. 8.28–30; Matt. 13.16–17*
Brooke Foss Westcott, Bishop of Durham, Teacher of the Faith, 1901

Green *or* White

DEL Wk 17	**EUCHARIST** CW		**MORNING PRAYER**	**EVENING PRAYER**
Psalms:	82 *or* Deut. 32.18–21		*1*; 2; 3 (Week 1 Ord)	*4*; 7
Readings:	Jer. 13.1–11; Matt. 13.31–35		1 Sam. 10.1–16; Luke 22.24–30	Ezek. 14.12–end; 2 Cor. 11.1–15
		AW	*Num. 23.1–12*	*1 Cor. 1.10–17*
	HOLY COMMUNION *BCP St Anne*		**MORNING PRAYER**	**EVENING PRAYER**
Psalms:	32		*120; 121; 122; 123; 124; 125*	*126; 127; 128; 129; 130; 131*
Readings:	Ecclus 2.1–6; Rev. 7.13–17; Mark 10.42–45		2 Kgs 1; 1 Cor. 4.1–17	2 Kgs 2.1–22; Luke 14.1–33
Hymns:	....		....	....

CW COLLECT
Lord God of Israel,
who bestowed such grace on Anne and Joachim
that their daughter Mary grew up
    obedient to your word
and made ready to be the mother of your Son:
help us to commit ourselves
    in all things to your keeping
and grant us the salvation you promised to
    your people;
through Jesus Christ your Son our Lord,
who is alive and reigns with you,
in the unity of the Holy Spirit,
one God, now and for ever.

POST COMMUNION
Father,
from whom every family in heaven and on earth
    takes its name,
your servants Anne and Joachim revealed your
goodness in a life of tranquillity and service:
grant that we who have gathered in faith
    around this table
may like them know the love of Christ
    that surpasses knowledge
and be filled with all your fullness;
through Jesus Christ our Lord.

BCP COLLECT
*Almighty God, who willest to be glorified in thy
Saints and didst raise up thy servant Anne to shine
as a light in the world: shine, we pray thee, in our
hearts, that we also in our generation may shew forth
thy praises, who hast called us out of darkness into
thy marvellous light, through Jesus Christ our Lord.*

Sunrise 05.13; Sunset 20.58

Green

	EUCHARIST CW	**MORNING PRAYER**	**EVENING PRAYER**
Psalms:	79.8–end	*5*; 6; (8)	*9*; 10*
Readings:	Jer. 14.17–end; Matt. 13.36–43	1 Sam. 10.17–end; Luke 22.31–38	Ezek. 18.1–20; 2 Cor. 11.16–end

		AW	*Prov. 12.1–12*	*Gal. 3.1–14*
	HOLY COMMUNION BCP		**MORNING PRAYER**	**EVENING PRAYER**
Psalms:			*132; 133; 134; 135*	*136; 137; 138*
Readings:			*2 Kgs 4.1–37;* *1 Cor. 4.18—end of 5*	*2 Kgs 5; Luke 15*
Hymns:	....		....	....

2021

January						February					March					April					May						June				
S		3	10	17	24	31	**S**		7	14	21	28	**S**		7	14	21	28	**S**		4	11	18	25	**S**		2	9	16	23	30	**S**		6	13	20	27
M		4	11	18	25		**M**	1	8	15	22		**M**	1	8	15	22	29	**M**		5	12	19	26	**M**		3	10	17	24	31	**M**		7	14	21	28
T		5	12	19	26		**T**	2	9	16	23		**T**	2	9	16	23	30	**T**		6	13	20	27	**T**		4	11	18	25		**T**	1	8	15	22	29
W		6	13	20	27		**W**	3	10	17	24		**W**	3	10	17	24	31	**W**		7	14	21	28	**W**		5	12	19	26		**W**	2	9	16	23	30
T		7	14	21	28		**T**	4	11	18	25		**T**	4	11	18	25		**T**	1	8	15	22	29	**T**		6	13	20	27		**T**	3	10	17	24	
F	1	8	15	22	29		**F**	5	12	19	26		**F**	5	12	19	26		**F**	2	9	16	23	30	**F**		7	14	21	28		**F**	4	11	18	25	
S	2	9	16	23	30		**S**	6	13	20	27		**S**	6	13	20	27		**S**	3	10	17	24		**S**	1	8	15	22	29	**S**	5	12	19	26	

Mary, Martha and Lazarus, Companions of our Lord   White *or* Green
CW Lesser Festival; EUCHARIST: Ps. 49.5–10, 16; Isa. 25.6–9; Heb. 2.10–15; John 12.1–8

	EUCHARIST	MORNING PRAYER	EVENING PRAYER
	CW		
Psalms	59.1–4, 18–end	*119.1–32*	*11*; 12; 13
Readings:	Jer. 15.10, 16–end;	1 Sam. 11;	Ezek. 18.21–32;
	Matt. 13.44–46	Luke 22.39–46	2 Cor. 12
AW		*Isa. 49.8–13*	*2 Cor. 8.1–11*

	HOLY COMMUNION	MORNING PRAYER	EVENING PRAYER
	BCP		
Psalms:		*139; 140; 141*	*142; 143*
Readings:		*2 Kgs 6.1–23;*	*2 Kgs 6.24—7.2;*
		1 Cor. 6	*Luke 16*
Hymns:	....	....	....

CW COLLECT
God our Father,
whose Son enjoyed the love of his friends,
Mary, Martha and Lazarus,
in learning, argument and hospitality:
may we so rejoice in your love
that the world may come to know the depths
of your wisdom, the wonder of your compassion, and
    your power to bring life out of death;
through the merits of Jesus Christ,
our friend and brother,
who is alive and reigns with you,
in the unity of the Holy Spirit,
one God, now and for ever.

POST COMMUNION
Father, from whom every family in heaven and on
    earth takes its name,
your servants Mary, Martha and Lazarus revealed
    your goodness in a life of tranquillity and service:
grant that we who have gathered in faith around this
    table may like them know the love of Christ
that surpasses knowledge and be filled with all your
    fullness; through Jesus Christ our Lord.

2020

	July	August	September	October	November	December
S	5 12 19 26	2 9 16 23 30	6 13 20 27	4 11 18 25	1 8 15 22 29	6 13 20 27
M	6 13 20 27	3 10 17 24 31	7 14 21 28	5 12 19 26	2 9 16 23 30	7 14 21 28
T	7 14 21 28	4 11 18 25	1 8 15 22 29	6 13 20 27	3 10 17 24	1 8 15 22 29
W	1 8 15 22 29	5 12 19 26	2 9 16 23 30	7 14 21 28	4 11 18 25	2 9 16 23 30
T	2 9 16 23 30	6 13 20 27	3 10 17 24	1 8 15 22 29	5 12 19 26	3 10 17 24 31
F	3 10 17 24 31	7 14 21 28	4 11 18 25	2 9 16 23 30	6 13 20 27	4 11 18 25
S	4 11 18 25	1 8 15 22 29	5 12 19 26	3 10 17 24 31	7 14 21 28	5 12 19 26

William Wilberforce, Social Reformer, Olaudah Equiano and   White *or* Green
Thomas Clarkson, anti-slavery campaigners, 1833, 1797 and 1846
(CW Readings see Common of the Saints also Job. 31.16–23; Gal. 3.26–29; 4.6–7; Luke 4.16–21)

	EUCHARIST CW	**MORNING PRAYER**	**EVENING PRAYER**
Psalms:	146.1–5	14; *15*; 16	*18**
Readings:	Jer. 18.1–6; Matt. 13.47–53	1 Sam. 12; Luke 22.47–62	Ezek. 20.1–20; 2 Cor. 13
	AW	*Hos. 14*	*John 15.1–17*

	HOLY COMMUNION BCP	**MORNING PRAYER**	**EVENING PRAYER**
Psalms:		*144; 145; 146*	*147; 148; 149; 150*
Readings:		2 Kgs 7.3–end; 1 Cor. 7	2 Kgs 8.1–15; Luke 17
Hymns:	....	....	....

CW COLLECT
God our deliverer,
who sent your Son Jesus Christ
to set your people free from the slavery of sin:
grant that, as your servant William Wilberforce
    toiled against the sin of slavery,
so we may bring compassion to all
and work for the freedom of all the children of God;
through Jesus Christ your Son our Lord,
who is alive and reigns with you,
in the unity of the Holy Spirit,
one God, now and for ever.

POST COMMUNION
God our redeemer,
who inspired William Wilberforce
    to witness to your love
and to work for the coming of your kingdom:
may we, who in this sacrament share
    the bread of heaven,
be fired by your Spirit to proclaim the gospel
    in our daily living
and never to rest content until your kingdom come,
on earth as it is in heaven;
through Jesus Christ our Lord.

2021

January					February					March					April					May					June				
S		3	10	17	24	31	S			7	14	21	28	S			7	14	21	28	S			4	11	18	25	S		2	9	16	23	30	S			6	13	20	27
M		4	11	18	25	M		1	8	15	22	M		1	8	15	22	29	M			5	12	19	26	M		3	10	17	24	31	M			7	14	21	28
T		5	12	19	26	T		2	9	16	23	T		2	9	16	23	30	T			6	13	20	27	T		4	11	18	25	T		1	8	15	22	29
W		6	13	20	27	W		3	10	17	24	W		3	10	17	24	31	W			7	14	21	28	W		5	12	19	26	W		2	9	16	23	30
T		7	14	21	28	T		4	11	18	25	T		4	11	18	25	T		1	8	15	22	29	T		6	13	20	27	T		3	10	17	24
F	1	8	15	22	29	F		5	12	19	26	F		5	12	19	26	F		2	9	16	23	30	F		7	14	21	28	F		4	11	18	25
S	2	9	16	23	30	S		6	13	20	27	S		6	13	20	27	S		3	10	17	24	S	1	8	15	22	29	S		5	12	19	26

Ignatius of Loyola, Founder of the Society of Jesus 1556 Green

	EUCHARIST	**MORNING PRAYER**	**EVENING PRAYER**
	CW	17; *19*	*22*
Psalms:	69.4–10		
Readings:	Jer. 26.1–9; Matt. 13.54–end	1 Sam. 13.5–18; Luke 22.63–end	Ezek. 20.21–38; Jas 1.1–11
	AW	*2 Sam. 18.18–end*	*Matt. 27.57–66*

	HOLY COMMUNION	**MORNING PRAYER**	**EVENING PRAYER**
	BCP	*144; 145; 146*	*147; 148; 149; 150*
Psalms:			
Readings:		*2 Kgs 9;* *1 Cor. 8*	*2 Kgs 11.1–20;* *Luke 18.1–14*
Hymns:			

2020

	July						August						September						October						November						December				
S		5	12	19	26	S		2	9	16	23	30	S		6	13	20	27	S		4	11	18	25	S	1	8	15	22	29	S		6	13	20	27
M		6	13	20	27	M		3	10	17	24	31	M		7	14	21	28	M		5	12	19	26	M	2	9	16	23	30	M		7	14	21	28
T		7	14	21	28	T		4	11	18	25		T	1	8	15	22	29	T		6	13	20	27	T	3	10	17	24		T	1	8	15	22	29
W	1	8	15	22	29	W		5	12	19	26		W	2	9	16	23	30	W		7	14	21	28	W	4	11	18	25		W	2	9	16	23	30
T	2	9	16	23	30	T		6	13	20	27		T	3	10	17	24		T	1	8	15	22	29	T	5	12	19	26		T	3	10	17	24	31
F	3	10	17	24	31	F		7	14	21	28		F	4	11	18	25		F	2	9	16	23	30	F	6	13	20	27		F	4	11	18	25	
S	4	11	18	25		S	1	8	15	22	29	S	5	12	19	26		S	3	10	17	24	31	S	7	14	21	28		S	5	12	19	26	

Lammas Day (BCP)

Green

	EUCHARIST CW	**MORNING PRAYER**	**EVENING PRAYER**
Psalms:	69.14–20	20; 21; *23*	*24*; 25
Readings:	Jer. 26.11–16, 24; Matt. 14.1–12	1 Sam. 13.19—14.15; Luke 23.1–12	Ezek. 24.15–end; Jas 1.12–end

AW   *Isa. 55.1–7*   *Mark 16.1–8*

	HOLY COMMUNION BCP	**MORNING PRAYER**	**EVENING PRAYER**
Psalms:		1; 2; 3; 4; 5	6; 7; 8
Readings:		2 Kgs 11.21—end of 12; 1 Cor. 9	2 Kgs 13; Matt. 20.1–16; E. Coll. (1) Trinity 8
Hymns:	....	....	....

THE EIGHTH SUNDAY AFTER TRINITY

(Green)

	PRINCIPAL SERVICE	**THIRD SERVICE**	**SECOND SERVICE**
	CW Proper 13		
Psalms:	*17.1–7, 16 [17.1–7];*	85	80 [80.1–8]
	145.8–9, 15–end [145.15–end]		
Readings:	*Gen. 32.22–31;*	*S. of Sol. 5.2–end or*	1 Kgs 10.1–13;
	Isa. 55.1–5; Rom. 9.1–5;	*1 Macc. 3.1–12;*	Acts 13.1–13;
	Matt. 14.13–21	*2 Pet. 1.1–15*	[John 6.24–35]

	HOLY COMMUNION	**MORNING PRAYER**	**EVENING PRAYER**
	BCP		
Psalms:	*31.1–6*	*85*	*80*
Readings:	*Jer. 23.16–24;*	*1 Kgs 10.1–13 or*	*1 Kgs 12 or*
	Rom. 8.12–17;	*Wisd. 6.12–end;*	*1 Kgs 13.1–32 or*
	Matt. 7.15–21	*Mark 10.1–31 or Phil. 2*	*Wisd. 7.15—8.1;*
			Matt. 10.24–end or
			Acts 17.16–end

Hymns: ....

....

....

....

....

....

....

....

....

....

....

....

....

....

....

....

....

....

....

....

2020

	July					August					September					October					November					December			
S		5	12	19	26		2	9	16	23	30		6	13	20	27		4	11	18	25		1	8	15	22	29		6	13	20	27
M		6	13	20	27		3	10	17	24	31		7	14	21	28		5	12	19	26		2	9	16	23	30		7	14	21	28
T		7	14	21	28		4	11	18	25		1	8	15	22	29		6	13	20	27		3	10	17	24		1	8	15	22	29
W	1	8	15	22	29		5	12	19	26		2	9	16	23	30		7	14	21	28		4	11	18	25		2	9	16	23	30
T	2	9	16	23	30		6	13	20	27		3	10	17	24		1	8	15	22	29		5	12	19	26		3	10	17	24	31
F	3	10	17	24	31		7	14	21	28		4	11	18	25		2	9	16	23	30		6	13	20	27		4	11	18	25
S	4	11	18	25		1	8	15	22	29		5	12	19	26		3	10	17	24	31		7	14	21	28		5	12	19	26

CW COLLECTS

Almighty Lord and everlasting God,
we beseech you to direct, sanctify and govern
   both our hearts and bodies
in the ways of your laws
   and the works of your commandments;
that through your most mighty protection,
both here and ever,
we may be preserved in body and soul;
through our Lord and Saviour Jesus Christ,
who is alive and reigns with you,
in the unity of the Holy Spirit,
one God, now and for ever.

or

Lord God,
your Son left the riches of heaven
and became poor for our sake:
when we prosper save us from pride,
when we are needy save us from despair,
that we may trust in you alone;
through Jesus Christ our Lord.

POST COMMUNION

Strengthen for service, Lord,
the hands that have taken holy things;
may the ears which have heard your word
   be deaf to clamour and dispute;
may the tongues which have sung your praise
   be free from deceit;
may the eyes which have seen the tokens of your
   love shine with the light of hope;
and may the bodies which have been fed
   with your body
be refreshed with the fullness of your life;
glory to you for ever.

BCP COLLECT

*O God, whose never-failing providence ordereth
all things both in heaven and earth: We humbly
beseech thee to put away from us all hurtful things,
and to give us those things which be profitable for
us; through Jesus Christ our Lord.*

2021

	January					February					March					April					May					June			
S		3	10	17	24	31		7	14	21	28		7	14	21	28		4	11	18	25		2	9	16	23	30		6	13	20	27
M		4	11	18	25		1	8	15	22		1	8	15	22	29		5	12	19	26		3	10	17	24	31		7	14	21	28
T		5	12	19	26		2	9	16	23		2	9	16	23	30		6	13	20	27		4	11	18	25		1	8	15	22	29
W		6	13	20	27		3	10	17	24		3	10	17	24	31		7	14	21	28		5	12	19	26		2	9	16	23	30
T		7	14	21	28		4	11	18	25		4	11	18	25		1	8	15	22	29		6	13	20	27		3	10	17	24	
F	1	8	15	22	29	5	12	19	26		5	12	19	26		2	9	16	23	30		7	14	21	28		4	11	18	25	
S	2	9	16	23	30	6	13	20	27		6	13	20	27		3	10	17	24		1	8	15	22	29		5	12	19	26	

Summer Bank Holiday (Scotland)

Green

DEL Wk 18	**EUCHARIST**	**MORNING PRAYER**	**EVENING PRAYER**
	CW		
Psalms	119.89–96	27; *30* (Ord. Week 2)	26; *28*; 29
Readings:	Jer. 28;	1 Sam. 14.24–46;	Ezek. 28.1–19;
	Matt. 14.13–21 *or* 14.22–end	Luke 23.13–25	Jas 2.1–13

AW *Joel 3.16–21* *Mark 4.21–34*

	HOLY COMMUNION	**MORNING PRAYER**	**EVENING PRAYER**
	BCP		
Psalms:		15; 16; 17	18
Readings:		2 Kgs 14;	2 Chr. 26;
		1 Cor. 10.1—11.1	Mark 10.32–end
Hymns:	....	....	....

Full Moon Sunrise 05.24; Sunset 20.46

2020

	July					August					September					October					November					December			
S		5	12	19	26		2	9	16	23	30		6	13	20	27		4	11	18	25		1	8	15	22	29		6	13	20	27
M		6	13	20	27		3	10	17	24	31		7	14	21	28		5	12	19	26		2	9	16	23	30		7	14	21	28
T		7	14	21	28		4	11	18	25		1	8	15	22	29		6	13	20	27		3	10	17	24		1	8	15	22	29
W	1	8	15	22	29		5	12	19	26	2	9	16	23	30		7	14	21	28		4	11	18	25		2	9	16	23	30
T	2	9	16	23	30		6	13	20	27	3	10	17	24		1	8	15	22	29		5	12	19	26		3	10	17	24	31
F	3	10	17	24	31		7	14	21	28	4	11	18	25		2	9	16	23	30		6	13	20	27		4	11	18	25
S	4	11	18	25	1	8	15	22	29	5	12	19	26		3	10	17	24	31		7	14	21	28		5	12	19	26

Jean-Baptiste Vianney, Curé d'Ars, Spiritual Guide, 1859

Green

	EUCHARIST	**MORNING PRAYER**	**EVENING PRAYER**
	CW		
Psalms:	102.6–21	32; *36*	*33*
Readings:	Jer. 30.1–2, 12–15, 18–22;	1 Sam. 15.1–23;	Ezek. 33.1–20;
	Matt. 14.22–end *or* 15.1–2, 10–14	Luke 23.26–43	Jas 2.14–end
		AW *Prov. 12.13–end*	*John 1.43–51*
	HOLY COMMUNION	**MORNING PRAYER**	**EVENING PRAYER**
	BCP		
Psalms:		19; 20; 21	*22; 23*
Readings:		2 Kgs 15.17–end;	*2 Kgs 16;*
		1 Cor. 11.2–end	*Luke 19.1–28*
Hymns:	....	....	....

Oswald, King of Northumbria, Martyr, 642 (CW Readings see Common of the Saints especially 1 Pet. 4.12–19; John 16.29–33)

Red *or* Green

	EUCHARIST CW	**MORNING PRAYER**	**EVENING PRAYER**
Psalms:	121	*34*	*119.33–56*
Readings:	Jer. 31.1–7; Matt. 15.21–28	1 Sam. 16; Luke 23.44–56a	Ezek. 33.21–end; Jas 3 *or* Eve of the Transfiguration Ps. 99, 110; Exod. 24.12–end; John 12.27–36a

| | | AW | *Isa. 55.8–end* | *2 Tim. 2.8–19* |

	HOLY COMMUNION BCP	**MORNING PRAYER**	**EVENING PRAYER**
Psalms:		24; 25; 26	27; 28; 29
Readings:		Isa. 7.1–17; 1 Cor. 12.1–27	Isa. 8.1–18; Luke 19.29–44 or *First Evensong of Transfiguration* Exod. 24.12–end; Luke 9.28–45
Hymns:	....	....	....

CW COLLECT

Lord God almighty,
who so kindled the faith of King Oswald
  with your Spirit
that he set up the sign of the cross in his kingdom
and turned his people to the light of Christ:
grant that we, being fired by the same Spirit,
may always bear our cross before the world
and be found faithful servants of the gospel;
through Jesus Christ your Son our Lord,
who is alive and reigns with you,
in the unity of the Holy Spirit,
one God, now and for ever.

POST COMMUNION

Eternal God,
who gave us this holy meal
in which we have celebrated the glory of the cross
and the victory of your martyr Oswald:
by our communion with Christ
in his saving death and resurrection,
give us with all your saints the courage to
  conquer evil
and so to share the fruit of the tree of life;
through Jesus Christ our Lord.

2020

	July				August				September				October				November				December			
S		5 12 19 26				2 9 16 23 30				6 13 20 27				4 11 18 25			1 8 15 22 29				6 13 20 27		
M		6 13 20 27				3 10 17 24 31				7 14 21 28				5 12 19 26			2 9 16 23 30				7 14 21 28		
T		7 14 21 28				4 11 18 25			1 8 15 22 29				6 13 20 27			3 10 17 24			1 8 15 22 29		
W	1 8 15 22 29				5 12 19 26			2 9 16 23 30				7 14 21 28			4 11 18 25			2 9 16 23 30		
T	2 9 16 23 30				6 13 20 27			3 10 17 24			1 8 15 22 29			5 12 19 26			3 10 17 24 31		
F	3 10 17 24 31				7 14 21 28			4 11 18 25			2 9 16 23 30			6 13 20 27			4 11 18 25		
S	4 11 18 25			1 8 15 22 29				5 12 19 26				3 10 17 24 31			7 14 21 28			5 12 19 26		

The Transfiguration of Our Lord

Gold *or* White

	PRINCIPAL SERVICE CW	THIRD SERVICE	SECOND SERVICE
Psalms:	97	27; 150	72
Readings:	Dan. 7.9–10, 13–14; 2 Pet. 1.16–19; Luke 9.28–36	Ecclus 48.1–10 *or* 1 Kgs 19.1–16; 1 John 3.1–3	Exod. 34.29–end; 2 Cor. 3

Displaced readings may be added to the previous or following day's portion:

Readings:	Jer. 31.31–34; Matt. 16.13–23	1 Sam. 17.1–30; Luke 23.56b–24.12;	Ezek. 34.1–16; Jas 4.1–12

	HOLY COMMUNION BCP The Transfiguration	MORNING PRAYER	EVENING PRAYER
Psalms:	84.1–7	30; 31	32; 33; 34
Readings:	Exod. 24.12–18; 1 John 3.1–3; Mark 9.2–7	Exod. 34.29–end; 2 Cor. 3	1 Kgs 19.1–6; 2 Pet. 1.12–end
Hymns:	....	....	....

CW COLLECTS

Father in heaven,
whose Son Jesus Christ was wonderfully
transfigured
before chosen witnesses upon the holy mountain,
and spoke of the exodus he would accomplish at
Jerusalem:
give us strength so to hear his voice and bear
our cross
that in the world to come we may see him as he is;
who is alive and reigns with you,
in the unity of the Holy Spirit,
one God, now and for ever.

POST COMMUNION

Holy God,
we see your glory in the face of Jesus Christ:
may we who are partakers at his table
reflect his life in word and deed,
that all the world may know
his power to change and save.
This we ask through Jesus Christ our Lord.

BCP COLLECT

*O God, who before the passion of thine only-
begotten Son didst reveal his glory upon the holy
mount: Grant unto us thy servants, that in faith
beholding the light of his countenance, we may be
strengthened to bear the cross, and be changed into
his likeness from glory to glory; through the same
Jesus Christ our Lord.*

2021

	January					February				March					April				May					June			
S		3	10	17	24	31			7	14	21	28			7	14	21	28		4	11	18	25		2	9	16	23	30			6	13	20	27
M		4	11	18	25		1	8	15	22		1	8	15	22	29		5	12	19	26		3	10	17	24	31			7	14	21	28
T		5	12	19	26		2	9	16	23		2	9	16	23	30		6	13	20	27		4	11	18	25		1	8	15	22	29
W		6	13	20	27		3	10	17	24		3	10	17	24	31		7	14	21	28		5	12	19	26		2	9	16	23	30
T		7	14	21	28		4	11	18	25		4	11	18	25		1	8	15	22	29		6	13	20	27		3	10	17	24
F	1	8	15	22	29		5	12	19	26		5	12	19	26		2	9	16	23	30		7	14	21	28		4	11	18	25
S	2	9	16	23	30		6	13	20	27		6	13	20	27		3	10	17	24		1	8	15	22	29		5	12	19	26

John Mason Neale, Priest, Hymn Writer 1866 Name of Jesus (BCP)

Green *or* White

	EUCHARIST	**MORNING PRAYER**	**EVENING PRAYER**
	CW		
Psalms:	137.1–6 *or* Deut. 32.35–36; 39; 41	*31*	*35*
Readings:	Nahum 2.1, 3, 3.1–3, 6–7; Matt. 16.24–end	1 Sam. 17.31–54; Luke 24.13–35	Ezek. 34.17–end; Jas 4.13—5.6
		AW Jer. 14.1–9	*Luke 8.4–15*

	HOLY COMMUNION	**MORNING PRAYER**	**EVENING PRAYER**
	BCP Naming of Jesus		
Psalms:	8	*35; 36*	*37*
Readings:	Jer. 14.7–9; Acts 4.8–12; Matt. 1.20–23	2 Kgs 18.1–8; 1 Cor. 14.1–19	2 Chr. 30; Matt. 22.1–22
Hymns:	....	....	....

BCP COLLECT
Almighty God, who hast taught us that in the name of Jesus Christ alone is salvation: Mercifully grant that thy faithful people, ever glorifying in his name, may make thy salvation known to all the world, through the same Jesus Christ our Lord.

2020

July				
S		5	12	19	26
M		6	13	20	27
T		7	14	21	28
W	1	8	15	22	29
T	2	9	16	23	30
F	3	10	17	24	31
S	4	11	18	25

August				
S		2	9	16	23	30
M		3	10	17	24	31
T		4	11	18	25
W		5	12	19	26
T		6	13	20	27
F		7	14	21	28
S	1	8	15	22	29

September				
S		6	13	20	27
M		7	14	21	28
T	1	8	15	22	29
W	2	9	16	23	30
T	3	10	17	24
F	4	11	18	25
S	5	12	19	26

October				
S		4	11	18	25
M		5	12	19	26
T		6	13	20	27
W		7	14	21	28
T	1	8	15	22	29
F	2	9	16	23	30
S	3	10	17	24	31

November				
S	1	8	15	22	29
M	2	9	16	23	30
T	3	10	17	24
W	4	11	18	25
T	5	12	19	26
F	6	13	20	27
S	7	14	21	28

December				
S		6	13	20	27
M		7	14	21	28
T	1	8	15	22	29
W	2	9	16	23	30
T	3	10	17	24	31
F	4	11	18	25
S	5	12	19	26

Dominic, Priest, Founder of the Order of Preachers, 1221 (CW Readings see Common of the Saints,   White *or* Green
also Ecclus 39.1–10)

	EUCHARIST	MORNING PRAYER	EVENING PRAYER
	CW		
Psalms:	9.7–11	41; *42*; 43	45; *46*
Readings:	Hab. 1.12—2.4;	1 Sam. 17.55—18.16;	Ezek. 36.16–36;
	Matt. 17.14–20	Luke 24.36–end	Jas 5.7–end

		AW	*Eccles. 5.10–19*	*1 Tim. 6.6–16*

	HOLY COMMUNION	MORNING PRAYER	EVENING PRAYER
	BCP	*38; 39; 40*	*41; 42; 43*
Readings:		2 Kgs 18.13–end;	2 Kgs 19;
		1 Cor. 14.20–end	Matt. 22.23–end;
			E. Coll. Trinity 9

Hymns: ....

CW COLLECTS
Almighty God,
whose servant Dominic grew
in the knowledge of your truth
and formed an order of preachers
to proclaim the faith of Christ:
by your grace give to all your people
a love for your word
and a longing to share the gospel,
so that the whole world may come to know you
and your Son Jesus Christ our Lord,
who is alive and reigns with you,
in the unity of the Holy Spirit,
one God, now and for ever.

POST COMMUNION
Merciful God,
who gave such grace to your servant Dominic
that he served you with singleness of heart
and loved you above all things:
help us, whose communion with you
has been renewed in this sacrament,
to forsake all that holds us back from following Christ
and to grow into his likeness from glory to glory;
through Jesus Christ our Lord.

2021

January						February					March					April					May						June				
S		3	10	17	24	31	S		7	14	21	28	S		7	14	21	28	S		4	11	18	25	S		2	9	16	23	30	S		6	13	20	27
M		4	11	18	25		M	1	8	15	22		M	1	8	15	22	29	M		5	12	19	26	M		3	10	17	24	31	M		7	14	21	28
T		5	12	19	26		T	2	9	16	23		T	2	9	16	23	30	T		6	13	20	27	T		4	11	18	25		T	1	8	15	22	29
W		6	13	20	27		W	3	10	17	24		W	3	10	17	24	31	W		7	14	21	28	W		5	12	19	26		W	2	9	16	23	30
T		7	14	21	28		T	4	11	18	25		T	4	11	18	25		T	1	8	15	22	29	T		6	13	20	27		T	3	10	17	24
F	1	8	15	22	29		F	5	12	19	26		F	5	12	19	26		F	2	9	16	23	30	F		7	14	21	28		F	4	11	18	25
S	2	9	16	23	30		S	6	13	20	27		S	6	13	20	27		S	3	10	17	24		S	1	8	15	22	29		S	5	12	19	26

THE NINTH SUNDAY AFTER TRINITY

(Green)

	PRINCIPAL SERVICE	THIRD SERVICE	SECOND SERVICE
	CW Proper 14		
Psalms:	*105.1–6, 16–22, 45b; 85.8–13*	88	86
Readings:	*Gen. 37.1–4, 12–28;*	S of Sol. 8.5–7 *or*	1 Kgs 11.41—12.20;
	1 Kgs 19.9–18;	1 Macc. 14.4–15;	Acts 14.8–20;
	Rom. 10.5–15;	2 Pet. 3.8–13	[John 6.35, 41–51]
	Matt. 14.22–33		

	HOLY COMMUNION	MORNING PRAYER	EVENING PRAYER
	BCP		
Psalms:	*95*	*88*	*86*
Readings:	*Num. 10.35—11.3;*	*1 Kgs 17* or	*1 Kgs 18* or *1 Kgs 19* or
	1 Cor. 10.1–13;	*Wisd. 11.21—12.2;*	*Wisd. 12.12–21;*
	Luke 16.1–9 or	*Luke 1.1–25 or Phil. 3*	*Matt. 11* or
	Luke 15.11–end		*Acts 20.17–end*
Hymns:	....	....	....

2020

	July					August						September					October					November					December				
S		5	12	19	26		2	9	16	23	30		6	13	20	27		4	11	18	25		1	8	15	22	29		6	13	20	27
M		6	13	20	27		3	10	17	24	31		7	14	21	28		5	12	19	26		2	9	16	23	30		7	14	21	28
T		7	14	21	28		4	11	18	25			1	8	15	22	29		6	13	20	27		3	10	17	24		1	8	15	22	29
W	1	8	15	22	29		5	12	19	26		2	9	16	23	30		7	14	21	28		4	11	18	25		2	9	16	23	30
T	2	9	16	23	30		6	13	20	27		3	10	17	24		1	8	15	22	29		5	12	19	26		3	10	17	24	31
F	3	10	17	24	31		7	14	21	28		4	11	18	25		2	9	16	23	30		6	13	20	27		4	11	18	25
S	4	11	18	25		1	8	15	22	29		5	12	19	26		3	10	17	24	31		7	14	21	28		5	12	19	26

CW COLLECTS

Almighty God,
who sent your Holy Spirit
to be the life and light of your Church:
open our hearts to the riches of your grace,
that we may bring forth the fruit of the Spirit
in love and joy and peace;
through Jesus Christ your Son our Lord,
who is alive and reigns with you,
in the unity of the Holy Spirit,
one God, now and for ever.

or

Gracious Father,
revive your Church in our day,
and make her holy, strong and faithful,
for your glory's sake
in Jesus Christ our Lord.

POST COMMUNION

Holy Father,
who gathered us here around the table of your Son
to share this meal with the whole household of God:
in that new world where you reveal the fullness of
    your peace,
gather people of every race and language
    to share in the eternal banquet
    of Jesus Christ our Lord.

BCP COLLECT

*Grant to us, Lord, we beseech thee, the spirit to think
and do always such things as be rightful; that we,
who cannot do any thing that is good without thee,
may by thee be enabled to live according to thy will;
through Jesus Christ our Lord.*

2021

	January						February						March						April						May						June			
S		3	10	17	24	31			7	14	21	28			7	14	21	28		4	11	18	25		2	9	16	23	30			6	13	20	27
M		4	11	18	25			1	8	15	22			1	8	15	22	29		5	12	19	26		3	10	17	24	31			7	14	21	28
T		5	12	19	26			2	9	16	23			2	9	16	23	30		6	13	20	27		4	11	18	25			1	8	15	22	29
W		6	13	20	27			3	10	17	24			3	10	17	24	31		7	14	21	28		5	12	19	26			2	9	16	23	30
T		7	14	21	28			4	11	18	25			4	11	18	25		1	8	15	22	29		6	13	20	27			3	10	17	24	
F	1	8	15	22	29		5	12	19	26			5	12	19	26			2	9	16	23	30		7	14	21	28			4	11	18	25	
S	2	9	16	23	30		6	13	20	27			6	13	20	27			3	10	17	24		1	8	15	22	29			5	12	19	26	

Laurence, Deacon at Rome, Martyr, 258 (CW Readings see Common of the Saints also 2 Cor. 9.6–10) *(also BCP)*   Red *or* Green

DEL Wk 19	**EUCHARIST**		**MORNING PRAYER**	**EVENING PRAYER**
	CW			
Psalms:	148.1–4		*44* (Week 3 Ord)	*47*; 49
Readings:	Ezek. 1.2–5, 24–end;		1 Sam. 19.1–18;	Ezek. 37.1–14;
	Matt. 17.22–end		Acts 1.1–14	Mark 1.1–13
		AW	Josh. 1.1–9	1 Cor. 9.19–end

	HOLY COMMUNION	**MORNING PRAYER**	**EVENING PRAYER**
	BCP Com. Martyr		
Psalms:	3	50; 51; 52	53; 54; 55
Readings:	Jer. 11.18–20; Heb. 11.32—12.2;	2 Kgs 20;	2 Chr. 33;
	Matt. 16.24–27	1 Cor. 15.1–34	Matt. 23
Hymns:	....	....	....

CW COLLECT

Almighty God,
who made Laurence a loving servant
    of your people
and a wise steward of the treasures of your Church:
fire us with his example to love as he loved
    and to walk in the way that leads to eternal life;
through Jesus Christ your Son our Lord,
who is alive and reigns with you,
in the unity of the Holy Spirit,
one God, now and for ever.

POST COMMUNION

God our redeemer,
whose Church was strengthened by the blood
    of your martyr Laurence:
so bind us, in life and death, to Christ's sacrifice
that our lives, broken and offered with his,
may carry his death and proclaim his resurrection in
    the world;
through Jesus Christ our Lord.

BCP COLLECT

*Almighty God, by whose grace and power thy
holy Martyr Laurence triumphed over suffering
and despised death: Grant, we beseech thee, that
enduring hardness and waxing valiant in fight,
we may with the noble army of martyrs receive
the crown of everlasting life; through Jesus Christ
our Lord.*

Sunrise 05.35; Sunset 20.33

2020

July						August						September						October						November						December					
S		5	12	19	26	S		2	9	16	23	30	S		6	13	20	27	S		4	11	18	25	S	1	8	15	22	29	S		6	13	20	27
M		6	13	20	27	M		3	10	17	24	31	M		7	14	21	28	M		5	12	19	26	M	2	9	16	23	30	M		7	14	21	28
T		7	14	21	28	T		4	11	18	25		T	1	8	15	22	29	T		6	13	20	27	T	3	10	17	24		T	1	8	15	22	29
W	1	8	15	22	29	W		5	12	19	26		W	2	9	16	23	30	W		7	14	21	28	W	4	11	18	25		W	2	9	16	23	30
T	2	9	16	23	30	T		6	13	20	27		T	3	10	17	24		T	1	8	15	22	29	T	5	12	19	26		T	3	10	17	24	31
F	3	10	17	24	31	F		7	14	21	28		F	4	11	18	25		F	2	9	16	23	30	F	6	13	20	27		F	4	11	18	25	
S	4	11	18	25		S	1	8	15	22	29		S	5	12	19	26		S	3	10	17	24	31	S	7	14	21	28		S	5	12	19	26	

Clare of Assisi, Founder of the Minoresses (Poor Clares), 1253 (CW readings see Common of the Saints
especially S. of Sol. 8.6–7) *John Henry Newman, Priest, Tractarian, 1890*   White *or* Green

	EUCHARIST	**MORNING PRAYER**	**EVENING PRAYER**
Psalms:	119.65–72	*48*; 52	*50*
Readings	Ezek. 2.8—3.4;	1 Sam. 20.1–17;	Ezek. 37.15–end;
	Matt. 18.1–5, 10, 12–14	Acts 1.15–end	Mark 1.14–20

		AW	*Prov. 15.1–11*		*Gal. 2.15–end*

	HOLY COMMUNION	**MORNING PRAYER**	**EVENING PRAYER**
	BCP		
Psalms:		56; 57; 58	59; 60; 61
Readings:		2 Kgs 22;	2 Kgs 23.1–20;
		1 Cor. 15.35–end	Mark 12.41—13.13
Hymns:	....	....	....

CW COLLECT
God of peace,
who in the poverty of the blessed Clare
gave us a clear light to shine in the darkness
    of this world:
give us grace so to follow in her footsteps
that we may, at the last, rejoice with her
    in your eternal glory;
through Jesus Christ your Son our Lord,
who is alive and reigns with you,
in the unity of the Holy Spirit,
one God, now and for ever.

POST COMMUNION
Merciful God,
who gave such grace to your servant Clare
that she served you with singleness of heart
and loved you above all things:
help us, whose communion with you
    has been renewed in this sacrament,
to forsake all that holds us back
    from following Christ
and to grow into his likeness from glory to glory;
through Jesus Christ our Lord

2021

	January						February					March					April					May					June			
S	3	10	17	24	31	S		7	14	21	28	S		7	14	21	28	S		4	11	18	25	S	2	9	16	23	30	S	6	13	20	27
M	4	11	18	25		M	1	8	15	22		M	1	8	15	22	29	M		5	12	19	26	M	3	10	17	24	31	M	7	14	21	28
T	5	12	19	26		T	2	9	16	23		T	2	9	16	23	30	T		6	13	20	27	T	4	11	18	25		T	1	8	15	22	29
W	6	13	20	27		W	3	10	17	24		W	3	10	17	24	31	W		7	14	21	28	W	5	12	19	26		W	2	9	16	23	30
T	7	14	21	28		T	4	11	18	25		T	4	11	18	25		T	1	8	15	22	29	T	6	13	20	27		T	3	10	17	24
F	1	8	15	22	29	F	5	12	19	26		F	5	12	19	26		F	2	9	16	23	30	F	7	14	21	28		F	4	11	18	25
S	2	9	16	23	30	S	6	13	20	27		S	6	13	20	27		S	3	10	17	24		S	1	8	15	22	29	S	5	12	19	26

Green

	EUCHARIST	MORNING PRAYER	EVENING PRAYER
	CW		
Psalms	113	*119.57–80*	*59*; 60 (67)
Readings:	Ezek. 9.1–7, 10.18–22;	1 Sam. 20.18–end;	Ezek. 39.21–end;
	Matt. 18.15–20	Acts 2.1–21	Mark 1.21–28

AW   *Isa. 49.1–7*   *1 John 1*

	HOLY COMMUNION	MORNING PRAYER	EVENING PRAYER
	BCP		
Psalms:		*62; 63; 64*	*65; 66; 67*
Readings:		*2 Kgs 23.21–35;*	*2 Kgs 23.36—24.17;*
		1 Cor. 16	*Mark 13.14–end*
Hymns:	....	....	....

2020

	July					August					September					October					November					December			
S		5	12	19	26		2	9	16	23	30		6	13	20	27		4	11	18	25		1	8	15	22	29		6	13	20	27
M		6	13	20	27		3	10	17	24	31		7	14	21	28		5	12	19	26		2	9	16	23	30		7	14	21	28
T		7	14	21	28		4	11	18	25		1	8	15	22	29		6	13	20	27		3	10	17	24		1	8	15	22	29
W	1	8	15	22	29		5	12	19	26		2	9	16	23	30		7	14	21	28		4	11	18	25		2	9	16	23	30
T	2	9	16	23	30		6	13	20	27		3	10	17	24		1	8	15	22	29		5	12	19	26		3	10	17	24	31
F	3	10	17	24	31		7	14	21	28		4	11	18	25		2	9	16	23	30		6	13	20	27		4	11	18	25
S	4	11	18	25		1	8	15	22	29		5	12	19	26		3	10	17	24	31		7	14	21	28		5	12	19	26

Jeremy Taylor, Bishop of Down and Connor, Teacher of the Faith, 1667 (CW Readings see
Common of the Saints also Titus 2.7–8, 11–14). *Florence Nightingale, Nurse, Social Reformer, 1910.*
Octavia Hill, Social Reformer, 1912

White *or* Green

	EUCHARIST CW	**MORNING PRAYER**	**EVENING PRAYER**
Psalms:	78.58–64	56; *57* (63*)	61; *62*; 64
Readings:	Ezek. 12.1–12; Matt. 18.21—19.1	1 Sam. 21.1—22.5; Acts 2.22–36	Ezek. 43.1–12; Mark 1.29–end

		AW	*Prov. 27.1–12*	*John 15.12–27*

	HOLY COMMUNION BCP	**MORNING PRAYER**	**EVENING PRAYER**
Psalms:		*68*	*69; 70*
Readings:		*2 Kgs 24.18—25.7;* *2 Cor. 1.1–22*	*2 Kgs 25.8–end;* *Matt. 25.1–30*
Hymns	....	....	....

CW COLLECT
Holy and loving God,
you dwell in the human heart
and make us partakers of the divine nature
in Christ our great high priest:
help us who remember your servant
      Jeremy Taylor
to put our trust in your heavenly promises
and follow a holy life in virtue and true godliness;
through Jesus Christ your Son our Lord,
who is alive and reigns with you,
in the unity of the Holy Spirit,
one God, now and for ever.

POST COMMUNION
God of truth,
whose Wisdom set her table
and invited us to eat the bread and drink the wine
      of the kingdom:
help us to lay aside all foolishness
and to live and walk in the way of insight,
that we may come with Jeremy Taylor to the eternal
      feast of heaven;
through Jesus Christ our Lord.

2021

January						February					March					April					May						June				
S		3	10	17	24	31	S		7	14	21	28	S		7	14	21	28	S		4	11	18	25	S		2	9	16	23	30	S		6	13	20	27
M		4	11	18	25		M	1	8	15	22		M	1	8	15	22	29	M		5	12	19	26	M		3	10	17	24	31	M		7	14	21	28
T		5	12	19	26		T	2	9	16	23		T	2	9	16	23	30	T		6	13	20	27	T		4	11	18	25	T	1	8	15	22	29
W		6	13	20	27		W	3	10	17	24		W	3	10	17	24	31	W		7	14	21	28	W		5	12	19	26	W	2	9	16	23	30
T		7	14	21	28		T	4	11	18	25		T	4	11	18	25		T	1	8	15	22	29	T		6	13	20	27	T	3	10	17	24
F	1	8	15	22	29		F	5	12	19	26		F	5	12	19	26		F	2	9	16	23	30	F		7	14	21	28	F	4	11	18	25
S	2	9	16	23	30		S	6	13	20	27		S	6	13	20	27		S	3	10	17	24		S	1	8	15	22	29	S	5	12	19	26

Maximilian Kolbe. Friar, Martyr 1941   Green

	EUCHARIST CW	**MORNING PRAYER**	**EVENING PRAYER**
Psalms:	118.14–18 *or Canticle:* Song of Deliverance	*51;* 54	*38*
Readings:	Ezek. 16.1–15, 60–end; Matt. 19.3–12	1 Sam. 22.6–end; Acts 2.37–end	Ezek. 44.4–16; Mark 2.1–12 *or* Eve of Blessed Virgin Mary: Ps. 72; Prov. 8.22–31; John 19.23–27

AW   *Isa. 59.8–end*   *Mark 15.6–20*

	HOLY COMMUNION BCP	**MORNING PRAYER**	**EVENING PRAYER**
Psalms:		*71; 72*	*73; 74*
Readings:		*Jer. 19;* *2 Cor. 1.23—end of 2*	*Jer. 21.1–10;* *Matt. 25.31–end*
Hymns:	....	....	....

2020

	July					August						September					October					November					December			
S		5	12	19	26	S		2	9	16	23	30	S		6	13	20	27	S		4	11	18	25	S	1	8	15	22	29	S		6	13	20	27
M		6	13	20	27	M		3	10	17	24	31	M		7	14	21	28	M		5	12	19	26	M	2	9	16	23	30	M		7	14	21	28
T		7	14	21	28	T		4	11	18	25		T	1	8	15	22	29	T		6	13	20	27	T	3	10	17	24		T	1	8	15	22	29
W	1	8	15	22	29	W		5	12	19	26		W	2	9	16	23	30	W		7	14	21	28	W	4	11	18	25		W	2	9	16	23	30
T	2	9	16	23	30	T		6	13	20	27		T	3	10	17	24		T	1	8	15	22	29	T	5	12	19	26		T	3	10	17	24	31
F	3	10	17	24	31	F		7	14	21	28		F	4	11	18	25		F	2	9	16	23	30	F	6	13	20	27		F	4	11	18	25	
S	4	11	18	25		S	1	8	15	22	29		S	5	12	19	26		S	3	10	17	24	31	S	7	14	21	28		S	5	12	19	26	

The Blessed Virgin Mary
White
(This Festival may be celebrated on September 8)

	PRINCIPAL SERVICE	**THIRD SERVICE**	**SECOND SERVICE**
	CW		
Psalms:	45.10–end	98; 138; 147.1–12	132
Readings:	Isa. 61.10–end *or*	Isa. 7.10–15;	S. of Sol. 2.1–7;
	Rev. 11.19—12.6, 10;	Luke 11.27–28	Acts 1.6–14
	Gal. 4.4–7; Luke 1.46–55		

Displaced readings may be added to the previous day's portion:

	EUCHARIST	**MORNING PRAYER**	**EVENING PRAYER**
Readings:	Ezek. 18.1–11a, 13b, 30, 32;	1 Sam. 23;	Ezek. 47.1–12;
	Matt. 19.13–15	Acts 3.1–10	Mark 2.13–22

	HOLY COMMUNION	**MORNING PRAYER**	**EVENING PRAYER**
	BCP		
Psalms:		75; 76; 77	78
Readings:		Jer. 22.20—23.8;	Jer. 24; Mark 14.1–26;
		2 Cor. 3	E. Coll. Trinity 10
Hymns:	....	....	....

CW COLLECT for the Blessed Virgin Mary
Almighty God, who looked upon the lowliness
    of the Blessed Virgin Mary and chose her
    to be the mother of your only Son:
grant that we who are redeemed by his blood
may share with her in the glory
    of your eternal kingdom;
through Jesus Christ your Son our Lord,
who is alive and reigns with you,
in the unity of the Holy Spirit,
one God, now and for ever.

POST COMMUNION
God most high,
whose handmaid bore the Word made flesh:
we thank you that in this sacrament of
    our redemption
you visit us with your Holy Spirit
and overshadow us by your power;
strengthen us to walk with Mary
    the joyful path of obedience
and so to bring forth the fruits of holiness;
through Jesus Christ our Lord.

2021

January					February					March					April					May					June				
S		3	10	17	24	31	S		7	14	21	28	S		7	14	21	28	S		4	11	18	25	S		2	9	16	23	30	S		6	13	20	27
M		4	11	18	25		M	1	8	15	22		M	1	8	15	22	29	M		5	12	19	26	M		3	10	17	24	31	M		7	14	21	28
T		5	12	19	26		T	2	9	16	23		T	2	9	16	23	30	T		6	13	20	27	T		4	11	18	25	T	1	8	15	22	29
W		6	13	20	27		W	3	10	17	24		W	3	10	17	24	31	W		7	14	21	28	W		5	12	19	26	W	2	9	16	23	30
T		7	14	21	28		T	4	11	18	25		T	4	11	18	25		T	1	8	15	22	29	T		6	13	20	27	T	3	10	17	24	
F	1	8	15	22	29		F	5	12	19	26		F	5	12	19	26		F	2	9	16	23	30	F		7	14	21	28	F	4	11	18	25	
S	2	9	16	23	30		S	6	13	20	27		S	6	13	20	27		S	3	10	17	24		S	1	8	15	22	29	S	5	12	19	26	

THE TENTH SUNDAY AFTER TRINITY

(Green)

	PRINCIPAL SERVICE CW Proper 15	**THIRD SERVICE**	**SECOND SERVICE**
Psalms:	*133; 67*	92	*90[90.1–12]*
Readings:	*Gen. 45.1–15;* *Isa. 56.1, 6–8;* *Rom. 11.1–2a, 29–32;* *Matt. 15.[10–20] 21–28*	Jonah 1 *or* Ecclus 3.1–15; 2 Pet. 3.14–end	2 Kgs 4.1–37; Acts 16.1–15; [John 6.51–58]

	HOLY COMMUNION BCP	**MORNING PRAYER**	**EVENING PRAYER**
Psalms:	*17.1–8*	*92*	*90*
Readings:	*Jer. 7.9–15;* *1 Cor. 12.1–11;* *Luke 19.41–47a*	*1 Kgs 21* or *Ecclus 3.17–29;* *Luke 1.29–56* or *Phil. 4*	*1 Kgs 22.1–40* or *2 Kgs 4.8–37* or *Ecclus 11.7–28;* *Matt. 13.24–52* or *Acts 27*
Hymns:	....	....	....

2020

	July					August						September					October					November					December			
S		5	12	19	26		2	9	16	23	30		6	13	20	27		4	11	18	25		1	8	15	22	29		6	13	20	27
M		6	13	20	27		3	10	17	24	31		7	14	21	28		5	12	19	26		2	9	16	23	30		7	14	21	28
T		7	14	21	28		4	11	18	25			1	8	15	22	29		6	13	20	27		3	10	17	24		1	8	15	22	29
W	1	8	15	22	29		5	12	19	26		2	9	16	23	30		7	14	21	28		4	11	18	25		2	9	16	23	30
T	2	9	16	23	30		6	13	20	27		3	10	17	24		1	8	15	22	29		5	12	19	26		3	10	17	24	31
F	3	10	17	24	31		7	14	21	28		4	11	18	25		2	9	16	23	30		6	13	20	27		4	11	18	25
S	4	11	18	25		1	8	15	22	29		5	12	19	26		3	10	17	24	31		7	14	21	28		5	12	19	26

CW COLLECTS

Let your merciful ears, O Lord,
be open to the prayers of your humble servants;
and that they may obtain their petitions
make them to ask such things as shall please you;
through Jesus Christ your Son our Lord,
who is alive and reigns with you,
in the unity of the Holy Spirit,
one God, now and for ever.

or

Lord of heaven and earth,
as Jesus taught his disciples to be persistent
    in prayer,
give us patience and courage never to lose hope,
but always to bring our prayers before you;
through Jesus Christ our Lord.

POST COMMUNION

God of our pilgrimage,
you have willed that the gate of mercy
should stand open for those who trust in you:
look upon us with your favour
that we who follow the path of your will
may never wander from the way of life;
through Jesus Christ our Lord.

BCP COLLECT

*Let thy merciful ears, O Lord, be open to the prayers
of thy humble servants; and that they may obtain
their petitions make them to ask such things as shall
please thee; through Jesus Christ our Lord.*

2021

January						February					March						April					May						June			
S		3	10	17	24	31	**S**			7	14	21	28	**S**			7	14	21	28	**S**			4	11	18	25	**S**			2	9	16	23	30	**S**			6	13	20	27
M		4	11	18	25		**M**	1	8	15	22		**M**	1	8	15	22	29	**M**		5	12	19	26	**M**		3	10	17	24	31	**M**		7	14	21	28
T		5	12	19	26		**T**	2	9	16	23		**T**	2	9	16	23	30	**T**		6	13	20	27	**T**		4	11	18	25	**T**	1	8	15	22	29
W		6	13	20	27		**W**	3	10	17	24		**W**	3	10	17	24	31	**W**		7	14	21	28	**W**		5	12	19	26	**W**	2	9	16	23	30
T		7	14	21	28		**T**	4	11	18	25		**T**	4	11	18	25		**T**	1	8	15	22	29	**T**		6	13	20	27	**T**	3	10	17	24
F	1	8	15	22	29		**F**	5	12	19	26		**F**	5	12	19	26		**F**	2	9	16	23	30	**F**		7	14	21	28	**F**	4	11	18	25
S	2	9	16	23	30		**S**	6	13	20	27		**S**	6	13	20	27		**S**	3	10	17	24		**S**	1	8	15	22	29	**S**	5	12	19	26

AUGUST
17 Monday

DEL Wk 20

	EUCHARIST CW		**MORNING PRAYER**	**EVENING PRAYER**
Psalms:	78.1–8		*71* (Week 4 Ord)	*72*; 75
Readings:	Ezek. 24.15–24; Matt. 19.16–22		1 Sam. 24; Acts 3.11–end	Prov. 1–19; Mark 2.23—3.6
		AW	*Judg. 13.1–23*	*Luke 10.38–42*

	HOLY COMMUNION BCP	**MORNING PRAYER**	**EVENING PRAYER**
Psalms:		*86; 87; 88*	*89*
Readings:		Jer. 25.1–14; 2 Cor. 4	Jer. 27.2–end; Mark 14.27–52
Hymns:	....	....	....

Sunrise 05.47; Sunset 20.19

2020

	July				August					September				October					November					December			
S		5	12	19	26		2	9	16	23	30		6	13	20	27		4	11	18	25		1	8	15	22	29		6	13	20	27
M		6	13	20	27		3	10	17	24	31		7	14	21	28		5	12	19	26		2	9	16	23	30		7	14	21	28
T		7	14	21	28		4	11	18	25		1	8	15	22	29		6	13	20	27		3	10	17	24		1	8	15	22	29
W	1	8	15	22	29		5	12	19	26		2	9	16	23	30		7	14	21	28		4	11	18	25		2	9	16	23	30
T	2	9	16	23	30		6	13	20	27		3	10	17	24		1	8	15	22	29		5	12	19	26		3	10	17	24	31
F	3	10	17	24	31		7	14	21	28		4	11	18	25		2	9	16	23	30		6	13	20	27		4	11	18	25
S	4	11	18	25		1	8	15	22	29		5	12	19	26		3	10	17	24	31		7	14	21	28		5	12	19	26

Green

	EUCHARIST	MORNING PRAYER	EVENING PRAYER
	CW		
Psalms:	107.1–3, 40, 43	*73*	*74*
Readings:	Ezek. 28.1–10; Matt. 19.23–end	1 Sam. 26; Acts 4.1–12	Prov. 1.20–end; Mark 3.7–19a

AW *Prov. 15.15–end* *Matt. 15.21–28*

	HOLY COMMUNION	MORNING PRAYER	EVENING PRAYER
	BCP		
Psalms:		*90; 91; 92*	*93; 94*
Readings:		*Jer. 28;* *2 Cor. 5*	*Jer. 29.1–20;* *Mark 14.53–end*
Hymns:	....	....	....

2021

January						February					March					April					May					June				
S		3	10	17	24	31	**S**		7	14	21	28	**S**		7	14	21	28	**S**		4	11	18	25	**S**		2	9	16	23	30	**S**		6	13	20	27
M		4	11	18	25		**M**	1	8	15	22		**M**	1	8	15	22	29	**M**		5	12	19	26	**M**		3	10	17	24	31	**M**		7	14	21	28
T		5	12	19	26		**T**	2	9	16	23		**T**	2	9	16	23	30	**T**		6	13	20	27	**T**		4	11	18	25	**T**	1	8	15	22	29
W		6	13	20	27		**W**	3	10	17	24		**W**	3	10	17	24	31	**W**		7	14	21	28	**W**		5	12	19	26	**W**	2	9	16	23	30
T		7	14	21	28		**T**	4	11	18	25		**T**	4	11	18	25		**T**	1	8	15	22	29	**T**		6	13	20	27	**T**	3	10	17	24	
F	1	8	15	22	29		**F**	5	12	19	26		**F**	5	12	19	26		**F**	2	9	16	23	30	**F**		7	14	21	28	**F**	4	11	18	25	
S	2	9	16	23	30		**S**	6	13	20	27		**S**	6	13	20	27		**S**	3	10	17	24		**S**	1	8	15	22	29	**S**	5	12	19	26	

Green

	EUCHARIST		**MORNING PRAYER**	**EVENING PRAYER**
	CW			
Psalms:	23		*77*	*119.81–104*
Readings:	Ezek. 34.1–11; Matt. 20.1–16		1 Sam. 28.3–end; Acts 4.13–31	Prov. 2; Mark 3.19b–end
		AW	*Isa. 45.1–7*	*Eph. 4.1–16*
	HOLY COMMUNION		**MORNING PRAYER**	**EVENING PRAYER**
	BCP			
Psalms:			*95; 96; 97*	*98; 99; 100; 101*
Readings:			*Jer. 32.1–25;* *2 Cor. 5.20—7.1*	*Jer. 32.26–end;* *Mark 15.1–41*
Hymns:	....		....	....

2020

July	August	September	October	November	December
S 5 12 19 26	S 2 9 16 23 30	S 6 13 20 27	S 4 11 18 25	S 1 8 15 22 29	S 6 13 20 27
M 6 13 20 27	M 3 10 17 24 31	M 7 14 21 28	M 5 12 19 26	M 2 9 16 23 30	M 7 14 21 28
T 7 14 21 28	T 4 11 18 25	T 1 8 15 22 29	T 6 13 20 27	T 3 10 17 24	T 1 8 15 22 29
W 1 8 15 22 29	W 5 12 19 26	W 2 9 16 23 30	W 7 14 21 28	W 4 11 18 25	W 2 9 16 23 30
T 2 9 16 23 30	T 6 13 20 27	T 3 10 17 24	T 1 8 15 22 29	T 5 12 19 26	T 3 10 17 24 31
F 3 10 17 24 31	F 7 14 21 28	F 4 11 18 25	F 2 9 16 23 30	F 6 13 20 27	F 4 11 18 25
S 4 11 18 25	S 1 8 15 22 29	S 5 12 19 26	S 3 10 17 24 31	S 7 14 21 28	S 5 12 19 26

Bernard, Abbot of Clairvaux, Teacher of the Faith, 1153 (CW Readings see Common of the Saints   White *or* Green
especially Rev. 19.5–9)   *William and Catherine Booth, Founders of the Salvation Army, 1912 and 1890*

	EUCHARIST CW	**MORNING PRAYER**	**EVENING PRAYER**
Psalms:	51.7–12	*78.1–39**	*78.40–end**
Readings:	Ezek. 36.23–28; Matt. 22.1–14	1 Sam. 31; Acts 4.32—5.11	Prov. 3.1–26; Mark 4.1–20
		AW *Jer. 16.1–15*	*Luke 12.35–48*

	HOLY COMMUNION BCP	**MORNING PRAYER**	**EVENING PRAYER**
Psalms:		*102; 103*	*104*
Readings:		*Jer. 33; 2 Cor. 7.2–end*	*Jer. 34.8–end; Luke 23.33–end*
Hymns:	....	....	....

CW COLLECT
Merciful redeemer,
who, by the life and preaching of your
    servant Bernard,
rekindled the radiant light of your Church:
grant us, in our generation,
to be inflamed with the same spirit
    of discipline and love
and ever to walk before you as children of light;
through Jesus Christ your Son our Lord,
who is alive and reigns with you,
in the unity of the Holy Spirit,
one God, now and for ever.

POST COMMUNION
God of truth,
whose Wisdom set her table
and invited us to eat the bread and drink
    the wine of the kingdom:
help us to lay aside all foolishness
and to live and walk in the way of insight,
that we may come with Bernard to the eternal
    feast of heaven;
through Jesus Christ our Lord.

2021

January				
S		3	10	17	24	31
M		4	11	18	25
T		5	12	19	26
W		6	13	20	27
T		7	14	21	28
F	1	8	15	22	29
S	2	9	16	23	30

February				
S			7	14	21	28
M	1	8	15	22
T	2	9	16	23
W	3	10	17	24
T	4	11	18	25
F	5	12	19	26
S	6	13	20	27

March				
S		7	14	21	28
M	1	8	15	22	29
T	2	9	16	23	30
W	3	10	17	24	31
T	4	11	18	25
F	5	12	19	26
S	6	13	20	27

April				
S		4	11	18	25
M		5	12	19	26
T		6	13	20	27
W		7	14	21	28
T	1	8	15	22	29
F	2	9	16	23	30
S	3	10	17	24

May				
S		2	9	16	23	30
M		3	10	17	24	31
T		4	11	18	25
W		5	12	19	26
T		6	13	20	27
F		7	14	21	28
S	1	8	15	22	29

June				
S		6	13	20	27
M		7	14	21	28
T	1	8	15	22	29
W	2	9	16	23	30
T	3	10	17	24
F	4	11	18	25
S	5	12	19	26

Green

	EUCHARIST	**MORNING PRAYER**	**EVENING PRAYER**
	CW		
Psalms:	107.1–8	*55*	*69*
Readings:	Ezek. 37.1–14;	2 Sam. 1;	Prov. 3.27—4.19;
	Matt. 22.34–40	Acts 5.12–26	Mark 4.21–34

AW *Jer. 18.1–11*   *Heb. 1.1–9*

	HOLY COMMUNION	**MORNING PRAYER**	**EVENING PRAYER**
	BCP		
Psalms:		*105*	*106*
Readings:		Jer. 37;	Jer. 38.1–13;
		2 Cor. 8	Mark 15.42—end of 16
Hymns:	....	....	....

2020

	July					August						September					October					November					December			
S		5	12	19	26		2	9	16	23	30		6	13	20	27		4	11	18	25	1	8	15	22	29		6	13	20	27
M		6	13	20	27		3	10	17	24	31		7	14	21	28		5	12	19	26	2	9	16	23	30		7	14	21	28
T		7	14	21	28		4	11	18	25		1	8	15	22	29		6	13	20	27	3	10	17	24		1	8	15	22	29
W	1	8	15	22	29		5	12	19	26		2	9	16	23	30		7	14	21	28	4	11	18	25		2	9	16	23	30
T	2	9	16	23	30		6	13	20	27		3	10	17	24		1	8	15	22	29	5	12	19	26		3	10	17	24	31
F	3	10	17	24	31		7	14	21	28		4	11	18	25		2	9	16	23	30	6	13	20	27		4	11	18	25
S	4	11	18	25		1	8	15	22	29		5	12	19	26		3	10	17	24	31	7	14	21	28		5	12	19	26

Green

	EUCHARIST CW	**MORNING PRAYER**	**EVENING PRAYER**
Psalms:	85.7–end	*76*; 79	81; *84*
Readings:	Ezek. 43.1–7; Matt. 23.1–12	2 Sam. 2.1–11; Acts 5.27–end	Prov. 6.1–19; Mark 4.35–end

AW *Jer. 26.1–19* *Eph. 3.1–13*

	HOLY COMMUNION BCP	**MORNING PRAYER**	**EVENING PRAYER**
Psalms:		107	108; 109
Readings:		*Jer. 38.14–end;* *2 Cor. 9*	*Jer. 39;* *Luke 24.13–end;* *E. Coll. Trinity 11*
Hymns:	....	....	....

THE ELEVENTH SUNDAY AFTER TRINITY

(Green)

	PRINCIPAL SERVICE	THIRD SERVICE	SECOND SERVICE
	CW Proper 16		
Psalms:	*124*; 138	104.1–25	95
Readings:	*Exod. 1.8—2.10;*	Jonah 2 *or* Ecclus 3.17–29;	2 Kgs 6.8–23;
	Isa. 51.1–6;	Rev. 1	Acts 17.15–end;
	Rom. 12.1–8;		[John 6.56–69]
	Matt. 16.13–20		*or* Eve of Bartholomew the Apostle:
			Ps. 97; Isa. 61.1–9; 2 Cor. 6.1–10

	HOLY COMMUNION	MORNING PRAYER	EVENING PRAYER
	BCP		
Psalms:	28	104.1–25	95
Readings:	*1 Kgs 3.5–15;*	*2 Kgs 5 or Ecclus 18.1–14;*	*2 Kgs 6.8–23 or 2 Kgs 17.1–23 or*
	1 Cor. 15.1–11;	Luke 1.57–end or	*Ecclus 38.24–end;*
	Luke 18.9–14	Col. 3.12—4.6	*Matt. 16.13–end or Acts 28 or First*
			Evensong of St Bartholomew:
			Gen. 28.10–17; John 1.43–end
Hymns:	....	....	....

CW COLLECTS

O God, you declare your almighty power
most chiefly in showing mercy and pity:
mercifully grant to us such a measure of your grace,
that we, running the way of your commandments,
may receive your gracious promises,
and be made partakers of your heavenly treasure;
through Jesus Christ your Son our Lord,
who is alive and reigns with you,
in the unity of the Holy Spirit,
one God, now and for ever.

or

God of glory,
the end of our searching,
help us to lay aside
all that prevents us from seeking your kingdom,
and to give all that we have
to gain the pearl beyond all price,
through our Saviour Jesus Christ.

POST COMMUNION

Lord of all mercy,
we your faithful people have celebrated that one
    true sacrifice which takes away our sins and brings
    pardon and peace:
by our communion keep us firm on the foundation of
    the gospel and preserve us from all sin;
through Jesus Christ our Lord.

BCP COLLECT

*O God, who declarest thy almighty power most
chiefly in shewing mercy and pity: Mercifully grant
unto us such a measure of thy grace, that we,
running the way of thy commandments, may obtain
thy gracious promises, and be made partakers of thy
heavenly treasure; through Jesus Christ our Lord.*

2021

January						February					March					April					May					June				
S		3	10	17	24	31	S		7	14	21	28	S		7	14	21	28	S		4	11	18	25	S		2	9	16	23	30	S		6	13	20	27
M		4	11	18	25		M	1	8	15	22		M	1	8	15	22	29	M		5	12	19	26	M		3	10	17	24	31	M		7	14	21	28
T		5	12	19	26		T	2	9	16	23		T	2	9	16	23	30	T		6	13	20	27	T		4	11	18	25	T	1	8	15	22	29
W		6	13	20	27		W	3	10	17	24		W	3	10	17	24	31	W		7	14	21	28	W		5	12	19	26	W	2	9	16	23	30
T		7	14	21	28		T	4	11	18	25		T	4	11	18	25		T	1	8	15	22	29	T		6	13	20	27	T	3	10	17	24	
F	1	8	15	22	29		F	5	12	19	26		F	5	12	19	26		F	2	9	16	23	30	F		7	14	21	28	F	4	11	18	25	
S	2	9	16	23	30		S	6	13	20	27		S	6	13	20	27		S	3	10	17	24		S	1	8	15	22	29	S	5	12	19	26	

Bartholomew the Apostle

Red

	PRINCIPAL SERVICE	THIRD SERVICE	SECOND SERVICE
	CW		
Psalms:	145.1–7	86; 117	91; 116
Readings:	Isa. 43.8–13; Acts 5.12–16;	Gen. 28.10–17	Ecclus 39.1–10 or
	Luke 22.24–30 or	[BCP Var. Isa. 43.8–13]	Deut. 18.15–19;
	Acts 5.12–16; 1 Cor. 4.9–15;	John 1.43–end	Matt. 10.1–22
	Luke 22.24–30		

Displaced readings may be added to the following day's portion:

	EUCHARIST	MORNING PRAYER	EVENING PRAYER
	CW		
Readings:	2 Thess. 1.1–5, 11–end;	2 Sam. 3.12–end;	Prov. 8.1.21;
	Matt. 23.13–22	Acts 6	Mark 5.1–20

	HOLY COMMUNION	MORNING PRAYER	EVENING PRAYER
	BCP St Bartholomew		
Psalms:	15	116; 117; 118	119.1–32
Readings:	Gen. 28.10–17;	Ecclus 39.1–10;	Deut. 18.15–19;
	Acts 5.12–16;	Matt. 10.1–15	Matt. 10.16–22
	Luke 22.24–30		
Hymns:	....	....	....

CW COLLECT
Almighty and everlasting God,
who gave to your apostle Bartholomew grace
    truly to believe and to preach your word:
grant that your Church
may love that word which he believed
and may faithfully preach and receive the same;
through Jesus Christ your Son our Lord,
who is alive and reigns with you,
in the unity of the Holy Spirit,
one God, now and for ever.

POST COMMUNION
Lord God, the source of truth and love,
keep us faithful to the apostles' teaching
    and fellowship,
united in prayer and the breaking of bread,
and one in joy and simplicity of heart,
in Jesus Christ our Lord.

BCP COLLECT
*O Almighty and everlasting God, who didst give to
thine Apostle Bartholomew grace truly to believe and
to preach thy Word: Grant, we beseech thee, unto
thy Church, to love that Word which he believed,
and both to preach and receive the same; through
Jesus Christ our Lord.*

Sunrise 05.58; Sunset 20.04

2020

	July					August					September					October					November					December			
S		5	12	19	26		2	9	16	23	30		6	13	20	27		4	11	18	25		1	8	15	22	29		6	13	20	27
M		6	13	20	27		3	10	17	24	31		7	14	21	28		5	12	19	26		2	9	16	23	30		7	14	21	28
T		7	14	21	28		4	11	18	25		1	8	15	22	29		6	13	20	27		3	10	17	24		1	8	15	22	29
W	1	8	15	22	29		5	12	19	26		2	9	16	23	30		7	14	21	28		4	11	18	25		2	9	16	23	30
T	2	9	16	23	30		6	13	20	27		3	10	17	24		1	8	15	22	29		5	12	19	26		3	10	17	24	31
F	3	10	17	24	31		7	14	21	28		4	11	18	25		2	9	16	23	30		6	13	20	27		4	11	18	25
S	4	11	18	25		1	8	15	22	29		5	12	19	26		3	10	17	24	31		7	14	21	28		5	12	19	26

Green

DEL Wk 21	**EUCHARIST**	**MORNING PRAYER**	**EVENING PRAYER**
	CW		
Psalms:	98	87; *89.1–18* (Week 5. Ord.)	*89.19–end*
Readings	2 Thess. 2.1–3a, 14–end;	2 Sam. 5.1–12;	Prov. 8.22–end;
	Matt. 23.23–26	Acts 7.1–16	Mark 5.21–34

		AW	*Prov. 16.1–11*	*Phil. 3.4b–end*

	HOLY COMMUNION	**MORNING PRAYER**	**EVENING PRAYER**
	BCP		
Psalms:		*119.33–72*	*119.73–104*
Readings:		*Jer. 42;*	*Jer. 43;*
		2 Cor. 11	*John 1.29–end*
Hymns:	....	....	....

2021

	January					February					March					April					May					June			
S		3	10	17	24	31		7	14	21	28		7	14	21	28		4	11	18	25		2	9	16	23	30		6	13	20	27
M		4	11	18	25		1	8	15	22		1	8	15	22	29		5	12	19	26		3	10	17	24	31		7	14	21	28
T		5	12	19	26		2	9	16	23		2	9	16	23	30		6	13	20	27		4	11	18	25		1	8	15	22	29
W		6	13	20	27		3	10	17	24		3	10	17	24	31		7	14	21	28		5	12	19	26		2	9	16	23	30
T		7	14	21	28		4	11	18	25		4	11	18	25		1	8	15	22	29		6	13	20	27		3	10	17	24
F	1	8	15	22	29	5	12	19	26		5	12	19	26		2	9	16	23	30		7	14	21	28		4	11	18	25
S	2	9	16	23	30	6	13	20	27		6	13	20	27		3	10	17	24		1	8	15	22	29		5	12	19	26

Green

	EUCHARIST	**MORNING PRAYER**	**EVENING PRAYER**
	CW		
Psalms:	128	*119.105–128*	*91*; 93
Readings:	2 Thess. 3.6–10, 16–end;	2 Sam. 6.1–19;	Prov. 9;
	Matt. 23.27–32	Acts 7.17–43	Mark 5.35–end

AW   *Deut. 11.1–21*   *2 Cor. 9.6–end*

	HOLY COMMUNION	**MORNING PRAYER**	**EVENING PRAYER**
	BCP		
Psalms:		*119.105–144*	*119.145–end*
Readings:		Jer. 44.1–14;	Jer. 44.15–end;
		2 Cor. 12.1–13	John 2
Hymns:	....	....	....

2020

	July					August					September					October					November					December			
S		5	12	19	26		2	9	16	23	30		6	13	20	27		4	11	18	25		1	8	15	22	29		6	13	20	27
M		6	13	20	27		3	10	17	24	31		7	14	21	28		5	12	19	26		2	9	16	23	30		7	14	21	28
T		7	14	21	28		4	11	18	25		1	8	15	22	29		6	13	20	27		3	10	17	24		1	8	15	22	29
W	1	8	15	22	29		5	12	19	26		2	9	16	23	30		7	14	21	28		4	11	18	25		2	9	16	23	30
T	2	9	16	23	30		6	13	20	27		3	10	17	24	1	8	15	22	29		5	12	19	26		3	10	17	24	31
F	3	10	17	24	31		7	14	21	28		4	11	18	25	2	9	16	23	30		6	13	20	27		4	11	18	25
S	4	11	18	25	1	8	15	22	29		5	12	19	26	3	10	17	24	31		7	14	21	28		5	12	19	26

Monica, mother of Augustine of Hippo, 387 (CW Readings see Common of the Saints   White *or* Green
also Ecclus 26.1–3, 13–16)

	EUCHARIST CW	**MORNING PRAYER**	**EVENING PRAYER**
Psalms:	145.1–7	90; *92*	*94*
Readings:	1 Cor. 1.1–9; Matt. 24.42–end	2 Sam. 7.1–17; Acts 7.44–53	Prov. 10.1–12; Mark 6.1–13

	AW	*Ecclus 2 or Eccles. 2.12–25*	*John 16.1–15*

	HOLY COMMUNION BCP	**MORNING PRAYER**	**EVENING PRAYER**
Psalms:		*120; 121; 123; 124; 125*	*126; 127; 128; 129; 130; 131*
Readings:		*Ezek. 2; 2 Cor. 12.14—end of 13*	*Ezek. 3.4–end; John 3.1–21*
Hymns:	....	....	....

CW COLLECT
Faithful God,
who strengthened Monica, the mother of Augustine,
    with wisdom,
and through her patient endurance
encouraged him to seek after you:
give us the will to persist in prayer
that those who stray from you may be brought to
    faith in your Son Jesus Christ our Lord,
who is alive and reigns with you,
in the unity of the Holy Spirit,
one God, now and for ever.

POST COMMUNION
Father,
from whom every family in heaven and on earth
    takes its name,
your servant Monica revealed your goodness
    in a life of tranquillity and service:
grant that we who have gathered in faith
    around this table
may like her know the love of Christ
    that surpasses knowledge
and be filled with all your fullness;
through Jesus Christ our Lord.

2021

	January						February					March						April					May						June			
S		3	10	17	24	31		7	14	21	28		7	14	21	28			4	11	18	25		2	9	16	23	30		6	13	20	27
M		4	11	18	25		1	8	15	22		1	8	15	22	29			5	12	19	26		3	10	17	24	31		7	14	21	28
T		5	12	19	26		2	9	16	23		2	9	16	23	30			6	13	20	27		4	11	18	25		1	8	15	22	29
W		6	13	20	27		3	10	17	24		3	10	17	24	31			7	14	21	28		5	12	19	26		2	9	16	23	30
T		7	14	21	28		4	11	18	25		4	11	18	25		1	8	15	22	29		6	13	20	27		3	10	17	24	
F	1	8	15	22	29		5	12	19	26		5	12	19	26		2	9	16	23	30		7	14	21	28		4	11	18	25	
S	2	9	16	23	30		6	13	20	27		6	13	20	27		3	10	17	24		1	8	15	22	29		5	12	19	26	

Augustine, Bishop of Hippo, Teacher of the Faith, 430 (CW Readings see Common of the Saints especially Ecclus 39.1–10, also Rom. 13.11–13) *(also BCP)*

White *or* Green

	EUCHARIST		MORNING PRAYER	EVENING PRAYER
	CW			
Psalms:	33.6–12		*88*; (95)	*102*
Readings:	1 Cor. 1.17–25; Matt. 25.1–13		2 Sam. 7.18–end; Acts 7.54—8.3	Prov. 11.1–12; Mark 6.14–29
		AW	*Obad. 1–10*	*John 19.1–16*

	HOLY COMMUNION	MORNING PRAYER	EVENING PRAYER
	BCP Com. Doctor		
Psalms:	37.30–35	132; 133; 134; 135	136; 137; 138
Readings:	Wisd. 7.7–14; 1 Cor. 2.6–13; Matt. 13.51–52	Ezek. 8; Rom. 1	Ezek. 9; John 3.22–end
Hymns:	....	....	....

CW COLLECT

Merciful Lord,
who turned Augustine from his sins
    to be a faithful bishop and teacher:
grant that we may follow him in penitence
    and discipline
till our restless hearts find their rest in you;
through Jesus Christ your Son our Lord,
who is alive and reigns with you,
in the unity of the Holy Spirit,
one God, now and for ever.

POST COMMUNION

God of truth,
whose Wisdom set her table
and invited us to eat the bread and drink the wine
    of the kingdom:
help us to lay aside all foolishness
and to live and walk in the way of insight,
that we may come with Augustine to the eternal feast
    of heaven;
through Jesus Christ our Lord.

BCP COLLECT

O God who hast enlightened thy Church by
the teaching of thy servant Augustine: Enrich it
evermore, we beseech thee, with thy heavenly grace,
and raise up faithful witnesses who by their life and
doctrine may set forth to all men the truth of thy
salvation; through Jesus Christ our Lord.

2020

July				August					September				October				November				December			
S	5 12 19 26			S	2 9 16 23 30				S	6 13 20 27			S	4 11 18 25			S	1 8 15 22 29			S	6 13 20 27	
M	6 13 20 27			M	3 10 17 24 31				M	7 14 21 28			M	5 12 19 26			M	2 9 16 23 30			M	7 14 21 28	
T	7 14 21 28			T	4 11 18 25				T	1 8 15 22 29			T	6 13 20 27			T	3 10 17 24			T	1 8 15 22 29	
W	1 8 15 22 29			W	5 12 19 26				W	2 9 16 23 30			W	7 14 21 28			W	4 11 18 25			W	2 9 16 23 30	
T	2 9 16 23 30			T	6 13 20 27				T	3 10 17 24			T	1 8 15 22 29			T	5 12 19 26			T	3 10 17 24 31	
F	3 10 17 24 31			F	7 14 21 28				F	4 11 18 25			F	2 9 16 23 30			F	6 13 20 27			F	4 11 18 25	
S	4 11 18 25			S	1 8 15 22 29				S	5 12 19 26			S	3 10 17 24 31			S	7 14 21 28			S	5 12 19 26	

The Beheading of John the Baptist   Red *or* Green (*or* Red)
CW Lesser Festival: Ps. 11; Jer. 1.4–10; Heb. 11.32—12.2; Matt. 14.1–12 *(also BCP)*

	EUCHARIST	**MORNING PRAYER**	**EVENING PRAYER**
	CW		
Psalms:	33.12–15, 20–end	96; *97*; 100	*104*
Readings:	1 Cor. 1.26–end;	2 Sam. 9;	Prov. 12.10–end;
	Matt. 25.14–30	Acts 8.4–25	Mark 6.30–44
	AW	*2 Kgs 2.11–14*	*Luke 24.36–end*

	HOLY COMMUNION	**MORNING PRAYER**	**EVENING PRAYER**
	BCP Beheading of St John Baptist		
Psalms:	*92.11–end*	*139; 140; 141*	*142; 143*
Readings:	*2 Chr. 24.17–21;*	*Ezek. 11.14–end;*	*Ezek. 33.21–end;*
	Heb. 11.32—12.2;	*Rom. 2.1–16*	*John 4.1–26;*
	Matt. 14.1–12		*E. Coll. Trinity 12*
Hymns:	....	....	....

CW COLLECT

Almighty God,
who called your servant John the Baptist
to be the forerunner of your Son in birth and death:
strengthen us by your grace
that, as he suffered for the truth,
so we may boldly resist corruption and vice
and receive with him the unfading crown of glory;
through Jesus Christ your Son our Lord,
who is alive and reigns with you,
in the unity of the Holy Spirit,
one God, now and for ever.

POST COMMUNION

Merciful Lord,
whose prophet John the Baptist
proclaimed your Son as the Lamb of God
    who takes away the sin of the world:
grant that we who in this sacrament have known
your forgiveness and your life-giving love
may ever tell of your mercy and your peace;
through Jesus Christ our Lord.

BCP COLLECT

*O God, who didst vouchsafe to thy servant John
Baptist to be in birth and death the forerunner of
thy Son: Grant that as he was slain for truth and
righteousness, so we may contend for the same unto
the end; for the love of thy Son Jesus Christ our Lord.*

THE TWELFTH SUNDAY AFTER TRINITY

(Green)

Harvest Thanksgiving may be kept on any Sunday provided it does not supersede any Principal Feast or Festival.
Readings Year A Common of the Saints

	PRINCIPAL SERVICE CW Proper 17	THIRD SERVICE	SECOND SERVICE
Psalms:	*105.1–6, 23–26, 45b [115]* *26.1–8*	*107.1–32*	*105.1–15*
Readings:	Exod. 3.1–15; Jer. 15.15–21; Rom. 12.9–end; Matt. 16.21–end	Jonah 3.1–9 *or* Ecclus 11.7–28 (*or* 19–28); Rev. 3.14–end	2 Kgs 6.24–25; 7.3–end; Acts 18.1–16; [Mark 7.1–8, 14, 15, 21–23]

	HOLY COMMUNION BCP	MORNING PRAYER	EVENING PRAYER
Psalms:	*34.1–10*	*107.1–32*	*105.1–15*
Readings:	Exod. 34.29–end; 2 Cor. 3.4–9; Mark 7.31–37	2 Kgs 18.13–end or *Mic. 6;* Luke 4.1–15 or Philemon	2 Kgs 19 or Isa. 38.1–20 or *Mic. 7;* Matt. 18.15–end or Eph. 1
Hymns:	....	....	....

2020

July				
S		5	12	19	26
M		6	13	20	27
T		7	14	21	28
W	1	8	15	22	29
T	2	9	16	23	30
F	3	10	17	24	31
S	4	11	18	25

August				
S		2	9	16	23	30
M		3	10	17	24	31
T		4	11	18	25
W		5	12	19	26
T		6	13	20	27
F		7	14	21	28
S	1	8	15	22	29

September				
S		6	13	20	27
M		7	14	21	28
T	1	8	15	22	29
W	2	9	16	23	30
T	3	10	17	24
F	4	11	18	25
S	5	12	19	26

October				
S		4	11	18	25
M		5	12	19	26
T		6	13	20	27
W		7	14	21	28
T	1	8	15	22	29
F	2	9	16	23	30
S	3	10	17	24	31

November				
S	1	8	15	22	29
M	2	9	16	23	30
T	3	10	17	24
W	4	11	18	25
T	5	12	19	26
F	6	13	20	27
S	7	14	21	28

December				
S		6	13	20	27
M		7	14	21	28
T	1	8	15	22	29
W	2	9	16	23	30
T	3	10	17	24	31
F	4	11	18	25
S	5	12	19	26

CW COLLECTS

Almighty and everlasting God,
you are always more ready to hear than we to pray
and to give more than either we desire or deserve:
pour down upon us the abundance of your mercy,
forgiving us those things
    of which our conscience is afraid
and giving us those good things
    which we are not worthy to ask
but through the merits and mediation
of Jesus Christ your Son our Lord,
who is alive and reigns with you,
in the unity of the Holy Spirit,
one God, now and for ever.

or

God of constant mercy,
who sent your Son to save us:
remind us of your goodness,
increase your grace within us,
that our thankfulness may grow,
through Jesus Christ our Lord.

POST COMMUNION

God of all mercy,
in this Eucharist you have set aside our sins
and given us your healing:
grant that we who are made whole in Christ
may bring that healing to this broken world,
in the name of Jesus Christ our Lord.

BCP COLLECT

*Almighty and everlasting God, who art always
more ready to hear than we to pray, and art wont
to give more than either we desire, or deserve:
Pour down upon us the abundance of thy mercy;
forgiving us those things whereof our conscience
is afraid, and giving us those good things which we
are not worthy to ask, but through the merits and
mediation of Jesus Christ, thy Son, our Lord.*

HARVEST THANKSGIVING COLLECTS (as required)

Eternal God,
you crown the year with your goodness
and you give us the fruits of the earth
    in their season:
grant that we may use them to your glory,
    for the relief of those in need
    and for our own well-being;
through Jesus Christ your Son our Lord,
who is alive and reigns with you,
in the unity of the Holy Spirit,
one God, now and for ever.

or

Creator God,
you made the goodness of the land,
the riches of the sea
and the rhythm of the seasons;
as we thank you for the harvest,
may we cherish and respect
this planet and its peoples,
through Jesus Christ our Lord.

POST COMMUNION

Lord of the harvest,
with joy we have offered thanksgiving
    for your love in creation
and have shared in the bread and the wine
    of the kingdom:
by your grace plant within us a reverence
    for all that you give us
and make us generous and wise stewards
of the good things we enjoy;
through Jesus Christ our Lord.

2021

	January						February					March						April					May						June			
S		3	10	17	24	31	S		7	14	21	28	S		7	14	21	28	S		4	11	18	25	S		2	9	16	23	30	S		6	13	20	27
M		4	11	18	25		M	1	8	15	22		M	1	8	15	22	29	M		5	12	19	26	M		3	10	17	24	31	M		7	14	21	28
T		5	12	19	26		T	2	9	16	23		T	2	9	16	23	30	T		6	13	20	27	T		4	11	18	25		T	1	8	15	22	29
W		6	13	20	27		W	3	10	17	24		W	3	10	17	24	31	W		7	14	21	28	W		5	12	19	26		W	2	9	16	23	30
T		7	14	21	28		T	4	11	18	25		T	4	11	18	25		T	1	8	15	22	29	T		6	13	20	27		T	3	10	17	24
F	1	8	15	22	29		F	5	12	19	26		F	5	12	19	26		F	2	9	16	23	30	F		7	14	21	28		F	4	11	18	25
S	2	9	16	23	30		S	6	13	20	27		S	6	13	20	27		S	3	10	17	24		S	1	8	15	22	29	S		5	12	19	26

Aidan, Bishop of Lindisfarne, Missionary, 651 (CW Readings see Common of the Saints also 1 Cor. 9.16–19)   White *or* Green
Bank Holiday (UK, except Scotland)

DEL Wk 22	**EUCHARIST**	**MORNING PRAYER**	**EVENING PRAYER**
	CW		
Psalms:	33.12–21	*98*; 99; 101 (Week 6 Ord.)	105* (or 103)
Readings:	1 Cor. 2.1–5;	2 Sam. 11;	Prov. 14.31—15.17;
	Luke 4.16–30	Acts 8.26–end	Mark 6.45–end
AW		*1 Sam. 17.32–50*	*Matt. 8.14–22*
	HOLY COMMUNION	**MORNING PRAYER**	**EVENING PRAYER**
	BCP		
Psalms:		144; 145; 146	147; 148; 149; 150
Readings:		Ezra 1;	Ezra 3;
		Rom. 2.17–end	John 4.27–end
Hymns:	....	....	....

CW COLLECT
Everlasting God,
you sent the gentle bishop Aidan
to proclaim the gospel in this land:
grant us to live as he taught
in simplicity, humility, and love for the poor;
through Jesus Christ your Son our Lord,
who is alive and reigns with you,
in the unity of the Holy Spirit,
one God, now and for ever.

POST COMMUNION
Holy Father,
who gathered us here around the table
   of your Son
to share this meal with the whole household of God:
in that new world where you reveal
   the fullness of your peace,
gather people of every race and language
to share with Aidan and all your saints
in the eternal banquet of Jesus Christ our Lord.

Sunrise 06.10; Sunset 19.48

2020

July	August	September	October	November	December
S 5 12 19 26	S 2 9 16 23 30	S 6 13 20 27	S 4 11 18 25	S 1 8 15 22 29	S 6 13 20 27
M 6 13 20 27	M 3 10 17 24 31	M 7 14 21 28	M 5 12 19 26	M 2 9 16 23 30	M 7 14 21 28
T 7 14 21 28	T 4 11 18 25	T 1 8 15 22 29	T 6 13 20 27	T 3 10 17 24	T 1 8 15 22 29
W 1 8 15 22 29	W 5 12 19 26	W 2 9 16 23 30	W 7 14 21 28	W 4 11 18 25	W 2 9 16 23 30
T 2 9 16 23 30	T 6 13 20 27	T 3 10 17 24	T 1 8 15 22 29	T 5 12 19 26	T 3 10 17 24 31
F 3 10 17 24 31	F 7 14 21 28	F 4 11 18 25	F 2 9 16 23 30	F 6 13 20 27	F 4 11 18 25
S 4 11 18 25	S 1 8 15 22 29	S 5 12 19 26	S 3 10 17 24 31	S 7 14 21 28	S 5 12 19 26

SEPTEMBER
2020
Tuesday **1**

Giles of Provence, Hermit c.710 (also BCP)

	EUCHARIST	MORNING PRAYER	EVENING PRAYER
	CW		
Psalms:	145.10–17	*106* (*or* 103)	*107*
Readings:	1 Cor. 2.10b–end;	2 Sam. 12.1–25;	Prov. 15.18–end;
	Luke 4.31–37	Acts 9.1–19a	Mark 7.1–13

| | | AW | Prov. 17.1–15 | Luke 7.1–17 |

	HOLY COMMUNION	MORNING PRAYER	EVENING PRAYER
	BCP Com. Abbot		
Psalms:	1	1; 2; 3; 4; 5	6; 7; 8
Readings:	Prov. 10.27–32; 1 John 2.15–17;	Ezra 4;	Hag. 1.1—2.9;
	Luke 6.20–23a	Rom. 3	John 5.1–23
Hymns:	....	....	....

BCP COLLECT
*O God, by whose grace the blessed Abbot Giles,
enkindled with the fire of thy love, became a burning
and a shining light in thy Church: Grant that we may
be inflamed with the same spirit of discipline and
love, and ever walk before thee as children of light;
through Jesus Christ our Lord.*

The Martyrs of Papua New Guinea, 1901 and 1942   Green

	EUCHARIST CW	**MORNING PRAYER**	**EVENING PRAYER**
Psalms	62	110; *111*; 112	*119.129–152*
Readings:	1 Cor. 3.1–9; Luke 4.38–end	2 Sam. 15.1–12; Acts 9.19b–31	Prov. 18.10–end; Mark 7.14–23

AW   *Jer. 5.20–end*   *2 Pet. 3.8–end*

	HOLY COMMUNION	**MORNING PRAYER**	**EVENING PRAYER**
Psalms:		9; 10; 11	12; 13; 14
Readings:		Zech. 1.1–17; Rom. 4	Zech. 1.18—end of 2; John 5.24–end
Hymns:	....	....	....

Full Moon

2020

	July						August						September						October						November						December				
S		5	12	19	26		2	9	16	23	30			6	13	20	27			4	11	18	25		1	8	15	22	29			6	13	20	27
M		6	13	20	27		3	10	17	24	31			7	14	21	28			5	12	19	26		2	9	16	23	30			7	14	21	28
T		7	14	21	28		4	11	18	25			1	8	15	22	29			6	13	20	27		3	10	17	24			1	8	15	22	29
W	1	8	15	22	29		5	12	19	26			2	9	16	23	30			7	14	21	28		4	11	18	25			2	9	16	23	30
T	2	9	16	23	30		6	13	20	27			3	10	17	24			1	8	15	22	29		5	12	19	26			3	10	17	24	31
F	3	10	17	24	31		7	14	21	28			4	11	18	25			2	9	16	23	30		6	13	20	27			4	11	18	25
S	4	11	18	25		1	8	15	22	29			5	12	19	26			3	10	17	24	31		7	14	21	28			5	12	19	26

Gregory the Great, Bishop of Rome, Teacher of the Faith, 604
(CW Readings see Common of the Saints also 1 Thess. 2.3–8)

White *or* Green

	EUCHARIST CW	**MORNING PRAYER**	**EVENING PRAYER**
Psalms:	24.1–6	113; *115*	114; *116*; 117
Readings:	1 Cor. 3.18–end; Luke 5.1–11	2 Sam. 15.13–end; Acts 9.32–end	Prov. 20.1–22; Mark 7.24–30

	AW	Dan. 2.1–23	Luke 10.1–20

	HOLY COMMUNION BCP	**MORNING PRAYER**	**EVENING PRAYER**
Psalms:		15; 16; 17	18
Readings:		Zech. 3; Rom. 5	Zech. 4; John 6.1–21
Hymns:	....	....	....

CW COLLECT
Merciful Father,
who chose your bishop Gregory
to be a servant of the servants of God:
grant that, like him,
we may ever long to serve you
by proclaiming your gospel to the nations,
and may ever rejoice to sing your praises;
through Jesus Christ your son our Lord,
who is alive and reigns with you,
in the unity of the Holy Spirit,
one God, now and for ever.

POST COMMUNION
God of truth,
whose Wisdom set her table
and invited us to eat the bread and drink the wine
    of the kingdom:
help us to lay aside all foolishness
and to live and walk in the way of insight,
that we may come with Gregory
to the eternal feast of heaven;
through Jesus Christ our Lord.

2021

	January					February				March					April					May					June				
S		3	10	17	24	31		7	14	21	28		7	14	21	28		4	11	18	25		2	9	16	23	30		6	13	20	27
M		4	11	18	25		1	8	15	22		1	8	15	22	29		5	12	19	26		3	10	17	24	31		7	14	21	28
T		5	12	19	26		2	9	16	23		2	9	16	23	30		6	13	20	27		4	11	18	25		1	8	15	22	29
W		6	13	20	27		3	10	17	24		3	10	17	24	31		7	14	21	28		5	12	19	26		2	9	16	23	30
T		7	14	21	28		4	11	18	25		4	11	18	25		1	8	15	22	29		6	13	20	27		3	10	17	24
F	1	8	15	22	29	5	12	19	26		5	12	19	26		2	9	16	23	30		7	14	21	28		4	11	18	25
S	2	9	16	23	30	6	13	20	27		6	13	20	27		3	10	17	24		1	8	15	22	29		5	12	19	26

Birinius, Bishop of Dorchester (Oxon.) Apostle of Wessex 650   Green

	EUCHARIST	**MORNING PRAYER**	**EVENING PRAYER**
	CW		
Psalms:	37.3–8	*139*	*130*; 131; 137
Readings:	1 Cor. 4.1–5;	2 Sam. 16.1–14;	Prov. 22.1–16;
	Luke 5.33–end	Acts 10.1–16	Mark 7.31–end

AW   *Dan. 3.1–28*   *Rev. 15*

	HOLY COMMUNION	**MORNING PRAYER**	**EVENING PRAYER**
	BCP		
Psalms:		*19; 20; 21*	*22; 23*
Readings:		Zech. 6.9–end;	Hag. 2.10–end;
		Rom. 6	John 6.22–40
Hymns:	....	....	....

2020

	July						August						September						October						November						December			
S		5	12	19	26	S		2	9	16	23	30	S		6	13	20	27	S		4	11	18	25	S	1	8	15	22	29	S		6	13	20	27
M		6	13	20	27	M		3	10	17	24	31	M		7	14	21	28	M		5	12	19	26	M	2	9	16	23	30	M		7	14	21	28
T		7	14	21	28	T		4	11	18	25		T	1	8	15	22	29	T		6	13	20	27	T	3	10	17	24		T	1	8	15	22	29
W	1	8	15	22	29	W		5	12	19	26		W	2	9	16	23	30	W		7	14	21	28	W	4	11	18	25		W	2	9	16	23	30
T	2	9	16	23	30	T		6	13	20	27		T	3	10	17	24		T	1	8	15	22	29	T	5	12	19	26		T	3	10	17	24	31
F	3	10	17	24	31	F		7	14	21	28		F	4	11	18	25		F	2	9	16	23	30	F	6	13	20	27		F	4	11	18	25	
S	4	11	18	25		S	1	8	15	22	29		S	5	12	19	26		S	3	10	17	24	31	S	7	14	21	28		S	5	12	19	26	

Green

	EUCHARIST	MORNING PRAYER	EVENING PRAYER
	CW		
Psalms:	145.18–end	120; *121*; 122	*118*
Readings:	1 Cor. 4.6–15;	2 Sam. 17.1–23;	Prov. 24.23–end;
	Luke 6.1–5	Acts 10.17–33	Mark 8.1–10

AW   *Dan. 6*   *Phil. 2.14–24*

	HOLY COMMUNION	MORNING PRAYER	EVENING PRAYER
	BCP		
Psalms:		*24; 25; 26*	*27; 28; 29*
Readings:		*Ezra 5;*	*Ezra 6;*
		Rom. 7	*John 6.41–end;*
			E. Coll. Trinity 13

Hymns: ....

THE THIRTEENTH SUNDAY AFTER TRINITY

(Green)

	PRINCIPAL SERVICE CW Proper 18	**THIRD SERVICE**	**SECOND SERVICE**
Psalms:	*149 or* *119.33–40*	119.17–32	108 [115]
Readings:	*Exod. 12.1–14;* *Ezek. 33.7–11;* *Rom. 13.8–end;* *Matt. 18.15–20*	Jonah 3.10—4.11; or Ecclus 27.30—28.9; Rev. 8.1–5	Ezek. 12.21—13.16; Acts 19.1–20; [BCP Var. Mark 7.24–end]

	HOLY COMMUNION BCP	**MORNING PRAYER**	**EVENING PRAYER**
Psalms:	*74.20–end*	*119.17–32*	*108 [115]*
Readings:	*Lev. 19.13–18;* *Gal. 3.16–22;* *or Heb. 13.1–6;* *Luke 10.23b–37*	*2 Kgs 22 or Hab. 2.1–14;* *Luke 4.31—5.11 or* *1 Tim. 6*	*2 Kgs 23.1–30 or 2 Chr. 36.1–21* *or Hab. 3.2–end;* *Matt. 20.1–28 or Eph. 2*
Hymns:	....	....	....

2020

	July				**August**					**September**				**October**				**November**				**December**			
S		5	12	19	26		2	9	16	23	30		6	13	20	27		4	11	18	25		1	8	15	22	29		6	13	20	27
M		6	13	20	27		3	10	17	24	31		7	14	21	28		5	12	19	26		2	9	16	23	30		7	14	21	28
T		7	14	21	28		4	11	18	25		1	8	15	22	29		6	13	20	27		3	10	17	24		1	8	15	22	29
W	1	8	15	22	29		5	12	19	26		2	9	16	23	30		7	14	21	28		4	11	18	25		2	9	16	23	30
T	2	9	16	23	30		6	13	20	27		3	10	17	24		1	8	15	22	29		5	12	19	26		3	10	17	24	31
F	3	10	17	24	31		7	14	21	28		4	11	18	25		2	9	16	23	30		6	13	20	27		4	11	18	25
S	4	11	18	25		1	8	15	22	29		5	12	19	26		3	10	17	24	31		7	14	21	28		5	12	19	26

CW COLLECTS

Almighty God,
who called your Church to bear witness
that you were in Christ
reconciling the world to yourself:
help us to proclaim the good news of your love,
that all who hear it may be drawn to you;
through him who was lifted up on the cross,
and reigns with you in the unity of the Holy Spirit,
one God, now and for ever.

or

Almighty God,
you search us and know us:
may we rely on you in strength
and rest on you in weakness,
now and in all our days;
through Jesus Christ our Lord.

POST COMMUNION

God our creator,
you feed your children with the true manna,
the living bread from heaven:
let this holy food sustain us through our earthly
    pilgrimage
until we come to that place
    where hunger and thirst are no more;
through Jesus Christ our Lord.

BCP COLLECT

*Almighty and merciful God, of whose only gift it
cometh that thy faithful people do unto thee true and
laudable service: Grant, we beseech thee, that we
may so faithfully serve thee in this life, that we fail
not finally to attain thy heavenly promises; through
the merits of Jesus Christ our Lord.*

2021

January						February					March					April					May					June				
S		3	10	17	24	31	S		7	14	21	28	S		7	14	21	28	S		4	11	18	25	S		2	9	16	23	30	S		6	13	20	27
M		4	11	18	25		M	1	8	15	22		M	1	8	15	22	29	M		5	12	19	26	M		3	10	17	24	31	M		7	14	21	28
T		5	12	19	26		T	2	9	16	23		T	2	9	16	23	30	T		6	13	20	27	T		4	11	18	25	T	1	8	15	22	29
W		6	13	20	27		W	3	10	17	24		W	3	10	17	24	31	W		7	14	21	28	W		5	12	19	26	W	2	9	16	23	30
T		7	14	21	28		T	4	11	18	25		T	4	11	18	26	T	1	8	15	22	29	T		6	13	20	27	T	3	10	17	24	
F	1	8	15	22	29	F	5	12	19	26		F	5	12	19	26	F	2	9	16	23	30	F		7	14	21	28	F	4	11	18	25	
S	2	9	16	23	30	S	6	13	20	27		S	6	13	20	27	S	3	10	17	24		S	1	8	15	22	29	S	5	12	19	26	

Evurtius, Bishop of Orleans (BCP)   Green (*or White*)

DEL Wk 23	**EUCHARIST**	**MORNING PRAYER**	**EVENING PRAYER**
	CW		
Psalms:	5.5–9a	123; 124; 125; *126* (Week 7 Ord)	*127*; 128; 129
Readings:	1 Cor. 5.1–8;	2 Sam. 18.1–18;	Prov. 25.1–14;
	Luke 6.6–11	Acts 10.34–end	Mark 8.11–21

	AW	2 Sam. 7.4–17	2 Cor. 5.1–10
	HOLY COMMUNION	**MORNING PRAYER**	**EVENING PRAYER**
	BCP Com. Bishop		
Psalms:	99	35; 36	37
Readings:	Ezek. 34.11–16; 1 Tim. 3.15–16;	Zech. 7;	Zech. 8;
	Matt. 4.26–32	Rom. 8.1–17	John 7.1–24
Hymns:	....	....	....

BCP COLLECT
*O God, the light of the faithful, and shepherd of souls,
who didst set blessed Evurtius to be a Bishop in the
Church, that he might feed thy sheep by his word and
guide them by his example: Grant us, we pray thee,
to keep the faith which he taught, and to follow in his
footsteps; through Jesus Christ our Lord.*

Sunrise 06.21; Sunset 19.32

2020

	July					August						September					October					November						December			
S		5	12	19	26	S		2	9	16	23	30	S		6	13	20	27	S		4	11	18	25	S	1	8	15	22	29	S		6	13	20	27
M		6	13	20	27	M		3	10	17	24	31	M		7	14	21	28	M		5	12	19	26	M	2	9	16	23	30	M		7	14	21	28
T		7	14	21	28	T		4	11	18	25		T	1	8	15	22	29	T		6	13	20	27	T	3	10	17	24		T	1	8	15	22	29
W	1	8	15	22	29	W		5	12	19	26		W	2	9	16	23	30	W		7	14	21	28	W	4	11	18	25		W	2	9	16	23	30
T	2	9	16	23	30	T		6	13	20	27		T	3	10	17	24		T	1	8	15	22	29	T	5	12	19	26		T	3	10	17	24	31
F	3	10	17	24	31	F		7	14	21	28		F	4	11	18	25		F	2	9	16	23	30	F	6	13	20	27		F	4	11	18	25
S	4	11	18	25	S	1	8	15	22	29		S	5	12	19	26	S	3	10	17	24	31	S	7	14	21	28	S	5	12	19	26

Birth of the Blessed Virgin Mary (CW Readings see Common of the Saints or see August 15)   Green *or* White

	EUCHARIST	MORNING PRAYER	EVENING PRAYER
	CW		
Psalms:	149.1–5	*132*; 133	(134); *135*
Readings:	1 Cor. 6.1–11;	2 Sam. 18.19—19.8a;	Prov. 25.15–end;
	Luke 6.12–19	Acts 11.1–18	Mark 8.22–26

		AW	*Prov. 18.10–21*	*Rom. 14.10–end*

	HOLY COMMUNION	MORNING PRAYER	EVENING PRAYER
	BCP Nativity of BVM		
Psalms:	45.11–18	38; 39; 40	41; 42; 43
Readings:	Gen. 3.9–15; Rom. 5.12–17;	Ezra 7;	Ezra 8.15–end;
	Luke 11.27–28	Rom. 8.18–end	John 7.25–end
Hymns:	....	....	....

CW COLLECT (Conception of BVM)
Almighty and everlasting God,
who stooped to raise fallen humanity
through the child-bearing of blessed Mary:
grant that we, who have seen your glory
    revealed in our human nature
and your love made perfect in our weakness,
may daily be renewed in your image
and conformed to the pattern of your Son,
Jesus Christ our Lord,
who is alive and reigns with you,
in the unity of the Holy Spirit,
one God, now and for ever.

POST COMMUNION
God most high,
whose handmaid bore the Word made flesh:
we thank you that in this sacrament
    of our redemption
you visit us with your Holy Spirit
and overshadow us by your power;
strengthen us to walk with Mary the joyful path of
obedience and so to bring forth the fruits of holiness;
    through Jesus Christ our Lord.

BCP COLLECT
O merciful God, hear the prayers of thy servants who
commemorate the Nativity of the Mother of the Lord;
and grant that by the incarnation of thy dear Son
we may indeed be made nigh unto him; who liveth
and reigneth with thee and the Holy Ghost, one God,
world without end.

2021

January						February					March					April					May						June				
S		3	10	17	24	31	S		7	14	21	28	S		7	14	21	28	S		4	11	18	25	S		2	9	16	23	30	S		6	13	20	27
M		4	11	18	25	M	1	8	15	22	M	1	8	15	22	29	M		5	12	19	26	M		3	10	17	24	31	M		7	14	21	28
T		5	12	19	26	T	2	9	16	23	T	2	9	16	23	30	T		6	13	20	27	T		4	11	18	25	T	1	8	15	22	29
W		6	13	20	27	W	3	10	17	24	W	3	10	17	24	31	W		7	14	21	28	W		5	12	19	26	W	2	9	16	23	30
T		7	14	21	28	T	4	11	18	25	T	4	11	18	25	T	1	8	15	22	29	T		6	13	20	27	T	3	10	17	24
F	1	8	15	22	29	F	5	12	19	26	F	5	12	19	26	F	2	9	16	23	30	F		7	14	21	28	F	4	11	18	25
S	2	9	16	23	30	S	6	13	20	27	S	6	13	20	27	S	3	10	17	24	S	1	8	15	22	29	S	5	12	19	26

Charles Fuge Lowder, Priest 1880   Green

	EUCHARIST	**MORNING PRAYER**	**EVENING PRAYER**
	CW		
Psalms:	45.11–end	*119.153–end*	*136*
Readings:	1 Cor. 7.25–31;	2 Sam. 19.8b–23;	Prov. 26.12–end;
	Luke 6.20–26	Acts 11.19–end	Mark 8.27—9.1
		AW *Judg. 4.1–10;*	*Rom. 1.8–17*

	HOLY COMMUNION	**MORNING PRAYER**	**EVENING PRAYER**
	BCP		
Psalms:		*44; 45; 46*	*47; 48; 49*
Readings:		*Ezra 9;*	*Ezra 10.1–19;*
		Rom. 9	*John 8.1–30*
Hymns:	....	....	....

2020

	July	August	September	October	November	December
S	5 12 19 26	2 9 16 23 30	6 13 20 27	4 11 18 25	1 8 15 22 29	6 13 20 27
M	6 13 20 27	3 10 17 24 31	7 14 21 28	5 12 19 26	2 9 16 23 30	7 14 21 28
T	7 14 21 28	4 11 18 25	1 8 15 22 29	6 13 20 27	3 10 17 24	1 8 15 22 29
W	1 8 15 22 29	5 12 19 26	2 9 16 23 30	7 14 21 28	4 11 18 25	2 9 16 23 30
T	2 9 16 23 30	6 13 20 27	3 10 17 24	1 8 15 22 29	5 12 19 26	3 10 17 24 31
F	3 10 17 24 31	7 14 21 28	4 11 18 25	2 9 16 23 30	6 13 20 27	4 11 18 25
S	4 11 18 25	1 8 15 22 29	5 12 19 26	3 10 17 24 31	7 14 21 28	5 12 19 26

	EUCHARIST	**MORNING PRAYER**	**EVENING PRAYER**
	CW		
Psalms:	139.1–9	*143*; 146	*138*; 140; 141
Readings:	1 Cor. 81–7, 11–end;	2 Sam. 19.24–end;	Prov. 27.1–22;
	Luke 6.27–38	Acts 12.1–17	Mark 9.2–13

AW Isa. *49.14–end* John *16.16–24*

	HOLY COMMUNION	**MORNING PRAYER**	**EVENING PRAYER**
	BCP		
Psalms:		50; 51; 52	53; 54; 55
Readings:		Neh. 1;	Neh. 2;
		Rom. 10	John 8.31–end
Hymns:	....	....	....

....

....

....

....

....

....

....

....

....

....

....

....

....

....

....

....

....

....

....

....

....

....

....

....

2021

	January						February					March					April					May						June			
S		3	10	17	24	31	S		7	14	21	28	S		7	14	21	28	S		4	11	18	25	S		2	9	16	23	30	S		6	13	20	27
M		4	11	18	25		M	1	8	15	22		M	1	8	15	22	29	M		5	12	19	26	M		3	10	17	24	31	M		7	14	21	28
T		5	12	19	26		T	2	9	16	23		T	2	9	16	23	30	T		6	13	20	27	T		4	11	18	25		T	1	8	15	22	29
W		6	13	20	27		W	3	10	17	24		W	3	10	17	24	31	W		7	14	21	28	W		5	12	19	26		W	2	9	16	23	30
T		7	14	21	28		T	4	11	18	25		T	4	11	18	25		T	1	8	15	22	29	T		6	13	20	27		T	3	10	17	24
F	1	8	15	22	29		F	5	12	19	26		F	5	12	19	26	F	2	9	16	23	30	F		7	14	21	28		F	4	11	18	25
S	2	9	16	23	30		S	6	13	20	27		S	6	13	20	27	S	3	10	17	24		S	1	8	15	22	29	S	5	12	19	26

SEPTEMBER
11 Friday

Green

	EUCHARIST		**MORNING PRAYER**	**EVENING PRAYER**
	CW			
Psalms:	84.1–6		142; *144*	*145*
Readings:	1 Cor. 9.16–19, 22–end;		2 Sam. 23.1–7;	Prov. 30.1–9, 24–31;
	Luke 6.39–42		Acts 12.18–end	Mark 9.14–29

AW   *Job 9.1–24*   *Mark 15.21–32*

	HOLY COMMUNION	**MORNING PRAYER**	**EVENING PRAYER**
	BCP		
Psalms:		*56; 57; 58*	*59; 60; 61*
Readings:		*Neh. 4;*	*Neh. 5;*
		Rom. 11.1–24	*John 9*
Hymns:	....	....	....

July				August					September				October				November				December			
S		5 12 19 26		S		2 9 16 23 30			S		6 13 20 27		S		4 11 18 25		S	1 8 15 22 29			S		6 13 20 27
M		6 13 20 27		M		3 10 17 24 31			M		7 14 21 28		M		5 12 19 26		M	2 9 16 23 30			M		7 14 21 28
T		7 14 21 28		T		4 11 18 25			T	1 8 15 22 29		T		6 13 20 27		T	3 10 17 24			T	1 8 15 22 29
W	1 8 15 22 29			W		5 12 19 26			W	2 9 16 23 30		W		7 14 21 28		W	4 11 18 25			W	2 9 16 23 30
T	2 9 16 23 30			T		6 13 20 27			T	3 10 17 24		T	1 8 15 22 29		T	5 12 19 26			T	3 10 17 24 31
F	3 10 17 24 31			F		7 14 21 28			F	4 11 18 25		F	2 9 16 23 30		F	6 13 20 27			F	4 11 18 25
S	4 11 18 25			S	1 8 15 22 29				S	5 12 19 26		S	3 10 17 24 31		S	7 14 21 28			S	5 12 19 26

Green

	EUCHARIST	MORNING PRAYER	EVENING PRAYER
	CW		
Psalms:	116.10–end	*147*	*148*; 149; 150
Readings:	1 Cor. 10.14–22;	2 Sam. 24;	Prov. 31.10–end;
	Luke 6.43–end	Acts 13.1–12	Mark 9.30–37

AW   *Exod. 19.1–9*   *John 20.12–18*

	HOLY COMMUNION	MORNING PRAYER	EVENING PRAYER
	BCP		
Psalms:		*62; 63; 64*	*65; 66; 67*
Readings:		*Neh. 6.1—7.4;*	*Neh. 8; John 10.1–21;*
		Rom. 11.25–end	*E. Coll. Trinity 14*
Hymns:	....	....	....

THE FOURTEENTH SUNDAY AFTER TRINITY

(Green)

Battle of Britain Sunday

	PRINCIPAL SERVICE CW Proper 19	THIRD SERVICE	SECOND SERVICE
Psalms:	*114, or Canticle: Exod. 15.1b–11, 20–21* *103.[1–7]8–13**	119.65–88	119.41–48[49–64]
Readings:	*Exod. 14.19–end;* *Gen. 50.15–21;* *Rom. 14.1–12;* *Matt. 18.21–35*	*Isa. 44.24—45.8;* *Rev. 12.1–12*	*Ezek. 20.1–8, 33–44;* *Acts 20.17–end;* *[Mark 8.27–end]* or Eve of Holy Cross Day: *Ps. 66; Isa. 52.13—end of 53;* *Eph. 2.11–end*

	HOLY COMMUNION BCP	MORNING PRAYER	EVENING PRAYER
Psalms:	*118.1–9*	*119.65–88*	*119.41–48[49–64]*
Readings:	*2 Kgs 5.9–16;* *Gal. 5.16–24;* *Luke 17.11–19*	*Ezra 1.1–8 and 3 or* *Zeph. 1;* *Luke 7.36–end or 1 Cor. 13*	*Neh. 1.1—2.8 or Dan. 1 or* *Zeph. 3;* *Matt. 21.23–end or Eph. 4.1–24*
Hymns:	....	....	....

2020

July				
S		5	12	19	26
M		6	13	20	27
T		7	14	21	28
W	1	8	15	22	29
T	2	9	16	23	30
F	3	10	17	24	31
S	4	11	18	25

August				
S		2	9	16	23	30
M		3	10	17	24	31
T		4	11	18	25
W		5	12	19	26
T		6	13	20	27
F		7	14	21	28
S	1	8	15	22	29

September				
S		6	13	20	27
M		7	14	21	28
T	1	8	15	22	29
W	2	9	16	23	30
T	3	10	17	24
F	4	11	18	25
S	5	12	19	26

October				
S		4	11	18	25
M		5	12	19	26
T		6	13	20	27
W		7	14	21	28
T	1	8	15	22	29
F	2	9	16	23	30
S	3	10	17	24	31

November				
S	1	8	15	22	29
M	2	9	16	23	30
T	3	10	17	24
W	4	11	18	25
T	5	12	19	26
F	6	13	20	27
S	7	14	21	28

December				
S		6	13	20	27
M		7	14	21	28
T	1	8	15	22	29
W	2	9	16	23	30
T	3	10	17	24	31
F	4	11	18	25
S	5	12	19	26

CW COLLECTS

Almighty God,
whose only Son has opened for us
a new and living way into your presence:
give us pure hearts and steadfast wills
to worship you in spirit and in truth;
through Jesus Christ your Son our Lord,
who is alive and reigns with you,
in the unity of the Holy Spirit,
one God, now and for ever.

or

Merciful God,
your Son came to save us
and bore our sins on the cross:
may we trust in your mercy
and know your love,
rejoicing in the righteousness that is ours
through Jesus Christ our Lord.

POST COMMUNION

Lord God, the source of truth and love,
keep us faithful to the apostles' teaching and
    fellowship,
united in prayer and the breaking of bread,
and one in joy and simplicity of heart,
in Jesus Christ our Lord.

BCP COLLECT

*Almighty and everlasting God, give unto us the
increase of faith, hope, and charity; and, that we may
obtain that which thou dost promise, make us to love
that which thou dost command; through Jesus Christ
our Lord.*

2021

	January					February					March					April					May					June			
S		3	10	17	24	31		7	14	21	28		7	14	21	28		4	11	18	25		2	9	16	23	30		6	13	20	27
M		4	11	18	25		1	8	15	22		1	8	15	22	29		5	12	19	26		3	10	17	24	31		7	14	21	28
T		5	12	19	26		2	9	16	23		2	9	16	23	30		6	13	20	27		4	11	18	25		1	8	15	22	29
W		6	13	20	27		3	10	17	24		3	10	17	24	31		7	14	21	28		5	12	19	26		2	9	16	23	30
T		7	14	21	28		4	11	18	25		4	11	18	25		1	8	15	22	29		6	13	20	27		3	10	17	24	
F	1	8	15	22	29	5	12	19	26		5	12	19	26		2	9	16	23	30		7	14	21	28		4	11	18	25	
S	2	9	16	23	30	6	13	20	27		6	13	20	27		3	10	17	24		1	8	15	22	29		5	12	19	26	

Holy Cross Day   White

	PRINCIPAL SERVICE	THIRD SERVICE	SECOND SERVICE
	CW		
Psalms:	22.23–28	2; 8; 146	110; 150
Readings:	Num. 21.4–9; Phil. 2.6–11; John 3.13–17	Gen. 3.1–15; John 12.27–36a	Isa. 63.1–16; 1 Cor. 1.18–25

Seasonal provisions on Saints Days: CW Book p 328

The following displaced readings may be added to the portions for the following day:

	EUCHARIST	MORNING PRAYER	EVENING PRAYER
	CW		
Readings:	1 Cor. 11.17–26, 33; Luke 7.1–10	1 Kgs 1.5–31; Acts 13.13–4	Wisd. 1 or 1 Chr. 10.1—11.9; Mark 9.38–end

	HOLY COMMUNION	MORNING PRAYER	EVENING PRAYER
	BCP Holy Cross		
Psalms:	67	71; 72	73; 74
Readings:	Num. 21.4–9; 1 Cor. 1.17–25; John 12.27–33	Neh. 9.1–23; Rom. 12	Neh. 9.24–end; John 10.22–end
Hymns:	....	....	....

CW COLLECT
Almighty God,
who in the passion of your blessed Son
made an instrument of painful death
to be for us the means of life and peace:
grant us so to glory in the cross of Christ
that we may gladly suffer for his sake;
who is alive and reigns with you,
in the unity of the Holy Spirit,
one God, now and for ever.

POST COMMUNION
Faithful God,
whose Son bore our sins in his body on the tree
and gave us this sacrament to show forth
his death until he comes:
give us grace to glory in the cross of our Lord Jesus
    Christ, for he is our salvation, our life and our hope,
who reigns as Lord, now and for ever.

BCP COLLECT
O God, who by the passion of thy blessed Son hast
made the instrument of shameful death to be unto us
the means of life and peace: Grant us so to glory in
the Cross of Christ that we may gladly suffer shame
and loss; for the sake of the same thy Son our Lord.

Sunrise 06.33; Sunset 19.16

2020

	July				August				September				October				November				December			
S		5	12	19	26		2	9	16	23	30			6	13	20	27			4	11	18	25			1	8	15	22	29			6	13	20	27
M		6	13	20	27		3	10	17	24	31			7	14	21	28			5	12	19	26			2	9	16	23	30			7	14	21	28
T		7	14	21	28		4	11	18	25			1	8	15	22	29			6	13	20	27			3	10	17	24		1	8	15	22	29
W	1	8	15	22	29		5	12	19	26			2	9	16	23	30			7	14	21	28		4	11	18	25			2	9	16	23	30
T	2	9	16	23	30		6	13	20	27			3	10	17	24		1	8	15	22	29			5	12	19	26			3	10	17	24	31
F	3	10	17	24	31		7	14	21	28			4	11	18	25		2	9	16	23	30			6	13	20	27			4	11	18	25
S	4	11	18	25		1	8	15	22	29			5	12	19	26		3	10	17	24	31			7	14	21	28			5	12	19	26

Cyprian, Bishop of Carthage, Martyr 258 (CW Readings see Common of the Saints especially 1 Pet. 4.12–19, also Matt. 18.18–22)

Green *or* Red

DEL Wk 24	**EUCHARIST** CW	**MORNING PRAYER**	**EVENING PRAYER**
Psalms:	100	*5*; 6; (8) (Week 1 Ord.)	*9*; 10*
Readings:	1 Cor. 12.12–14, 27–end; Luke 7.11–17	1 Kgs 1.32—2.4; 2.10–12; Acts 13.44—14.7	Wisd. 2 *or* 1 Chr. 13; Mark 10.1–16

	AW	*Prov. 21.1–18*	*Mark 6.30–44*

	HOLY COMMUNION BCP	**MORNING PRAYER**	**EVENING PRAYER**
Psalms:		75; 76; 77	*78*
Readings:		Neh. 13; Rom. 13	*Dan. 2.1–24; John 11.1–44*
Hymns:	....	....	....

CW COLLECT

Holy God,
who brought Cyprian to faith in Christ,
made him a bishop in the Church
and crowned his witness with a martyr's death:
grant that, after his example,
we may love the Church and her teachings,
find your forgiveness within her fellowship
and so come to share the heavenly banquet
  you have prepared for us;
through Jesus Christ your Son our Lord,
who is alive and reigns with you,
in the unity of the Holy Spirit,
one God, now and for ever.

POST COMMUNION

God our redeemer,
whose Church was strengthened by the blood
  of your martyr Cyprian:
so bind us, in life and death, to Christ's sacrifice
that our lives, broken and offered with his,
may carry his death and proclaim his resurrection
  in the world;
through Jesus Christ our Lord.

2021

	January					February					March					April					May					June			
S		3	10	17	24	31		7	14	21	28		7	14	21	28		4	11	18	25		2	9	16	23	30		6	13	20	27
M		4	11	18	25		1	8	15	22		1	8	15	22	29		5	12	19	26		3	10	17	24	31		7	14	21	28
T		5	12	19	26		2	9	16	23		2	9	16	23	30		6	13	20	27		4	11	18	25		1	8	15	22	29
W		6	13	20	27		3	10	17	24		3	10	17	24	31		7	14	21	28		5	12	19	26		2	9	16	23	30
T		7	14	21	28		4	11	18	25		4	11	18	25		1	8	15	22	29		6	13	20	27		3	10	17	24
F	1	8	15	22	29		5	12	19	26		5	12	19	26		2	9	16	23	30		7	14	21	28		4	11	18	25
S	2	9	16	23	30		6	13	20	27		6	13	20	27		3	10	17	24		1	8	15	22	29		5	12	19	26

Ninian, Bishop of Galloway, Apostle of the Picts, 432 (CW Readings see Common of the Saints
especially Acts 13.46–49; Mark 16.15–end).
Edward Bouverie Pusey, Priest Tractarian, 1882 Ember Day (BCP)

White *or* Green (*or Red*)

	EUCHARIST	MORNING PRAYER	EVENING PRAYER
	CW		
Psalms:	33.1–12	*119.1–32*	*11*; 12; 13
Readings:	1 Cor. 12.31b—end of 13;	1 Kgs 3;	Wisd. 3.1–9 *or* 1 Chr. 15.1—16.3;
	Luke 7.31–35	Acts 14.8–end	Mark 10.17–31
AW		*Hos. 11.1–11*	*1 John 4.9–end*

	HOLY COMMUNION	MORNING PRAYER	EVENING PRAYER
	BCP Ember CEG see Dec 18		
Psalms:		79; 80; 81	82; 83; 84; 85
Readings:		Dan. 2.25–end;	Dan. 4.1–18;
		Rom. 14	John 11.45–end
Hymns:	....	....	....

CW COLLECT
Almighty and everlasting God,
who called your servant Ninian to preach the
    gospel to the people of northern Britain:
raise up in this and every land
heralds and evangelists of your kingdom,
that your Church may make known
    the immeasurable riches
    of your Son our Saviour Jesus Christ,
who is alive and reigns with you,
in the unity of the Holy Spirit,
one God, now and for ever.

POST COMMUNION
Holy Father,
who gathered us here around the table
    of your Son to share this meal
with the whole household of God:
in that new world where you reveal
    the fullness of your peace,
gather people of every race and language
    to share with Ninian and all your saints
in the eternal banquet of Jesus Christ our Lord.

For Ember Days
*Almighty God, the giver of all good gifts, who of
thy divine providence hast appointed divers Orders
in thy Church: Give thy grace, we humbly beseech
thee, to all those who are to be called to any office
or administration in the same; and so replenish them
with the truth of thy doctrine, and endue them with
innocency of life, that they may faithfully serve before
thee, to the glory of thy great name, and the benefit
of thy Holy Church; through Jesus Christ our Lord.*

2020

	July					August						September					October					November					December			
S		5	12	19	26	S		2	9	16	23	30	S		6	13	20	27	S		4	11	18	25	S	1	8	15	22	29	S		6	13	20	27
M		6	13	20	27	M		3	10	17	24	31	M		7	14	21	28	M		5	12	19	26	M	2	9	16	23	30	M		7	14	21	28
T		7	14	21	28	T		4	11	18	25	T	1	8	15	22	29	T		6	13	20	27	T	3	10	17	24	T	1	8	15	22	29
W	1	8	15	22	29	W		5	12	19	26	W	2	9	16	23	30	W		7	14	21	28	W	4	11	18	25	W	2	9	16	23	30
T	2	9	16	23	30	T		6	13	20	27	T	3	10	17	24	T	1	8	15	22	29	T	5	12	19	26	T	3	10	17	24	31
F	3	10	17	24	31	F		7	14	21	28	F	4	11	18	25	F	2	9	16	23	30	F	6	13	20	27	F	4	11	18	25
S	4	11	18	25	S	1	8	15	22	29	S	5	12	19	26	S	3	10	17	24	31	S	7	14	21	28	S	5	12	19	26

Hildegard, Abbess of Bingen, Visionary, 1179 (CW Readings see Common of the Saints   Green *or* White (*or Red*)
especially 1 Cor. 2.9–13 and Luke 10.21–24). *Lambert, Bishop & Martyr, 709 (BCP)*

	EUCHARIST CW	**MORNING PRAYER**	**EVENING PRAYER**
Psalms:	118.1–2, 17–20	14; *15*; 16	*18**
Readings:	1 Cor. 15.1–11; Luke 7.36–end	1 Kgs 4.29—5.12; Acts 15.1–21	Wisd. 4.7–end *or* 1 Chr. 17; Mark 10.32–34
		AW *Lam. 3.34–48*	*Rom. 7.14–end*

	HOLY COMMUNION BCP *Com. Martyr*	**MORNING PRAYER**	**EVENING PRAYER**
Psalms:	3	86; 87; 88	89
Readings:	*Jer. 11.18–20; Heb. 11.32—12.2; Matt. 16.24–27*	*Dan. 4.19–end; Rom. 15.1–13*	*Dan. 7.9–end; John 12.1–19*
Hymns:	....	....	....

CW COLLECT
Most glorious and holy God,
whose servant Hildegard, strong in the faith,
was caught up in the vision
of your heavenly courts:
by the breath of your Spirit
open our eyes to glimpse your glory
and our lips to sing your praises
with all the angels;
through Jesus Christ your Son our Lord,
who is alive and reigns with you,
in the unity of the Holy Spirit,
one God, now and for ever.

POST COMMUNION
Merciful God,
who gave such grace to your servant Hildegard
that she served you with singleness of heart
and loved you above all things:
help us, whose communion with you
   has been renewed in this sacrament,
to forsake all that holds us back
   from following Christ
and to grow into his likeness from glory to glory;
through Jesus Christ our Lord.

BCP COLLECT
*Almighty God, by whose grace and power thy
holy Martyr Lambert triumphed over suffering
and despised death: Grant, we beseech thee, that
enduring hardness and waxing valiant in fight,
we may with the noble army of martyrs receive
the crown of everlasting life; through Jesus Christ
our Lord.*

2021

January					February					March					April					May					June				
S		3	10	17	24	31			7	14	21	28			7	14	21	28			4	11	18	25		2	9	16	23	30			6	13	20	27
M		4	11	18	25			1	8	15	22			1	8	15	22	29			5	12	19	26		3	10	17	24	31			7	14	21	28
T		5	12	19	26			2	9	16	23			2	9	16	23	30			6	13	20	27		4	11	18	25			1	8	15	22	29
W		6	13	20	27			3	10	17	24			3	10	17	24	31			7	14	21	28		5	12	19	26			2	9	16	23	30
T		7	14	21	28			4	11	18	25			4	11	18	25			1	8	15	22	29		6	13	20	27			3	10	17	24	
F	1	8	15	22	29			5	12	19	26			5	12	19	26		2	9	16	23	30		7	14	21	28			4	11	18	25	
S	2	9	16	23	30			6	13	20	27			6	13	20	27		3	10	17	24		1	8	15	22	29			5	12	19	26	

SEPTEMBER
18 Friday

Ember Day (BCP)

Green (*or Red*)

	EUCHARIST	MORNING PRAYER	EVENING PRAYER
	CW		
Psalms:	17.1–8	17; *19*	*22*
Readings:	1 Cor. 15.12–20; Luke 8.1–3	1 Kgs 6.1, 11–28; Acts 15.22–35	Wisd. 5.1–16 *or* 1 Chr. 21.1—22.1; Mark 10.35–45

AW | | *1 Kgs 19.4–18* | *1 Thess. 3* |

	HOLY COMMUNION	MORNING PRAYER	EVENING PRAYER
	BCP For Ember CEG see Dec 18		
Psalms:		90; 91; 92	93; 94
Readings:		Dan. 9.1–19; Rom. 15.14–end	Dan. 9.20–end; John 12.20–end
Hymns:	....	....	....

	July					August					September					October					November					December			
S		5	12	19	26		2	9	16	23	30		6	13	20	27		4	11	18	25		1	8	15	22	29		6	13	20	27
M		6	13	20	27		3	10	17	24	31		7	14	21	28		5	12	19	26		2	9	16	23	30		7	14	21	28
T		7	14	21	28		4	11	18	25		1	8	15	22	29		6	13	20	27		3	10	17	24		1	8	15	22	29
W	1	8	15	22	29		5	12	19	26		2	9	16	23	30		7	14	21	28		4	11	18	25		2	9	16	23	30
T	2	9	16	23	30		6	13	20	27		3	10	17	24		1	8	15	22	29		5	12	19	26		3	10	17	24	31
F	3	10	17	24	31		7	14	21	28		4	11	18	25		2	9	16	23	30		6	13	20	27		4	11	18	25
S	4	11	18	25		1	8	15	22	29		5	12	19	26		3	10	17	24	31		7	14	21	28		5	12	19	26

Theodore of Tarsus, Archbishop of Canterbury, 690 Ember Day (BCP)   Green

	EUCHARIST	**MORNING PRAYER**	**EVENING PRAYER**
	CW		
Psalms:	30.1–5	20; 21; *23*	*24*; 25
Readings:	1 Cor. 15.35–37, 42–49;	1 Kgs 8.1–30;	Wisd. 5.17—6.11 *or* 1 Chr. 22.2–end;
	Luke 8.4–15	Acts 15.36—16.5	Mark 10.46–end

	AW	*Ecclus 4.11–28* or *Deut. 29.2–15*	2 Tim. 3.10–end
	HOLY COMMUNION	**MORNING PRAYER**	**EVENING PRAYER**
	BCP For Ember CEG see Dec 18		
Psalms:		*95; 96; 97*	*98; 99; 100; 101*
Readings:		*Dan. 10;*	*Dan. 12;*
		Rom. 16	*John 13;*
			E. Coll. Trinity 15
Hymns:	....	....	....

2021

January					February				March				April				May					June			
S		3	10	17	24	31	S		7	14	21	28	S		7	14	21	28	S		4	11	18	25	S		2	9	16	23	30	S		6	13	20	27
M		4	11	18	25	M	1	8	15	22	M	1	8	15	22	29	M		5	12	19	26	M		3	10	17	24	31	M		7	14	21	28
T		5	12	19	26	T	2	9	16	23	T	2	9	16	23	30	T		6	13	20	27	T		4	11	18	25	T	1	8	15	22	29
W		6	13	20	27	W	3	10	17	24	W	3	10	17	24	31	W		7	14	21	28	W		5	12	19	26	W	2	9	16	23	30
T		7	14	21	28	T	4	11	18	25	T	4	11	18	25	T	1	8	15	22	29	T		6	13	20	27	T	3	10	17	24
F	1	8	15	22	29	F	5	12	19	26	F	5	12	19	26	F	2	9	16	23	30	F		7	14	21	28	F	4	11	18	25
S	2	9	16	23	30	S	6	13	20	27	S	6	13	20	27	S	3	10	17	24	S	1	8	15	22	29	S	5	12	19	26

THE FIFTEENTH SUNDAY AFTER TRINITY

(Green)

	PRINCIPAL SERVICE	**THIRD SERVICE**	**SECOND SERVICE**
	CW Proper 20		
Psalms:	*105.1–6, 37–end**	*119.153–176*	*119.113–136**
	145.1–8		
Readings:	*Exod. 16.2–15;*	*Isa. 45.9–22;*	*Ezek. 33.23, 30—34.10;*
	Jonah 3.10—end of 4;	*Rev. 14.1–5*	*Acts 26.1, 9–25;*
	Phil. 1.21–end; Matt. 20.1–16		*HC Mark 9.30–37*
			or Eve of Matthew, Apostle and
			Evangelist: Ps. 34; Isa. 33.13–17;
			Matt. 6.19–end
			[BCP Var. Prov. 3.3–18]

	HOLY COMMUNION	**MORNING PRAYER**	**EVENING PRAYER**
	BCP		
Psalms:	*92.1–6*	*119.153–176*	*119.113–136**
Readings:	*Josh. 24.14–25;*	*Dan. 3;*	*Dan. 5 or Dan. 6;*
	Gal. 6.11–end;	*Luke 9.57—10.24 or*	*Matt. 28 or Eph. 4.25—5.21*
	Matt. 6.24–end	*2 Tim. 1*	*or First Evensong of St Matthew:*
			1 Kgs 19.15–end;
			Matt. 6.19–end
Hymns:	....	....	....

2020

July					August					September					October					November					December			
S		5	12	19	26	S		2	9	16	23	30	S		6	13	20	27	S		4	11	18	25	S	1	8	15	22	29	S		6	13	20	27
M		6	13	20	27	M		3	10	17	24	31	M		7	14	21	28	M		5	12	19	26	M	2	9	16	23	30	M		7	14	21	28
T		7	14	21	28	T		4	11	18	25	T	1	8	15	22	29	T		6	13	20	27	T	3	10	17	24	T	1	8	15	22	29
W	1	8	15	22	29	W		5	12	19	26	W	2	9	16	23	30	W		7	14	21	28	W	4	11	18	25	W	2	9	16	23	30
T	2	9	16	23	30	T		6	13	20	27	T	3	10	17	24	T	1	8	15	22	29	T	5	12	19	26	T	3	10	17	24	31
F	3	10	17	24	31	F		7	14	21	28	F	4	11	18	25	F	2	9	16	23	30	F	6	13	20	27	F	4	11	18	25
S	4	11	18	25	S	1	8	15	22	29	S	5	12	19	26	S	3	10	17	24	31	S	7	14	21	28	S	5	12	19	26

CW COLLECTS

God, who in generous mercy sent the Holy Spirit
   upon your Church in the burning fire of your love:
grant that your people may be fervent
   in the fellowship of the gospel
that, always abiding in you,
they may be found steadfast in faith
   and active in service;
through Jesus Christ your Son our Lord,
who is alive and reigns with you,
in the unity of the Holy Spirit,
one God, now and for ever.

or

Lord God,
defend your Church from all false teaching
and give to your people knowledge of your truth,
that we may enjoy eternal life
in Jesus Christ our Lord.

POST COMMUNION

Keep, O Lord, your Church,
   with your perpetual mercy;
and, because without you our human frailty
   cannot but fall,
keep us ever by your help from all things hurtful,
and lead us to all things profitable to our salvation;
through Jesus Christ our Lord.

BCP COLLECT

Keep, we beseech thee, O Lord, thy Church with thy perpetual mercy; and, because the frailty of man without thee cannot but fall, keep us ever by thy help from all things hurtful, and lead us to all things profitable to our salvation; through Jesus Christ our Lord.

2021

	January					February					March					April					May						June			
S		3	10	17	24	31	S		7	14	21	28	S		7	14	21	28	S		4	11	18	25	S		2	9	16	23	30	S		6	13	20	27
M		4	11	18	25		M	1	8	15	22		M	1	8	15	22	29	M		5	12	19	26	M		3	10	17	24	31	M		7	14	21	28
T		5	12	19	26		T	2	9	16	23		T	2	9	16	23	30	T		6	13	20	27	T		4	11	18	25	T	1	8	15	22	29
W		6	13	20	27		W	3	10	17	24		W	3	10	17	24	31	W		7	14	21	28	W		5	12	19	26	W	2	9	16	23	30
T		7	14	21	28		T	4	11	18	25		T	4	11	18	25		T	1	8	15	22	29	T		6	13	20	27	T	3	10	17	24
F	1	8	15	22	29		F	5	12	19	26		F	5	12	19	26		F	2	9	16	23	30	F		7	14	21	28	F	4	11	18	25
S	2	9	16	23	30		S	6	13	20	27		S	6	13	20	27		S	3	10	17	24		S	1	8	15	22	29	S	5	12	19	26

Matthew, Apostle and Evangelist   Red

	PRINCIPAL SERVICE	THIRD SERVICE	SECOND SERVICE
Psalms:	119.65–72	49; 117	119.33–40, 89–96
Readings:	Prov. 3.13–18;	1 Kgs 19.15–end;	Eccles. 5.4–12;
	2 Cor. 4.1–6;	2 Tim. 3.14–end	Matt. 19.16–end
	Matt. 9.9–13		

Displaced readings may be added to the following day's portion:

	EUCHARIST	MORNING PRAYER	EVENING PRAYER
	CW		
Readings:	Prov. 3.27–34;	1 Kgs 8.31–62;	Wisd. 6.12–23 *or* 1 Chr. 28.1–10;
	Luke 8.16–18	Acts 16.6–24	Mark 11.1–11

	HOLY COMMUNION	MORNING PRAYER	EVENING PRAYER
	BCP St Matthew		
Psalms:	*119.65–72*	*105*	*106*
Readings:	*Isa. 33.13–17; 2 Cor. 4.1–6;*	*Prov. 3.1–18;*	*1 Chr. 29.9–17;*
	Matt. 9.9–13	*Matt. 19.16–end*	*1 Tim. 6.6–19*
Hymns:	....	....	....

CW COLLECT
O Almighty God,
whose blessed Son called Matthew the tax collector
to be an apostle and evangelist:
give us grace to forsake the selfish pursuit of gain
    and the possessive love of riches
that we may follow
in the way of your Son Jesus Christ,
who is alive and reigns with you,
in the unity of the Holy Spirit,
one God, now and for ever.

POST COMMUNION
Almighty God,
who on the day of Pentecost
sent your Holy Spirit to the apostles
with the wind from heaven and in tongues of flame,
filling them with joy and boldness
    to preach the gospel:
by the power of the same Spirit
strengthen us to witness to your truth
and to draw everyone to the fire of your love;
through Jesus Christ our Lord.

BCP COLLECT
O Almighty God, who by thy blessed Son didst
call Matthew from the receipt of custom to be an
Apostle and Evangelist: Grant us grace to forsake all
covetous desires, and inordinate love of riches, and
to follow the same thy Son Jesus Christ, who liveth
and reigneth with thee and the Holy Ghost, one God,
world without end.

Sunrise 06.44; Sunset 18.59

2020

	July					August						September					October					November					December				
S		5	12	19	26		2	9	16	23	30		6	13	20	27		4	11	18	25		1	8	15	22	29			6	13	20	27
M		6	13	20	27		3	10	17	24	31		7	14	21	28		5	12	19	26		2	9	16	23	30			7	14	21	28
T		7	14	21	28		4	11	18	25		1	8	15	22	29		6	13	20	27		3	10	17	24		1	8	15	22	29
W	1	8	15	22	29		5	12	19	26		2	9	16	23	30		7	14	21	28		4	11	18	25		2	9	16	23	30
T	2	9	16	23	30		6	13	20	27		3	10	17	24		1	8	15	22	29		5	12	19	26		3	10	17	24	31
F	3	10	17	24	31		7	14	21	28		4	11	18	25		2	9	16	23	30		6	13	20	27		4	11	18	25
S	4	11	18	25		1	8	15	22	29		5	12	19	26		3	10	17	24	31		7	14	21	28		5	12	19	26

Green

DEL Wk 25	**EUCHARIST**	**MORNING PRAYER**	**EVENING PRAYER**
	CW		
Psalms:	119.1–8	32; *36* (Week 2 Ord.)	*33*
Readings:	Prov. 21.1–6, 10–13;	1 Kgs 8.63—9.9;	Wisd. 7.1–14 *or* 1 Chr. 28.11–end;
	Luke 8.19–21	Acts 16.25–end	Mark 11.12–26

AW   *Prov. 8.1–11*   *Luke 6.39–end*

	HOLY COMMUNION	**MORNING PRAYER**	**EVENING PRAYER**
	BCP		
Psalms:		*107;*	*108; 109*
Readings:		*Esther 3;*	*Esther 4;*
		Phil. 1.12–end	*John 14.15–end*
Hymns:	....	....	....

SEPTEMBER
23 Wednesday

Ember Day (CW see Common of the Saints)

	EUCHARIST	**MORNING PRAYER**	**EVENING PRAYER**
	CW		
Psalms:	119.105–112	*34*	*119.33–56*
Readings:	Prov. 30.5–9;	1 Kgs 10.1–25;	Wisd. 7.15—8.4 *or* 1 Chr. 29.1–9;
	Luke 9.1–6	Acts 17.1–15	Mark 11.27–end
AW		*Prov. 2.1–15*	*Col. 1.9–20*

	HOLY COMMUNION	**MORNING PRAYER**	**EVENING PRAYER**
	BCP		
Psalms:		*110; 111; 112; 113*	*114; 115*
Readings:		*Esther 5;*	*Esther 6 and 7;*
		Phil. 2.1–11	*John 15*
Hymns:	....	....	....

2020

	July					August						September					October					November					December			
S		5	12	19	26		2	9	16	23	30		6	13	20	27		4	11	18	25		1	8	15	22	29		6	13	20	27
M		6	13	20	27		3	10	17	24	31		7	14	21	28		5	12	19	26		2	9	16	23	30		7	14	21	28
T		7	14	21	28		4	11	18	25			1	8	15	22	29		6	13	20	27		3	10	17	24		1	8	15	22	29
W	1	8	15	22	29		5	12	19	26		2	9	16	23	30		7	14	21	28		4	11	18	25		2	9	16	23	30
T	2	9	16	23	30		6	13	20	27		3	10	17	24		1	8	15	22	29		5	12	19	26		3	10	17	24	31
F	3	10	17	24	31		7	14	21	28		4	11	18	25		2	9	16	23	30		6	13	20	27		4	11	18	25
S	4	11	18	25		1	8	15	22	29		5	12	19	26		3	10	17	24	31		7	14	21	28		5	12	19	26

Green

	EUCHARIST	MORNING PRAYER	EVENING PRAYER
	CW		
Psalms:	Ps. 90.1–6	*37***	39; *40*
Readings:	Eccles. 1.2–11;	1 Kgs 11.1–13;	Wisd. 8.5–18 *or* 1 Chr. 29.10–20;
	Luke 9.7–9	Acts 17.16–end	Mark 12.1–12

		MORNING PRAYER	EVENING PRAYER
AW		*Baruch 3.4–end* or *Gen. 1.1–13*	*John 1.1–18*

	HOLY COMMUNION	MORNING PRAYER	EVENING PRAYER
	BCP		
Psalms:		116; 117; 118	119.1–32
Readings:		1 Macc. 1.1–19;	1 Macc. 1.20–40;
		Phil. 2.12–end	John 16.1–15
Hymns:	....	....	....

Lancelot Andrewes, Bishop of Winchester, Spiritual Writer 1626 (CW Readings see common of the Saints   Green *or* White
Especially Isa. 6.1–8) Ember Day (CW see Common of the Saints)
Sergei of Radonezh, Russian Monastic Reformer, Teacher of the Faith 1392

	EUCHARIST	MORNING PRAYER	EVENING PRAYER
	CW		
Psalms:	144.1–4	*31*	*35*
Readings:	Eccles. 3.1–11;	1 Kgs 11.26–end;	Wisd. 8.21—end of 9
	Luke 9.18–22	Acts 18.1–21	*or* 1 Chr. 29.21–end;
			Mark 12.13–17

		AW	*Ecclus 1.1–20* or *Deut. 7.7–16*	1 Cor. 1.18–end

	HOLY COMMUNION		MORNING PRAYER	EVENING PRAYER
	BCP			
Psalms:			*119.33–72*	*119.73–104*
Readings:			1 Macc. 1.41–end;	1 Macc. 2.1–28;
			Phil. 3	John 16.16–end
Hymns:			....	....

CW COLLECT
Lord God,
who gave to Lancelot Andrewes
   many gifts of your Holy Spirit,
making him a man of prayer
and a pastor of your people:
perfect in us that which is lacking in your gifts,
   of faith, to increase it,
   of hope, to establish it,
   of love, to kindle it,
that we may live in the light
of your grace and glory;
through Jesus Christ your Son our Lord,
who is alive and reigns with you,
in the unity of the Holy Spirit,
one God, now and for ever.

POST COMMUNION
God, shepherd of your people,
whose servant Lancelot Andrewes revealed the
   loving service of Christ in his ministry
   as a pastor of your people:
by this eucharist in which we share
awaken within us the love of Christ
and keep us faithful to our Christian calling;
through him who laid down his life for us,
but is alive and reigns with you, now and for ever.

2020

SEPTEMBER
Saturday 26

Wilson Carlile, Founder of the Church Army, 1942; Ember Day (CW see Common of the Saints)   Green *or* Red (*or* Red)
St Cyprian, Archbishop of Carthage, Martyr, 258 (BCP)

	EUCHARIST	MORNING PRAYER	EVENING PRAYER
	CW		
Psalms:	90; 1–2, 12–end	41; *42*; 43	45; *46*
Readings:	Eccles. 11.9—12.8; Luke 9.43b–45	1 Kgs 12.1–24; Acts 18.22—19.7	Wisd. 10.15—11.10 *or* 2 Chr. 1.1–13; Mark 12.18–27

AW		*Wisd. 9.1–12* or *Jer. 1.4–10*	*Luke 2.41–end*
	HOLY COMMUNION	MORNING PRAYER	EVENING PRAYER
	BCP Com. Martyr		
Psalms:	3	119.105–144	119.145–end
Readings:	Jer. 11.18–20; Heb. 11.32—12.2; Matt. 16.24–27	1 Macc. 2.29–48; Phil. 4	1 Macc. 2.49–end; John 17; E. Coll. Trinity 16
Hymns:	....	....	....

BCP COLLECT
Almighty God, by whose grace and power thy holy Martyr Cyprian triumphed over suffering and despised death: Grant, we beseech thee, that enduring hardness and waxing valiant in fight, we may with the noble army of martyrs receive the crown of everlasting life; through Jesus Christ our Lord.

2021

	January	February	March	April	May	June
S	3 10 17 24 31	7 14 21 28	7 14 21 28	4 11 18 25	2 9 16 23 30	6 13 20 27
M	4 11 18 25	1 8 15 22	1 8 15 22 29	5 12 19 26	3 10 17 24 31	7 14 21 28
T	5 12 19 26	2 9 16 23	2 9 16 23 30	6 13 20 27	4 11 18 25	1 8 15 22 29
W	6 13 20 27	3 10 17 24	3 10 17 24 31	7 14 21 28	5 12 19 26	2 9 16 23 30
T	7 14 21 28	4 11 18 25	4 11 18 25	1 8 15 22 29	6 13 20 27	3 10 17 24
F	1 8 15 22 29	5 12 19 26	5 12 19 26	2 9 16 23 30	7 14 21 28	4 11 18 25
S	2 9 16 23 30	6 13 20 27	6 13 20 27	3 10 17 24	1 8 15 22 29	5 12 19 26

THE SIXTEENTH SUNDAY AFTER TRINITY

(Green)

	PRINCIPAL SERVICE	THIRD SERVICE	SECOND SERVICE
	Proper 21		
Psalms:	*78.1–4, 12–16* [78.1–7] 25.1–8*	125; 126; 127	[120; 123] 124
Readings:	*Exod. 17.1–7 Ezek. 18.1–4, 25–end; Phil. 2.1–13; Matt. 21.23–32*	Isa. 48.12–21; Luke 11.37–54	Ezek. 37.15–28; 1 John 2.22–end; [Mark 9.38–end]

	HOLY COMMUNION	MORNING PRAYER	EVENING PRAYER
	BCP		
Psalms:	*102.12–17*	*125; 126; 127*	*[120; 123] 124*
Readings:	*1 Kgs 17.17–end; Eph. 3.13–end; Luke 7.11–17*	*Jer. 5.1–19; Luke 11.1–28 or Titus 2.1—3.7*	*[120; 123] 124* *Jer. 5.20–end or Jer. 7.1–15; John 8.12–30 or Eph. 5.22—6.9*
Hymns:	....	....	....

2020

	July					August						September					October					November					December			
S		5	12	19	26		2	9	16	23	30		6	13	20	27		4	11	18	25		1	8	15	22	29		6	13	20	27
M		6	13	20	27		3	10	17	24	31		7	14	21	28		5	12	19	26		2	9	16	23	30		7	14	21	28
T		7	14	21	28		4	11	18	25			1	8	15	22	29		6	13	20	27		3	10	17	24		1	8	15	22	29
W	1	8	15	22	29		5	12	19	26		2	9	16	23	30		7	14	21	28		4	11	18	25		2	9	16	23	30
T	2	9	16	23	30		6	13	20	27		3	10	17	24		1	8	15	22	29		5	12	19	26		3	10	17	24	31
F	3	10	17	24	31		7	14	21	28		4	11	18	25		2	9	16	23	30		6	13	20	27		4	11	18	25
S	4	11	18	25		1	8	15	22	29		5	12	19	26		3	10	17	24	31		7	14	21	28		5	12	19	26

CW COLLECTS

O Lord, we beseech you mercifully to hear
the prayers of your people who call upon you;
and grant that they may both perceive and know
    what things they ought to do,
and also may have grace and power
    faithfully to fulfil them;
through Jesus Christ your Son our Lord,
who is alive and reigns with you,
in the unity of the Holy Spirit,
one God, now and for ever.

or

Lord of creation,
whose glory is around and within us:
open our eyes to your wonders,
that we may serve you with reverence
and know your peace at our lives' end,
through Jesus Christ our Lord.

POST COMMUNION

Almighty God,
you have taught us through your Son
that love is the fulfilling of the law:
grant that we may love you with our whole heart
and our neighbours as ourselves;
through Jesus Christ our Lord.

BCP COLLECT

*O Lord, we beseech thee, let thy continual pity
cleanse and defend thy Church; and, because it
cannot continue in safety without thy succour,
preserve it evermore by thy help and goodness;
through Jesus Christ our Lord.*

2021

January						February					March					April					May					June				
S		3	10	17	24	31	S		7	14	21	28	S		7	14	21	28	S		4	11	18	25	S		2	9	16	23	30	S		6	13	20	27
M		4	11	18	25		M	1	8	15	22		M	1	8	15	22	29	M		5	12	19	26	M		3	10	17	24	31	M		7	14	21	28
T		5	12	19	26		T	2	9	16	23		T	2	9	16	23	30	T		6	13	20	27	T		4	11	18	25	T	1	8	15	22	29
W		6	13	20	27		W	3	10	17	24		W	3	10	17	24	31	W		7	14	21	28	W		5	12	19	26	W	2	9	16	23	30
T		7	14	21	28		T	4	11	18	25		T	4	11	18	25		T	1	8	15	22	29	T		6	13	20	27	T	3	10	17	24	
F	1	8	15	22	29		F	5	12	19	26		F	5	12	19	26		F	2	9	16	23	30	F		7	14	21	28	F	4	11	18	25
S	2	9	16	23	30		S	6	13	20	27		S	6	13	20	27		S	3	10	17	24		S	1	8	15	22	29	S	5	12	19	26

Green

		MORNING PRAYER	**EVENING PRAYER**
DEL Wk 26	**EUCHARIST** CW		
Psalms:	17.1–11	*44*; (Week 3 Ord.)	*47*; 49
Readings:	Job 1.6–end; Luke 9.46–50	1 Kgs 12.25—13.10; Acts 19.8–20	Wisd. 11.21—12.2 *or* 2 Chr. 2.1–16; Mark 12.28–34 *or* Eve of Michael & All Angels: Ps. 91; 2 Kgs 6.8–17; Matt. 18.1–6, 10 [BCP Var. John 1.47–51]

		AW	*Gen. 21.1–13*	*Luke 1.26–38*

		MORNING PRAYER	**EVENING PRAYER**
	HOLY COMMUNION BCP		
Psalms		*132; 133; 134; 135*	*136; 137; 138*
Readings		*1 Macc. 3.1–26;* *Col. 1.1–20*	*1 Macc. 3.27–41;* *John 18.1–27* or *First Evensong of* *St Michael & All Angels:* *Ezek. 10.8–end; Rev. 5*
Hymns:	....	....	....

Sunrise 06.56; Sunset 18.43

2020

	July						August						September						October						November						December			
S		5	12	19	26	S		2	9	16	23	30	S		6	13	20	27	S		4	11	18	25	S	1	8	15	22	29	S		6	13	20	27
M		6	13	20	27	M		3	10	17	24	31	M		7	14	21	28	M		5	12	19	26	M	2	9	16	23	30	M		7	14	21	28
T		7	14	21	28	T		4	11	18	25		T	1	8	15	22	29	T		6	13	20	27	T	3	10	17	24		T	1	8	15	22	29
W	1	8	15	22	29	W		5	12	19	26		W	2	9	16	23	30	W		7	14	21	28	W	4	11	18	25		W	2	9	16	23	30
T	2	9	16	23	30	T		6	13	20	27		T	3	10	17	24		T	1	8	15	22	29	T	5	12	19	26		T	3	10	17	24	31
F	3	10	17	24	31	F		7	14	21	28		F	4	11	18	25		F	2	9	16	23	30	F	6	13	20	27		F	4	11	18	25	
S	4	11	18	25		S	1	8	15	22	29	S		5	12	19	26	S		3	10	17	24	31	S	7	14	21	28		S	5	12	19	26

Michael and All Angels Ember Day (CW see Common of the Saints) White

	PRINCIPAL SERVICE CW	THIRD SERVICE	SECOND SERVICE
Psalms:	103.19–end	34; 150	138; 148
Readings:	Gen. 28.10–17; Rev. 12.7–12; John 1.47–end or Rev. 12.7–12; Heb. 1.5–end; John 1.47–end	Tobit 12.6–end or Dan. 12.1–4; Acts 12.1–11	Dan. 10.4–end [BCP Var. Gen. 28.10–17] Rev. 5

Seasonal provisions CW Book p 328

Displaced readings may be added to the previous or following day's portion:

	EUCHARIST CW	MORNING PRAYER	EVENING PRAYER
Readings:	Job 3.1–3, 11–17, 20–23; Luke 9.51–56	1 Kgs 13.11–end; Acts 19.21–end	Wisd. 12.12–21 or 2 Chr. 3; Mark 12.35–end

	HOLY COMMUNION BCP St Michael & All Angels	MORNING PRAYER	EVENING PRAYER
Psalms:	103.17–22	139; 140; 141	142; 143
Readings:	Dan. 10.10–19a; Rev. 12.7–12; Matt. 18.1–10	2 Kgs 6.8–17; Acts 12.1–11	Dan. 10.4–end; Matt. 13.24–30, 36–43
Hymns:	....	....	....

CW COLLECT
Everlasting God,
you have ordained and constituted the ministries
 of angels and mortals in a wonderful order:
grant that as your holy angels
 always serve you in heaven,
so, at your command,
 they may help and defend us on earth;
through Jesus Christ your Son our Lord,
who is alive and reigns with you,
in the unity of the Holy Spirit,
one God, now and for ever.

POST COMMUNION
Lord of heaven,
in this eucharist you have brought us near
 to an innumerable company of angels
 and to the spirits of the saints made perfect:
as in this food of our earthly pilgrimage
 we have shared their fellowship,
so may we come to share their joy in heaven;
through Jesus Christ our Lord.

BCP COLLECT
*O everlasting God, who hast ordained and
constituted the services of Angels and men in a
wonderful order: Mercifully grant, that as thy holy
Angels alway do thee service in heaven, so by thy
appointment they may succour and defend us on
earth; through Jesus Christ our Lord.*

Jerome, Translator of the Scriptures, Teacher of the Faith 420 (also BCP)

Green (*or White*)

	EUCHARIST	MORNING PRAYER	EVENING PRAYER
	CW		
Psalms:	88.1–6, 14–16	*119.57–80*	*59*; 60 [67]
Readings:	Job 9.1–12, 14–16;	1 Kgs 17;	Wisd. 13.1–9 *or* 2 Chr. 5;
	Luke 9.57–end	Acts 20.1–16	Mark 13.1–13

AW		*2 Kgs 4.1–7*	*John 2.1–11*

	HOLY COMMUNION	MORNING PRAYER	EVENING PRAYER
	BCP Com. Doctor		
Psalms:	37.30–35	*144; 145; 146*	*147; 148; 149; 150*
Readings:	Wisd. 7.7–14; 1 Cor. 2.6–13;	1 Macc. 4.26–35;	1 Macc. 4.36–end;
	Matt. 13.51–52	Col. 2.8–19	John 19.1–30
Hymns:	....	....	....

BCP COLLECT

O God, who hast enlightened thy Church by the teaching of thy servant Jerome: Enrich it evermore, we beseech thee, with thy heavenly grace, and raise up faithful witnesses, who by their life and doctrine may set forth to all men the truth of thy salvation; through Jesus Christ our Lord.

2020

	July					August						September					October					November					December			
S		5	12	19	26		2	9	16	23	30		6	13	20	27		4	11	18	25		1	8	15	22	29		6	13	20	27
M		6	13	20	27		3	10	17	24	31		7	14	21	28		5	12	19	26		2	9	16	23	30		7	14	21	28
T		7	14	21	28		4	11	18	25			1	8	15	22	29		6	13	20	27		3	10	17	24		1	8	15	22	29
W	1	8	15	22	29		5	12	19	26		2	9	16	23	30		7	14	21	28		4	11	18	25		2	9	16	23	30
T	2	9	16	23	30		6	13	20	27		3	10	17	24		1	8	15	22	29		5	12	19	26		3	10	17	24	31
F	3	10	17	24	31		7	14	21	28		4	11	18	25		2	9	16	23	30		6	13	20	27		4	11	18	25
S	4	11	18	25		1	8	15	22	29		5	12	19	26		3	10	17	24	31		7	14	21	28		5	12	19	26

Remigius, Bishop of Rheims, Apostle of the Franks, 533 (also BCP)
Anthony Ashley Cooper, Earl of Shaftsbury, Social Reformer, 1885.

Green *(or White)*

	EUCHARIST	**MORNING PRAYER**	**EVENING PRAYER**
	CW		
Psalms:	27.13–16	56; *57*; (63*)	61; *62*; 64
Readings:	Job 19.21–27a;	1 Kgs 18.1–20;	Wisd. 16.15—17.1 *or* 2 Chr. 6.1–21;
	Luke 10.1–12	Acts 20.17–end	Mark 13.14–23
	AW	*2 Kgs 4.25b–37*	*Mark 3.19b–35*
	HOLY COMMUNION	**MORNING PRAYER**	**EVENING PRAYER**
	BCP Com. Missionary		
Psalms:	96.7–13	1; 2; 3; 4; 5	6; 7; 8
Readings:	Isa. 61.1–3; 2 Cor. 4.5–10;	1 Macc. 6.1–17;	1 Macc. 6.18–47;
	Matt. 28.16–20	Col. 2.20—3.11	John 19.31–end
Hymns:	....	....	....

BCP COLLECT
O Lord Jesus Christ, who callest to thee whom thou willest and sendest them whither thou dost choose: we thank thee for calling thy servant Remigius to preach thy gospel to the nations; and we humbly pray thee to raise up among us those who shall be heralds and evangelists of thy kingdom, and shall build up thy church in every land; who livest and reignest with the Father and the Holy Spirit, one God, world without end.

Full Moon

2021

January					February					March					April					May					June				
S		3	10	17	24	31	S			7	14	21	28	S		7	14	21	28	S		4	11	18	25	S		2	9	16	23	30	S		6	13	20	27
M		4	11	18	25	M	1	8	15	22	M	1	8	15	22	29	M		5	12	19	26	M	3	10	17	24	31	M		7	14	21	28
T		5	12	19	26	T	2	9	16	23	T	2	9	16	23	30	T		6	13	20	27	T	4	11	18	25	T	1	8	15	22	29
W		6	13	20	27	W	3	10	17	24	W	3	10	17	24	31	W		7	14	21	28	W	5	12	19	26	W	2	9	16	23	30
T	7	14	21	28	T	4	11	18	25	T	4	11	18	25	T	1	8	15	22	29	T	6	13	20	27	T	3	10	17	24
F	1	8	15	22	29	F	5	12	19	26	F	5	12	19	26	F	2	9	16	23	30	F	7	14	21	28	F	4	11	18	25
S	2	9	16	23	30	S	6	13	20	27	S	6	13	20	27	S	3	10	17	24	S	1	8	15	22	29	S	5	12	19	26

Green

	EUCHARIST	MORNING PRAYER	EVENING PRAYER
	CW		
Psalms:	139.6–11	*51*; 54	*38*
Readings:	Job 38.1, 12–21, 40.3–5; Luke 10.13–16	1 Kgs 18.21–end; Acts 21.1–16	Wisd. 18.6–19 *or* 2 Chr. 6.22–end; Mark 13.24–31

AW *Judith 8.9–17, 28–36 or Ruth 1.1–8*   *John 19.25b–30*

	HOLY COMMUNION	MORNING PRAYER	EVENING PRAYER
	BCP		
Psalms:		9; 10; 11	12; 13; 14
Readings:		1 Macc. 7.1–20; Col. 3.12—4.1	1 Macc. 7.21–end; John 20
Hymns:	....	....	....

2020

	July					August						September					October					November					December			
S		5	12	19	26		2	9	16	23	30		6	13	20	27		4	11	18	25		1	8	15	22	29		6	13	20	27
M		6	13	20	27		3	10	17	24	31		7	14	21	28		5	12	19	26		2	9	16	23	30		7	14	21	28
T		7	14	21	28		4	11	18	25		1	8	15	22	29		6	13	20	27		3	10	17	24		1	8	15	22	29
W	1	8	15	22	29		5	12	19	26		2	9	16	23	30		7	14	21	28		4	11	18	25		2	9	16	23	30
T	2	9	16	23	30		6	13	20	27		3	10	17	24		1	8	15	22	29		5	12	19	26		3	10	17	24	31
F	3	10	17	24	31		7	14	21	28		4	11	18	25		2	9	16	23	30		6	13	20	27		4	11	18	25
S	4	11	18	25		1	8	15	22	29		5	12	19	26		3	10	17	24	31		7	14	21	28		5	12	19	26

George Bell, Bishop of Chichester, Ecumenist, Peacemaker 1958   Green

	EUCHARIST	**MORNING PRAYER**	**EVENING PRAYER**
	CW		
Psalms:	119.169–end	*68*	65; *66*
Readings:	Job 42.1–3, 6, 12–end; Luke 10.17–24	1 Kgs 19; Acts 21.17–36	Wisd. 19 *or* 2 Chr. 7; Mark 13.32–end *or* Eve of Dedication (if required) Ps. 24, 2 Chr. 7.11–16; John 4.19–29

		AW	*Exod. 15.19–27*	*Acts 1.6–14*

	HOLY COMMUNION	**MORNING PRAYER**	**EVENING PRAYER**
	BCP		
Psalms:		*15; 16; 17*	*18*
Readings:		*1 Macc. 9.1–22;* *Col. 4.2–end*	*1 Macc. 13.41–end; 14.4–15;* *John 21;* *E. Coll. Trinity 17*
Hymns:	....	....	....

THE SEVENTEENTH SUNDAY AFTER TRINITY

(Green *or* Gold *or* White for Dedication)

	PRINCIPAL SERVICE CW Proper 22	THIRD SERVICE	SECOND SERVICE
Psalms:	*19** [*or 19.7–end*] *80.9–17*	128; 129; 134	136*
Readings:	*Exod. 20.1–4, 7–9, 12–20;* *Isa. 5.1–7;* *Phil. 3.4b–14;* *Matt. 21.33–end*	Isa. 49.13–23; Luke 12.1–12	Prov. 2.1–11; 1 John 2.1–17; [Mark 10.2–16]

DEDICATION FESTIVAL

If date unknown – the first Sunday in October or alternatively last Sunday after Trinity (Oct. 29th)

	PRINCIPAL SERVICE CW	THIRD SERVICE	SECOND SERVICE
Psalms:	122	48; 150	132
Readings:	1 Kgs 8.22–30 *or* Rev. 21.9–14; Heb. 12.18–24; Matt. 21.12–16	Hag. 2.6–9; Heb. 10.19–25	Jer. 7.1–11; 1 Cor. 3.9–17 [Luke 19.1–10]

	HOLY COMMUNION *BCP Trinity 17 (for Dedication use CW provision)*	MORNING PRAYER	EVENING PRAYER
Psalms:	*33.6–12*	128; 129; 134	*136**
Readings:	*Prov. 25.6–14;* *Eph. 4.1–6;* *Luke 14.1–11*	*Jer. 17.5–14;* *Luke 11.29–end or* *1 Pet. 1.1–21*	*Jer. 18.1–17 or Jer. 22.1–19;* *John 8.31–end or* *Eph. 6.10–end*
Hymns:	....	....	....

2020

	July					August						September					October					November					December			
S		5	12	19	26		2	9	16	23	30		6	13	20	27		4	11	18	25		1	8	15	22	29		6	13	20	27
M		6	13	20	27		3	10	17	24	31		7	14	21	28		5	12	19	26		2	9	16	23	30		7	14	21	28
T		7	14	21	28		4	11	18	25		1	8	15	22	29		6	13	20	27		3	10	17	24		1	8	15	22	29
W	1	8	15	22	29		5	12	19	26		2	9	16	23	30		7	14	21	28		4	11	18	25		2	9	16	23	30
T	2	9	16	23	30		6	13	20	27		3	10	17	24		1	8	15	22	29		5	12	19	26		3	10	17	24	31
F	3	10	17	24	31		7	14	21	28		4	11	18	25		2	9	16	23	30		6	13	20	27		4	11	18	25
S	4	11	18	25		1	8	15	22	29		5	12	19	26		3	10	17	24	31		7	14	21	28		5	12	19	26

CW COLLECTS

Almighty God,
you have made us for yourself,
and our hearts are restless
till they find their rest in you:
pour your love into our hearts
and draw us to yourself,
and so bring us at last to your heavenly city
where we shall see you face to face;
through Jesus Christ your Son our Lord,
who is alive and reigns with you,
in the unity of the Holy Spirit,
one God, now and for ever.

or

Gracious God,
you call us to fullness of life:
deliver us from unbelief
and banish our anxieties
with the liberating love of Jesus Christ our Lord.

POST COMMUNION

Lord, we pray that your grace
   may always precede and follow us,
and make us continually to be given to all good works;
through Jesus Christ our Lord.

BCP COLLECT

*Lord, we pray thee that thy grace may always
prevent and follow us, and make us continually to
be given to all good works; through Jesus Christ our
Lord.*

CW COLLECT Dedication Festival

Almighty God,
to whose glory we celebrate the dedication
   of this house of prayer:
we praise you for the many blessings
you have given to those who worship you here:
and we pray that all who seek you in this place
   may find you,
and, being filled with the Holy Spirit,
may become a living temple acceptable to you;
through Jesus Christ your Son our Lord,
who is alive and reigns with you,
in the unity of the Holy Spirit,
one God, now and for ever.

POST COMMUNION

Father in heaven,
whose Church on earth is a sign of your heavenly peace,
an image of the new and eternal Jerusalem:
grant to us in the days of our pilgrimage
that, fed with the living bread of heaven,
and united in the body of your Son,
we may be the temple of your presence,
the place of your glory on earth,
and a sign of your peace in the world;
through Jesus Christ our Lord.

BCP COLLECT for Consecration or Dedication

*O God, by whose providence we celebrate again the
consecration [or dedication] of this church: Send down upon
us, we beseech thee, thy heavenly blessing; and, because
holiness becometh thine house for ever, make us living
temples, holy and acceptable unto thee; through Jesus Christ
our Lord.*

2021

January						February						March						April						May						June				
S		3	10	17	24	31	S			7	14	21	28	S			7	14	21	28	S		4	11	18	25	S		2	9	16	23	30	S		6	13	20	27
M		4	11	18	25		M	1	8	15	22			M	1	8	15	22	29		M		5	12	19	26	M		3	10	17	24	31	M		7	14	21	28
T		5	12	19	26		T	2	9	16	23			T	2	9	16	23	30		T		6	13	20	27	T		4	11	18	25		T	1	8	15	22	29
W		6	13	20	27		W	3	10	17	24			W	3	10	17	24	31		W		7	14	21	28	W		5	12	19	26		W	2	9	16	23	30
T		7	14	21	28		T	4	11	18	25			T	4	11	18	25		T	1	8	15	22	29	T		6	13	20	27		T	3	10	17	24
F	1	8	15	22	29		F	5	12	19	26			F	5	12	19	26		F	2	9	16	23	30	F		7	14	21	28		F	4	11	18	25
S	2	9	16	23	30		S	6	13	20	27			S	6	13	20	27		S	3	10	17	24		S	1	8	15	22	29	S		5	12	19	26

Green

DEL Wk 27	**EUCHARIST**		**MORNING PRAYER**	**EVENING PRAYER**
	CW			
Psalms:	111.1–6		*71* (Week 4 Ord.)	*72*; 75
Readings:	Gal. 1.6–12;		1 Kgs 21;	1 Macc. 1.1–19 *or* 2 Chr. 9.1–12;
	Luke 10.25–37		Acts 21.37—22.21	Mark 14.1–11
		AW	*Exod. 19.16–end*	*Heb. 12.18–end*
	HOLY COMMUNION		**MORNING PRAYER**	**EVENING PRAYER**
	BCP			
Psalms:			*24; 25; 26*	*27; 28; 29*
Readings:			*Job 1;*	*Job 2;*
			Philem.	*Luke 1.1–23*
Hymns:	....		....	....

Sunrise 07.08; Sunset 18.27

2020

	July					August						September					October					November					December			
S		5	12	19	26	S		2	9	16	23	30	S		6	13	20	27	S		4	11	18	25	S	1	8	15	22	29	S		6	13	20	27
M		6	13	20	27	M		3	10	17	24	31	M		7	14	21	28	M		5	12	19	26	M	2	9	16	23	30	M		7	14	21	28
T		7	14	21	28	T		4	11	18	25		T	1	8	15	22	29	T		6	13	20	27	T	3	10	17	24		T	1	8	15	22	29
W	1	8	15	22	29	W		5	12	19	26		W	2	9	16	23	30	W		7	14	21	28	W	4	11	18	25		W	2	9	16	23	30
T	2	9	16	23	30	T		6	13	20	27		T	3	10	17	24		T	1	8	15	22	29	T	5	12	19	26		T	3	10	17	24	31
F	3	10	17	24	31	F		7	14	21	28		F	4	11	18	25		F	2	9	16	23	30	F	6	13	20	27		F	4	11	18	25	
S	4	11	18	25		S	1	8	15	22	29		S	5	12	19	26		S	3	10	17	24	31	S	7	14	21	28		S	5	12	19	26	

William Tyndale, Translator of the Scriptures, Reformation Martyr, 1536
(CW Readings see Common of the Saints also Prov. 8.4–11; 2 Tim. 3.12–17).
Faith of Aquitaine, Virgin and Martyr, c.304 (BCP)

Red *or* Green (*or Red*)

	EUCHARIST CW	MORNING PRAYER	EVENING PRAYER
Psalm	139.1–9	*73*	*74*
Readings:	Gal. 1.13–end; Luke 10.38–end	1 Kgs 22.1–28; Acts 22.22—23.11	1 Macc. 1.20–40 *or* 2 Chr. 10.1—11.4; Mark 14.12–25

	AW	*1 Chr. 16.1–13*	*Rev. 11.15–end*
	HOLY COMMUNION BCP Com. Virgin and Martyr	MORNING PRAYER	EVENING PRAYER
Psalms:	131	*30; 31*	*32; 33; 34*
Readings:	Ecclus 51.1–10; Phil. 3.7–14; Matt. 25.1–13	Job 3; Eph. 1.1–14	Job 4; Luke 1.24–56
Hymns:	....	....	....

CW COLLECT
Lord, give to your people grace
  to hear and keep your word
that, after the example
  of your servant William Tyndale,
we may not only profess your gospel
but also be ready to suffer and die for it,
to the honour of your name;
through Jesus Christ your Son our Lord,
who is alive and reigns with you,
in the unity of the Holy Spirit,
one God, now and for ever.

POST COMMUNION
Eternal God,
who gave us this holy meal
in which we have celebrated the glory of the cross
and the victory of your martyr William Tyndale:
by our communion with Christ
in his saving death and resurrection,
give us with all your saints the courage
  to conquer evil
and so to share the fruit of the tree of life;
through Jesus Christ our Lord.

BCP COLLECT for St Faith
*O God, who didst endue the holy Virgin Faith with
grace to witness a good confession (and to suffer
gladly for thy sake): Grant that we, after her example,
may be found ready when the Bridegroom cometh
and enter with him to the marriage feast; through the
same thy Son Jesus Christ our Lord.*

2021

January					February				March					April				May					June			
S		3	10	17	24	31	S		7	14	21	28	S		7	14	21	28	S		4	11	18	25	S		2	9	16	23	30	S		6	13	20	27
M		4	11	18	25		M	1	8	15	22		M	1	8	15	22	29	M		5	12	19	26	M		3	10	17	24	31	M		7	14	21	28
T		5	12	19	26		T	2	9	16	23		T	2	9	16	23	30	T		6	13	20	27	T		4	11	18	25	T	1	8	15	22	29
W		6	13	20	27		W	3	10	17	24		W	3	10	17	24	31	W		7	14	21	28	W		5	12	19	26	W	2	9	16	23	30
T		7	14	21	28		T	4	11	18	25		T	4	11	18	25		T	1	8	15	22	29	T		6	13	20	27	T	3	10	17	24
F	1	8	15	22	29		F	5	12	19	26		F	5	12	19	26		F	2	9	16	23	30	F		7	14	21	28	F	4	11	18	25
S	2	9	16	23	30		S	6	13	20	27		S	6	13	20	27		S	3	10	17	24	S	1	8	15	22	29	S	5	12	19	26

Green

	EUCHARIST	MORNING PRAYER	EVENING PRAYER
	CW		
Psalms:	117	*77*	*119.81–104*
Readings:	Gal. 2.1–2, 7–14;	1 Kgs 22.29–45;	1 Macc. 1.41–end *or* 2 Chr. 12;
	Luke 11.1–4	Acts 23.12–end	Mark 14.26–42

| | | *AW* | *1 Chr. 29.10–19* | *Col. 3.12–17* |

	HOLY COMMUNION	MORNING PRAYER	EVENING PRAYER
	BCP		
Psalms:		*35; 36*	*37*
Readings:		*Job 5;*	*Job 6;*
		Eph. 1.15–end	*Luke 1.57–end*
Hymns:	....	....	....

2020

	July					August						September					October					November					December			
S		5	12	19	26		2	9	16	23	30		6	13	20	27		4	11	18	25		1	8	15	22	29		6	13	20	27
M		6	13	20	27		3	10	17	24	31		7	14	21	28		5	12	19	26		2	9	16	23	30		7	14	21	28
T		7	14	21	28		4	11	18	25			1	8	15	22	29		6	13	20	27		3	10	17	24		1	8	15	22	29
W	1	8	15	22	29		5	12	19	26		2	9	16	23	30		7	14	21	28		4	11	18	25		2	9	16	23	30
T	2	9	16	23	30		6	13	20	27		3	10	17	24			1	8	15	22	29		5	12	19	26		3	10	17	24	31
F	3	10	17	24	31		7	14	21	28		4	11	18	25			2	9	16	23	30		6	13	20	27		4	11	18	25
S	4	11	18	25		1	8	15	22	29		5	12	19	26			3	10	17	24	31		7	14	21	28		5	12	19	26

Green

	EUCHARIST	**MORNING PRAYER**	**EVENING PRAYER**
	CW		
Psalms:	*Canticle:* Benedictus	*78.1–39**	*78.40–end**
Readings:	Gal. 3.1–5;	2 Kgs 1.2–17;	1 Macc. 2.1–28 *or* 2 Chr. 13.1—14.1
	Luke 11.5–13	Acts 24.1–23	Mark 14.43–52

		AW	*Neh. 8.1–12*	*1 Cor. 14.1–12*

	HOLY COMMUNION	**MORNING PRAYER**	**EVENING PRAYER**
	BCP		
Psalms:		*38; 39; 40*	*41; 42; 43*
Readings:		*Job 7;*	*Job 8;*
		Eph. 2.1–10	*Luke 2.1–21*
Hymns:	....	....	....

2021

	January					February					March					April					May					June			
S		3	10	17	24	31		7	14	21	28		7	14	21	28		4	11	18	25		2	9	16	23	30		6	13	20	27
M		4	11	18	25		1	8	15	22		1	8	15	22	29		5	12	19	26		3	10	17	24	31		7	14	21	28
T		5	12	19	26		2	9	16	23		2	9	16	23	30		6	13	20	27		4	11	18	25		1	8	15	22	29
W		6	13	20	27		3	10	17	24		3	10	17	24	31		7	14	21	28		5	12	19	26		2	9	16	23	30
T		7	14	21	28		4	11	18	25		4	11	18	25		1	8	15	22	29		6	13	20	27		3	10	17	24
F	1	8	15	22	29		5	12	19	26		5	12	19	26		2	9	16	23	30		7	14	21	28		4	11	18	25
S	2	9	16	23	30		6	13	20	27		6	13	20	27		3	10	17	24		1	8	15	22	29		5	12	19	26

Denys, Bishop of Paris, and his Companions, Martyrs, c.250. St Denys (BCP)
Robert Grosseteste, Bishop of Lincoln, Philosopher, Scientist, 1253

Green (*or Red*)

	EUCHARIST	MORNING PRAYER	EVENING PRAYER
	CW		
Psalms:	111.4–end	*55*	*69*
Readings:	Gal. 3.7–14;	2 Kgs 2.1–18;	1 Macc. 2.29–48 *or* 2 Chr. 14.2–end;
	Luke 11.15–26	Acts 24.24—25.12	Mark 14.53–65

AW *Isa. 1.10–17* *Mark 12.28–34*

	HOLY COMMUNION	MORNING PRAYER	EVENING PRAYER
	BCP Com Martyr		
Psalms:	*3*	*44; 45; 46*	*47; 48; 49*
Readings:	*Jer. 11.18–20; Heb. 11.32—12.2;*	*Job 9;*	*Job 10;*
	Matt. 16.24–27	*Eph. 2.11–end*	*Luke 2.22–end*
Hymns:	....	....	....

BCP COLLECT
*Almighty God, by whose grace and power thy holy
Martyr Denys triumphed over suffering and despised
death: Grant, we beseech thee, that enduring
hardness and waxing valiant in fight, we may with
the noble army of martyrs receive the crown of
everlasting life; through Jesus Christ our Lord.*

2020

July					August						September					October					November					December				
S		5	12	19	26	S		2	9	16	23	30	S		6	13	20	27	S		4	11	18	25	S	1	8	15	22	29	S		6	13	20	27
M		6	13	20	27	M		3	10	17	24	31	M		7	14	21	28	M		5	12	19	26	M	2	9	16	23	30	M		7	14	21	28
T		7	14	21	28	T		4	11	18	25	T	1	8	15	22	29	T		6	13	20	27	T	3	10	17	24	T	1	8	15	22	29
W	1	8	15	22	29	W		5	12	19	26	W	2	9	16	23	30	W		7	14	21	28	W	4	11	18	25	W	2	9	16	23	30
T	2	9	16	23	30	T		6	13	20	27	T	3	10	17	24	T	1	8	15	22	29	T	5	12	19	26	T	3	10	17	24	31
F	3	10	17	24	31	F		7	14	21	28	F	4	11	18	25	F	2	9	16	23	30	F	6	13	20	27	F	4	11	18	25
S	4	11	18	25	S	1	8	15	22	29	S	5	12	19	26	S	3	10	17	24	31	S	7	14	21	28	S	5	12	19	26

Paulinus, Bishop of York, Missionary, 644 (CW Readings see Common of the Saints especially   White *or* Green
Matt. 28.16–20)   *Thomas Traherne, Poet, Spiritual Writer, 1674*

	EUCHARIST CW	MORNING PRAYER	EVENING PRAYER
Psalms:	105.1–7	*76*; 79	81; *84*
Readings:	Gal. 3.22–end; Luke 11.27–28	2 Kgs 4.1–37; Acts 25.13–end	1 Macc. 2.49–end *or* 2 Chr. 15.1–15; Mark 14.66–end
AW		*Dan. 6.6–23*	*Rev. 12.7–12*

	HOLY COMMUNION BCP	MORNING PRAYER	EVENING PRAYER
Psalms:		*50; 51; 52*	*53; 54; 55*
Readings:		*Job 11;* *Eph. 3*	*Job 12;* *Luke 3.1–22*
Hymns:	....	....	....

CW COLLECT
God our saviour,
who sent Paulinus to preach and to baptise,
and so to build up your Church in this land:
grant that, inspired by his example,
we may tell all the world of your truth,
that with him we may receive
the reward you prepare for all your faithful servants;
through Jesus Christ your Son our Lord,
who is alive and reigns with you,
in the unity of the Holy Spirit,
one God, now and for ever.

POST COMMUNION
Holy Father, who gathered us here around
the table of your Son to share this meal
with the whole household of God:
in that new world where you reveal
    the fullness of your peace,
gather people of every race and language
to share with Paulinus and all your saints
in the eternal banquet of Jesus Christ our Lord.

2021

January					
S		3	10	17	24	31
M		4	11	18	25
T		5	12	19	26
W		6	13	20	27
T		7	14	21	28
F	1	8	15	22	29
S	2	9	16	23	30

February				
S		7	14	21	28
M	1	8	15	22
T	2	9	16	23
W	3	10	17	24
T	4	11	18	25
F	5	12	19	26
S	6	13	20	27

March				
S		7	14	21	28
M	1	8	15	22	29
T	2	9	16	23	30
W	3	10	17	24	31
T	4	11	18	25
F	5	12	19	26
S	6	13	20	27

April				
S		4	11	18	25
M		5	12	19	26
T		6	13	20	27
W		7	14	21	28
T	1	8	15	22	29
F	2	9	16	23	30
S	3	10	17	24

May				
S		2	9	16	23	30
M		3	10	17	24	31
T		4	11	18	25
W		5	12	19	26
T		6	13	20	27
F		7	14	21	28
S	1	8	15	22	29

June				
S		6	13	20	27
M		7	14	21	28
T	1	8	15	22	29
W	2	9	16	23	30
T	3	10	17	24
F	4	11	18	25
S	5	12	19	26

THE EIGHTEENTH SUNDAY AFTER TRINITY

(Green)

	PRINCIPAL SERVICE CW Proper 23	**THIRD SERVICE**	**SECOND SERVICE**
Psalms:	*106.1–6, 19–23** 23	138; 141	139.1–18*
Readings:	*Exod. 32.1–14;* Isa. 25.1–9; Phil. 4.1–9; Matt. 22.1–14	Isa. 50.4–10; Luke 13.22–30	Prov. 3.1–18; 1 John 3.1–15 [Mark 10.17–31]

	HOLY COMMUNION BCP Trinity 18	**MORNING PRAYER**	**EVENING PRAYER**
Psalms:	122	*138; 141*	*139.1–18**
Readings:	*Deut. 6.4–9;* 1 Cor. 1.4–8; Matt. 22.34–end	*Jer. 26;* Luke 12.1–34 or 1 Pet. 1.22—2.10	*Jer. 30.1–3, 10–22* or *Jer. 31.1–20;* John 13 or 1 John 1.1—2.11
Hymns:	....	....	....

2020

July					August						September					October					November					December			
S	5	12	19	26	S		2	9	16	23	30	S		6	13	20	27	S		4	11	18	25	S	1	8	15	22	29	S		6	13	20	27
M	6	13	20	27	M		3	10	17	24	31	M		7	14	21	28	M		5	12	19	26	M	2	9	16	23	30	M		7	14	21	28
T	7	14	21	28	T		4	11	18	25		T	1	8	15	22	29	T		6	13	20	27	T	3	10	17	24		T	1	8	15	22	29
W	1	8	15	22	29	W		5	12	19	26	W	2	9	16	23	30	W		7	14	21	28	W	4	11	18	25	W	2	9	16	23	30
T	2	9	16	23	30	T		6	13	20	27	T	3	10	17	24		T	1	8	15	22	29	T	5	12	19	26	T	3	10	17	24	31
F	3	10	17	24	31	F		7	14	21	28	F	4	11	18	25		F	2	9	16	23	30	F	6	13	20	27	F	4	11	18	25
S	4	11	18	25	S	1	8	15	22	29	S	5	12	19	26		S	3	10	17	24	31	S	7	14	21	28	S	5	12	19	26

CW COLLECTS

Almighty and everlasting God,
increase in us your gift of faith
that, forsaking what lies behind
and reaching out to that which is before,
we may run the way of your commandments
and win the crown of everlasting joy;
through Jesus Christ your Son our Lord,
who is alive and reigns with you,
in the unity of the Holy Spirit,
one God, now and for ever.

or

God, our judge and saviour,
teach us to be open to your truth
and to trust in your love,
that we may live each day
with confidence in the salvation which is given
    through Jesus Christ our Lord.

POST COMMUNION

We praise and thank you, O Christ,
for this sacred feast:
for here we receive you,
here the memory of your passion is renewed,
here our minds are filled with grace,
and here a pledge of future glory is given,
when we shall feast at that table where you reign
with all your saints for ever.
through Jesus Christ thy Son our Lord,
who liveth and reigneth with thee,
in the unity of the Holy Spirit,
one God, now and for ever.

BCP COLLECT

*Lord, we beseech thee, grant thy people grace to
withstand the temptations of the world, the flesh, and
the devil, and with pure hearts and minds to follow
thee the only God; through Jesus Christ our Lord.*

2021

January						February					March					April					May					June				
S		3	10	17	24 31	S		7	14	21 28	S		7	14	21 28	S		4	11	18 25	S		2	9	16 23 30	S		6	13	20 27
M		4	11	18	25	M	1	8	15	22	M	1	8	15	22 29	M		5	12	19 26	M		3	10	17 24 31	M		7	14	21 28
T		5	12	19	26	T	2	9	16	23	T	2	9	16	23 30	T		6	13	20 27	T		4	11	18 25	T	1	8	15	22 29
W		6	13	20	27	W	3	10	17	24	W	3	10	17	24 31	W		7	14	21 28	W		5	12	19 26	W	2	9	16	23 30
T		7	14	21	28	T	4	11	18	25	T	4	11	18	25	T	1	8	15	22 29	T		6	13	20 27	T	3	10	17	24
F	1	8	15	22	29	F	5	12	19	26	F	5	12	19	26	F	2	9	16	23 30	F		7	14	21 28	F	4	11	18	25
S	2	9	16	23	30	S	6	13	20	27	S	6	13	20	27	S	3	10	17	24	S	1	8	15	22 29	S	5	12	19	26

Wilfrid, of Ripon, Bishop, Missionary, 709 (CW Readings see Common of the Saints especially   White *or* Green
Luke 1.5–11 also 1 Cor. 1.18–25)   *Elizabeth Fry, Prison Reformer, 1845. Edith Cavell, Nurse, 1915*

DEL Wk 28	**EUCHARIST** CW	**MORNING PRAYER**	**EVENING PRAYER**
Psalms:	113	*80*; 82 (Week 5 Ord.)	*85*; 86
Readings:	Gal. 4.21–24, 26–27, 31, 5.1; Luke 11.29–32	2 Kgs 5; Acts 26.1–23	1 Macc. 3.1–26 *or* 2 Chr. 17.1–12; Mark 15.1–15
AW		*2 Sam. 22.4–7, 17–20*	*Heb. 7.26—8.6*
	HOLY COMMUNION BCP	**MORNING PRAYER**	**EVENING PRAYER**
Psalms:		*62; 63; 64*	*65; 66; 67*
Readings:		*Job 13; Eph. 4.1–16*	*Job 14; Luke 4.1–30*
Hymns:			

CW COLLECT
Almighty God,
who called our forebears to the light of the gospel
    by the preaching of your servant Wilfrid:
help us, who keep his life and labour in
    remembrance,
to glorify your name by following the example
    of his zeal and perseverance;
through Jesus Christ your Son our Lord,
who is alive and reigns with you,
in the unity of the Holy Spirit,
one God, now and for ever.

POST COMMUNION
Holy Father,
who gathered us here around the table of your Son
to share this meal with the whole household of God:
in that new world where you reveal
    the fullness of your peace,
gather people of every race and language
to share with Wilfrid and all your saints
in the eternal banquet of Jesus Christ our Lord.

Sunrise 07.20; Sunset 18.11

Edward the Confessor, King of England, 1066 (CW Readings see Common of the Saints   White *or* Green
also 2 Sam. 23.1–5; 1 John 4.13–16) *Translated 1163 (BCP)*

	EUCHARIST	MORNING PRAYER	EVENING PRAYER
	CW		
Psalms:	119.41–48	87; *89.1–18*	*89.19–end*
Readings:	Gal. 5.1–6;	2 Kgs 6.1–23;	1 Macc. 3.27–41 *or* 2 Chr. 18.1–27;
	Luke 11.37–41	Acts 26.24–end	Mark 15.16–32

		AW	*Prov. 22.17–end*	*2 Cor. 12.1–10*

	HOLY COMMUNION	MORNING PRAYER	EVENING PRAYER
	BCP Com. Confessor		
Psalms:	*37.30–35*	*68*	*69; 70*
Readings:	*Wisd. 7.7–14; 1 Cor. 2.6–13;*	*Job 15.1–16;*	*Job 16.1—17.2;*
	Matt. 13.51–52	*Eph. 4.17–30*	*Luke 4.31–end*
Hymns:	....	....	....

CW COLLECT

Sovereign God,
who set your servant Edward
    upon the throne of an earthly kingdom
and inspired him with zeal
    for the kingdom of heaven:
grant that we may so confess the faith of Christ
    by word and deed,
that we may, with all your saints,
inherit your eternal glory;
through Jesus Christ your Son our Lord,
who is alive and reigns with you,
in the unity of the Holy Spirit,
one God, now and for ever.

POST COMMUNION

God our redeemer,
who inspired Edward to witness to your love
and to work for the coming of your kingdom:
may we, who in this sacrament share the bread
    of heaven,
be fired by your Spirit to proclaim the gospel in
    our daily living and never to rest content until
    your kingdom come, on earth as it is in heaven;
through Jesus Christ our Lord.

BCP COLLECT

*O God, who hast enlightened thy Church by the
teaching of thy servant Edward: Enrich it evermore,
we beseech thee, with thy heavenly grace, and raise
up faithful witnesses, who by their life and doctrine
may set forth to all men the truth of thy salvation;
through Jesus Christ our Lord.*

Green

	EUCHARIST	**MORNING PRAYER**	**EVENING PRAYER**
	CW		
Psalms:	1	*119.105–128*	*91*; 93
Readings:	Gal. 5.18–end;	2 Kgs 9.1–16;	1 Macc. 3.42–end
	Luke 11.42–46	Acts 27.1–26	*or* 2 Chr. 18.28—end of 19;
			Mark 15.33–41

AW   *Hos. 14*   *Jas 2.14–26*

	HOLY COMMUNION	**MORNING PRAYER**	**EVENING PRAYER**
	BCP		
Psalms:		*71; 72*	*73; 74*
Readings:		Job 17.3–end;	Job 18;
		Eph. 4.31—5.21	Luke 5.1–16
Hymns:	....	....	....

2020

	July					August						September					October					November					December			
S		5	12	19	26	S		2	9	16	23	30	S		6	13	20	27	S		4	11	18	25	S	1	8	15	22	29	S		6	13	20	27
M		6	13	20	27	M		3	10	17	24	31	M		7	14	21	28	M		5	12	19	26	M	2	9	16	23	30	M		7	14	21	28
T		7	14	21	28	T		4	11	18	25		T	1	8	15	22	29	T		6	13	20	27	T	3	10	17	24		T	1	8	15	22	29
W	1	8	15	22	29	W		5	12	19	26		W	2	9	16	23	30	W		7	14	21	28	W	4	11	18	25		W	2	9	16	23	30
T	2	9	16	23	30	T		6	13	20	27		T	3	10	17	24		T	1	8	15	22	29	T	5	12	19	26		T	3	10	17	24	31
F	3	10	17	24	31	F		7	14	21	28		F	4	11	18	25		F	2	9	16	23	30	F	6	13	20	27		F	4	11	18	25	
S	4	11	18	25		S	1	8	15	22	29		S	5	12	19	26		S	3	10	17	24	31	S	7	14	21	28		S	5	12	19	26	

Teresa of Avila, Teacher of the Faith, 1582 (CW Readings see Common of the Saints also Rom. 8.22–27)   *White or Green*

	EUCHARIST	**MORNING PRAYER**	**EVENING PRAYER**
	CW		
Psalms:	98.1–4	90; *92*	*94*
Readings:	Eph. 1.1–10;	2 Kgs 9.17–end;	1 Macc. 4.1–25 *or* 2 Chr. 20.1–23;
	Luke 11.47–end	Acts 27.27–end	Mark 15.42–end

AW   *Isa. 24.1–15*   *John 16.25–33*

	HOLY COMMUNION	**MORNING PRAYER**	**EVENING PRAYER**
	BCP		
Psalms:		*75; 76; 77*	*78*
Readings:		*Job 19;*	*Job 21;*
		Eph. 5.22–end	*Luke 5.17–end*
Hymns:	....	....	....

CW COLLECT

Merciful God,
who by your Spirit raised up your servant
    Teresa of Avila
    to reveal to your Church the way of perfection:
grant that her teaching
may awaken in us a longing for holiness,
until we attain to the perfect union of love
in Jesus Christ your Son our Lord,
who is alive and reigns with you,
in the unity of the Holy Spirit,
one God, now and for ever.

POST COMMUNION

God of truth
whose Wisdom set her table
and invited us to eat the bread
and drink the wine of the kingdom:
help us to lay aside all foolishness
and to live and walk in the way of insight,
that we may come with Teresa of Avila to
    the eternal feast of heaven;
through Jesus Christ our Lord.

2021

January						February					March					April					May					June			
S		3	10	17	24	31	S			7	14	21	28	S			7	14	21	28	S		4	11	18	25	S		2	9	16	23	30	S		6	13	20	27
M		4	11	18	25	M	1	8	15	22	M	1	8	15	22	29	M		5	12	19	26	M		3	10	17	24	31	M		7	14	21	28
T		5	12	19	26	T	2	9	16	23	T	2	9	16	23	30	T		6	13	20	27	T		4	11	18	25	T	1	8	15	22	29
W		6	13	20	27	W	3	10	17	24	W	3	10	17	24	31	W		7	14	21	28	W		5	12	19	26	W	2	9	16	23	30
T		7	14	21	28	T	4	11	18	25	T	4	11	18	25	T	1	8	15	22	29	T		6	13	20	27	T	3	10	17	24
F	1	8	15	22	29	F	5	12	19	26	F	5	12	19	26	F	2	9	16	23	30	F		7	14	21	28	F	4	11	18	25
S	2	9	16	23	30	S	6	13	20	27	S	6	13	20	27	S	3	10	17	24	S	1	8	15	22	29	S	5	12	19	26

Nicholas Ridley, Bishop of London, and Hugh Latimer, Bishop of Worcester, Reformation Martyrs, 1555   Green

	EUCHARIST	**MORNING PRAYER**	**EVENING PRAYER**
	CW		
Psalms:	33.1–6	*88*; (95)	*102*
Readings:	Eph. 1.11–14;	2 Kgs 12.1–19;	1 Macc. 4.26–35
	Luke 12.1–7	Acts 28.1–16	*or* 2 Chr. 22.10—end of 23;
			Mark 16.1–8

AW   *Jer. 14.1–9*   *Luke 23.44–56*

	HOLY COMMUNION	**MORNING PRAYER**	**EVENING PRAYER**
	BCP		
Psalms:		*79; 80; 81*	*82; 83; 84; 85*
Readings:		*Job 22;*	*Job 23;*
		Eph. 6.1–9	*Luke 6.1–19*
Hymns:	....	....	....

2020

	July					August						September					October					November					December			
S		5	12	19	26		2	9	16	23	30		6	13	20	27		4	11	18	25		1	8	15	22	29		6	13	20	27
M		6	13	20	27		3	10	17	24	31		7	14	21	28		5	12	19	26		2	9	16	23	30		7	14	21	28
T		7	14	21	28		4	11	18	25			1	8	15	22	29		6	13	20	27		3	10	17	24		1	8	15	22	29
W	1	8	15	22	29		5	12	19	26		2	9	16	23	30		7	14	21	28		4	11	18	25		2	9	16	23	30
T	2	9	16	23	30		6	13	20	27		3	10	17	24		1	8	15	22	29		5	12	19	26		3	10	17	24	31
F	3	10	17	24	31		7	14	21	28		4	11	18	25		2	9	16	23	30		6	13	20	27		4	11	18	25
S	4	11	18	25		1	8	15	22	29		5	12	19	26		3	10	17	24	31		7	14	21	28		5	12	19	26

Ignatius, Bishop of Antioch, Martyr, c.107 (CW Readings see Common of the Saints
also Phil. 3.7–12; John 6.52–58) *Etheldreda, Virgin, Ely, 697 (BCP)*

Green *or* Red

	EUCHARIST	**MORNING PRAYER**	**EVENING PRAYER**
	CW		
Psalms:	8	96; *97*; 100	*104*
Readings:	Eph. 1.15–end;	2 Kgs 17.1–23;	1 Macc. 4.36–end *or* 2 Chr. 24.1–22;
	Luke 12.8–12	Acts 28.17–end	Mark 16.9–end *or* Eve of Luke:
			Ps. 33; Hos. 6.1–3; 2 Tim. 3.10–end

		AW	*Zech. 8.14–end*	*John 20.19–end*

	HOLY COMMUNION	**MORNING PRAYER**	**EVENING PRAYER**
	BCP Com. Virgin		
Psalms:	*131*	*86; 87; 88*	*89*
Readings:	*Ecclus 51.10–12; Phil. 3.7–14;*	*Job 24;*	*Job 25.1–26.end;*
	Matt. 25.1–13	*Eph. 6.10–end*	*Luke 6.20–38 or First Evensong of*
			St Luke: Isa. 55; Luke 1.1–4;
Hymns:	....	....	....

CW COLLECT
Feed us, O Lord, with the living bread
and make us drink deep of the cup of salvation
that, following the teaching of your bishop Ignatius
and rejoicing in the faith
    with which he embraced a martyr's death,
we may be nourished for that eternal life
    for which he longed;
through Jesus Christ your Son our Lord,
who is alive and reigns with you,
in the unity of the Holy Spirit,
one God, now and for ever.

POST COMMUNION
Eternal God,
who gave us this holy meal
in which we have celebrated the glory of the cross
and the victory of your martyr Ignatius:
by our communion with Christ
in his saving death and resurrection,
give us with all your saints the courage
    to conquer evil
and so to share the fruit of the tree of life;
through Jesus Christ our Lord.

BCP COLLECT
*O God, who didst endue thy Holy Virgin Etheldreda
to witness a good confession: Grant that we, after her
example, may be found ready when the Bridegroom
cometh, and enter with him into the marriage feast;
through the same thy Son Jesus Christ our Lord.*

2021

	January						February					March					April					May					June			
S		3	10	17	24	31		7	14	21	28		7	14	21	28		4	11	18	25		2	9	16	23	30		6	13	20	27
M		4	11	18	25		1	8	15	22		1	8	15	22	29		5	12	19	26		3	10	17	24	31		7	14	21	28
T		5	12	19	26		2	9	16	23		2	9	16	23	30		6	13	20	27		4	11	18	25		1	8	15	22	29
W		6	13	20	27		3	10	17	24		3	10	17	24	31		7	14	21	28		5	12	19	26		2	9	16	23	30
T		7	14	21	28		4	11	18	25		4	11	18	25		1	8	15	22	29		6	13	20	27		3	10	17	24
F	1	8	15	22	29		5	12	19	26		5	12	19	26		2	9	16	23	30		7	14	21	28		4	11	18	25
S	2	9	16	23	30		6	13	20	27		6	13	20	27		3	10	17	24		1	8	15	22	29		5	12	19	26

LUKE THE EVANGELIST

(Red)

	PRINCIPAL SERVICE	**THIRD SERVICE**	**SECOND SERVICE**
	CW		
Psalms:	147.1–7	145; 146	103
Readings:	Isa. 35.3–6 *or* Acts 16.6–12a; 2 Tim. 4.5–17; Luke 10.1–9	Isa. 55; Luke 1.1–4	Ecclus 38.1–14 *or* Isa. 61.1–6; Col. 4.7–end [Luke 24.44–end*]

Seasonal provisions on Saints Days: CW Book p 328

Luke the Evangelist may be celebrated on Monday in which case use:

	CW Proper 24		
Psalms:	*99*; *96.1–9[10–end]*	145, 149 [BCP Var: 138]	142 [143.1–11]
Readings:	*Exod. 33.12–end*; *Isa. 45.1–7*; *1 Thess. 1.1–10*; *Matt. 22.15–22*	Isa. 54.1–14; Luke 13.31–35	Prov. 4.1–18 1 John 3.16—4.6; [Mark 10.35–45] *or* First Evensong of St Luke PS. 33; Hos. 6.1–3; 2 Tim. 3.1–17

	HOLY COMMUNION	**MORNING PRAYER**	**EVENING PRAYER**
	BCP St Luke		
Psalms:	*147.1–6*	*145; 146*	*103*
Readings:	*Isa. 35.3–6; 2 Tim. 4.5–15; Luke 10.1–9* or *Luke 7.36–50*	*Isa. 61.1–6*; *Acts 16.6–18*	*Ecclus 38.1–14*; *Col. 4.7–end*
Hymns:	....	....	....

CW COLLECT

Almighty God,
you called Luke the physician,
whose praise is in the gospel,
to be an evangelist and physician of the soul:
by the grace of the Spirit
and through the wholesome medicine of the gospel,
give your Church the same love and power to heal;
through Jesus Christ your Son our Lord,
who is alive and reigns with you,
in the unity of the Holy Spirit,
one God, now and for ever.

POST COMMUNION

Almighty God,
who on the day of Pentecost
sent your Holy Spirit to the apostles
with the wind from heaven and in tongues of flame,
filling them with joy and boldness
    to preach the gospel:
by the power of the same Spirit
strengthen us to witness to your truth
and to draw everyone to the fire of your love;
through Jesus Christ our Lord

BCP COLLECT

*Almighty God, who calledst Luke the Physician, whose praise
is in the Gospel, to be an Evangelist, and Physician of the soul;
May it please thee, that, by the wholesome medicines of the
doctrine delivered by him, all the diseases of our souls may be
healed; through the merits of thy Son Jesus Christ our Lord.*

CW COLLECTS for Trinity 19

O God, forasmuch as without you
we are not able to please you;
mercifully grant that your Holy Spirit
may in all things direct and rule our hearts;
through Jesus Christ your Son our Lord,
who is alive and reigns with you,
in the unity of the Holy Spirit,
one God, now and for ever.

or

Faithful Lord,
whose steadfast love never ceases
and whose mercies never come to an end:
grant us the grace to trust you
and to receive the gifts of your love,
new every morning,
in Jesus Christ our Lord.

POST COMMUNION

*Holy and blessed God,
you have fed us with the body and blood of your Son
and filled us with your Holy Spirit:
may we honour you,
not only with our lips
but in lives dedicated to the service
of Jesus Christ our Lord.*

BCP COLLECT

*O God, forasmuch as without thee we are not able to please
thee: Mercifully grant, that thy Holy Spirit may in all things
direct and rule our hearts; through Jesus Christ our Lord.*

2021

January						
S		3	10	17	24	31
M		4	11	18	25	
T		5	12	19	26	
W		6	13	20	27	
T		7	14	21	28	
F	1	8	15	22	29	
S	2	9	16	23	30	

February				
S		7	14	21	28
M	1	8	15	22
T	2	9	16	23
W	3	10	17	24
T	4	11	18	25
F	5	12	19	26
S	6	13	20	27

March					
S		7	14	21	28
M	1	8	15	22	29
T	2	9	16	23	30
W	3	10	17	24	31
T	4	11	18	25	
F	5	12	19	26	
S	6	13	20	27	

April				
S		4	11	18	25
M		5	12	19	26
T		6	13	20	27
W		7	14	21	28
T	1	8	15	22	29
F	2	9	16	23	30
S	3	10	17	24	

May				
S		2	9	16	23	30
M		3	10	17	24	31
T		4	11	18	25
W		5	12	19	26
T		6	13	20	27
F		7	14	21	28
S	1	8	15	22	29

June				
S		6	13	20	27
M		7	14	21	28
T	1	8	15	22	29
W	2	9	16	23	30
T	3	10	17	24	
F	4	11	18	25	
S	5	12	19	26	

Henry Martyn, Translator of the Scriptures, Missionary in India and Persia 1812   Green *or* White
(CW Readings see Common of the Saints especially Mark 16.15–20; also Isa. 55.6–11)

DEL Wk 29	EUCHARIST CW	MORNING PRAYER	EVENING PRAYER
Psalms:	100	*98*; 99; 101 (Week 6 Ord.)	*105** (or 103)
Readings:	Eph. 2.1–10; Luke 12.13–21	2 Kgs 17.24–end; Phil. 1.1–11	1 Macc. 6.1–17 *or* 2 Chr. 26.1–21; John 13.1–11
		AW *1 Kgs 3.3–14*	*1 Tim. 3.14—4.8*

	HOLY COMMUNION BCP	MORNING PRAYER	EVENING PRAYER
Psalms:		95; 96; 97	98; 99; 100; 101
Readings:		Job 27; 1 Tim. 1.1–17	Job 28; Luke 6.39—7.10
Hymns			

CW COLLECT
Almighty God,
who by your Holy Spirit gave Henry Martyn
a longing to tell the good news of Christ
and skill to translate the Scriptures:
by the same Spirit give us grace to offer you our gifts,
wherever you may lead, at whatever the cost;
through Jesus Christ your Son our Lord,
who is alive and reigns with you,
in the unity of the Holy Spirit,
one God, now and for ever.

POST COMMUNION
Holy Father,
who gathered us here around the table of your Son
to share this meal with the whole household of God:
in that new world where you reveal
   the fullness of your peace,
gather people of every race and language
to share with Henry Martyn and all your saints
in the eternal banquet of Jesus Christ our Lord.

Sunrise 07.32; Sunset 17.56

2020

	July					August						September					October					November					December			
S		5	12	19	26		2	9	16	23	30		6	13	20	27		4	11	18	25	S	1	8	15	22	29		6	13	20	27
M		6	13	20	27		3	10	17	24	31		7	14	21	28		5	12	19	26	M	2	9	16	23	30		7	14	21	28
T		7	14	21	28		4	11	18	25			1	8	15	22	29		6	13	20	27	T	3	10	17	24		1	8	15	22	29
W	1	8	15	22	29		5	12	19	26		2	9	16	23	30		7	14	21	28	W	4	11	18	25		2	9	16	23	30
T	2	9	16	23	30		6	13	20	27		3	10	17	24		1	8	15	22	29	T	5	12	19	26		3	10	17	24	31
F	3	10	17	24	31		7	14	21	28		4	11	18	25		2	9	16	23	30	F	6	13	20	27		4	11	18	25
S	4	11	18	25		1	8	15	22	29		5	12	19	26		3	10	17	24	31	S	7	14	21	28		5	12	19	26

Green

	EUCHARIST	MORNING PRAYER	EVENING PRAYER
	CW		
Psalms:	85.7–end	*106** (*or* 103)	*107**
Readings:	Eph. 2.12–end;	2 Kgs 18.1–12;	1 Macc. 6.18–47 *or* 2 Chr. 28;
	Luke 12.35–38	Phil. 1.12–end	John 13.12–20

AW		*Prov. 27.11–end*	*Gal. 6.1–10*

	HOLY COMMUNION	MORNING PRAYER	EVENING PRAYER
	BCP		
Psalms:		102; 103	104
Readings:		Job 29.1—30.1;	Job 31.13–end;
		1 Tim. 1.18—end of 2	Luke 7.11–35
Hymns	....	....	....

Green

	EUCHARIST	**MORNING PRAYER**	**EVENING PRAYER**
	CW		
Psalms:	98	110; *111*; 112	*119.129–152*
Readings:	Eph. 3.2–12;	2 Kgs 18.13–end;	1 Macc. 7.1–20 *or* 2 Chr. 29.1–19;
	Luke 12.39–48	Phil. 2.1–13	John 13.21–30

AW   *Isa. 51.1–6*   *2 Cor. 1.1–11*

	HOLY COMMUNION	**MORNING PRAYER**	**EVENING PRAYER**
	BCP		
Psalms:		*105*	*106*
Readings:		*Job 32;*	*Job 33;*
		1 Tim. 3	*Luke 7.36–end*
Hymns:	....	....	....

2020

	July					August						September					October					November						December			
S		5	12	19	26	S		2	9	16	23	30	S		6	13	20	27	S		4	11	18	25	S	1	8	15	22	29	S		6	13	20	27
M		6	13	20	27	M		3	10	17	24	31	M		7	14	21	28	M		5	12	19	26	M	2	9	16	23	30	M		7	14	21	28
T		7	14	21	28	T		4	11	18	25		T	1	8	15	22	29	T		6	13	20	27	T	3	10	17	24		T	1	8	15	22	29
W	1	8	15	22	29	W		5	12	19	26		W	2	9	16	23	30	W		7	14	21	28	W	4	11	18	25		W	2	9	16	23	30
T	2	9	16	23	30	T		6	13	20	27		T	3	10	17	24		T	1	8	15	22	29	T	5	12	19	26		T	3	10	17	24	31
F	3	10	17	24	31	F		7	14	21	28		F	4	11	18	25		F	2	9	16	23	30	F	6	13	20	27		F	4	11	18	25	
S	4	11	18	25		S	1	8	15	22	29		S	5	12	19	26		S	3	10	17	24	31	S	7	14	21	28		S	5	12	19	26	

Green

	EUCHARIST	MORNING PRAYER	EVENING PRAYER
	CW		
Psalms:	33.1–6	113; *115*	114; *116*; 117
Readings:	Eph. 3.14–end; Luke 12.49–53	2 Kgs 19.1–19; Phil. 2.14–end	1 Macc. 7.21–end *or* 2 Chr. 29.20–end; John 13.31–end

AW   *Ecclus 18.1–14* or *Job 26*   *1 Cor. 11.17–end*

	HOLY COMMUNION	MORNING PRAYER	EVENING PRAYER
	BCP		
Psalms:		107	108; 109
Readings:		*Job 38.1–21;* *1 Tim. 4*	*Job 38.22–end;* *Luke 8.1–21*
Hymns:	....	....	....

Green

	EUCHARIST		**MORNING PRAYER**	**EVENING PRAYER**
	CW			
Psalms:	24.1–6		*139*	*130*; 131; 137
Readings:	Eph. 4.1–6; Luke 12.54–end		2 Kgs 19.20–36; Phil. 3.1—4.1	1 Macc. 9.1–22 *or* 2 Chr. 30; John 14.1–14
		AW	*Ecclus 28.2–12* or *Job 19.21–end*	*Mark 15.33–47*
	HOLY COMMUNION		**MORNING PRAYER**	**EVENING PRAYER**
	BCP			
Psalms:			*110; 111; 112; 113*	*114; 115*
Readings:			*Job 39;* *1 Tim. 5*	*Job 40;* *Luke 8.22–end*
Hymns:	....		....	....

2020

	July					August						September					October					November					December			
S		5	12	19	26		2	9	16	23	30		6	13	20	27		4	11	18	25		1	8	15	22	29		6	13	20	27
M		6	13	20	27		3	10	17	24	31		7	14	21	28		5	12	19	26		2	9	16	23	30		7	14	21	28
T		7	14	21	28		4	11	18	25			1	8	15	22	29		6	13	20	27		3	10	17	24		1	8	15	22	29
W	1	8	15	22	29		5	12	19	26			2	9	16	23	30		7	14	21	28		4	11	18	25		2	9	16	23	30
T	2	9	16	23	30		6	13	20	27			3	10	17	24		1	8	15	22	29		5	12	19	26		3	10	17	24	31
F	3	10	17	24	31		7	14	21	28			4	11	18	25		2	9	16	23	30		6	13	20	27		4	11	18	25	
S	4	11	18	25		1	8	15	22	29			5	12	19	26		3	10	17	24	31		7	14	21	28		5	12	19	26	

Green

	EUCHARIST	**MORNING PRAYER**	**EVENING PRAYER**
	CW		
Psalms:	122	120; *121*; 122	*118*
Readings:	Eph. 4.7–16;	2 Kgs 20;	1 Macc. 13.41–end, 14.4–15
	Luke 13.1–9	Phil. 4.2–end	*or* 2 Chr. 32.1–22;
			John 14.15–end

		AW	*Isa. 44.21–end*	*John 21.15–end*

	HOLY COMMUNION	**MORNING PRAYER**	**EVENING PRAYER**
	BCP		
Psalms:		*116; 117; 118*	*119.1–32*
Readings:		*Job 41;*	*Job 42;*
		1 Tim. 6	*Luke 9.1–17*
Hymns:	....	....	....

2021

	January					February					March					April					May					June			
S		3	10	17	24	31		7	14	21	28		7	14	21	28		4	11	18	25		2	9	16	23	30		6	13	20	27
M		4	11	18	25		1	8	15	22		1	8	15	22	29		5	12	19	26		3	10	17	24	31		7	14	21	28
T		5	12	19	26		2	9	16	23		2	9	16	23	30		6	13	20	27		4	11	18	25		1	8	15	22	29
W		6	13	20	27		3	10	17	24		3	10	17	24	31		7	14	21	28		5	12	19	26		2	9	16	23	30
T		7	14	21	28		4	11	18	25		4	11	18	25		1	8	15	22	29		6	13	20	27		3	10	17	24
F	1	8	15	22	29	5	12	19	26		5	12	19	26		2	9	16	23	30		7	14	21	28		4	11	18	25
S	2	9	16	23	30	6	13	20	27		6	13	20	27		3	10	17	24		1	8	15	22	29		5	12	19	26

THE LAST SUNDAY AFTER TRINITY
Trinity 20

(Green)

Bible Sunday   *British Summer time ends. Clocks go back one hour*

	PRINCIPAL SERVICE	**THIRD SERVICE**	**SECOND SERVICE**
	CW		
Psalms:	119.9–16	119.137–152	119.89–104
Readings:	Neh. 8.1–4a [5–6], 8–12;	Deut. 17.14–15, 18–end;	Isa. 55.1–11;
	Col. 3.12–17;	John 5.36b–end	Luke 4.14–30
	Matt. 24.30–35		

Seasonal provisions CW Book pp 326–327

Dedication Festival can take place on this day in which case use Readings for First Sunday in October

	HOLY COMMUNION	**MORNING PRAYER**	**EVENING PRAYER**
	BCP		
Psalms:	145.15–end	119.137–152	119.89–104
Readings:	*Prov. 9.1–6;*	*Ezek. 2;*	*Ezek. 3.4–21* or *Ezek. 13.1–16;*
	Eph. 5.15–21;	*Luke 13* or *1 Pet. 3.8—4.6*	*John 15* or *1 John 3*
	Matt. 22.1–14		
Hymns:	....	....	....

CW COLLECTS FOR BIBLE SUNDAY

Blessed Lord,
who caused all holy scriptures
  to be written for our learning:
help us so to hear them,
to read, mark, learn and inwardly digest them
that, through patience,
  and the comfort of your holy word,
we may embrace and for ever hold fast
  the hope of everlasting life,
which you have given us
in our Saviour Jesus Christ,
who is alive and reigns with you,
in the unity of the Holy Spirit,
one God, now and for ever.

or

Merciful God,
teach us to be faithful in change and uncertainty,
that trusting in your word
and obeying your will
we may enter the unfailing joy of Jesus Christ
  our Lord.

POST COMMUNION

God of all grace,
your Son Jesus Christ fed the hungry
with the bread of his life
and the word of his kingdom:
renew your people with your heavenly grace,
and in all our weakness
sustain us by your true and living bread;
who is alive and reigns, now and for ever.

BCP COLLECT for TRINITY 20

O Almighty and most merciful God, of thy bountiful goodness keep us, we beseech thee, from all things that may hurt us; that we, being ready both in body and soul, may cheerfully accomplish those things that thou wouldest have done; through Jesus Christ our Lord.

2021

January					February					March					April					May					June				
S		3	10	17	24	31		7	14	21	28		7	14	21	28		4	11	18	25		2	9	16	23	30		6	13	20	27
M		4	11	18	25		1	8	15	22		1	8	15	22	29		5	12	19	26		3	10	17	24	31		7	14	21	28
T		5	12	19	26		2	9	16	23		2	9	16	23	30		6	13	20	27		4	11	18	25		1	8	15	22	29
W		6	13	20	27		3	10	17	24		3	10	17	24	31		7	14	21	28		5	12	19	26		2	9	16	23	30
T		7	14	21	28		4	11	18	25		4	11	18	25		1	8	15	22	29		6	13	20	27		3	10	17	24
F	1	8	15	22	29	5	12	19	26		5	12	19	26		2	9	16	23	30		7	14	21	28		4	11	18	25
S	2	9	16	23	30	6	13	20	27		6	13	20	27		3	10	17	24		1	8	15	22	29		5	12	19	26

Alfred the Great, King of the West Saxons, Scholar, 899 (CW Readings see Common of the Saints   *White or Green*
also 2 Sam. 23.1–5; John 18.33–37) *Cedd, Abbott of Lastingham, Bishop of the East Saxons, 664*
Chad may be celebrated today with Cedd (see readings and collect for March 2)

DEL Wk 30	EUCHARIST CW		MORNING PRAYER	EVENING PRAYER
Psalms:	1		123; 124; 125; *126* (Week 7 Ord.)	*127*; 128; 129
Readings:	Eph. 4.32—5.8; Luke 13.10–17		2 Kgs 21.1–18; 1 Tim. 1.1–17	2 Macc. 4.7–17 or 2 Chr. 33.1–13; John 15.1–11
		AW	*Isa. 42.14–21*	*Luke 1.5–25*

	HOLY COMMUNION BCP	MORNING PRAYER	EVENING PRAYER
Psalms:		*119.105–144*	*119.145–end*
Readings:		*Prov. 1.1–19; Titus 1.1—2.8*	*Prov. 1.20–end; Luke 9.18–50*
Hymns:	....	....	....

CW COLLECT

God, our maker and redeemer,
we pray you of your great mercy
and by the power of your holy cross
to guide us by your will and to shield us
    from our foes:
that, after the example of your servant Alfred,
we may inwardly love you above all things;
through Jesus Christ your Son our Lord,
who is alive and reigns with you,
in the unity of the Holy Spirit,
one God, now and for ever.

POST COMMUNION

God our redeemer,
who inspired Alfred to witness to your love
and to work for the coming of your kingdom:
may we, who in this sacrament share
    the bread of heaven,
be fired by your Spirit to proclaim the gospel
in our daily living
and never to rest content until your kingdom come,
on earth as it is in heaven;
through Jesus Christ our Lord.

Sunrise 06.45; Sunset 16.41

2020

	July					August					September					October					November					December				
S		5	12	19	26		2	9	16	23	30		6	13	20	27		4	11	18	25		1	8	15	22	29		6	13	20	27
M		6	13	20	27		3	10	17	24	31		7	14	21	28		5	12	19	26		2	9	16	23	30		7	14	21	28
T		7	14	21	28		4	11	18	25		1	8	15	22	29		6	13	20	27		3	10	17	24		1	8	15	22	29
W	1	8	15	22	29		5	12	19	26	2	9	16	23	30		7	14	21	28		4	11	18	25		2	9	16	23	30
T	2	9	16	23	30		6	13	20	27	3	10	17	24		1	8	15	22	29		5	12	19	26		3	10	17	24	31
F	3	10	17	24	31		7	14	21	28	4	11	18	25		2	9	16	23	30		6	13	20	27		4	11	18	25
S	4	11	18	25	1	8	15	22	29	5	12	19	26		3	10	17	24	31		7	14	21	28		5	12	19	26

Green

	EUCHARIST	**MORNING PRAYER**	**EVENING PRAYER**
	CW		
Psalms:	128	*132*; 133	(134) *135*
Readings:	Eph. 5.21–end;	2 Kgs 22.1—23.3;	2 Macc. 6.12–end *or* 2 Chr. 34.1–18;
	Luke 13.18–21	1 Tim. 1.18—end of 2	John 15.12–17
			or Eve of Simon and Jude:
			Ps. 124, 125, 126; Deut. 32.1–4;
			John 14.15–26

| | | *AW* | *1 Sam. 4.12–end* | *Luke 1.57–80* |

	HOLY COMMUNION	**MORNING PRAYER**	**EVENING PRAYER**
	BCP		
Psalms:		*120; 121; 122; 123; 124; 125*	*126; 127; 128; 129; 130; 131*
Readings:		*Prov. 2;*	*Prov. 3.1–26;*
		Titus 2.9—end of 3	*Luke 9.51–end*
			or First Evensong of St Simon
			and St Jude:
			Isa. 28.9–16; Eph. 2.11–end

Hymns: ....

Simon and Jude, Apostles   Red

	PRINCIPAL SERVICE CW	THIRD SERVICE	SECOND SERVICE
Psalms:	119.89–96	116; 117 [BCP Var. 119.89–96]	119.1–16
Readings:	Isa. 28.14–16; Eph. 2.19–end; John 15.17–end	Wisd. 5.1–16 *or* Isa. 45.18–end; Luke 6.12–16	1 Macc. 2.42–66 *or* Jer. 3.11–18; Jude 1–4, 17–end [BCP Var. Eph. 2.19–end]

Seasonal provisions CW Book p 328

Displaced readings may be added to the previous or following day's portion

Readings:	Eph. 6.1–9; Luke 13.22–30	2 Kgs 23.4–25; 1 Tim. 3	2 Macc. 7.1–19 *or* 2 Chr. 34.19–end; John 15.18–end

	HOLY COMMUNION BCP St Simon and St Jude	MORNING PRAYER	EVENING PRAYER
Psalms:	*116.11–end*	*132; 133; 134; 135*	*136; 137; 138*
Readings:	*Isa. 28.9–16; Jude 1–8 or Rev. 21.9–14; John 15.17–27*	*Ecclus 2; Luke 6.12–23*	*1 Macc. 2.42–66; Jude 17–end*
Hymns:	....	....	....

CW COLLECT
Almighty God,
who built your Church upon the foundation
  of the apostles and prophets,
with Jesus Christ himself as the chief cornerstone:
so join us together in unity of spirit by their doctrine,
that we may be made a holy temple acceptable
  to you;
through Jesus Christ your Son our Lord,
who is alive and reigns with you,
in the unity of the Holy Spirit,
one God, now and for ever.

POST COMMUNION
Lord God, the source of truth and love,
keep us faithful to the apostles' teaching
  and fellowship,
united in prayer and the breaking of bread,
and one in joy and simplicity of heart,
in Jesus Christ our Lord.

BCP COLLECT
*O Almighty God, who hast built thy Church upon the
foundation of the Apostles and Prophets, Jesus Christ
himself being the head corner-stone: Grant us so to
be joined together in unity of spirit by their doctrine,
that we may be made an holy temple acceptable unto
thee; through Jesus Christ our Lord.*

2020

	July					August					September					October					November					December			
S		5	12	19	26		2	9	16	23	30		6	13	20	27		4	11	18	25		1	8	15	22	29		6	13	20	27
M		6	13	20	27		3	10	17	24	31		7	14	21	28		5	12	19	26		2	9	16	23	30		7	14	21	28
T		7	14	21	28		4	11	18	25		1	8	15	22	29		6	13	20	27		3	10	17	24		1	8	15	22	29
W	1	8	15	22	29		5	12	19	26		2	9	16	23	30		7	14	21	28		4	11	18	25		2	9	16	23	30
T	2	9	16	23	30		6	13	20	27		3	10	17	24		1	8	15	22	29		5	12	19	26		3	10	17	24	31
F	3	10	17	24	31		7	14	21	28		4	11	18	25		2	9	16	23	30		6	13	20	27		4	11	18	25
S	4	11	18	25		1	8	15	22	29		5	12	19	26		3	10	17	24	31		7	14	21	28		5	12	19	26

James Hannington, Bishop of Eastern Equatorial Africa, Martyr in Uganda, 1885
(CW Readings see Common of the Saints especially Matt. 10.28–39)

Red *or* Green

	EUCHARIST CW	**MORNING PRAYER**	**EVENING PRAYER**
Psalms:	144.1–2, 9–11	143; 146	138; 140; 141
Readings:	Eph. 6.10–20; Luke 13.31–end	2 Kgs 23.36—24.17; 1 Tim. 4	2 Macc. 7.20–41 *or* 2 Chr. 35.1–19; John 16.1–15

		AW	*Isa. 35*	*Matt. 11.2–19*

	HOLY COMMUNION BCP	**MORNING PRAYER**	**EVENING PRAYER**
Psalms:		*139; 140; 141*	*142; 143*
Readings:		*Prov. 6.1–19; 2 Tim. 2*	*Prov. 8; Luke 10.25–end*
Hymns:	....	....	....

CW COLLECT
Most merciful God,
who strengthened your Church by the steadfast
    courage of your martyr James Hannington:
grant that we also,
thankfully remembering his victory of faith,
may overcome what is evil
and glorify your holy name;
through Jesus Christ your Son our Lord,
who is alive and reigns with you,
in the unity of the Holy Spirit,
one God, now and for ever.

POST COMMUNION
Eternal God,
who gave us this holy meal
in which we have celebrated the glory of the cross
and the victory of your martyr James Hannington:
by our communion with Christ
in his saving death and resurrection,
give us with all your saints the courage to
    conquer evil
and so to share the fruit of the tree of life;
through Jesus Christ our Lord.

2021

	January					February				March				April				May					June			
S		3	10	17	24	31		7	14	21	28		7	14	21	28		4	11	18	25		2	9	16	23	30		6	13	20	27
M		4	11	18	25		1	8	15	22		1	8	15	22	29		5	12	19	26		3	10	17	24	31		7	14	21	28
T		5	12	19	26		2	9	16	23		2	9	16	23	30		6	13	20	27		4	11	18	25		1	8	15	22	29
W		6	13	20	27		3	10	17	24		3	10	17	24	31		7	14	21	28		5	12	19	26		2	9	16	23	30
T		7	14	21	28		4	11	18	25		4	11	18	25		1	8	15	22	29		6	13	20	27		3	10	17	24
F	1	8	15	22	29		5	12	19	26		5	12	19	26		2	9	16	23	30		7	14	21	28		4	11	18	25
S	2	9	16	23	30		6	13	20	27		6	13	20	27		3	10	17	24		1	8	15	22	29		5	12	19	26

Green

	EUCHARIST	MORNING PRAYER	EVENING PRAYER
	CW		
Psalms:	111	142; *144*	*145*
Readings:	Phil. 1.1–11; Luke 14.1–6	2 Kgs 24.18—25.12; 1 Tim. 5.1–16	Tobit 1 *or* 2 Chr. 35.20—36.10; John 16.16–22

AW		*2 Sam. 11.1–17*	*Matt. 14.1–12*

	HOLY COMMUNION	MORNING PRAYER	EVENING PRAYER
	BCP		
Psalms:		*144; 145; 146*	*147; 148; 149; 150*
Readings:		*Prov. 9;* *2 Tim. 3*	*Prov. 10.1–22;* *Luke 11.1–28*
Hymns:	....	....	....

Martin Luther, Reformer, 1546   Green

	EUCHARIST	MORNING PRAYER	EVENING PRAYER
	CW		
Psalms:	42.1–7	*147*	1; 5
Readings:	Phil. 1.18–26; Luke 14.1, 7–11	2 Kgs 25.22–end; 1 Tim. 5.17–end	First Evensong of All Saints Ps. 1, 5; Ecclus 44.1–15 *or* Isa. 40.27–end; Rev. 19.6–10

	AW	*Isa. 43.15–21*	*Acts 19.1–10*
	HOLY COMMUNION	MORNING PRAYER	EVENING PRAYER
	BCP		
Psalms:		144; 145; 146	*147; 148; 149; 150*
Readings:		*Prov. 11.1–25;* *2 Tim. 4*	*Prov. 12.10–end;* *Luke 11.29–end;* or *First Evensong of All Saints:* *Wisd. 3.1–9; Heb. 11.32—12.2* *E. Coll. All Saints*
Hymns:	....	....	....

Full Moon

2021

	January					February				March				April				May					June			
S		3	10	17	24	31			7	14	21	28			7	14	21	28			4	11	18	25			2	9	16	23	30			6	13	20	27
M		4	11	18	25			1	8	15	22		1	8	15	22	29			5	12	19	26			3	10	17	24	31			7	14	21	28
T		5	12	19	26			2	9	16	23		2	9	16	23	30			6	13	20	27			4	11	18	25		1	8	15	22	29
W		6	13	20	27			3	10	17	24		3	10	17	24	31			7	14	21	28			5	12	19	26		2	9	16	23	30
T		7	14	21	28			4	11	18	25		4	11	18	25		1	8	15	22	29			6	13	20	27		3	10	17	24
F	1	8	15	22	29			5	12	19	26		5	12	19	26		2	9	16	23	30			7	14	21	28		4	11	18	25
S	2	9	16	23	30			6	13	20	27		6	13	20	27		3	10	17	24		1	8	15	22	29		5	12	19	26

ALL SAINTS' DAY
Trinity 21

(White *or* Gold)

	PRINCIPAL SERVICE	**THIRD SERVICE**	**SECOND SERVICE**
	CW		
Psalms:	34.1–10	15; 84; 149	148; 150
Readings:	Rev. 7.9–end;	Isa. 35;	Isa. 65.17–end;
	1 John 3.1–3;	Luke 9.18–27	Heb. 11.32—12.2
	Matt. 5.1–12		[Luke 6.20–31*]

Seasonal provisions for All Saints' Day: CW Book pp 324–5

	HOLY COMMUNION	**MORNING PRAYER**	**EVENING PRAYER**
	BCP All Saints		
Psalms:	33.1–5	15; 84; 149	148; 150
Readings:	Isa. 66.20–23;	Wisd. 5.1–16;	Ecclus 44.1–15;
	Rev. 7.2–4,[5–8], 9–12;	Rev. 19.6–10	Rev. 7.9–end
	Matt. 5.1–12		
Hymns:	....	....	....

2020

	July	August	September	October	November	December
S	5 12 19 26	2 9 16 23 30	6 13 20 27	4 11 18 25	1 8 15 22 29	6 13 20 27
M	6 13 20 27	3 10 17 24 31	7 14 21 28	5 12 19 26	2 9 16 23 30	7 14 21 28
T	7 14 21 28	4 11 18 25	1 8 15 22 29	6 13 20 27	3 10 17 24	1 8 15 22 29
W	1 8 15 22 29	5 12 19 26	2 9 16 23 30	7 14 21 28	4 11 18 25	2 9 16 23 30
T	2 9 16 23 30	6 13 20 27	3 10 17 24	1 8 15 22 29	5 12 19 26	3 10 17 24 31
F	3 10 17 24 31	7 14 21 28	4 11 18 25	2 9 16 23 30	6 13 20 27	4 11 18 25
S	4 11 18 25	1 8 15 22 29	5 12 19 26	3 10 17 24 31	7 14 21 28	5 12 19 26

CW COLLECTS

Almighty God,
you have knit together your elect
in one communion and fellowship
    in the mystical body of your Son Christ our Lord:
grant us grace so to follow your blessed saints
in all virtuous and godly living
that we may come to those inexpressible joys
that you have prepared for those who truly love you;
through Jesus Christ your Son our Lord,
who is alive and reigns with you,
in the unity of the Holy Spirit,
one God, now and for ever.

or

God of holiness,
your glory is proclaimed in every age:
as we rejoice in the faith of your saints,
inspire us to follow their example
with boldness and joy;
through Jesus Christ our Lord.

POST COMMUNION

God, the source of all holiness
    and giver of all good things:
may we who have shared at this table
    as strangers and pilgrims here on earth
be welcomed with all your saints
    to the heavenly feast on the day of your kingdom;
through Jesus Christ our Lord.

BCP COLLECT

*O Almighty God, who hast knit together thine elect
in one communion and fellowship, in the mystical
body of thy Son Christ our Lord; Grant us grace so
to follow thy blessed Saints in all virtuous and godly
living, that we may come to those unspeakable joys,
which thou hast prepared for them that unfeignedly
love thee; through Jesus Christ our Lord.*

2021

	January						February						March						April						May						June			
S		3	10	17	24	31		7	14	21	28			7	14	21	28			4	11	18	25		2	9	16	23	30			6	13	20	27
M		4	11	18	25		1	8	15	22		1	8	15	22	29			5	12	19	26		3	10	17	24	31			7	14	21	28
T		5	12	19	26		2	9	16	23		2	9	16	23	30			6	13	20	27		4	11	18	25			1	8	15	22	29
W		6	13	20	27		3	10	17	24		3	10	17	24	31			7	14	21	28		5	12	19	26			2	9	16	23	30
T		7	14	21	28		4	11	18	25		4	11	18	25		1	8	15	22	29		6	13	20	27			3	10	17	24
F	1	8	15	22	29		5	12	19	26		5	12	19	26		2	9	16	23	30		7	14	21	28		4	11	18	25
S	2	9	16	23	30		6	13	20	27		6	13	20	27		3	10	17	24		1	8	15	22	29		5	12	19	26

Commemoration of the Faithful Departed (All Souls' Day)   Red *or* Green *or* Purple
CW Lesser Festival; EUCHARIST: Ps. 23 *or* 27.1–6, 16–end Lam. 3.17–26, 31–33 *or*
Wisd. 3.1–9; Rom. 5.5–11 *or* 1 Pet. 1.3–9; John 5.19–25 *or* John 6.37–40

DEL Wk 31	EUCHARIST		MORNING PRAYER	EVENING PRAYER
	CW			
Psalms:	131		*2*; 146	*92*; 96; 97
Readings:	Phil. 2.1–4;		Dan. 1;	Isa. 1.1–20;
	Luke 14.12–14		Rev. 1	Matt. 1.18–end
		AW	*Esther 3.1–11, 4.7–17*	*Matt. 18.1–10*

	HOLY COMMUNION	MORNING PRAYER	EVENING PRAYER
	BCP to celebrate All Souls' Day use CW provision		
Psalms:		9; 10; 11	12; 13; 14
Readings:		Prov. 14.9–27;	Prov. 15.18–end;
		Luke 12.1–34	Luke 12.35–53
Hymns:	....	....	....

CW COLLECT

Eternal God, our maker and redeemer,
grant us, with all the faithful departed,
the sure benefits of your Son's saving passion
    and glorious resurrection
that, in the last day,
when you gather up all things in Christ,
we may with them enjoy
    the fullness of your promises;
through Jesus Christ your Son our Lord,
who is alive and reigns with you,
in the unity of the Holy Spirit,
one God, now and for ever.

POST COMMUNION

God of love,
may the death and resurrection of Christ
which we have celebrated in this eucharist
bring us, with all the faithful departed,
into the peace of your eternal home.
We ask this in the name of Jesus Christ,
our rock and our salvation,
to whom be glory for time and for eternity.

Sunrise 06.58; Sunset 16.28

2020

July						August						September					October					November					December				
S		5	12	19	26	S		2	9	16	23	30	S		6	13	20	27	S		4	11	18	25	S	1	8	15	22	29	S		6	13	20	27
M		6	13	20	27	M		3	10	17	24	31	M		7	14	21	28	M		5	12	19	26	M	2	9	16	23	30	M		7	14	21	28
T		7	14	21	28	T		4	11	18	25		T	1	8	15	22	29	T		6	13	20	27	T	3	10	17	24		T	1	8	15	22	29
W	1	8	15	22	29	W		5	12	19	26		W	2	9	16	23	30	W		7	14	21	28	W	4	11	18	25		W	2	9	16	23	30
T	2	9	16	23	30	T		6	13	20	27		T	3	10	17	24		T	1	8	15	22	29	T	5	12	19	26		T	3	10	17	24	31
F	3	10	17	24	31	F		7	14	21	28		F	4	11	18	25		F	2	9	16	23	30	F	6	13	20	27		F	4	11	18	25
S	4	11	18	25		S	1	8	15	22	29	S	5	12	19	26		S	3	10	17	24	31	S	7	14	21	28		S	5	12	19	26

Richard Hooker, Priest, Anglican Apologist, Teacher of the Faith, 1600   Red *or* Green *or* White
(CW Readings see Common of the Saints especially John 16.12–15; also Ecclus 44.10–15).
Martin of Porres, Friar, 1639

	EUCHARIST	**MORNING PRAYER**	**EVENING PRAYER**
	CW		
Psalms:	22.22–27	5; 147.1–12	98; 99; *100*
Readings:	Phil. 2.5–11;	Dan. 2.1–24;	Isa. 1.21–end;
	Luke 14.15–24	Rev. 2.1–11	Matt. 2.1–15
		AW *Ezek. 18.21–end*	*Matt. 18.12–20*
	HOLY COMMUNION	**MORNING PRAYER**	**EVENING PRAYER**
	BCP		
Psalms:		*15; 16; 17*	*18*
Readings:		*Prov. 16.31—17.17;*	*Prov. 18.10–end;*
		Luke 12.54—13.9	*Luke 13.10–end*
Hymns:	....	....	....

CW COLLECT

God of peace, the bond of all love,
who in your Son Jesus Christ have made the
    human race your inseparable dwelling place:
after the example of your servant Richard Hooker,
give grace to us your servants ever to rejoice
    in the true inheritance of your adopted children
and to show forth your praises now and ever;
through Jesus Christ your Son our Lord,
who is alive and reigns with you,
in the unity of the Holy Spirit,
one God, now and for ever.

POST COMMUNION

God of truth,
whose Wisdom set her table
and invited us to eat the bread and drink the wine
    of the kingdom:
help us to lay aside all foolishness
and to live and walk in the way of insight,
that we may come with Richard Hooker
    to the eternal feast of heaven;
through Jesus Christ our Lord.

Red *or* Green

	EUCHARIST CW	**MORNING PRAYER**	**EVENING PRAYER**
Psalms:	27.1–5	*9*; 147.13–end	111; *112*; 116
Readings:	Phil. 2.12–18; Luke 14.25–33	Dan. 2.25–end; Rev. 2.12–end	Isa. 2.1–11; Matt. 2.16–end

AW *Prov. 3.27–end* *Matt. 18.21–end*

	HOLY COMMUNION BCP	**MORNING PRAYER**	**EVENING PRAYER**
Psalms:		*19; 20; 21*	*22; 23*
Readings:		*Prov. 20.1–22;* *Luke 14.1–24*	*Prov. 22.1–16;* *Luke 14.25—15.10*
Hymns:	....	....	....

2020

	July					August						September					October					November					December			
S		5	12	19	26		2	9	16	23	30		6	13	20	27		4	11	18	25		1	8	15	22	29		6	13	20	27
M		6	13	20	27		3	10	17	24	31		7	14	21	28		5	12	19	26		2	9	16	23	30		7	14	21	28
T		7	14	21	28		4	11	18	25		T	1	8	15	22	29		6	13	20	27		3	10	17	24		1	8	15	22	29
W	1	8	15	22	29		5	12	19	26		2	9	16	23	30		7	14	21	28		4	11	18	25		2	9	16	23	30
T	2	9	16	23	30		6	13	20	27		3	10	17	24		1	8	15	22	29		5	12	19	26		3	10	17	24	31
F	3	10	17	24	31		7	14	21	28		4	11	18	25		2	9	16	23	30		6	13	20	27		4	11	18	25
S	4	11	18	25		1	8	15	22	29		5	12	19	26		3	10	17	24	31		7	14	21	28		5	12	19	26

Red *or* Green

	EUCHARIST CW	**MORNING PRAYER**	**EVENING PRAYER**
Psalms:	105.1–7	11; *15*; 148	*118*
Readings:	Phil. 3.3–8a; Luke 15.1–10	Dan. 3.1–18; Rev. 3.1–13	Isa. 2.12–end; Matt. 3

		AW	*Exod. 23.1–9*	*Matt. 19.1–15*

	HOLY COMMUNION BCP	**MORNING PRAYER**	**EVENING PRAYER**
Psalms:		*24; 25; 26*	*27; 28; 29*
Readings:		*Prov. 24.23–end;* *Luke 15.11–end*	*Prov. 25;* *Luke 16*
Hymns:	....	....	....

Leonard, Hermit, 6th century (BCP)
William Temple, Archbishop of Canterbury, Teacher of the Faith, 1944

Red, Green (*or White*)

	EUCHARIST	MORNING PRAYER	EVENING PRAYER
	CW		
Psalms:	122	*16*; 149	137; 138; *143*
Readings:	Phil. 3.17—4.1; Luke 16.1–8	Dan. 3.19–end; Rev. 3.14–end	Isa. 3.1–15; Matt. 4.1–11

	AW	Prov. 3.13–18	Matt. 19.16–end
	HOLY COMMUNION	MORNING PRAYER	EVENING PRAYER
	BCP Com Abbot		
Psalms:	1	30; 31	32; 33; 34
Readings:	Prov. 10.27–32; 1 John 2.15–17; Luke 6.20–23a	Prov. 26.12–end; Luke 17.1–19	Prov. 27.1–22; Luke 17.20–end
Hymns:	....	....	....

BCP COLLECT
O God, by whose grace the blessed Abbot Leonard enkindled with the fire of thy love, became a burning and a shining light in thy Church: Grant that we may be inflamed with the same spirit of discipline and love, and ever walk before thee as children of light; through Jesus Christ our Lord.

2020

	July					August						September					October					November					December			
S		5	12	19	26		2	9	16	23	30		6	13	20	27		4	11	18	25		1	8	15	22	29		6	13	20	27
M		6	13	20	27		3	10	17	24	31		7	14	21	28		5	12	19	26		2	9	16	23	30		7	14	21	28
T		7	14	21	28		4	11	18	25			1	8	15	22	29		6	13	20	27		3	10	17	24		1	8	15	22	29
W	1	8	15	22	29		5	12	19	26		2	9	16	23	30		7	14	21	28		4	11	18	25		2	9	16	23	30
T	2	9	16	23	30		6	13	20	27		3	10	17	24		1	8	15	22	29		5	12	19	26		3	10	17	24	31
F	3	10	17	24	31		7	14	21	28		4	11	18	25		2	9	16	23	30		6	13	20	27		4	11	18	25
S	4	11	18	25		1	8	15	22	29		5	12	19	26		3	10	17	24	31		7	14	21	28		5	12	19	26

Willibrord of York, Bishop, Apostle of Frisia, 739 (CW Readings see Common of the Saints   Red, Green *or* White
especially Isa. 52.7–10; Matt. 28.16–end)

	EUCHARIST	**MORNING PRAYER**	**EVENING PRAYER**
	CW		
Psalms:	112	*18.31–end*; 150	*145*
Readings:	Phil. 4.10–19;	Dan. 4.1–18;	Isa. 4.2—5.7;
	Luke 16.9–15	Rev. 4	Matt. 4.12–22
	AW	*Deut. 28.1–6*	*Matt. 20.1–16*
	HOLY COMMUNION	**MORNING PRAYER**	**EVENING PRAYER**
	BCP		
Psalms:		*35; 36*	*37*
Readings		*Prov. 30.1–16;*	*Prov. 31.10–end;*
		Luke 18.1–30	*Luke 18.31—19.10;*
			E. Coll. Trinity 22
Hymns:	....	....	....

CW COLLECT
God, the saviour of all,
you sent your bishop Willibrord from this land
to proclaim the good news to many peoples
and confirm them in their faith:
help us also to witness to your steadfast love
    by word and deed
so that your Church may increase
    and grow strong in holiness;
through Jesus Christ your Son our Lord,
who is alive and reigns with you,
in the unity of the Holy Spirit,
one God, now and for ever.

POST COMMUNION
Holy Father,
who gathered us here around the table of your Son
to share this meal with the whole household of God:
in that new world where you reveal
    the fullness of your peace,
gather people of every race and language
to share with Willibrord and all your saints
in the eternal banquet of Jesus Christ our Lord.

2021

January	February	March	April	May	June
S 3 10 17 24 31	S 7 14 21 28	S 7 14 21 28	S 4 11 18 25	S 2 9 16 23 30	S 6 13 20 27
M 4 11 18 25	M 1 8 15 22	M 1 8 15 22 29	M 5 12 19 26	M 3 10 17 24 31	M 7 14 21 28
T 5 12 19 26	T 2 9 16 23	T 2 9 16 23 30	T 6 13 20 27	T 4 11 18 25	T 1 8 15 22 29
W 6 13 20 27	W 3 10 17 24	W 3 10 17 24 31	W 7 14 21 28	W 5 12 19 26	W 2 9 16 23 30
T 7 14 21 28	T 4 11 18 25	T 4 11 18 25	T 1 8 15 22 29	T 6 13 20 27	T 3 10 17 24
F 1 8 15 22 29	F 5 12 19 26	F 5 12 19 26	F 2 9 16 23 30	F 7 14 21 28	F 4 11 18 25
S 2 9 16 23 30	S 6 13 20 27	S 6 13 20 27	S 3 10 17 24	S 1 8 15 22 29	S 5 12 19 26

THE THIRD SUNDAY BEFORE ADVENT
Trinity 22

(Red or Green)

Remembrance Sunday

	PRINCIPAL SERVICE CW	**THIRD SERVICE**	**SECOND SERVICE**
Psalms:	*Canticle:* Wisd. 6.17–20 *or* Ps. 70	91	[20] 82
Readings:	Wisd. 6.12–16; 1 Thess. 4.13–end; Matt. 25.1–13 *or* Ps. 70 Amos 5.18–24; 1 Thess. 4.13–end; Matt. 25.1–13	Deut. 17.14–end; 1 Tim. 2.1–7	Judg. 7.2–22; John 15.9–17

Seasonal provisions: CW Book pp 326–327

	HOLY COMMUNION BCP	**MORNING PRAYER**	**EVENING PRAYER**
Psalms:	133	91	[20] 82
Readings:	Gen. 45.1–7, 15; Phil. 1.3–11; Matt. 18.21–end For Remembrance Sunday	Ezek. 34.1–16; Luke 14.25—15.10 or 2 Pet. 1 Mic. 4.1–5; Rom. 8.31–end;	Ezek. 34.17–end or Ezek. 37.15–end; John 17 or 1 John 5 Ecclus 51.1–12; 1 Cor. 15.50–end

Or any of the following: John 14.1–8; John 15.9–17; Rom. 8.31–39; 1 Thess. 4.13–18; 2 Thess. 2.13–16; Rev. 21.1–7

Hymns: ....

2020

	July					August						September					October					November					December			
S		5	12	19	26			2	9	16	23	30			6	13	20	27			4	11	18	25		1	8	15	22	29			6	13	20	27
M		6	13	20	27			3	10	17	24	31			7	14	21	28			5	12	19	26		2	9	16	23	30			7	14	21	28
T		7	14	21	28			4	11	18	25			1	8	15	22	29			6	13	20	27		3	10	17	24		1	8	15	22	29
W	1	8	15	22	29			5	12	19	26			2	9	16	23	30			7	14	21	28		4	11	18	25	2	9	16	23	30
T	2	9	16	23	30			6	13	20	27			3	10	17	24		1	8	15	22	29		5	12	19	26	3	10	17	24	31
F	3	10	17	24	31			7	14	21	28		4	11	18	25		2	9	16	23	30		6	13	20	27	4	11	18	25
S	4	11	18	25		1	8	15	22	29		5	12	19	26		3	10	17	24	31		7	14	21	28	5	12	19	26

CW COLLECTS

Almighty Father,
whose will is to restore all things
in your beloved Son, the King of all:
govern the hearts and minds of those in authority,
and bring the families of the nations,
divided and torn apart by the ravages of sin,
to be subject to his just and gentle rule;
who is alive and reigns with you,
in the unity of the Holy Spirit,
one God, now and for ever.

or

God, our refuge and strength,
bring near the day when wars shall cease
and poverty and pain shall end,
that earth may know the peace of heaven
through Jesus Christ our Lord.

POST COMMUNION

God of peace,
whose Son Jesus Christ proclaimed the kingdom
and restored the broken to wholeness of life:
look with compassion on the anguish of the world,
and by your healing power
make whole both people and nations;
through our Lord and Saviour Jesus Christ.

BCP COLLECT

*Lord, we beseech thee to keep thy household the
Church in continual godliness; that through thy
protection it may be free from all adversities, and
devoutly given to serve thee in good works, to the
glory of thy name; through Jesus Christ our Lord.*

2021

January					
S		3	10	17	24	31
M		4	11	18	25
T		5	12	19	26
W		6	13	20	27
T		7	14	21	28
F	1	8	15	22	29
S	2	9	16	23	30

February				
S		7	14	21	28
M	1	8	15	22
T	2	9	16	23
W	3	10	17	24
T	4	11	18	25
F	5	12	19	26
S	6	13	20	27

March				
S		7	14	21	28
M	1	8	15	22	29
T	2	9	16	23	30
W	3	10	17	24	31
T	4	11	18	25
F	5	12	19	26
S	6	13	20	27

April				
S		4	11	18	25
M		5	12	19	26
T		6	13	20	27
W		7	14	21	28
T	1	8	15	22	29
F	2	9	16	23	30
S	3	10	17	24

May				
S		2	9	16	23	30
M		3	10	17	24	31
T		4	11	18	25
W		5	12	19	26
T		6	13	20	27
F		7	14	21	28
S	1	8	15	22	29

June				
S		6	13	20	27
M		7	14	21	28
T	1	8	15	22	29
W	2	9	16	23	30
T	3	10	17	24
F	4	11	18	25
S	5	12	19	26

Margery Kempe, Mystic, c.1440

Red *or* Green

DEL Wk 32	**EUCHARIST** CW		**MORNING PRAYER**	**EVENING PRAYER**
Psalms:	24.1–6		19; *20*	*34*
Readings:	Titus 1.1–9; Luke 17.1–6		Dan. 4.19–end; Rev. 5	Isa. 5.8–24; Matt. 4.23—5.12
		AW	*Isa. 40.21–end*	*Rom. 11.25–end*
	HOLY COMMUNION BCP		**MORNING PRAYER**	**EVENING PRAYER**
Psalms:			*44; 45; 46*	*47; 48; 49*
Readings:			*Eccles. 1; Luke 19.11–28*	*Eccles. 2.1–23; Luke 19.29–end*
Hymns:				

Sunrise 07.10; Sunset 16.16

2020

	July					August						September					October					November					December			
S		5	12	19	26			2	9	16	23	30			6	13	20	27			4	11	18	25		1	8	15	22	29			6	13	20	27
M		6	13	20	27		3	10	17	24	31			7	14	21	28			5	12	19	26		2	9	16	23	30			7	14	21	28
T		7	14	21	28		4	11	18	25		1	8	15	22	29			6	13	20	27		3	10	17	24		1	8	15	22	29
W	1	8	15	22	29		5	12	19	26		2	9	16	23	30		7	14	21	28		4	11	18	25		2	9	16	23	30
T	2	9	16	23	30		6	13	20	27		3	10	17	24		1	8	15	22	29		5	12	19	26		3	10	17	24	31
F	3	10	17	24	31		7	14	21	28		4	11	18	25		2	9	16	23	30		6	13	20	27		4	11	18	25
S	4	11	18	25		1	8	15	22	29		5	12	19	26		3	10	17	24	31		7	14	21	28		5	12	19	26

Leo the Great, Bishop of Rome, Teacher of the Faith, 461 (CW Readings see   Red, Green *or* White
Common of the Saints also 1 Pet. 5.1–11)

	EUCHARIST CW	**MORNING PRAYER**	**EVENING PRAYER**
Psalms:	37.3–5, 30–32	*21*; 24	36; *40*
Readings:	Titus 2.1–8, 11–14; Luke 17.7–10	Dan. 5.1–12; Rev. 6	Isa. 5.25–end; Matt. 5.13–20
		AW *Ezek. 34.20–end*	*John 10.1–18*
	HOLY COMMUNION BCP	**MORNING PRAYER**	**EVENING PRAYER**
Psalms:		50; 51; 52	53; 54; 55
Readings:		*Eccles. 3.1–15;* *Luke 20.1–26*	*Eccles. 3.16—4.6;* *Luke 20.27—21.4*
Hymns:	....	....	....

CW COLLECT
God our Father,
who made your servant Leo strong in the defence of
   the faith:
fill your Church with the spirit of truth
that, guided by humility and governed by love,
she may prevail against the powers of evil;
through Jesus Christ your Son our Lord,
who is alive and reigns with you,
in the unity of the Holy Spirit,
one God, now and for ever.

POST COMMUNION
God of truth,
whose Wisdom set her table
and invited us to eat the bread and drink the wine
   of the kingdom:
help us to lay aside all foolishness
and to live and walk in the way of insight,
that we may come with Leo to the
   eternal feast of heaven;
through Jesus Christ our Lord.

2021

January					
S		3	10	17	24	31
M		4	11	18	25
T		5	12	19	26
W		6	13	20	27
T		7	14	21	28
F	1	8	15	22	29
S	2	9	16	23	30

February					
S			7	14	21	28
M	1	8	15	22
T	2	9	16	23
W	3	10	17	24
T	4	11	18	25
F	5	12	19	26
S	6	13	20	27

March					
S			7	14	21	28
M	1	8	15	22	29
T	2	9	16	23	30
W	3	10	17	24	31
T	4	11	18	25
F	5	12	19	26
S	6	13	20	27

April					
S			4	11	18	25
M		5	12	19	26
T		6	13	20	27
W		7	14	21	28
T	1	8	15	22	29
F	2	9	16	23	30
S	3	10	17	24

May					
S		2	9	16	23	30
M		3	10	17	24	31
T		4	11	18	25
W		5	12	19	26
T		6	13	20	27
F		7	14	21	28
S	1	8	15	22	29

June					
S		6	13	20	27
M		7	14	21	28
T	1	8	15	22	29
W	2	9	16	23	30
T	3	10	17	24
F	4	11	18	25
S	5	12	19	26

Armistice Day   Martin, Bishop of Tours, 397 (CW Readings see Common of the Saints   Red, Green *or* White
also 1 Thess. 5.1–11; Matt. 25.34–40) *(also BCP)*

	EUCHARIST	MORNING PRAYER	EVENING PRAYER
	CW		
Psalms:	23	*23*; 25	*37*
Readings:	Titus 3.1–7;	Dan. 5.13–end;	Isa. 6;
	Luke 17.11–19	Rev. 7.1–4, 9–end	Matt. 5.21–37
AW		*Lev. 26.3–13*	*Titus 2.1–10*

	HOLY COMMUNION	MORNING PRAYER	EVENING PRAYER
	BCP Com. Confessor		
Psalms:	*37.30–35*	*56; 57; 58*	*59; 60; 61*
Readings:	*Wisd. 7.7–14; 1 Cor. 2.6–13;*	*Eccles. 4.7–end;*	*Eccles. 5;*
	Matt. 13.51–52	*Luke 21.5–end*	*Luke 22.1–38*
Hymns:	....	....	....

CW COLLECT

God all powerful,
who called Martin from the armies of this world
to be a faithful soldier of Christ:
give us grace to follow him
in his love and compassion for the needy,
and enable your Church to claim for all people
their inheritance as children of God;
through Jesus Christ your Son our Lord,
who is alive and reigns with you,
in the unity of the Holy Spirit,
one God, now and for ever.

POST COMMUNION

God, shepherd of your people,
whose servant Martin revealed the loving service of
   Christ in his ministry
as a pastor of your people:
by this eucharist in which we share
awaken within us the love of Christ
and keep us faithful to our Christian calling;
through him who laid down his life for us,
but is alive and reigns with you, now and for ever.

BCP COLLECT

*O God, who hast enlightened thy Church by the
teaching of thy servant Martin: Enrich it evermore,
we beseech thee, with thy heavenly grace, and raise
up faithful witnesses, who by their life and doctrine
may set forth to all men the truth of thy salvation;
through Jesus Christ our Lord.*

A REMEMBRANCE COLLECT

Almighty and eternal God,
from whose love in Christ we cannot be parted,
either by death or life:
Hear our prayers and thanksgivings for all whom
   we remember this day;
fulfil in them the purpose of your love;
and bring us all, with them, to your eternal joy;

2020

July					August					September					October					November					December				
S		5	12	19	26	S		2	9	16	23	30	S		6	13	20	27	S		4	11	18	25	S	1	8	15	22	29	S		6	13	20	27
M		6	13	20	27	M		3	10	17	24	31	M		7	14	21	28	M		5	12	19	26	M	2	9	16	23	30	M		7	14	21	28
T		7	14	21	28	T		4	11	18	25	T	1	8	15	22	29	T		6	13	20	27	T	3	10	17	24	T	1	8	15	22	29
W	1	8	15	22	29	W		5	12	19	26	W	2	9	16	23	30	W		7	14	21	28	W	4	11	18	25	W	2	9	16	23	30
T	2	9	16	23	30	T		6	13	20	27	T	3	10	17	24	T	1	8	15	22	29	T	5	12	19	26	T	3	10	17	24	31
F	3	10	17	24	31	F		7	14	21	28	F	4	11	18	25	F	2	9	16	23	30	F	6	13	20	27	F	4	11	18	25
S	4	11	18	25	S	1	8	15	22	29	S	5	12	19	26	S	3	10	17	24	31	S	7	14	21	28	S	5	12	19	26

Red *or* Green

	EUCHARIST	MORNING PRAYER	EVENING PRAYER
	CW		
Psalms:	146.4–end	*26*; 27	42; *43*
Readings:	Philem. 7–20;	Dan. 6;	Isa. 7.1–17;
	Luke 17.20–25	Rev. 8	Matt. 5.38–end

AW		*Hos. 6.1–6*	*Matt. 9.9–13*

	HOLY COMMUNION	MORNING PRAYER	EVENING PRAYER
	BCP		
Psalms:		*62; 63; 64*	*65; 66; 67*
Readings:		*Eccles. 6;*	*Eccles. 7.1–14;*
		Luke 22.39–53	*Luke 22.54–end*
Hymns:	....	....	....

Charles Simeon, Priest, Evangelical Divine, 1836 (CW Readings see Common of the Saints   Red, Green *or* White
especially Mal. 2.5–7, also Col. 1.3–8; Luke 8.4–8)   *Britius, Bishop (BCP)*

	EUCHARIST CW	MORNING PRAYER	EVENING PRAYER
Psalms:	119.1–8	28; *32*	*31*
Readings:	2 John 4–9; Luke 17.26–end	Dan. 7.1–14; Rev. 9.1–12	Isa. 8.1–15; Matt. 6.1–18

AW   *Mal. 4*   *John 4.5–26*

	HOLY COMMUNION BCP Com Bishop	MORNING PRAYER	EVENING PRAYER
Psalms:	99	*68*	*69; 70*
Readings:	Ezek. 34.11–16; 1 Tim. 3.15–16; Mark 4.26–32	Eccles. 7.15–end; Luke 23.1–25	Eccles. 8; Luke 23.26–49
Hymns:	....	....	....

CW COLLECT
Eternal God,
who raised up Charles Simeon
to preach the good news of Jesus Christ
and inspire your people in service and mission:
grant that we with all your Church may worship
    the Saviour,
turn in sorrow from our sins and walk in the way
    of holiness;
through Jesus Christ your son our Lord,
who is alive and reigns with you in the unity of the
    Holy Spirit,
one God now and forever

POST COMMUNION
God, shepherd of your people,
whose servant Charles Simeon revealed
the loving service of Christ
in his ministry as a pastor of your people:
by this eucharist in which we share
awaken within us the love of Christ
and keep us faithful to our Christian calling:
through him who laid down his life for us
but is alive and resigns with you, now and forever

BCP COLLECT for St Britius
*O God, the light of the faithful, and shepherd of
souls, who didst set blessed Britius to be a Bishop in
the Church, that he might feed thy sheep by his word
and guide them by his example: Grant us, we pray
thee, to keep the faith which he taught, and to follow
in his footsteps; through Jesus Christ our Lord.*

2020

	July					August					September					October					November					December			
S		5	12	19	26		2	9	16	23	30		6	13	20	27		4	11	18	25		1	8	15	22	29		6	13	20	27
M		6	13	20	27		3	10	17	24	31		7	14	21	28		5	12	19	26		2	9	16	23	30		7	14	21	28
T		7	14	21	28		4	11	18	25		1	8	15	22	29		6	13	20	27		3	10	17	24		1	8	15	22	29
W	1	8	15	22	29		5	12	19	26		2	9	16	23	30		7	14	21	28		4	11	18	25		2	9	16	23	30
T	2	9	16	23	30		6	13	20	27		3	10	17	24		1	8	15	22	29		5	12	19	26		3	10	17	24	31
F	3	10	17	24	31		7	14	21	28		4	11	18	25		2	9	16	23	30		6	13	20	27		4	11	18	25
S	4	11	18	25		1	8	15	22	29		5	12	19	26		3	10	17	24	31		7	14	21	28		5	12	19	26

Samuel Seabury, First Anglican Bishop of North America, 1796   Red *or* Green

	EUCHARIST	**MORNING PRAYER**	**EVENING PRAYER**
	CW		
Psalms:	112	*33*	84; *86*
Readings:	3 John 5–8;	Dan. 7.15–end;	Isa. 8.16—9.7;
	Luke 18.1–8	Rev. 9.13–end	Matt. 6.19–end

| | | AW | *Mic. 6.6–8* | *Col. 3.12–17* |

	HOLY COMMUNION	**MORNING PRAYER**	**EVENING PRAYER**
	BCP		
Psalms:		*71; 72*	*73; 74*
Readings:		*Eccles. 9;*	*Eccles. 10.5–18;*
		Luke 23.50—24.12	*Luke 24.13–end;*
			E. Coll. Trinity 23
Hymns:	....	....	....

THE SECOND SUNDAY BEFORE ADVENT
Trinity 23

(Red *or* White)

	PRINCIPAL SERVICE CW	**THIRD SERVICE**	**SECOND SERVICE**
Psalms:	90.1–8 [9–11] 12*	98	89.19–37*
Readings:	Zeph. 1.7, 12–end; 1 Thess. 5.1–11; Matt. 25.14–30	Dan. 10.19–end; Rev. 4	1 Kgs 1.15–40 (*or* 1–40); Rev. 1.4–18; [Luke 9.1–6]

Seasonal provisions: CW Book pp 326–327

	HOLY COMMUNION BCP	**MORNING PRAYER**	**EVENING PRAYER**
Psalms:	44.1–9	98	89.19–37*
Readings:	Isa. 11.1–10; Phil. 3.17–end; Matt. 22.15–22	Prov. 1.20–end or 1 Macc. 2.1–28; Luke 16 or 1 Cor. 1.1–25	Prov. 2 or Prov. 3.1–26 or 1 Macc. 2.29–48; John 9 or 1 Cor. 13
Hymns:	....	....	....

2020

	July					August						September					October					November					December			
S		5	12	19	26		2	9	16	23	30		6	13	20	27		4	11	18	25		1	8	15	22	29		6	13	20	27
M		6	13	20	27		3	10	17	24	31		7	14	21	28		5	12	19	26		2	9	16	23	30		7	14	21	28
T		7	14	21	28		4	11	18	25			1	8	15	22	29		6	13	20	27		3	10	17	24		1	8	15	22	29
W	1	8	15	22	29		5	12	19	26		2	9	16	23	30		7	14	21	28		4	11	18	25		2	9	16	23	30
T	2	9	16	23	30		6	13	20	27		3	10	17	24		1	8	15	22	29		5	12	19	26		3	10	17	24	31
F	3	10	17	24	31		7	14	21	28		4	11	18	25		2	9	16	23	30		6	13	20	27		4	11	18	25
S	4	11	18	25		1	8	15	22	29		5	12	19	26		3	10	17	24	31		7	14	21	28		5	12	19	26

CW COLLECTS

Heavenly Father,
whose blessed Son was revealed
   to destroy the works of the devil
and to make us the children of God
   and heirs of eternal life:
grant that we, having this hope,
may purify ourselves even as he is pure;
that when he shall appear in power and great glory
we may be made like him
   in his eternal and glorious kingdom;
where he is alive and reigns with you,
in the unity of the Holy Spirit,
one God, now and for ever.

or

Heavenly Lord,
you long for the world's salvation:
stir us from apathy,
restrain us from excess
and revive in us new hope
that all creation will one day be healed
in Jesus Christ our Lord.

POST COMMUNION

Gracious Lord,
in this holy sacrament
you give substance to our hope:
bring us at the last
to that fullness of life for which we long;
through Jesus Christ our Saviour.

BCP COLLECT for TRINITY 23

*O God, our refuge and strength, who art the author
of all godliness: Be ready, we beseech thee, to hear
the devout prayers of thy Church; and grant that
those things which we ask faithfully we may obtain
effectually; through Jesus Christ our Lord.*

2021

January						February					March					April					May						June				
S		3	10	17	24 31	S		7	14	21 28	S		7	14	21 28	S		4	11	18 25	S		2	9	16	23 30	S		6	13	20 27
M		4	11	18	25	M	1	8	15	22	M	1	8	15	22 29	M		5	12	19 26	M		3	10	17	24 31	M		7	14	21 28
T		5	12	19	26	T	2	9	16	23	T	2	9	16	23 30	T		6	13	20 27	T		4	11	18	25	T	1	8	15	22 29
W		6	13	20	27	W	3	10	17	24	W	3	10	17	24 31	W		7	14	21 28	W		5	12	19	26	W	2	9	16	23 30
T		7	14	21	28	T	4	11	18	25	T	4	11	18	25	T	1	8	15	22 29	T		6	13	20	27	T	3	10	17	24
F	1	8	15	22	29	F	5	12	19	26	F	5	12	19	26	F	2	9	16	23 30	F		7	14	21	28	F	4	11	18	25
S	2	9	16	23	30	S	6	13	20	27	S	6	13	20	27	S	3	10	17	24	S	1	8	15	22	29	S	5	12	19	26

Margaret, Queen of Scotland, Philanthropist, Reformer of the Church, 1093
(CW Readings see Common of the Saints also Prov. 31.10–12, 20, 26–31; 1 Cor. 12.13—13.3;
Matt. 25.34–end)   *Edmund Rich of Abingdon, Archbishop of Canterbury, 1240*

Red, Green *or* White

DEL Wk 33	EUCHARIST CW	MORNING PRAYER	EVENING PRAYER
Psalms:	1	46; *47*	70; *71*
Readings:	Rev. 1.1–4, 2.1–5; Luke 18.35–end	Dan. 8.1–14; Rev. 10	Isa. 9.8—10.4; Matt. 7.1–12
		AW Mic. 7.1–7	Matt. 10.24–39

	HOLY COMMUNION BCP	MORNING PRAYER	EVENING PRAYER
Psalms:		79; 80; 81	82; 83; 84; 85
Readings:		Ecclus 1.1–10; Acts 1	Ecclus 1.11–end; Acts 2.1–21
Hymns:			

CW COLLECT
God, the ruler of all,
who called your servant Margaret to an
   earthly throne
and gave her zeal for your Church and love for
   your people
that she might advance your heavenly kingdom:
mercifully grant that we who commemorate
   her example
may be fruitful in good works
and attain to the glorious crown of your saints;
through Jesus Christ your Son our Lord,
who is alive and reigns with you,
in the unity of the Holy Spirit,
one God, now and forever.

POST COMMUNION
God our redeemer,
who inspired Margaret to witness to your love
and to work for the coming of your kingdom:
may we, who in this sacrament share the bread
   of heaven,
be fired by your Spirit to proclaim the gospel in our
   daily living
and never to rest content until your kingdom come,
on earth as it is in heaven;
through Jesus Christ our Lord.

Sunrise 07.23; Sunset 16.06

2020

	July					August					September					October					November					December			
S		5	12	19	26		2	9	16	23	30		6	13	20	27		4	11	18	25		1	8	15	22	29		6	13	20	27
M		6	13	20	27		3	10	17	24	31		7	14	21	28		5	12	19	26		2	9	16	23	30		7	14	21	28
T		7	14	21	28		4	11	18	25		1	8	15	22	29		6	13	20	27		3	10	17	24		1	8	15	22	29
W	1	8	15	22	29		5	12	19	26		2	9	16	23	30		7	14	21	28		4	11	18	25		2	9	16	23	30
T	2	9	16	23	30		6	13	20	27		3	10	17	24		1	8	15	22	29		5	12	19	26		3	10	17	24	31
F	3	10	17	24	31		7	14	21	28		4	11	18	25		2	9	16	23	30		6	13	20	27		4	11	18	25
S	4	11	18	25		1	8	15	22	29		5	12	19	26		3	10	17	24	31		7	14	21	28		5	12	19	26

Hugh, Bishop of Lincoln, 1200 (CW Readings see Common of the Saints also 1 Tim. 6.11–16) *(Also BCP)*   Red, Green *or* White

	EUCHARIST	MORNING PRAYER	EVENING PRAYER
	CW		
Psalms:	15	48; *52*	*67*; 72
Readings:	Rev. 3.1–6, 14–end;	Dan. 8.15–end;	Isa. 10.5–19;
	Luke 19.1–10	Rev. 11.1–14	Matt. 7.13–end

		AW	*Hab. 3.1–19a*	*1 Cor. 4.9–16*

	HOLY COMMUNION	MORNING PRAYER	EVENING PRAYER
	BCP Com. Bishop		
Psalms:	*99*	*86; 87; 88*	*89*
Readings:	*Ezek. 34.11–16; 1 Tim. 3.15–16;*	*Ecclus 2;*	*Ecclus 3.17–29;*
	Mark 4.26–32	*Acts 2.22–end*	*Acts 3.1—4.4*
Hymns:	....	....	....

CW COLLECT
O God,
who endowed your servant Hugh
with a wise and cheerful boldness
and taught him to commend to earthly rulers
    the discipline of a holy life:
give us grace like him to be bold
    in the service of the gospel,
putting our confidence in Christ alone,
who is alive and reigns with you,
in the unity of the Holy Spirit,
one God, now and for ever.

POST COMMUNION
God, shepherd of your people,
whose servant Hugh revealed the loving service of
    Christ in his ministry as a pastor of your people: by
    this eucharist in which we share
awaken within us the love of Christ
and keep us faithful to our Christian calling;
through him who laid down his life for us,
but is alive and reigns with you, now and for ever.

BCP COLLECT
*O God, the light of the faithful, and shepherd of
souls, who didst set blessed Hugh to be a Bishop in
the Church, that he might feed thy sheep by his word
and guide them by his example: Grant us, we pray
thee, to keep the faith which he taught, and to follow
in his footsteps; through Jesus Christ our Lord.*

Elizabeth of Hungary, Princess of Thuringia, Philanthropist, 1231   Red, Green *or* White
(CW Readings see Common of the Saints especially Matt. 25.31–end; also Prov. 31.10–31)

	EUCHARIST	MORNING PRAYER	EVENING PRAYER
	CW		
Psalms:	150	*56*; 57	*73*
Readings:	Rev. 4; Luke 19.11–28	Dan. 9.1–19; Rev. 11.15–end	Isa. 10.20–32; Matt. 8.1–13
		AW *Zech. 8.1–13*	*Mark 13.3–8*
	HOLY COMMUNION	MORNING PRAYER	EVENING PRAYER
	BCP		
Psalms:		90; 91; 92	93; 94
Readings:		*Ecclus 4.11–28;* *Acts 4.5–31*	*Ecclus 4.29—6.1;* *Acts 4.32—5.11*
Hymns:	....	....	....

CW COLLECT
Lord God,
who taught Elizabeth of Hungary
   to recognize and reverence Christ
   in the poor of this world:
by her example strengthen us to love and serve
   the afflicted and the needy
and so to honour your Son, the servant king,
who is alive and reigns with you,
in the unity of the Holy Spirit,
one God, now and for ever.

POST COMMUNION
Faithful God,
who called Elizabeth of Hungary to serve you
and gave her joy in walking the path of holiness:
by this eucharist
   in which you renew within us the vision of
   your glory,
strengthen us all to follow the way of perfection
until we come to see you face to face;
through Jesus Christ our Lord.

Hilda, Abbess of Whitby, 680 (CW Readings see Common of the Saints especially Isa. 61.10—62.5)   Red, Green *or* White
Mechtild, Béguine of Magdeburg, Mystic, 1280

	EUCHARIST	MORNING PRAYER	EVENING PRAYER
	CW		
Psalms:	149.1–5	61; *62*	74; *76*
Readings:	Rev. 5.1–10;	Dan. 9.20–end;	Isa. 10.33—11.9;
	Luke 19.41–44	Rev. 12	Matt. 8.14–22
		AW Zech. 10.6–end	*1 Pet. 5.1–11*

	HOLY COMMUNION	MORNING PRAYER	EVENING PRAYER
	BCP		
Psalms:		95; 96; 97	98; 99; 100; 101
Readings:		Ecclus 6.14–31;	Ecclus 7.27–end;
		Acts 5.12—6.7	Acts 6.8—7.16
Hymns:	....	....	....

CW COLLECT
Eternal God,
who made the abbess Hilda
 to shine like a jewel in our land
and through her holiness and leadership
 blessed your Church with new life and unity:
help us, like her, to yearn for the gospel of Christ
and to reconcile those who are divided;
through him who is alive and reigns with you,
in the unity of the Holy Spirit,
one God, now and for ever.

POST COMMUNION
Merciful God,
who gave such grace to your servant Hilda
that she served you with singleness of heart
and loved you above all things:
help us, whose communion with you
 has been renewed in this sacrament,
to forsake all that holds us back from following Christ
and to grow into his likeness from glory to glory
through Jesus Christ our Lord

Edmund, King of the East Angles, Martyr 870 (CW Readings see Common of the Saints
also Prov. 20.28; 21.1–4, 7) *Priscilla Lydia Sellon, a Restorer of the Religious Life in the
Church of England, 1876 Edmund, King and Martyr 870 (BCP)*

Red *or* Green (*or Red*)

	EUCHARIST	MORNING PRAYER	EVENING PRAYER
	CW		
Psalms:	119.65–72	*63*; 65	*77*
Readings:	Rev. 10.8–11;	Dan. 10.1—11.1;	Isa. 11.10—end of 12;
	Luke 19.45–48	Rev. 13.1–10	Matt. 8.23–end

	AW	*Mic. 4.1–5*	*Luke 9.28–36*

	HOLY COMMUNION	MORNING PRAYER	EVENING PRAYER
	BCP Com. Martyr		
Psalms:	3	102; 103	104
Readings:	Jer. 11.18–20; Heb. 11.32—12.2;	Ecclus 10.6–8, 12–24;	Ecclus 11.7–28;
	Matt. 16.24–27	Acts 7.17–34	Acts 7.35—8.4
Hymns:	....	....	....

CW COLLECT
Eternal God,
whose servant Edmund kept faith to the end,
both with you and with his people,
and glorified you by his death:
grant us such steadfastness of faith
that, with the noble army of martyrs,
we may come to enjoy the fullness
of the resurrection life;
through Jesus Christ your Son our Lord,
who is alive and reigns with you,
in the unity of the Holy Spirit,
one God, now and for ever.

POST COMMUNION
Eternal God,
who gave us this holy meal
in which we have celebrated the glory of the cross
and the victory of your martyr Edmund:
by our communion with Christ
in his saving death and resurrection,
give us with all your saints the courage
to conquer evil and so to share
the fruit of the tree of life;
through Jesus Christ our Lord.

BCP COLLECT
*Almighty God, by whose grace and power thy holy
Martyr Edmund triumphed over suffering and
despised death:
Grant, we beseech thee, that enduring hardness
and waxing valiant in fight, we may
with the noble army of martyrs received the crown of
everlasting life; through Jesus Christ our Lord.*

2020

July					August					September					October					November					December			
S	5	12	19	26	S	2	9	16	23	30	S	6	13	20	27	S	4	11	18	25	S	1	8	15	22	29	S	6	13	20	27
M	6	13	20	27	M	3	10	17	24	31	M	7	14	21	28	M	5	12	19	26	M	2	9	16	23	30	M	7	14	21	28
T	7	14	21	28	T	4	11	18	25	T	1	8	15	22	29	T	6	13	20	27	T	3	10	17	24	T	1	8	15	22	29
W	1	8	15	22	29	W	5	12	19	26	W	2	9	16	23	30	W	7	14	21	28	W	4	11	18	25	W	2	9	16	23	30
T	2	9	16	23	30	T	6	13	20	27	T	3	10	17	24	T	1	8	15	22	29	T	5	12	19	26	T	3	10	17	24	31
F	3	10	17	24	31	F	7	14	21	28	F	4	11	18	25	F	2	9	16	23	30	F	6	13	20	27	F	4	11	18	25
S	4	11	18	25	S	1	8	15	22	29	S	5	12	19	26	S	3	10	17	24	31	S	7	14	21	28	S	5	12	19	26

Red *or* Green

EUCHARIST	MORNING PRAYER	EVENING PRAYER
CW		

Psalms: 144.1–9   *78.1–39*   *78.40–end*

Readings: Rev. 11.4–12;   Dan. 12;   Isa. 13.1–13;
Luke 20.27–40   Rev. 13.11–end   Matt. 9.1–17
or Eve of Christ the King:
Ps. 99, 100; Isa. 10.33—11.9;
1 Tim. 6.11–16

AW: At Evening Prayer the Readings for the Eve of Christ the King are used.
At other services the following readings are used:
Exod. 16.1–21   John 6.3–15

HOLY COMMUNION	MORNING PRAYER	EVENING PRAYER
BCPCom		

Psalms: *105*   *106*

Readings: *Ecclus 14.20—15.10;*   *Ecclus 15.11–end;*
Acts 8.4–25   *Acts 8.26–end;*
E. Coll: Sunday next before Advent.

Hymns: ....

2021

	January				February				March				April				May				June		
S		3 10 17 24 31	S		7 14 21 28	S		7 14 21 28	S		4 11 18 25	S		2 9 16 23 30	S		6 13 20 27
M		4 11 18 25	M	1	8 15 22	M	1	8 15 22 29	M		5 12 19 26	M		3 10 17 24 31	M		7 14 21 28
T		5 12 19 26	T	2	9 16 23	T	2	9 16 23 30	T		6 13 20 27	T		4 11 18 25	T	1	8 15 22 29
W		6 13 20 27	W	3	10 17 24	W	3	10 17 24 31	W		7 14 21 28	W		5 12 19 26	W	2	9 16 23 30
T		7 14 21 28	T	4	11 18 25	T	4	11 18 25	T	1	8 15 22 29	T		6 13 20 27	T	3	10 17 24
F	1	8 15 22 29	F	5	12 19 26	F	5	12 19 26	F	2	9 16 23 30	F		7 14 21 28	F	4	11 18 25
S	2	9 16 23 30	S	6	13 20 27	S	6	13 20 27	S	3	10 17 24	S	1	8 15 22 29	S	5	12 19 26

CHRIST THE KING
Sunday next before Advent

(Red *or* White)

	PRINCIPAL SERVICE	**THIRD SERVICE**	**SECOND SERVICE**
	CW		
Psalms:	95.1–7	29; 110	93 [97]
Readings:	Ezek. 34.11–16, 20–24; Eph. 1.15–end; Matt. 25.31–end	Isa. 4.2—5.7; Luke 19.29–38	2 Sam. 23.1–7 *or* 1 Macc. 2.15–29; Matt. 28.16–end

Seasonal provisions: CW Book pp 326–327

	HOLY COMMUNION	**MORNING PRAYER**	**EVENING PRAYER**
	BCP to celebrate Christ the King see CW provision		
Psalms:	*85.8–end*	*29; 110*	*93 [97]*
Readings:	*Jer. 23.5–8;* *Col. 1.13–20;* *John 6.5–14*	*Eccles. 11 and 12;* *John 19.13–end* or *Heb. 11.1–16*	*Hag. 2.1–9* or *Mal. 3 and 4;* *John 20* or *Heb. 11.17—12.2* or *Luke 15.11–end*
Hymns:	....	....	....

CW COLLECTS

Eternal Father,
whose Son Jesus Christ ascended to the throne of
heaven that he might rule over all things
  as Lord and King:
keep the Church in the unity of the Spirit
  and in the bond of peace,
and bring the whole created order to worship
at his feet; who is alive and reigns with you,
in the unity of the Holy Spirit,
one God, now and for ever.

or

God the Father,
help us to hear the call of Christ the King
and to follow in his service,
whose kingdom has no end;
for he reigns with you and the Holy Spirit,
one God, one glory.

POST COMMUNION

Stir up, O Lord,
the wills of your faithful people;
that they, plenteously bringing forth the fruit
  of good works,
may by you be plenteously rewarded;
through Jesus Christ our Lord.
*This Post Communion may be used as the Collect at
Morning and Evening Prayer during this week*

BCP COLLECT for Sunday next before Advent
*Stir up, we beseech thee, O Lord, the wills of thy
faithful people; that they, plenteously bringing forth
the fruit of good works, may of thee be plenteously
rewarded; through Jesus Christ our Lord.*

2021

	January	February	March	April	May	June
S	3 10 17 24 31	7 14 21 28	7 14 21 28	4 11 18 25	2 9 16 23 30	6 13 20 27
M	4 11 18 25	1 8 15 22	1 8 15 22 29	5 12 19 26	3 10 17 24 31	7 14 21 28
T	5 12 19 26	2 9 16 23	2 9 16 23 30	6 13 20 27	4 11 18 25	1 8 15 22 29
W	6 13 20 27	3 10 17 24	3 10 17 24 31	7 14 21 28	5 12 19 26	2 9 16 23 30
T	7 14 21 28	4 11 18 25	4 11 18 25	1 8 15 22 29	6 13 20 27	3 10 17 24
F	1 8 15 22 29	5 12 19 26	5 12 19 26	2 9 16 23 30	7 14 21 28	4 11 18 25
S	2 9 16 23 30	6 13 20 27	6 13 20 27	3 10 17 24	1 8 15 22 29	5 12 19 26

Clement, Bishop of Rome, Martyr, c.100 (CW Readings see Common of the Saints
also Phil. 3.17—4.3; Matt. 16.13–19) *(Also BCP)*

Red *or* Green (*or Red*)

DEL Wk 34	**EUCHARIST**	**MORNING PRAYER**	**EVENING PRAYER**
	CW		
Psalms:	24.1–6	92; *96*	*80*; 81
Readings:	Rev. 14.1–5;	Isa. 40.1–11;	Isa. 14.3–20;
	Luke 21.1–4	Rev. 14.1–13	Matt. 9.18–34
	AW	*Jer. 30.1–3, 10–17*	*Rom. 12.9–21*
	HOLY COMMUNION	**MORNING PRAYER**	**EVENING PRAYER**
	BCP Com. Martyr		
Psalms:	3	*110; 111; 112; 113*	*114; 115*
Readings:	*Jer. 11.18–20; Heb. 11.32—12.2;*	*Wisd. 1;*	*Wisd. 2;*
	Matt. 16.24–27	*Rev. 1*	*Rev. 2*
Hymns:	....	....	....

CW COLLECT

Creator and Father of eternity,
whose martyr Clement bore witness with his blood
to the love he proclaimed
and the gospel that he preached:
give us thankful hearts
    as we celebrate your faithfulness
      revealed to us in the lives of your saints
and strengthen us in our pilgrimage
    as we follow your Son, Jesus Christ our Lord,
who is alive and reigns with you,
in the unity of the Holy Spirit,
one God, now and for ever.

POST COMMUNION

Eternal God,
who gave us this holy meal
in which we have celebrated the glory of the cross
and the victory of your martyr Clement:
by our communion with Christ
in his saving death and resurrection,
give us with all your saints the courage to
    conquer evil
and so to share the fruit of the tree of life;
through Jesus Christ our Lord.

BCP COLLECT

*Almighty God, by whose grace and power thy holy
Martyr Clement triumphed over suffering and
    despised death:
Grant, we beseech thee, that enduring hardness
and waxing valiant in fight, we may
with the noble army of martyrs receive the crown
of everlasting life; through Jesus Christ our Lord.*

Sunrise 07.35; Sunset 15.57

2020

	July					August						September					October					November					December			
S		5	12	19	26	S		2	9	16	23	30	S		6	13	20	27	S		4	11	18	25	S	1	8	15	22	29	S		6	13	20	27
M		6	13	20	27	M		3	10	17	24	31	M		7	14	21	28	M		5	12	19	26	M	2	9	16	23	30	M		7	14	21	28
T		7	14	21	28	T		4	11	18	25		T	1	8	15	22	29	T		6	13	20	27	T	3	10	17	24		T	1	8	15	22	29
W	1	8	15	22	29	W		5	12	19	26		W	2	9	16	23	30	W		7	14	21	28	W	4	11	18	25		W	2	9	16	23	30
T	2	9	16	23	30	T		6	13	20	27		T	3	10	17	24		T	1	8	15	22	29	T	5	12	19	26		T	3	10	17	24	31
F	3	10	17	24	31	F		7	14	21	28		F	4	11	18	25		F	2	9	16	23	30	F	6	13	20	27		F	4	11	18	25
S	4	11	18	25		S	1	8	15	22	29		S	5	12	19	26		S	3	10	17	24	31	S	7	14	21	28		S	5	12	19	26

Red *or* Green

	EUCHARIST	MORNING PRAYER	EVENING PRAYER
	CW		
Psalms:	96	*97*; 98; 100	99; *101*
Readings:	Rev. 14.4–19;	Isa. 40.12–26;	Isa. 17;
	Luke 21.5–11	Rev. 14.14—end of 15	Matt. 9.35—10.15

		AW	Jer. 30.18–24	John 10.22–30

	HOLY COMMUNION	MORNING PRAYER	EVENING PRAYER
	BCP		
Psalms:		116; 117; 118	119.1–32
Readings:		Wisd. 3.1–9;	Wisd. 4.7–end;
		Rev. 3	Rev. 4
Hymns:	....	....	....

NOVEMBER
25 Wednesday

Catherine of Alexandria, Martyr, 4th Century (also BCP). Isaac Watts, Hymn Writer, 1748 Red *or* Green (*or* Red)

	EUCHARIST	MORNING PRAYER	EVENING PRAYER
	CW		
Psalms:	98	110; 111; *112*	121; *122*; 123; 124
Readings:	Rev. 15.1–4;	Isa. 40.27—41.7;	Isa. 19;
	Luke 21.12–19	Rev. 16.1–11	Matt. 10.16–33

AW   *Jer. 31.1–9*   *Matt. 15.21–31*

	HOLY COMMUNION	MORNING PRAYER	EVENING PRAYER
	BCP Com Virgin Martyr		
Psalms:	*131*	*119.33–72*	*119.73–104*
Readings:	*Ecclus 51.10–12; Phil. 3.7–14;*	*Wisd. 5.1–16;*	*Wisd. 6.1–21;*
	Matt. 25.1–13	*Rev. 5*	*Rev. 6*
Hymns:	....	....	....

BCP COLLECT
O God, who didst endue the holy Virgin Catherine with grace to witness a good confession (and to suffer gladly for thy sake): Grant that we, after her example, may be found ready when the Bridegroom cometh and enter with him to the marriage feast; through the same thy Son Jesus Christ our Lord.

	July	August	September	October	November	December
S	5 12 19 26	2 9 16 23 30	6 13 20 27	4 11 18 25	1 8 15 22 29	6 13 20 27
M	6 13 20 27	3 10 17 24 31	7 14 21 28	5 12 19 26	2 9 16 23 30	7 14 21 28
T	7 14 21 28	4 11 18 25	1 8 15 22 29	6 13 20 27	3 10 17 24	1 8 15 22 29
W	1 8 15 22 29	5 12 19 26	2 9 16 23 30	7 14 21 28	4 11 18 25	2 9 16 23 30
T	2 9 16 23 30	6 13 20 27	3 10 17 24	1 8 15 22 29	5 12 19 26	3 10 17 24 31
F	3 10 17 24 31	7 14 21 28	4 11 18 25	2 9 16 23 30	6 13 20 27	4 11 18 25
S	4 11 18 25	1 8 15 22 29	5 12 19 26	3 10 17 24 31	7 14 21 28	5 12 19 26

Red *or* Green

	EUCHARIST	**MORNING PRAYER**	**EVENING PRAYER**
	CW		
Psalms:	100	*125*; 126; 127; 128	131; 132; *133*
Readings:	Rev. 18.1–2, 21–23, 19.1–3, 9;	Isa. 41.8–20;	Isa. 21.1–12;
	Luke 21.20–28	Rev. 16.12–end	Matt. 10.34—11.1

AW   *Jer. 31.10–17*   *Matt. 16.13–end*

	HOLY COMMUNION	**MORNING PRAYER**	**EVENING PRAYER**
	BCP		
Psalms:		119.105–144	119.145–end
Readings:		Wisd. 7.15—8.4;	Wisd. 8.5–18;
		Rev. 7	Rev. 10 and 11.1–14
Hymns:	....	....	....

Red *or* Green

	EUCHARIST	**MORNING PRAYER**	**EVENING PRAYER**
	CW		
Psalms:	84.1–6	*139*	*146*; 147
Readings:	Rev. 20.1–4, 11—21.2;	Isa. 41.21—42.9;	Isa. 22.1–14;
	Luke 21.29–33	Rev. 17	Matt. 11.2–19

		AW	*Jer. 31.31–37*	*Heb. 10.11–18*

	HOLY COMMUNION	**MORNING PRAYER**	**EVENING PRAYER**
	BCP		
Psalms:		*120; 121; 122; 123; 124; 125*	*126; 127; 128; 129; 130; 131*
Readings:		*Wisd. 8.21—end of 9;*	*Wisd. 10.15—11.10;*
		Rev. 11.5—end of 12	*Rev. 14.1–13*
Hymns:	....	....	....

2020

	July					August						September					October					November					December			
S		5	12	19	26	S		2	9	16	23	30	S		6	13	20	27	S		4	11	18	25	S	1	8	15	22	29	S		6	13	20	27
M		6	13	20	27	M		3	10	17	24	31	M		7	14	21	28	M		5	12	19	26	M	2	9	16	23	30	M		7	14	21	28
T		7	14	21	28	T		4	11	18	25	T	1	8	15	22	29	T		6	13	20	27	T	3	10	17	24	T	1	8	15	22	29
W	1	8	15	22	29	W		5	12	19	26	W	2	9	16	23	30	W		7	14	21	28	W	4	11	18	25	W	2	9	16	23	30
T	2	9	16	23	30	T		6	13	20	27	T	3	10	17	24	T	1	8	15	22	29	T	5	12	19	26	T	3	10	17	24	31
F	3	10	17	24	31	F		7	14	21	28	F	4	11	18	25	F	2	9	16	23	30	F	6	13	20	27	F	4	11	18	25
S	4	11	18	25	S	1	8	15	22	29	S	5	12	19	26	S	3	10	17	24	31	S	7	14	21	28	S	5	12	19	26

Red *or* Green

	EUCHARIST CW	MORNING PRAYER	EVENING PRAYER
Psalms:	95.1–7	*145*	148; 149; *150*
Readings:	Rev. 22.1–7; Luke 21.34–36	Isa. 42.10–17; Rev. 18	Isa. 24; Matt. 11.20–end

AW Isa. 51.17—52.2 Eph. 5.1–20

	HOLY COMMUNION BCP	MORNING PRAYER	EVENING PRAYER
Psalms:		*132; 133; 134; 135*	*136; 137; 138*
Readings:		*Wisd. 11.21—12.2; Rev. 18*	*Wisd. 12.12–21; Rev. 19.1–16; E. Coll. Advent Sunday*
Hymns:	....	....	....

2021

	January					February					March					April					May					June				
S		3	10	17	24	31		7	14	21	28		7	14	21	28		4	11	18	25		2	9	16	23	30		6	13	20	27
M		4	11	18	25		1	8	15	22		1	8	15	22	29		5	12	19	26		3	10	17	24	31		7	14	21	28
T		5	12	19	26		2	9	16	23		2	9	16	23	30		6	13	20	27		4	11	18	25		1	8	15	22	29
W		6	13	20	27		3	10	17	24		3	10	17	24	31		7	14	21	28		5	12	19	26		2	9	16	23	30
T		7	14	21	28		4	11	18	25		4	11	18	25		1	8	15	22	29		6	13	20	27		3	10	17	24
F	1	8	15	22	29		5	12	19	26		5	12	19	26		2	9	16	23	30		7	14	21	28		4	11	18	25
S	2	9	16	23	30		6	13	20	27		6	13	20	27		3	10	17	24		1	8	15	22	29		5	12	19	26

29 Sunday   **ADVENT SUNDAY**   Church Book and Desk Diary 2021 begins here   **CW Year B**   **DEL Year 1**

30 Monday

1 Tuesday

2021

	January					February					March					April					May					June			
S		3	10	17	24	31		7	14	21	28		7	14	21	28		4	11	18	25		2	9	16	23	30		6	13	20	27
M		4	11	18	25		1	8	15	22		1	8	15	22	29		5	12	19	26		3	10	17	24	31		7	14	21	28
T		5	12	19	26		2	9	16	23		2	9	16	23	30		6	13	20	27		4	11	18	25		1	8	15	22	29
W		6	13	20	27		3	10	17	24		3	10	17	24	31		7	14	21	28		5	12	19	26		2	9	16	23	30
T		7	14	21	28		4	11	18	25		4	11	18	25		1	8	15	22	29		6	13	20	27		3	10	17	24
F	1	8	15	22	29		5	12	19	26		5	12	19	26		2	9	16	23	30		7	14	21	28		4	11	18	25
S	2	9	16	23	30		6	13	20	27		6	13	20	27		3	10	17	24		1	8	15	22	29		5	12	19	26

Wednesday 2

Thursday 3

Friday 4

Saturday 5

2021

	July					August					September					October						November					December			
S		4	11	18	25	S	1	8	15	22	29	S		5	12	19	26	S		3	10	17	24	31	S		7	14	21	28	S		5	12	19	26
M		5	12	19	26	M	2	9	16	23	30	M		6	13	20	27	M		4	11	18	25		M	1	8	15	22	29	M		6	13	20	27
T		6	13	20	27	T	3	10	17	24	31	T		7	14	21	28	T		5	12	19	26		T	2	9	16	23	30	T		7	14	21	28
W		7	14	21	28	W	4	11	18	25		W	1	8	15	22	29	W		6	13	20	27		W	3	10	17	24		W	1	8	15	22	29
T	1	8	15	22	29	T	5	12	19	26		T	2	9	16	23	30	T		7	14	21	28		T	4	11	18	25		T	2	9	16	23	30
F	2	9	16	23	30	F	6	13	20	27		F	3	10	17	24		F	1	8	15	22	29		F	5	12	19	26		F	3	10	17	24	31
S	3	10	17	24	31	S	7	14	21	28		S	4	11	18	25		S	2	9	16	23	30		S	6	13	20	27		S	4	11	18	25	

6 Sunday   Advent 2

7 Monday

8 Tuesday

2021

	January	February	March	April	May	June
S	3 10 17 24 31	7 14 21 28	7 14 21 28	4 11 18 25	2 9 16 23 30	6 13 20 27
M	4 11 18 25	1 8 15 22	1 8 15 22 29	5 12 19 26	3 10 17 24 31	7 14 21 28
T	5 12 19 26	2 9 16 23	2 9 16 23 30	6 13 20 27	4 11 18 25	1 8 15 22 29
W	6 13 20 27	3 10 17 24	3 10 17 24 31	7 14 21 28	5 12 19 26	2 9 16 23 30
T	7 14 21 28	4 11 18 25	4 11 18 25	1 8 15 22 29	6 13 20 27	3 10 17 24
F	1 8 15 22 29	5 12 19 26	5 12 19 26	2 9 16 23 30	7 14 21 28	4 11 18 25
S	2 9 16 23 30	6 13 20 27	6 13 20 27	3 10 17 24	1 8 15 22 29	5 12 19 26

Wednesday 9

Thursday 10

Friday 11

Saturday 12

13 Sunday   Advent 3

....
....
....
....
....
....
....
....
....
....
....
....
....
....
....

14 Monday

....
....
....
....
....
....

15 Tuesday

....
....
....
....
....
....
....

2021

January						February					March					April					May						June				
S		3	10	17	24	31	S		7	14	21	28	S		7	14	21	28	S		4	11	18	25	S		2	9	16	23	30	S		6	13	20	27
M		4	11	18	25		M	1	8	15	22		M	1	8	15	22	29	M		5	12	19	26	M		3	10	17	24	31	M		7	14	21	28
T		5	12	19	26		T	2	9	16	23		T	2	9	16	23	30	T		6	13	20	27	T		4	11	18	25	T	1	8	15	22	29
W		6	13	20	27		W	3	10	17	24		W	3	10	17	24	31	W		7	14	21	28	W		5	12	19	26	W	2	9	16	23	30
T		7	14	21	28		T	4	11	18	25		T	4	11	18	25	T	1	8	15	22	29	T		6	13	20	27	T	3	10	17	24
F	1	8	15	22	29	F	5	12	19	26		F	5	12	19	26	F	2	9	16	23	30	F		7	14	21	28	F	4	11	18	25
S	2	9	16	23	30	S	6	13	20	27		S	6	13	20	27	S	3	10	17	24	S	1	8	15	22	29	S	5	12	19	26

O Sapientia (BCP) (Beginning of 8 days of prayer before Christmas) **Wednesday 16**

O Sapientia (CW) **Thursday 17**

Friday 18

Saturday 19

2021

	July					August					September					October					November					December			
S		4	11	18	25	S	1	8	15	22	29	S		5	12	19	26	S		3	10	17	24	31	S		7	14	21	28	S		5	12	19	26
M		5	12	19	26	M	2	9	16	23	30	M		6	13	20	27	M		4	11	18	25	M	1	8	15	22	29	M		6	13	20	27
T		6	13	20	27	T	3	10	17	24	31	T		7	14	21	28	T		5	12	19	26	T	2	9	16	23	30	T		7	14	21	28
W		7	14	21	28	W	4	11	18	25		W	1	8	15	22	29	W		6	13	20	27	W	3	10	17	24		W	1	8	15	22	29
T	1	8	15	22	29	T	5	12	19	26		T	2	9	16	23	30	T		7	14	21	28	T	4	11	18	25		T	2	9	16	23	30
F	2	9	16	23	30	F	6	13	20	27		F	3	10	17	24		F	1	8	15	22	29	F	5	12	19	26		F	3	10	17	24	31
S	3	10	17	24	31	S	7	14	21	28		S	4	11	18	25		S	2	9	16	23	30	S	6	13	20	27		S	4	11	18	25	

20 Sunday   Advent 4

21 Monday

22 Tuesday

Wednesday 23

Christmas Eve　**Thursday 24**

BANK HOLIDAY　　　　　　　　**Christmas Day**　Friday **25**

Stephen　**Saturday 26**

2021

	July					August					September					October						November					December			
S		4	11	18	25	S	1	8	15	22	29	S		5	12	19	26	S		3	10	17	24	31	S		7	14	21	28	S		5	12	19	26
M		5	12	19	26	M	2	9	16	23	30	M		6	13	20	27	M		4	11	18	25	M	1	8	15	22	29	M		6	13	20	27
T		6	13	20	27	T	3	10	17	24	31	T		7	14	21	28	T		5	12	19	26	T	2	9	16	23	30	T		7	14	21	28
W		7	14	21	28	W	4	11	18	25		W	1	8	15	22	29	W		6	13	20	27	W	3	10	17	24		W	1	8	15	22	29
T	1	8	15	22	29	T	5	12	19	26		T	2	9	16	23	30	T		7	14	21	28	T	4	11	18	25		T	2	9	16	23	30
F	2	9	16	23	30	F	6	13	20	27		F	3	10	17	24		F	1	8	15	22	29	F	5	12	19	26		F	3	10	17	24	31
S	3	10	17	24	31	S	7	14	21	28		S	4	11	18	25		S	2	9	16	23	30	S	6	13	20	27		S	4	11	18	25	

Forward Planner

27 Sunday   Christmas 1   John

28 Monday   The Holy Innocents   BANK HOLIDAY

29 Tuesday

2021

January					February				March				April				May				June			
S		3	10	17	24	31	S		7	14	21	28	S		7	14	21	28	S		4	11	18	25	S		2	9	16	23	30	S		6	13	20	27
M		4	11	18	25		M	1	8	15	22		M	1	8	15	22	29	M		5	12	19	26	M		3	10	17	24	31	M		7	14	21	28
T		5	12	19	26		T	2	9	16	23		T	2	9	16	23	30	T		6	13	20	27	T		4	11	18	25	T	1	8	15	22	29
W		6	13	20	27		W	3	10	17	24		W	3	10	17	24	31	W		7	14	21	28	W		5	12	19	26	W	2	9	16	23	30
T		7	14	21	28		T	4	11	18	25		T	4	11	18	25		T	1	8	15	22	29	T		6	13	20	27	T	3	10	17	24	
F	1	8	15	22	29		F	5	12	19	26		F	5	12	19	26		F	2	9	16	23	30	F		7	14	21	28	F	4	11	18	25	
S	2	9	16	23	30		S	6	13	20	27		S	6	13	20	27		S	3	10	17	24		S	1	8	15	22	29	S	5	12	19	26	

Wednesday 30

Thursday 31

BANK HOLIDAY   Naming of Jesus   **Friday 1**

Saturday 2

2021

	July					August					September					October					November					December			
S		4	11	18	25	**S**	1	8	15	22	29	**S**		5	12	19	26	**S**		3	10	17	24	31	**S**		7	14	21	28	**S**		5	12	19	26
M		5	12	19	26	**M**	2	9	16	23	30	**M**		6	13	20	27	**M**		4	11	18	25	**M**	1	8	15	22	29	**M**		6	13	20	27
T		6	13	20	27	**T**	3	10	17	24	31	**T**		7	14	21	28	**T**		5	12	19	26	**T**	2	9	16	23	30	**T**		7	14	21	28
W		7	14	21	28	**W**	4	11	18	25		**W**	1	8	15	22	29	**W**		6	13	20	27	**W**	3	10	17	24		**W**	1	8	15	22	29
T	1	8	15	22	29	**T**	5	12	19	26		**T**	2	9	16	23	30	**T**		7	14	21	28	**T**	4	11	18	25		**T**	2	9	16	23	30
F	2	9	16	23	30	**F**	6	13	20	27		**F**	3	10	17	24		**F**	1	8	15	22	29	**F**	5	12	19	26		**F**	3	10	17	24	31
S	3	10	17	24	31	**S**	7	14	21	28		**S**	4	11	18	25		**S**	2	9	16	23	30	**S**	6	13	20	27		**S**	4	11	18	25	

ACCOUNTS
December

Date	Income	£	p	Date	Expenditure	£	p

January

Date	Income	£	p	Date	Expenditure	£	p

February

Date	Income	£	p	Date	Expenditure	£	p

March

Date	Income	£	p	Date	Expenditure	£	p

April Tax Year Begins—6 April

Date	Income	£	p	Date	Expenditure	£	p

May

Date	Income	£	p	Date	Expenditure	£	p

ACCOUNTS
June

Date	Income	£	p	Date	Expenditure	£	p

July

Date	Income	£	p	Date	Expenditure	£	p

August

Date	Income	£	p	Date	Expenditure	£	p

ACCOUNTS
September

Date	Income	£	p	Date	Expenditure	£	p

October

Date	Income	£	p	Date	Expenditure	£	p

November

Date	Income	£	p	Date	Expenditure	£	p

Names and Addresses

	Telephone
	Mobile
	E-mail
	Telephone
	Mobile
	E-mail
	Telephone
	Mobile
	E-mail
	Telephone
	Mobile
	E-mail
	Telephone
	Mobile
	E-mail
	Telephone
	Mobile
	E-mail
	Telephone
	Mobile
	E-mail
	Telephone
	Mobile
	E-mail
	Telephone
	Mobile
	E-mail
	Telephone
	Mobile
	E-mail
	Telephone
	Mobile
	E-mail
	Telephone
	Mobile
	E-mail
	Telephone
	Mobile
	E-mail

	Telephone
	Mobile
	E-mail
	Telephone
	Mobile
	E-mail
	Telephone
	Mobile
	E-mail
	Telephone
	Mobile
	E-mail
	Telephone
	Mobile
	E-mail
	Telephone
	Mobile
	E-mail
	Telephone
	Mobile
	E-mail
	Telephone
	Mobile
	E-mail
	Telephone
	Mobile
	E-mail
	Telephone
	Mobile
	E-mail
	Telephone
	Mobile
	E-mail
	Telephone
	Mobile
	E-mail
	Telephone
	Mobile
	E-mail
	Telephone
	Mobile
	E-mail

Names and Addresses

	Telephone
	Mobile
	E-mail
	Telephone
	Mobile
	E-mail
	Telephone
	Mobile
	E-mail
	Telephone
	Mobile
	E-mail
	Telephone
	Mobile
	E-mail
	Telephone
	Mobile
	E-mail
	Telephone
	Mobile
	E-mail
	Telephone
	Mobile
	E-mail
	Telephone
	Mobile
	E-mail
	Telephone
	Mobile
	E-mail
	Telephone
	Mobile
	E-mail
	Telephone
	Mobile
	E-mail
	Telephone
	Mobile
	E-mail

	Telephone
	Mobile
	E-mail
	Telephone
	Mobile
	E-mail
	Telephone
	Mobile
	E-mail
	Telephone
	Mobile
	E-mail
	Telephone
	Mobile
	E-mail
	Telephone
	Mobile
	E-mail
	Telephone
	Mobile
	E-mail
	Telephone
	Mobile
	E-mail
	Telephone
	Mobile
	E-mail
	Telephone
	Mobile
	E-mail
	Telephone
	Mobile
	E-mail
	Telephone
	Mobile
	E-mail
	Telephone
	Mobile
	E-mail

Notes

Notes

Notes

Notes

Notes

Notes

Notes

Notes

Notes

Notes

Notes

Notes

Notes

Notes

1 F	The Naming of Jesus	BANK HOLIDAY
2 Sa		
3 S	Christmas 2	
4 M		BANK HOLIDAY (Scotland)
5 Tu		
6 W	**The Epiphany**	
7 Th		
8 F		
9 Sa		
10 S	Baptism of Christ	
11 M		
12 Tu		
13 W		
14 Th		
15 F		
16 Sa		
17 S	Epiphany 2	
18 M		
19 Tu		
20 W		
21 Th		
22 F		
23 Sa		
24 S	Epiphany 3	
25 M	The Conversion of Paul	
26 Tu		
27 W		
28 Th		
29 F		
30 Sa		
31 S	Epiphany 4	

1 M	
2 Tu	**The Presentation** (Candlemas)
3 W	
4 Th	
5 F	
6 Sa	
7 **S**	2nd before Lent
8 M	
9 Tu	
10 W	
11 Th	
12 F	
13 Sa	
14 **S**	Sunday next before Lent
15 M	
16 Tu	
17 W	**Ash Wednesday**
18 Th	
19 F	
20 Sa	
21 **S**	Lent 1
22 M	
23 Tu	
24 W	
25 Th	
26 F	
27 Sa	
28 **S**	Lent 2

1 M	St David, Patron of Wales
2 Tu	
3 W	
4 Th	
5 F	
6 Sa	
7 **S**	Lent 3
8 M	
9 Tu	
10 W	
11 Th	
12 F	
13 Sa	
14 **S**	Lent 4, Mothering Sunday
15 M	
16 Tu	
17 W	St Patrick, Patron of Ireland BANK HOLIDAY (N. Ireland)
18 Th	
19 F	Joseph of Nazareth
20 Sa	
21 **S**	Lent 5, Passiontide begins
22 M	
23 Tu	
24 W	
25 Th	**Annunciation of Our Lord**
26 F	
27 Sa	
28 **S**	**Palm Sunday**
29 M	Monday of Holy Week
30 Tu	Tuesday of Holy Week
31 W	Wednesday of Holy Week

Forward Planner

1 Th	**Maundy Thursday**	
2 F	**Good Friday**	BANK HOLIDAY
3 Sa	Easter Eve	
4 S	**Easter Day**	
5 M	Monday of Easter Week	BANK HOLIDAY (not Scotland)
6 Tu	Tuesday of Easter Week	
7 W	Wednesday of Easter Week	
8 Th	Thursday of Easter Week	
9 F	Friday of Easter Week	
10 Sa	Saturday of Easter Week	
11 S	Easter 2	
12 M		
13 Tu		
14 W		
15 Th		
16 F		
17 Sa		
18 S	Easter 3	
19 M		
20 Tu		
21 W		
22 Th		
23 F	George, Martyr	
24 Sa		
25 S	Easter 4	
26 M	Mark the Evangelist (transferred)	
27 Tu		
28 W		
29 Th		
30 F		

1	Sa	Philip and James, Apostles	
2	S	Easter 5	
3	M		BANK HOLIDAY
4	Tu		
5	W		
6	Th		
7	F		
8	Sa		
9	S	Easter 6	
10	M		
11	Tu		
12	W		
13	Th	**Ascension Day**	
14	F	Matthias the Apostle	
15	Sa		
16	S	Easter 7	
17	M		
18	Tu		
19	W		
20	Th		
21	F		
22	Sa		
23	S	**Pentecost**	
24	M		
25	Tu		
26	W		
27	Th		
28	F		
29	Sa		
30	S	**Trinity Sunday**	
31	M	Visitation of the BVM to Elizabeth	BANK HOLIDAY

Forward Planner

1 Tu	
2 W	
3 Th	Corpus Christi
4 F	
5 Sa	
6 S	Trinity 1
7 M	
8 Tu	
9 W	
10 Th	
11 F	Barnabas the Apostle
12 Sa	
13 S	Trinity 2
14 M	
15 Tu	
16 W	
17 Th	
18 F	
19 Sa	
20 S	Trinity 3
21 M	
22 Tu	
23 W	
24 Th	Birth of John the Baptist
25 F	
26 Sa	
27 S	Trinity 4
28 M	
29 Tu	Peter and Paul, Apostles
30 W	

1 Th	
2 F	
3 Sa	Thomas the Apostle
4 **S**	Trinity 5
5 M	
6 Tu	
7 W	
8 Th	
9 F	
10 Sa	
11 **S**	Trinity 6
12 M	BANK HOLIDAY (N. Ireland)
13 Tu	
14 W	
15 Th	
16 F	
17 Sa	
18 **S**	Trinity 7
19 M	
20 Tu	
21 W	
22 Th	Mary Magdalene
23 F	
24 Sa	
25 **S**	James the Apostle
26 M	
27 Tu	
28 W	
29 Th	
30 F	
31 Sa	

1 **S**	Trinity 9	
2 M		BANK HOLIDAY (Scotland)
3 Tu		
4 W		
5 Th		
6 F	The Transfiguration	
7 Sa		
8 **S**	Trinity 10	
9 M		
10 Tu		
11 W		
12 Th		
13 F		
14 Sa		
15 **S**	The Blessed Virgin Mary	
16 M		
17 Tu		
18 W		
19 Th		
20 F		
21 Sa		
22 **S**	Trinity 12	
23 M		
24 Tu	Bartholomew the Apostle	
25 W		
26 Th		
27 F		
28 Sa		
29 **S**	Trinity 13	
30 M		BANK HOLIDAY (not Scotland)
31 Tu		

1 W	
2 Th	
3 F	
4 Sa	
5 **S**	Trinity 14
6 M	
7 Tu	
8 W	
9 Th	
10 F	
11 Sa	
12 **S**	Trinity 15
13 M	
14 Tu	Holy Cross Day
15 W	
16 Th	
17 F	
18 Sa	
19 **S**	Trinity 16
20 M	
21 Tu	Matthew, Apostle and Evangelist
22 W	
23 Th	
24 F	
25 Sa	
26 **S**	Trinity 17
27 M	
28 Tu	
29 W	Michael and All Angels
30 Th	

1 F	
2 Sa	
3 **S**	
4 M	Trinity 18
5 Tu	
6 W	
7 Th	
8 F	
9 Sa	
10 **S**	Trinity 19
11 M	
12 Tu	
13 W	
14 Th	
15 F	
16 Sa	
17 **S**	Trinity 20
18 M	Luke the Evangelist
19 Tu	
20 W	
21 Th	
22 F	
23 Sa	
24 **S**	Last Sunday after Trinity
25 M	
26 Tu	
27 W	
28 Th	Simon and Jude, Apostles
29 F	
30 Sa	
31 **S**	4th before Advent

1	M	**All Saints**
2	Tu	All Souls
3	W	
4	Th	
5	F	
6	Sa	
7	**S**	3rd before Advent
8	M	
9	Tu	
10	W	
11	Th	
12	F	
13	Sa	
14	**S**	2nd before Advent, Remembrance Sunday
15	M	
16	Tu	
17	W	
18	Th	
19	F	
20	Sa	
21	**S**	Christ the King
22	M	
23	Tu	
24	W	
25	Th	
26	F	
27	Sa	
28	**S**	**Advent Sunday**
29	M	
30	Tu	Andrew the Apostle BANK HOLIDAY (Scotland)

1 W	
2 Th	
3 F	
4 Sa	
5 **S**	Advent 2
6 M	
7 Tu	
8 W	
9 Th	
10 F	
11 Sa	
12 **S**	Advent 3
13 M	
14 Tu	
15 W	
16 Th	
17 F	
18 Sa	
19 **S**	Advent 4
20 M	
21 Tu	
22 W	
23 Th	
24 F	
25 Sa	**Christmas Day**
26 **S**	Stephen, Deacon, First Martyr
27 M	John, Apostle and Evangelist — BANK HOLIDAY
28 Tu	The Holy Innocents — BANK HOLIDAY
29 W	
30 Th	
31 F	

Forward Planner 2022

MAY	JUNE	JULY	AUGUST
1 S Easter 3	1 W	1 F	1 M
2 M Philip and James (transferred)	2 Th	2 Sa	2 Tu
3 Tu	3 F	3 S Thomas	3 W
4 W	4 Sa	4 M	4 Th
5 Th	5 S **Pentecost**	5 Tu	5 F
6 F	6 M	6 W	6 Sa Transfiguration
7 Sa	7 Tu	7 Th	7 S Trinity 8
8 S Easter 4	8 W	8 F	8 M
9 M	9 Th	9 Sa	9 Tu
10 Tu	10 F	10 S Trinity 4	10 W
11 W	11 Sa Barnabas	11 M	11 Th
12 Th	12 S **Trinity Sunday**	12 Tu	12 F
13 F	13 M	13 W	13 Sa
14 Sa Matthias	14 Tu	14 Th	14 S Trinity 9
15 S Easter 5	15 W	15 F	15 M The Blessed Virgin Mary
16 M	16 Th Corpus Christi	16 Sa	16 Tu
Tu	17 F	17 S Trinity 5	17 W
W	18 Sa	18 M	18 Th
Th	19 S Trinity 1	19 Tu	19 F
	20 M	20 W	20 Sa
a	21 Tu	21 Th	21 S Trinity 10
Easter 6	22 W	22 F Mary Magdalene	22 M
	23 Th	23 Sa	23 Tu
	24 F Birth of John the Baptist	24 S Trinity 6	24 W Bartholomew
	25 Sa	25 M James	25 Th
Ascension Day	26 S Trinity 2	26 Tu	26 F
	27 M	27 W	27 Sa
	28 Tu	28 Th	28 S Trinity 11
aster 7	29 W Peter and Paul	29 F	29 M
	30 Th	30 Sa	30 Tu
sit of BVM		31 S Trinity 7	31 W

Forward Planner 2022

See 2021 Planner on pp 501–512

JANUARY	FEBRUARY	MARCH	APRIL
1 Sa The Naming of Jesus	1 Tu	1 Tu	1 F
2 **S** Christmas 2	2 **W** **Presentation of Christ** (Candlemas)	2 **W** **Ash Wednesday**	2 Sa
3 M	3 Th	3 Th	3 **S** Lent 5, Passiontide begins
4 Tu	4 F	4 F	4 M
5 W	5 Sa	5 Sa	5 Tu
6 Th **The Epiphany**	6 **S** 4th before Lent	6 **S** Lent 1	6 W
7 F	7 M	7 M	7 Th
8 Sa	8 Tu	8 Tu	8 F
9 **S** Baptism of Christ	9 W	9 W	9 Sa
10 M	10 Th	10 Th	10 **S** Palm Sunday
11 Tu	11 F	11 F	11 M Monday of Holy Week
12 W	12 Sa	12 Sa	12 Tu Tuesday of Holy Week
13 Th	13 **S** 3rd before Lent	13 **S** Lent 2	13 W Wednesday of Holy Week
14 F	14 M	14 M	14 Th **Maundy Thursday**
15 Sa	15 Tu	15 Tu	15 F **Good Friday**
16 **S** Epiphany 2	16 W	16 W	16 Sa Easter Eve
17 M	17 Th	17 Th Patrick	17 **S** **Easter Day**
18 Tu	18 F	18 F	18 M Monday of Easter Week
19 W	19 Sa	19 Sa Joseph of Nazareth	19 Tu Tuesday of Easter Week
20 Th	20 **S** 2nd before Lent	20 **S** Lent 3	20 W Wednesday of Easter Week
21 F	21 M	21 M	21 Th Thursday of Easter Week
22 Sa	22 Tu	22 Tu	22 F Friday of Easter Week
23 **S** Epiphany 3	23 W	23 W	23 Sa Saturday of Easter Week
24 M	24 Th	24 Th	24 **S** Easter 2
25 Tu Conversion of Paul	25 F	25 F **Annunciation**	25 M Mark (tr)
26 W	26 Sa	26 Sa	26 Tu George
27 Th	27 **S** Sunday next before Lent	27 **S** Lent 4, Mothering Sunday	27 W
28 F	28 M	28 M	28 Th
29 Sa		29 Tu	29 F
30 **S** Epiphany 4		30 W	30 Sa
31 M		31 Th	31 Tu